CANADA

A NATION OF REGIONS

BRETT McGILLIVRAY

OXFORD
UNIVERSITY PRESS

OXFORD

UNIVERSITY PRESS

70 Wynford Drive, Don Mills, Ontario M3C 1J9
www.oup.com/ca

Oxford University Press is a department of the University of Oxford. It furthers the University's objective of
excellence in research, scholarship, and education by publishing worldwide in

Oxford New York

Auckland   Cape Town   Dar es Salaam   Hong Kong   Karachi   Kuala Lumpur   Madrid   Melbourne
Mexico City   Nairobi   New Delhi   Shanghai   Taipei   Toronto

With offices in

Argentina   Austria   Brazil   Chile   Czech Republic   France   Greece   Guatemala   Hungary   Italy
Japan   Poland   Portugal   Singapore   South Korea   Switzerland   Thailand   Turkey   Ukraine   Vietnam

Oxford is a trade mark of Oxford University Press in the UK and in certain other countries

Published in Canada by Oxford University Press

Library and Archives Canada Cataloguing in Publication

McGillivray, Brett, 1944–
Canada : a nation of regions / Brett McGillivray.

Includes bibliographical references and index.
ISBN-13: 978-0-19-542326-6
ISBN-10: 0-19-542326-7

1. Canada—Geography—Textbooks. I. Title.

FC76.M33 2006   917.1   C2005-907391-8

Cover Design: Sonya Thursby/OPUS House
Cover Image: Photodisc/Getty Images

3 4 – 09 08
This book is printed on permanent (acid-free) paper ∞
Printed in Canada

Contents

List of Tables

List of Figures

Preface

Canada is a large and extremely diverse country. In fact, it is a nation of regions. *Canada: A Nation of Regions* is intended to help students understand the processes—both physical and human—that have shaped those regions and continue to modify them. It is the product of three decades' experience teaching the geography of Canada at Capilano College in North Vancouver. Like most of the texts I have used in that time, it is based on the core–periphery or heartland–hinterland model. Where it differs from those books is in its organization and its emphasis on the insights offered by an interdisciplinary approach. *Canada: A Nation of Regions* tells the story of Canada's regions through the stories of their peoples and landscapes, and the interactions between them.

There are three parts to the book. Part I focuses on the national and international scales, Part II on the regional, and Part III on some of the most important issues—regional and global—confronting the nation today. The seven regional divisions—Quebec, Ontario, the Maritimes, Newfoundland and Labrador, the Prairies, British Columbia, and the North—are based largely on political boundaries, to facilitate the use of statistical information. But these divisions are not rigid by any means. Ontario and Quebec, for example, are treated in separate chapters, as two distinct regions, but in terms of the country as a whole their southern portions function as a single region: the dominant core.

Part I, 'Canada: Past and Present', sets the stage for the detailed regional discussions to follow, providing the background information that is necessary in order to understand how developments in individual regions reflect and influence developments elsewhere. Chapter 1 offers a general introduction to geographical concepts and two theoretical frameworks that have proved particularly helpful in explaining Canada's development: staples theory and the core–periphery model. Chapter 2 introduces Canada's physical landscapes—including geomorphology, climate, soils, and vegetation patterns—and the physical processes responsible for them, and concludes with a look at some of the 'natural hazards' created by the interplay of physical processes and human activities.

The first part of Chapter 3 provides a broad overview of Canada's history, from the arrival of its first people through European colonization to the political and economic developments leading to Confederation. The second part focuses on the evolution of Aboriginal rights, particularly with respect to the land—from marginalization and systematic dispossession to reclamation through the modern-day treaty process. Finally, Chapter 4 focuses on Canada's economic and spatial development within a global system of trade and commerce. Major themes in this chapter—and throughout the book—are the consequences of technological innovation (including the replacement of human workers by machines, compression of time and space, and fragmentation of production processes), the shift from manufacturing industries to services as the most important component of the global economy, and the various ways in which demography reflects changing conditions over time.

The order of the chapters in Part II, 'Canada from a Regional Perspective', roughly follows the sequence of European colonization and settlement. Although Europeans had been fishing in the Atlantic region for some time before the fur trade began, early settlement efforts there were generally small-scale and short-lived. It was not until fur traders began moving inland that the French established a permanent colony. For this reason Quebec is the first region examined in detail (Chapter 5), followed by Ontario, which began as part of Quebec and shared a long history with it (Chapter 6). Both chapters examine in detail how the southern parts of these provinces emerged as the dominant core; at the same time they emphasize that the territories to the north in both cases remain resource hinterlands. The focus moves to the Atlantic periphery in Chapter 7, on the Maritimes, and Chapter 8, on Newfoundland and Labrador. The Prairies and British Columbia are covered in Chapters 9 and 10, and the section concludes with Canada's most recently developed region, the North (Chapter 11).

Each of these chapters begins with a look at the region's physical characteristics, including its resource base, followed by a comprehensive overview of its history, especially with regard to settlement and economic development. After that, the discussion focuses on whatever the most salient issues are for each region. In the case of Quebec, for example, those issues include not only the historic tensions between French-speaking majority and the English-speaking elite, the Quiet Revolution, the rise of Quebec nationalism, and the independence movement, but the massive James Bay hydroelectric projects, which have raised a number of questions about Aboriginal rights.

In fact, Aboriginal rights, especially in the context of resource development, are an important theme throughout this book. In the Maritimes the immediate bone of contention in conflicts like the one that erupted at Burnt Church in 2000 may be lobster traps, but the question of fishing rights has its roots in the historic treaties of peace and friendship negotiated by the British with the Mi'kmaq in the 1700s. On the Prairies, the numbered treaties were specifically designed to move the First Nations out of the way so that agricultural settlement could proceed, and it was threats to the land rights of the Métis that sparked both the Red River (1870) and North-West (1885) uprisings. In British Columbia the existence of Aboriginal title was not recognized until the late twentieth century. Today the North is leading the way in the modern-day treaty process.

In the case of Ontario, a particularly important theme is the air, water, and soil pollution associated with industrial manufacturing. The chapter on the Maritimes examines how a region with so much promise in the nineteenth century was reduced to relying on transfer payments by the 1960s. Not surprisingly, the fishing industry is highlighted in Chapter 8, on Newfoundland and Labrador. For the Prairies, a major theme is economic diversification, from an almost exclusive dependence on agriculture, specifically wheat, to other resource industries, especially oil and gas. The chapter on British

Columbia emphasizes the growing core–periphery divide between Vancouver, with its expanding role in the international service economy, and the rest of the province, which continues to depend on resource extraction. Finally, the chapter on the North draws particular attention to the precedents that northern Aboriginal peoples have set in asserting their rights to the land in the context of resource development.

Part III, 'Canadian Issues from a Geographic Perspective', consists of only one chapter, but it brings together many threads. Returning from the regional to the national scale, it begins with a brief summary of Canada's evolution as a nation that draws attention to ongoing regional issues. It then considers some of the most important challenges that the country as a whole faces today, both internal and external.

Acknowledgments

Many people helped to bring this book to completion. Capilano College has been extremely supportive over the years. It is an institution that stresses the importance teaching and encourages research. I am particularly grateful for a one-year paid educational leave that provided me with the time to research and write many of the chapters as well as to travel across Canada, visit other universities and geography departments, and simply experience the many different landscapes and people that make up Canada.

Many individuals at Capilano College deserve credit for their time and suggestions including librarians and my colleagues in the Social Sciences. Gordon Bailey and Charles Greenberg reviewed parts of the manuscript, making encouraging remarks and helpful modifications, while Karen Ewing and Cheryl Schreader made valuable suggestions regarding the chapter on the processes responsible for the physical geography of Canada.

I am also grateful to many individuals I met while travelling across Canada as well as to those geography departments that gave me the opportunity to present a lecture on British Columbia at their institution—all provided insights into their regions and their issues. The following deserve special thanks: Darren Bardati, Rick Baydeck, John Briggs, John Everitt, Jeremy Frith, Jim and Marcella Hladik, Audrey Kobyashi, Derek and Heather McGillivray, Robert MacKinnon, John Meligrana, Orest Murawsky, Keith Nicol, Tim Noel, Jeff Ollerhead, Bob Patrick, and Keith Storey. I would also like to thank the students who offered suggestions on earlier drafts used as course texts.

At a more personal level, thanks go to my son, Jake, who shared the driving across Canada as well as his insights into the landscapes and people. Finally, my wife and partner, Carolann Glover, who also made the cross-country trip, performed the time-consuming task of editing earlier drafts. I am forever grateful for her time and patience.

Of course, none of this would be in print without the able assistance of Oxford University Press where Sally Livingston and Eric Sinkins shaped the manuscript. Interactive Composition Corporation was responsible for the professional maps.

For any errors or omissions, I am responsible.

To Carolann, Jake, and Meegan

Part *I*

Viewing Canada, Past and Present

Canada in Geographic Perspective

Geography may be very broadly defined as the study of the surface of the earth. One geographer has described it as the study of 'where things are, and why they are where they are' (McCune, 1970: 454). Those things can be virtually anything on the landscape, from physical features such as mountains, lakes, or continents to human creations such as towns, mines, or railways.

There are two ways of approaching the 'where'—or **location**—question. One is to establish the **absolute location** of the thing you are interested in by identifying its outermost points and specifying their **latitude** and **longitude**. In the case of Canada, Figure 1.1 shows the northern tip of Ellesmere Island at 83°00′ north latitude, the southernmost point of Pelee Island at 41°41′, the eastern edge of Newfoundland's Avalon Peninsula (Cape Spear) at 52°37′ west longitude, and the western boundary of the Yukon Territory at 141° west longitude. Once those coordinates have been established, they can be used to calculate both distance and area. Canada stretches more than 7,200 kilometres from north to south, and more than 5,000 from east to west; its area is nearly 10 million square kilometres, and it covers four-and-a-half time zones.

In addition, Figure 1.1 shows the political divisions within Canada: the provincial and territorial boundaries imposed on the land by its human inhabitants over the last few hundred years. Four of the regions that are the subject of this book—Quebec, Ontario, British Columbia, and Newfoundland and Labrador—correspond exactly to these units, while three regions—the Maritimes, Prairies, and North—encompass three units each. Since latitude has an obvious effect on climate (see p. 39 below), simply identifying the absolute location of a place can tell us a lot about the conditions of life there.

The second way of answering the 'where' question is to establish where the thing is in relation to other things. Thus Figure 1.1 also shows Canada's **relative location** with respect to its closest neighbours. Adjoining three oceans—Atlantic, Pacific, and Arctic—Canada shares the continent of North America with the United States; the total extent of the border is 8,890 kilometres (Natural Resources Canada, 2001). Of Canada's other neighbours, the nearest are the French islands of St Pierre and Miquelon, the Danish territory of Greenland, and Russia. Within Canada, the locations of the various regions in relation to the oceans goes a long way towards explaining the historic sequence of exploration, resource development, and settlement.

geography
the study of the surface of the earth as the home of humankind.

location
the specific part of the earth's surface where a particular thing is situated; **absolute** location is identified by reference to latitude and longitude, whereas **relative** location is identified in terms of the location of other things.

latitude
a measure of absolute distance north or south of the equator (0°). Lines of latitude run around the globe, an equal distance apart, parallel to the equator and perpendicular to lines of longitude. There are 180 degrees of latitude in all, 90 north and 90 south of the equator.

longitude
a measure of absolute distance east or west of the Prime (or first) Meridian (also known as Greenwich Meridian). Lines of longitude run through the north and south poles, parallel to the Prime Meridian and perpendicular to lines of latitude. There are 180 degrees east or west of the Prime Meridian. The distance between lines of longitude is greatest at the equator (approximately 111 km) and narrows to nothing at the poles.

Figure 1.1   Absolute and relative location of Canada

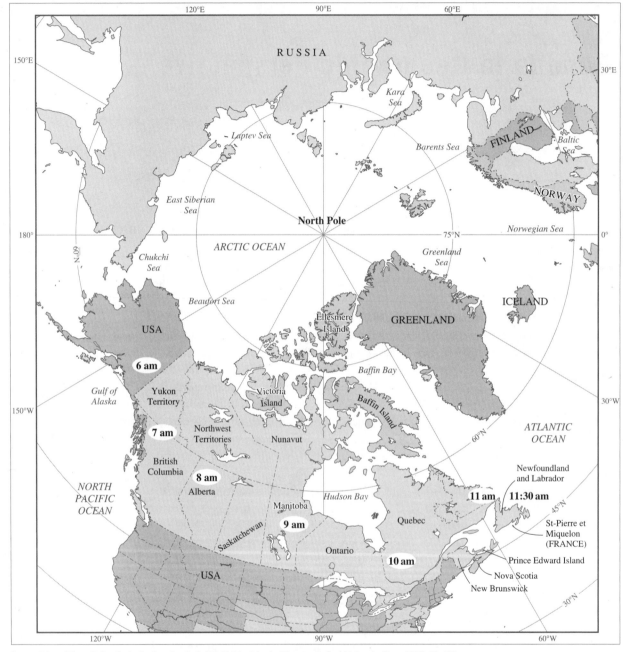

Sources: Adapted from Q. Stanford, ed., *Canadian Oxford World Atlas,* 5th edn (Toronto: Oxford University Press, 2003), 59, 109.

population density
the size of a population in relation to the space it occupies; calculated by dividing the number of people in a defined region by the area of the region.

The various provinces and territories differ greatly not only in area but in number of residents and **population density** (Table 1.1). The vast expanses of the Northwest Territories and Nunavut are very sparsely populated, while the smallest province—Prince Edward Island—has the highest population density of all. According to Natural Resources Canada, nearly 89 per cent of the country 'has never been permanently settled' (2001, #31). Figure 1.2 shows the distribution of Canada's population—projected to reach a total of 32,228,600 in 2006 (Statistics Canada, n.d.)—across the country. By far the largest portion of the Canadian ecumene, or inhabited land, is located in close proximity to the southern border with the United States, which has a population nearly ten times the size of Canada's.

Understanding how these patterns evolved is a large part of the purpose of this book, and it is here that the 'why' question comes to the forefront. 'Why' questions are far more challenging than 'where' questions, partly because there is rarely just one cause, and partly because every answer generates a new series of 'whys'. Why are some regions more likely than others to experience earthquakes? Why did the Canadian Pacific Railway choose a southern route across the Prairies? Why was the James Bay hydro project important to Quebec nationalism? Why has free trade changed manufacturing in North America and challenged Canada's sovereignty over its resources? Why did the east coast cod disappear, and why are west coast salmon in jeopardy today? Why do some First Nations still have outstanding land claims?

Table 1.1 Provinces and territories by area, population, and density, 2001

Province/Territory	Area (sq. km)	Population	Density (pop./sq. km)
Newfoundland/Labrador	405,212	512,930	1.4
Prince Edward Island	5,660	135,294	23.8
Nova Scotia	55,284	908,007	17.2
New Brunswick	72,908	729,498	10.2
Quebec	1,542,056	7,237,479	5.3
Ontario	1,076,395	11,410,046	12.6
Manitoba	647,797	1,119,583	2.0
Saskatchewan	651,036	978,933	1.7
Alberta	661,848	2,974,807	4.6
British Columbia	944,735	3,907,738	4.2
Yukon	482,443	28,674	0.1
Northwest Territories	1,346,106	37,360	0.0
Nunavut	2,093,190	26,745	0.0
Canada	9,970,610	**30,007,094**	3.3

Sources: Natural Resources Canada, 'Facts About Canada' (http://atlas.gc.ca/site/index.html); and Statistics Canada, CANSIM Series 93F0051XIE.

Figure 1.2 The Canadian ecumene

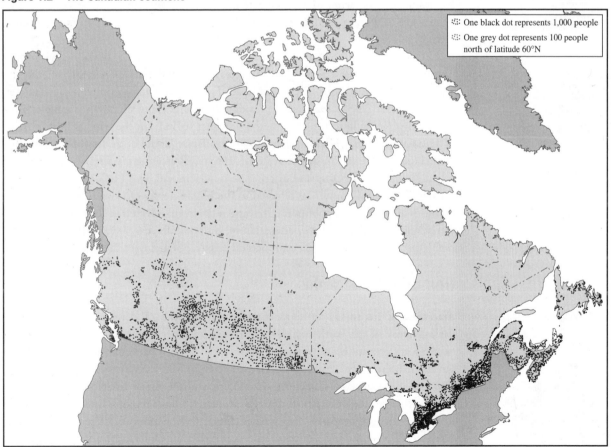

Source: Atlas of Canada, 'Population Distribution, 2001' (http://atlas.gc.ca/site/english/maps/peopleandsociety/population/population2001/distribution2001). Reprinted by permission of Geomatics for Connecting Canadians, Earth Sciences Sector, Natural Resources Canada.

Some geographers add a third type of question, centred on 'what'. What is the significance of a particular locational pattern (Renwick and Rubenstein, 1995: 5)? What consequences will follow from the decision to dam a river or clearcut a forest? What influence do people have on the environment? What influence does the environment have on people? These are not easy questions, and answering them means exploring much more than basic physical geography. History, politics, and economics are only some of the other fields that studying geography can involve.

The idea that the physical environment has profoundly affected human activity in Canada may seem too obvious even to mention. Latitude, climate, geomorphology, soils, vegetation, distribution of resources such as fish, forests, minerals, and energy sources, river systems, access to maritime trade—clearly all these physical factors have affected patterns of settlement and economic development in Canada. For centuries, in fact, it was a fundamental assumption of geography that physical characteristics such as these not only distinguished one region of the earth's surface from another, but determined human behaviour within those regions. This assumption reached its height in the late nineteenth century, when it was expressed in a philosophical perspective known as **environmental determinism**. By the 1940s, however, it was generally recognized that political, economic, and cultural factors tend to play much more important roles in human behaviour than any aspect of the physical environment on its own. Environmental determinism was rejected, and since then students of geography have been wary of words like 'determine' and 'cause', especially when they refer to a single factor.

environmental determinism
the assumption that physical environment determines human behaviour; for a brief history of this perspective see Livingstone (2000: 212–15).

To reject environmental determinism is not to suggest that the physical environment is unimportant. Physical geography is an integral part of the discipline, and some notable writers on the regional geography of Canada have focused mainly on physical characteristics: Robinson (1989), for example, divided the country into six physiographic regions. Warkentin (1997), however, identified 39 distinct regions on the basis of both physical and human features, while McCann (1982) and Bone (2000) both stressed the historical factors that led the various regions of Canada to develop along the lines of what has been called the heartland–hinterland or core–periphery model. This book takes a similar approach. Although Chapter 2 is devoted to the physiography of Canada, and a recurring theme is the way the distribution of resources has been reflected in the country's historical development, much of the discussion in this book has less to do with physical geography than with the human, economic, and political branches of the discipline.

Regional Geography

Traditionally, the essence of regional geography was the effort to describe what makes various areas of the earth unique—to identify distinct geographic spaces by finding 'some sort of unity or organizing principle(s)' within a particular region 'that distinguishes it from other regions' (Gregory, 2000: 687). Many distinctive landscapes within Canada—the Canadian Shield, the Cordillera, and the Great Interior Plains, to name only three—are the products of physical processes. Other regions, however, are identified on the basis of human factors such as culture (e.g., a common language or religion), political organization (e.g., division into counties, as in Ontario, or regional districts, as in British Columbia), economic factors (e.g., fishing zones or agricultural regions), or social factors (e.g., average income, unemployment rates, or prevalence of suicide). Provincial boundaries represent the organization of space based on political considerations, whereas tourist areas, forestry regions, newspaper circulation areas, and ethnic television broadcast zones are defined in terms of their economic and social functions. For many people who live in a particular area and share historical experiences, such as First Nations, Québécois, Acadians, or Newfoundlanders, there is a powerful sense of place—even of 'nationalism'—that comes with a close and longstanding connection to the land. Certainly, through the traditional regional geography approach, important distinctions are made that bring some meaning to large and diverse landscapes such as Canada.

Yet other geographers criticize the traditional approach. They point out that regions are not islands unto themselves, and maintain that to emphasize what makes each region unique is to ignore the relationships between them. Moreover, they say, a description of a given region may be accurate at a particular moment, but nothing is static: therefore any regionalization will need to be reassessed and reconfigured as conditions change.

Regional geography as it is practised today has been described as 'reconstructed' (Pudup, 1988). The new approach takes into account both the many complex and dynamic relationships within any landscape, and the many complex and dynamic ways in which different regions may interact with one another. This new regional geography also recognizes the fact that the configuration of regions can change over time. Historically, for example, the northern half of North America was inhabited by semi-nomadic Aboriginal peoples, each occupying a more or less distinct territory. From time to time the boundaries of those territories changed as a result of changes in the availability of resources, warfare, or the adoption of new technology (such as the use of the horse). The greatest change of all, however, came with the arrival of Europeans, who reorganized the landscape in ways that had nothing to do with indigenous patterns. The political boundaries of Canada have been drawn and redrawn many times, but only the most recent political unit—the territory of Nunavut, created out of the eastern portion of the Northwest Territories in 1999—has come anywhere near reflecting the historic pattern of occupation by the region's Aboriginal people, the Inuit.

Regional geography must also take into account changes in external conditions. Part of what is now Quebec was colonized by France for a century and a half before it was conquered and handed over to Britain. Confederation created a new independent nation state; but as the colonial ties to Britain were loosened, the rapidly growing and economically powerful United States exerted increasing neocolonial influence on the development of both the manufacturing and the resource-producing regions of Canada. More recently, the signing of the Canada–US Free Trade Agreement (1989) and North American Free Trade Agreement (1994) formalized new regional alignments in the framework of an economic system that is now global in scale, and in so doing marked a radical departure from Canada's traditional emphasis on national economic development.

Historical Perspectives

Another recurring theme throughout this text is the importance of historical perspective. For example, some parts of Canada were profoundly affected by European colonialism. On the east coast, the history of European resource exploitation dates back more than four centuries, and the eastern Arctic has an equally long history of exploration, mainly devoted to the search for the Northwest Passage. Yet the west coast remained untouched by Europeans until nearly two centuries later. In the interior of Canada, exploration, development, and settlement moved overland from east to west and then north.

The history of Aboriginal peoples in Canada is much longer, however. Conservative estimates date the earliest human occupation of northern North America to somewhere between 10,000 and 12,000 years ago (Muckle, 1999), but many archaeologists and anthropologists have suggested that the first people may have arrived long before that. Physical geography, of course, uses a very different time-scale, tracing changes to the landscape over hundreds of millions—in some cases even billions—of years.

territory
the area occupied by any person, group, or state, particularly in the context of control or sovereignty.

From the perspective of human geography, there are several basic concepts that need to be defined. Although the term **territory** may be used to refer to any 'portion of space occupied by a person, group, local economy or state' (Agnew, 2000: 824), in this text 'territory' is used mainly in the context of political control or sovereignty—for example, to refer to the area of land traditionally occupied by a certain Aboriginal group. The boundaries of territories such as these are defined both by historic use of the land as the source of food, clothing, and shelter, and by cultural heritage as expressed in traditional songs, dances, stories, and ceremonies tying a particular people to a particular landscape. Europeans, by contrast, initially staked their claims to new territories simply by documenting the 'discoveries' of the early explorers in their ships' logbooks. Once they went ashore, they either established forts on the territory and defended 'their turf'

Champlain's map of New France, 1632.   *Library and Archives Canada, NMC-15661.*

by force of arms or tried to seize territories already claimed by other Europeans. It was through these conflicts that the territory of British North America and then Canada evolved. Most such conflict in Canada today involves the division of powers between the federal and provincial levels of government. Still, the issue of separation—whether on the part of Quebec or of the west—is a clear example of territorial conflict. In other words, the forms that territorial conflict takes can change significantly over time.

Movement over the landscape is another important theme in geography. **Time–space convergence** refers to the shrinking of time and space through changes in the technologies of movement. In 1790 it took nearly seven months to sail from London, England, around the tip of South America to the Pacific northwest. By 1890 steam-driven vessels and the Canadian Pacific Railway had reduced the time required for that trip to just three weeks. Today a flight from London to Vancouver takes approximately nine hours. These changes in transportation have had major implications, not only for settlement patterns but also for resource development—particularly as reductions in travelling time frequently led to reductions in freight rates. Similarly, the advent of the telegraph in 1890 made it possible for information to travel from London to Vancouver in just three days (Harris, 1997). Today satellite systems allow instantaneous communication around the world. As a result, goods and services can now be produced virtually anywhere, and large corporations are able to organize their operations on a global scale.

Yet time and space are not shrinking at the same rate in every location. The highways that make rapid transport possible are located mainly in southern Canada; most northern and coastal communities have only secondary roads, and some have no roads at all. The same is true of airports, railways, canals, and pipelines. Unequal distribution of infrastructure means that some regions face significant economic disadvantages.

Also related to movement is the concept of **spatial diffusion**: the spread or movement from one location to another of virtually anything, from diseases (e.g., the smallpox that devastated Aboriginal populations in the early contact era) to people (e.g., the French Canadians who left Quebec to settle in western Canada), innovations (e.g., new agricultural practices), goods (e.g., farm equipment, or computer software), services (e.g., medical services), or ideas (e.g., that genetically modified food is unhealthy). Spatial diffusion is influenced by both 'carriers', which promote the spread of the phenomenon in question, and 'barriers', which prevent or block it (Gould, 1969).

In the case of human migration (sometimes referred to as relocation diffusion), the decision to relocate often reflects both **'push' and 'pull' factors**. A push factor is something that makes people want to leave their homes, such as religious persecution, warfare, overcrowding, or lack of employment opportunities. A pull factor is a positive feature that attracts people to a particular location, such as the hope of striking gold (as in the Klondike in the 1890s), the chance to own land (as on the Prairies in the early 1900s), or employment opportunities (as in cities like Vancouver or Toronto today). The variations in Canada's history of immigration and emigration (Fig. 1.3) represent a wide range of push and pull factors—and help to explain the multiculturalism that has become a distinguishing feature of Canada today.

Historically, as different European states laid claim to different parts of what is now Canada, they encouraged settlement by people from the home country. Those immigrants

time–space convergence (time–space compression; time–space collapse) the shrinking of time and space as a result of technological advances in transportation and communications.

spatial diffusion spread or movement through space and over time.

'push' and 'pull' factors the negative ('push') and positive ('pull') factors that may influence the decision to leave one location and migrate to another.

Figure 1.3   Immigration and emigration, Canada, 1851–2001

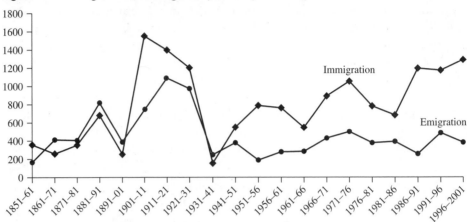

Source: Adapted from the Statistics Canada website ⟨http://www.40.statcan.ca/101/cst01/demo03.htm⟩.

'tragedy of the commons'

a parable about the destructive nature of unchecked capitalism, in which two tribes measured their wealth in cattle that fed on the grassland—the Commons—they shared. For years, wars and poaching kept the numbers of people and cattle in some equilibrium. Then came peace. Without the controls formerly provided by war and poaching, individual cattle owners saw the opportunity to increase their wealth by adding more cows to their herds. But of course the grassland that fed the cattle was finite, and so overgrazing eventually brought ruin to all.

externalities

consequences—i.e., social or environmental costs—of industrial or commercial activity that are not included in the price of the goods or services produced by that activity. For example, a pulp mill that provides jobs for a community will also produce contaminants that pollute the water, and it is the community rather than the mill's owners that must pay for water treatment.

brought with them beliefs and value systems shaped by their homelands, including particular concepts of what constituted 'civilization' and images of what the landscape of the new world should look like—usually much the same as the world they had left behind. The specific details would have varied over time, but since most early immigrants to Canada were Europeans, they shared a set of fundamental beliefs in private land ownership, capital accumulation, the rule of law, and, increasingly, the ability of science and technology to overcome any problem presented by 'nature'. Thus equipped, they set out to reap the new land's resources to fuel ever-increasing growth.

Many of the beliefs imported to the new world were myths, but that did not stop the newcomers from acting on them as if they were true. The consequences were often disastrous. One common European myth saw Canada as an empty vessel waiting to be filled by surplus populations displaced from their overcrowded homelands. This is not to say that Europeans ignored the indigenous population; to the contrary, they depended on Aboriginal people first as suppliers of furs, later as a pool of cheap labour, and Christian missionaries worked hard to convert the 'uncivilized heathens'. Because most Native groups did not live in permanent settlements or practise agriculture, however, Europeans did not regard them as using the land in a way that gave them any rights to it. If Aboriginal people stood in the way of development, therefore, Europeans felt justified in moving them out of the way and onto reserves.

Another myth saw Canada as a land so bountiful that its resources could be exploited at will without fear that they would ever run out. But of course unregulated exploitation resulted in a host of environmental conflicts along the lines of the **'tragedy of the commons'**. In this famous scenario, outlined by Garrett Hardin (1968), the individual pursuit of wealth through resource exploitation inevitably ends in destruction of the resource and ruin for all concerned. Even today, consequences such as the extinction or near-extinction of animal species, the destruction of forests, the deterioration of soils, the loss of fertile land to urban and industrial uses, and the pollution of air, water, and soil, along with the damage that pollution does to human health, tend to be treated as mere side-effects or **externalities**.

A modern parallel to the 'bountiful land' myth is the belief that there is a technological solution to every problem. If demand for electricity is outstripping supply, an 'enduring faith in science' (Glavin, 2000: 8) means that government is often more likely to build another hydro dam than to seek out ways to reduce demand. Similarly, those involved in extractive industries tend to seek out the most cost-effective technologies, even at the risk of destroying the resource altogether: clearcutting forests, for instance, or using electronic fish-finders to locate schools of fish and then encircling them with nets so gigantic that few, if any, individuals are left to reproduce.

Nor are the species identified as resources the only ones that have been endangered by the relentless drive for profit. Unfortunately, until recent times 'resource' species such as beaver, cod, salmon, or white pine were never regarded as components in an intricate web of relationships on which many other species also depend. Far from recognizing the complexity of predator–prey relationships, governments have made it standard policy to destroy unwanted species; British Columbia, for example, has offered bounties on seals and sea lions, and sanctioned the shooting of bears in salmon-spawning waters, in order to increase the commercial salmon harvest. The same tendency to deny the existence of natural systems and relationships is evident wherever single-aged stands of a single commercially valuable tree species replace biologically diverse forests, or fish hatcheries replace natural spawning streams.

The history of the transitions that the Canadian landscape has undergone is particularly important in light of the current interest in **sustainable development**: the idea that resources should not be exploited to the extent that they will not be available for future generations. Introduced in the 1980s and popularized by the Brundtland Commission (World Commission on Environment and Development, 1987) in its report (*Our Common Future*, 2000: 812), the concept of sustainable development is not easy to put into practice. One problem, as McManus points out, is ongoing disagreement about where the emphasis should be placed: on sustaining development (and hence the standard of living the public is accustomed to) or on sustaining ecological processes (2000: 813). Another is that, as the Brundtland Commission noted, sustainability must be considered in a global perspective. In other words, decisions about resource use must take into account the implications for the world as a whole, not just for one nation or group of nations. The same is true at the level of regions within a country like Canada.

sustainable development
defined by the UN Department of Social and Economic Affairs (n.d.) as follows: 'Development that meets the needs of the present without compromising the ability of future generations to meet their own needs'.

Canadian Economic Development

Staples Theory

Historically, natural resources played a crucial role in Canada's development, and they are still the main engine of economic activity in many regions today. Resources were also the basis of an influential theory developed by Harold Innis of the University of Toronto (1930, 1940, 1956). Based on the assumption of pre-existing external demand, first in Europe and later in the US, the **staples theory** proposed that the economic and political development of the colonies that became Canada was shaped by their early roles as suppliers of certain staple commodities to those markets. To harvest, process, and transport staple commodities, workers are essential, and workers in turn require food, clothing, shelter, and services of various kinds. In the beginning those needs were filled

staples theory
the theory that Canada's economic and political development was shaped by its role as supplier of staple commodities—fish, furs, timber, wheat, and minerals—first to Britain and then to the United States and other countries.

from outside, but gradually local suppliers established themselves. Meanwhile technologies and infrastructure were developing, and in time local businesses emerged to meet the demands for services such as banking and insurance.

Innis identified five staples as particularly crucial for Canada: fish, furs, timber, wheat, and minerals. The first four represent a progression in time and space as the development frontier moved across the country from east to west. Commercial cod-fishing on the shallow banks off Newfoundland and the Maritimes began in the late 1400s, when fishermen from several European countries would cross the Atlantic to spend their summers fishing and preserving their catch, and then return home in the fall. Eventually small year-round communities were established along the coastlines of Newfoundland and the Maritimes, and a coastal economy developed based on fishing and related activities: boat repairing, fish processing, barrelling, and shipping, along with the importation of whatever goods the communities required.

Demand for the second staple emerged in the early seventeenth century, when felt hats made from beaver fur became the fashion in Europe. European entrepreneurs began trading with Aboriginal suppliers for beaver skins, and as the trade developed, port facilities, packaging, and warehousing were required, first along the St Lawrence and later on Hudson Bay. Integral to the fur trade was a network of trading forts connected by rivers, lakes, and overland trails that gradually expanded ever farther to the west and the north. The central purpose of the forts was to trade for furs, but they also served a variety of other functions: as centres for colonial administration, the maintenance of law and order, and the spread of Christianity. As Innis noted, 'It is no mere accident that the present Dominion coincides roughly with the fur-trading areas of northern North America' (1930: 56, 392).

Water sawmills like this one at King's Landing, New Brunswick, were common before the advent of the steam engine.   *Photo B. McGillivray.*

International events stimulated demand for both timber and wheat. Britain had imported much of the timber it needed from the Baltics, but conflict with France in the late 1700s and early 1800s cut off its access to that region for several decades. As a result the British turned to the forests of the North American colonies. Logging camps, sawmills, transportation routes, and port facilities were soon established in the Maritimes and along the St Lawrence, and by the 1860s the young colony of British Columbia was establishing its own forest industry. Wheat was also in short supply in Britain by the early 1800s, resulting in a substantial increase in demand for grain and flour from the North American colonies. Some came from the farms of the Maritimes, but the greatest quantities were produced in the fertile St Lawrence lowlands and Niagara Peninsula. (It was only in the later part of the century that the Prairies became Canada's principal wheat-growing region.) Once again, increasing demand for a particular commodity meant increasing demand for the relevant inputs—in this case, seed and farm equipment—along with processing, packing, and transportation facilities.

The fifth category, minerals, is the one exception to the east-to-west pattern. For example, coal mining began in the Maritimes in the 1820s, but the next major coal region to be developed was on Vancouver Island. The discovery of particular mineral deposits led to the establishment of many communities, transportation routes, and processing facilities, as well as jobs. Mining communities are particularly vulnerable, however, in part because mineral resources are non-renewable, and in part because demand for minerals can change rapidly with new technological developments.

Building on the rather loose theoretical framework provided by Innis, Mel Watkins (1963, 1977) identified various components of the economic investment—and by implication, the nature of the employment—associated with resource extraction. The facilities necessary to export a resource are called **backward linkages**. In the case of resource industries, the most important backward linkages involve transportation facilities, because they stimulate so many other economic activities. When the country was first developed, this meant building and running port facilities with warehouses, boat repairs, and all the employment related to loading resources onto ships for export. Over time, ports were connected to canals, railways, and road systems. Backward linkages include the employment that goes into building all these facilities and manufacturing all the equipment—boats, trains, rails, and so on—required to ship the commodity to the export market.

Processes that add value to a commodity prior to export are known as **forward linkages**. In the case of timber, for instance, a forward linkage would be created if the raw material—logs—destined for Europe were first sent to a Canadian sawmill for processing into lumber. Much greater value could be added by transforming that lumber into doors, furniture, or musical instruments, with many more benefits in the form of job creation and revenue for the government.

The third type of linkage develops over time as communities are established in association with a particular export resource, whether at the point of origin or at the port from which the commodity is shipped to market. With the accumulation of backward and forward linkages, these communities grow, stimulating demand for new consumer goods and services. At first these may have to be imported, but as the population grows, local sources are established. It is this sequence of events that the term **final demand linkage** refers to.

backward linkages
the facilities necessary to export a resource back to the source of the initial investment (in Canada's case, first Britain and later the US). The most important backward linkages involve transportation, because it influences so many other economic activities. For example, investment in a railway to access a particular body of ore may also stimulate development in other areas such as forestry or tourism, or other types of mining. Backward linkages include the jobs created to construct these facilities, along with all the other inputs—rails, boats, trains, and so on—required to export the resource.

forward linkages
the processes involved in transforming raw materials into more refined products. The term 'value-added' refers to the degree of processing required to turn raw materials into consumer goods—and therefore the prices that manufacturers can charge. Goods categorized as 'low value-added', such as lumber or newsprint, sell for only a little more than the wood used to make them, whereas 'high value-added' goods such as furniture or snowboards sell for significantly more.

final demand linkage
the local economic activity that develops around a particular resource and the forward and backward linkages associated with it. As the population grows, so does the opportunity for the development of local industry in the form of bakeries, breweries, furniture manufacturers, and so on. In this way the imported goods on which the community initially relies are gradually replaced by locally produced goods.

multiplier effect
all the additional jobs and economic activity that are indirect
consequences of direct investment
in some productive industry: in
the case of a new auto assembly
plant, these effects might include
not only a new auto parts plant
but increased demand for housing, retail outlets, and services in
the community.

Together, all these linkages produce what is known as the **multiplier effect.** For example, suppose that a new pulp mill adds 500 workers to the population of the local community (forward linkage). Those workers require housing, food, and much else, from necessities to luxuries, and consequently the local economy expands to meet this increased demand (final demand linkages). One additional pulp mill in the region may be all it takes to persuade some other company to start manufacturing pulp-machine components nearby (backward linkages). Over time, all this additional economic activity will create jobs for many more than the original 500 people.

It is important to emphasize once again that underlying all these scenarios is the assumption of external demand. Past experiences of recession and depression are reminders that external demand is not always sustained. If the pulp mill shuts down, the multiplier effect will work in reverse and the mill employees won't be the only ones to lose their jobs. And if the mill is the only major employer, its closure may put the entire community in jeopardy.

In the case of Canada, a country abounding in resources and largely 'empty' of people, the export of staples explains a great deal. Regions with more than one major export resource were able to capitalize on multiple linkages to continue expanding and diversifying their economies. At the same time, some resources naturally produced more linkages than others. Catching and barrelling codfish, for example, created comparatively few linkages. By contrast, grain production required many different backward linkages: from seed, fertilizer, tools, equipment, and machinery to transportation—initially by horse and cart, then railways, and eventually trucks on asphalt-paved roads. Agricultural products also lend themselves to numerous forward linkages through processing prior to export: wheat to flour, milk to dairy products, cattle to beef or leather products. Final demand linkages, particularly in the favourable agricultural areas of southern Ontario and southern Quebec, which attracted thousands of farmers in the early 1800s, represented a significant market for the production of local goods and services. Agriculture—notably wheat cultivation—has the potential to create more linkages than any other activity.

Staples theory is still considered a useful framework for understanding the importance of resources to regional growth and development (Barnes, 1993; Barnes and Hayter, 1997; Bone, 2000; Hutton, 1997; Sitwell and Seifried, 1984). Nevertheless, it is limited in its scope. As Harris comments, Innis did not begin 'to theorize other sources of power: government, the military, ideology, culture. He did not understand how pre-industrial European society was hinged together and so could not, in any comprehensive way, consider how it rehinged itself outside of Europe' (1993: 357). Others have pointed out that natural resources are not the only stimulus for economic development, as resource-poor countries such as Switzerland and Japan show (Economic Council of Canada, 1977: 24)

site
in the context of location theory,
the internal characteristics of a
place. For example, the site of
Quebec City included bluffs for
defence, the St Lawrence for
transport, and proximity to good
agricultural land.

situation
the external context (relative
location) of a place. Thus Quebec
City served both as a fortress
defending New France and the
French fur trade, and as a shipping centre. Later, when developments in transportation infrastructure favoured Montreal,
Quebec City's economic
importance diminished.

It is also important to recognize that resource extraction and exports in themselves cannot explain the development of a city like Vancouver. Local factors, both physical and human, must also be taken into account, as well as **site** and **situation**—in the case of Vancouver, a natural harbour and a wealth of forests nearby, with the potential for trade across the Pacific and a railway providing transport across the continent. Political decisions can also play a significant role. For example, the decision to locate the western terminal of the transcontinental railway in Vancouver reflected the power of the Canadian Pacific Railway. When the CPR decided to extend the line another 20 kilometres past the planned terminus of Port Moody, the province granted it more than

2,500 hectares of land at the new site. As a result, the CPR controlled much of the new city's real estate and played a major role in shaping its landscape. Among the other factors that may have played a part in Vancouver's development were decisions made by individual entrepreneurs, the advantages of central location (**agglomeration economies**), and the tendency, once the transportation, industrial, and commercial infrastructure was in place, to build on this framework. A similar review of the factors contributing to development could be conducted for any urban centre in Canada. In short, there are many things besides staples theory that a regional geography must consider.

agglomeration economies
the advantages that come with locating in close proximity to other productive activities.

The Core-Periphery Model

Like the staples theory, the **core–periphery model** of development focuses on the relationship between resource-producing regions and the manufacturing or industrial regions to which they supply raw materials. Where it differs is in its emphasis on the spatial character of that relationship. As the terms suggest, a core (also known as a metropolis or heartland) is a region at the centre of the system, the one that dominates—politically, economically, and socially—over all the others, whereas a periphery (or margin, or hinterland) is a region on the outer fringes, subservient to and dependent on the core. From the sixteenth century to the early nineteenth, Britain was the core and its North American colonies were the periphery whose **primary industries**—fishing, lumbering, agriculture—supplied it with resources; then over time the Great Lakes–St Lawrence region emerged as Canada's own industrial heartland.

core–periphery model
an economic model in which the system consists of two parts: a dominant central core and a subservient, dependent periphery.

primary industry
activities such as fishing, farming, and lumbering, which provide the raw materials for manufacturing.

Core areas have significant advantages over peripheries. Southern Quebec and Ontario had not only favourable physical conditions for agriculture but enough good

Fertile land and modern agricultural techniques allowed many farmers in southern Ontario to establish substantial homesteads. *Photo B. McGillivray.*

secondary industry
manufacturing.

tertiary industry
sales and service activities.

quaternary industry
knowledge-based services
that do not involve direct
contact with the public (included
as part of the tertiary category
until 1961).

agricultural land to attract a large population and therefore stimulate the development of numerous linkages. The natural transportation network provided by the St Lawrence and Great Lakes was gradually expanded with the addition first of canals and then of roads, railways, and eventually of freeways and airports, creating important backward linkages. Increasing population and manufacturing (**secondary industry**) attracted even more people and jobs, not only because of the industrial activity itself but also because of all the activities associated with manufacturing—banking and finance, insurance, research and development, legal services, warehousing, wholesaling, and so on. Another major engine of economic growth in the core was the **tertiary industry**—retail and services—that supplied the needs not only of the core itself but also, through catalogue sales, of the periphery. Friedmann (1973) argues that the defining characteristic of cores is innovation: the creation of new technologies, goods, ideas, or approaches to management reflected in the concentration of head offices, stock markets, research and development programs (both at universities and within corporations), and government bureaucracies in core regions. Regions that innovate are regions of power and control. Much of the work done in these regions involves what is now often described as **quaternary industry**: research and development, consulting, information services, and so on. The sheer diversity of the economic activities associated with core areas helps to protect them against the most extreme troughs of recession and depression.

Another characteristic of core regions is that their urban centres are concentrated in a relatively small geographic area and are highly integrated in the sense that one urban centre will perform functions necessary to the production of goods and services in another centre. Montreal and Toronto led the way, but other important urban centres emerged from Windsor to Quebec City. Figure 1.4 maps the locations of the main urban centres in this core region. Table 1.2 gives the rank order for the largest 25 urban centres in Canada from the 2001 census and traces these populations back 130 years. Of the 17 urban centres that existed across the country in 1871, all but five were located in the relatively small geographic region of southern Ontario and southern Quebec. The fact that by 2001 the same region contained nearly half of the country's largest urban centres (12 of 25) underlines the point: even today, the Great Lakes–St Lawrence region contains approximately 55 per cent of Canada's population. Finally, Table 1.3 suggests the political clout that Quebec and Ontario have enjoyed ever since Confederation: even though both have federal ridings outside the core area, they hold the controlling interest in a democratic system based on representation by population. As the 1988 federal election over the Canada–US Free Trade Agreement showed, the interests of the core region dominate the political, economic, and social agendas for the whole of Canada.

Peripheries are the opposite of cores in virtually every way. Most jobs are in primary industries—fish, forests, metals, energy resources, agriculture—with only limited processing of the primary resource. In many cases the physical characteristics of the region either restrict access to it or limit the potential for activities such as agriculture. Urban communities do arise to serve regional interests, but they have little in common with one another; they are neither concentrated nor well integrated, and the businesses that operate in them tend to be branch offices or chain stores. Peripheries are on the receiving end of innovations developed in the core, which often involve technologies intended specifically to reduce the need for labour. Dependent on the core for investment, and subject to the decisions made by head offices there, peripheries have insufficient population to sway political and economic decisions at the national scale.

Figure 1.4   The core region of Canada and major urban centres

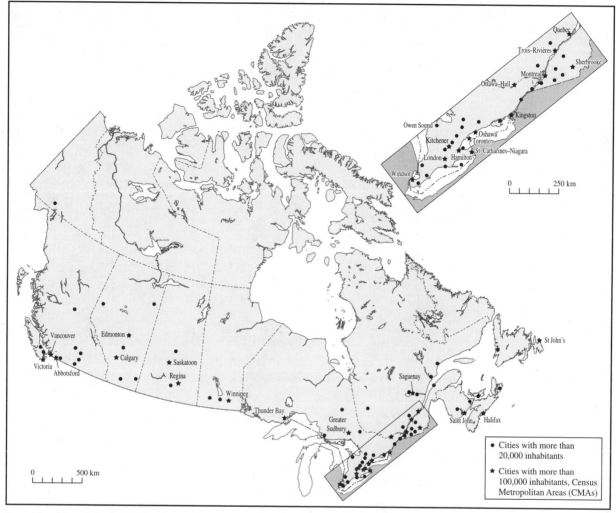

Source: Adapted from Q. Stanford, ed., *Canadian Oxford World Atlas,* 5th edn (Toronto: Oxford University Press, 2003), 34.

The core–periphery model operates at various geographic scales above and below that of the nation. Globally, for instance, Canada functions largely as a periphery in relation to the United States, Japan, and Europe. And if southern Ontario and southern Quebec constitute the core region for Canada on the national scale, on the provincial scale centres such as Halifax, Winnipeg, and Vancouver function as cores for their respective regions.

Some commentators, such as Rostow (1960, 1978), have justified the hierarchical relationship between nations by suggesting that investment flowing from cores to peripheries will eventually enable all regions of the world to attain core status. Others, however, have suggested quite a different view. For example, Frank (1967), Wallerstein (1979), and Gonic (1987) have argued that core regions remain dominant because they exploit other regions. As Frank put it: 'economic development and underdevelopment are the opposite faces of the same coin' (1967: 9). In short, cores need to exploit peripheries in order to continue functioning as cores. Friedmann, on the other hand, pointed out that core–periphery relationships change. Writing of Venezuela, he suggested that

Table 1.2   Canada's 25 largest urban centres (× 1,000), 1871–2001

CMA	1871	1881	1891	1901	1911	1921	1931	1941	1951	1961	1971	1981	1991	2001
Toronto	56.1	86.4	174.4	208.0	376.5	521.9	631.2	667.5	1,210.4	1,824.5	2,628.0	2,998.9	3,893.0	4,907.0
Montreal	107.2	140.7	216.7	267.7	468.0	618.5	818.6	903.0	1,471.9	2,109.5	2,743.2	2,828.3	3,127.2	3,511.8
Vancouver	–	–	13.7	29.4	120.8	163.2	246.6	275.4	562.0	790.2	1,082.4	1,268.2	1,602.5	2,099.4
Ottawa–Hull[1]	25.3	34.3	50.2	73.9	105.3	131.9	156.3	187.9	292.5	429.8	602.5	718.0	920.9	1,063.7
Calgary	–	–	–	4.4	43.7	63.3	83.8	88.9	142.3	279.1	403.3	592.7	754.0	969.6
Edmonton	–	–	–	2.6	24.9	58.8	79.2	93.8	176.8	337.6	495.7	657.1	839.9	954.1
Quebec City	59.7	62.4	63.1	68.8	78.1	95.2	130.6	150.8	276.2	357.6	480.5	576.1	645.6	694.0
Winnipeg	0.2	8.0	25.6	42.3	136.0	179.1	218.8	222.0	356.8	476.0	540.3	584.8	652.4	684.3
Hamilton	26.7	36.0	47.2	52.6	82.0	114.2	155.5	166.3	280.3	395.2	498.5	542.1	599.8	680.0
Kitchener	2.7	4.1	7.4	9.7	15.2	21.8	30.8	35.7	107.5	154.9	226.8	287.8	356.4	431.2
London	15.8	19.7	27.9	39.9	46.3	61.0	71.1	78.3	129.0	181.3	286.0	283.7	381.5	425.2
St Catharines[2]	9.5	11.9	12.5	14.1	21.7	34.7	43.8	50.9	108.2	150.2	303.4	304.4	364.6	391.9
Halifax	29.3	36.1	38.4	40.8	46.6	58.4	59.3	70.5	133.9	183.9	222.6	277.7	320.5	359.1
Victoria	4.2	5.9	16.8	20.9	31.7	38.7	39.1	44.1	113.2	154.2	195.8	233.5	287.9	319.4
Windsor	4.3	6.6	10.3	12.2	17.8	38.6	63.1	105.3	163.6	193.4	258.6	246.1	262.1	313.7
Oshawa	3.2	4.0	4.1	4.4	7.4	11.9	23.4	26.8	50.2	80.9	120.3	154.2	240.1	304.6
Saskatoon	–	–	–	0.1	12.0	25.7	43.3	43.0	53.3	95.5	126.4	154.2	210.0	231.5
Regina	–	–	–	2.2	30.2	34.4	53.2	58.2	71.3	112.1	140.7	164.3	191.7	198.3
St John's	n.a.	n.a.	n.a.	n.a.	32.3	36.4	39.95	n.a.	68.6	90.8	131.8	154.8	171.9	176.4
Chicoutimi[3]	1.4	1.9	2.3	3.8	8.3	13.8	21.3	29.8	44.7	60.3	133.7	135.2	160.9	158.8
Sudbury	–	–	–	2.0	4.2	8.6	18.5	32.2	73.8	110.7	155.4	149.9	157.6	157.0
Sherbrooke	4.4	7.2	10.1	11.8	16.4	23.5	28.9	36.0	54.5	70.3	84.6	117.3	139.2	155.0
Trois-Rivières	7.6	8.7	8.3	10.0	13.7	22.4	35.5	42.0	65.9	83.7	97.9	111.5	136.3	141.2
Saint John	41.3	41.4	39.2	40.7	42.5	47.2	47.5	51.7	78.3	95.6	106.7	114.0	125.0	127.3
Thunder Bay[4]	–	2.0	4.9	6.8	27.7	35.4	46.1	55.0	68.1	93.3	112.1	121.4	124.4	125.7

[1]Ottawa and Hull were shown separately in the census until 1951, but are combined here for consistency.

[2]Includes Niagara Falls.

[3]Includes Jonquière.

[4]Port Arthur and Fort William were shown separately in the census until 1961, when they were joined to form Thunder Bay.

[5]From the 1935 Census of Newfoundland.

Sources: Statistics Canada, Census of Canada 1871–1981; Community Profiles (1991, 2001).

Table 1.3   Federal political representation, 1871–2004 (number of seats)

Year	Cda	BC	Alta	Sask.	Man.	Ont.	Que.	NB	NS	PEI	Nfld	Yukon	NWT[1]
1871	181	–	–	–	–	82	65	15	19	–	–	–	–
1881	206	6	–	–	4	88	65	16	21	6	–	–	–
1891	215	6	–	–	5	92	65	16	21	6	–	–	4
1901	213	6	–	–	7	92	65	14	20	5	–	–	4
1911	221	7	7	10	10	86	65	13	18	4	–	–	1
1921	235	13	12	16	15	82	65	11	16	4	–	–	1
1931	245	14	16	21	17	82	65	11	14	4	–	–	1
1941	243	16	17	21	17	82	65	10	11	3	–	–	1
1951	260	18	17	20	16	83	73	10	12	3	7	–	1
1961	263	22	17	17	14	85	75	10	11	3	7	1	1
1971	264	23	19	13	13	88	74	10	11	4	7	1	1
1981	282	28	21	14	14	95	75	10	11	4	7	1	2
1991	295	32	26	14	14	99	75	10	11	4	7	1	2
2001	301	34	26	14	14	103	75	10	11	4	7	1	2
2004	308	36	28	14	14	106	75	10	11	4	7	1	2

[1]For the 2000 and 2004 elections the NWT was divided between the Northwest Territories and Nunavut; each region had one representative.

Sources: Statistics Canada, Historical Statistics of Canada, Cat. no. 11-516-XIE, Series Y199-210 (1871-1971); Elections Canada (1981–2004).

neither core nor peripheral regions were static (1966). To accurately reflect spatial relationships, therefore, the model must be dynamic, describing how peripheral regions struggle to gain the advantages enjoyed by the core, while the core exerts its own pressures on peripheries to consolidate even more power and control.

It is also important to recognize that industrial capitalism has changed fundamentally since the 1970s. For nearly 200 years, manufacturing was the main engine driving economic growth and giving core regions the advantage over peripheries. At the heart of the industrial economy were the resources that provided the raw materials for manufacturing. Today the situation is fundamentally different in that manufacturing is no longer the largest component of the global economy (see Table 1.4). The emergence of the service economy has been accompanied by profound changes in the ways goods and services are produced. It has also brought radical changes in the location of production activities. Manufacturing industries have taken advantage of new technologies that allow them to break up the production process, manufacturing different components of a product in different parts of the world (e.g., using regions with low labour costs to produce labour-intensive components and regions with low energy costs for stages of the process that require a lot of energy). The result has been a massive restructuring of cores and peripheries, both spatially and in terms of the relationships between them, nationally and globally.

As early as 1977, the Economic Council of Canada recognized that 'the overall growth of employment is no longer tied to the opening up of new areas for agriculture, forestry or mining, although from time to time there may be surges of activity in particular areas associated with the tapping of natural resources' (1977: 8). The advent of the service economy shifts the focus away from both resource exploitation and manufacturing: now the emphasis is on providing services in the context of the global economic order. Among the

Table 1.4 Employment by industry, 2000–2004

	2000	2001	2002	2003	2004
	(thousands)				
All industries	**14,758.6**	**14,946.7**	**15,307.9**	**15,665.1**	**15,949.7**
Goods-producing sector	3,826.0	3,779.4	3,881.4	3,930.6	3,992.7
Agriculture	373.7	322.7	324.2	328.3	324.1
Forestry, fishing, mining, oil and gas	276.0	279.6	271.0	281.1	285.7
Utilities	113.7	122.3	131.0	130.4	133.0
Construction	808.7	825.4	864.3	907.4	952.8
Manufacturing	2,253.9	2,229.5	2,291.0	2,283.4	2,297.0
Services-producing sector	10,932.6	11,167.3	11,426.5	11,734.4	11,957.0
Trade	2,303.3	2,363.9	2,401.6	2,457.6	2,503.6
Transportation and warehousing	773.8	779.3	760.3	789.3	809.3
Finance, insurance, real estate, and leasing	861.2	878.2	891.1	912.2	955.0
Professional, scientific, and technical services	937.4	985.5	985.5	1,000.7	1,010.1
Business, building, and other support services[1]	533.0	535.7	579.6	607.9	630.1
Educational services	973.5	981.3	1,008.5	1,029.3	1,038.4
Health care and social assistance	1,499.6	1,543.1	1,622.2	1,683.2	1,736.7
Information, culture, and recreation	664.9	711.6	714.2	714.2	732.7
Accommodation and food services	935.4	944.3	984.9	1,006.8	1,006.8
Other services	685.6	665.1	685.5	713.0	705.1
Public administration	765.0	779.2	793.0	820.3	829.2

[1]Formerly Management of companies, administrative and other support services.

Source: Statistics Canada, CANSIM Table 282-0008 and Catalogue no. 71F0004XCB.

Table 1.5   Population by province/territory (× 1,000), 1851–2001

Year	Canada[1]	BC	Alta	Sask.[2]	Man.	Ont.	Que.	NB	NS	PEI	Nfld[3]	Yukon	NWT[4]	
1851	2,436.3	55.0	–	–	–	952.0	890.3	193.8	276.9	62.7	96.3	–	–	
1861	3,229.6	51.5	–	–	–	1,396.1	1,111.6	252.1	330.9	80.9	124.3	–	1.0	
1871	3,689.3	36.2	–	–	25.2	1,620.9	1,191.5	285.6	387.8	94.0	146.5	–	48.0	
1881	4,324.8	49.5	–	–	62.3	1,926.9	1,359.0	321.2	440.6	108.9	197.3	–	56.4	
1891	4,833.2	98.2	25.3	11.2	152.5	2,114.3	1,488.5	321.3	450.4	109.1	–	–	62.6	
1901	5,371.3	178.7	65.9	25.7	255.2	2,182.9	1,648.9	331.1	459.6	103.3	221.0	27.2	25.5	
1911	7,206.6	392.5	374.3	492.4	461.4	2,527.3	2,005.8	351.9	492.3	93.7	242.6	8.5	6.5	
1921	8,787.9	524.6	588.5	757.5	610.1	2,933.7	2,360.5	387.9	523.8	88.6	263.0	4.2	8.1	
1931	10,376.8	694.3	731.6	921.8	700.1	3,431.7	2,874.7	408.2	512.8	88.0	289.6	4.2	9.3	
1941	11,506.7	817.9	796.2	896.0	729.7	3,787.7	3,331.9	457.4	578.0	95.0	321.8	4.9	12.0	
1951	13,984.3	1,165.2	939.5	831.7	776.5	4,597.5	4,055.7	515.7	642.6	98.4	361.4	9.1	16.0	
1961	18,200.6	1,629.1	1,331.9	925.2	921.7	6,236.1	5,259.2	597.9	737.0	104.6	457.9	14..6	23.0	
1971	21,515.1	2,184.6	1,627.9	926.2	988.3	7,703.1	6,027.8	634.6	789.0	111.6	522.1	18.4	34.8	
1981	24,343.2	2,744.5	2,237.7	968.3	1,026.2	8,625.1	6,438.4	696.4	847.9	122.5	567.2	23.2	45.7	
1991	27,296.9	3,282.1	2,545.6	988.9	1,091.9	10,084.9	6,896.0	723.9	899.9	129.8	568.5	27.8	57.6	
2001	31,021.3	4,078.4	3,056.7	1,000.1	1,151.3	11,897.6	7,397.0	749.9	932.4	136.7	522.0	30.1	40.8	28.1

[1]Does not include Newfoundland until 1951.

[2]Part of the North–West Territories until 1905.

[3]The data shown are for census years 1845, 1857, 1869, 1884, 1901, 1911, 1921, 1935, and 1945.

[4]NWT and Nunavut (created in 1999) in 2001..

Sources: Statistics Canada, Census of Canada, 1851–1991; CANSIM table 051–0001 (for 2001); Newfoundland and Labrador Census 1845–1945.

most important activities in the service economy are banking and finance, marketing, accounting, advertising, telecommunications, research and development, tourism, and head office management. Fuelled by knowledge and information, the service economy is chiefly urban in nature; thus the largest metropolitan areas, with the most modern communications and transportation infrastructure, attain the greatest growth. The expanding populations and economies of Vancouver, Edmonton, and Calgary reflect the growing importance of the service economy and represent a challenge to the traditional core–periphery structure within Canada.

Of course restructuring of the production of goods and services does not mean that industrial production has stopped: companies will continue to produce manufactured goods as long as it is economically feasible to do so. What restructuring does mean is that regions whose economies have been based on resources or manufacturing must now face increasing global competition and rapidly fluctuating world market prices. The transition from the industrial economy to the service economy also widens the gap between the core and the periphery. The core, which by definition is urban and densely populated, can readily adjust to the dynamics of the service economy, capturing the knowledge and information-based service industries. This is not the case for the periphery: regions that continue to rely on resource extraction, processing, and transporting are vulnerable to the same external threats as core regions, but it is much more difficult for them to attract service industries because they lack the necessary concentration of population, transportation infrastructure (freeways, railways, international airports), convention centres, head offices of banks and financial services, government and administrative structures, and universities, which channel research and development.

Population, employment, and urbanization are all related. Thus changes in these areas over time serve as important indicators of core–periphery relationships. Rapid population

Table 1.6 Primary,[1] secondary,[2] tertiary–quaternary[3] occupations, by region (%), 1901–2001

Year		Cda	BC	Alta[4]	Sask. [4]	Man.	Ont.	Que.	NB	NS	PEI	Nfld	Yukon	NWT[5]	
1901	Prim.	44.2	35.9			55.8	42.2	40.0	48.1	50.3	66.8			68.8	
	Sec.	21.8	21.2			11.3	23.7	25.2	18.0	17.0	11.0			7.3	
	Ter.	34.0	42.9			32.9	34.1	34.8	33.9	32.7	22.2			23.9	
1911	Prim.	39.4	27.3	54.0	65.2	40.1	34.1	34.6	45.0	48.3	66.3				
	Sec.	19.2	19.4	10.6	7.5	14.4	23.1	22.7	14.6	19.2	10.2				
	Ter.	41.4	53.3	35.4	27.3	45.5	42.8	42.7	40.4	32.5	23.5				
1921	Prim.	36.5	28.6	57.2	65.8	40.6	28.1	30.6	41.3	42.3	63.6				
	Sec.	17.9	17.4	7.8	5.6	12.1	22.8	21.7	13.1	15.2	8.9				
	Ter.	45.6	54.0	35.0	28.6	47.3	49.1	47.7	45.6	42.5	27.5				
1931	Prim.	32.7	24.9	56.1	61.3	36.8	24.9	25.2	39.1	40.2	61.7				
	Sec.	17.8	17.6	8.4	5.9	13.2	22.4	21.4	12.2	13.6	8.5				
	Ter.	49.5	58.5	35.5	33.8	50.0	52.7	53.4	48.7	46.2	29.8				
1941	Prim.	30.7	24.3	53.1	60.8	38.1	21.7	25.5	40.6	35.7	59.1				
	Sec.	22.0	21.3	9.8	6.2	15.4	27.5	26.2	14.2	17.2	8.1				
	Ter.	47.3	54.4	37.1	33.0	46.5	50.8	48.3	45.2	47.1	32.8				
1951	Prim.	20.9	15.5	36.9	52.1	26.9	13.5	17.8	28.7	24.7	43.7	33.9			
	Sec.	30.6	28.4	14.8	7.5	20.2	38.2	35.7	22.5	22.1	13.6	18.2			
	Ter.	49.5	56.1	49.3	40.4	52.9	48.3	47.5	48.8	53.2	42.7	47.9			
1961	Prim.	13.8	9.7	24.6	38.3	19.6	9.5	11.3	15.7	14.2	33.3	18.8			
	Sec.	28.4	25.9	16.3	10.0	19.8	33.3	33.6	22.1	21.0	15.4	19.3			
	Ter.	57.8	64.4	59.1	51.7	60.6	57.2	55.1	62.2	64.8	51.3	61.9			
1971	Prim.	8.3	7.5	16.8	29.4	13.6	5.4	5.7	8.5	7.7	18.9	10.4			
	Sec.	26.0	23.1	16.7	10.2	19.2	30.5	28.6	23.2	21.9	16.3	22.4			
	Ter.	65.7	69.4	66.5	60.4	67.2	64.1	65.7	68.3	70.4	64.8	67.2			
1981	Prim.	7.0	7.2	13.7	22.4	10.4	4.5	4.5	8.0	7.2	16.2	9.9	12.5	13.3	
	Sec.	25.3	22.4	19.7	13.1	19.2	29.2	26.8	23.6	21.2	18.6	23.8	10.1	7.6	
	Ter.	67.7	70.4	66.6	64.5	70.4	66.3	68.7	68.4	71.6	65.2	66.3	77.4	79.1	
1991	Prim.	5.2	5.2	13.5	21.3	9.6	3.3	3.6	6.5	6.7	15.7	9.1	7.9	7.4	
	Sec.	23.0	19.9	13.5	9.8	14.8	23.7	22.9	17.9	16.9	16.5	15.4	11.2	8.8	
	Ter.	71.8	74.9	73.0	68.9	75.6	73.0	73.5	75.6	76.4	67.8	75.5	70.9	83.8	
2001	Prim.	4.3	4.2	6.9	15.9	7.0	2.7	2.9	5.7	5.6	13.1	7.8	3.0	4.4	1.7
	Sec.	21.7	19.1	20.8	17.9	21.2	22.3	23.1	23.9	20.4	21.4	23.7	17.5	17.6	19.6
	Ter.	74.0	76.7	72.3	66.2	71.8	75.0	74.0	70.4	74.0	65.5	68.5	79.5	77.0	78.7

[1]Primary industry includes agriculture, fishing and trapping, logging, mining and quarrying.

[2]Secondary industry includes manufacturing and construction.

[3]Tertiary–quaternary includes all other categories.

[4]Alberta and Saskatchewan are included with the Northwest Territories.

[5]NWT and Nunavut in 2001.

Sources: Statistics Canada, Historical Statistics of Canada, Cat. no. 11-516-XIE, Series D8-85 (1901–1971); CANSIM Table 282-0012 (1981–2001).

growth correlates well with employment opportunities that attract people to a region, while slow or negative growth reflects poor economic conditions leading to outmigration. Table 1.5 traces population growth in Canada by region since 1851. In central Canada, Ontario and Quebec start out fairly even and show similar growth rates until 1961, when Ontario begins to pull ahead. The Maritime provinces have a much slower growth rate overall, although there are considerable differences between the provinces. The western provinces grew extremely rapidly from the early 1900s until the 1930s; by the 1920s, all four had larger populations than any of the Maritime provinces.

Table 1.6 shows the percentages employed in the various sectors from 1901 to 2001 (quaternary-sector employment is included in the 'tertiary' category). Figure 1.5

Figure 1.5   Employment by sector (%), British Columbia and Ontario, 1901–2001

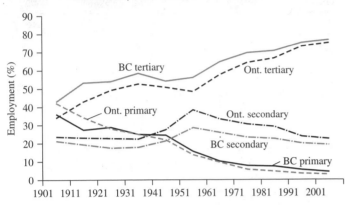

graphs the figures for two provinces only (British Columbia and Ontario) as an example. Employment in primary industry has declined significantly, while tertiary–quaternary employment has made significant gains. The reasons behind these changes lie in the changes that Canada's economy has undergone over time. Where is secondary industry concentrated? Which regions had the most and the least primary industry employment by 2001? Provincial variations do occur, but there is a common pattern, which may lead us to ask whether the core region is substantially different from peripheral regions. A partial answer can be found through further analysis of the statistics. For example, automobile production and high-value-added consumer manufacturing dominate secondary industry in core regions such as Ontario. In peripheral regions, secondary industry tends to be limited to simple processing of resource commodities—milling logs, baling pulp, concentrating metals, processing fish. The similarities between the two provinces appear even more striking in tertiary–quaternary employment. The precise nature of the activities in this sector can vary widely, however. The majority of head offices, research and development organizations, and stock markets—in other words, the innovators and controllers—are located in the core; thus tertiary employment in peripheral regions is more likely to involve sales and service activity at the branch-office level. (In the cases of Ontario and Quebec, keep in mind that the core region is confined to the south, and that each of those provinces itself contains a periphery as well as a core.)

The proportions of people living in rural and urban areas also vary widely (Table 1.7, p. 23). Many primary industries are based in rural settings, whereas manufacturing and services are based in urban centres. The rural-to-urban trend apparent in Table 1.7 corresponds to the employment trends shown in Table 1.6, where the shift is from primary employment to secondary and tertiary. Saskatchewan and the four Maritime provinces—accounting for roughly 20 per cent of the total population—are notable exceptions.

The statistical data presented in Tables 1.5 and 1.6 offer an overview, but a great deal more can be learned by taking into account other kinds of information and analysis. Global events such as the depressions of late 1800s and the 1930s, the two world wars, the 1970s energy crisis, the Asian economic recession that began in 1997, and the terrorist attacks of 2001 may have profound political and economic implications in some regions of the country and little impact elsewhere. Similarly, the discovery of resources, the development of transportation infrastructure, and technological innovation that makes resource exploitation and processing economically feasible can have dramatic consequences for regional development. For example, the opening up of the Prairies to agriculture in the late 1800s and early 1900s is reflected in accelerated population increases, high rural population growth, and high levels of employment in primary industry. In the case of Quebec, the threat of separation creates a climate of economic uncertainty, which helps to explain why that province's population growth rate is lower than Ontario's. In the same way, the

Table 1.7   Urban–rural population distribution (%), 1901–2001[1]

Year		Cda	BC	Alta[2]	Sask.[2]	Man.	Ont.	Que.	NB	NS	PEI	Nfld	Yukon	NWT
1901	Urban	37.5	50.5	25.3	15.7	27.6	42.9	39.4	23.3	28.1	14.5		33.5	
	Rural	62.5	49.5	74.7	84.3	72.4	57.1	60.6	76.7	71.9	85.5		66.5	
1911	Urban	45.4	51.9	36.8	26.7	43.4	52.6	48.2	28.3	37.8	16.0		45.9	
	Rural	54.6	48.1	63.2	73.3	56.6	47.4	51.8	71.7	62.2	84.0		54.1	
1921	Urban	49.5	47.2	37.9	28.9	42.9	58.2	56.0	32.1	43.3	21.6		31.0	
	Rural	50.5	52.8	62.1	71.1	57.1	41.8	44.0	67.9	56.7	78.4		69.0	
1931	Urban	53.7	43.1	38.1	31.6	45.1	61.1	63.1	31.6	45.2	23.2		32.6	
	Rural	46.3	56.9	61.9	68.4	54.9	38.9	26.9	68.4	54.8	76.8		67.4	
1941	Urban	54.3	54.2	38.5	32.9	44.1	61.7	63.3	31.4	46.3	25.6		36.7	
	Rural	45.7	45.8	61.5	67.1	55.9	38.3	26.7	68.6	53.7	74.4		63.3	
1951	Urban	61.6	52.8	48.0	30.4	56.6	73.4	67.0	42.6	55.3	25.1	42.7	28.6	16.9
	Rural	38.4	47.2	52.0	69.6	43.4	26.6	33.0	57.4	44.7	74.9	55.3	71.4	83.1
1961	Urban	69.6	72.6	63.3	43.0	63.9	77.3	74.3	53.5	54.3	32.4	50.7	34.2	38.7
	Rural	30.4	27.4	36.7	57.0	36.1	22.7	25.7	46.5	45.7	67.6	49.3	65.8	61.3
1971	Urban	76.1	75.7	68.8	49.0	67.1	80.3	78.3	50.6	58.1	36.6	54.1	44.2	40.1
	Rural	23.9	24.3	31.2	51.0	32.9	19.7	21.7	49.4	41.9	63.4	45.9	55.8	59.9
1981	Urban	75.7	78.0	77.2	58.2	71.1	81.7	77.6	50.7	55.1	36.3	58.6	64.1	48.0
	Rural	24.3	22.0	22.8	41.8	28.9	18.2	22.4	49.3	44.9	63.7	41.4	35.9	52.0
1991	Urban	76.6	80.4	79.8	63.0	72.1	81.8	77.6	47.7	53.5	39.9	53.6	58.8	36.7
	Rural	23.4	19.6	20.2	37.0	27.9	18.2	22.4	52.3	46.5	60.1	46.4	41.2	63.3
2001	Urban	79.7	84.7	80.9	64.3	71.9	84.7	80.4	50.4	55.8	44.8	57.7	58.7	58.4
	Rural	20.3	15.3	19.1	35.7	28.1	15.3	19.6	49.6	44.2	55.2	42.3	41.3	41.6[2]

[1]Until 1961 the 'urban' category consists of all incorporated cities, towns, and villages, regardless of size. After that date it includes all incorporated and unincorporated cities, towns, and villages of 1,000 and over, as well as fringe parts of metropolitan areas.

[2]Nunavut: 20.3 urban and 79.7 rural.

Sources: Statistics Canada, Historical Statistics of Canada, Cat. no. 11-516-XIE, Tables A2-14 (1901–1971); Census of Canada 1981, 1991, and 2001.

moratorium imposed on cod fishing in the early 1990s has been a major factor in Newfoundland's population decline.

Summary

Chapter 1 is the first of four chapters providing a broad overview of the issues to be explored in detail in Chapters 5 to 11. In addition to defining some key geographical terms and concepts, it introduces the central theoretical framework for the regional analysis to come: the core–periphery model. Based on Innis's staples theory—that Canada's economic development was powered by the exploitation of staple commodities for export to external markets and the various backward, forward, and final demand linkages generated in the process—the core–periphery model is particularly valuable because it incorporates historical perspectives, is flexible enough to be used at a variety of geographic scales, and focuses attention on the relationships between regions and how they have evolved in response to capitalism's need for continuous growth and consumption.

Nevertheless, it is important to recognize that economic activity is not the only factor in Canada's development. Nor are economic values the only motivation for human activity, as a number of the issues to be examined in this text will show. Among those issues are Aboriginal rights, Quebec nationalism, and environmental concerns.

References

Agnew, J. 2000. 'Territory'. P. 824 in Johnston et al. (2000).

'Atlas Quiz'. N.d. atlas.gc.ca: english: quiz: Canada_superlatives_a.php3?

Barnes, T.J., ed. 1993. 'Focus: A Geographical Appreciation of Harold A. Innis'. *Canadian Geographer* 37, 4 (Winter): 352–64.

———, and R. Hayter, eds. 1997. *Troubles in the Rainforest: British Columbia's Forest Economy in Transition*. Canadian Western Geographical Series, vol. 33. Victoria: Western Geographical Press.

Bone, R.M. 2000. *The Regional Geography of Canada*. 1st edn. Toronto: Oxford University Press.

———. 2005. *The Regional Geography of Canada*. 3rd edn. Toronto: Oxford University Press.

Economic Council of Canada. 1977. *Living Together: A Study of Regional Disparities*. Ottawa: Ministry of Supply and Services Canada.

Frank, A.G. 1967. *Capitalism and Underdevelopment in Latin America*. New York: Monthly Review Press.

Friedmann, J. 1973. *Urbanization, Planning and Natural Development*. Beverly Hills: Saga.

———. 1966. *Regional Development Policy: A Case Study of Venezuela*. Cambridge: MIT Press.

Glavin, T. 2000. *The Last Great Sea: A Voyage through the Human and Natural History of the North Pacific Ocean*. Vancouver: Greystone.

Gonic, C. 1987. *The Great Economic Debate*. Toronto: Lorimer.

Gould, P.R. 1969. *Spatial Diffusion*. Resource Paper No. 4. Washington: Association of American Geographers.

Gregory, D. 2000. 'Regions and Regional Geography'. Pp. 687–90 in Johnston et al. (2000).

Haggett, P. 1986. In Johnston et al. (1986).

Hardin, G. 1968. 'The Tragedy of the Commons'. *Science* 162: 1243–8.

Harris, C. 1993. 'Innis on Early Canada'. Pp. 355–7 in Barnes (1993).

———. 1997. *The Resettlement of British Columbia: Essays on Colonialism and Geographical Change*. Vancouver: University of British Columbia Press.

Hutton, T.A. 1997. 'The Innisian Core-Periphery Revisited: Vancouver's Changing Relationships with British Columbia's Staple Economy'. *BC Studies* 113 (Spring): 69–98.

Innis, H.A. 1930/1956. *The Fur Trade in Canada*. Revised edn. Toronto: University of Toronto Press.

———. 1940/1954. *The Cod Fisheries: The History of an International Economy*. Revised edn. Toronto: University of Toronto Press.

———. 1956. *Essays in Canadian Economic History*. Toronto: University of Toronto Press.

Johnston, R.J., D. Gregory, and D.M. Smith, eds. 1986. *The Dictionary of Human Geography*. 2nd edn. Oxford: Blackwell.

———. 2000. *The Dictionary of Human Geography*. 4th edn. Oxford: Blackwell.

Livingstone, D. 2000. In Johnston et al. (2000).

McCune, S. 1970. 'Geography: Where? Why? So What?'. *Journal of Geography* 7, 69: 454–7.

McManus, P. 2000. 'Sustainable Development'. Pp. 812–16 in Johnston et al. (2000).

Muckle, R.J. 1998. *The First Nations of British Columbia*. Vancouver: University of British Columbia Press.

Natural Resources Canada. N.d. 'Facts About Canada'. atlas.gc.ca: english: facts: faq.html.

Pudup, M.B. 1988. 'Arguments within Regional Geography'. *Progress in Human Geography* 12: 369–90.

Renwick, W.H., and J.M. Rubenstein. 1995. *An Introduction to Geography: People, Places, and Environment*. Englewood Cliffs, NJ: Prentice Hall.

Robinson, J.L. 1989. *Concepts and Themes in the Regional Geography of Canada*. 2nd edn. Vancouver: Talon Books.

Rostow, W.W. 1960. *The Stages of Economic Growth*. New York: Cambridge University Press.

———. 1978. *The World Economy: History and Prospect*. Austin: University of Texas Press.

Sitwell, O.F.G., and N.R.M. Seifried. 1984. *The Regional Structure of the Canadian Economy*. Toronto: Methuen.

Statistics Canada. N.d. 40.statcan.ca/101/cst01/demo23a.htm. Accessed 12 Oct. 2005.

UN Department of Social and Economic Affairs. N.d. http://www.un.org/esa/sustdev/. Accessed 8 November 2005.

Wallerstein, I. 1979. *The Capitalist World-Economy*. Cambridge: Cambridge University Press.

Warkentin, J. 1997. *Canada: A Regional Geography*. Scarborough: Prentice-Hall.

Watkins, M.H. 1963. 'A Staple Theory of Economic Growth'. *Canadian Journal of Economic and Political Science* 29, 2: 141–58.

———. 1977. 'The Staple Theory Revisited'. *Journal of Canadian Studies* (Winter).

2

Canada's Physical Characteristics

Canada is a country of extraordinary physical contrasts: from the oldest rock formations known in the world to some of the youngest; from towering mountains to flat-lying plains; from rain forests to deserts; from vast coniferous forests to treeless tundra and permafrost. Weather and climate also vary widely from north to south and between coastal and interior regions. Together, these physical characteristics have affected both the distribution of resources and the patterns of settlement in Canada. The first two parts of this chapter offer an introduction to the physical processes that have shaped (and continue to modify) the country's physiographic and climatic regions. The third part looks at vegetation and soils, while the fourth and last part examines a number of hazards created by the interplay of physical processes and human activities.

Geomorphology

Geomorphology is the study of the physical features of the surface of the earth, their underlying structures, and the processes that created and continue to modify them. The age of a rock formation is a direct indication of the processes that formed it. The most basic age division is between Phanerozoic rock, which contains fossilized evidence of life forms consisting of more than a single cell, and rock from the preceding epoch, known as the Precambrian. Whereas the earliest Phanerozoic rocks date from at most 545 million years ago, Precambrian rock may be as much as 4.6 billion years old. Table 2.1 shows the standard divisions within those two categories.

Under the crust of the earth is a molten material called magma. When magma is brought to, or close to, the surface of the earth, it cools and solidifies

Table 2.1   The geologic time scale

Eon	Era	Period	Years before present
	Cenozoic	Quaternary	
		Holocene	Present
		Pleistocene	1,800,000
		Tertiary	
		Pliocene	5,800,000
		Miocene	23,800,000
		Oligocene	33,700,000
		Eocene	54,800,000
Phanerozoic		Paleocene	65,000,000
	Mesozoic	Cretaceous	146,000,000
		Jurassic	208,000,000
		Triassic	248,000,000
	Paleozoic	Permian	280,000,000
		Carboniferous	360,000,000
		Devonian	408,000,000
		Silurian	438,000,000
		Ordovician	505,000,000
		Cambrian	545,000,000
Precambrian			
Proterozoic			2,500,000,000
Archean			3,800,000,000
Hadean			4,600,000,000

into igneous rock. The size of the minerals in igneous rock reflects the rate at which the magma cooled. If it cooled relatively quickly (in a matter of days, years, or even decades), the crystals are so small that they cannot be seen without a microscope. These rapidly cooled rocks, of which basalt is a common type, are dark and heavy, containing iron and other heavy minerals. Usually produced by volcanic activity, they are known as extrusive or volcanic igneous rocks. Most of the rocks on the floor of the world's oceans are of this type.

Magma that cools at greater depths below the earth's surface may take millions of years to solidify. This time period allows the crystals to grow to a size where they can be seen by the human eye. These intrusive or plutonic igneous rocks, of which granite is an example, are lighter in weight and colour than basalt, and typically make up the continental plates (see p. 28 below). Although these ancient rocks were formed deep within the earth, in some regions forces have pushed them close to the surface, and if the more recent rock formations overlying them are stripped off through weathering and erosion, they will be exposed to the same processes. **Weathering** is the process in which solid rock is disintegrated through exposure to things such as water and wind, temperature change, and vegetation growth. Some of these agents break the rock down into progressively smaller fragments; others dissolve the minerals in it (these dissolved minerals are what makes water 'hard' and the oceans salty). The sediments and dissolved minerals produced through weathering may then be moved—by streams, waves, wind, glaciers, or gravity—to a new location in a process known as **erosion**. When the sediments are eventually deposited, they often form layers, one on top of another. As the sedimentary layers accumulate, those on the bottom are pushed deeper into the earth's crust, resulting in compaction and heating. The sediments can also be infiltrated by ground water, which may precipitate (turn back into solid form) some of the dissolved minerals in the spaces between the sediments.

These precipitated minerals can act as a cement, bonding the sediments together. Compaction, heating, and cementing transform the sediments into a different kind of rock called—not surprisingly—sedimentary. There are three types of sedimentary rock. Sandstone (made from sand-sized sediments) and shale (made from clay and silt-sized sediments) are examples of the clastic variety. Precipitated minerals form a second type of sedimentary rock, of which minerals like rock salt and potash are examples: these 'evaporatives' form in the shallow regions of warm oceans as the water evaporates. The third type of sedimentary rock consists of hydrocarbon compounds, formed from the remains of organic material, both plant and animal. Coal, for example, is the product of plant remains, while limestone is formed from the remains of tiny organisms that in life used minerals dissolved in lakes and oceans to form their shells and skeletons (in the same way that humans extract calcium from milk to make bones). When those organisms die, their shells and skeletons sink to the bottom and accumulate to form limestone.

Besides igneous and sedimentary rock, there is a third category called metamorphic. When rock is exposed to extreme pressures and temperatures, or to chemical infusions from nearby magma bodies, the minerals within it change in shape and chemistry. The original rock does not melt; instead, it 'metamorphoses' (changes) into a new rock. For example, limestone will metamorphose into marble, and coal will metamorphose into diamonds. Metamorphic rocks are very hard and are usually found in mountainous regions, since they are produced by the extreme pressure, heat, and chemical activity associated with mountain building.

weathering
the process in which solid rock is broken down or decomposed through exposure to various physical, biological, or chemical agents.

erosion
the process in which the sediments and minerals produced through weathering are moved to a different location by gravity, wind, water, and so on.

The **rock cycle** (Fig. 2.1) reminds us that even rocks are not static in geologic time, and that all rocks are related. Beginning in the molten state, as magma, all rock is 'born' igneous. Sedimentary rock is then formed over time, through weathering and erosion. Both sedimentary and igneous rock, if subjected to intense heating, pressure, and chemical action, can become metamorphic rock. And rock of all three types may eventually return to the molten form.

The forces that created the continents originate far below the earth's surface. Figure 2.2 shows a cross-section of the earth. At the centre is a solid inner core ringed by a liquid outer core. This core in turn is ringed by the mantle, which is solid but behaves like a plastic substance because of the extreme pressures and temperatures it is subjected to.

The mantle itself is made up of several layers, each with its own characteristics. Close to the top is the asthenosphere, which has temperatures and pressures high enough to partially melt the mantle rocks. Because the asthenosphere is in a semi-molten state, convection currents develop as a result of radioactive decay. The moving plumes of molten material (magma) put pressure on the solid rocks above, forcing them to break and shift position. The brittle rocks above the asthenosphere belong to a layer known as the lithosphere. The lower part of the lithosphere consists of rocks from the upper mantle, while the upper part of the lithosphere contains ocean crust and continental crust. The lithosphere is thinnest beneath the oceanic crust (5 to 10 km in some locations), and it is here that rising convection plumes from the asthenosphere can force the lithosphere to fracture and move. The broken parts of the lithosphere are known as plates, and most volcanic and earthquake activity occurs at their edges.

The theory now usually referred to as **plate tectonics** was first proposed in the

Figure 2.1   The rock cycle

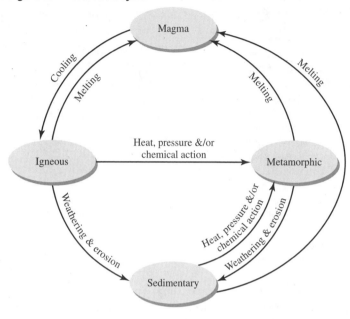

Figure 2.2   Cross-section of the Earth

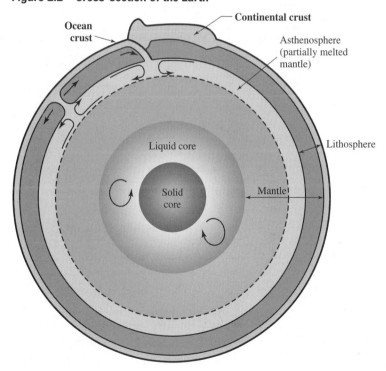

plate tectonics

the theory that the crust of the earth consists of rigid plates floating on a plastic-like mantle. There are two types of plates: thick continental plates and thinner but denser oceanic plates. Forces deep within the earth cause these plates to collide. In some cases they move laterally against one another, creating transform faults. In others, where an oceanic plate collides with a continental one, the denser, heavier oceanic plate is forced down and under the continental plate (subduction). In other regions of the world, known as rift zones, the plates are spreading apart. These tectonic activities are the forces responsible for mountain building, earthquakes, volcanoes, and tsunamis.

subduction

the process in which an oceanic plate is forced down and under a continental plate.

early 1900s, but was not generally accepted until the 1960s, when technological developments in the drilling and dating of rock, and the discovery of the mid-Atlantic ridge and sea-floor spreading, confirmed that the continents do indeed 'drift' and sometimes collide. Today the term 'plate tectonics' has largely replaced 'continental drift' because it places the emphasis on the tectonic activity that is responsible for the plates' movement. Tectonic activity can also bend and break the continental crust, push oceanic sediments into mountain chains, and create volcanic eruptions and earthquakes.

The lithosphere consists of both continental and oceanic plates of varying sizes; some, such as the North and South American continental plates and the Pacific oceanic plate, are very large, and others, such as the Juan de Fuca oceanic plate, are considerably smaller. The main plates making up North and South America are shown in Figure 2.3. Sea-floor spreading, shown in Figure 2.3 at the Mid-Atlantic ridge, is separating North and South America from Europe and Africa. The pushing apart of these plates creates movement in other parts of the globe, causing other plates to collide.

The Juan de Fuca plate, off the west coast of British Columbia, is an oceanic plate in collision with a continental plate (Fig. 2.4). The thinner but heavier oceanic plate is forced down and under the thicker but lighter continental plate in a process called **subduction**. The major subduction zones for North and South America are shown in Figure 2.3. The subducting plate forms a trench in the ocean floor that can be up to five kilometres deep. As the plate subducts deeper, it becomes warmer until eventually the temperature is high enough for some of the plate to melt. If enough magma is produced, it will flow upwards towards the crust, producing volcanic eruptions at the surface.

The various movements of plates—separating, sliding past each other, or colliding—are the forces responsible for mountain-building. Some mountains are the product of volcanic eruptions in subduction zones. Others, including chains such as the Rockies, are formed through compression, which folds flat-lying sediments into towering mountains. In other regions mountains are created through faulting, in which the tectonic pressure fractures the brittle rock of the crust and forces one side to be lifted, or thrown over the other, producing cliffs and sharp walls of rock. Another type of tectonic movement can cause fragments of crust (oceanic, continental, or both), known as terranes, to collide with a section of continental crust, resulting in folding, faulting, and uplifting of the edge of the crust.

Tectonic activity and weathering have gone on for hundreds of millions, even billions, of years. Glaciation, however, is a relatively recent phenomenon. In the past 1.5 million years there have been four glacial periods, each lasting approximately 100,000 years, when large expanses of Europe, Asia, and North America were covered by vast sheets of ice. The last glacial age ended roughly 12,000 years ago.

During these periods of glaciation huge accumulations of ice 1,500 to 2,000 metres in height covered most of Canada; the only exceptions were the upper levels of the Cypress Hills (on the southern border between Alberta and Saskatchewan), a portion of the Yukon, and perhaps the Queen Charlotte Islands and some of the Arctic.

As the ice sheets moved, they carved through the landscape like bulldozers, rounding off the tops of smaller mountains (under 2,000 metres) and scouring out the existing V-shaped river valleys and turning them into U-shapes. Nor did glacial movement end at the coastline: the scouring continued along the ocean floor. In the periods between the ice ages, when temperatures were considerably warmer, the glaciers melted,

Figure 2.3   Major oceanic and continental plates

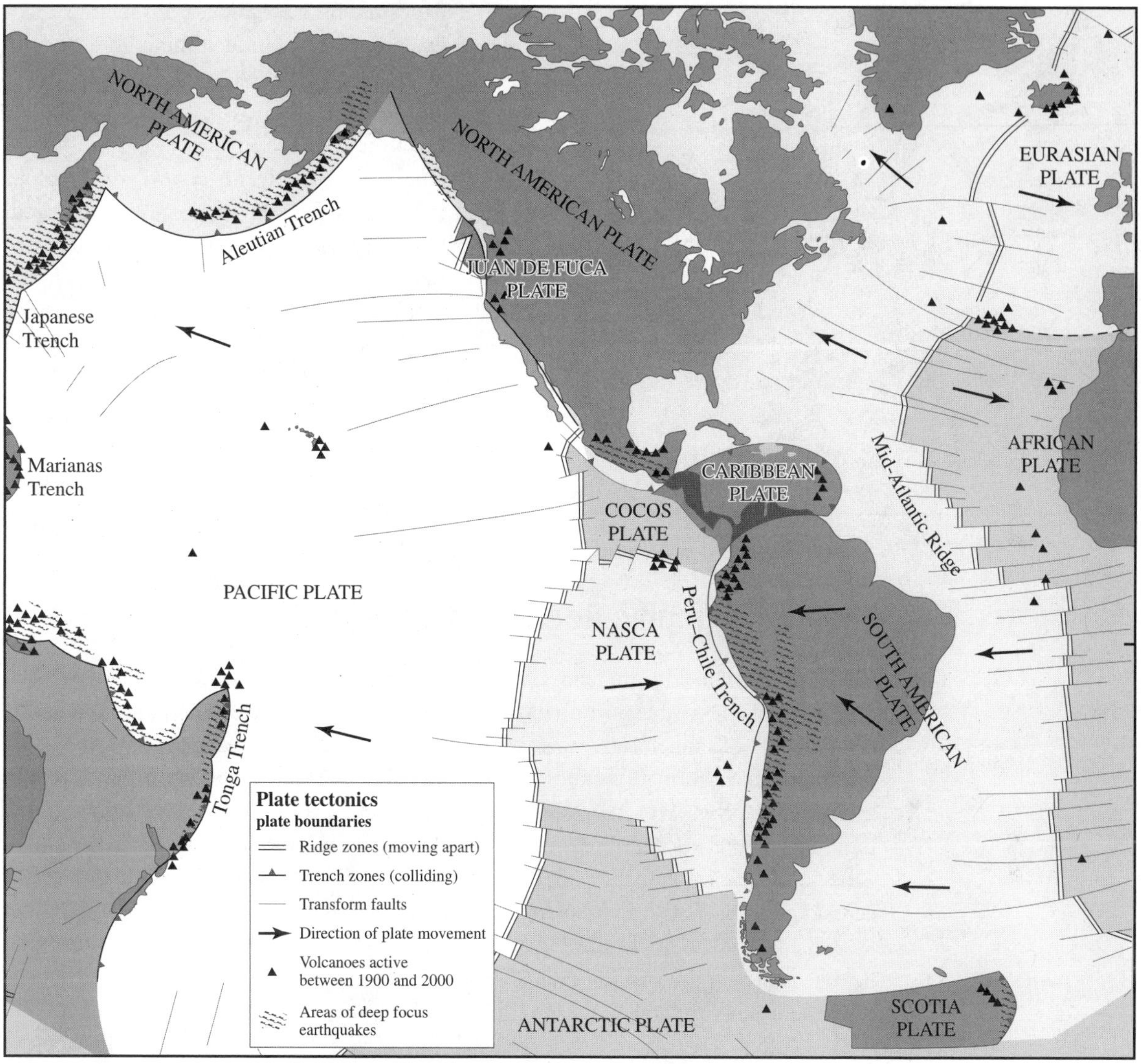

NORTH AMERICAN PLATE

NORTH AMERICAN PLATE

Aleutian Trench

JUAN DE FUCA PLATE

EURASIAN PLATE

Japanese Trench

AFRICAN PLATE

Mid-Atlantic Ridge

Marianas Trench

CARIBBEAN PLATE

COCOS PLATE

PACIFIC PLATE

NASCA PLATE

SOUTH AMERICAN PLATE

Peru–Chile Trench

Tonga Trench

Plate tectonics
plate boundaries

Ridge zones (moving apart)

Trench zones (colliding)

Transform faults

Direction of plate movement

Volcanoes active between 1900 and 2000

Areas of deep focus earthquakes

ANTARCTIC PLATE

SCOTIA PLATE

Source: Q. Stanford, ed., *Canadian Oxford World Atlas,* 5th edn (Toronto: Oxford University Press, 2003), 123.

causing sea levels to rise and large lakes to form, particularly in flat-lying regions such as the Prairies. At the same time the earth itself rose, in a process called **isostatic rebound**, once it was no longer pressed down by the weight of the glaciers. Together, glacial scouring and isostatic rebound created a coastal landscape of fjords—a significant asset for deep harbour ports and coastal navigation.

Glacial bulldozing was also responsible for several other common features of the Canadian landscape. Erratics are large boulders picked up and transported by glaciers; they are particularly obvious on flat landscapes. Moraines are large linear piles of unconsolidated sediments deposited around the edges of melting glaciers; some are several kilometres in length. Drumlins are smaller oval mounds formed under the glaciers.

isostatic rebound
the process in which land that has been compressed by the weight of glaciers rises again as the glaciers recede.

Figure 2.4   Subduction off the south coast of British Columbia

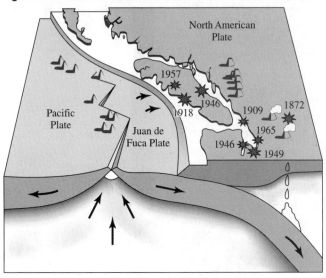

Source: Mines and Resources Canada, 'Geofacts: Earthquakes in Southwest British Columbia' (Geological Survey of Canada, n.d).

Eskers are long, narrow ridges, mainly of sand and gravel, deposited by the run-off from melting glaciers. Today, the glaciers found at the high elevations in alpine areas (such as the Cordilleran mountains) and the high Arctic are the last remnants of the ice that once covered the country.

In the far north, however, even in regions where the ice cover itself eventually disappeared, the ground that had been covered by glaciers remained almost entirely frozen to depths of as much as 400 metres. Only the topmost layer (1 to 4 metres) thaws and becomes 'active' for a brief period in the summer. Figure 2.5 shows the extent of glaciation in Canada in the Pleistocene era and today. In addition it distinguishes between the zone of continuous permafrost and the 'discontinuous' zone where permafrost occurs only in patches.

The Physiographic Regions of Canada

The Canadian Shield is the core on and around which the rest of the North American plate formed. The visible portion of the Shield covers roughly half the country, but in fact it is only part of a much larger formation. Surrounding the exposed area of the Shield are four more recent formations known as the Great Lakes–St Lawrence, Hudson, Arctic, and Interior Platforms (Fig. 2.6). While those platform regions were being formed, three mountain complexes emerged on their peripheries, adding continental crust to the North American plate: the Appalachian, Innuitian, and Cordilleran ranges. Finally, the most recent additions were three continental or oceanic shelves: the Atlantic, Arctic, and Pacific.

The Canadian Shield was formed during the Precambrian epoch; some of its rock has been dated at 3.96 billion years (Statistics Canada, 2003). By the end of the Precambrian, some 545 million years ago, the Shield had become what is called a craton—a stable geologic formation. But it took billions of years to reach that state. In fact, the Canadian Shield began as an amalgam of many high mountain ranges formed and cemented together at different stages by many different tectonic processes over that vast expanse of time. For this reason the Shield is an extremely complex geological formation, containing many different kinds of rock—mainly igneous and metamorphic, but also sedimentary. One of its most interesting components, visible in belts throughout the region, is greenstone: old, mainly metamorphosed sedimentary and igneous rock that is greenish in colour and high in metals such as gold, silver, nickel, copper, and iron.

Over further billions of years, weathering and erosion reduced towering mountains to what are now mostly rolling hills. The outer rim of the Shield is highest at the Torngat Mountains (Mont d'Iberville, 1,729 metres) on the boundary between northern Quebec and Labrador; much of Ontario is less than 700 metres high. There is little soil for agriculture, although forests of pine and spruce grow as far north as climatic conditions allow (see p. 43 below). Thousands of lakes connected by rivers and streams make the Shield region ideal habitat for fur-bearing animals.

Figure 2.5   (a) Glaciation and permafrost zones; (b) Permafrost profile

(a)

Glaciation
- Present
- 15,000 years BP
- Unglaciated areas
- —— Southern limit of continuous permafrost
- - - - Southern limit of discontinuous permafrost

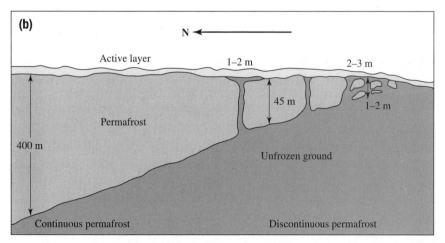

(b)

N ←——

Active layer

1–2 m   2–3 m

45 m   1–2 m

400 m   Permafrost

Unfrozen ground

Continuous permafrost   Discontinuous permafrost

Sources: Adapted from Q. Stanford, ed., *Canadian Oxford World Atlas,* 5th edn (Toronto: Oxford University Press, 2003), 12, 54.

Figure 2.6   Physiographic regions of Canada

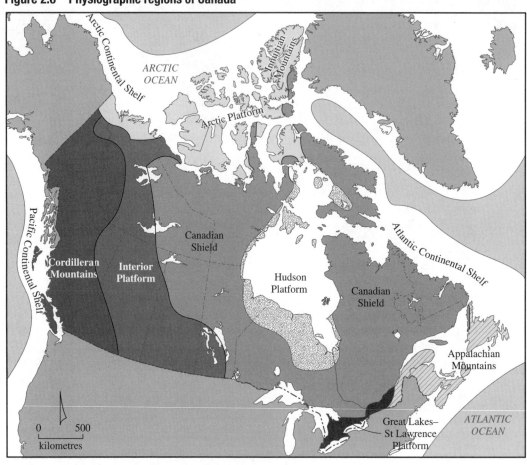

Source: Adapted from R. Bone, *The Regional Geography of Canada* (Toronto: Oxford University Press, 2005), 46.

Surrounding the Shield are four distinct 'platforms' of sediments left behind after the outermost portions of the Shield were submerged by shallow seas at various times. When those seas retreated, at different stages in the last 545 million years, they left behind sediments that eventually stabilized as separate physiographic regions.

At the centre of the craton is the Hudson Platform, a region encompassing Foxe Basin, James Bay, Hudson Bay, and the Hudson Bay Lowlands, into which the rivers of the surrounding uplands flow. The product of post-glacial flooding, most of this platform was covered by water (known as the Tyrrell Sea), and it is only within the past 8,000 years that isostatic rebound has caused the Hudson Bay Lowlands to emerge—a process that continues today. This is exceedingly swampy land and difficult for humans to navigate, but excellent wildlife habitat.

To the south of the Shield is the Great Lakes–St Lawrence Platform. Although this is the smallest of the four platforms, it is the one where the majority of Canadians live. With the melting of the glaciers the St Lawrence Lowlands were inundated by what is known as the Champlain Sea. Isostatic rebound played a significant role in this region, uplifting the Great Lakes and reversing the drainage pattern so that instead of flowing south into the Mississippi system they flow northeast to the St Lawrence. Various layers of sediment have resulted in fertile soils that support deciduous as well as coniferous forests, and where the forests have been cleared, the land is ideal for agriculture.

To the north and west of the Shield is the Arctic Platform. This broad region consists largely of islands—including Banks, Victoria, and King William, and parts of Somerset, Ellesmere, and Baffin—and the ocean floor under the waterways between them. This platform consists mainly of flat-lying sedimentary layers in which deposits of oil and gas are known to exist, particularly in the northerly Sverdrup Basin. Relatively few species live in this cold, treeless permafrost zone, and human settlement is limited.

The fourth region is the Interior Platform, sometimes called the Great Interior Plains. Bordering the western and southern edges of the Canadian Shield, this vast platform covers much of the North American continent. Within Canada's borders, the layering of sediments began in the east and gradually moved west, with corresponding increases in elevation. Three distinct Prairie plains are identifiable. The First Prairie Plain, or Manitoba Plain, is the oldest and the lowest in elevation (approximately 300 metres). Although elevations begin to rise in the western portion, most of the Manitoba Plain is very flat, especially in the south; at the end of the last glacial age, this region was covered by an enormous lake known as Lake Agassiz. The Second Prairie Plain (Saskatchewan Plain) rises to approximately 600 metres and continues north to include northern Alberta, the Peace River region of British Columbia, and the Mackenzie corridor. Finally, the Third Prairie Plain (Alberta Plain) is the most recent and the highest in elevation, at about 1,000 metres.

At various periods in geologic history the climate of the Interior Plains was actually tropical and supported many kinds of plants and animals whose remains were eventually buried in different layers of sediments. As a consequence, the Devonian layer (408 to 360 million years ago) is rich in deposits of oil and natural gas, while the Cretaceous layer (146 to 65 million years ago) contains coal and, in northern Alberta, tar sands. At other

The Badlands near Drumheller, Alberta. Fossilized remains of more than 30 dinosaur species have been found in this region. *Photo B. McGillivray.*

times the Interior Plains were covered by warm shallow seas, which left behind sedimentary evaporates such as salt, potash, and gypsum.

The landscape of the Interior Platform has been profoundly affected by glaciation. The giant bulldozers of ice moved huge quantities of material known as **till**—from boulders to gravel, sand, clay, and silt—which they deposited as moraines. As the continental ice sheets of the last glacial period receded, only 12,000 years ago, numerous lakes formed, some large (e.g., Lake Agassiz) and some small. Many of these glacial lakes overflowed their banks and became spillways that carved deep channels out of the soft sedimentary layers. Only the Cypress Hills, spanning the border between Alberta and Saskatchewan, were not affected by glaciation. Here in the south the ice sheet was not nearly as thick as it was in the north, and the more elevated areas, or nunataks, remained free of ice, becoming places of refuge for a variety of plants (including lodgepole pine and fescue grass), birds, and mammals (including the pronghorn antelope).

To the east of the Shield are the Appalachian Mountains. Though not as ancient as the Shield, this region is still very old, formed between 600 and 400 million years ago when tectonic pressures brought together pieces of continental and oceanic crust. A complex geological region of mountains, valleys, uplands, lowlands, and submerged land, it includes Quebec's Gaspé region, where the highest mountain is Mont Jacques-Cartier (1,268 metres); all three Maritime provinces; the Gulf of St Lawrence (including the Îles de la Madeleine); and most of Newfoundland (the exception is a thin strip on the western edge of the island that contains ancient Shield rock). During the Carboniferous period (360 to 280 million years ago) great forests grew here that were later covered by sediments. Over time, the compacted vegetation was transformed into the coal that would become a cornerstone of the economies of Nova Scotia and New Brunswick. This landscape was subject to repeated periods of glaciation, which rounded off its mountains, created fjords, and deposited glacial till.

till
unconsolidated sediments—from clay to boulders—deposited by ice sheets.

The Tablelands in Gros Morne National Park, in western Newfoundland, were formed when tectonic forces pushed a section of the Earth's mantle to the surface.   *Photo B. McGillivray.*

In the far north, Ellesmere, Axel Heiberg, and Devon Islands are the visible portions of the Innuitian Mountains. Although covered in a permanent ice cap, these mainly folded sedimentary mountains exceed 2,500 metres in elevation. The tectonic activity that initiated the folding of sedimentary layers began some 400 to 350 million years ago; much more recently (approximately 65 million years ago) major volcanic activity put additional pressure on existing structures, creating 'effective traps' for deposits of oil and gas that were explored in the 1970s and 1980s but so far have not been exploited. The Cordilleran Mountains, which make up the westernmost portion of the Canadian land mass, may be the most complex geologic structure of all. Along the eastern edge are the Rocky Mountains (Mount Robson, 3,954 metres) and, farther north and marking the border between Yukon and the Northwest Territories, the Mackenzie Mountains (Keele Peak, 2,975 metres). To the west of these spectacular ranges are other north–south chains, including the Rockies and the Coast Range, which contains Canada's highest mountain (Mount Logan, Yukon, at 5,959 metres). These two ranges are separated by plateaus consisting of lava over top of sedimentary layers. Finally, the westernmost range consists of the Insular Mountains on Vancouver Island and the Queen Charlottes. The geologic complexity of this region is the product of many tectonic processes, some of which continue today.

In early geologic time, the sedimentary layers of the Interior Platform, which include the fossilized remains of vegetation and marine animals, were covered by a shallow sea that extended to the interior of British Columbia. Then, about 170 million years ago, tectonic forces pushed a series of islands lying to the west of the North American plate eastward, joining these islands (**terranes**) to the continental crust. The collision created the Columbia and Omineca Mountain chains (exposing ancient craton rock) and began the process of lifting the sedimentary layers of the Rocky Mountains and draining the shallow sea. By approximately 85 million years ago, a second set of terranes was attached to the continent, and the force of the collision pushed the Rockies even higher (Cameron, 2003). These forces of compression were the product of subduction in a zone east of the Juan de Fuca plate's present-day location off the coast of Vancouver Island. Over the 40 to 60 million years since that time, the Juan de Fuca plate has added many more terranes to the landscape of British Columbia, Yukon, and Alaska, and it is possible that more terranes will be added to the BC mainland in the future (Foster Learning, 1997–2004).

Meanwhile, the volcanic activity associated with subduction zones has also contributed to the mountain-building process. North of Vancouver Island, there is a transform fault where the plates are slipping past each other, but at the junction of British Columbia, Yukon, and Alaska, the oceanic plate again subducts under the continental plate and is actively pushing up the St Elias range—the highest mountains on the continent—'at the remarkable rate of 4 centimetres a year' (Cannings and Cannings, 2004: 25).

British Columbia and much of Yukon are vertical landscapes that, along with Alaska, have been added to the North American plate at various stages in geologic time. The accretion (adding on) of terranes formed individually at different times resulted in folding, faulting, and compaction of earlier continental margins (Fig. 2.7). The mountains of the Cordillera are the youngest in Canada, and therefore the weathering and erosion processes have had relatively little time to wear them down. Nevertheless, the bulldozer effect of glaciation is evident throughout the region, rounding off mountains under 2,500 metres, and creating U-shaped valleys, moraines, erratics, and fjords. The Cordillera is rich in metals (including gold) and hydrocarbons (oil and gas).

terrane

a fragment of an oceanic or continental plate that has been attached to an adjacent continental plate. Terranes consist of rock with a distinctive structure and geological history, and are separated from the surrounding rock by faultlines.

Figure 2.7   Cordilleran terranes and major fault lines

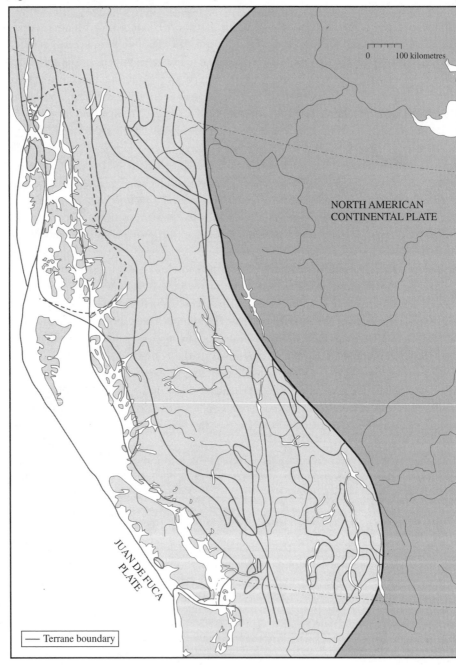

Sources: Adapted from S. Cannings and R. Cannings, *British Columbia: A Natural History* (Vancouver: Greystone, 2004), 15; E.J. Tarbuck and F.K. Lutgens, *The Earth: An Introduction to Physical Geology,* 4th edn (New York: Macmillan, 1992), 531.

continental shelves
shallow offshore ledges formed by sediments washed into the ocean from the adjacent land

The last three physiographic regions are the **continental shelves** off the Atlantic, Arctic, and Pacific coasts. These are shallow oceanic ledges or terraces formed by sediments washed into the water from the adjacent land. The Atlantic Shelf, which includes the Grand Banks, stretching some 480 kilometres off Newfoundland, is relatively young, formed after the North American plate separated from the European plate some

200 million years ago. The Arctic Shelf does not extend so far offshore, but is very shallow. The Pacific Shelf is unusually narrow, because ongoing subduction activity in the area continues to return oceanic crust to molten form. The sediments of all three continental shelves contain layers of hydrocarbons.

Weather and Climate

Weather is the set of atmospheric conditions—including temperature, precipitation (rain, snow, or hail), wind, and cloud cover—in a particular place at a particular time. **Climate** is the general pattern of such conditions over the long term. This section will examine the atmospheric processes that influence the climate of any region, beginning with the circulation of air (Fig. 2.8).

The driving force behind weather and climate variations throughout the world is the radiation generated by the sun. Solar radiation is most intense at the equator, where it causes huge volumes of air to rise thousands of metres. Meanwhile, at the surface, this

Figure 2.8 The global circulation of air

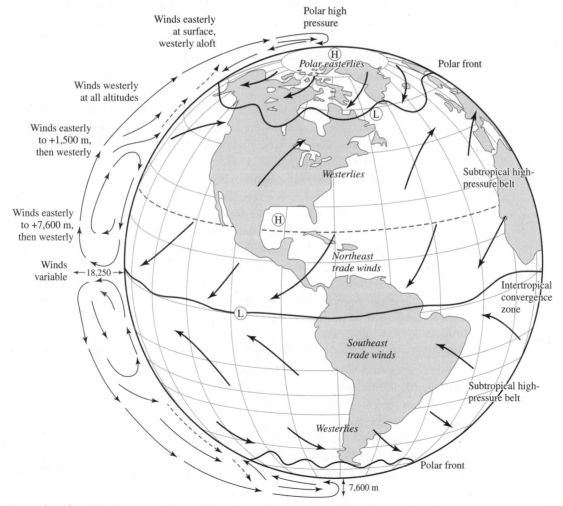

Source: Adapted from J. Welsted, J. Everitt, and C. Stadel, *The Geography of Manitoba: Its Land and Its People* (Winnipeg: University of Manitoba Press, 1996).

displacement creates a low-pressure zone that is characterized by precipitation: as the warm moist air rises, it expands and cools, causing clouds and condensation to form. High above the surface, the rising air diverges to the north and south poles. At latitudes approximately 30 degrees north and south of the equator, these air masses descend and compress, producing high-pressure zones. These subtropical high-pressure belts are the driest regions of the world.

Air moves from high-pressure regions toward low-pressure regions. Thus some of that descending air moves back along the surface towards the low-pressure zone at the equator, although some continues moving towards the pole. The surface air mass then collides with an air mass driven towards the equator from the polar high-pressure zone. Where these collisions take place, a low-pressure zone is produced, referred to as a polar front. Thousands of metres (9 to 12 kilometres) above the polar front is a high-velocity, easterly moving wind known as the jet stream.

The locations of high- and low-pressure regions change with the seasons of the year, especially in countries (like Canada) located towards the poles. On the summer solstice (21–22 June) the sun is directly over the Tropic of Cancer, whereas on the winter solstice (21–22 December) it is over the Tropic of Capricorn. This seasonal shift modifies the latitudinal location of high- and low-pressure zones shown in Figure 2.8: in the northern hemisphere, the high-pressure zone shifts north in summer and south in winter.

High- and low-pressure zones are also responsible for wind, because air will always flow from a high-pressure zone to a low-pressure zone until the two reach a state of equilibrium. However, because the earth is a sphere rotating from west to east (counter-clockwise when viewed from the north pole), winds moving over its surface are deflected to the right in the northern hemisphere (to the left in the southern); this effect is known as the Coriolis force. Thus as air masses move from the mid-latitude high-pressure zone to the polar-front, low-pressure zone, most Canadians experience the winds commonly called westerlies. This is the prevailing wind pattern for most of Canada except the far north, where the Arctic high-pressure winds (polar easterlies) move in the opposite direction (Fig. 2.9).

The prevailing wind patterns shown in Figure 2.9 are influenced by flows of air between high- and low-pressure zones, the rotation of the earth, and the seasons of the year. During summer in the northern hemisphere, the days are longer, the sun is higher in the sky, and the jet stream of the polar front shifts northward. During the winter there is less sun and the jet stream shifts southward.

The world is made up of large continents and even larger oceans, which are much slower to heat up and cool down than the continents. The description of climates as either maritime or continental is a reflection of this difference. Communities such as Vancouver and Halifax, which are close to large bodies of water, are said to have a maritime climate, characterized by relatively low summer temperatures and relatively mild winter temperatures. Communities such as Edmonton and Winnipeg, by contrast, have continental climates, with much greater extremes between summer and winter.

Ocean currents also play a role in determining temperature, particularly in coastal areas. On Canada's east coast, the Labrador Current flowing out of Davis Strait brings cold water (and icebergs) down the coast of Labrador to Newfoundland and the Maritimes. As a result, winters are colder on the east coast than they are at similar latitudes on the west coast, where a much warmer current flows across the Pacific from Japan and circulates up the coast to Alaska.

Figure 2.9   Air masses

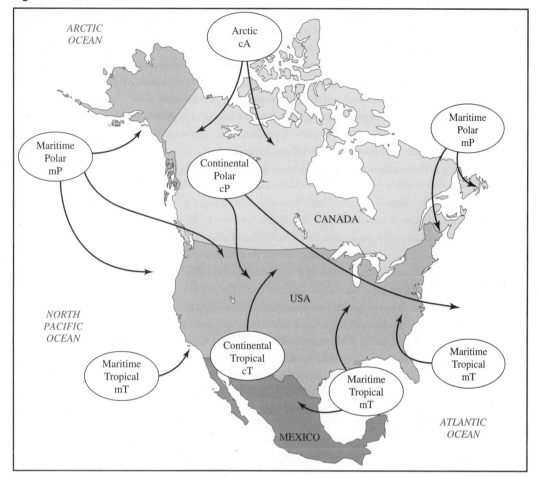

Sources: Adapted from E. Aguado and J.E. Burt, *Understanding Weather & Climate*, 3rd edn (Upper Saddle River, NJ: Prentice Hall, 2004), 267; and F.K. Lutgens and E.J. Tarbuck, *The Atmosphere: An Introduction to Meteorology*, 8th edn (Upper Saddle River, NJ: Prentice Hall, 2001), 202, 222.

Another important influence on weather and climate is latitude, which affects both temperature and precipitation and produces great variations between communities in southern Canada and those in the North. The distance from the southernmost point in Ontario to the northern tip of Ellesmere Island is more than 4,600 kilometres, and this makes a considerable difference to the length of daylight hours: from the Arctic Circle (66.5°) north to the pole there are 24 hours of daylight on the summer solstice and 24 hours of darkness on the winter solstice, whereas southern Ontario will have 16 and 9 hours of daylight on the same dates. Different latitudes also experience wide variations in the angle of the sun—hence the intensity of incoming solar radiation—over the year. Allowing 23.5° for the tilt of the earth, the angle of the sun for Inuvik (68°N) at noon on the summer solstice is 45.5° ($90° - 68° + 23.5° = 45.5°$) whereas on the same day in Toronto (44°N) the sun is at 69.5° ($90° - 44° + 23.5° = 69.5°$). On the winter solstice there is no daylight at Inuvik, but the angle of the sun for Toronto at noon is 22.5° ($90° - 44° - 23.5° = 22.5°$).

Topography is another significant climatic factor, particularly in regions such as the Cordillera, where high mountains force the prevailing westerly air mass to rise and then descend into the river valleys. These are the same westerly air masses that descend the east side of the Rockies to produce the chinook winds (see p. 43 below) in Alberta. Mountainous topography can also present a barrier to the movement of air masses. For example, the Rockies often serve as a barrier preventing the polar easterlies that bring frigid Arctic air south in the winter from entering the interior of British Columbia. Bodies of water such as the Great Lakes are large enough to moderate the climate of the surrounding area in the same way that the oceans influence the adjacent land.

The map in Figure 2.10 divides Canada into seven climatic regions, while Table 2.2 designates a community for each zone and lists its average monthly temperature, average monthly precipitation, and annual average of growing degree-days (a measure of the growing season; see p. 42 below). In the Pacific region, Vancouver's relatively high

Figure 2.10   Climatic regions of Canada

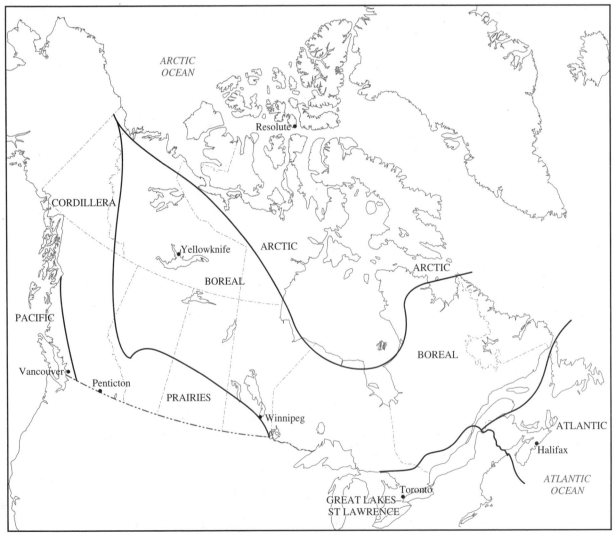

Source: Adapted from K. Hare and J. Thomas, *Climate Canada* (Toronto: John Wiley, 1974).

Table 2.2 Climate data for selected Canadian communities (averages), 1971–2000

Vancouver, UBC: Latitude: 49°15′N; Longitude: 123°15′W; Elevation: 76.00 m

	J	F	M	A	M	J	J	A	S	O	N	D	Year
T	3.6	4.9	6.6	9.1	12.3	14.7	16.9	17.1	14.5	10.3	6.1	3.8	10.0
P	162.7	137.5	121.9	89.6	68.3	55.5	39.3	48.1	58.6	113.6	198.9	183.5	1277.4
>5°	23.6	32.8	59.6	122.3	224.9	291.7	367.6	373.5	285.2	165.0	56.0	24.6	2026.8

Penticton: Latitude: 49°27′N; Longitude: 119°36′W; Elevation: 344.10 m

	J	F	M	A	M	J	J	A	S	O	N	D	Year
T	−1.7	0.7	4.7	9.0	13.6	17.4	20.4	20.1	14.9	8.7	3.1	−1.1	9.2
P	26.8	22.5	22.3	26.6	37.3	38.9	27.9	30.7	24.7	19.7	27.1	28.4	332.7
>5°	2.0	5.8	32.7	123.2	267.5	371.3	477.9	467.9	296.7	123.6	26.1	3.1	2197.8

Winnipeg: Latitude: 49°55′N; Longitude: 97°13′W; Elevation: 238.70 m

	J	F	M	A	M	J	J	A	S	O	N	D	Year
T	−17.8	−13.6	−6.1	4.0	12.0	17.0	19.5	18.5	12.3	5.3	−5.3	−14.4	2.6
P	19.7	14.9	21.5	31.9	58.8	89.5	70.6	75.1	52.3	36.0	25.0	18.5	513.7
>5°	0.0	0.0	1.7	58.7	225.1	359.9	450.5	418.0	221.9	66.5	4.1	0.0	1806.3

Toronto: Latitude: 43°40′N; Longitude: 79°24′W; Elevation: 112.50 m

	J	F	M	A	M	J	J	A	S	O	N	D	Year
T	−4.2	−3.2	1.3	7.6	14.2	19.2	22.2	21.3	17.0	10.6	4.8	−0.9	9.2
P	61.2	50.5	66.1	69.6	73.3	71.5	67.5	79.6	83.4	64.7	75.7	71.0	834.0
>5°	2.2	2.8	24.1	102.3	285.3	424.4	533.0	506.1	360.0	177.4	49.4	7.2	2474.0

Halifax, International Airport: Latitude: 44°52′N; Longitude: 63°31′W; Elevation: 145.40 m

	J	F	M	A	M	J	J	A	S	O	N	D	Year
T	−6.0	−5.6	−1.4	4.0	9.8	15.0	18.6	18.4	14.1	8.3	3.1	−2.8	6.3
P	149.2	114.4	134.5	118.3	109.7	98.3	102.2	92.7	103.6	128.7	146.0	154.8	1452.2
>5°	1.6	1.3	3.9	29.4	152.1	299.5	420.7	416.4	272.3	112.9	31.1	5.2	1746.3

Yellowknife: Latitude: 62°27′N; Longitude: 114°26′W; Elevation: 205.70 m

	J	F	M	A	M	J	J	A	S	O	N	D	Year
T	−26.8	−23.4	−17.3	−5.3	5.6	13.5	16.8	14.2	7.1	−1.7	−13.8	−23.7	−4.6
P	14.1	12.9	13.4	10.8	19.1	26.9	35.0	40.9	32.9	35.0	23.5	16.3	280.7
>5°	0.0	0.0	0.0	4.0	76.3	253.8	364.9	286.6	87.8	3.6	0.0	0.0	1077.0

Resolute: Latitude: 74°43′N; Longitude: 94°58′W; Elevation: 67.40 m

	J	F	M	A	M	J	J	A	S	O	N	D	Year
T	−32.4	−33.1	−30.7	−22.8	−10.9	−0.1	4.3	1.5	−4.7	−14.9	−23.6	−29.2	−16.4
P	4.3	3.4	6.5	6.1	9.5	14.7	20.2	34.3	25.0	13.8	7.6	4.7	150.0
>5°	0.0	0.0	0.0	0.0	0.0	2.7	23.9	5.5	0.1	0.0	0.0	0.0	32.2

T: Average temperature in °C.

P: Average precipitation including rain and snowfall in mm.

>5°: Growing degree-days in excess of 5°C.

Source: Environment Canada, 'Canadian Climate Normals or Averages 1971–2000' ⟨http://www.weatheroffice.ec.gc.ca/canada_e.html⟩.

winter temperatures—above zero even in January—reflect the influence of westerly winds flowing over an ocean that is considerably warmer than the Atlantic. It is important to note the limitations of such mean data, however: mean monthly temperatures, for example, are calculated by recording the daily maximum and minimum temperatures and averaging these out over the month. In fact, Vancouver can experience much colder temperatures when a very strong Arctic front ('polar easterly') brings a cold air mass over the Rockies. Further, the figures in this set of data are averages over three decades (1971–2000). Thus the average temperature listed for Vancouver in August—barely over 17°—is considerably less than the daytime temperatures that most people living in the city experience.

In the Pacific region there are several influences on precipitation. The orographic effect occurs where saturated air is forced (pushed by westerly winds) to rise over mountains such as the Insular range on Vancouver Island or in the Coast range. Forcing the body of air up causes cooling and condensation, with the result that precipitation on the west coast of British Columbia often amounts to more than 3,000 millimetres per year. By contrast, in Vancouver the average annual precipitation (though still high compared to many other places) is only 1,277 mm—because of the rain shadow effect created by the mountains on Vancouver Island. The body of air forced up and over the mountains behaves like a saturated sponge that is squeezed as it rises, producing precipitation; however, when it descends down the east side of the mountains it warms up (the sponge expands) and is able to absorb and hold more moisture until it is once again forced to rise by the Coast Mountains to the east of Vancouver.

Vancouver receives considerably more precipitation in winter than in summer. This pattern is related to seasonal variations in the position of the wavy line representing the low-pressure zone of the polar front shown in Figure 2.8 (p. 37) and the high-pressure zone to the south of this line. In summer, when there is far greater incoming solar radiation, this line shifts mainly to the north of Vancouver, leaving the city under the influence of a high-pressure zone that usually means warm, sunny weather. In the winter the low-pressure zone of the polar front is far to the south, and as a result Vancouver experiences considerably more cloud and rain.

growing degree-days
a measure calculated from daily temperature averages and based on the assumption that plants need a minimum temperature of 5°c in order to grow. Thus if the average temperature for a day is 10°c, then that day is recorded as representing 5 growing-degree days.

Table 2.2 also includes the growing season as represented by **growing degree-days**. The greater the number of growing degree-days throughout the year, the greater the range of crops it is possible to grow in that location. This measure allows us to compare the seven communities with respect to climate conditions affecting agricultural capability. Vancouver's relatively mild climate means that the city enjoys more growing degree-days in the winter months than Penticton (in the Cordilleran climate region) or Toronto (Great Lakes–St Lawrence); yet the higher average summer temperatures in Penticton and Toronto mean that these locations have higher annual totals.

Located at the south end of the Okanagan Valley, Penticton is surrounded by mountains. Although its latitude is similar to Vancouver's, its elevation is somewhat higher. Temperatures in the winter fall below freezing, but relatively mild Pacific air masses tend to influence temperatures even this far inland, particularly in winter. Summer temperatures in Penticton are not moderated to the same extent, however, and therefore are considerably higher than in Vancouver.

A more significant contrast emerges with respect to precipitation. The Okanagan Valley, including Penticton, is on the eastern side of the Coast Mountains: thus the orographic effect has extracted most of the moisture out of the westerly flowing air masses before they descend into the valley. In winter there is plenty of snow for skiing in the surrounding mountains, but the valley itself is so dry that it is nearly a desert. Most of the precipitation that the Okanagan receives comes in summer, as a result of convection. In convection precipitation, the intense incoming solar energy in summer causes evaporation and transpiration, and this moisture cools as it rises, forming thunderheads and showers. Warm summer temperatures also give this region a fairly high total of growing degree-days for crops, although the limited precipitation makes irrigation a necessity.

The Prairie climate zone is truly continental. In winter there are no physical barriers to prevent frigid Arctic air masses from flowing far into the southern interior of North America. Overall, winters are cold, as the mean January temperature of Winnipeg indicates (keep in mind that Winnipeg's latitude is similar to that of Vancouver and Penticton). On the western Prairies, however, occasional 'chinook' winds (warm westerly winds descending the Rockies) can raise temperatures from −10°C 'to nearly 20° . . . in just a couple of hours' (Cornish, n.d.). Summers can be hot because of the tropical air masses coming up from the Gulf of Mexico. Although most of the Prairies are relatively dry, Winnipeg can receive a fair amount of precipitation in summer, mainly as a result of convection, although frontal precipitation also occurs. In frontal precipitation, a warm body of air collides with a cold one and the warm air is forced up, causing condensation and precipitation. Growing degree-days for Winnipeg are limited by cold weather from September until May.

Moving east, the next climate zone is the Great Lakes–St Lawrence. The most southerly region in Canada, it is subject to the same air masses as Winnipeg, but the moderating effect of the Great Lakes means that winter temperatures are not nearly so cold. Average summer temperatures are among the highest in Canada, and in Toronto the proximity of the Great Lakes means that high temperatures are usually accompanied by high humidity. Frontal precipitation gives a fairly even distribution throughout the year. Together, hot summers and only moderately cold winters give this region a large number of growing degree-days.

The Atlantic zone, like its Pacific counterpart, has a maritime climate. However, it receives air masses coming across the continent in addition to the maritime masses coming from the north (primarily in winter) and from the south (in summer). Because the Labrador Current is a much colder body of water than the Pacific Ocean, winter in Halifax is colder than in Toronto and much colder than in Vancouver, even though Halifax is considerably farther south than Vancouver. Summer temperatures in Halifax are slightly higher than in Vancouver. The combination of relatively cold winters and only moderately warm summers gives Halifax even fewer growing degree-days than Winnipeg. Much of Halifax's precipitation is frontal and occurs in the winter months.

The vast Boreal climate zone consists mainly of coniferous forest. Latitude is the biggest influence in this continental climatic regime, where solar radiation is severely restricted in the winter months, and the sharp angle of the sun during the brief period of daylight allows very little warming. The average temperature of Yellowknife in January (−32°C) indicates the presence of extremely cold Arctic air masses. In summer, by contrast, the warmth accumulated during the long hours of sunlight is enough for trees and other vegetation to grow. Yellowknife is relatively dry, although there is more precipitation in summer because the increased solar radiation allows convection precipitation to occur. Other parts of the Boreal climate region, especially those near Hudson Bay and James Bay, receive considerably more precipitation.

The last climate zone is the Arctic. Latitude plays a particularly important role in this region. From the Arctic Circle (66°33′N) to the pole there is no solar radiation at all for much of the winter. Because the Arctic Ocean is frozen in winter, the climate of Resolute (at nearly 75°N) is more continental than maritime, and temperatures are never very warm even though the region receives 24 hours of sunlight per day in the summer. At noon on the summer solstice, the angle of the sun is only 38.5°, and it is progressively reduced after that date. Solar radiation has to pass through a great quantity of the earth's atmosphere before striking the earth. Much of it is deflected, reflected, and absorbed on the way, and of the limited amount that does reach the Arctic surface, some is lost because it comes in at such a low angle and is deflected by the white surface of snow. By late spring enough solar energy does get through to melt the snow and the top layer of the earth, but growing degree-days are negligible, and the only plants that can grow under these conditions are a few specially adapted species such as lichens. In summer the sea-ice recedes and there is considerable moisture present for convection precipitation; however, as the data for Resolute indicate, this is a polar desert.

Vegetation and Soils

The connection between climate and vegetation is obvious, but soils, in combination with different slopes and elevations as well as other landscape features such as drainage, also help to shape Canada's natural vegetation regions. The basic ingredients of any soil are rock particles (produced through weathering) and decayed organic matter, along with air and water. Different types of rock and organic material, in different quantities and combinations, produce many different soil types.

The map in Figure 2.11 shows the country's major vegetation zones. Moving from west to east, the first zone is the narrow band of the Pacific Coast Forest. Here mild winters and plentiful moisture support the largest coniferous trees in Canada. Douglas fir, western hemlock, and western red cedar, along with some Sitka spruce and balsam fir, grow to enormous size in this region, where the forest industry has been an important part of the economy since the late 1800s.

Vegetation in the Western Mountain zone reflects differences in elevation, latitude, and moisture. The Subalpine Forest zone covers moderately high elevations in both the coastal and interior mountains. The most common trees in the coastal area are alpine fir, hemlock, and yellow cedar; in the interior, lodgepole pine and white and black spruce. At higher elevations, however, where climatic conditions are more extreme and soil is scarce, trees give way to Tundra plants such as mosses and lichens. At lower elevations the Montane Forest covers much of the south and central interior. Considerably drier than the coast, with much greater extremes in temperatures, this region is much more prone to forest fires. To the south, Ponderosa pine is the dominant species; to the north, various spruces. In the grasslands of the Interior plateau and arid southern valleys, sagebrush is now the most common vegetation, largely because the region's natural bunch grass has been overused for cattle grazing. The mountainous Kootenay region, which has considerably more moisture than the Montane Forest region, is characterized as Columbian Forest: here hemlock, cedar, and Douglas fir again appear, although they do not grow nearly so large as those on the coast. Many of the moist forest regions of Canada have podzolic soils, which are essentially acidic because of the needles from coniferous trees.

Figure 2.11 Vegetation regions of Canada

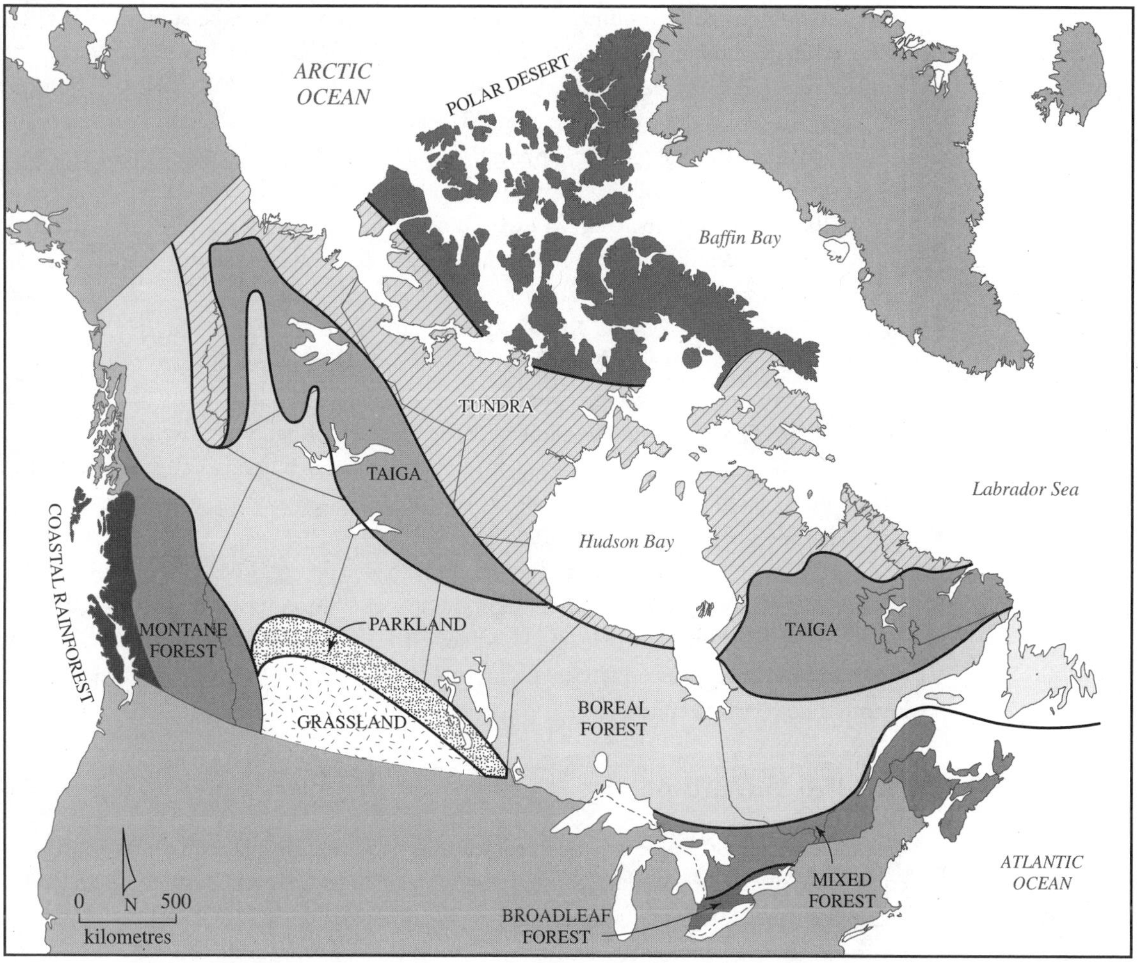

Source: Adapted from R. Bone, *The Regional Geography of Canada,* 3rd edn (Toronto: Oxford University Press, 2005), 68.

The Prairie region takes the form of an arc stretching from Alberta to southern Manitoba, with an outpost in the Peace River region of Alberta and British Columbia. Most of this region is grassland (the exception is the Park Belt, the transitional area between the Prairie and the Boreal Forest to the north). The Prairie has become known as the 'bread basket' of Canada because of its wheat production. The soil is generally chernozemic, although fertility is greatest in the moister northern regions and somewhat lower in the dry southern regions of Alberta and Saskatchewan. The northern slopes of the grasslands have stands of trembling aspen, while the Park Belt has forests of poplar, aspen, and birch interspersed with conifers (pine and spruce) in the north.

From southeastern Manitoba across the lower portion of Ontario and along the St Lawrence to the Maritimes is the Mixed Forest region (some classification systems treat the Maritimes as a separate 'Acadian' forest zone). Deciduous trees include aspen, maple, birch, beech, ash, and elm; the main conifers balsam fir and spruce, along with cedar in wetter regions and larch on sandy soils. For centuries, portions of this Mixed Forest zone have been logged for timber and cleared for agriculture.

A unique feature of southern Ontario is a small area that represents the northern-most extension of the Carolinian Forest. This zone begins far to the south and is characterized by a number of distinctly southern deciduous species such as 'tulip tree, cucumber tree, pawpaw, red mulberry, Kentucky coffee tree, sassafras, black oak and pin oak', with 'scattered . . . eastern white pine, Tamarack, eastern red cedar and eastern hemlock' (Canadian Forestry Association, n.d.). With an exceptional number of growing degree-days and good soil, this region is highly valued for agriculture.

To the north, the Sub-Arctic is a region of discontinuous permafrost and many rock outcroppings, covered by Boreal Forest: mainly conifers—white and black spruce, larch, jack pine, and balsam fir—with a few deciduous trees such as birch. The transitional zone between the Boreal and Arctic regions, known as the Taiga, is characterized by stunted trees (mainly spruce) and has been significantly modified by forest fires.

The Arctic is a treeless region of permafrost. Vegetation is limited to Tundra species: mosses, lichens, sedges, grasses, and shrubs. Soils are mainly cryosolic, with 'huge amounts of organic matter, mostly in the frozen subsoil where surface soil has been moved by frost action' (Saskatchewan Interactive, 2002). Farther still to the north, and in high elevations, there is year-round ice cap.

Not shown in Figure 2.11 are the wetlands that make up much of the Hudson Bay Lowlands and also occur in other vegetation zones throughout Canada. Consisting mainly of muskeg and peat bogs interspersed with both coniferous and deciduous trees, these areas are highly productive wildlife habitat, but in southern Canada many have been drained for agriculture.

Natural Hazards

The earlier parts of this chapter looked at the processes, from plate tectonics to the circulation of water and air, that over billions of years have formed Canada's natural landscape. The same forces continue to operate today, sometimes with serious consequences for the earth's human inhabitants. In 2004–5 alone, two events underlined the magnitude of those consequences: the tsunami, caused by an earthquake off the coast of Sumatra, that killed more than 200,000 people in the Indian Ocean, and the hurricane that devastated much of the US Gulf Coast, including the city of New Orleans. Although it has been suggested that the increasing frequency and severity of tropical storms may be partly attributable to human-induced global warming, in itself Hurricane Katrina was just as natural an event as the tsunami. 'Extreme' geophysical events such as hurricanes and tsunamis, earthquakes, floods, droughts, and landslides may be relatively rare, but they are still products of natural processes. It is only when they threaten human beings and their property that these phenomena become 'hazards' (see Fig. 2.12).

When a river overflows and washes away the community situated on its flood plain, is it the fault of the natural processes that caused the water to rise, or of the human use system that made the decision to build in that location? De Loë

Figure 2.12   Natural hazards model

suggests that the answer is clear: 'flooding is a hazard only because humans have chosen to occupy flood-vulnerable areas' (2000: 355).

Such decisions are not hard to understand. Historically, rivers offered not only transportation but irrigation, while river flood plains provided both fertile soil for agriculture and flat land for housing. When people decided to settle in these locations, however, the determining factors were usually economic; adequate attention was rarely paid to the physical conditions that cause floods. The larger the concentration of human inhabitants in any location, the greater the potential for harm as a result of natural hazards. Today, therefore, land-use planning is more urgent than ever.

Working on 'the assumption that nature could be controlled' (University of Toronto, 2002), humans have historically responded to natural hazards by looking for technological 'solutions'. Once it is recognized that a particular area is prone to flooding, for example, the most common reaction is to build a dike—even though the complex dynamics of river systems mean that diking technology is never infallible. Thus it is not enough to seek technological solutions: education is also essential, and regulations (e.g., zoning) may be required to reduce the numbers of people in hazardous locations.

Natural disasters, especially large and expensive ones, are commonly described as 'acts of God'. Insurance companies normally do not insure against them, and those affected usually count on government compensation as a matter of right. In this simplistic way, people put extreme geophysical events into a category of things that they have no control over—as if they had learned nothing from experience, knew nothing about physical processes, and bore no responsibility for their location decisions. The hazards model underlines the active role that human decisions play in creating a hazard, encouraging us to look beyond economic considerations to the natural/physical system and take whatever steps are necessary to reduce any risks to the lowest possible level.

Extreme geophysical events can be classified in three categories: tectonic, gravitational, and climatic. Earthquakes, volcanic eruptions, and tsunamis are tectonic events produced when crustal plates collide, subduct, or slide past one another. Gravitational hazards include snow avalanches, rock- and mudslides, and debris flows—any sort of surface material that can be discharged down slope under the force of gravity. Finally, climatic hazards arise from unusual weather conditions, whether too little moisture (drought) or too much (floods), lightning and forest fires, hail, ice storms, or violent winds (hurricanes and tornadoes). According to Environment Canada (2003), the most expensive natural disasters in Canada to date were as follows:

1. 2001–2 drought (British Columbia, Prairies, Ontario, Quebec, Nova Scotia): preliminary estimate, $5 billion.
2. 1998 ice storm (Ontario and Quebec): $4.2 billion.
3. 1979–80 drought (Prairies): $2.5 billion.
4. 1988 drought (Prairies): $1.8 billion.
5. 1984 drought (Prairies): $1 billion
6. 1996 flood (Saguenay, Quebec): $1 billion

The risks posed by geophysical events are not uniform across Canada. In Saskatchewan, for example, the chance of an earthquake is low and of an avalanche nonexistent, but the risks of tornadoes, snowstorms, and drought are quite high. The risk associated with a given event can be assessed in terms of five factors: magnitude (how

Table 2.3   Major flood events in the twentieth century

Year	Location	Year	Location
1928	Rideau, Chaudière, & Quyon R., Que.	1979	Red River, Man.
		1979	Dawson, Yukon
1937	London, Ont.	1980	Squamish River, BC
1948	Fraser River, BC	1986	N. Sask. River, Sask.
1950	Red River, Man.	1987	Montreal, Que.
1954	Toronto, Ont.	1989	Essex County, Ont.
1973	Saint John River, NB	1993	Canadian Midwest
1974	Grand R. & Cambridge, Ont.	1996	Saguenay River, Que.
1974	Prairies	1997	Red River, Man.

Sources: S.E. Brun, 'Atmospheric, Hydrologic and Geophysical Hazards', in 'Coping with Natural Hazards in Canada: Scientific, Government and Insurance Industry Perspectives' (1996) ⟨http://www.utoronto.ca/env/nh/tab2-11.htm⟩; and K. Hewitt, 'Safe Place or "Catastrophic Society"? Perspectives on Hazards and Disasters in Canada', *The Canadian Geographer* 44, 4 (Winter 2000): 331.

strong), frequency (how often), duration (how long it lasts), speed of onset (how much warning is possible), and spatial pattern (where it occurs). Analysis of spatial patterns that takes into account the magnitude and frequency of past events makes it possible to assess the statistical probability of particular events in particular places. Thus the Red River flood of 1997 is described as a '500-year flood', meaning that a flood of that magnitude may be expected to occur only once in 500 years.

The risk of flood is fairly high across the country because most communities are located near water (Table 2.3). As well, there are many physical reasons for flooding to occur. Many of the floods listed in Table 2.3 resulted from the spring snowmelt and ice jams that caused water to overtop river banks; the Red River in Manitoba is particularly susceptible to spring floods of this kind. By contrast, flash floods are the result of intense precipitation, such as occurred in the Saguenay River region in 1996, when 290 millimetres of rain fell in less than 36 hours, causing approximately $1 billion in damages and at least ten deaths (Natural Resources Canada, 2004). Toronto experienced disastrous flash flooding in 1954 as a result of Hurricane Hazel, in which 81 people died and 'damages were estimated at $25 million [$146.9 million in 1998 dollars]' (Environment Canada, 2000). Tsunamis and storm surges threaten communities in coastal locations.

Most communities subject to flooding have flood plain maps available through joint provincial and federal government programs. Identifying the regions at highest risk, these maps can be very helpful in planning appropriate preventive and corrective measures. Most flood-prone regions have constructed diking systems, which—if properly built and maintained—can be effective in combatting this hazard. Winnipeg, for example, has a floodway, or canal, that diverts water around the city. Other measures include watershed management to reduce the rate of snowmelt, dams on rivers, zoning that restricts development and, in some areas, regulations requiring that houses and other structures be built with flood-resistant materials. Global warming obviously increases the risk of flooding for coastal communities, where a one-metre rise in ocean levels could spell disaster.

Four of the six most expensive disasters in Canada have involved drought. Inadequate moisture has always posed a risk for farmers, especially on the Prairies but also in the south-central interior of British Columbia and southern Ontario (Gardner, 1976: 52), and today global warming is only increasing that risk. The fact that the southern Prairies on average receive only 300 to 400 millimetres of precipitation per year makes this region semi-arid and therefore marginal for agriculture from the start. What is worse is that precipitation there has often fallen short of the expected average: 'In the past 200 years, 40 severe droughts have occurred in western Canada' (Brun, 1996). The problem of drought is compounded on the Prairies by wind, which not only dries the soil but can blow the topsoil away.

Of course farmers cannot do anything to change the weather itself. But there are many corrective and preventative measures they can take to reduce the risk that drought

The low elevation of Tuktoyaktuk, NWT, makes this small community vulnerable to any rise in sea level. *Photo B. McGillivray.*

poses to their crops. They can erect snow fences to trap vital moisture for spring planting; they can plant shelter belts of trees to act as windbreaks; and they can create 'dugouts'—ponds to collect groundwater for animals and irrigation. There are also farming practices that conserve moisture, such as summer fallow (planting only every second year), zero-tillage (planting without turning the soil over), conservation tillage (leaving crop residue such as straw on the ground as a protective covering), and crop diversification. Agriculture and Agri-Foods Canada provides an information service during the growing season, including digital satellite data, information on the probability of precipitation for various regions, and historical data, including maps (Agriculture and Agri-Food Canada, 2004).

Drought is not the only weather-related hazard in Canada. Ice storms have affected all regions from time to time, causing power outages and making roads too icy to drive. The worst ice storm on record, however, was the one that hit Quebec and eastern Ontario in 1998. 'Over a period of six days 100mm of freezing rain fell intermittently. As a result more than 4 million Canadians were displaced and nearly three million households were without electricity' (Institute for Catastrophic Loss Reduction, 2004). Bringing down not only power lines but major transmission towers, the 1998 storm set off a chain reaction in which other 'essential infrastructures'—including 'telecommunications, transportation, the banking and financial system, [and] drinking-water supplies' also were unable to function (Nicolet Commission Report, 2001). As well, the 1998 ice storm was responsible for 30 deaths.

In its report on the event, the Nicolet Commission made a number of technical recommendations regarding power transmission and urged the Quebec government to establish an emergency preparedness policy for communities to follow in dealing with immediate needs, such as organizing communications, transportation, shelters, food and

Table 2.4   Canada's worst tornadoes

- Regina, Saskatchewan, 30 June 1912: 28 dead, hundreds injured
- Edmonton, Alberta, 31 July 1987: 27 dead, hundreds injured
- Windsor, Ontario, 17 June 1946: 17 dead, hundreds injured
- Pine Lake, Alberta, 14 July 2000: 12 dead, 140 injured
- Valleyfield, Quebec, 16 August 1888: 9 dead, 14 injured
- Windsor, Ontario, 3 April 1974: 9 dead, 30 injured
- Barrie, Ontario, 31 May 1985: 8 dead, 155 injured
- Sudbury, Ontario, 20 August 1970: 6 dead, 200 injured
- St-Rose, Quebec, 14 June 1892: 6 dead, 26 injured
- Buctouche, New Brunswick, 6 August 1879: 5 dead, 10 injured

Source: Environment Canada, 'Tornadoes' (http://www.mb.ec.gc.ca/air/summersevere/ae00s02.en.html).

water supplies, and medical aid and facilities. It is equally important that individual citizens be prepared to cope for some time without the services they normally take for granted.

Other weather-related disasters include forest fires, hailstorms, and tornadoes. In the summer of 2003 alone, fires started by lightning strikes and human carelessness in British Columbia resulted in more than $500 million in damages. Crop damage caused by hailstorms amounts to millions of dollars every year. And according to Environment Canada (2004), 'during an average year, 80 tornadoes cause two deaths and 20 injuries, plus tens of millions of dollars in property damage'; for Canada's worst tornadoes, see Table 2.4 and Figure 2.13. In winter, large accumulations of snow in the high mountains of the Cordillera often generate avalanches, which have claimed more lives in British Columbia than any other natural hazard (Fig. 2.13).

Figure 2.13 and Table 2.5 offer an overview of earthquake activity in Canada. Earthquakes of up to five to six on the Richter scale are not uncommon in the Great Lakes–St Lawrence and Maritime regions. The far north has also experienced quakes, some exceeding magnitude seven, although the small population in this region means that the risk for humans is relatively low. On the east coast, the 1929 Grand Banks earthquake generated a tsunami that killed 28 people on the Burin Peninsula of Newfoundland. And in 1964 Port Alberni, on Vancouver Island, was seriously damaged by a tsunami that followed a major earthquake in Alaska, although no one was killed.

As Table 2.5 shows, the west coast has experienced several earthquakes of catastrophic magnitude in the last century. Today there is increasing concern that subduction of the Juan de Fuca plate could result in a mega-thrust quake exceeding nine on the Richter scale (Heaton and Hartzell, 1987; Charlwood and Atkinson, 1983; Koppel, 1989; Mayse, 1992). A documentary called *Quake Hunters* (Raincoast, 1998) identifies the date of the last mega-thrust quake—26 January 1700—and points out that a similar event can be expected once every 300 to 800 years.

Although earthquakes cannot be predicted in time to permit evacuation, statistical probability can be calculated. In addition, it is known that greater movement can be expected of structures located on unconsolidated till than of those situated on bedrock.

Table 2.5   Significant earthquakes in Canada since 1900

#	Year	Magnitude	Location	#	Year	Magnitude	Location
1	2004	6.8	N. of Queen Charlotte Is., BC	9	1946	7.3	Vancouver Is., BC
2	1989	6.3	Ungava, Que.	10	1944	5.6	Cornwall, Ont.
3	1988	5.9	Saguenay, Que.	11	1935	6.2	Que.–Ont. border
4	1985	6.6, 6.9	Nahanni, NWT	12	1933	7.3	Baffin Bay, NWT
5	1982	5.7 & 5.4	Miramichi, NB	13	1929	7.2	Atlantic, S. of Nfld
6	1979	7.2	S. Yukon	14	1929	7.0	S. of Queen Charlotte Is., BC
7	1970	7.4	S. of Queen Charlotte Is., BC	15	1925	6.2	Charlevoix, Que.
8	1949	8.1	Queen Charlotte Is., BC	16	1918	7.0	Vancouver Is., BC

Source: Natural Resources Canada, 'Major Earthquakes in Canada—20th century', 2003 (http://www.seismo.nrcan.gc.ca/major_eq/majoreq_e.php).

Figure 2.13 Earthquake, tornado, and avalanche activity in Canada

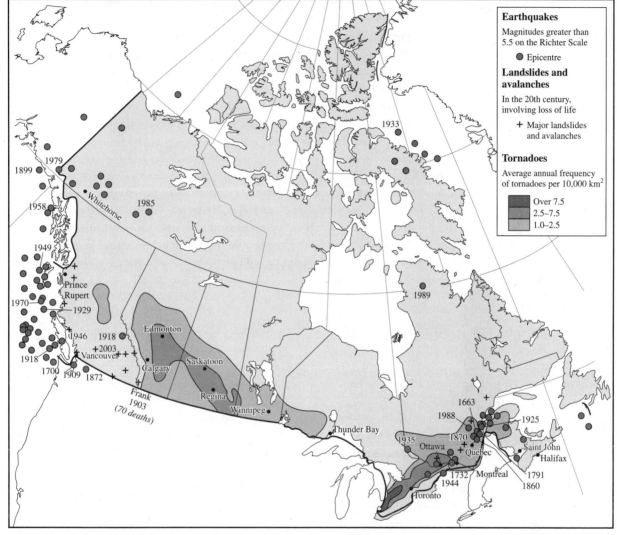

Source: Q. Stanford, ed., *Canadian Oxford World Atlas,* 5th edn (Toronto: Oxford University Press, 2003), 24.

This understanding makes it possible to develop appropriate building codes for various regions and if necessary retrofit structures such as bridges and dams. As Kenneth Hewitt puts it, 'who lives or dies in earthquakes depends more directly upon land use and, especially, the siting and design of buildings' (2000: 333).

Summary

The 11 physiographic regions of Canada emerged over billions of years. The foundation of the North American continental plate is the Canadian Shield. The Precambrian rock of the Shield was already old by the time the other regions began to form around its edges. Eventually, the retreat of shallow seas on the outer part of the Shield left accumulations of sediment that formed four distinct platforms, while tectonic activity added mountain ranges on the far edges of the continental plate. Together, these different landscapes have yielded a wide range of valuable resources, including metals (gold, silver, nickel), non-metals (potash, diamonds), and fossil fuels (coal, oil, natural gas).

Weather and climate have also helped to shape distinct regional landscapes. Differences in temperature, precipitation and growing degree-day patterns reflect a variety of influences—from latitude and prevailing winds to topography and proximity to water—and these differences in turn are reflected in distinct patterns of vegetation. These patterns have been a major influence on settlement as well as on economic activity, particularly with respect to agriculture and forestry.

Finally, our discussion of natural hazards was a reminder that the geophysical forces behind these diverse landscapes continue to operate, and can have serious consequences for human populations. Those forces are not random, however. It may not be possible to predict exactly when a particular place will be hit by an earthquake, a flood, or a hurricane, but in most cases there is enough information available to substantially reduce the danger to life and property. Therefore it is the responsibility of human decision-makers to take those forces into account, informing themselves and taking whatever steps are necessary to minimize risks.

References

Agriculture and Agri-Food Canada. 2004. 'Drought Watch'. http://www.agr.gc.ca/pfra/drought/cliprof_e.htm.

Aguado, E., and J.E. Burt. 2004. *Understanding Weather & Climate*. 3rd edn. Upper Saddle River, NJ: Prentice Hall.

Atlas of Canada. 'Land and Freshwater Resources'. http://atlas.gc.ca/site/english/learningresources/facts/surfareas.html.

———. 'Age of Rocks'. http://atlas.gc.ca/site/english/maps/environment/geology/ageofrocks/1.

Brun, S.E. 1996. 'Atmospheric, Hydrologic and Geophysical Hazards'. In *Coping with Natural Hazards in Canada: Scientific, Government and Insurance Industry Perspective*. http://www.utoronto.ca/env/nh/tab2-11.htm.

Burton, I., R.W. Kates, and G.F. White. 1978. *The Environment as Hazard*. New York: Oxford.

Cameron, W. 2003. 'The Formation of the Rocky Mountains'. http://www.mountainnature.com/Geology/platetectonics.htm.

Canadian Forestry Association. N.d. 'Forest Regions of Canada'. http://www.canadianforestry.com/html/forest/forest_regions_e.html#top.

Cannings, R., and S. Cannings. 2004. *British Columbia: A Natural History*. 2nd edn. Vancouver: Greystone.

Charlwood, R.G. and G.M. Atkinson. 1983. 'Earthquake Hazards in British Columbia'. *The BC Professional Engineer*, December: 13–16.

Cornish, J. N.d. 'Chinook Winds; The Snow-eaters'. http://www.cdli.ca/CITE/chinook.pdf.

de Loë, R. 2000. 'Floodplain Management in Canada: Overview and Prospects'. *The Canadian Geographer* 44, 4 (Winter): 355–68.

Environment Canada. N.d. 'Canadian Climate Normals or Averages 1971–2000'. http://www.climate.weatheroffice.ec.gc.ca/climate_normals/index_e.html?Province=ALL&StationName=Yellowknife&SearchType=BeginsWith&LocateBy=Province&Proximity=25&ProximityFrom=City&StationNumber=&IDType=MSC&CityName=&ParkName=&LatitudeDegrees=&LatitudeMinutes=&LongitudeDegrees=&LongitudeMinutes=&NormalsClass=A&SelNormals=&StnId=1706&.

———. 2000. 'Flooding Events in Canada–Ontario'. http://www.ec.gc.ca/water/en/manage/floodgen/e_ont.htm.

———. 2003. 'Natural Disasters on the Rise'. http://www.ec.gc.ca/science/sandefeb03/a3_e.html.

———. 2004. 'Tornadoes'. http://www.mb.ec.gc.ca/air/summersevere/ae00s02.en.html.

Foster Learning Inc. 1997–2004. 'An Overview: The Shaping of Western Canada'. http://www.lloydminsterheavyoil.com/geooverview.htm.

Gardner, J.S. 1976. 'Natural Hazards of Climatic Origin in Canada'. Pp. 42–68 in G.R. McBoyle and E. Sommerville, eds,

Canada's Natural Environment: Essays in Applied Geography. Toronto: Methuen.

Heaton, T.H., and S.H. Hartzell. 1987. 'Earthquake Hazards on the Cascadia Subduction Zone'. *Science* 236: 162–8.

Hewitt, K. 2000. 'Safe Place or "Catastrophic Society"? Perspectives on Hazards and Disasters in Canada'. *The Canadian Geographer* 44, 4 (Winter): 325–41.

Institute for Catastrophic Loss Reduction. 2004. 'Understanding Winter Storms'. http://www.iclr.org/hazards/winter.htm.

Klivo, L. 1999. 'Geology and Origin of the Niagara Escarpment'. http://www4.vc-net.ne.jp/~klivo/gen/geology.htm.

Koppel, T. 1989. 'Earthquake: A Major Quake Is Overdue on the West Coast'. *Canadian Geographic* 109, 4: 46–55.

Kump, L.R., J.F. Kasting, and R.G. Crane. 1999. *The Earth System*. Upper Saddle River, NJ: Prentice Hall.

Lutgens, F.K., and E.J. Tarbuck 2001. *The Atmosphere: An Introduction to Meteorology*. 8th edn. Upper Saddle River: Prentice Hall.

McGillivray, B.P. 2000. *Geography of British Columbia: People and Landscapes in Transition*. Vancouver: University of British Columbia Press.

Mayse, S. *Earthquake: Surviving the Big One*. Edmonton: Lone Pine, 1992.

Natural Resources Canada. 2003. 'Major Earthquakes in Canada—20th century'. http://www.seismo.nrcan.gc.ca/major_eq/majoreq_e.php.

———. 2004. 'Major Floods'. http://atlas.gc.ca/site/english/maps/environment/naturalhazards/majorfloods/1.

Nicolet Commission Report. 2001. '1998 Ice Storm'. http://www.msp.gouv.qc.ca/secivile/dossiers/verglas/nicolet/section3_en.htm#top.

Raincoast Storylines Ltd for the Canadian Broadcasting Corporation. 1998. 'Quake Hunters: Tracking a Monster in the Subduction Zone'. Videorecording. Producer: Terence McKeown.

Saskatchewan Interactive. 2002. 'Soil Order'. 'Soil Classification'. http://interactive.usask.ca/ski/agriculture/soils/soilclass/soilclass_can.html.

Statistics Canada. 2003. 'The Land: The Canadian Shield'. http://142.206.72.67/01/01a/01a_002a_e.htm.

University of Toronto 2002 'Natural Hazards Workshop'. http://www.geology.utoronto.ca/basinanalysis/admwebnathazworkshop.pdf.

University of Waterloo. 'What Is the Niagara Escarpment?' http://www.science.uwaterloo.ca/earth/waton/niagara.html.

Welstead, J., J. Everitt, and C. Stadel. 1996. *The Geography of Manitoba: Its Land and Its People*. Winnipeg: University of Manitoba Press.

Weyman, D., and V. Weyman. 1977. *Landscape Processes: An Introduction to Geomorphology*. London: Allen & Unwin.

Whittow, J. 1980. *Disasters: The Anatomy of Environmental Hazards*. Markham, ON: Penguin.

3

Conflict and Conquest: The Historic Shaping of the Canadian Landscape

This chapter outlines the human history of the northern half of North America, beginning with the most widely accepted theory about the arrival of the first human occupants, more than 10,000 years ago, and a very brief review of Aboriginal cultures and societies in the pre-contact era. The largest part of the chapter is devoted to an overview of European colonization and political and economic developments up to Confederation (material that will be discussed in more detail in Chapters 5–11). The last two sections look at recent developments in the area of Aboriginal rights, especially with regard to the land.

Aboriginal History to c. 1500

The human history of the northern half of North America began sometime before the end of the last ice age with the Paleolithic ancestors of modern Aboriginal peoples. When did they arrive? Where did they come from, and what route did they take? What were the conditions that made their journey possible?

The archaeological evidence is sparse, partly because much of the land where traces of human occupation might have been found was eventually submerged by rising seas as the glaciers melted. Some scholars have proposed an arrival date as early as 40,000 BP ('before the present'), but most focus on the period between 15,000 and 25,000 years ago. As for possible routes, one scenario envisions migrants from the south Pacific arriving in South America and gradually making their way north. The most widely accepted theory, however, suggests that the first people travelled from northern Asia to what is now Alaska.

When the last ice age was at its peak, some 20,000 years ago, vast quantities of sea water were locked in the ice sheets that covered most of northern North America. Hence sea level was approximately 120 metres lower than it is today (Aquado and Burt 2001: 441), and the area that is known as the Bering Strait was exposed as a relatively flat plain extending from present-day Siberia to the Mackenzie delta. Free of ice because of its dry climate, this area was known as **Beringia**. Archaeologists suggest that early hunter-gatherers in search of food crossed Beringia to North America and gradually made their way south either along the coast or via an ice-free corridor through the mountains (see Figure 3.1).

Beringia
the strip of land (or 'land bridge'), now covered by the Bering Sea, that was exposed during the last ice age and is thought to have allowed Canada's first human inhabitants to cross from what is now Siberia to North America

Figure 3.1   Beringia and possible migration routes, c. 15,000–12,000 BP

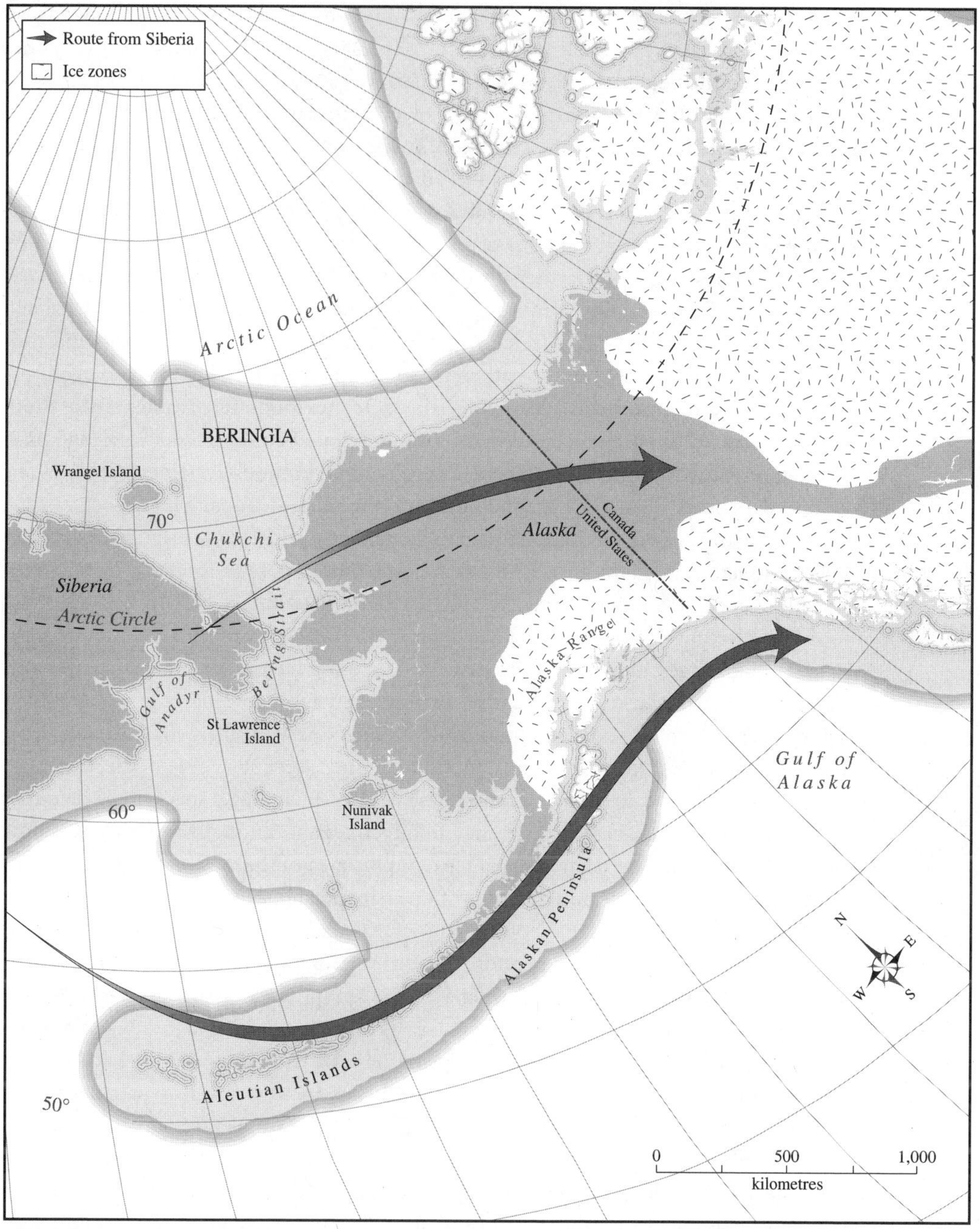

Source: Adapted from J.M. Bumsted, *A History of the Canadian Peoples,* 2nd edn (Toronto: Oxford University Press, 2003), 4.

Beringia facilitated the diffusion of many species besides humans, from plants to animals such as caribou, bison, musk ox, and mammoth (the extinct long-haired elephant with huge curved tusks). Other species migrated east to west. The ancestor of the modern horse, for example, originated in North America, and although that species eventually went extinct on this continent, its descendants on the other side of the world survived, to be reintroduced to North America by Spanish conquistadors thousands of years later.

A crucial factor in these events was climate change. An overall warming trend began roughly 15,000 years ago, but it was interrupted more than once by cooler periods, the last of which began about 6000 BP and lasted 2,000 to 3,000 years before temperatures once again rose (Kump et al., 1999: 235). Warmer periods resulted in the flooding of large expanses of land by glacial meltwater, rising ocean levels, isostatic rebound, and major changes both in flora and fauna and in the conditions of life for the people who lived off the land.

In most of Canada, the glaciers had receded to their present locations in the far north and the alpine Cordilleran regions by about 4000 BCE, although those in the northeastern region took another 1,000 years or so. The climate at that time was unusually warm. The boreal forest extended farther north than it does today, salmon swam in the rivers flowing to the Pacific and Atlantic, and other plants and animals established habitats throughout Canada. The Paleo-Indians who adjusted and adapted to the changing conditions began as **nomadic** hunter-gatherers. But as the ice melted and the land stabilized, they became **semi-nomadic,** returning to the same sites for hundreds and perhaps thousands of years. In this way each cultural group developed an intimate knowledge of its own regional environment and adapted accordingly. Over time, refinements in tools and technologies made survival easier, and population numbers gradually increased.

nomadic peoples
hunting and gathering groups who moved from region to region in search of food without establishing permanent camps

semi-nomadic peoples
groups that stayed within a defined region, moving from one site to another on a seasonal basis as different sources of food became available. In this way the same sites were used for hundreds and even thousands of years, and detailed knowledge of local flora, fauna, and landscapes was developed, along with specialized technologies.

On the west coast the transition to a semi-nomadic way of life took place approximately 5,000 years ago, around the same time that a number of important tools and technologies were developed, including pointed weapons, ground slate knives, barbed harpoons, fish hooks, and weights for fishing nets (McGhee, 1985: 1467). It was in this period that the Haida people of the Queen Charlotte Islands began using dugout canoes (crafted from the region's giant red cedar trees) to hunt sea mammals, including whales. The exceptionally rich environment of the coastal region made it unnecessary for the people to travel long distances in search of food. With the adoption of a more sedentary way of life, the Haida developed complex political and economic structures, including a strict social hierarchy and division of labour; elaborate art and architecture; and distinctive social institutions such as the potlatch. The relatively small geographic area of the west coast contained the highest population density and the greatest diversity of language groups in Canada.

On the Interior Plains, life continued to revolve around the hunt—caribou in the north and bison in the south. Therefore the Plains peoples had to remain fairly mobile. McGhee suggests that the most important change around 5,000 years ago was the development of communal hunting techniques based on the use of buffalo jumps and pounds. Use of these techniques required knowledge of the animals' migration routes and became the basis of semi-nomadic territories on the Plains for the ancestors of Algonquian groups such as the Plains Cree, Blackfoot, Peigan, Blood, Gros Ventre, and Sarcee as well as Siouan groups such as the Assiniboine. To the north, Athapaskan language groups such as the Beaver and Chipewyan carved out territories based on the movements of caribou and woodlands buffalo. Further improvements in hunting came with the adoption of the bow and arrow (about 2,000 years ago) and especially the horse, which was reintroduced to America by the Spanish and French and arrived on the plains in the early 1700s.

A more sedentary way of life began to develop in south–central Canada about 7,000 years ago. The Iroquoian peoples of the Great Lakes–St Lawrence region began planting corn (acquired from more southerly peoples who were already farming) around 500 CE and by 1350 they were also growing beans and squash. Since crops—the responsibility of women—required regular attention, settlements became more permanent, at least

Haida village at Skidegate on the Queen Charlotte Islands, 1878. The photographer, George M. Dawson, conducted the first survey of northern British Columbia and the Yukon. *Library and Archives Canada, PA-037756.*

during the growing season, though hunting was still a necessity during the winter. By 1500 smaller groups were coming together to form large palisaded villages of up to 3,000 people, and social organization accordingly became more complex. Some of the more southerly Algonquian groups also grew crops, but in the north life continued to depend on hunting, fishing, and gathering. The most important technological innovations in that region had to do with transportation: by snowshoe and toboggan in winter, by canoe (made either from birchbark or from the hide of animals such as moose) in summer.

On the east coast, archaeological evidence has been hard to find because early settlements were flooded when melting glaciers caused sea levels to rise. However, McGhee suggests that life there was becoming semi-nomadic by about 5000 BP. Some 2,500 years ago the original inhabitants were displaced by Paleoeskimo invaders from the Arctic—the Dorset (see below)—who occupied the region for roughly a millennium before they in turn were replaced by the Beothuk in Newfoundland and the Naskapi in Labrador.

The first human inhabitants of the Arctic probably arrived via the Bering Strait about 4,000 years ago. Over the next 1,000 to 1,500 years their Paleoeskimo culture developed into what is known as the Dorset culture, characterized by more permanent housing (built of snow and turf and heated with soapstone lamps) and improvements in tools and techniques that allowed them to hunt animals as large as walruses. Although a few scattered groups appear to have survived until about 500 years ago, the Dorset were largely replaced by the Thule about 1000 CE, during a period when the climate

Figure 3.2   Aboriginal language groups in Canada

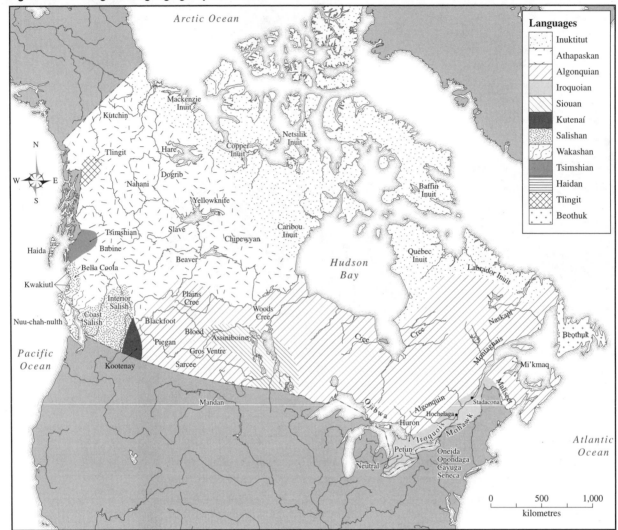

Sources: Adapted from O.P. Dickason, *Canada's First Nations,* 3rd edn (Toronto: Oxford University Press, 2002), 14, 47.

was unusually warm. The ancestors of the present-day Inuit, the Thule were a whale-hunting people who moved into the Canadian Arctic from Alaska. There is only so much that archaeology can tell us about Aboriginal cultures prior to the arrival of Europeans. However, evidence of extensive trading networks, as well as exchanges of ideas and technologies, indicates that sophisticated Aboriginal societies existed throughout North America by 1500 CE.

Figure 3.2 maps the language families within Canada, and Table 3.1 lists the specific languages in each group—a total of 53. The existence of so many distinct languages suggests significant cultural differences. In other ways, though, there were many similarities. All Aboriginal societies relied to

Table 3.1   Aboriginal language groups in Canada

Language Family	Languages	Language Family	Languages
Algonquian	9 languages	Salishan	11 (1 extinct)
Athapaskan	16 (1 extinct)	Siouan	1 language
Haidan	1 language	Tlingit	1 language
Inuktitut	1 language	Tsimshian	3 languages
Iroquoian	8 (2 extinct)	Wakashan	5 languages
Kutenai	1 language	Beothuk	Unknown

Source: 'Languages of Canada' ⟨http://www.ethnologue.com/show_country.asp?name=Canada⟩

some extent on hunting and gathering. All lived and travelled within well-defined regions. All were oral cultures. All had clearly defined roles for their various members, strong social and cultural traditions, and established governance structures. Finally, all had powerful spiritual connections to the natural world on which their lives depended: the land was the culture.

European Colonialism

The first Europeans known to have reached North America were Norse sailors. Originating in Scandinavia, the Norse had already established a colony on Iceland, and in the late tenth century—during the same unusually warm period when the Thule were making their way across the Arctic—they began settling on Greenland. Accounts of further voyages to the west and south describe a land of rock and ice thought to have been Baffin Island; a wooded land that was probably southern Labrador; and a place where fruit grew that they called 'Vinland' (thought to be either Nova Scotia or New Brunswick). In addition, a remarkable archaeological find at L'Anse aux Meadows, a present-day heritage site on the tip of Newfoundland's Northern Peninsula, indicates that the Norse established a small settlement there. Consisting of eight buildings of the same style as those at other Norse sites, the settlement was abandoned after just a few years, possibly because of hostilities with the local people. Apparently no other Europeans were to make a similar attempt for nearly 500 years.

By the 1400s in Europe a thriving trade had been established in silks, spices, and precious metals imported from the far east, creating a prosperous merchant class that was determined to improve its access to those treasures. Growing recognition that the earth was round (in defiance of medieval Christian teachings) suggested that it might be possible to reach the east more quickly by sailing west. But several technological developments were necessary before that could happen: sailing vessels had to be large and strong enough to withstand heavy winds, and navigators had to be able to fix latitude. Another important technological innovation was the development of guns and firepower capable of overcoming any resistance on the part of indigenous populations. The moral right of Europeans to invade and exploit lands occupied by other peoples was unquestioned: as Christians, they considered themselves to be naturally superior, and the Church itself welcomed any opportunity to convert the heathen to the 'true faith'. In short, all other lands and resources were Europe's for the taking.

Portuguese sailors were first off the mark, making a number of voyages in the late 1400s that led their European competition to fear they would soon control the source of wealth. Spain quickly followed suit, sending Christopher Columbus west to find Asia in 1492. When he reached Haiti he thought he had succeeded: thus the Caribbean islands became the 'West Indies', and their indigenous people became 'Indians'. However, further voyages soon made it clear that the way to Asia was barred by the Americas. Undaunted, Portugal and Spain in 1494 signed the Treaty of Tordesillas, dividing the world between themselves: Portugal claimed Brazil, Africa, the Middle East, India, and virtually all of Asia, leaving Spain with the Philippines and all the rest of the Americas.

In the Caribbean the Spanish first plundered Haiti, Puerto Rico, Jamaica, and Cuba, enslaving the Aboriginal peoples and forcing them to work in gold mines. From there the conquistadors moved to the mainland, conquering Central and then South

America, before gaining a foothold in Mexico. These wealthy colonies were firmly under Spanish control, but the vessels taking the booty back to Europe were much less secure. In order to catch the ocean currents and prevailing winds that would carry them back across the Atlantic, ships carrying Mexican gold and silver would round the tip of the Florida peninsula and sail north, hugging the coast, until they caught the westerly winds. This made Florida a prime location for French and British pirates, and therefore Spain had to gain control of that territory as well.

These activities may appear unrelated to events in the northern half of North America. But European **colonialism** was a global phenomenon, and in the years to come, the various European powers would use their colonies as pawns in their own competition for ascendancy, trading them off as necessary. At the same time, the period of European colonialism represented the beginning of global trade and investment, in which the resources of distant hinterlands became critical to the economies of Europe.

Thus other European countries were not about to be shut out of North America. In 1497 King Henry VII of England commissioned the Italian navigator known as John Cabot to undertake a voyage of discovery. Cabot returned from the west with reports of 'new founde landes' and waters abounding in fish. But he vanished in the course of a return expedition in 1498, and the British did not attempt any further exploration in the area until the latter part of the 1500s. In the meantime several European nations developed a seasonal fishery in the waters around Newfoundland.

Among those nations was France. In 1534 the king of France commissioned Jacques Cartier to sail in search of treasure in the waters to the west of the fishing grounds. In the end Cartier made three such voyages, the last of which, in 1541, was supposed to establish a colony in the fertile St Lawrence valley. That attempt failed, and the 'treasure' that Cartier took back to France turned out to be worthless iron pyrites ('fool's gold') and quartz. The king lost interest in the region and for several decades the only Frenchmen to visit the new world were the fishers working off Newfoundland.

The seasonal migration of fishers coincided with the seasonal migration of the cod: 'during winter and spring sea life withdraws to deep water, but with the retreat of the ice the cod follows the capelin and comes to spawn from May to September in the gulfs and fjords and in the shallower layer of water which covers the Banks' (Innis, 1954: 5-6). As Table 3.2 shows, a number of European nations were interested in Newfoundland's cod from an early date, but French fishers from the port of La Rochelle were clearly dominant.

By the end of the 1500s, the French and British still did not know very much about North America apart from its east coast and the section of the St Lawrence that Cartier had explored. Some considered the continent little more than an obstruction blocking their access to the riches of 'the Orient'. Hopes of finding a shortcut inspired many unsuccessful voyages in search of the supposed Northwest Passage (see Fig. 3.3), and many lives were lost to hypothermia, scurvy, and starvation. Still, the sailors who survived were able to add to a growing body of information about the physical geography of the region and its inhabitants.

Other Europeans, however, were increasingly interested in the resources of the new land. By the late 1500s both French and British cod fishers had established posts along the shore of Newfoundland where the catch could be spread out to dry ('wet' or 'green' curing

---

colonialism
The subjugation and control of a people and their land by a wealthier power. Among the characteristics of colonialism as Michael Watts describes it are 'political and legal domination over an alien society, relations of economic and political dependence and exploitation between imperial power and colony, and racial and cultural inequality' (2000: 93).

Table 3.2   Vessels sailing to Newfoundland before 1550

English only	11
English–Portuguese	3
Portuguese	12
Spanish	9
French from La Rochelle	71
French from other French ports	22
Total	128

Source: H.A. Innis, *The Cod Fishery: The History of an International Economy*, rev. edn (Toronto: University of Toronto Press, 1954), 19.

Figure 3.3   North and South America in 1569, by Gerard Mercator

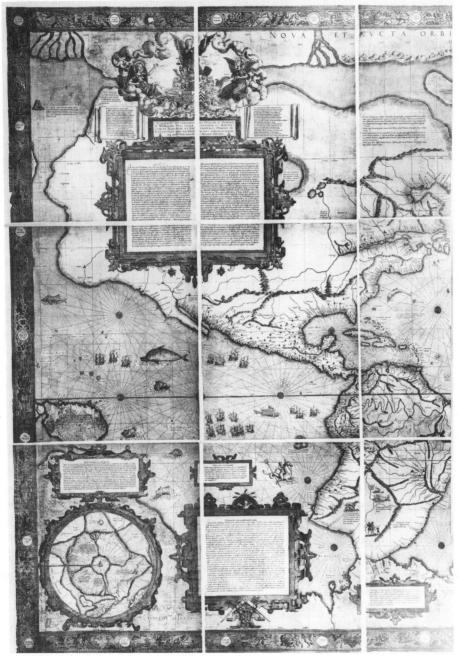

Source: Library and Archives Canada, NMCO 17080.

in salt or brine was done at sea). During the weeks they spent on land, fishermen began trading with the local people, who offered furs in exchange for metal goods. The Europeans soon found that they could sell the furs for a healthy profit at home.

Meanwhile in Britain population pressures were building, especially as increasing numbers of landowners shifted away from labour-intensive agriculture to wool production.

The need to relocate displaced farm workers with nowhere to go and no work to do provided a significant 'push' to establish agricultural colonies in the 'empty' territory along the eastern seaboard of North America. Moreover, England by now was officially Protestant and was anxious to spread its version of Christianity to the heathens of the New World.

By the end of 1500s, European demand for beaver pelts to be made into felt hats had made the fur trade profitable enough to be worth pursuing on its own. The French then returned to the St Lawrence, establishing trading posts at Tadoussac (1600), Quebec City (1608), and later Montreal (1642). From this base, French traders gradually moved west and then south along the Mississippi and its tributaries, laying claim to 'Louisiana' in 1701 (Fig. 3.4).

By this time the beaver was not the only fur-bearing animal of interest to traders. In the south, deer hides were particularly prized. Still, the most valuable furs by far were beaver pelts trapped in winter, when the fur was thickest. The Canadian Shield, with its myriad of lakes and waterways, and cold winter temperatures, provided the ideal conditions and came to be regarded as the richest region for furs.

The colonies of New France—the St Lawrence, the Great Lakes, plus Acadia—were well located to exploit this valuable resource. But they did not have a monopoly. Early challenges came not only from the English colonies to the south, but also from Dutch and Swedish traders based on the Delaware River. Then, with the creation of the Hudson's Bay Company in 1670, the British claimed ownership of all the vast territory draining into Hudson Bay and James Bay (see Fig. 5.5, p. 130).

There were many battles for control of the fur trade. The Dutch chased out the Swedes in 1655, and the British annexed the Dutch possessions in 1664. This left the main competition to French and British interests, and the conflict between them escalated after the two mother countries went to war. The War of the League of Augsburg (1689–97) was the first in a series of major European conflicts that were to continue for a good part of the next seven decades.

The next instalment in that series was the War of the Spanish Succession (1702–13). Under the terms of the peace agreement, the Treaty of Utrecht, the British took over much of Acadia, which they renamed Nova Scotia. In addition France surrendered its claim to Newfoundland, although for the time being it retained Île St-Jean (the future Prince Edward Island) and Île Royale (Cape Breton Island). Figure 3.5 outlines some of resources at stake in the Atlantic-based rivalry. Using the northeast trade winds, Europeans sailed down the coast of Africa picking up slaves for the plantations in South America, the Caribbean, and the southern colonies of North America. Having exchanged the slaves for agricultural produce—sugar, cotton, rice, and tobacco—the traders would then head north to pick up additional cargoes of furs and fish before catching the westerlies back across the Atlantic and home.

Peace between France and Britain lasted until 1744, during which time the French secured their hold on Louisiana and bolstered the defences of New France and Acadia by building a fortified naval base at Louisbourg on Île Royale. Renewed warfare in 1744–8 saw limited military action in North America. In 1749, however, nearly forty years after it had gained formal control of Nova Scotia, Britain made its first serious effort to colonize the territory, establishing Halifax as a British counterbalance to Louisbourg. Six years later, in 1755, the British decided that the time had come to expel

Figure 3.4   European colonial interest in North and Central America, c. 1650

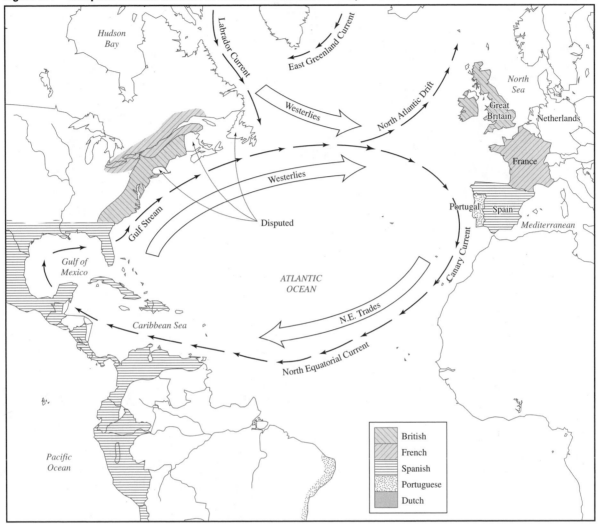

Nova Scotia's Acadian residents. Some managed to escape, but the majority were forced onto ships and deported to the thirteen English-speaking American colonies. The following year war broke out again, and this time most of Europe was involved. In North America the British captured Île Saint-Jean and Île Royale, including the fortress of Louisbourg. Then the islands' Acadian inhabitants, some of whom had fled there from Nova Scotia, were rounded up and deported. In 1759 British troops under General James Wolfe captured Quebec. The following year they took Montreal—and with it New France.

The agreement that ended the Seven Years War—The Treaty of Paris (1763)—caused many territories to change hands: in Africa, India, and the Mediterranean as well as North America. In addition to losing New France to Britain, the French were forced to cede Louisiana to Spain, which in exchange for the return of Cuba agreed to give Florida to the British. Now Britain had formal control of all the disparate societies from Florida north to Hudson Bay and east to Newfoundland.

Figure 3.5   European colonial interest in North and Central America, c. 1750

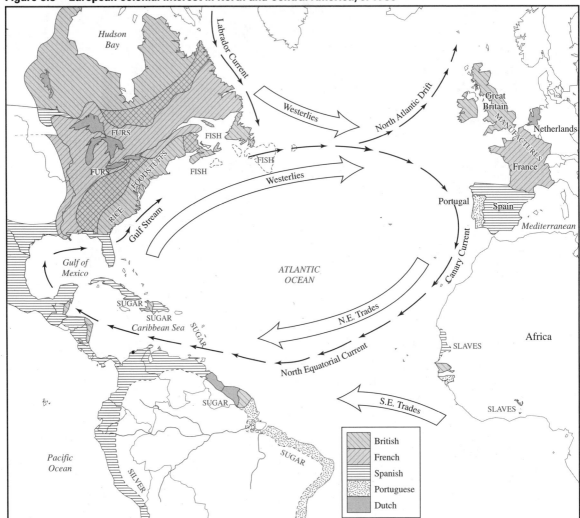

That control did not last very long. Within a few years the thirteen American colonies began demanding their independence, and in 1783 they achieved it, with significant consequences for Britain's remaining colonies in North America. Yet not everyone in the American colonies supported the revolution: some 80,000 to 100,000 of them became political refugees. About half of the Loyalists fled to Britain. Of the rest, approximately 35,000 went to the Maritimes—so many that in 1784 Nova Scotia was twice divided to create the new colonies of New Brunswick and Cape Breton Island. Other Loyalists went to Quebec: some to the Eastern Townships, and some to the western region between the Ottawa River and Niagara, which until then had remained virtually untouched by European settlement. Under the pressure of this influx, in 1791 Britain passed the Constitutional Act, dividing Quebec into the two separate colonies of Upper and Lower Canada and giving each its own elective assembly. Figure 3.6 shows British North America following the Constitutional Act.

Figure 3.6   British North America after the Constitutional Act (1791)

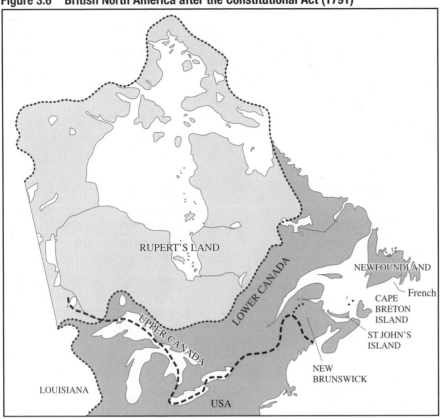

RUPERT'S LAND

LOWER CANADA

UPPER CANADA

NEWFOUNDLAND

French

CAPE
BRETON
ISLAND

ST JOHN'S
ISLAND

NEW
BRUNSWICK

LOUISIANA

USA

Source: Q. Stanford, ed., *Canadian Oxford World Atlas,* 5th edn (Toronto: Oxford University Press, 2003), 37.

On the other side of the continent, the Pacific Northwest remained uncharted by Europeans until well into the 1700s—nearly three centuries after Spain had conquered Mexico. The first to explore the northern region were the Russians, who undertook two voyages in the first half of the century and soon realized that the region's sea otters represented a highly profitable resource. By the 1770s Russian traders were

Captain James Cook's ships *Resolution* and *Discovery* at Nootka Sound, Vancouver Island, 1778.
Library and Archives Canada, c-011201.

active in Alaska, and the Spanish—whose northernmost fort was at San Francisco—were becoming concerned. In 1774 one Spanish expedition explored as far north as the Queen Charlotte Islands. The next year Captain Juan Francisco de la Bodega y Quadra tried to stake a claim for Spain on what is now the Alaska panhandle, but the cross he erected was torn down by the local Aboriginal people.

Four years later Captain James Cook sailed up the same coast in search of a western entrance to the Northwest Passage, hoping to collect the £20,000 reward offered by the British parliament for its discovery. Cook was no more successful than his predecessors. However, on the way north he and his men had spent a month at Nootka Sound (on Vancouver Island), trading with the local people for sea-otter pelts. Less than a year later Cook was dead, killed in a dispute on the Sandwich Islands (Hawaii). On their way home his men stopped in China, where they found that the otter pelts were extremely valuable as trade goods—especially since Chinese traders were not interested in European products and would normally accept only gold or silver in exchange for their tea, porcelain, and silk.

Although the Spanish were initially incensed at Britain's intrusion into territory they considered their own, in the early 1790s the two powers agreed that neither would stake an exclusive claim to the region. Before long, the Spanish had effectively withdrawn from the region, leaving little trace of their presence apart from more than a hundred Spanish names such as Quadra, Galiano, Texada (islands), and Juan de Fuca (strait). To the north, the Treaty of St Petersburg (1825) confirmed Russia's claim to Alaska and defined its boundaries. By 1815 the sea otters had been trapped to near-extinction.

Other explorers in this period made their way to the northwest not by sea but over-land, across the rugged Cordillera. In the 1780s a group of French and Scottish fur traders in competition with the HBC had established themselves in Montreal as the North West Company. Between 1792 and 1810 three employees of the 'Nor'Westers'—Alexander Mackenzie, Simon Fraser, and David Thompson—had effectively extended the reach of British North America as far north as the Arctic Ocean and as far west as the Pacific, although the southern boundary was in dispute.

To the east, the border between the United States and the British colonies of Upper and Lower Canada was also disputed, as it had been ever since the end of the American War of Independence. It took the War of 1812 to bring definition to this boundary. In that year, at the height of the Napoleonic Wars, the US declared war on Britain and attacked both Upper and Lower Canada. Even though they were outnumbered by the Americans, a combined force of British regulars, Upper and Lower Canadians, and Aboriginal allies successfully defended the colonies. Although the treaty that followed the war did not set-tle the boundary issue, the peace negotiations laid the groundwork for agreement a few years later. The convention of 1818 confirmed the boundary that had been established in 1783—which ran through Lakes Huron and Superior and then west as far as Lake of the Woods—and extended it to the Rockies along the 49th parallel, while leaving the dis-puted 'Oregon Territory'—from the continental divide to the coast, south to the Mexican border and north to the Russian boundary at 54°40′—open for another ten years.

By the mid-1840s, however, numerous Americans had settled in the area of the Columbia River and were demanding that the United States annex the territory. Americans generally endorsed a New York journalist's argument that it was their nation's mission and 'manifest destiny to . . . possess the whole of the continent'. The Democratic presidential candidate in 1844, James K. Polk, made his intentions clear when he took as his campaign slogan the phrase '54°40′ or Fight'. But in the end no fighting was necessary. The two parties accepted a compromise: the Oregon Boundary Treaty (1846) simply extended the border along the 49th parallel from the Rockies to the Pacific, with a small detour south around the bottom of Vancouver Island, the site of the HBC's main Northwest trading post, established at Fort Victoria in 1843. The island became a British colony in 1849, while the mainland region called New Caledonia was made a Crown colony in 1858 and renamed British Columbia (to avoid confusion with a French colony also called New Caledonia). By 1846 the borders defining Canada were established, although they would be challenged more than once in the years to come.

Figure 3.7   The Oregon Territory in the 1840s

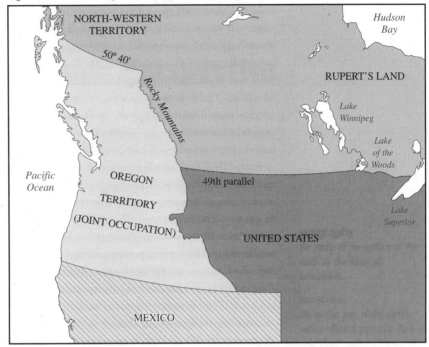

Source: Adapted from R.D. Francis, R. Jones, and D.B. Smith, *Origins: Canadian History to Confederation,* 4th edn (Toronto: Harcourt, 2000), 456.

Economic and Political Development

Behind the drive to define and defend the boundaries of the colonies was their economic potential. In the early 1800s the British North American economy was still driven by two staples: fish and fur. A handful of towns served the population—a total of perhaps 350,000 across seven colonies—as centres for trade and commerce. None of them were large—in 1800 Quebec and Halifax each numbered about 8,000, Montreal 6,000, and St John's and Saint John 3,000—and together their residents made up less than 10 per cent of the colonies' total population. Although agriculture was the principle activity, 'directly support[ing] some three-quarters of the non-Native population in 1800' (Harris, 1987: 196), very little of the food produced was exported. Soon, however, as more land was settled, wheat production increased. By the 1820s agricultural products were becoming important exports, and the many linkages they created—flour, breweries, leather goods—as well as demand for agricultural inputs such as seed, fertilizer, and equipment, along with improved overland transportation, in turn stimulated both agricultural settlement and urbanization as the new industries linked to agriculture established themselves in Montreal, Toronto, and, increasingly, other towns in southern Ontario (Upper Canada).

Another new staple was added to the export list around the same time. Wood was a essential resource, required not only for building and furniture but for heating, cooking, and tools. It was also the most important component in shipbuilding. Before the Napoleonic Wars, Britain had obtained much of its timber from the Baltic, but the conflict cut off that source of supply, forcing Britain to turn to its colonies. The sudden increase in export demand for spruce and pine, initially from the Maritimes and then from the St Lawrence and its tributaries, also created new linkages in the form of lumber production and shipbuilding. Even so, forest products did not create as many linkages as agriculture did.

From the early 1800s to Confederation in 1867, the population of British North America grew dramatically. Technologies developed (especially in the area of transportation), the region became more urban, and political decisions were made in Canada and elsewhere that affected the economy in both positive and negative ways. In short, the world was becoming much more complex, and British North America would no longer serve only as a supplier of raw materials for Britain.

The figures presented in Tables 3.3 and 3.4 indicate significant increases in both population and urbanization over the first half of the nineteenth century. But not every part of British North America was affected to the same degree. Population growth was greatest in Upper Canada (officially known as Canada West after 1841), which had overtaken Lower Canada (Canada East) by 1851. For the region as a whole, however, Montreal was the dominant urban centre, and its chief rival was Quebec City; of the 14 other towns in the future Quebec, none had a population over 5,000. Even though the future Ontario did not have the largest centre, with 33 communities of various sizes it was considerably more urbanized than its eastern counterpart (Fig. 3.8).

A host of interrelated factors account for those dynamics. Among them were innovations and investments in transportation infrastructure (Fig. 3.9). The St Lawrence made it possible to penetrate far inland, but rapids prevented ocean-going vessels from sailing beyond Quebec City; from that point, smaller craft (including canoes) were necessary. Beginning in the early 1800s, canals were built at various places along the St Lawrence

Table 3.3 Populations in British North America, 1806–1851

Year	Upper Canada	Lower Canada	Canadas total	PEI	NS[1]	NB	Maritimes total	NF
1806	70,718	250,000	320,718	9,676		35,000		26,505
1807					65,000		109,676	
1814	95,000	335,000	430,000					52,672
1816								
1817					81,351			
1822		427,465		24,600				
1824	150,066					74,176		
1825	157,923							55,719
1827	177,174	473,475	650,649		123,630			
1828								60,088
1833	295,863			32,292				
1834	321,145					119,457		
1836	374,099							73,705
1838	399,422				202,575			
1840	432,159					156,162		
1841	455,688			47,042				
1844		697,084						
1845								96,295
1851	952,004	890,261	1,842,265	62,678	276,854	193,800	533,332	101,600

[1]Includes Cape Breton as of 1819.

Source: Adapted from Statistics Canada, 'Introduction to Censuses of Canada, 1665 to 1871', Cat. no. 98-187 〈http://www.statcan.ca/english/freepub/98-187-XIE/1800s.htm〉.

Table 3.4   Urban population of British North America, 1851

Population	Canada West		Canada East		Maritimes[1]	
	Urban centres	Population	Urban centres	Population	Urban centres	Population
Over 25,000	1	30,775	2	99,767	–	
10,000–24,999	2	25,679	–		2	43,594
5,000–9,999	2	14,795	–		1	9,200
2,500–4,999	7	26,788	6	20,981	2	9,175[2]
1,000–2,499	21	34,872	8	10,531	n.a.	n.a.
Total	33	132,927	16	131,279	5	61,969

[1]Excludes Newfoundland

[2]Calculated using a population figure for Charlottetown (4,717) from 1848, not 1851.

Sources: G.A. Nader, *Cities of Canada*, vol. I, *Theoretical, Historical and Planning Perspectives* (Toronto: Macmillan, 1975), 172, 186–90; Statistics Canada, 'Introduction to Censuses of Canada, 1665 to 1871', Cat. no. 98-187.

(and between the Great Lakes), and by 1848 ocean shipping was able to reach Montreal. Railway construction also got underway, often in areas where canals were inadequate. But most lines were trivial in comparison to those in the US. 'By 1840 only 16 miles [26 km] of steam railway had been completed in British North America, compared to 2,800 [4,480 km] in the United States; by 1850 the respective figures were 66 [106 km] and 9,000 [14,000 km]' (Nader, 1975: 149). Canals and railways offered important economic benefits to those communities able to take advantage of them. Thus the St Lawrence canals favoured Montreal over Quebec City—but a far more serious competitor for both cities was New York, which had access both to canals (the Erie Canal,

Figure 3.8   Urban centres with populations over 2,500, 1851

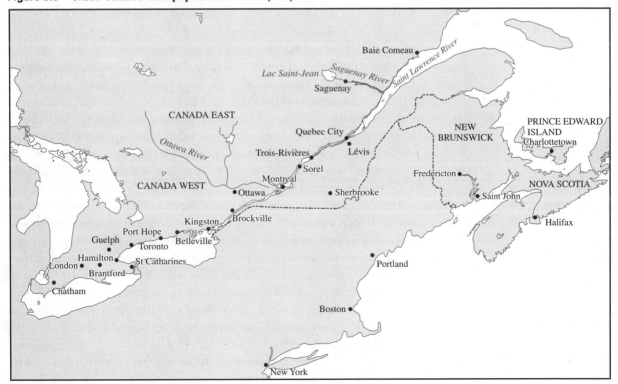

Figure 3.9   Main railways and canals, 1850s

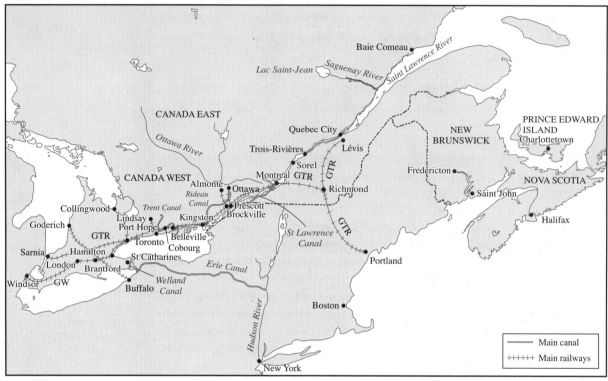

Source: Adapted from R.D. Francis, R. Jones, and D.B. Smith, *Origins: Canadian History to Confederation,* 4th edn (Toronto: Harcourt, 2000), 349.

between Lake Erie and the Hudson River, as well as others linking to Lake Champlain) and to the rapidly expanding American rail network. New York won out and became the gateway to and from the Canadian west as well as its American counterpart.

Global politics also played an important role in New York's ascendancy. Ever since it had become a major colonial power in the 1600s, Britain had based its trade policy on an economic theory called **mercantilism**. Mercantilist theory suggested that, to maximize its wealth and power, the state should encourage exports, especially of manufactured goods, while restricting imports. Thus Britain expected its colonies, including Canada, to concentrate on producing raw materials for Britain, and—instead of developing its own secondary industries—to rely on Britain to provide whatever manufactured goods they might need; it even required that all shipping be handled by British vessels. This core–periphery relationship left no question as to the dependent status of colonies. In the 1840s, however, Britain abandoned these protectionist policies in favour of free trade. This meant greater economic freedom for the colonies of British North America. But it also meant that they could no longer count on receiving preferential treatment for their goods in Britain. Even worse, goods from the Great Lakes region no longer had to be transported by British ships: now those goods could be—and were—exported mainly through New York. These changes in British policy forced the British North American colonies into a much closer economic relationship with the United States.

As long as the Canadas' principal exports were high-value, low-bulk furs, the cost of transporting them was not a major consideration, and there was little need to improve

mercantilism

the economic theory based on the principle that trade generates wealth. The dominant school of economic thought in the colonial period, mercantilism encouraged the state to play an active role in promoting exports and limiting imports.

the St Lawrence–Great Lakes transportation system. In 1821, however, after years of expensive rivalry, the North West Company merged with the Hudson's Bay Company. With the disappearance of the NWC, Montreal declined as a fur entrepôt. Now two different staples became increasingly important for the Canadas: timber and wheat. Unlike furs, these high-bulk, low-value commodities did require less expensive modes of transportation, such as railways and canals capable of accommodating large sailing vessels.

The timber trade was an important source of employment, even though exports were confined mainly to squared timbers (as opposed to finished lumber). To transport the large quantities of wood that the 'mother country' required, sailing vessels were needed, and the costs of shipbuilding were significantly lower in the colonies than in Britain. Both Montreal and Quebec City responded to this new demand, building ships specifically to transport lumber to Britain.

The booms in timber exports and shipbuilding in turn encouraged immigration from the British Isles. As more ships were built to carry timber to Britain, their owners— anxious to make sure the vessels' holds were not empty on the return trip to the colonies— began to encourage British immigration to Canada, charging only about one-fifth of the standard fare from Britain to US ports (Sitwell and Seifried, 1984: 36–7). The availability of affordable transportation made it possible to respond to the 'pull' that North America represented for people who by the late 1820s were experiencing at least two significant 'push' factors at home: a shortage of agricultural land and a growing pool of agricultural workers left unemployed by the industrial revolution. Between 1828 and 1837 some 300,000 British immigrants, mainly Scots and Irish, came to Canada.

Most of the new immigrants headed for Upper Canada, where good agricultural land was still available. By the 1840s its population numbers were comparable to those of its partner to the east, but it was far ahead of Lower Canada in agricultural production, especially wheat.

The discussion of staples theory in Chapter 1 pointed out that agriculture has the potential to create more linkages than any of the other staple industries. Thus Upper Canada soon acquired flour mills, tanneries, breweries, and tool manufacturers, as well as improvements in the transportation facilities necessary to move its agricultural products to the United States and Britain as well as to local markets, Lower Canada, and the Maritime colonies. Warehouses, packaging plants, insurance companies, and financial institutions were established, along with educational and political institutions. These economic, educational, and political functions were the beginnings of urbanization.

Politically, both Upper and Lower Canada experienced increasingly bitter conflict in the early decades of the 1800s. In Upper Canada, reform-minded members of the elected assembly objected to the political control exercised by a group of wealthy, conservative men known as the 'Family Compact'. In Lower Canada, the political division was similar, but reinforced by an ethnic dimension in that the conservative elite who held the political reins, the 'Château Clique', were mainly English-speaking, whereas the assembly was almost exclusively francophone. Finally, in 1837 both provinces erupted in armed rebellion. Although the uprisings were soon quashed, they signalled an urgent need for political restructuring.

Britain responded by sending a new governor general, Lord Durham, who recommended encouraging the assimilation of the French Canadians by joining the two Canadas in a 'legislative union . . . in which an English-speaking majority would dominate' (Mills, 1985: 525). Thus in 1841 the Act of Union created a single Province of

Canada consisting of two sections, Canada West and Canada East, with an elected assembly in which each section would have the same number of members. At that time Canada East had nearly twice as many people as Canada West, and naturally it demanded proportional representation. To grant Canada East more representatives, however, would have defeated the assimilation plan. Only when Canada West surpassed Canada East in size, in 1851, did its politicians begin to argue against the equal-representation rule—and by then Canada East had no desire to see 'rep by pop' introduced. As a result, the two sections of the legislature remained in a state of deadlock, and no party was able to form a majority government. The need for a new arrangement, in which the two sections would be separate entities, was to become one of the more persuasive arguments for Confederation in the Canadas.

In the Maritime colonies, meanwhile, urbanization was concentrated at the main ports and administration centres of Halifax, Saint John, Fredericton, and Charlottetown. Maritime economies were dominated by the fisheries rather than the fur trade. And it was the export of fish to the British West Indies (particularly after the American Revolution led the British to ban American traders) that promoted shipbuilding in centres such as Halifax. Therefore most settlements were located along the coastlines. Britain's demand for timber had its greatest impact on New Brunswick, where it stimulated the development of shipbuilding.

Unlike the Canadas, the Maritimes had no large base of good agricultural land, so most farming was concentrated in the fertile river valleys. Prince Edward Island had potential for agriculture, but the land had been divided into 67 lots of 20,000 acres (8,000 ha) that were sold to absentee landlords in Britain; since few farmers were content to be tenants on the land that they worked, agricultural settlement on the Island was delayed. Agricultural produce was exported to Britain, the US, and the West Indies, as were some staple-based processed goods such as flour and leather. The economic infrastructure required by agriculture, forestry, and shipbuilding—including banking, finance, insurance, and transportation facilities, along with government administration and military services—was concentrated in a handful of centres, the largest of which at mid-century were Halifax (population 20,749 in 1851) and Saint John (22,745). The next largest centres, Charlottetown (4,717 in 1848) and Fredericton (4,458), were considerably smaller.

International events and conditions that affected shipping were critical to the Maritime economy. Here too the Napoleonic Wars gave an important boost to the timber trade, and with the War of 1812 Halifax boomed as a naval centre and trans-shipment point. For a time Britain's mercantilist policies encouraged Maritime shipping and provided a protected market for the Maritime colonies. Thus Britain's adoption of free trade in the 1840s was a setback. However, by the 1850s the Maritimes' population and economy were both expanding, and in 1854 the signing of the Reciprocity Treaty opened the way to increased trade with the US.

Steel ships driven by steam engines rapidly replaced wooden vessels powered by wind, and the steam engine became the main energy source. Coal and iron ore were in demand and so were steel rails. From a paltry 66 miles (106 km) of track in 1850, railway mileage increased to 2,065 miles (3,304 km) by 1860 and 2,617 (4,187 km) by 1870 (Nader, 1975: 150). Much of the track was laid in the emerging core region in response to the expansion of commerce in agricultural products, timber, and manufactured

Table 3.5   Population by region, 1851–1871

Year	CW/Ont.	CE/Que.	Canadas total	PEI	NS	NB	Mar. total	NF
1851	952,004	890,261	1,842,265	62,678	276,854	193,800	533,332	101,600
1861	1,396,091	1,111,566	2,507,657	80,857	330,858	252,047	663,762	122,638[1]
1871	1,620,851	1,191,516	2,812,367	94,021	387,800	285,594	767,415	146,536[2]

[1]1857 Census. [2]1869 Census.

Source: Adapted from Statistics Canada, 'Introduction to Censuses of Canada, 1665 to 1871', Cat. no. 98-187 ⟨http://www.statcan.ca/english/freepub/98-187-XIE/1800s.htm⟩.

goods. The railways, upgraded canals, and telegraph lines—modern transportation and communications infrastructure—helped to integrate the economies of the two Canadas, and in 1858 the government of the united province adopted tariffs 'of a distinctly protectionist character', which stimulated manufacturing and hence further growth of urban populations (Census of Canada, 1931: 467). At the same time the two competed fiercely for the major share of industrial growth, trade, and investment. Montreal and Toronto were still the dominant centres, although other towns, especially in Canada West, were growing rapidly. The regional population figures in Table 3.5, from the censuses of 1861 and 1871, show Canada West/Ontario gaining over Canada East/Quebec, while Table 3.6 shows the corresponding trend in urbanization.

Changing technology had both positive and negative consequences for the Maritime colonies. Coal mining expanded and a steel plant, which imported iron ore from Newfoundland's Bell Island, was constructed at Sydney on Cape Breton Island. But even as the growth of the steel industry expanded Nova Scotia's economic base, it undermined the shipbuilding industry based on wood and wind. Similarly, water wheels were replaced by steam engines, which had the advantage of not being tied to a specific location. Even though the Maritime colonies had no specific industrial strategy, their populations continued to grow, especially in urban centres.

Events on the political front had economic repercussions. Britain's involvement in the Crimean War (1853–6) increased the demand for wood from its North American colonies. Closer to home, the American Civil War (1861–4) increased trade for the Maritime colonies as well as Britain, which backed the southern states. With the end of the Civil War, however, trade fell off, and to make matters worse, the Reciprocity Treaty was terminated in 1866. The Canadas feared reprisals and even annexation, because Britain had backed the southern states. Another threat to the colonies' security was the Fenian brotherhood—a group of Irish nationalists in the United States agitating for their home country's independence from Britain. In 1866 Fenians mounted raids into both New Brunswick and Canada West.

Concerned by the increasing cost of defending its North American colonies, Britain was more than willing to see them unite and assume responsibility for themselves. When the legislation creating the Dominion of Canada—the British North America Act (now known as the Constitution Act, 1867)—was presented to the members of the

Table 3.6   Urban centres with populations of 5,000 or more, 1851–1871

	1851	1861	1871
Cda East/Quebec			
Montreal	57,715	90,323	107,225
Quebec City	42,052	51,990	59,699
Trois–Rivières	4,936	6,058	7,570
Lévis	–	5,333	6,691
Sorel	–	–	5,636
Sherbrooke	2,998	5,899	4,432
Cda West/Ontario			
Toronto	30,775	44,821	56,092
Hamilton	14,112	19,096	26,716
Ottawa (Bytown)	7,760	14,669	21,545
London	7,035	11,555	15,826
Kingston	11,585	13,743	12,407
Brantford	3,877	6,251	8,107
St Catharines	4,368	6,284	7,864
Belleville	4,569	6,277	7,305
Guelph	1,860	5,076	6,878
Chatham	2,070	4,466	5,873
Port Hope	2,476	4,162	5,114
Brockville	3,246	4,112	5,102
Maritimes			
Saint John	22,745	39,317	41,325
Halifax	20,749	25,026	29,582
Portland[1]	9,200	–	–
Charlottetown	–	6,706	7,872
Fredericton	–	5,652	6,006

[1]A residential suburb of Saint John, amalgamated in 1861.

Source: Adapted from Statistics Canada, 'Introduction to Censuses of Canada, 1665 to 1871', Cat. no. 98-187 ⟨http://www.statcan.ca/english/freepub/98-187-XIE/1800s.htm⟩.

British Parliament in March 1867, they passed it without amendment, and on 1 July that year the new country was born.

The Boundaries of Canada: 1867–1999

Geographically, the new Dominion of Canada was relatively small in 1867, consisting only of Ontario, Quebec, New Brunswick, and Nova Scotia (Fig. 3.10). But its boundaries expanded rapidly.

Before the end of the year, the new Canadian parliament had voted to purchase Rupert's Land from the Hudson's Bay Company and govern it as a colony. Ottawa was forced to revise its plans when the Métis people of Red River, led by Louis Riel, declared their own provisional government and drew up a list of demands. One man was killed in the course of the Red River resistance, and Riel was eventually forced into exile, but the delegates he sent to Ottawa succeeded in achieving much of what the Métis wanted—including full provincial status for the area around the Red River settlement. The new province of Manitoba was created in 1870.

By that time the Fraser and Cariboo gold rushes were long over. The colony of British Columbia was piling up debt, and Britain was strongly in favour of seeing it join

Figure 3.10   Canada, 1867

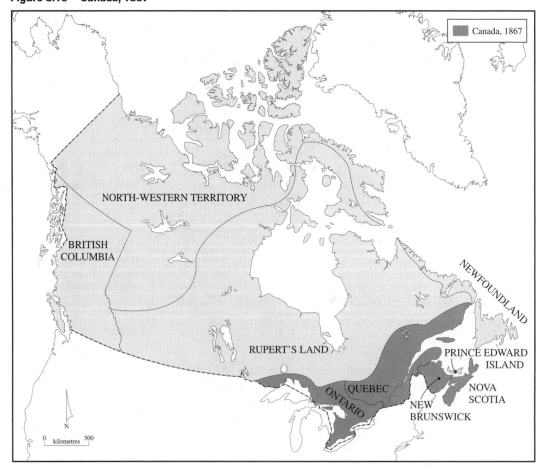

Figure 3.11 Canada, 1873

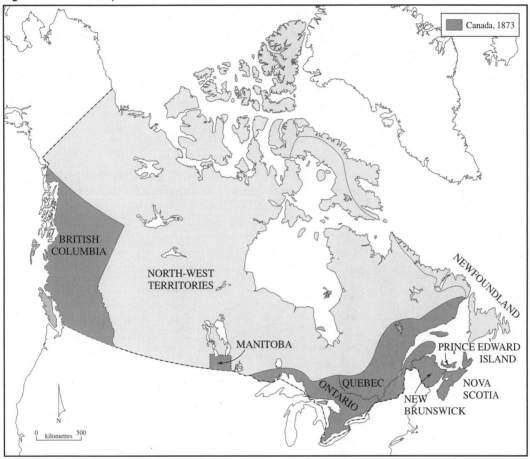

the new dominion to the east. Most residents were not overly anxious for union, and Americans living there would have preferred to join the US. Canada, however, was so keen that it had already included a clause in the BNA Act providing for BC's admission. When a delegation from the colony met with Canadian officials to discuss terms, the Canadians not only agreed to all BC's demands (including relief from its debt), but offered to build a transcontinental railway. British Columbia joined Confederation in 1871. Two years after that, in 1873, the promise of relief from railway debt persuaded Prince Edward Island to join as well. Figure 3.11 shows Canada in 1873.

In 1882 Britain transferred the Arctic Islands to Canada, and a decade later the Klondike gold rush led to the creation of the Yukon as a distinct territory, separate from the NWT. By the beginning of the new century, thousands of settlers had moved to the new agricultural frontier of the prairies and were pushing for provincial status. Manitoba's borders had been extended somewhat in 1881. In 1905 Alberta and Saskatchewan were carved out of the North-West Territories and granted provincial status, with their northern borders set at the 60th parallel, and in 1912 Manitoba's northern boundary was finally extended to the same level. Meanwhile, Ontario and

Figure 3.12   Canada, 1905

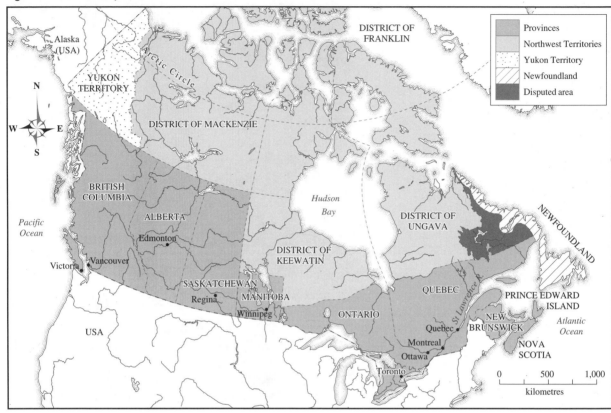

Source: Adapted from J.M. Bumsted, *A History of the Canadian Peoples,* 2nd edn (Toronto: Oxford University Press, 2003), 272.

Quebec had also been pushing to gain control of their resource-rich hinterlands. In 1889 Ontario prevailed over Manitoba and had its western border extended to Lake of the Woods. Eleven years later the northern boundaries of both Quebec and Ontario moved up to the level of James Bay, and the two provinces acquired their current configurations in 1912 (Fig. 3.12).

Newfoundland and Labrador became part of Canada in 1949. The referendum process through which the union plan was approved may seem straightforward: only the people of Newfoundland voted (not the people of Canada), and only a simple majority (fifty per cent plus one) was required for the proposal to pass. In recent decades, however, the precedent established in 1949 has come back to haunt Ottawa—for if a province can join Canada through a simple majority vote, then the reverse might also be possible.

The most recent modification of the map of Canada took place in 1999, when the new territory of Nunavut was created in the eastern Arctic and the largest land claim in Canada's history was settled, transferring ownership of roughly 375,000 square kilometres of that land to the Inuit. The following section will examine how, after more than 400 years of colonization, Canada's Aboriginal peoples have managed to reclaim at least some of the lands and rights that were taken from them.

The Treaty Process

As was noted earlier in this chapter, the primary motivation for the European invasion of North America was the desire for various resources. A number of historians have suggested that the Europeans' treatment of indigenous populations depended to some extent on the nature of the resources they were seeking and whether the local people represented a help or a hindrance in that effort (Innis, 1956; Billington, 1960; Harris, 1987; Frideres, 1988, 1998).

In the eyes of the early European cod fishermen who used coastal Newfoundland as a land base to dry their catch, mend their nets, and repair their boats, the local Beothuk people 'were of no use' (Frideres, 1988: 45). Rather, they were considered pilferers and thieves. It has been estimated that the Beothuk population at the time of first contact with Europeans may have been as high as 50,000 (Winter, 1975). Over the following centuries the Beothuk were exterminated: many likely died of European diseases, and those who survived were driven into the remote interior of the island. Starving, hunted down for sport or for bounty, the population continued to shrink until 1829, when the last known Beothuk—a young woman named Shanandithit or Shawnadithit, who had been captured in 1823—died of tuberculosis in St John's.

For the Europeans involved in the fur trade, by contrast, the local indigenous peoples were essential in every way: as the suppliers of furs, as allies in the competition for control of the trade, as guides, and as sources of knowledge about how to survive in a harsh and alien environment. In the early years especially, the Europeans—French and British alike— needed the Native people far more than the Native people needed them. There were benefits to forming partnerships: European trade goods were desirable; European weapons represented a tremendous advantage in battle with traditional enemies; and European alliances gave Aboriginal middlemen a certain power in relation to more distant groups. In time, however, the benefits would pale in comparison to the damage done by disease, war, and loss of land to European settlement. Even by the latter part of the 1600s, Iroquoians along the St Lawrence had been displaced from their traditional lands to reserves.

A century later, the Treaty of Paris formally transferred control of New France to Britain. The Crown then moved quickly to establish a framework for the administration of its newly acquired territories. Recognizing that the Aboriginal peoples of the vast 'Indian Territory' west of Quebec and the Thirteen Colonies had certain rights with respect to the land they had occupied before the arrival of Europeans, the Royal Proclamation of 1763 declared that they should be permitted to continue governing themselves, and should be compensated for the use of their land (Tennant, 1990; Frideres, 1988). It was this last point in particular that defined a new geographic relationship between Native and non-Native populations.

By the late twentieth century, the Royal Proclamation had come to be recognized as the legal basis of both **Aboriginal title**—the legal term for the right of a tribe or band to a particular area of land that it has historically used and defined as its territory— and the treaty process through which the Crown alone would have the right to negotiate with Aboriginal groups for the cession of that land in return for compensation. At the time, these provisions applied only in the 'Indian Territory': Quebec and Rupert's Land were specifically exempt; the Maritime colonies were not mentioned; and the British were in no hurry to begin making treaties in any case. It was only when the

Aboriginal title
the legal right of a tribe or band to a particular area of land that it has historically used and defined as its territory.

American Revolution provided the 'push' for thousands of Loyalists to move to British-held territory that it became necessary to begin negotiating with Native people to acquire the land to settle the immigrants on.

The early treaties were made in haste, with little care for formalities. It was not until 1850 that a formula was established in the Robinson Treaties, negotiated to secure land for resource development around Lakes Huron and Superior. From that point on, provisions were made for 'annuities, Indian reserves, and freedom for the Indians to hunt and fish on any unconceded Crown lands' (Frideres, 1988: 66).

By the 1870s the Canadian landscape had become much more complex. The fur trade was in serious decline, Rupert's Land no longer existed, the Prairies were being seen as the new agricultural frontier, demand for forest and mineral resources was growing, railways were being built, and manufacturing industry was attracting increasing numbers of people to the rapidly urbanizing southern Quebec–Ontario core. Under these circumstances, Aboriginal people themselves were of little use to the dominant society. Their lands, however, were highly desirable, for purposes of both settlement and economic development.

numbered treaties
The eleven treaties negotiated between 1871 and 1921 in order to acquire land (mainly on the prairies, but also in northern Ontario and the NWT) for settlement and development while fulfilling the legal obligation set down in the Royal Proclamation of 1763 that Aboriginal groups must be compensated for surrendering their traditional lands.

Thus following the purchase of Rupert's Land, the Robinson formula was applied in a series of **numbered treaties** (Fig. 3.13) covering the Prairies as well as portions of northern Ontario and the Northwest Territories. The first was negotiated in 1871, the last in 1921, following the discovery of oil at Norman Wells, NWT. Fulfilling the legal obligation, set down in the Royal Proclamation of 1763, that Aboriginal peoples must be compensated for surrendering their lands, the numbered treaties had many elements in common, providing land (reserves), cash, and gifts such as blankets, clothes, tools, and hunting supplies. Most also included provisions allowing the people concerned to continue hunting, fishing, and trapping in their traditional territories, although Treaties 1 and 2 made no such allowances and Treaty 5 included some restrictions on those rights. There were also differences, however. For example, Treaties 1, 2, and 5 provided only a quarter-section of land, or 160 acres (65 ha), for a family of five, whereas the others offered a full section. The cash allotment also varied, and Treaty 6 included a medicine chest.

To the west, a few small treaties (the Douglas Treaties) were established on Vancouver Island in the 1850s, just before the stampede of gold seekers, and the northeast corner of British Columbia was included in Treaty 8. In the rest of the province, however, reserves were established without treaties. Aboriginal title was neither recognized nor compensated for in British Columbia, most of the Yukon, a major portion of the Northwest Territories, northern Quebec, or Labrador.

Were these historic treaties fair? Not many Aboriginal people could read or write English at the time, and it is possible they did not understand they were extinguishing their rights to the land forever. From the non-Native perspective, the Native people did not use the land productively. If they represented barriers to settlement and development, therefore, they should be removed: it was simply good business practice to ensure that development could proceed without risk of competing claims. The reserve lands provided through treaties were owned not by individuals but by the federal government. They varied in size. For the numbered treaties, a common standard was based on the typical homestead: a quarter section, or 160 acres (71 hectares) of land. Thus the size of a given reserve would be determined by counting the families in question (usually assuming five people to a family) and multiplying that number by 160 acres. Occasionally, as in Treaty 8, the allotment was a full section, or 640 acres (285 ha), per family. But in the untreatied portions of British Columbia only 10 to 20 acres (4–8 ha) were allotted per family. The situation in the Maritimes was similar, and in the North reserves were generally considered unnecessary (Treaty 11 included a provision for reserves, but it was never acted on). Northern Quebec and Labrador, likewise, did not provide reserves.

Under the terms of Confederation, the federal government alone is responsible for Aboriginal affairs, and has a **fiduciary obligation** to look after the best interests of First Nations. Under the BNA Act, however, most Crown land came under provincial juris-diction; thus the federal government was in the difficult position of having to persuade the various provinces to give up their land for reserves. The Atlantic provinces, Quebec, and British Columbia all insisted that Aboriginal title had been extinguished, and strongly objected to the idea of providing land for reserves.

The policies that Ottawa put in place after Confederation were designed to assim-ilate Aboriginal people to the dominant culture. To that end, the Indian Act of 1876 not only abolished the tradition of hereditary chiefs and imposed a band system, centred on an elected chief and council, but appointed a non-Native 'Indian agent' to relay the needs of each band to Ottawa. In the mid-1880s the Act was amended to ban traditional ceremonies such as the potlatch.

Another tactic in Ottawa's assimilation campaign was to offer status Indians 'en-franchisement' if they would leave the reserve and give up the privileges (such as ex-emption from taxation) granted to registered Indians. Until the law was changed in 1985, a status woman who married a non-Native man forfeited both her status and that of her children; by contrast, when a status man married a non-Native woman, she automatically gained 'Indian' status.

One key element in the government's assimilation policy was to persuade Aborig-inal people to give up traditional hunting and gathering in favour of agriculture; the numbered treaties often included guarantees of farm equipment and seed—but not the knowledge needed to practise agriculture successfully. Another element of that policy, and perhaps the most enduring, was to remove children from their families and send them to residential schools. The main objective of these schools, most of which were run by religious institutions, was to strip Native children of their language and culture and, as Tennant (1990: 80) puts it, 'transform [them] into an unskilled or semi-skilled work-force while forcing them into the mould of Anglo-Canadian identity'. In recent years, horrific stories have emerged of physical and sexual abuse in some residential schools, and even children who were not physically harmed were severely deprived emotionally and psychologically. It is now widely recognized that the residential schools played a large part in the breakdown of the family unit in some Native societies.

Cole Harris (1997) uses the concepts of deterritorialization and reterritorialization to describe what was done to Native peoples. Disease annihilated some bands alto-gether, and alcohol exacted an enormous toll. Reserves, residential schools, and assimi-lationist policies destroyed traditional ways of life, social organization, and relationships with the land. Meanwhile, a new set of values was imposed on the land and the peo-ple: English or French in place of Native languages, Christianity in place of Aboriginal spirituality, British common law in place of traditional governance structures, agricul-ture in place of hunting and gathering, and private land ownership in place of com-munal occupation and use. For four hundred years, Aboriginal peoples were pressured to abandon their values and accept European ones, and for four hundred years they have resisted.

fiduciary obligation
a legal obligation to act in the best interests of the other party. Canada's fiduciary obligation with respect to First Nations and the lands reserved for them is enshrined in section 91(24) of the Constitution Act.

Cree children from the Lac La Ronge First Nation at an Anglican mission school in Saskatchewan, 1945.   *Photo Bud Glunz. Library and Archives Canada* PA-134110.

Claiming back the land: Modern-day treaties

mega-projects
huge investments in resource development and processing based on technologies such as open-pit mining, clear-cutting, and the flooding of vast expanses of land to create hydro dams (one of the latter projects created British Columbia's largest lake, Lake Williston). The radical changes to the landscape caused by such projects became a focus of attention for the environmental movement of the 1970s and after.

White Paper on Indian Policy (1969)
a federal government proposal intended to ensure Aboriginal assimilation to the mainstream by abolishing the Indian Act along with official Indian status and its privileges.

After the Second World War, public attitudes towards discrimination against minorities changed rapidly, and these changes were reflected in new policies. Status Indians in BC were allowed to vote in provincial elections starting in 1949; the bans on the potlatch, dances, and ceremonies were lifted in 1951; status Indians were permitted to vote in federal elections without renouncing their status in 1960; and residential schools were phased out in the 1960s. These were all positive steps; but powerful new threats were emerging. The 1950s and 1960s were the era of **mega-projects**: multi-million and even –billion dollar investments in areas such as metal mining, forestry, hydroelectricity, and energy resources, often carried out by foreign corporations. The technologies associated with these projects permanently altered large parts of the landscape and directly threatened those who continued to make their living from the land.

In the late 1960s and early 1970s, however, two events changed the course of history for Aboriginal people in Canada. Having assumed office in 1968, the government of Prime Minister Pierre Elliott Trudeau was struggling to come to terms with the Indian Act and the growing Aboriginal resistance to it. The result was a **White Paper on Indian Policy** (1969), that proposed radical changes: the Indian Act would be abolished, reserve lands would be divided into private parcels for band members, and special Indian status would be eliminated. In other words, there would be no recognition of Aboriginal title, no compensation for past injustices or expropriation of land, and none of the special rights associated with Indian status. The intention of the White Paper was to turn all Aboriginal people into 'ordinary Canadians'—the ultimate in assimilation. Harold Cardinal, then president of the Indian Association of Alberta, commented:

> For the Indian to survive, says the government in effect, he must become a good little brown white man. The Americans to the south of us have a saying: 'the only good Indian is a dead Indian'. The [Canadian] doctrine would amend this, but slightly, to: 'The only good Indian is a non-Indian' (1969: 1).

Aboriginal people across Canada responded by forming their largest national organization ever, the National Indian Brotherhood, to argue against the proposed policy. The federal government backed down and in 1973 withdrew the White Paper.

The second event involved a decision handed down by the Supreme Court of Canada in 1973. At issue in the Calder case was the claim of the Nisga'a people that their Aboriginal title to their traditional territory on the northwest coast of British Columbia had never been surrendered. The Supreme Court was unanimous in ruling that Aboriginal title existed historically: 'Aboriginal Title is rooted in the long-time occupation, possession and use of traditional territories. As such, Title existed at the time of original contact with Europeans, regardless of whether or not Europeans recognized it' (British Columbia, Ministry of Aboriginal Affairs, 1994). On the question of whether Aboriginal title still existed, six judges split evenly and a seventh dismissed the case on a technicality. Even though there was no decision, the fact that three judges recognized the continuation of Aboriginal title produced an abrupt change in federal policy, and Ottawa began negotiating **comprehensive claims** for unsurrendered lands.

Comprehensive claims opened the door for modern-day treaties, which have included land, resource management rights (including hunting, fishing, and trapping rights), cash compensation, education opportunities, and economic development, but initially did not include self-government. It took constitutional debates and military stand-offs as well as court challenges before self-government was included as a possibility. Comprehensive claims are distinct from **specific claims**, which involve non-fulfilment or breach of government's responsibilities under existing treaties or agreements (for example, neglect in fulfilling a treaty clause, or use of established reserve lands for roads, airports, or other functions).

The concept of Aboriginal title is nested in the overarching concept of **Aboriginal rights**. The existence of Aboriginal rights is recognized in section 35 of the Canadian Constitution (1982). Even today, however, it is not clear exactly what those rights include; this question will be discussed at more length in Chapter 10.

The first of the modern-day treaties was negotiated in order to permit construction of Quebec's James Bay I hydroelectric project (see Chapter 5). Although it was not called a treaty, the James Bay and Northern Quebec Agreement (1975) accomplished the same purpose, obtaining the right to flood the lands historically occupied by the Cree and Inuit in exchange for cash, land, and hunting rights, as well as 'indirect financial compensation in the form of a "guaranteed annual income"' (Frideres, 1988: 130).

The James Bay Agreement established the precedent for modern-day treaties. The second such arrangement, the Northeastern Quebec Agreement of 1978, involved the Naskapi people of the Schefferville region, where iron ore was being mined. Treaty negotiations then shifted to the north, where traditional Aboriginal ways of life were threatened by oil and gas exploration. The creation of the separate territory of Nunavut, in 1999, as a result of the modern-day treaty process, was a significant change to the political landscape of Canada. Finally, the provincial government of British Columbia accepted the existence of Aboriginal title in 1991 and the Nisga'a treaty, the first modern-day treaty in that province, was ratified in 2000.

comprehensive claims
claims regarding lands where no treaty has been signed and there is a broad range of issues to be negotiated (e.g., land title, fishing or hunting rights, financial compensation).

specific claims
grievances involving non-fulfilment or breach of government's responsibilities under existing treaties or other agreements.

Aboriginal rights
rights derived from Aboriginal peoples' historic occupancy and use of the land. Section 35 of the Canadian Constitution recognizes the existence of such rights but does not specify what they include. Thus the courts and the treaty process continue to play a central role in defining the rights of individual First Nations.

Figure 3.13   Treaties concluded in Canada to 1923

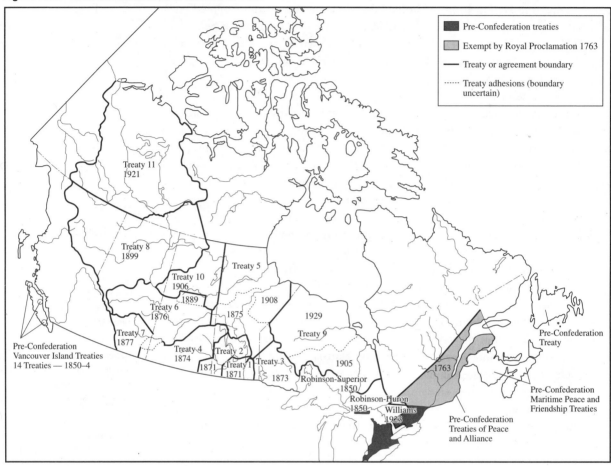

Source: Adapted from O. Dickason, *Canada's First Nations,* 3rd edn (Toronto: Oxford University Press, 2005), 254.

The regional chapters (5–11) of this text will explore the specific experiences of Aboriginal peoples across the country. The present discussion is intended simply to provide an overview of the way 'Aboriginal people in Canada have been marginalized spatially and imaginatively' by colonialism (Peters, 2000: 45). The consequences of this marginalization are clear: even today, many Aboriginal communities experience high unemployment, inadequate housing, high rates of suicide and substance abuse, high infant mortality, low education and skills attainment, and below-average incomes (DiFrancesco, 2000; Royal Commission on Aboriginal Peoples, 1996; Frideres, 1998).

These problems are not characteristic of all First Nations, nor of all geographic locations, and the modern-day treaty process is helping to improve socio-economic conditions (Saku and Bone, 2000). DiFrancesco (2000: 131) points to the unique political structure of Nunavut, 'which includes a fully elected Inuit legislature, the power to extract economic rents from resource developments on lands in the settlement area, a share of royalty payments stemming from resource activity on Crown Lands in the settlement area, as well as some regulatory authority over the location, pace, nature and scale of resource projects'. This self-government model has the potential to help the

Inuit of Nunavut enhance and improve their way of life and exert far greater control over the land.

Finally, it should be emphasized that many First Nations in the West and the North have never been party to any treaty, historic or modern. But treaty-making is an essential part of many economic development schemes. Thus rising prices for oil and gas, and increasing interest in Canada's northern hydrocarbon resources, will likely see the treaty process extended to a number of currently untreatied regions, especially if a pipeline is to be built down the Mackenzie River corridor.

The modern-day treaty process is only beginning in British Columbia; negotiations are underway in Labrador; the Maritimes have many issues that need to be addressed; and even existing numbered treaties are subject to revision (Treaty 11, for example, has now been renegotiated into several modern-day treaties). Furthermore, because First Nations reserves are not covered under the Municipalities Act, they do not benefit from the revenue-sharing arrangements under which the provinces share the revenue from resource industries such as mining or lumbering with the municipalities where those industries operate. For First Nations, treaties are not the end of the story; they are the beginning.

Summary

This introductory chapter has provided a broad overview of the various ways in which different peoples have occupied, modified, and organized the physical landscape of Canada. By the time Europeans arrived, territorial boundaries and land-use patterns were well established. In their quest for resources—fish, furs, agricultural land, forests, minerals—Europeans for the most part ignored those traditional boundaries and patterns. In the struggle for control of the northern half of North America, territorial maps were drawn and re-drawn many times before Canada emerged as an independent nation.

By the 1870s the country's population was growing rapidly and urbanization and industrialization were increasing, at least in some regions. Central Canada, with its base of good agricultural land, made the greatest gains in terms of population, urbanization, and industry, but the Maritime provinces, with their economies based on local resources and international trade, were not far behind. The rest of the land was still sparsely populated and relatively undeveloped. But as more and more of it was brought under the control of the Dominion, more resources were tapped, attracting settlement and development. Finally, in the mid-twentieth century Canada's territorial boundaries were extended to include Newfoundland and Labrador. The historic territories of Aboriginal peoples reflected intimate relationships with the land. European colonization eradicated those territories and created new ones from which Aboriginal people were excluded. As population growth and resource exploitation proceeded, Aboriginal people were further marginalized, and government explicitly attempted to eliminate all traces of their traditional cultures. Nevertheless, in the 1960s Aboriginal resistance began to gain strength. With political and legal acknowledgement of Aboriginal land title, the first comprehensive claims were established. Since then the modern-day treaty process has provided a way for Native peoples to negotiate fair compensation, self-governing arrangements, and improvements in social and economic conditions. For many, the treaty process today offers renewed connections with the land and hope for a better future.

References

Aguado, E., and Burt, J.E. 2001. *Understanding Weather and Climate*. 2nd edn. Upper Saddle River, NJ: Prentice Hall.

Billington, R.A. 1960. *Westward Expansion: A History of the American Frontier*. 2nd edn. Galt, Ont.: Brett-Macmillan.

Bone, R.M. 1992. *The Geography of the Canadian North: Issues and Challenges*. Toronto: Oxford University Press.

British Columbia, Ministry of Aboriginal Affairs. 1994. 'Landmark Court Cases'. Victoria: Communication Branch.

Cardinal, H. 1969. *The Unjust Society*. Edmonton: Hurtig.

Census of Canada. 1931. 'The Growth of Rural and Urban Population in Canada, 1851 to 1931'. Ottawa. Vol. XIII, 467–70.

DiFrancesco, R.J. 2000. 'A Diamond in the Rough?: An Examination of the Issues Surrounding the Development of the Northwest Territories'. *The Canadian Geographer* 44, 2 (Summer): 114–34.

Easterbrook, W.T., and M.H. Watkins, eds. *Approaches to Canadian Economic History*. Toronto: McClelland and Stewart.

Frideres, J.S. 1988. *Native Peoples in Canada: Contemporary Conflicts*. 3rd edn. Scarborough: Prentice Hall.

———. 1998. *Native Peoples in Canada: Contemporary Conflicts*. 5th edn. Scarborough: Prentice Hall.

Hamelin, L.-E. 1973. *Canada: A Geographical Perspective*. Toronto: Wiley.

Hammond, B. 1967. 'Banking in Canada before Confederation, 1792–1867'. Pp. 127–68 in Easterbrook and Watkins (1967).

Harris, C. 1987. 'The Pattern of Early Canada'. *The Canadian Geographer*, 31, 4 (Winter): 290–8.

———. 1997. *The Resettlement of British Columbia: Essays on Colonialism and Geographical Change*. Vancouver. University of British Columbia Press.

Innis, H.A. 1954. *The Cod Fishery: The History of an International Economy*. Revised edn. Toronto: University of Toronto Press.

———. 1956. *Essays in Canadian Economic History*. Toronto: University of Toronto Press.

Kump, L.R., J.F. Kasting, and R.G. Crane. 1999. *The Earth System*. Upper Saddle River, NJ: Prentice Hall.

'Languages of Canada'. N.d. http://www.ethnologue.com/show_country.asp?name= Canada.

McGhee, R. 1985. 'Prehistory'. Pp. 1466–9 in *The Canadian Encyclopedia*. Edmonton: Hurtig.

Mills, D. 1985. 'Durham Report'. Pp. 525–6 in *The Canadian Encyclopedia*. Edmonton: Hurtig.

Morland, R.E. 1985. 'Beringia'. Pp. 164–5 in *The Canadian Encyclopedia*. Edmonton: Hurtig.

Muckle, R. 1998. *The First Nations of British Columbia*. Vancouver: University of British Columbia Press.

Nader, G.A. 1975. *Cities of Canada: Volume One: Theoretical, Historical and Planning Perspectives*. Toronto: Macmillan.

Peters, E.J. 2000. 'Aboriginal People and Canadian Geography: A Review of the Recent Literature'. *The Canadian Geographer* 44, 1 (Spring): 44–55.

Royal Commission on Aboriginal Peoples. 1996. *Report of the Royal Commission on Aboriginal Peoples*. Ottawa: Canada Communications Group.

Saku, J.C., and R.M. Bone. 2000. 'Looking for Solutions in the Canadian North: Modern Treaties as a New Strategy'. *The Canadian Geographer* 44, 3 (Fall), 259–70.

Sitwell, O.F.G., and N.R.M. Seifried. 1984. *The Regional Structure of the Canadian Economy*. Agincourt, ON: Methuen.

Tennant, P. 1990. *Aboriginal People and Politics: The Indian Land Question in British Columbia*. Vancouver: University of British Columbia Press.

Watts, M. 2000. 'Colonialism'. Pp. 93–5 in R.J. Johnston, D. Gregory, G. Pratt, and M. Watts, eds. *The Dictionary of Human Geography*. 4th edn. Oxford: Blackwell.

Winter, K. 1975. *Shananditti: The Last of the Beothucks*. North Vancouver: J.J. Douglas.

4

Canada Within the World Economy

> ... the 1970s will likely prove to have been the last decade in which the
> exploitation of natural resources played a major role in shaping the
> geography of Canada's national economy.
> —Iain Wallace (2002: 1)

The last chapter underlined two central aspects of Canada's history. First, this country has been part of a global system of trade and investment for more than five hundred years. Second, the course of its development during that time has been largely directed by decisions made outside its borders. This chapter builds on those points, placing national issues in the global context and drawing attention to the economic and political decisions through which the heartland of Canada gained its dominant position.

Southern Ontario and southern Quebec did not become the core region overnight. It is true that they enjoyed a number of physical advantages, including a wealth of export commodities, from the start. But many of the factors that influenced their development were external, including political decisions at both national and international levels; international events such as wars and economic recessions; changes in foreign markets and competition; and technological innovation.

By 1970, after nearly thirty years of good economic times following the Second World War, the southern Quebec–Ontario region had consolidated its position as the economic and political centre of Canada. The key was the region's success in acquiring most of the country's manufacturing and related service industries. In short, the core had not only staple commodities themselves but also many backward, forward, and final demand linkages.

In Chapter 1 the distinction was made between the industrial economy and the service economy. The industrial economy is a direct outgrowth of the resource economy described by staples theory, in which the production of resource commodities for export to an external market led to distinctive local, regional, and national patterns of settlement and development. Today resource-related activities, from harvesting or extraction to manufacturing, are still the cornerstones of many regional economies. A fundamental change has taken place, however, with increasing globalization and the shift in emphasis from manufacturing to services. Today many of the spatial barriers that used to constrain the production of goods and services have been broken down. A global economic shift from Europe to the Asia–Pacific region accompanied these changes, and the formation of regional free-trade agreements eroded many political barriers to trade and investment. This new economy has constantly adjusted in response to the dynamics of globalization, leaving producers and nations alike in a state of uncertainty. At the same time, the growing importance of services has meant that regions outside the traditional core are developing their own core–periphery dynamics, with metropolitan centres such as Vancouver, Edmonton, and Halifax becoming cores with their own peripheries.

At the beginning of the twentieth century, most Canadians worked in primary industries: farming, fishing, logging, mining, trapping. Today, most Canadians live in large urban centres and earn their living in service-oriented occupations. This chapter focuses on the processes through which this transition came about. It examines the period—roughly a century, from Confederation to the 1970s—during which the industrial heartland became the political and economic centre of Canada. Most important, it focuses on the dynamics of the international service economy since the 1970s and how these have affected regional patterns of life and work for all Canadians.

The First Kondratieff Wave: 1867–1895

Kondratieff waves
long-term boom-and-bust cycles in capitalist economies. Booms are generally thought to begin with technological breakthroughs and the economic investments they attract. For a more detailed discussion, see Johnston et al., 2000.

In the 1920s the Russian economist Nikolai Kondratieff proposed that capitalist economies are subject to boom-and-bust cycles. Many writers (Dicken, 1998; Knox and Agnew, 1998; Lee, 2000; Wallace 2002) have recognized these **Kondratieff waves**: cycles of 40 to 60 years in which economic development oscillates between growth and stagnation, depression, or recession, with consequences that reverberate throughout society. 'Boom' periods are generally believed to begin with technological breakthroughs and the economic investments they attract. Figure 4.1 identifies three Kondratieff waves corresponding to five phases of economic development from the mid-1800s to the 1970s, along with the technological innovations that launched them and the geographical regions that dominated the world system at each phase. Within these longer cycles, of course, shorter-term recessions and recovery phases also occur.

The first Kondratieff wave began towards the end of the Industrial Revolution, when the primary source of power was coal, and steel rails were being laid around the

Figure 4.1   Kondratieff waves, 1845–1970

Year	1845	1873	1895	1914	1939	1970
Economic devel.	Late phase of Industrial Rev.	Depression	Recovery phase	WWI to 1930s Depression	WWII and post-war boom
Technol. innovation	Coal, steel, and railways		Assembly line, electricity		Automobiles, electronics, and petrochemicals
Dominant core	Britain	Britain Northwest Europe United States	Britain Northwest Europe United States	United States	United States

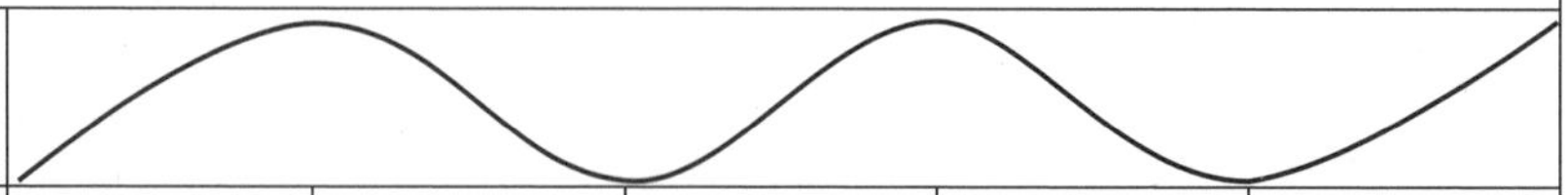

Source: Adapted from R. Lee, 'Kondratieff cycles', in R. J. Johnston, D. Gregory, G. Pratt, and M. Watts, eds, *The Dictionary of Human Geography* (Oxford: Blackwell, 2000), 414.

world, connecting resource locations, industrial centres, and shipping ports. These technological innovations not only required new skills of workers but also led to important shifts in the geographic location of employment opportunities. Because railways made it possible to move high-bulk, low-value goods such as agricultural products, lumber, and minerals long distances at relatively low cost, they encouraged the opening of new hinterland regions to resource development. Meanwhile, locations that specialized in industries based on outmoded materials (such as wooden shipbuilding) or sources of power (such as water wheels) inevitably lost jobs.

These technological innovations, and the investments that financed them, originated in Britain, which led the Industrial Revolution and, with its powerful navy, exerted its colonial influence over much of the world. By mid-century, however, other European countries, such as France, Germany, and the Netherlands, were catching up and increasingly exerting their own global influence. At the same time on the other side of the Atlantic, the United States was also industrializing and becoming involved in world trade and investment, while aggressively seeking to enlarge its territorial share of North America. It was during this initial wave that the world economic core expanded to include the United States as well as Britain and northwestern Europe.

What was the position of British North America during the first Kondratieff wave? Before Confederation, the colonies were under the political control of Britain. Economically, however, they were increasingly drawn into the American sphere of influence after Britain's shift to free trade in the 1840s eliminated the system of colonial preference. The colonies responded to this loosening of their economic ties to the 'mother country' by seeking a closer economic relationship with the United States. The signing of the Reciprocity Treaty in 1854 created an important economic alliance, and many British North Americans were apprehensive that it marked a step towards possible political integration with the United States. The threat of political integration receded somewhat with the conclusion of the American Civil War, in which Britain and its North American colonies had tended to support the South, and Washington's decision not to renew the Reciprocity Treaty in 1865. Trade with the US continued, however, albeit on less favourable terms for the colonies. The core region's need to find new markets within British North America was one of several considerations that made the idea of political union attractive.

Britain also played a role in pushing its North American colonies towards confederation. For one thing, an independent country would have to assume responsibility for its own military and infrastructure expenditures, relieving Britain of a significant financial burden. At the same time, a single unified country would represent a more stable environment for private investment.

From a global perspective, the British North American colonies before 1867 were resource peripheries first to Britain alone, then to the increasingly powerful United States as well. Confederation did nothing to change this reality. The new nation continued to play the subservient role of a resource hinterland, supplying the two cores with furs, fish, timber, agricultural products, minerals, and whale oil. Before long, though, massive changes did occur, both in core–periphery relationships and in economic conditions around the world.

As was noted above, Britain's economic supremacy was increasingly challenged as other nations established their own core–periphery relationships. Not unrelated to these changes was a fundamental downturn in the global economy that reflected the aging of many of the innovations that had powered the Industrial Revolution (many of which had originated in Britain): once a new technology, such as the steam engine, had been generally adopted and new applications became hard to find, its ability to stimulate growth started to decline. The result was an international depression that lasted roughly twenty years, from 1873 to the mid-1890s.

To protect their domestic industries during this difficult time, many countries imposed tariffs on imported goods. Among them was Canada. In 1879 the Conservative government of Sir John A. Macdonald introduced what it called the **National Policy**: a system of tariffs designed to promote Canadian manufacturing by excluding American imports, which in many cases were less expensive than Canadian-made goods. But the Americans were not shut out of Canada. The National Policy allowed American manufacturers to cross the border and establish branch plants in Canada, which were then free to sell their products without paying tariffs. In this way the National Policy secured additional factory jobs for Canadians; but there were costs: reliance on American technology discouraged Canadian innovation, and profits were lost to the US.

In time the National Policy came to cover a much broader range of initiatives. One of the most important was the support it provided for the completion of the transcontinental railway and the settlement of the west. South of the 49th parallel, the US west was rapidly filling up, and Canadians aware of the American doctrine of Manifest Destiny were concerned about the possibility of annexation. A Canadian railway was therefore perceived as essential not only to fulfilling Canada's promise to British Columbia, but to preserving the country's sovereignty. At the same time, westward expansion and settlement were expected to give a significant boost to the Canadian economy. Thus in addition to protecting Canadian manufacturers from foreign competition, the National Policy helped to stimulate demand for everything from steel rails and steam locomotives to housing construction materials and farm equipment.

The decline in international trade that began in the 1870s affected the various regions of Canada in different ways. In the Maritimes, Halifax was linked to central Canada with the completion of the Intercolonial Railway in 1876. Since all goods shipped via the Intercolonial enjoyed subsidized rates, the line was a boost to the land-based portion of the Maritime economies—especially the steel industry located in Sydney, Nova Scotia, which produced steel rails and even locomotives—through trade to central Canada. The larger portion of those economies, however, was based on the sea, and the international depression severely curtailed the Atlantic trade. Population figures for the Maritimes show an increase of more than 100,000 between 1871 and 1881, and much smaller increases for the next 20 years (Table 4.1).

Central Canada, by contrast, had a diverse economy based on agriculture and forestry, with multiple backward, forward, and final demand linkages. The southern portions of Quebec and Ontario were well connected by canals, railways, and telegraph lines, and the combined population of the two provinces was more than three times that of the Maritimes. The boost that the National Policy gave to manufacturing benefited southern Ontario in particular because of its proximity to industrial centres such as Chicago and Detroit. Montreal retained its supremacy as the largest urban centre, however. It was also the main shipping and rail centre and had a substantial industrial base, including flour mills, foundries, and footwear, as well as cotton, textile, and clothing goods.

The population of the vast landscape west of Ontario was very small until the railway construction boom of the 1880s encouraged an influx of settlers. Once the rail lines were

National Policy
the protectionist policy introduced in 1879 to promote Canadian manufacturing by making American imports prohibitively expensive (although it also allowed American manufacturers to establish branch plants in Canada to sell to Canadians). Over time, the term came to be applied to other policies promoting national economic development, such as the construction of the CPR.

Table 4.1   Population and population change, 1871–1901

Region	Year 1871	1881	1891	1901
Canada	3,689,257	4,324,810	4,833,239	5,371,315
10 yr change		635,553	508,429	538,076
Maritimes	767,415	870,696	880,737	893,953
10 yr change		103,281	10,041	13,216
PEI	94,021	108,891	109,078	103,259
10 yr change		14,870	187	(–5,819)
NS	387,800	440,572	450,369	459,574
10 yr change		52,772	9,824	9,178
NB	285,594	321,233	321,263	331,120
10 yr change		35,639	30	9,857
Central	2,812,367	3,285,949	3,602,856	3,831,845
10 yr change		473,582	316,907	228,989
Quebec	1,191,516	1,359,027	1,488,535	1,648,898
10 yr change		167,511	129,408	160,363
Ontario	1,620,851	1,926,922	2,114,321	2,182,947
10 yr change		306,071	187,399	68,626
West [1]	109,475	168,165	349,646	598,169
10 yr change		58,690	181,481	248,523
Manitoba	25,228	62,260	152,506	255,211
10 yr change		37,032	90,246	102,705
Saskatchewan [1]	–	–	–	91,279
10 yr change				
Alberta [1]	–	–	–	73,022
10 yr change				
BC	36,247	49,459	98,173	178,657
10 yr change		13,212	48,714	80,484
North [1]	–	–	–	47,348
10 yr change				
Yukon	–	–	–	27,219
10 yr change				
NWT	–	–	–	20,129
10 yr change				

[1] The totals for the West include the Northwest Territories from 1871 to 1891.

Source: Adapted from Statistics Canada, 'Historical Statistics of Canada', 1983, Cat. no. 11-516, 29 July 1999, Series A2-14.

in place, economies could begin to develop on the basis of staples: wheat on the Prairies, and timber, fish, minerals, and some agricultural products in British Columbia. New immigrants, mostly from Great Britain, accounted for approximately 35 per cent of the population increase west of Ontario between 1881 and 1891. But this was not rapid growth, and part of the reason was that prospective settlers were more attracted to the American west, where homesteads were available, land was more accessible, and the costs of agricultural inputs such as equipment, bank loans, seed, fertilizer, and transportation were lower. In addition, many French Canadians, instead of moving west, were attracted to work in cotton factories in the New England states (Maine, New Hampshire) and New York. As Table 4.2 shows, many immigrants spent only a short time in Canada before moving on to the United States. Immigration did not surpass emigration until the turn of the twentieth century.

Table 4.2   Net migration, 1871–1901 (× 1,000)

Decade	Immigration	Emigration	Net migration
1871–1881	350	404	–54
1881–1891	680	826	–146
1891–1901	250	380	–130

Source: Adapted from Statistics Canada, 'Historical Statistics of Canada', 1983, Cat. no. 11-516, 29 July 1999, Series A350.

The Second Kondratieff Wave: 1896 to 1939

The definition of Kondratieff waves on p. 86 suggested that innovation is the catalyst for economic expansion. By the mid-1890s, the stagnant world economy had been kick-started into recovery by two related technological innovations: electrical power and the assembly line.

Initially electricity was used mainly for lighting, but before long many new appliances had been invented to run on electrical power. Increasing demand both for those goods themselves and for the necessary infrastructure—dams, transformers, transmission lines—created many new jobs. At the same time electricity facilitated the production of those goods using the assembly line.

The assembly line became synonymous with **Fordism**: the mass production of standardized goods in central locations by workers specializing in individual tasks. Fundamental to this mode of production was the concept of **economies of scale**: the idea that producing large quantities of a particular commodity reduces the cost of each individual unit. Henry Ford put that concept into practice in 1913 when he began mass-producing his Model T—a basic, no-frills model, standardized right down to the colour (as Ford was reported to have put it: 'You can have any colour you want as long as it's black')—using an assembly line.

Until that time automobiles had been rare, too expensive for most people to own, but the assembly line made it possible to produce many more vehicles at significantly lower cost. Ford was inspired to develop the assembly line by seeing how meat was handled at a stockyard: a beef carcass on a trolley would pass along a line of butchers, each of whom would remove a specific part. Beginning at his Detroit plant in 1908, Ford continued to refine the assembly line model, and **productivity** increased accordingly: 'Production increased by approximately 100 per cent in each of the first three years, from 19,000 in 1910, to 34,000 in 1911, to a staggering 78,440 in 1912' ('Henry Ford and the Model T': n.d.).

As production increased, Ford was able to reduce the price of the Model T from $575 in 1912 to $290 by the mid-1920s (in the same way, new electronic equipment today is expensive when it is first introduced, but prices drop over time). For employees, however, working on the assembly line meant performing one isolated task over and over and over—in effect, becoming machines. Although Charlie Chaplin's film 'Modern Times' (1936) offered a comic view of the assembly line, the reality was that Ford workers in 1913 earned just $2.38 for a nine-hour day of mind-numbing repetition. Employee turnover was so high that productivity suffered. Rather than stand by and watch workers unionize to gain improvements in wages and working conditions, Ford in 1914 introduced his own reforms, reducing the work day to eight hours, increasing wages to $5.00 per day, and introducing a profit-sharing plan—revolutionary for the time ('Henry Ford and the Model T': n.d.). Turnover was reduced, productivity increased, and the threat of unionization was forestalled. Before long, higher wages and falling prices made it possible for Ford workers to purchase their own Model Ts. 'Between 1914 and 1916, the company's profits doubled from $30 million to $60 million' ('Henry Ford and the Model T': n.d.).

The importance of the automobile to the North American economy cannot be overstated. It spurred investment in roads, gas stations, repairs, parts, and insurance, while increasing demand for raw materials both for automobiles themselves and for all the other goods and services associated with them. As well, by facilitating the movement of

Fordism
the industrial strategy based on the mass production of standardized goods in large factories (rather than in the home) using assembly lines. While the assembly line increased productivity, it deskilled workers by requiring each one to do a single repetitive task, using them as little more than machines. In fact, many workers were eventually replaced by machines. Use of robots was becoming common on assembly lines as early as the 1970s.

economies of scale
the principle that producing large quantities of a particular commodity reduces the cost of each individual unit. The Canada–US Auto Pact (1965–2001) was an example: producing for the entire North American market reduced the manufacturing costs attached to each vehicle. Bigger is not necessarily better, however: at a certain point, increasing size may also mean increasing costs for management, inputs, and so on.

productivity
a measure of the costs of producing a good or service in relation to its value. The concept of 'value-added'—the increase in value over the costs of production (labour, energy, transportation, raw materials, and capital equipment)—is often synonymous with productivity: the greater the value-added, the greater the productivity. Conversely, low productivity means a low margin of profit and the risk of business failure.

both goods and people, automobile and truck transportation made a major contribution to time–space convergence.

Outside North America, however, other forces were at work. For much of Europe the years around the turn of the century were a difficult period of labour surpluses, land shortages, and political turbulence. These 'push' factors helped to propel millions of emigrants towards North America. Meanwhile the competition for territory, both in Europe and around the world, increased, eventually erupting into what was known at the time as the Great War (1914–18). Fordist technologies were used to manufacture weapons of mass destruction; millions of lives were lost (including those of more than 116,000 Canadians and Newfoundlanders), much of Europe was destroyed, and a revolution in Russia set that massive country on a political and economic path that was to have profound repercussions for the rest of the world.

Following the Great War, the European countries set about rebuilding their devastated landscapes. Trade and investment increased globally through the 1920s (assisted by the reduced shipping costs that came with the opening of the Panama Canal in 1914), as did dependence on electricity and petroleum products. The world system formerly centred on northern Europe shifted, and the United States emerged as 'the world's foremost industrial and financial economy' (Galois and Mabin, 1987: 44). Many of the investments made during the 1920s were speculative, however, and on 'Black Tuesday' (29 October 1929) the New York stock market collapsed. The production of goods and services dropped dramatically, along with world market prices for most staple commodities. Unemployment soared, raising fundamental questions about the institutional structures of capitalist systems. What role should governments play in providing employment or relief for the unemployed? Should governments provide education and health care for people who have no income? Should governments stick to the gold standard to regulate the value of their currencies?

Different countries tried different strategies, but currencies were in chaos, particularly in those countries without large reserves of gold. Some banks declared bankruptcy; others became disinclined to loan money on the basis of assets that might prove to be worthless. To protect their domestic manufacturing, some countries, including the United States, imposed tariffs that served to further reduce international trade. The loss of confidence in investment and a downward economic spiral continued until the Second World War broke the cycle.

Governments, which had been reluctant to invest in creating employment during the 1930s, did not hesitate to spend money on manufacturing implements of war, which in turn revived demand for staples. Together, military service and the increase in manufacturing largely solved the unemployment problem. In this way, ironically, the war performed a valuable service, proving that government spending could jump-start an economy out of a depression.

How were the events of the second Kondratieff wave reflected in Canada? The adoption of electricity and assembly-line production provided the boost that allowed the economy to recover and expand from the late 1890s through the early 1900s. Corporations increased in size and power not only through buy-outs, takeovers, and mergers, but through diversification into other areas of economic activity. American branch plants expanded their operations, again mainly in southern Ontario, and Canadian businesses based in the core region—especially Toronto and Montreal—established their

The Bank of New Brunswick in Saint John. Chartered in 1820, the Bank of New Brunswick was the first bank in the Maritimes. *Photo B. McGillivray.*

own branch plants across the country. The trend towards mergers, often motivated by the 'economies of scale' principle, significantly reduced competition and was particularly damaging to the Maritimes, which were reduced to hinterland status. From the perspective of central Canada, it made more economic sense to have a single large rope factory in Montreal or Toronto than a medium-sized factory in the centre and a small one in the Maritimes. In this way the Maritimes lost industry after industry along with the jobs they had provided. Nor were the mergers confined to manufacturing: by the early 1900s central Canadian interests had also moved into Maritime banking, as well as wholesale and retail operations, and they had taken control of resources such as coal. These losses would create lasting bitterness towards central Canada.

Canada's economic recovery was marked by a major increase in immigration around the turn of the twentieth century. As Table 4.3 shows, the only decade in the first half of the century when immigration did not outpace emigration was the 1930s—the decade of the Depression. With the end of the Second World War immigration rebounded. Table 4.4 shows population changes between 1901 and 1941. In that time the population of Canada more than doubled, going from 5.3 million to 11.5 million. The distribution of the increases reflected political policies, technological changes (Fordism in particular) and new resource discoveries, as well as international events.

Railway expansion, mainly in central and western Canada, encouraged settlement and resource development. Farming increased substantially: by 1913 agricultural products (especially wheat) accounted for roughly 60 per cent of Canada's exports (Economic Council of Canada, 1977: 6). Forest activities, which until the turn of the century had been confined mainly to logging and saw milling, expanded with the development of new technology for the conversion of wood fibre into pulp and paper: by 1910, new mills had been established throughout the southern Shield region of central Canada, in New Brunswick, and along the British Columbia coast. A shortage of newsprint in the United States led to the removal of duties on exports to that country in 1911, and by 1921 the price of newsprint had jumped to $137 a ton. Just 13 years later, however, the Depression had driven that price down to $40 a ton (Wallace, 1987: 451).

Mining also expanded from the early 1900s on, though it was not nearly so widespread as the forest industry. Investors were particularly interested in the gold and silver of the Canadian Shield, Yukon, and British Columbia. A major barrier in **lode mining** was overcome with the development of smelter technology to concentrate the valuable metals (nickel, copper, lead, zinc) extracted from complex ores by smashing the rock. By the 1920s smelters were in place across southern Canada—though (with the exception of those processing gold) they would soon be idled by low prices and over-capacity.

Increasing use of petroleum products (initially imported from California) also affected staple industries in Canada. By the 1920s, most shipping was diesel-powered, and the coal industry declined. Coal mining fell dramatically in the 1920s, as diesel-powered vessels took over most shipping: Vancouver Island production declined from 1 million tons at the turn of the century to 350,000 tons in 1922 and just

lode mining
mining in which the metal is embedded in rock, which must be smashed into fragments so that the metal can be removed and refined; also known as hard rock mining.

Table 4.3   Net migration, 1901–1951 (× 1,000)

	Immigration	Emigration	Net migration
1901–1911	1,550	739	811
1911–1921	1,400	1,089	311
1921–1931	1,200	971	229
1931–1941	149	241	–92
1941–1951	548	379	169

Source: Adapted from Statistics Canada, 'Historical Statistics of Canada', 1983, Cat. no. 11-516, 29 July 1999, Series A350.

Table 4.4   Population and population change, 1901–1941

Region	Year				
	1901	1911	1921	1931	1941
Canada	5,371,315	7,206,643	8,787,949	10,376,786	11,506,655
10 yr change		1,835,328	1,581,306	1,588,837	1,129,869
Maritimes	893,953	937,955	1,000,328	1,009,103	1,130,410
10 yr change		44,002	62,373	8,775	121,307
PEI	103,259	93,728	88,615	88,038	95,047
10 yr change		(–9,531)	(–5,113)	(–577)	7,009
NS	459,574	492,338	523,837	512,846	577,962
10 yr change		32,764	31,499	(–11,091)	65,116
NB	331,120	351,889	387,876	408,219	457,401
10 yr change		20,769	35,997	20,343	49,182
Central	3,831,845	4,533,068	5,294,172	6,306,345	7,119,537
10 yr change		701,213	761,104	1,012,173	813,192
Quebec	1,648,898	2,005,776	2,360,510	2,874,662	3,331,882
10 yr change		356,878	354,734	514,152	457,220
Ontario	2,182,947	2,527,292	2,933,662	3,431,683	3,787,655
10 yr change		344,345	406,370	498,021	355,972
West	598,169	1,720,601	2,480,664	3,047,789	3,239,766
10 yr change		1,122,432	760,063	567,125	191,974
Manitoba	255,211	461,394	610,118	700,139	729,744
10 yr change		206,183	148,724	90,021	29,605
Saskatchewan	91,279	492,432	757,510	921,785	895,992
10 yr change		401,153	265,078	164,275	(–25,793)
Alberta	73,022	374,295	588,454	731,605	796,169
10 yr change		301,273	214,159	143,151	64,564
BC	178,657	392,480	524,582	694,263	817,861
10 yr change		213,823	132,102	69,681	123,598
North	47,348	15,019	12,300	13,546	16,942
10 yr change		(–32,329)	(–2,719)	1,246	3,396
Yukon	27,219	8,512	4,157	4,230	4,914
10 yr change		(–18,707)	(–4,355)	73	684
NWT	20,129	6,507	8,143	9,316	12,028
10 yr change		(–13,622)	1,636	1,173	2,712

Source: Adapted from Statistics Canada, 'Historical Statistics of Canada', 1983, Cat. no. 11-516, 29 July 1999, Series A2-14.

50,000 tons in 1930 (Belshaw and Mitchell, 1996: 315). Petroleum was also instrumental in destroying the whaling industry on Vancouver Island, which had flourished when manufacturers depended on whale oil to lubricate their machinery: 812 whales were taken off the island's west coast alone in 1911, but ten years later the industry was finished (Belshaw and Mitchell, 1996: 315).

Central Canada accounted for more than half of the country's population growth between 1901 and 1941 (3.3 million of 6.2 million people). Increases in staple production created many jobs, but many more were created through the expansion of manufacturing. Southern Ontario led the way in the manufacturing of automobiles and all the products requiring electricity—from toasters to vacuum cleaners to electric motors. These industries in turn increased demand for the iron and steel produced mainly in Hamilton and Sault Ste Marie. The collapse of this market in the 1930s was particularly

Table 4.5 Urban–rural population distribution (%), 1901–1941

		1901	1911	1921	1931	1941
Canada	Urban	37.5	45.4	49.5	53.7	54.3
	Rural	62.5	54.6	50.5	46.3	45.7
British Columbia	Urban	50.5	51.9	47.2	43.1	54.2
	Rural	49.5	48.1	52.8	56.9	45.8
Alberta[1]	Urban	25.3	36.8	37.9	38.1	38.5
	Rural	74.7	63.2	62.1	61.9	61.5
Saskatchewan[1]	Urban	15.7	26.7	28.9	31.6	32.9
	Rural	84.3	73.3	71.1	68.4	67.1
Manitoba	Urban	27.6	43.4	42.9	45.1	44.1
	Rural	72.4	56.6	57.1	54.9	55.9
Ontario	Urban	42.9	52.6	58.2	61.1	61.7
	Rural	57.1	47.4	41.8	38.9	38.3
Quebec	Urban	39.4	39.4	56.0	63.1	63.3
	Rural	60.6	60.6	44.0	26.9	26.7
New Brunswick	Urban	23.3	28.3	32.1	31.6	31.4
	Rural	76.7	71.7	67.9	68.4	68.6
Nova Scotia	Urban	28.1	37.8	43.3	45.2	46.3
	Rural	71.9	62.2	56.7	54.8	53.7
Prince Edward Island	Urban	14.5	16.0	21.6	23.2	25.6
	Rural	85.5	84.0	78.4	76.8	74.4
Yukon	Urban	33.5	45.9	31.0	32.6	36.7
	Rural	66.5	54.1	69.0	67.4	63.3
Northwest Territories	Urban	–	–	–	–	–
	Rural	–	–	–	–	–

[1]Part of the Northwest Territories until 1905.

Source: Adapted from Statistics Canada, 'Historical Statistics of Canada', 1983, Cat. no. 11-516, 29 July 1999, Series A67-69.

hard on Sault Ste Marie, though it also hurt the steel mill in Sydney, Nova Scotia (Sitwell and Seifried, 1984: 68).

Growth in manufacturing also stimulated growth in urban-based service activities such as finance, banking, and insurance, as well as wholesale and retail sales. In the process the urbanization of Quebec and Ontario (highlighted in Table 4.5) intensified.

The gain in the Maritime provinces' populations between 1901 and 1941 amounted to less than 2 per cent of Canada's overall increase. Prince Edward Island actually lost population during these years. Most employment was in staples, primarily fish and forest products, though the Sydney steel plant was a notable exception. The First World War made Halifax an important naval base, but it also interrupted shipping to the St Lawrence, and as a result Cape Breton coal suppliers lost their Quebec and Ontario markets to cheaper, higher quality coal from the central United States. The demand for Nova Scotia steel did not recover after the end of the war. And although new pulp mills created some jobs in New Brunswick, depressed prices for dried cod in the 1920s and stiff competition from superior European vessels brought hard times for the fishery and maritime shipping (Wynn, 1987: 195). The completion of the Panama Canal was another setback for the Maritimes, as it allowed lumber and fish from British

Columbia to compete for markets in the east. The Depression of the 1930s only made hard times harder. As Table 4.5 shows, the Maritime population remained predominantly rural. By 1941 only Halifax and Saint John had populations of more than 30,000.

In western Canada, by contrast, the population increased fivefold between 1901 and 1941, from just under 600,000 to more than 3 million. The Prairies alone gained nearly two million. Among the factors that encouraged settlement was the construction of spurs off the CPR mainline into the fertile belt, where 160-acre (68-ha) homesteads were still relatively inexpensive. The building of a second national railway, the Canadian Northern, along with the Grand Trunk Pacific (absorbed by the Canadian government in 1919 to become the Canadian National Railway) offered a more northerly route across the Prairies, and facilitated both settlement and the movement of agricultural products. At the same time, technological innovations such as the self-binding reaper and the threshing machine made wheat cultivation less risky, providing further encouragement to settle the Prairies. Unfortunately, the 1930s brought not only low prices for crops but ten years of drought, forcing many farmers to give up their land.

British Columbia's population also grew quite dramatically in the first four decades of the century. The province's fertile river valleys attracted some farmers, but the greatest increase occurred in Vancouver, with its national railhead and international port. The initial boost for the Vancouver region came with the completion of the CPR, which made it easy to transport forest products and tinned salmon; expansion in those industries then stimulated growth in a number of coastal locations. Elsewhere in the province the key industry was mining. In particular, the discovery of silver in the Kootenay region (in the southeastern corner of the province) in the 1890s led to a major extension of the CPR. In exchange for federal financial assistance in building a line through Lethbridge and the Crowsnest Pass into the Kootenays, the CPR agreed to charge a reduced rate (the 'Crow Rate') for western grain travelling east and farm implements westbound. The same agreement allowed the CPR to acquire vast tracts of mineral-rich land on which to lay its tracks in BC, where it diversified its corporate activities to include coal mining, lead–zinc smelting, and hydroelectricity generation.

The opening of the Panama Canal for the first time made it economically feasible to ship BC lumber and fish to the east. The completion of the Grand Trunk Pacific (later absorbed into the Canadian National Railways) from Winnipeg to Prince Rupert established the latter as an alternative port to Vancouver. Other private railways also assisted in the opening up of the province and expanding employment in farming, mining, and forestry. Dependence on these staples for jobs meant that when markets collapsed in the 1930s, unemployment levels were staggering; only relief camps kept many men from starving.

As for the North, until the very end of the nineteenth century it was generally seen as a remote wilderness where the only ways of making a living were hunting, fishing, and trapping. The Klondike gold rush changed this perception. Some 30,000 gold-seekers rushed to the Dawson City region in 1897–9; with this stampede, new communities were built, transportation systems were established (including a narrow-gauge railway between Whitehorse and Skagway, Alaska), and the Yukon was created as a separate territory. Most important, the landscape was carefully explored in the hope of finding other mineral resources to exploit; it was in this way that oil was discovered at Norman Wells in 1920. Even by 1941, however, the North was still very sparsely populated.

By the beginning of the Second World War, southern Ontario and southern Quebec were highly urbanized and economically integrated, with many linkages related to its staple industries, especially agriculture. The St Lawrence and Great Lakes provided a significant natural advantage, and improvements in transportation facilitated the movement of goods, services, and people. The concentration of population within a relatively small geographic area made it practical for corporations to merge and extend branch plants to the periphery—in effect, all the rest of the country. By 1939 core–periphery relationships were solidly established within Canada.

Gold-seekers climbing the Chilkoot Pass, 1898–9. Some had to make the same trip 20 times to carry in all the required supplies.
Library and Archives Canada, c-33462.

The Third Kondratieff Wave: 1945 to the Present

> The dominant social order that emerged in the West after the World War II and flourished in the period 1945–72 was based on a Fordist production regime.
> —Iain Wallace (2002: 5)

At the end of the Second World War, the United States emerged as the world's foremost financial, industrial, and military nation. With no wartime damage on its own soil to repair, the US wanted to continue its economic expansion and create new outlets for its industrial capacity. But that would not be possible until the western countries that had been ravaged by the war achieved stable currencies and reversed the protective economic measures they had adopted during the Depression. To facilitate the process of economic recovery, in July 1944 delegates from all the Allied nations met at Bretton Woods, New Hampshire, and established three major international institutions: the World Bank, the International Monetary Fund (IMF), and the General Agreement on Tariffs and Trade (GATT). The initial purpose of the World Bank (1945) was to provide long-term loans to help war-ravaged capitalist countries repair the damages, though later it would make long-term loans for infrastructure and other economic improvements. The IMF (1946) was responsible for maintaining international currencies and exchange rates that essentially made the US dollar (based on the gold standard) the world's principal medium of exchange. The GATT (1947–94) and its successor, the World Trade

Organization (WTO; 1995–) were established to break down the barriers to trade liberalization by persuading member countries to reduce or eliminate tariffs. In this way the US became the centre of an international system of trade and investment that increasingly extended beyond national boundaries.

The Second World War did not put an end to military friction; it merely changed the players. At its conclusion, the world was divided between two political and economic poles, one centred on the United States, the other on the Soviet Union. The 'Cold War' between the capitalist and communist blocs led both sides to stockpile weapons of mass destruction that could be delivered from distant points of the globe (more time–space convergence). Much of the investment necessary for military research, development, and manufacturing came from the governments concerned. In this way, governments continued to finance industrial expansion long after 1945.

The Cold War was not cold for countries like Korea and Vietnam, which saw intense military conflict. Nor was it the only source of political tension in the world. In the 1950s and 1960s especially, peoples colonized for decades and even centuries by the imperialist powers were struggling to break free. In the end most succeeded, though rarely without resorting to violence.

On the economic front, one of the most significant changes in this period was the industrialization of several Asian states. American aid to Japan following the devastation of 1945, and, later, investment in Korea and Taiwan (intended to prevent the spread of communism) jump-started their transformation from agrarian to industrial economies. Hong Kong and Singapore also industrialized, though in their cases the main influence was Britain rather than the United States. Through the Bretton Woods agreements, some of the products of this new industrial capacity found their way to Canadian markets, and Canada in turn traded goods, mainly resources, to markets in Asia. This new trade represented a significant step away from the protectionism that had been characteristic of Canada since the days of the National Policy.

Another important step away from protectionism came with the signing of the Canada–US Auto Pact in 1965. This agreement essentially dissolved the border between Canada and the United States with respect to the production of automobiles and their parts. Economically, this move was justified by the economies of scale that producing for a larger market allowed; politically, however, it was controversial because it meant closer ties to the US.

North America's economic boom lasted until the early 1970s, powered by developments at both the international and national levels. Global trade and investment were expanding rapidly. Meanwhile at home the post-war baby boom sparked a demand for new housing construction. Increasing disposable income made it possible to purchase more consumer goods, and owning a car became a necessity for most people. Immigration also increased (Table 4.6) with the adoption of less restrictive policies based on a points system (fully adopted by 1967) that made education and skills important criteria; thus new arrivals were 'much more likely' than their predecessors 'to be professionals or skilled workers' (Crompton and Vickers, 2000: 6). Locating mainly in urban settings, they too contributed to the increasing demand for housing, automobiles, and consumer goods.

Table 4.6 Total population growth, immigration, and emigration (× 1,000), 1941–1971[1]

Period	Population[2]	Total pop. growth	Immigration	Emigration	Total migration
1941–51	13,648	2,141	548	379	169
1951–61	18,238	4,590	1,543	463	1,080
1961–71	21,568	3,330	1,429	707	722

[1]Newfoundland/Labrador included from 1951 on.

[2]Calculated for the end of the period shown.

Source: Adapted from Statistics Canada, 'Historical Statistics of Canada', 1983, Cat. no. 11-516, 29 July 1999, Series A350.

The manufacturing plants that used Fordist technologies to mass-produce standardized consumer goods were located mainly in the southern Ontario and southern Quebec heartland, and increasing numbers of them were owned by American firms. Hinterland regions also boomed as rail and road systems pushed deeper into remote areas to exploit the energy, mineral, and forest resources required by southern manufacturers. Mega-projects such as open-pit mines, hydroelectric dams, and clear-cut forestry operations cost billions, and the communities built around them were expected to remain long into the future. Table 4.7 traces population changes for the 1941–71 period. Canada's total population nearly doubled in these years. While manufacturing and related services fuelled growth in central Canada, particularly Ontario, the substantial increases in the western provinces, especially Alberta and British Columbia, were related primarily to the increase in demand for their resources. The population of the North more than doubled, and Atlantic Canada grew steadily, although the rate of growth there was the lowest in the country.

Overall, Canada was already more than 50 per cent urban in 1941 (Table 4.8). By 1971 the urban component had grown to more than 75 per cent, and the only provinces that were still predominantly rural were Prince Edward Island and Saskatchewan. Even in the northern hinterland, by 1971 the rural majority accounted for only 60 per cent of the population.

Table 4.7 Population and population change (× 1,000), 1941–1971

Region	Year			
	1941	1951	1961	1971
Canada	11,506.7	13,984.3	18,200.6	21,515.1
10 yr change		2,477.6	4,216.3	3,314.5
Atlantic	1,452.2	1,618.1	1,897.4	2,057.3
10 yr change		165.9	279.3	159.9
PEI	95.0	98.4	104.6	111.6
10 yr change		3.4	6.2	7.0
NS	578.0	642.6	737.0	789.0
10 yr change		64.6	94.4	52.0
NB	457.4	515.7	597.9	634.6
10 yr change		58.3	82.2	36.7
Nfld.	321.8	361.4	457.9	522.1
10 yr change		39.6	96.5	64.2
Central	7,119.6	8,653.2	11,495.3	13,730.9
10 yr change		1,533.6	2,842.1	2,235.6
Quebec	3,331.9	4,055.7	5,259.2	6,027.8
10 yr change		723.8	1,203.5	768.6
Ontario	3,787.7	4,597.5	6,236.1	7,703.1
10 yr change		809.8	1,638.6	1,467.0
West	3,239.8	3,712.9	4,807.9	5,727.0
10 yr change		473.1	1,095.0	919.1
Manitoba	729.7	776.5	921.7	988.3
10 yr change		46.8	145.2	66.6
Saskatchewan	896.0	831.7	925.2	926.2
10 yr change		−64.3	93.5	1.0
Alberta	796.2	939.5	1,331.9	1,627.9
10 yr change		143.3	392.4	296.0
BC	817.9	1,165.2	1,629.1	2,184.6
10 yr change		347.3	463.9	555.5
North	16.9	25.1	37.6	43.2
10 yr change		8.2	12.5	5.6
Yukon	4.9	9.1	14.6	18.4
10 yr change		4.2	5.5	3.8
NWT	12.0	16.0	23.0	34.8
10 yr change		4.0	7.0	11.8

Source: Adapted from Statistics Canada, 'Historical Statistics of Canada', 1983, Cat. no. 11-516, 29 July 1999, Series A2-14.

Table 4.8   Urban–rural population distribution (%), 1941–1971

		1941	1951	1961	1971
Canada	Urban	54.3	61.6	69.6	76.1
	Rural	45.7	38.4	30.4	23.9
British Columbia	Urban	54.2	52.8	72.6	75.7
	Rural	45.8	47.2	27.4	24.3
Alberta[1]	Urban	38.5	48.0	63.3	68.8
	Rural	61.5	52.0	36.7	31.2
Saskatchewan[1]	Urban	32.9	30.4	43.0	49.0
	Rural	67.1	69.6	57.0	51.0
Manitoba	Urban	44.1	56.6	63.9	67.1
	Rural	55.9	43.4	36.1	32.9
Ontario	Urban	61.7	73.4	77.3	80.3
	Rural	38.3	26.6	22.7	19.7
Quebec	Urban	63.3	67.0	74.3	78.3
	Rural	26.7	33.0	25.7	21.7
New Brunswick	Urban	31.4	42.6	53.5	50.6
	Rural	68.6	57.4	46.5	49.4
Nova Scotia	Urban	46.3	55.3	54.3	58.1
	Rural	53.7	44.7	45.7	41.9
Prince Edward Island	Urban	25.6	25.1	32.4	36.6
	Rural	74.4	74.9	67.6	63.4
Newfoundland	Urban	–	42.7	50.7	54.1
	Rural	–	55.3	49.3	45.9
Yukon	Urban	36.7	28.6	34.2	44.2
	Rural	63.3	71.4	65.8	55.8
Northwest Territories	Urban	–	16.9	38.7	40.1
	Rural	–	83.1	61.3	59.9

[1]The definition of 'urban' changes after 1951. From 1961 on, the 'urban' category includes all incorporated and unincorporated cities, towns and villages of 1,000 and over, as well as fringe parts of metropolitan areas. Prior to 1961, 'urban' consists of all incorporated cities, towns and villages, regardless of size.

Sources: Statistics Canada, Census of Canada 1961, 92–536 (1901–61); 1971.

horizontal integration
the corporate strategy of buying out, taking over, or merging with other firms dealing in similar products or services. In the auto industry, Chevrolet, Cadillac, Oldsmobile, and Buick were competitors until they came together in the early years of the twentieth century to form a single giant corporation, General Motors. By the 1930s the North American auto industry had been reduced to three players (General Motors, Ford, and Chrysler).

vertical integration
the strategy in which a single corporation controls many stages of production, from the acquisition of raw materials through processing and product research and development to production and retailing. Thus Weyerhaeuser has acquired tenure in forests across Canada, and can use the trees to produce any number of wood or paper products—lumber, pulp, plywood, newsprint, or glossy paper. Kraft Foods owns the dairies that produce the milk it uses to manufacture processed cheese.

diversification
the strategy of investing in a number of unrelated areas, so that trouble in one area will not mean trouble for others. Corporations that follow this strategy of not putting all their eggs in one basket are known as **conglomerates**, as in the definition of sedimentary rock: unrelated stones cemented together. Thus the CPR, which began as a railway company, invested in a wide variety of fields, including mining, forestry, and real estate, in many countries.

In the corporate world, the strongest firms grew stronger by reducing competition (**horizontal integration**); taking control of all stages in the production process (**vertical integration**); and investing in a broad range of unrelated activities (**diversification**). Examples of these corporate strategies could be found in a wide range of industries by the 1960s, including forest products, mining, and fish processing. 'Scientific management' principles, aimed at maximizing workers' productivity, and capital-intensive technology such as robots made it possible to produce ever-greater quantities of goods with ever-fewer people.

Governments at both the provincial and federal levels helped to shape the economic landscape in several ways. They encouraged large (often foreign) corporations to invest by providing incentives such as infrastructure (roads, rail lines, pipelines, port facilities), tax deductions, and direct subsidies. New investment brought new capital, new technologies ('technology transfer'), and new jobs. As long as new plants were being opened, the multiplier effect brought further increases in employment and more tax revenue for government. Once the plant and equipment were in place, however, new capital-intensive technologies tended to reduce the numbers of workers required, and eventually it would fall to government to assist displaced workers by providing unemployment insurance and retraining programs. Until the early 1970s, however, almost all of Canada was booming, and governments had money to spend.

Unions, for their part, were caught in a dilemma. In order to stay in business, employers had to be competitive: remaining competitive meant increasing productivity, which in turn required the use of new technologies. These realities made it hard for unions to oppose the introduction of new technologies, even if they displaced union members, since there would be no jobs left to protect if the firm went out of business. As a trade-off, unions worked to ensure better working conditions and wages for those workers who remained. Figure 4.2 illustrates the intersecting relationships between corporations, government, and unions. For example, a corporation's decision to introduce robots on the assembly line may increase its productivity but leave many workers needing government assistance in the form of (un)employment insurance or retraining, while the loss of jobs leaves the union with fewer members.

Worker displacement was not the only source of friction in this period. By the 1970s, the environmental movement was beginning to attract wide public attention to the dangers of clear-cut logging, open-pit mining, over-harvesting of fish, massive hydro projects, toxic wastes, and disappearing farm land. At the same time First Nations were gathering strength in their opposition to the industrial and commercial activities taking place on 'their land'.

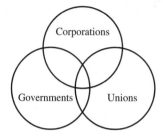

Figure 4.2 Intersecting relationships of corporations, governments, and unions

Globalization, Structural Change, and Uncertainty: From the 1970s to the Present

> If you think the system is working, ask someone who isn't.
> — Anonymous

Time–space convergence, described in the 1990s as the 'death of distance', has been one of the most important factors in the profound changes that economies around the world have experienced during the most recent Kondratieff wave (Cairncross, 1995: 5). Technological innovations in the movement of goods, people, ideas, information, and capital have shrunk weeks to days, days to hours, and in some cases hours to instants. By reducing the cost of overcoming distance, these innovations have radically changed the way business is conducted (how and where goods and services are produced). As important as these changes have been, however, other factors have also helped to place Canada in its present economic and political orbit.

The world economy took a dramatic turn in the early 1970s, from seemingly endless growth and optimism to uncertainty. One of the cornerstones of the Bretton Woods agreement was dislodged when the United States abandoned the gold standard in 1971 (Borthwick, 1998: 508). Exchange rates were left to float, with the result that currencies around the world were destabilized, and international trade and investment suffered accordingly. Interest in gold mining revived as the price of gold, pegged at US$35 an ounce in 1934, soared to $612 in 1980.

Worse, in 1973 the price of oil began to rise in response to an embargo imposed by Arab members of Organization of Petroleum Exporting Countries (OPEC)—from approximately three dollars per barrel to more than thirty by the end of the decade. Fear loomed that supplies would be inadequate for future demand, or even cut off entirely. The rich nations of the world had become dependent upon oil not only as an energy source for everything from transportation to the generation of hydro power, but also for the vast range of petrochemical products—from paints to polyesters. The leap in oil prices became a major contributor to a massive wave of inflation that continued into the early 1980s.

By 1980, goods and services worth $1.00 in 1970 cost $2.17 (Crompton and Vickers, 2000: 9); unemployment increased, and interest rates reached an all-time high (over 20 per cent) as the Bank of Canada tried to curb inflation. The federal government, in an attempt to delay the pain of paying the full market price, implemented the National Energy Program, fixing the price of oil for Canadians below the world market price. At the same time it introduced incentives to explore for new sources of oil and gas as well as alternative energy sources, in the hope that Canada would be able to supply all its own energy needs. The National Energy Program provided a buffer for all regions of Canada. As the country's largest oil producer, however, the province of Alberta objected strongly to this federal intrusion—especially since resources were (and are still) constitutionally supposed to be the exclusive preserve of the provinces.

A major worldwide recession, beginning in 1981, was a frightening reminder of the 1930s depression. World prices for many goods and services, including oil, collapsed. Businesses that had relied on the old Fordist model, mass-producing standardized goods in central locations, had to restructure if they hoped to survive in the new international context. The United States was losing its competitive edge in many areas of production to challengers in Asia and Europe, and responded by imposing new restrictions on imports from those regions.

Although Asia was not immune to events such as the recession of the early 1980s, countries like Japan, South Korea, Taiwan, Singapore, and Hong Kong were among the most rapidly growing economies in the world. In the past Canada's 'front door' to trade and investment had been the Atlantic region, with its strong links to British and other European markets; the west coast was the 'back door'. By the 1980s many nations of the world were coming to prefer trading with the Asia–Pacific region. For Canada, British Columbia became the front door to this economic activity.

In 1989 another significant event took place: the tearing down of the Berlin Wall represented the end of the Cold War. Communist economies, for the most part, adopted capitalism and the global economic system expanded. With more countries signing on to the GATT, freer trade was embraced on the global scale. Other economic arrangements were being contracted on a regional scale, however.

In the North American region, the signing of the Free Trade Agreement (FTA) in 1989 created closer economic ties between Canada and the United States, and five years later the North America Free Trade Agreement (NAFTA) brought Mexico into the relationship. Similar arrangements were being made in other regions of the world as well, the formation of the European Union (EU) in 1992 being the most significant. The purpose of these agreements was to promote trade and employment within regional boundaries while diminishing trade outside them. Thus Commonwealth nations such as Canada, Australia, and New Zealand lost their traditional markets in Britain. From a global perspective, therefore, 'free' trade was anything but free. The advent of another global recession in 1991–2 reined in investments and led corporations to try to reduce their production costs, often by laying off workers. Meanwhile, mounting debts and deficits led governments to reduce their services to the public. Then in 1997 many of the Asian economies collapsed. Trade and investment in that part of the world plummeted, and western Canada was particularly hard hit.

By the late 1990s, meetings of the World Trade Organization were attracting major protests. Police efforts to suppress protests resulted in riots at WTO meetings in Seattle (1999), Genoa (2000), and Quebec City (2001). Criticism has been directed at many aspects of the world economic system as it operates today: among them are the way it appears to reinforce global inequalities, and the power of the WTO and **transnational corporations** to control the internal affairs of nation-states. In the case of Canada, that power may include the ability to dictate policy in areas such as natural resources and health care. In effect, critics charge that major economic interests put the private good ahead of the public good.

The final entry in the list of events that have contributed to the prevailing climate of uncertainty must be the events of September 2001. Their tragic human consequences aside, the terrorist attacks on New York and Washington have disrupted economies around the world, both through the military interventions that followed and through the erection of additional barriers to the movement of goods and people.

Meanwhile, in the midst of this economic and political turbulence, services have replaced manufacturing as the largest component of the world economy, and the rigid Fordist production system is increasingly giving way to a much more flexible system that functions with little regard for national borders. Many writers have seen these changes as part of a general trend that they call globalization (Wallace, 2002; Norcliffe, 2001; Dicken, 1998). Driven by the power of transnational corporations, globalization has three components: economic, cultural, and political. Economically, transnational corporations such as Nike, Coca-Cola, Pepsi, McDonalds, Guess Jeans, and Walt Disney Films have the power to control virtually all aspects of production and consumption. These same corporations also exercise a powerful cultural influence. Meanwhile, free trade agreements and global institutions such as the World Trade Organization, the International Monetary Fund, and the World Bank have made it possible for them to transcend national borders in what amounts to a process of political globalization.

How did transnational corporations become so dominant? There were two related innovations that transformed the world economy: time–space convergence and fragmentation of the production process. The revolution in transportation and communications achieved with advent of super tankers, jet air-cargo carriers, coaxial cables, satellites, cell phones, fax machines, and the Internet effectively conquered the problem of distance, permitting rapid (in the case of communications, virtually instantaneous) movement of goods, capital, and information. Not all locations are equally well connected by these technologies, of course, since they require the kind of infrastructure—sophisticated communication systems, major financial institutions, international airports, universities— usually found only in large urban centres.

Fragmentation of the production process is the strategy of separating the various phases in the production process and assigning them to whatever geographic locations can carry them out in the most cost-effective manner. Together, time–space convergence and fragmentation of the production process have produced the truly transnational corporation. A classic example is IBM. Writing in the 1980s, Galois and Mabin pointed out that IBM had not one 'single plant outside the United States in which a complete product is manufactured'. Typically, every stage of the production process—'from management

transnational (multinational) corporations (TNC; MNC) corporations that control the production of goods and services in more than one country. The head offices of most TNCs are located in the United States, the European Union, or Japan, but 'they are also typically involved in a spider's web of collaborative relationships with other legally independent firms across the globe' (Dicken, 1998: 8).

Despite its remote location, a farmhouse near Smithers, BC, is connected to the world via satellite dish. *Photo B. McGillivray.*

control and raw material production, through simple and more complex component manufacture, to research, design, and final assembly' took place in a different location, 'with the market perhaps in still another country' (1987: 10). The same practices are standard in the manufacture of automobiles, computers, electronic equipment, and many other products. The service industry has also followed this fragmenting, decentralizing strategy. Steve Lohr describes how the New York Life Insurance Company in 1988 decided to 'farm out' to Ireland the processing of insurance claims. Mailed-in claims were sent by air to Ireland, where computer-literate operators—'well-educated young people who need jobs and are willing to work for wages lower than those that must be paid in the United States'—processed them and transferred the necessary information to the head office in Clinton, New Jersey, via the Internet. With a turnaround time of less than a week, this system reduced the company's labour costs substantially.

This global reordering has resulted in an international division of labour. Labour is the least mobile factor in production, and labour-intensive components tend to be manufactured in 'cheap' labour regions such as Mexico and China. Other regions of the world are chosen for their inexpensive supplies of resources such as energy or minerals, or their legal climate, or their willingness to provide tax shelters. Traditional Fordist manufacturing—producing standardized products in a central location—was particularly hard hit by technological change and unpredictable global events. This fatal combination resulted in a great deal of uncertainty in trade and investment decisions. Another major challenge to Fordism's one-size-fits-all principle was the move towards **flexible specialization**: producing goods tailored to meet individual consumer demands, often by contracting out or out-sourcing to small firms throughout the world.

In Canada, the need to respond to these emerging challenges became all the more urgent in the face of the 1980s recessions and the move towards free trade, which made

flexible specialization using a variety of suppliers around the world to produce goods tailored to individual needs, as opposed to the Fordist practice of producing standardized goods in one central location.

many American branch plants redundant. In order to survive, many firms began **restructuring** their operations to reduce costs and thereby increase profits: adopting flexible work regimes to cut down on over-time, disintegrating vertically integrated production processes by contracting-out various phases to independent suppliers, introducing new capital-intensive equipment that required fewer workers, moving to non-unionized locations. What almost all these approaches had in common was that they involved downsizing: reducing the size of the workforce. It was not long before the term 'restructuring' came to be widely seen as a euphemism for cutting costs on the backs of workers. The consequences of restructuring for individuals and communities were often devastating, as Michael Moore's *Roger and Me* (1989)—a documentary about the impact of General Motors's decision to reduce the workforce at its Flint, Michigan, plant by 40,000 workers—showed.

The service industries were also subject to cost-cutting. Bank tellers were replaced by automatic teller machines (ATMs), public transit service was contracted out to part-time, non-union employees, and all levels of public services experienced massive reductions as governments embarked on their own restructuring programs.

Both federal and provincial governments continued to encourage investment by transnational corporations by making land available, offering tax incentives, or promising infrastructure improvements (roads, convention centres, port facilities, etc.); by supporting the GATT and, later, the WTO; and by signing on to the FTA and NAFTA. But these were hard times for government: revenues were insufficient to cover the rising costs of services, from resource management to health care and education. The national debt, and the interest payments on it, had reached a state of crisis by the mid-1990s, soaring from '$20 billion in 1971 to over $545 billion in 1995' (*Canada Year Book*, 2001). Major cuts to such expenditures allowed Ottawa to record a surplus in 1997–8—the first in 28 years (ibid.). But this was accomplished only through significant reductions in transfer payments to the provinces and territories. As Figure 4.3 shows, unemployment increased dramatically in the late twentieth century as a result of events such as the energy crisis and recessions of the 1980s and 1990s. In other words, the government was dismantling the social safety net at the very time when the need for it was increasing.

restructuring
reorganizing corporate operations to cut costs and increase profits, usually by reducing the size of the workforce

Figure 4.3   Unemployment rates, 1969–2003

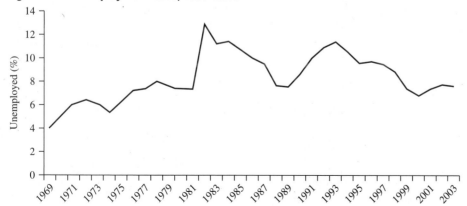

Source: Adapted in part from Statistics Canada, CANSIM database (http://cansim2.statcan.ca), Table 109-5204 (2002–2003 data).

Figure 4.4   Service-producing versus goods-producing employment, 1961–2003

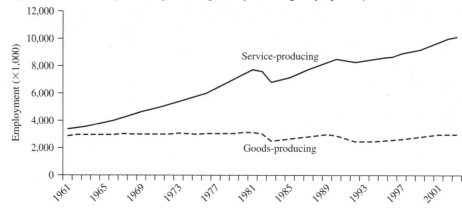

Sources: Adapted from S. Crompton and M. Vickers, 'One Hundred Years of Labour Force', *Canadian Social Trends* (Statistics Canada, Catalogue no. 11-008, Summer 2000): 8; Statistics Canada, CANSIM Tables 281-0005 and 281-0024.

Meanwhile the third sphere (unions) was under siege in both the private and public sectors as corporations and governments alike restructured and downsized their work forces. As the size of the work force shrank, so did the power of unions.

Not all the changes of the 1970s and 1980s were negative, however. Employment in services expanded rapidly, and the fastest-growing transnational corporations were those offering information and knowledge-based services in areas such as advertising, marketing, consulting, engineering, computer programming and servicing, public administration, financial and legal advice, tourism, entertainment, and retail. 'Services are currently the fastest increasing sector of multinationals' investments in both developed and developing countries, outperforming manufacturing production. The export of managerial skills, information and organizational techniques is a major form of intrafirm cross-border trade of multinationals' (Short and Kim, 1999: 17). Figure 4.4 shows the increase in service-related employment. Many of these occupations pay well for the high levels of education and training they require. Unfortunately, other service jobs, particularly at the retail level, pay only minimum wages.

The fact that most new service jobs are located in large urban centres is reflected in population data. Table 4.9 shows that the population increased by nearly 10 million between 1971 and 2001—slightly less than the gain in the previous 30 years (just over 10 million). The baby boom is over, and as Table 4.10 shows, it is through immigration that the greatest population increases now occur. Whereas in the past most immigrants to Canada came from Europe and the United States, today most come from Asian countries, and these newcomers 'have settled overwhelmingly in a handful of large metropolitan areas' (Hiebert, 2000: 26), mainly Toronto, Vancouver, Montreal, and Calgary.

The regional break-down in Table 4.9 shows that Atlantic Canada has experienced the slowest growth rates. The shift in trade and investment from Europe to the Asia–Pacific region, along with the collapse of the cod fishery, has been hard on this part of Canada, particularly Newfoundland.

Central Canada received more than half of the population increase, although there were considerable differences between Quebec and Ontario. Quebec, which has a greater number of labour-intensive industries than Ontario, felt more of an impact from global competition. As well, Quebec's political struggle to separate from Canada created a climate of uncertainty that has discouraged investment. In southern Ontario, a number of Fordist-style operations and American branch plants folded; but a substantial amount of manufacturing has survived, including the auto industry, and service employment has offset job losses in manufacturing.

In the west, Alberta and British Columbia made substantial gains in population. In Alberta, new tar-sands and petro-chemical technologies, together with head-office management in the hydrocarbon industry, have been powerful employment magnets. Asia–Pacific trade, investment, and immigration were major 'pull' factors increasing the population of British Columbia. And although the North is still lightly populated, continued interest in minerals has contributed to a substantial increase.

Table 4.11 records the populations of Canada's twenty largest cities in ten-year intervals from 1971 to 2001. While urban growth generally reflects a combination of natural increase and immigration (from inside the country as well as outside), in some cases it also reflects amalgamation with neighbouring communities (also known as annexation or restructuring boundaries). Halifax, Toronto, and Montreal are just some of the larger centres in Canada that extended their boundaries between the 1991 and 2001 censuses.

Ten of the 16 largest CMAs (Census Metropolitan Areas) are located in the core region. It is an indication of the extent of regional disparities in Canada that the city of Vancouver has almost

Table 4.9 Population and population change (× 1,000), 1971–2001

Region	1971	1981	1991	2001
Canada	21,962.1	24,342.6	27,296.9	31,110.6
10 yr change		2,380.5	2,953.7	3,813.7
Atlantic	2,083.3	2,233.5	2,322.1	2,371.6
10 yr change		150.2	88.1	49.5
PEI	112.6	122.5	129.8	138.9
10 yr change		9.9	7.3	9.1
NS	797.3	847.4	899.9	942.9
10 yr change		50.1	52.0	43.0
NB	642.5	696.4	723.9	756.0
10 yr change		53.9	27.5	32.1
Nfld.	530.9	567.2	568.5	533.8
10 yr change		36.3	1.3	−34.7
Central	13,986.4	15,063.5	16,980.9	19,312.6
10 yr change		1,077.1	1,917.4	2,331.7
Quebec	6,137.4	6,438.4	6,896.0	7,417.7
10 yr change		301.0	457.6	521.7
Ontario	7,849.0	8,625.1	10,084.9	11,894.9
10 yr change		776.1	1,459.8	1,810.0
West[1]	5,837.1	6,976.7	7,908.5	9,329.1
10 yr change		1,139.6	931.8	1,420.6
Manitoba	998.9	1,026.2	1,091.9	1,150.7
10 yr change		27.3	65.7	58.8
Saskatchewan	932.0	968.3	988.9	1,017.7
10 yr change		36.3	20.6	28.8
Alberta	1,665.7	2,237.7	2,545.6	3,059.1
10 yr change		572.0	307.9	513.5
BC	2,240.5	2,744.5	3,282.1	4,101.6
10 yr change		504.0	537.6	819.5
North[1]	55.4	68.9	85.4	99.5
10 yr change		13.5	16.5	14.1
Yukon	19.0	23.2	27.8	30.2
10 yr change		4.2	4.6	2.4
NWT	36.4	45.7	57.6	41.2
10 yr change		9.7	11.9	−16.4
Nunavut				28.1

[1]The totals for the West include the Northwest Territories from 1871 to 1891.

Source: Adapted from Statistics Canada, CANSIM database ⟨http://cansim2.statcan.ca⟩, Table 051-0001.

Table 4.10 Total population growth, immigration, and emigration (× 1,000), 1971–2001

Period	Population[1]	Total pop. growth	Immigration	Emigration	Total migration
1971–81	24,820	3,253	1,824	636	1,188
1981–91	28,031	3,210	1,876	491	1,385
1991–2001	31,111	3,080	2,187	520	1,667

[1]Calculated for the end of the period shown.

Source: Adapted from Statistics Canada, CANSIM database ⟨http://cansim2.statcan.ca⟩, Table 051-0001.

Table 4.11   Largest 20 Census Metropolitan Areas, 1971–2003

	1971		1981		1991		2001		2003
Toronto	2,628.0	2	2,998.9	1	3,898.9	1	4,682.9	1	5,101.6
Montreal	2,743.2	1	2,828.3	2	3,209.0	2	3,426.4	2	3,574.5
Vancouver	1,082.4	3	1,268.2	3	1,602.6	3	1,987.0	3	2,134.3
Ottawa–Hull	602.5	4	717.8	4	941.8	4	1,063.7	4	1,132.2
Calgary	495.7	7	657.1	5	754.0	6	951.4	5	1,016.7
Edmonton	403.3	9	592.7	6	841.1	5	937.8	6	990.5
Subtotal	8,094.9		9,063.0		11,247.4		13,049.2		13,949.8
% of Canada	37.6		37.2		41.2		41.9		
Quebec	480.5	8	576.0	8	645.6	8	682.8	7	705.9
Hamilton	498.5	6	542.1	9	599.8	9	662.4	9	702.9
Winnipeg	540.3	5	584.8	7	660.5	7	671.3	8	698.2
London	286.0	1	283.7	12	381.5	10	432.5	10	457.2
Kitchener	226.8	3	287.8	11	356.4	12	414.3	11	444.1
St Catharines–Niagara	303.4	0	304.4	10	364.5	11	377.0	12	393.6
Halifax	222.6	4	277.7	13	320.5	13	359.2	13	377.9
Windsor	258.6	2	246.1	14	262.1	15	307.9	15	329.0
Victoria	195.8	5	233.5	15	287.9	14	311.9	14	326.7
Oshawa	120.3	[2]	154.2	18	240.1	16	296.3	16	319.3
Saskatoon	126.4	0	154.2	19	210.9	17	225.9	17	233.9
Regina	140.7	7	164.3	16	191.7	18	192.8	18	197.0
St John's	131.8	9	154.8	17	171.8	19	172.9	19	179.7
Sherbrooke	80.7	[2]	74.1	[2]	140.7	[2]	157.0	20	160.9
Total	11,642.2		13,176.5		16,098.3		18,312.0		19,476.1
% of Canada	54.1		54.1		59.0		58.9		61.6

[1] Calculated for the top 6 CMAs.

[2] Not among the largest 20 CMAs.

Source: Adapted from Statistics Canada, CANSIM database (http://cansim2.statcan.ca), Table 051-0034.

as many people as the entire Atlantic region, while Toronto and Montreal are both considerably larger. It is also interesting to compare the population changes in the largest centres with the changes for their provinces. For example, although Newfoundland and Labrador lost some 34,000 people between 1991 and 2001, the province's capital, St John's, recorded an increase in its population, albeit a small one. Halifax gained more than 38,000 people over this period, accounting for almost all of Nova Scotia's increase. Saskatoon and Regina each gained population in a province that recorded only a small overall gain. The major urban centres are growing largely because of the job opportunities they offer. Smaller communities and rural areas, where employment is based on resource extraction and processing, are the big losers in a globalized economy.

Table 4.12 shows interprovincial migration between 1996 and 2003. These data reinforce some of the points made above. In the case of Newfoundland and Labrador, out-migration consistently outweighed in-migration throughout the period, and the out-migration numbers were especially high between 1996 and 1998—no doubt because of the collapse of the cod fishery in 1992. British Columbia too experienced significant out-migration from 1998 on, as a result of the economic slump in Asia, especially Japan, and the crisis in softwood lumber sales. Conversely, Alberta's boom in oil and natural gas industries may have helped to attract immigrants.

Another worthwhile comparison is between urban and rural populations (Table 4.13). As early as 1971 even Saskatchewan was virtually half urban, and by 2001 only Prince

Table 4.12   Interprovincial net migration, 1996–2004

	1996	1997	1998	1999	2000	2001	2002	2003	2004
BC	22,025	9,880	−10,029	−14,484	−14,610	−12,689	−8,556	−1,037	7,333
Alta	7,656	26,282	43,089	25,191	22,674	25,748	26,235	11,903	10,902
Sask.	−2,161	−2,794	−1,940	−4,333	−7,947	−10,453	−8,820	−5,141	−2,901
Man.	−3,566	−5,873	−5,276	−2,113	−3,456	−3,094	−4,344	−2,875	−2,095
Ont.	−2,822	1,977	9,231	16,706	22,369	17,877	5,354	637	−8,793
Que.	−12,626	−17,436	−16,958	−13,065	−12,146	−11,782	−4350	−1,829	−1,474
NB	−369	−1,263	−3,192	−1,244	−1,183	−81	−1,218	−843	−691
NS	−1,245	−1,648	−2,569	201	−270	−824	−898	510	−842
PEI	638	136	−416	193	104	71	62	165	299
NL	−7,436	−8,134	−9,490	−5,695	−4,263	−3,541	−3,352	−1,683	−1,980
Yukon	564	−54	−1,024	−747	−691	−846	−221	149	400
NWT	−542	−696	−1,316	−555	−651	−606	84	242	−31
Nun.	−116	−377	−110	−55	70	220	24	−198	−127

Source: Adapted from Statistics Canada, CANSIM database (http://cansim2.statcan.ca), Table 051-0012.

Table 4.13   Urban–rural population distribution (%), 1971–2001

		1971	1981	1991	2001
Canada	Urban	76.1	75.7	76.6	79.7
	Rural	23.9	24.3	23.4	20.3
British Columbia	Urban	75.7	78.0	80.4	84.7
	Rural	24.3	22.0	19.6	15.3
Alberta	Urban	68.8	77.2	80	80.9
	Rural	31.2	22.8	20	19.1
Saskatchewan	Urban	49.0	58.2	63	64.3
	Rural	51.0	41.8	37	35.7
Manitoba	Urban	67.1	71.1	72	71.9
	Rural	32.9	28.9	28	28.1
Ontario	Urban	80.3	81.7	82	84.7
	Rural	19.7	18.2	18	15.3
Quebec	Urban	78.3	77.6	78	80.4
	Rural	21.7	22.4	22	19.6
New Brunswick	Urban	50.6	50.7	48	50.4
	Rural	49.4	49.3	52	49.6
Nova Scotia	Urban	58.1	55.1	54	55.8
	Rural	41.9	44.9	46	44.2
Prince Edward Island	Urban	36.6	36.3	40	44.8
	Rural	63.4	63.7	60	55.2
Newfoundland/ Labrador	Urban	54.1	58.6	54	57.7
	Rural	45.9	41.4	46	42.3
Yukon	Urban	44.2	64.1	59	58.7
	Rural	55.8	35.9	41	41.3
Northwest Territories	Urban	40.1	48.0	37	58.4
	Rural	59.9	52.0	63	41.6
Nunavut	Urban				20.3
	Rural				79.7

Sources: Statistics Canada, Census of Canada, 1971, 1981, 1991, 2001.

Edward Island and Nunavut were still predominantly rural. The move to globalized world trade and investment, the shift to service-oriented employment, and the ever-greater uncertainty in resource-based employment do not favour these locations.

Across Canada, communities are facing issues that represent opportunities for students contemplating urban studies or urban planning. The largest centres must address all the problems of growth: inadequate housing and transportation, aging infrastructure, suburban sprawl, crime, homelessness, poverty, and drugs. These large cities are also keenly aware of the need to present a dynamic, up-to-date image if they are to attract new economic activity. Supporting professional sports franchises, bidding to host international events like the Olympics, and providing locations for Hollywood films all help to publicize a city and project the kind of image required to attract the interest of major corporations.

At the opposite end of the scale are small communities dependent on resource harvesting and perhaps some processing of these resources. Because these communities are so vulnerable to downturns in the industries they depend on, it is particularly important that they work to re-invent themselves, mainly as tourist or retirement destinations. Here the challenge for planners is to maintain the existing population.

Demographic Change: Using the Past to Predict the Future

> The baby boomers—those born in the two decades after the Second World War—will have the most profound impact on the nation's demographics in the next 25 years.
> — Statistics Canada (2001: 1)

crude birth and death rates
numbers of births and deaths per 1,000 population. Crude rates do not take into account the age and sex structure of the population.

Population change is a product of natural increase (births minus deaths), net migration (immigration minus emigration) and, occasionally, territorial expansion. Table 4.14 summarizes the population and migration data presented in Tables 4.2, 4.3, 4.6 and 4.9. It also documents **crude birth and death rates**: numbers of births and deaths per 1,000 population in a given period. The term 'crude' indicates that these measures do not take into account factors such as the numbers of women of child-bearing age, or of females versus males. Nevertheless, they do give a rough idea of what is happening in Canada today: namely, that birth and death rates have both declined.

Many factors influence fertility, including religion, culture, and economic conditions. The post-war 'baby boom' was a reversal in the downward trend for birth rates that lasted for approximately twenty years. Today the fertility rate is exceptionally low for a variety of reasons: both parents working and establishing careers, higher levels of education, the high costs of raising children, availability of birth control, and perhaps a reluctance to bring children into the world at a time when the future looks so uncertain. On the other hand, death rates have fallen, largely because of improvements in medicine, heath care, and public education. Infant mortality is now very low, and life expectancy has increased (Table 4.15).

Traditionally, natural increase has been the main factor in total population growth; net migration has accounted for a relatively small portion in most census periods, and in a few instances a negative portion (Table 4.14). Since the 1981 census, however, net migration has played a more prominent role, and this trend will likely

Table 4.14   Components of Canadian population growth,[1] 1871–2001

Year	Crude birth rate[2]	Crude death rate[2]	Births (× 1000)	Deaths (× 1000)	Natural increase (× 1000)	Immig- ration (× 1000)	Emig- ration (× 1000)	Net migration (× 1000)	Total growth
1861–71	37.1	20.6	1,370	760	610	260	411	−151	459
1871–81	34.2	18.3	1,480	790	690	350	404	−54	636
1881–91	31.5	18.0	1,524	870	654	680	826	−146	508
1891–01	28.1	16.4	1,548	880	668	250	380	−130	538
1901–11	26.7	12.5	1,925	900	1,025	1,550	739	811	1,836
1911–21	29.3	11.6	2,340	1,070	1,270	1,400	1,089	311	1,581
1921–31	23.2	10.2	2,415	1,055	1,360	1,200	971	229	1,589
1931–41	22.4	10.1	2,294	1,072	1,222	149	241	−92	1,130
1941–51	27.2	9.0	3,186	1,214	1,972	548	379	169	2,141
1951–61	26.1	7.7	4,468	1,320	3,148	1,543	462	1,081	4,229
1961–71	16.8	7.3	4,105	1,497	2,608	1,429	707	722	3,330
1971–81	15.3	7.0	3,575	1,667	1,908	1,824	858	966	2,874
1981–91	14.3	7.0	3,805	1,831	1,974	1,876	639	1,237	3,211
1991–01	11.7	6.8	3,643	2,130	1,513	2,187	520	1,667	3,180

[1]Includes Newfoundland/Labrador since 1951.

[2]For the last year shown.

Source: Statistics Canada, 'Historical Statistics of Canada', Cat. no. 11-516-XIE: Series B1-14 and B15-22, and CANSIM Tables 051–0002 and 051–0013.

continue. Until the mid-twentieth century, Canadian policy encouraged immigrants from Europe and the United States, while actively discriminating against non-whites; head taxes were imposed on immigrants from China (1886, 1901, and 1904), and from 1923 to 1947 the Chinese Exclusion Act prevented all but 15 Chinese immigrants from entering Canada. With the introduction of a points-based system in 1967, people of any nationality were eligible to immigrate to Canada. Canadian society became increasingly multicultural, and further revisions in the late 1980s brought substantial increases in the numbers of newcomers admitted each year (Hiebert, 2000: 26). Table 4.16 shows the major changes in immigration since 1871.

Age–sex pyramids are another indicator of population dynamics, and can be a powerful tool for predicting future population characteristics and societal needs. Essentially an age–sex pyramid is a graph that shows the structure of a population for any given year.

Figure 4.5 shows the age–sex pyramids for Canada in 1901, 1971, 2001, and (projected) 2021. In 1901 most families were quite large. Most Canadians lived in a rural setting; very few people lived to the age of 85, and life expectancy was less than 60 years for both men and women. By 1971 the outline of the pyramid had changed substantially. The decline in birth rates beginning around the turn of the twentieth century is evident, as is the 'baby boom', which made the pyramid broader in the 10–30 age range than at the base. The 2001 pyramid is strikingly different from both 1901 and 1971: now that the broadest segment has moved up to the 45-to-64 age range, the aging of Canada's population is obvious.

Table 4.15   Life expectancy at birth by sex, 1920–1999

Year of birth	Men	Women	Year of birth	Men	Women
1920–22	58.8	60.6	1975–77	70.3	77.7
1925–27	60.5	62.3	1980–82	71.9	79.1
1930–32	60.0	62.1	1985–87	73.0	79.7
1935–37	61.3	63.7	1990–92	74.6	80.9
1940–42	63.0	66.3	1993	74.8	80.9
1945–47	65.1	68.6	1994	75.0	81.0
1950–52	66.4	70.9	1995	75.1	81.1
1955–57	67.7	73.0	1996	75.5	81.2
1960–62	68.4	74.3	1997	75.8	81.3
1965–67	68.7	75.3	1998	76.0	81.5
1970–72	69.4	76.5	1999	76.3	81.7

Sources: Statistics Canada, Cat. no. 84–210–XIB and CANSIM Table 102–0025.

age–sex pyramid
a graph showing the distribution of a population by sex and age for a given year. The shape of the 'pyramid' is a powerful indicator of demographic trends. (For an animated population pyramid illustrating Canada's changing age structure, see Statistics Canada's site '2001 Census: Multimedia' at ⟨http://www12.statcan.ca/english/census01/products/analytic/Multimedia. cfm?M=1⟩. The same site offers several other audiovisual presentations of demographic data).

Table 4.16 Immigration by place of birth (%) and period of immigration, 1871–2001

	1871	1901–1911	1961–1970	1971–1980	1981–1990	1991–2001
Europe	88.9	65.5	69.0	35.8	25.7	19.0
United States	10.9	31.8	6.4	7.4	4.2	2.7
Asia		2.3	12.3	33.0	46.9	59.7
Africa			3.3	5.8	5.9	7.6
Caribbean and Bermuda			5.7	9.6	6.6	4.5
Central and South America			2.2	6.8	9.7	5.6
Other	0.2	0.4	1.2	1.5	0.9	0.9

Sources: G.J. Matthews and R. Morrow, *Canada and the World: An Atlas Resource* (Scarborough: Prentice–Hall, 1995: 13); Statistics Canada Cat. no. 93F0020XCB.

Figure 4.5 Population pyramids, 1901, 1971, 2001, and 2021

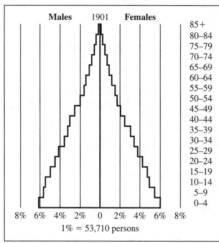

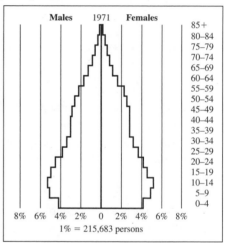

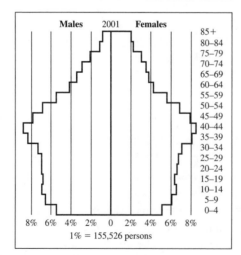

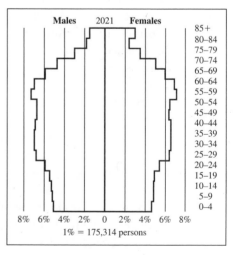

Sources: Statistics Canada, CANSIM Table 052-0001, and 2001 Census Multimedia ⟨www12.statcan.ca/english/census01/products/analytic/Multimedia.cfm?M=1⟩.

Future age–sex pyramids can be predicted on the basis of current life expectancy and fertility rates. Thus in 2021 the population is expected to be older still; as in 2001, women will tend to outlive men, with no significant increase in the number of children at the base of the pyramid. Predicting future population characteristics is important because it allows planners to anticipate the needs of society. Older populations will need more facilities such as hospitals, extended care, and seniors' complexes; and more prescription drugs, hip replacement operations, eye care, and so on. These needs represent enormous additional costs and challenges for the health care system. At the same time many people will be retiring, opening up positions for younger workers. There will be increased demand for housing that is all on one floor, without stairs. Recreational activities such as golf, curling, old-timers hockey, carpet bowling, gardening, and square dancing will increase, as will tourism in the form of cruises, package tours, elder hostelling, and RV outings. There will also be many seniors without sufficient income to live on, and this will present other challenges for the social safety net.

Summary

This chapter has focused on the economic transformation of Canada within the world system of trade and investment. The concept of Kondratieff cycles highlights the links between economic change and technological innovations, recessions and depressions, and other political and social upheavals, including wars.

The Canadian Confederation was formed near the top of the first Kondratieff wave. The new country faced many challenges: to connect distant regions with rail lines, promote settlement, facilitate economic development, and ward off the threat of American annexation in the west. The National Policy, introduced in 1879 during a major international depression, was designed to promote Canadian manufacturing, and it set the course for Canada's economic development for more than a century. Although the National Policy also encouraged the establishment of American branch plants in Canada, economic nationalism would remain the country's preferred approach until the signing of the Free Trade Agreement with the United States in 1989. The impact of economic and political events is evident in demographic data (population growth, immigration, regional distribution, rural versus urban distribution). These data also reflect core–periphery relationships. By 1901, for example, the core region had captured much of Canada's manufacturing and related service functions. With 70 per cent of the country's total population, Ontario and Quebec were already well on their way to becoming more urban than rural. The Maritimes, with nearly 17 per cent of the population—down from 22 per cent in 1871—was already losing ground; and although the west was beginning to attract settlers, the population west of Manitoba was still sparse.

The second Kondratieff wave was powered by the new technologies, such as electricity and the assembly line, that became synonymous with Fordism. Industry, resource extraction, trade, and investment all suffered during the Depression of the 1930s, but the two world wars boosted manufacturing and increased demand for resources.

Census data reflect both the good and the bad times. Despite periods of limited immigration during the Depression and world wars, Canada's total population grew from 5.4 million in 1901 to 14 million by 1951. Population patterns changed significantly over this period. While Ontario and Quebec continued to dominate, the west grew rapidly, and by 1951 accounted for 27 per cent of the national total. Atlantic Canada, even with the addition of Newfoundland and Labrador in 1949, had less than 12 per cent of the population by 1951. The economic boom after the Second World War was a prosperous time for most of Canada, and marked the beginning of the third Kondratieff cycle. Most people were employed, and governments had the revenue for social programs, including universal health care, that did not exist in the 1930s. Statistically, the 1951 to 1971 census indicated a steady growth in Atlantic Canada, continued dominant growth in the central core, and significant increases in the west.

Manufacturing, structured along Fordist lines, continued as the main engine of Canada's economy until the 1970s. Thereafter the world became more complex, largely as a result of technological innovations that made it possible for large corporations to operate on a global scale. New methods of production turned the American industrial belt into the 'rust belt'. Many industries in Canada suffered a similar fate. The main engine of the economy after the 1970s was service industries, and these tended to be located in large urban centres.

At the same time, economies around the world had to deal with the stresses of the energy crisis of the 1970s, a series of recessions in the 1980s and 1990s, and, after 2001, increasing fear of terrorist attacks. The result has been a climate of increasing uncertainty, which has affected the various regions of Canada in different ways.

Ottawa's response to the energy crisis was to set a 'made-in-Canada' price for oil, through the National Energy Program, and to adopt energy self-sufficiency as a goal. The recession of 1981 forced Fordist industries to restructure or go out of business. The focus of trade and investment shifted from Europe to the Pacific region, which favoured British Columbia and the western provinces. Regional alliances such as the Canada–US Free Trade Agreement and, later, NAFTA were formed in an effort to promote cross-border trade and investment, but they threatened the integrity of national borders and policies, and led to the closure of many branch plants. Further recessions in the 1990s and, after 2001, the 'war on terrorism' only increased the general uncertainty that dampened enthusiasm for trade and investment. These dynamics were reflected in census data indicating growth in the major urban centres where knowledge- and information-based service industries preferred to locate, while smaller communities and rural areas struggled to keep their remaining populations.

The last section of the chapter looked in more detail at the way key demographic indicators have reflected the ups and downs of national and international events. Finally, we noted the importance of age–sex pyramids in predicting future societal needs.

This chapter has examined Canada as a region within the international system. The following chapters will trace how the individual regions of Canada itself have evolved within the national framework.

References

Belshaw, J.D., and D.J. Mitchell. 1996. 'The Economy since the Great War'. Pp. 313–42 in H.J.M. Johnston, ed. *The Pacific Province: A History of British Columbia*. Vancouver: Douglas and McIntyre.

Berry, B.J.L., E.C. Conkling, and D. M. Ray 1997. *The Global Economy in Transition*. 2nd edn. Toronto: Prentice Hall.

Borthwick, M. 1998. *Pacific Century*. 2nd edn. Boulder: Westview Press.

Cairncross, F. 1995. 'The Death of Distance'. *The Economist* 336 (7934): 5–6.

Canada Year Book. 2001. Catalogue no. 11-402-XPE.

Crompton, S., and M. Vickers 2000. 'One Hundred Years of Labour Force'. *Canadian Social Trends*. Statistics Canada. Catalogue no. 11-008. Summer.

Dicken, P. 1998. *Global Shift: Transforming the World Economy*. 3rd edn. London: Paul Chapman.

Economic Council of Canada 1977. *Living Together: A Study of Regional Disparities*. Ottawa: Ministry of Supply and Services Canada.

Galois, R.M., and A. Mabin. 1987. 'Canada, the United States, and the World-System: The Metropolis–Hinterland Paradox'. In McCann (1987).

Glavin, T. 2000. *The Last Great Sea*. Vancouver: Greystone.

Hiebert, D. 2000. 'Immigration and the Changing Canadian City'. *Canadian Geographer* 44, 1 (Spring): 25–43.

Knox, P., and J. Agnew 1998. *The Geography of the World Economy*. 3rd edn. New York: Wiley.

Lee, R. 2000. 'Kondratieff cycles'. Pp. 412–15 in R.J. Johnston, D. Gregory, G. Pratt, and M. Watts, eds. *The Dictionary of Human Geography*. Oxford: Blackwell.

Lohr, S. 1988. 'Global Office'. *Vancouver Sun*. 29 October: B9–10.

McCann, L.D. 1990. 'Metropolitanism and Branch Businesses in the Maritimes, 1881–1931'. Pp. 233–46 in G. Wynn, ed. *People, Places, Patterns, Processes: Geographical Perspectives on the Canadian Past*. Toronto: Copp Clark Pitman.

———, ed. 1987. *Heartland and Hinterland*. 2nd edn. Scarborough: Prentice-Hall.

Matthews, G. J., and R. Morrow. 1995. *Canada and the World: An Atlas Resource*. Scarborough: Prentice-Hall.

Moore, M. 1989. *Roger and Me*. Warner Bros. Michael Moore, Producer.

Norcliffe, G. 2001. 'Canada in a Global Economy'. *Canadian Geographer* 45: 14–30.

Short, J.R., and Y.-H. Kim. 1999. *Globalization and the City*. New York: Addison Wesley Longman.

Sitwell, O.F.G., and N.R.M. Seifried. 1984. *The Regional Structure of the Canadian Economy*. Toronto: Methuen.

Wallace, I. 2002. *The Geography of the Canadian Economy*. Toronto: Oxford University Press.

——— 1987. 'The Canadian Shield: The Development of a Resource Frontier'. Pp. 443–81 in McCann (1987).

Wynn, G. 1987. 'The Maritimes: The Geography of Fragmentation and Underdevelopment'. Pp. 174–245 in McCann (1987).

Part *II*

Canada from a Regional Perspective

5

Quebec: Maintaining a Distinct Society

In its present configuration Quebec is Canada's largest province, bounded to the south by New Brunswick and several American states, to the east by Labrador, to the west by Ontario, and to the north by Nunavut.

Within those boundaries are four distinct physiographic regions: the Canadian Shield, which covers most of the province; the St Lawrence Lowlands, where most of the people live; the Hudson Bay Lowlands in the northwest; and the Appalachian Mountains to the south and east. In the 10,000 years since the glaciers retreated, a landscape has emerged that is rich in all the physical attributes essential to development: lakes, rivers, forests, fur-bearing animals, minerals, and, in the south, fertile agricultural land.

The province of Quebec as it exists today is the product of a long history of French–British conflict. Although the British acquired control of New France in 1763, the French-speaking population retained the rights to their own language and religion, as well as their own civil law. As a result, Québécois have maintained a strong sense of identity as a nation and successfully resisted assimilation into the English-speaking mainstream of the country.

Southern Quebec and southern Ontario together constitute the economic core, or heartland, of Canada, and their economies are closely integrated. Nevertheless, they developed in quite different ways. Innis's staples theory provides a good overall explanation of Quebec's development, particularly when the various linkages are taken into account. Montreal attracted many more manufacturing firms than other urban centres in the province, partly because of heavy investment in transportation, and partly because it was home to the anglophones who controlled the banks and finance companies. Quebec's core gained far more labour-intensive industries than its counterpart in southern Ontario. Since the 1960s, however, the pressures imposed by changing global conditions, combined with the uncertainty arising from the politics of separation, have hampered the expansion of both the province's economy and its population.

Settlement in Quebec's periphery was directly related to resource development. As a result, much of the province's hinterland is still dependent on resources, and many communities are vulnerable to the ups and downs of resource industries. Today Quebec's

Figure 5.1   Map of Quebec

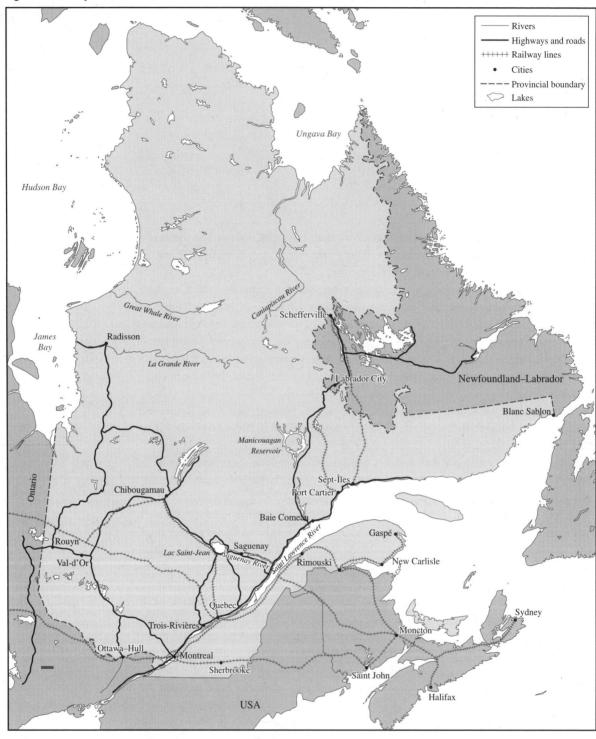

most important resource industry is the generation of hydroelectric power. The giant James Bay hydro project was the catalyst for Canada's first modern-day treaty, signed with the Cree and Inuit people of the region in 1975.

Physical Characteristics and Resources

Quebec encompasses a major portion of the Canadian Shield. After hundreds of thousands of years, weathering and erosion have worn down what once were mountains, reducing them to rugged hills. The exception is in the remote northeast corner, on the Labrador border, where Mount D'Iberville reaches to 1,729 metres. The mainly granitic rocks of the Shield, interspersed with volcanic intrusions, have proven to be rich in deposits of gold, silver, nickel, copper, lead, zinc, and iron, among other minerals. In addition, the province's forests—mixed coniferous and deciduous in the south, spruce and pine in the central portion—have been important economic assets. Quebec's many rivers and lakes and cold winter climate make it ideal habitat not only for fur-bearing animals, especially beaver, but for caribou, deer, moose, waterfowl, and fish, all of which are still abundant.

Along the edges of Hudson Bay and James Bay are the Hudson Bay Lowlands: a flat, low-lying area made up mainly of sedimentary deposits exposed through isostatic rebound over the last 8,000 years. The marshlands of this relatively small region are habitat for fish, birds, and water-oriented animals.

During the last ice age the whole of Quebec was covered by glaciers. As they moved south, the glaciers acted as giant bulldozers, scraping much of the soil from the Canadian Shield and depositing it in the St Lawrence Lowlands. Then, as the glaciers retreated, the Lowlands were flooded with enormous quantities of sediment-carrying water—so much that for approximately 2,500 years the entire region was submerged by what is known today as the Champlain Sea. As the land gradually rose through isostatic rebound and water levels dropped, the Lowlands were left with quantities of unusually fertile soil and the occasional whale fossil—in the summer of 2001, a farmer near Joliette uncovered an almost complete fossilized skeleton of a 10,000-year-old beluga whale (*Vancouver Sun*, 2002: A5).

The mountains of the Appalachian range, in the south and east of the province, are not as old as the Canadian Shield, but they are much older and more weathered than the mountains of Canada's west coast. Since the mountains mark a tectonic boundary, earthquakes are not unknown: settlers in the Quebec City area were terrified by a quake in 1663, and the same region was hit twice in the last century, in 1925 (magnitude between 6.5 and 7.0 on the Richter Scale) and 1997 (magnitude 5.2). The area to the south and east of Montreal has rolling hills, mixed coniferous and deciduous forests, and some fertile land for agriculture. The Gaspé peninsula to the east is much more rugged—Mount Jacques Cartier ascends to 1,248 metres—and although it has forests and some minerals, its agricultural land is limited to the shoreline fringe and river valleys.

Weather and climate in Quebec are mainly continental. Neither the Shield nor the Appalachian range is sufficiently elevated to deflect prevailing winds. Thus cold Arctic air descends in the winter, bringing freezing temperatures and snow. Maritime influences can produce variations, however. In the northwest, the land around Hudson Bay and James Bay experiences large deposits of snow; in the southwest the moderating influence of the Great Lakes gives Montreal more frost-free days (150) than Quebec City (130); and in the winter, dry, cold Arctic air sometimes collides with warm moist air coming from the south, resulting in freezing rain: the 'ice storm' of January 1998 was the worst on record, collapsing transmission lines, bringing transportation to a halt for days, and leaving some parts of the province without power for nearly a month. Finally, in the eastern part of the province the Atlantic Ocean, the cold Labrador Current, and frigid Arctic air masses have an influence in winter, while in summer hot air from the Gulf of Mexico can bring stifling heat.

Rivers have played a crucial role in the economy of Quebec, both as transportation routes and, more recently, as sources of hydroelectric power. Some rivers also have considerable economic value as tourist destinations: the mouth of the Saguenay, for example, offers spectacular scenery and excellent whale-watching. In fact, the diversity of the physical landscape means that the province lends itself to a host of tourism and recreation opportunities throughout the year.

Aboriginal Peoples and Early European Activities

By 1500 the region that is now central Canada was home to numerous Aboriginal groups. In the far north, above the tree line, were the ancestors of the modern Inuit, but farther south were First Nations belonging to two distinct language families: Algonquian to the north and Iroquoian to the south (see Figure 3.2, p. 58). Although tribes of the same group spoke mutually intelligible dialects, they occupied distinct territories and there were often fierce rivalries between them. One of the bitterest was between the Five Nations Iroquois (a confederacy of the Seneca, Cayuga, Onondaga, Oneida, and Mohawk peoples, formed sometime before the sixteenth century), who lived mainly south of the St Lawrence in the area that is now northern New York state, and another Iroquoian confederacy based farther west, between Lake Ontario and Georgian Bay. The members of this confederacy called themselves Wendat but came to be better known as Huron (the name the French called them).

The fertile soils and temperate climate of the St Lawrence Lowlands made it possible to supplement the basic hunter-gatherer diet by growing corn, squash, and beans. The Iroquoians would move to a new location every 15 or 20 years, when the soil they were farming became exhausted, but the relative stability provided by agriculture allowed them to develop highly sophisticated political and cultural institutions. The Algonquian peoples such as the Ottawa, Abenaki, Maliseet and Micmac who occupied the far larger and harsher territory to the north and east lived a less settled life centred on hunting and fishing, although some of the more southerly groups also grew some crops. By the time the first European intruders arrived, the various peoples were already connected by long-established trading relationships.

As Chapter 3 pointed out, the first European expeditions to North America were motivated by the desire for fish, gold, and a more direct route to the precious spices of Asia. In 1534 Jacques Cartier sailed around Newfoundland, establishing that it was an island; charted the Gulf of St Lawrence; and went ashore at Gaspé harbour, where he erected a cross and claimed the land for his king, François I. He then sailed for France, taking with him two sons of an Iroquois chief named Donnacona.

The following year Cartier returned to search for gold and other precious minerals. With the guidance of his Native captives, he travelled up the river to Donnacona's base at Stadacona, near the site of the present-day Quebec City. It is generally thought to have been this place, which the local people also referred to as 'kanata' ('village'), that gave Canada its name.

Continuing upriver, Cartier reached another Iroquois village called Hochelaga before returning to winter over at Stadacona. By the spring 25 of the 110 French sailors had died of scurvy, though many others were saved by the local remedy: a tea made of white cedar. In May 1536 the survivors sailed for France, taking with them Donnacona as well as his sons and several other members of the tribe. Only one of the captives was still alive five years later, when Cartier set out on his last voyage to Canada. Including a number of prospective settlers expecting to establish a French colony at Stadacona, this expedition was much larger than its predecessors, but it was no more successful. Cartier himself returned to France in 1542 with a quantity of supposed gold and diamonds that turned out to be worthless quartz and fool's gold, and the would-be colonists abandoned their settlement the following year. For the rest of the century France took little interest in Canada, except for the fishery off its coast.

Interest in land-based resources was renewed only when the new fashion for felt hats created a sudden demand for North American furs, especially beaver. In 1603 Samuel de Champlain visited the first French trading post on the mainland, established three years

Iroquoian women preparing corn. From Father François Du Creux, *Historiae Canadensis* (Paris, 1664).
Library and Archives Canada.

earlier at Tadoussac, where the Saguenay flows into the St Lawrence. On a second trip, in 1604–5, he helped establish the first successful French settlement in Acadia, and in 1608 he was commissioned by a private company to open a post farther upriver, near the former site of Stadacona. Champlain soon established close relationships both with nearby Algonquian groups such as the Montagnais and with the Huron to the west, who traded with more distant groups for furs and acted as middlemen in the trade. These alignments only intensified the hostility of the Iroquois, who had not forgotten how Cartier treated their ancestors seventy years earlier and were longstanding enemies of both the Huron and the Montagnais. Thus the French and their Native colleagues in the fur trade became military allies as well. At first the French guns provided an advantage over the bows and arrows of the Iroquois. But it was not long before the Iroquois found their own European allies, first Dutch and later British, who supplied them with similar weapons of mass destruction.

No doubt the Aboriginal people saw the Europeans as intruders, but they welcomed the tools and technologies they received in exchange for furs, as well as the military aid and protection that the newcomers offered against their traditional enemies. Conversely, both the French and the British needed their Aboriginal allies to supply furs and to serve as mercenaries in the competition for control of the fur-trade territory.

The consequences of these partnerships were far-reaching. They even extended to Europe, where manufacturing activities received a boost from the increasing demand for trade goods such as kettles, needles, knives, axes, blankets, guns, and ammunition. Far more significant, however, were the consequences for Native North Americans. The introduction of guns changed the nature of Aboriginal warfare from largely ritualistic skirmishes to battles of annihilation. The use of alcohol as a trade good created debilitating dependency, while the increasing demand for furs substantially reduced the time that Native trappers and traders spent hunting for food, and as a consequence many people became increasingly dependent on European foods. Europeans brought with them diseases to which Aboriginal people had no immunity, and they rapidly spread even to districts where no European had yet set foot, resulting in horrendous losses; it has been estimated that a pre-contact population of 20,000 to 30,000 Huron and Petun (another Iroquoian people who were neighbours of the Huron in southern Ontario) was reduced by disease to 12,000 by 1634—only a century after Cartier's first voyage (Heidenreich, 1987: Plate 35). The Christian missionaries who followed the traders and soon established themselves in Huronia contributed to the spread of disease; they also undermined not only traditional spiritual beliefs but also the social bonds between those Hurons who converted and those who did not. When the Iroquois invaded Huronia in the 1648–9, therefore, a society that had already been severely weakened was effectively destroyed. Over the following decades, as French settlement along the St Lawrence gradually increased, several reserves were established to house the Native people displaced by the colonists (Patterson, 1972: 71).

By the beginning of the next century the expansion of the fur trade had taken the French deep into the interior of the continent, and a few small settlements were beginning to take root around missions and trading forts as far south as Louisiana. To the east there was Acadia and a scattering of French settlers on the north coast of Newfoundland. Of all these colonies, the one centred on the St Lawrence—Canada—was the largest. Nevertheless, the 'Canadiens' were vastly outnumbered by the rapidly growing population of the British colonies to the south.

New France

Ten years after establishing the fur-trading fort at Quebec City, Champlain presented the French Crown with a detailed plan for colonization and commercial expansion beyond furs into other commodities such as fish and timber. Finally in 1627 the king's chief minister, Cardinal Richelieu, created the Compagnie des Cent-Associés (Company of One Hundred Associates) and gave it a monopoly of trade from Florida to the Arctic, in return for promoting settlement and missionary activity among the Native population. War between England and France prevented the company from establishing itself in Canada until 1632, by which time the associates had already lost much of their capital. In addition, the costs of fulfilling the Crown's conditions went well beyond those of transporting settlers and missionaries, since the company also had to provide housing, education, hospitals, and defence. In 1645 the associates transferred effective responsibility for the colony to its male residents (the Communauté des Habitants), and in 1663 the king of France himself, Louis XIV, took direct control.

Part of the reason the Crown decided to intervene was that population growth had been extremely slow. In 1663 the colony still had only about 2,500 residents, most of them single men. Thus in addition to dispatching troops to defend the colony, over the next decade France gave small dowries to impoverished young women who became known as the 'filles du roi' ('daughters of the king') and sent them to Canada in the hope that they would marry and raise families there. Although not all the new settlers stayed, the colony's fortunes did improve, and by the early 1670s there were approximately 7,000 non-Native people living along the shores of the St Lawrence. Furs continued to be the principal export, but the economy was beginning to diversify to include 'shipbuilding, trade with the West Indies, commercial crops like flax and hemp, fishing industries, and brewing' (Mathieu, 1985: 1239).

Officially, the economic, political, and social organization of the colony was based on France's own seigneurial system: an essentially feudal model in which the king granted land to the seigneurs (lords), who divided it up and rented it out to tenant farmers. The latter paid taxes to the seigneurs and were required to perform a certain amount of labour on projects such as road-building, and the seigneurs in turn had an obligation to provide facilities such as mills and bake ovens for the community. In practice, however, the seigneurial system in New France served mainly to impose a distinctive geometry on the landscape. To maximize access to the colony's main transportation network—the St Lawrence and its tributaries—seigneurial lands were divided into long, narrow lots, each with a small river frontage. Measuring approximately 180 by 600 metres, each 'long lot' amounted to 30.5 hectares (about 75 acres). Figure 5.2 is a detail from a 1709 map of the Quebec City region, showing the division of land on the Île d'Orléans and the two shores of the St Lawrence The land shown as unoccupied would remain so as long as land with water access was available. By the mid-1700s there were 250 seigneuries in Canada.

Economically, there were fundamental differences in the way the seigneurial system functioned in the old world and the new. France had plenty of people and a limited supply of land, whereas the new colony had an abundance of land, but few labourers to clear and cultivate it. Moreover, in Canada there was little or no market for whatever the land might produce because there were few towns. Low commodity prices and high transportation costs meant that the land along the St Lawrence had little value for the seigneurs. Another important difference was that, in order to attract settlers, taxes were kept much lower in the colony than in France. Thus in theory the peasant land owner ('habitant') in Canada was considerably better off than his French counterpart—though in fact it would take many years of hard work just to clear the land, let alone to establish any kind of economic security.

The Crown's efforts to encourage immigration were successful up to a point, but many of the newcomers did not stay. According to Cole Harris (1966: 110-11), only 10,000 people settled in New France during the colony's first 150 years (1550–1700). Thus most of the population growth shown in Table 5.1 can be attributed to natural increase.

Figure 5.2   Land division in the Quebec City region, 1709

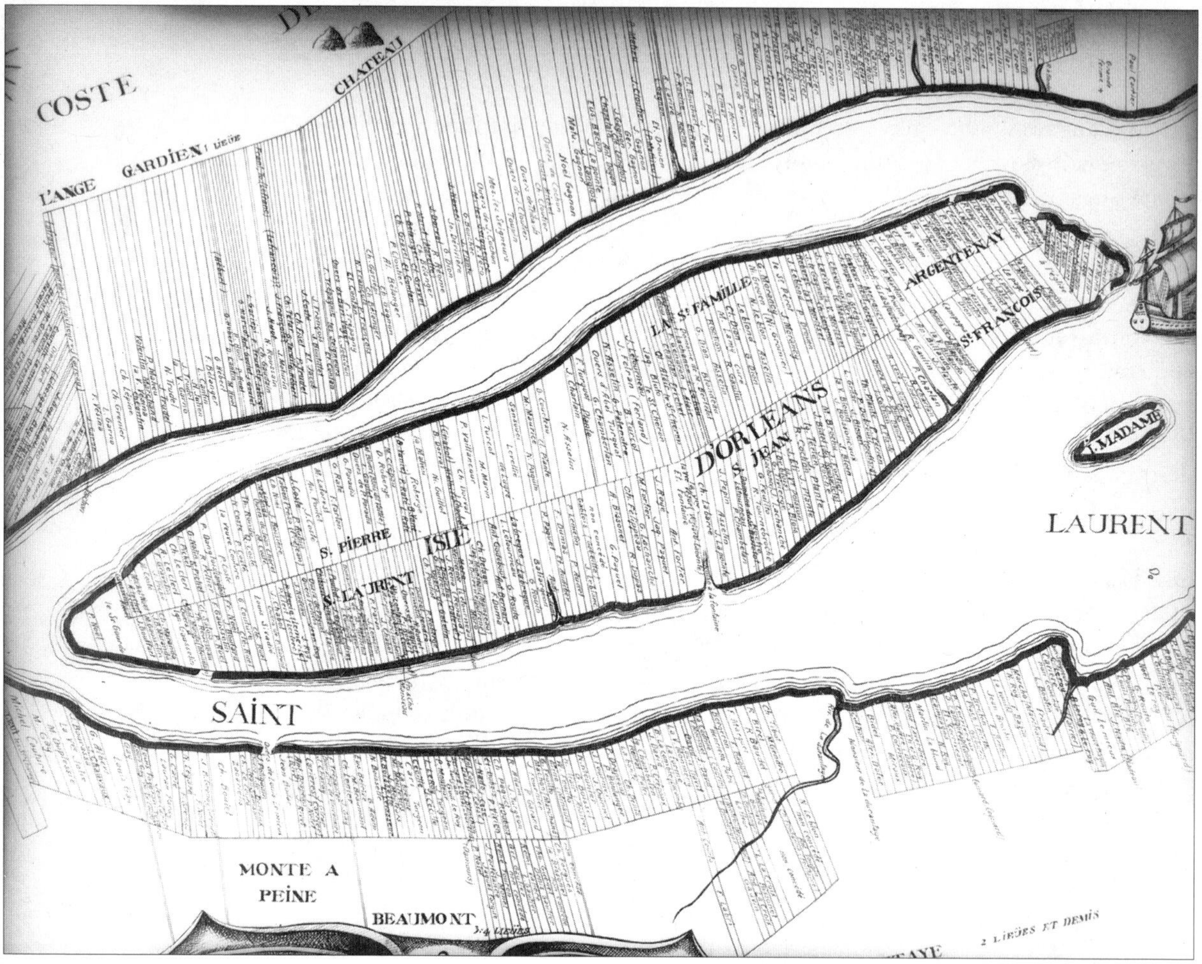

Source: Library and Archives Canada, NMC-0048248.

Table 5.1   Approximate population, New France, 1608–1760

Year	Population	Year	Population
1608	few	1706	16,417
1628	76	1716	20,531
1641	240	1730	33,682
1665	3,215	1737	39,970
1672	7,600	1760	70,000

Source: Adapted from Statistics Canada, 'Introduction to Censuses of Canada, 1665 to 1871', Cat. no. 98-187 (http://www.statcan.ca/english/freepub/98-187-XIE/earlyfre.htm).

Of those 10,000 settlers, Harris estimates that approximately one-third (3,500) were soldiers who came to the colony on contracts and accepted the Crown's offer of a small plot of land if they chose to stay on. One thousand were women, mainly 'filles du roi'. Some 4,500 were indentured servants ('engagés') hired by seigneurs to work for three years, after which they (like the soldiers) could choose either to return to France or to remain in Canada as independent farmers. Of the remaining 1,500, perhaps 500 were seigneurs, clergy, and merchants. The rest were prisoners (often salt smugglers) sent from France as a much-needed labour force to clear away the rocks and trees and create farmland. (New France was not the only distant European outpost to serve as a penal colony.)

In short, most of the settlers were people who arrived with little or nothing and had to work hard for everything they acquired. Once they had cleared enough land to

Figure 5.3 Population distribution along the St Lawrence, 1692 and 1763

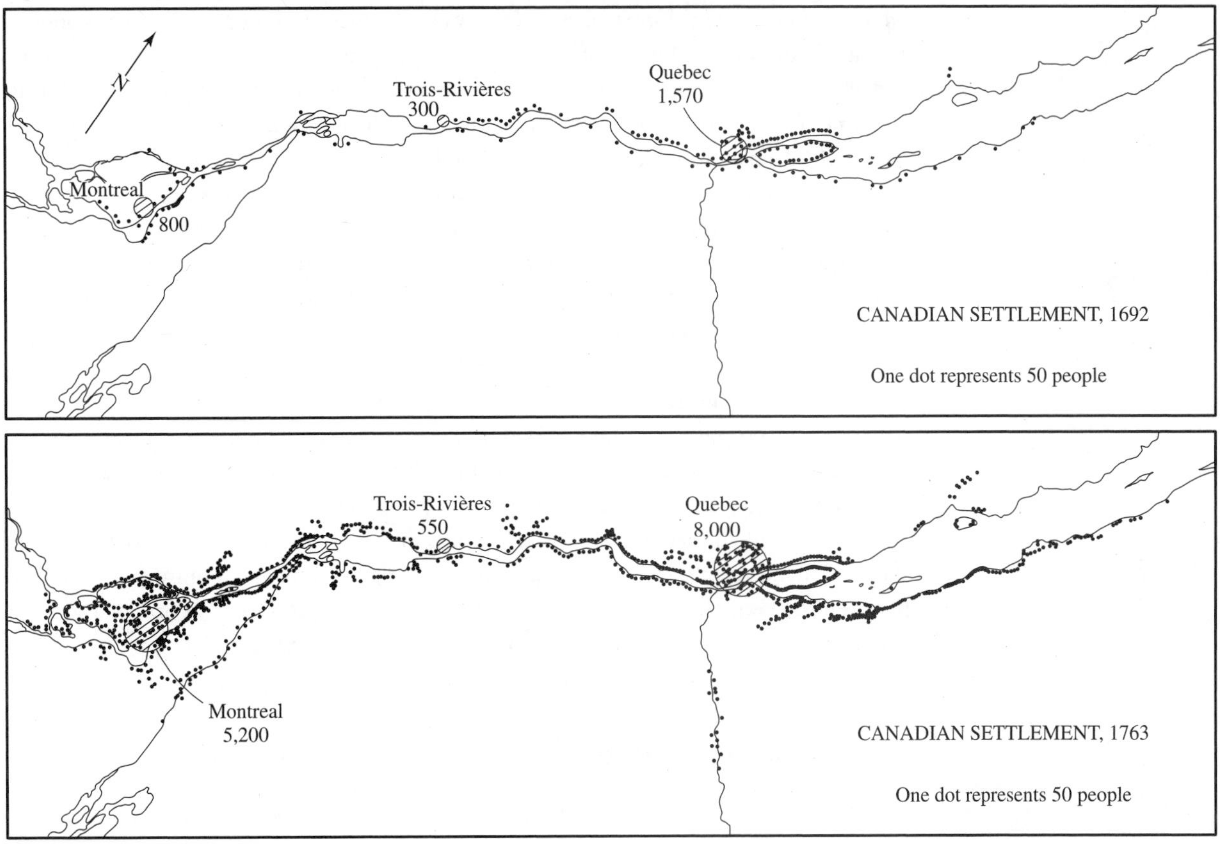

Source: R.C. Harris and J. Warkentin, *Canada Before Confederation: A Study in Historical Geography* (Ottawa: Carleton University Press, 1991). Reprinted by permission of McGill–Queen's University Press.

support a family, most habitants stopped. Harris suggests that 'only a handful of habitant farms' contained more than 34 hectares (84 acres), 'and much the same family farm passed from generation to generation' (1990: 103).

There were advantages to the seigneurial system as it operated in New France. By offering poor people the chance to raise a family on their plot of land, it encouraged immigration. It provided an orderly way of dividing up and distributing land. In addition, the long lots brought neighbours close to one another, which was important for defence, and gave everyone access to water. Other aspects of the system were not so favourable, however. The residential pattern that it imposed did nothing to promote village development. As self-sufficient farmers in a society with no need for commercial agriculture, the habitants had little incentive to invest in new farming practices that might have improved their yields. Finally, the long lots were usually too small to divide among family members: thus in most cases the land would be left to the eldest son, and younger sons would have to move away from the family in order to find land for themselves (see Hamelin, 1969: 56).

Table 5.2 Population of urban centres on the St Lawrence, 1665–1763

Year	Quebec City	Trois-Rivières	Montreal
1665	2,100	455	635
1692	1,570	300	800
1740	4,600	378	4,200
1763	8,000	550	5,200

Sources: Canadian Museum of Civilization, 'New France: A New World' (http://www.civilization.ca); Statistics Canada; R.C. Harris and J. Warkentin, *Canada Before Confederation: A Study in Historical Geography* (Ottawa: Carleton University Press, 1991), 76.

By 1700 three of every four families in New France were farming and the fur trade, which had been the colony's raison d'être, was only its second most important economic activity. With more and more of the river frontage around Quebec taken up, new settlers and younger sons of established habitants increasingly moved upriver towards Trois-Rivières (founded in 1634) and Montreal (founded in 1642 as a missionary colony), where good agricultural land was still available (Figure 5.5).

At the same time the urban population was gradually increasing. Quebec City's location, at the point where the St Lawrence narrows, was ideal both for repelling intruders and for receiving ocean-going vessels; thus all goods entering and leaving the colony continued to move through its port. The centre of the fur trade, however, soon shifted to Montreal. This shift reflected the fact that the trade itself was moving ever deeper into the continent—east, north, and south.

One reason the traders had to keep moving was that the animal populations they depended on, both for furs and for food, were becoming depleted, especially as the competition increased. The first rivals that the French had faced were the Dutch based in the Hudson Valley, but in 1664 they were driven out by the British. By 1670 the British had laid claim to all the lands draining into Hudson Bay and granted this territory, called Rupert's Land, to the newly created Hudson's Bay Company (Figure 5.4). Conflict between the rival empires escalated with the outbreak, in 1689, of the first in a series of European wars that would continue for most of the next seven decades.

French Landscape, British Territory: 1760–1867

In 1759 British troops defeated the French at the battle of the Plains of Abraham, and within a year Britain had nominal control of the eastern half of North America. In reality its control was far from complete.

The Treaty of Paris (1763) marked the end of the Seven Years War, but it did not end the challenges that Britain faced in North America: in some cases it intensified them. One major problem was the vast 'Indian Territory' to the west of the settler colonies. For many years Aboriginal people had been essential partners to one or the other of the European rivals, and this had given them a certain amount of bargaining power. Now, with the disappearance of the French, that power had vanished as well. Always less courteous than the French towards their Native allies, the British put an end to the gift-giving that had been a central feature of French trading practice, and prohibited the sale of ammunition to Aboriginal people, who by now had become accustomed to hunting with guns. Fearing worse to come, a number of Aboriginal leaders in the Ohio Valley organized an armed resistance and in the spring of 1763 launched the first in a series of attacks on British forts that came to be known as Pontiac's uprising.

When news of the uprising reached the British officials who at the time were drafting Britain's policy for its new territory, they recognized the importance of including some conciliating measures for Aboriginal peoples. Thus the Royal Proclamation issued in the fall of 1763 included a number of provisions that in the twentieth century would become central elements in the struggle for Aboriginal rights. It also clearly set the 'Indian Territory' aside for the sole use of Aboriginal people: non-Natives were forbidden to settle there, and only the Crown would have the right to purchase Aboriginal land.

Figure 5.4 British and French in North America after the Treaty of Utrecht (1713)

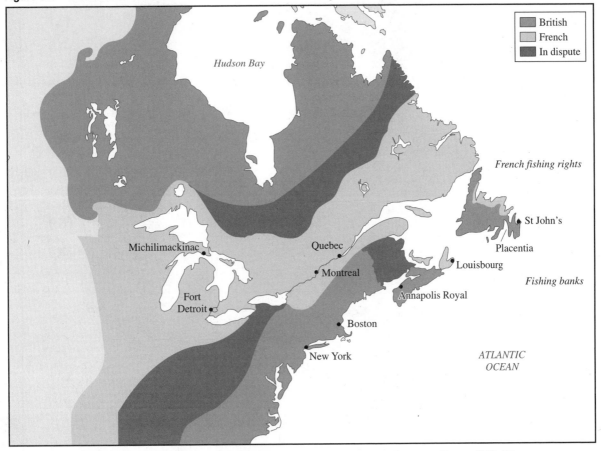

Source: Adapted from R.D. Francis, R. Jones, and D.B. Smith, *Origins: Canadian History to Confederation,* 4th edn (Toronto: Harcourt, 2000), 124.

Land-hungry speculators and settlers in the Thirteen Colonies were not pleased by these provisions, and they were outraged eleven years later, when the Quebec Act (1774) extended the boundaries of Quebec south to the Ohio River and west to the Missis-sippi. Advocates of independence added this legislation to the list of 'intolerable acts' justifying rebellion. A year later the American Revolutionary War began.

In the Royal Province of Quebec, however, the Quebec Act helped to secure the loyalty of more than 70,000 French-speaking people. In addition to extending the province's boundaries, the Quebec Act guaranteed the Canadiens the right to keep their cultural institutions: the French language, the Roman Catholic religion, the French civil law, and the seigneurial system. In this way Britain also managed to retain the crucial support both of the church and of the seigneurs, and Quebec became a society distinct from the rest of British North America.

The American rebels gained their independence in 1783. Of the approximately 35,000 Loyalists—both civilians and disbanded soldiers—who fled to the remaining British colonies during and after the Revolutionary War, the largest group went to the Maritimes, but substantial numbers settled in Quebec, especially in the western region

Figure 5.5   Quebec boundaries before and after the Quebec Act (1774)

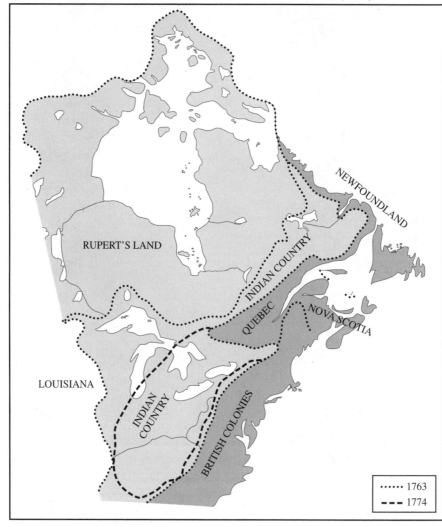

Source: Adapted from Q. Stanford, ed., *Canadian Oxford World Atlas,* 5th edn (Toronto: Oxford University Press, 2003).

between Montreal and Niagara. Having been accustomed to representative government in the Thirteen Colonies, the Loyalists in Quebec were not content to be ruled by a governor, as provided under the Quebec Act. For its part, Britain recognized that, with two very different populations, the vast territory of Quebec would be increasingly difficult to govern; it was also anxious to let the colonies themselves take on some of the financial burden of administration. Thus in 1791 Britain passed the Constitutional Act, creating the separate colonies of Upper and Lower Canada and giving each its own elected assembly with the power to impose taxes.

For the habitant farmers in the St Lawrence Valley it made little difference whether the territory was called Canada, the Royal Province of Quebec, or Lower Canada, but conditions had changed all the same. Lower Canada was no longer exclusively French-speaking. In the years following the American Revolution, the British authorities encouraged English-speakers—both Loyalists from the United States and new immigrants from Great Britain—to settle in Lower Canada. The south coast of the Gaspé, on the Bay of Chaleur, became known as the 'English Coast' as hundreds of Loyalists settled there and established towns such as Carleton, New Carlisle, and New Richmond. Other Loyalists went to the Appalachian region south and east of Montreal: still dotted with place names such as Sherbrooke, Windsor, and Richmond, this region is known today as the Eastern Townships.

Other English-speaking newcomers went mainly to Montreal, where a number of French and Scottish competitors in the fur trade had joined forces in the early 1780s to form the North West Company. By the 1790s the Nor'Westers were presenting a serious challenge to the Hudson's Bay Company. At the same time Montreal was playing an increasingly important role in the timber trade and as a supply centre for Loyalists and others coming into Lower and Upper Canada to farm.

By 1812 relations between the United States and Britain had become increasingly strained. There were two major sources of dispute: Britain's efforts to prevent the Americans from trading with the French, with whom the British were yet again at war, and Britain's support for Aboriginal resistance to American rule in the territory south of the Great Lakes. Believing that many of their former compatriots now living in the Canadas would support them, the Americans declared war on Britain in June 1812. The war was fought on both sides of the border, as well as on the Great Lakes, with Upper Canada bearing the brunt of the action. Nevertheless, Lower Canadian militias did their part—along with British regulars, Upper Canadian militiamen, and Britain's Aboriginal allies—in repelling the invaders. However much Lower Canadians might have resented their province's status as a British colony, at least under British rule they retained the essentials of their distinct society.

The War of 1812 brought French and English Canadians together against a common enemy. Within Lower Canada, however, tensions were soon on the rise. The province's population was growing rapidly and agricultural land was becoming scarce. In the 1820s wheat crops were devastated by the wheat midge (a pest) and rust (a disease), and a slump in the price of wheat from 1835 to 1837 hit marginal farmers—notably the habitants—especially hard. At the same time political discontent was increasing in the elected assembly, which remained virtually powerless compared to the legislative council appointed by the British governor. Although Upper Canada faced the same problem, in Lower Canada the situation was aggravated by an ethnic dimension: the assembly consisted mainly of middle-class French–Canadians, while the appointed elite—the body with the decision-making power—consisted almost exclusively of English-speaking Montreal merchants, with a few wealthy francophones. This elite, known as the Château Clique, preferred to use taxpayers' money for projects such as canals, which benefited themselves, rather than for roads, which would have benefited the struggling farmers (Morton, 1992).

In 1834 the assembly submitted to London a long list of demands for political reform prepared by its dominant party: the nationalist Parti Patriote, led by Louis-Joseph Papineau. The British government did not respond until 1837, and then not only rejected the demands but further restricted the power of the assembly. Meanwhile rural discontent was increasing. Fearing outright rebellion, in mid-November the British authorities decided to arrest the Patriote leaders. Papineau fled to the United States (as did his counterpart in Upper Canada, William Lyon Mackenzie; see Chapter 6) and over the following month more than 300 people were killed in fighting between inexperienced, poorly armed Patriotes and the British army.

Before the end of the year a new governor general had been appointed for British North America. Charged with investigating the causes of the rebellions, Lord Durham arrived in May 1838 and left after just six months, having spent most of that time in Canada East. Nevertheless, his findings had far-reaching consequences.

The Durham Report made three major recommendations: that the system of colonial government be reformed to put more power in the hands of the colonists; that Upper and Lower Canada be reunited; and that the allegedly backward people of French Canada be assimilated as quickly as possible to the culture of the English-speaking majority. Accordingly, in 1840 the Act of Union was passed, and in 1841 Upper and Lower Canada were reunited to form a single 'united province' known as Canada. The two sections were renamed Canada East and Canada West, and an elected assembly was established in which both sections had the same number of representatives—even though Canada East had the larger population at the time.

By mid-century the limits to agricultural settlement in the St Lawrence Lowlands had been reached. Now most aspiring farmers would be forced to move, either to a less favourable location inside the province or somewhere else altogether. Even long-established farms were not doing well. The long lots prescribed by the seigneurial system were not large enough either to subdivide or to support commercial-scale operations, and after generations of subsistence-level cultivation without the benefit of fertilizer or practices such as crop rotation, the soil was exhausted. (The seigneurial system, which had led to the subdivision of farmland into smaller and smaller lots, was seen as part of the problem and was officially abolished in 1854 to encourage the more efficient large-scale farming practised in English Canada.)

Canada West, by contrast, was growing rapidly. With a larger base of good agricultural land to begin with, it continued to attract settlers, and by 1851 its population had surpassed that of Canada East (see Chapter 3, Table 3.2). At this point many in Canada West began calling for representation by population, and the calls for reform grew more insistent as it became clear that no party from either side could win enough seats to form a majority government. By 1864 the need to break this political deadlock had become a major argument in favour of forming a new union of all the British North American colonies.

The French-Canadian Diaspora

The term 'diaspora' originally referred to the dispersion of the Jews among the Gentiles in the 8th–6th centuries BCE, and in recent times it has been applied to the Jews and Jewish communities scattered throughout the world outside the state of Israel. It is also used to refer to any group of people dispersed from their **cultural hearth**: the geographic centre where their culture developed.

cultural hearth
the location where a particular culture evolved.

In the case of French Canada, that hearth is located in the St Lawrence Valley, where the first French colonists settled in the early 1600s. Here the foundations on which French-Canadian society was built are still visible. The long lots bordering the St Lawrence are reminders of the seigneurial system a century and a half after that system was abandoned. The Roman Catholic churches that dot the landscape, and the many places named after saints, recall the central role that the church played in French-Canadian society until the latter half of the twentieth century. The maintenance of the French civil code and, above all, the special status of French as the official language continue to set Quebec apart from the rest of Canada and North America.

It was in the mid-1800s, when the shortage of agricultural land in the St Lawrence Valley became acute, that French-Canadians began to leave their cultural hearth in large numbers. Of course the diffusion of French-Canadian culture had started much earlier, with the young men who left their homes on the St Lawrence to work in the fur trade—some as unlicensed 'coureurs de bois', others as licensed 'voyageurs' employed by the North West Company in Montreal. In the course of exploring, trapping, and trading in the hinterland, many of these men formed relationships with Aboriginal women and eventually settled down to raise families. For the most part their children were brought up as French-speaking Roman Catholics. In this way a number of Métis communities developed in the west, the largest of which was centred in the Red River region of southern Manitoba.

By the 1850s the fur trade was in decline and no longer offered an outlet for those pushed away from the hearth by the land crisis. However, commercial agriculture began to increase once the seigneurial system was abolished (1854), and demand for lumber was rising as well. The manufacturing industry was taking off, and transportation improvements in the form of canals, rail lines, and roads made it increasingly easy to move

Figure 5.6 Diffusion of French Canadians from the cultural hearth

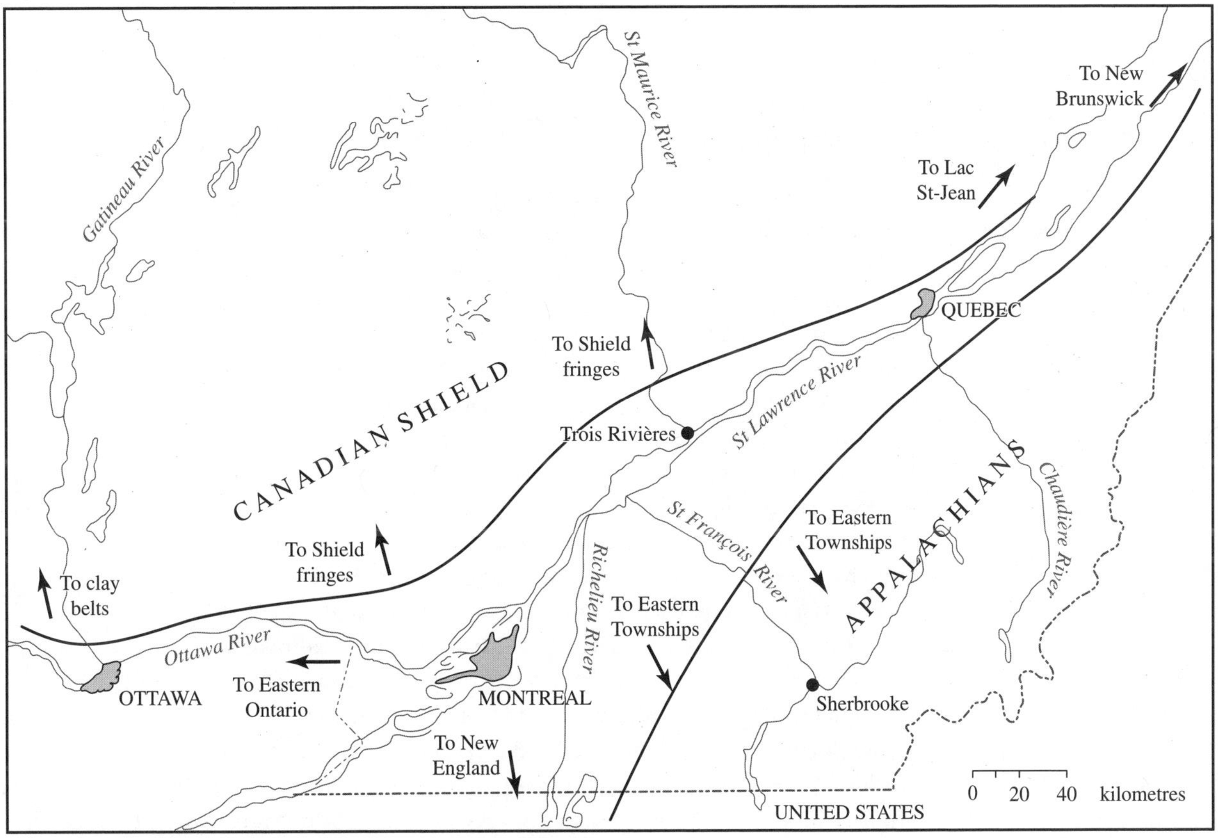

Source: Adapted from J.L. Robinson, *Concepts and Themes in the Regional Geography of Canada*, 2nd edn (Vancouver: Talon Books, 1989), 104.

both people and goods. French Canadians who were determined to continue farming spread out in all directions: south to the Appalachians (Eastern Townships); north to the clay belts of the upper Ottawa River, Lac Témiscamingue, and the Lac Saint-Jean–Saguenay River region; east to the Gaspé and northern New Brunswick; and west to Ontario (Fig. 5.8). Others found work in forestry and mining. By far the largest group, however, headed across the border into the New England states, where textile plants in particular were eager to hire entire families: men, women and children.

The Catholic Church played a major role in the French-Canadian diaspora. On the one hand, it fostered a sense of French-Canadian nationalism, encouraging the faithful to see themselves as a 'chosen people'. On the other, it was well aware of the pressures on the land, and priests often encouraged their parishioners to leave their homes and establish new parishes in other regions; by the 1860s, the church was promoting resettlement to the marginal agricultural land of the northern clay belts and by the end of that century French Canadians had spread across North America. Wherever French Canadians went—the Prairies, British Columbia, the United States—the church accompanied them. In fact, it became even more central to community life outside the cultural hearth, fulfilling a broad range of social and economic functions that in Quebec would have been performed by other institutions.

French Canadians outside Quebec frequently met with opposition to their efforts to maintain their culture, especially through French-language education. Over successive generations, physical distance and pressure to conform to the English-speaking majority culture tended to weaken the diaspora's ties to the cultural hearth, even as the hearth itself grew stronger.

The Quebec Half of the Core: 1867–Present

Canada's core or heartland consists of both southern Quebec and southern Ontario. By the time of Confederation these two provinces were already well integrated economically and poised to dominate the rest of Canada.

Staples theory provides a useful framework for analyzing the evolution of Quebec's industrial heartland. The overlapping sequence of resources—furs, timber, and wheat—stimulated settlement, investment, and demand for consumer goods. As Bertram (1967: 76) points out, however, all staples were not equal in terms of their linkages or economic spin-offs. For example, while the fur trade required the development of port facilities and some warehousing, it did little to encourage settlement. Timber had a far greater multiplier effect, creating a wide range of jobs not only in logging itself but in sawmilling and transportation. As well, the timber trade stimulated shipbuilding in Quebec City and Montreal and as indirectly encouraged immigration (see Chapter 3).

Agriculture, as has been noted, has the potential to generate more linkages—backward, forward, and final demand—than any other industry. In the case of Quebec, the farmland of the St Lawrence Valley attracted thousands of settlers in the first half of the nineteenth century. As the lots with river frontage filled up, roads had to be built to more distant farmlands, and in time these roads facilitated additional settlement. Inputs such as farm equipment and seed became important backward linkages and sources of employment. Among the forward linkages associated with farming are both processing industries (e.g., flour milling, dairy production, tanning) and manufacturing (e.g., leather

Table 5.3   Population of Quebec, Ontario, and Canada (× 1,000), 1871–1891

	1871		1881		1891	
Region	Pop.[1]	% of Cda	Pop.	% of Cda	Pop. %	of Cda
Quebec	1,191.5	32.3	1,359.0	31.4	1,488.5	30.8
Ontario	1,620.9	43.9	1,926.9	44.6	2,114.3	43.7
Canada	3,689.3	100.0	4,324.8	100.0	4,833.2	100.0

Source: Adapted from Statistics Canada, 'Historical Statistics of Canada', 1983, Cat. no. 11-516, 29 July 1999, Series A2-14.

goods). Agricultural land was never as plentiful in Quebec as it was in southern Ontario, however. Nor was it as viable economically. As agricultural land became increasingly scarce, more and more people looking for work either moved away from the core area altogether or relocated to labour-intensive factories, mainly in Montreal. Table 5.3 shows comparative population data for Quebec, Ontario, and Canada as a whole between 1871 and 1891, while Table 5.4 presents data on urban development over the same period.

Many factors besides good soil contributed to Quebec's becoming a core region of Canada. The St Lawrence was the major 'highway' that gave Montreal the advantage as a supply centre for the fur trade, agricultural settlers, and the forest industry. And even though the merger of the North West Company and the Hudson Bay Company in 1821 meant that Montreal's portion of fur-trade activity moved to Hudson Bay, by that time the city was already well on its way to becoming a major centre for banking (the Bank of Montreal was established in 1817), wholesaling, and transportation. By 1820 Montreal's population (19,000) had surpassed that of Quebec City (15,237 in 1819; Nader, 1976: 83, 123).

Maintaining Montreal's dominant position required considerable investment in transportation. To allow large ships to travel up the St Lawrence and into the Great Lakes, new canals had to be built (Lachine Canal, 1825; Welland Canal, 1829) and old ones up-graded. At the same time, the introduction of steam-powered vessels by the 1880s reduced sailing times as well as freight and insurance rates, while the availability of hydraulic power allowed for expansion of manufacturing.

The greatest challenge to the St Lawrence transportation system came from American investments in facilities such as the Erie Canal, which in 1825 linked southern Ontario and the American midwest to New York City. Even though this route took longer than the St Lawrence, lower costs gave it the advantage. Meanwhile, the navigational hazards and three- to four-month annual freeze-up of the river between Montreal and Quebec City raised the costs of both transportation and insurance.

On the other hand, Montreal's position as a transportation and manufacturing centre was reinforced with the construction of rail lines radiating west from Montreal to southern Ontario, east along the south bank of the St Lawrence in the 1850s and, by 1860, south to Portland, Maine. Over the next three decades the Canadian Pacific Railway (CPR) and the Canadian National Railway (CNR; an amalgam of many private railways bought by the federal government in 1919) made Montreal, with its international port, the national rail centre. These transportation advantages were also important factors in the

Table 5.4   Urban population (× 1,000), Quebec and Canada, 1871–1891

	1871	1881	1891
Canada % urban	19.6	25.7	31.8
Quebec % urban	19.9	23.8	33.6
Montreal	107.2	140.7	216.7
Quebec City	59.2	62.4	63.1
Ottawa–Hull	25.3	34.3	50.2
Sherbrooke	4.4	7.2	10.1
Trois-Rivières	7.6	8.7	8.3
Toronto	56.1	86.4	174.4

Source: Statistics Canada, Census of Canada 1871, 1881, 1891.

Table 5.5   Population (× 1,000), Quebec, Ontario, and Canada, 1901–1951

		Quebec	Ontario	Canada
1901	Population	1,648.9	2,182.9	5,371.3
	% of Canada	30.7	40.6	100.0
1911	Population	2,005.8	2,527.3	7,206.6
	% of Canada	27.8	35.1	100.0
1921	Population	2,360.5	2,933.7	8,788.0
	% of Canada	26.9	33.4	100.0
1931	Population	2,874.7	3,431.7	10,376.8
	% of Canada	27.7	33.1	100.0
1941	Population	3,331.9	3,787.7	11,506.7
	% of Canada	29.0	32.9	100.0
1951	Population	4,055.7	4,597.5	14,009.4
	% of Canada	28.9	32.8	100.0

Source: Adapted from Statistics Canada, 'Historical Statistics of Canada', 1983, Cat. no. 11-516, 29 July 1999, Series A2-14.

location of manufacturing, which by the 1880s included railway cars, clothing, and food processing.

Manufacturing and the commercial activities related to it—banking, finance, accounting, insurance, warehousing, wholesaling, retailing—all encouraged urbanization. Montreal was the largest city in Canada in the 1870s and 1880s, with Quebec City a distant second, and Montreal manufacturing in 1881 accounted for 52 per cent of the province's manufacturing (Sitwell and Seifried, 1984: 49).

With the significant exception of the 1930s, the years from the end of the 1800s to the 1950s were relatively prosperous for Canada and the world. Technological advances in a wide range of fields, from electricity to assembly-line production, pulp and paper, and smelting, all played their part. Tables 5.5 and 5.6 track important changes in population and urbanization over the first half of the twentieth century.

Quebec's share of Canada's population steadily declined, but so did Ontario's share, particularly as the west opened up. More revealing was the population shift from rural to urban locations. Even in the core region, there was a trend towards consolidation of farms, and by 1951 technology was making it possible for fewer farmers to produce more agricultural commodities (Table 5.7). Southern Quebec and southern Ontario, the undisputed industrial core of Canada, retained more than three-quarters of the manufacturing jobs in the country (Table 5.8).

Quebec's overall share of manufacturing employment was less than Ontario's because regional specialization meant that manufacturing industries were spread across various Ontario cities, whereas manufacturing in Quebec continued to be concentrated in the vicinity of Montreal. Nevertheless, as Table 5.9 shows, by 1951 Quebec had captured many labour-intensive industries, including textiles, leather, clothing, and wood products.

Ethnicity was another factor in the urban growth of Quebec. Most of the money for investment was in Montreal and it was controlled by anglophones, who were reluctant to

Table 5.6   Urban population, Canada, Quebec, and selected cities (× 1,000), 1901–1951

	1901	1911	1921	1931	1941	1951
Canada % urban	37.5	45.4	49.5	53.7	54.3	61.6
Quebec % urban	39.4	48.2	56.0	63.1	63.3	67.0
Montreal	267.7	468.0	618.5	818.6	903.0	1,471.9
Quebec City	68.8	78.1	95.2	130.6	150.8	276.2
Ottawa–Hull	73.9	105.3	131.9	156.3	187.9	292.5
Sherbrooke	11.8	16.4	23.5	28.9	36.0	54.5
Trois-Rivières	10.0	13.7	22.4	35.5	42.0	65.9
Toronto	208.0	376.5	521.9	631.2	667.5	1,210.4

Source: Statistics Canada, Census of Canada 1901, 1911, 1921, 1931, 1941, 1951.

Table 5.7   Quebec farms, farm size, and farm employment, 1901–1951

Year	Farm	Average farm size (acres)	Farms employment
1901	140,110	103.1	195,921
1911	149,701	104.3	204,616
1921	137,619	125.4	220,036
1931	135,957	127.3	230,547
1941	154,669	116.8	255,083
1951	134,336	125.0	192,072

Source: Adapted from Statistics Canada, 'Historical Statistics of Canada', 1983, Cat. no. 11-516, 29 July 1999, Series M12-22.

venture into regions where English-speakers were few. Thus, as Table 5.6 shows, growth was concentrated in Montreal. With declining demand for ships and squared-off timber, growth in Quebec City was slow, although pulp production and labour-intensive industries such as shoe manufacturing provided some economic advantages, as did the city's position as an administrative centre and port. Growth in the Ottawa–Hull region was somewhat more rapid, largely because Ottawa was the national capital, although pulp and paper and manufacturing were also responsible for some population increases.

From the 1961 to 2001, Quebec's share of the overall Canadian population fell from 28.9 per cent to 23.8, while Ontario's rose from 34.3 per cent to 38.2 (Table 5.10). Although Quebec had a considerably slower growth rate than Ontario, its urban component increased from 74.3 per cent to 80.4. Meanwhile, Toronto surpassed Montreal in population by the beginning of the 1980s (Table 5.11).

Many factors contributed to these population dynamics. Among them were changes in transportation that altered some long-standing spatial patterns. As highway-based trucking increasingly replaced rail service, Montreal's transport role was diminished. At the same time, highway construction allowed industrial and urban expansion to the fringes of Montreal and beyond. In 1959 the completion of the St Lawrence Seaway—a major infrastructure project, shared by Canada and the United States, that

Table 5.8   Manufacturing employment as % of total, Quebec and Ontario, 1911–1951

Year	Quebec	Ontario	Total (Quebec and Ontario)
1911	30.48	46.97	77.45
1941	34.05	45.36	79.41
1951	32.99	44.58	77.57

Source: O.F.G. Sitwell and N.R.M. Seifried, *The Regional Structure of the Canadian Economy* (Agincourt, Ont.: Methuen, 1984), 62.

Table 5.9   Manufacturing employment by industry (%), Quebec and Ontario, 1951

Industrial group	Que.	Ont.	Industrial group	Que.	Ont.
Food and beverages	10.2	11.6	Printing, publishing, and allied industries	4.1	5.5
Tobacco prod.	1.9	0.3	Iron and steel and non-ferrous	14.0	24.2
Rubber prod.	1.7	2.6	Transportation equipment	7.4	11.7
Leather prod.	4.0	2.2	Electrical apparatus	4.5	8.0
Textile prod.	11.2	5.0	Non-metallic mineral prod.	2.2	2.8
Clothing	15.9	6.5	Petroleum and coal prod.	0.8	1.3
Wood prod.	7.9	5.4	Chemicals and allied prod.	4.4	3.8
Paper prod.	7.9	5.4	Miscellaneous industries	2.0	3.0

Source: O.F.G. Sitwell and N.R.M. Seifried, *The Regional Structure of the Canadian Economy* (Agincourt, Ont.: Methuen, 1984), 63.

Table 5.10   Population (× 1,000), Quebec, Ontario, and Canada, 1961–2001

	Region	Quebec	Ontario	Canada
1961	Population	5,259.2	6,236.1	18,200.6
	% of Canada	28.9	34.3	100.0
1971	Population	6,027.8	7,703.1	21,515.1
	% of Canada	28.0	35.8	100.0
1981	Population	6,438.4	8,625.1	24,343.2
	% of Canada	26.4	35.4	100.0
1991	Population	6,896.0	10,084.9	27,296.9
	% of Canada	25.3	36.9	100.0
2001	Population	7,417.7	11,894.9	31,110.6
	% of Canada	23.8	38.2	100.0

Sources: Statistics Canada, 'Historical Statistics of Canada', Cat. no. 11-516-XIE, Series A2–14 to 1971; CANSIM Table 051–0001 for 1981–2001.

Table 5.11   Urban population (× 1,000), Canada, Quebec, and selected cities, 1961–2001

Location	1961	1971	1981	1991	2001
Canada % urban	69.6	76.0	76.0	77.0	79.7
Quebec % urban	74.3	78.0	78.0	78.0	80.4
Montreal	2,109.5	2,743.2	2,828.3	3,209.0	3,426.4
Quebec City	357.6	480.5	576.0	645.6	682.8
Ottawa–Hull	429.8	602.5	717.8	941.8	1,063.7
Sherbrooke	70.3	84.6	117.3	139.2	153.8
Trois-Rivières	83.7	97.9	111.5	136.3	137.5
Chicoutimi	60.3	133.7	135.2	160.9	154.9
Toronto	1,824.5	2,628.0	2,998.9	3,898.9	4,682.9

Sources: Statistics Canada, Census of Canada 1961, 1971, 1981; 'Community Profiles' for 1991 and 2001 ⟨http://www12.statcan.ca/english/profil01/CP01/Index.cfm?Lang=E⟩.

facilitated the movement of ocean-going vessels up the St Lawrence to the Great Lakes—benefited peripheral regions such as northeastern Quebec, with its iron ore industry (see p. 142), but did nothing for Montreal. With the assistance of icebreakers, however, after 1970 Montreal was able to establish itself as a year-round port specializing in container handling.

Politics, both provincial and national, also affected Quebec's demographic and economic development. The Quiet Revolution of the 1960s (discussed in greater detail later in this chapter) inspired a new Québécois nationalism that was reinforced when the sovereignist Parti Québécois was elected to form the provincial government in 1976. The number of English-speaking Quebecers who left the province over next two decades has been estimated at more than 400,000 (UNI, 1999). With them went 'some 300 significant business firms', most of which relocated in Ontario (McKnight, 2001: 141), including the head offices of companies such as Sun Life Insurance. At the same time the province was not faring well in many of the changes associated with globalization, Canada–US free trade, and the shift from manufacturing to service industries as the main source of employment. The loss of American branch plants was not as extensive in Quebec as in Ontario, but only because Quebec had fewer branch plants to begin with. Quebec's labour-intensive industries were hardest hit because they were not able to compete with low-wage regions of the world.

Nevertheless, manufacturing, including forest products such as pulp and paper, is still an important component of Quebec's core economy. A number of labour-intensive industries have also survived, including food processing, textile and clothing manufacturing, and woodworking. Aerospace, snowmobiles, and medical supplies (pharmaceuticals) are other important industries, many of which are still located near Montreal. The graph in Figure 5.7, comparing manufacturing in Quebec and Ontario for 2003, reveals some substantial differences. Whereas automotive products clearly account for the largest share of manufacturing jobs in Ontario, the picture in Quebec is more varied, with jobs distributed across a broader range of product areas.

Many more people are employed in service industries in Quebec's core than in its periphery. While most of these services are business-oriented (marketing, research and development, accounting, real estate, engineering, legal, financial), government services are particularly important in the Ottawa–Hull area and

Tourism is now an important part of Quebec City's economy.
Photo B. McGillivray.

Figure 5.7   Manufacturing as % of total employment, Quebec and Ontario, 2003

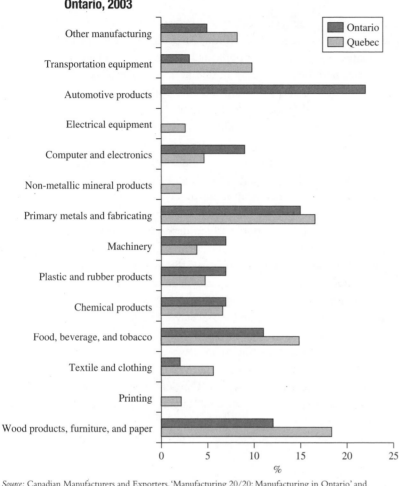

Source: Canadian Manufacturers and Exporters, 'Manufacturing 20/20: Manufacturing in Ontario' and 'Manufacturing in Québec' (http://www.cme-mec.ca/mfg2020/dates/ONReport.pdf); (http://www.cme-mec.ca/mfg2020/dates/QCReport.pdf).

Quebec City. The film industry, computer services, and tourism are other major areas of employment.

Quebec City is not only the province's capital and main administrative centre, but a major tourist destination. Its historic quarter—the only walled city in North America —was designated a UNESCO world heritage site in 1985. Tourists are also attracted to events such as the Winter Carnival, with its famous symbolic figure, the snowman 'Bonhomme'.

Montreal, with nearly half of the province's population, is a vibrant, cosmopolitan city with many service industries, including banking and finance as well as television and film, although as Iain Wallace points out, these services are 'increasingly . . . geared towards the provincial and regional market rather than the national one' (2002: 202). Expo '67 and the 1976 Summer Olympics made Montreal an international destination, and it remains the province's dominant urban centre.

Quebec's Peripheries: 1867–2005

Quebec has two distinct peripheral areas: the Canadian Shield to the north of the St Lawrence Lowlands, and the Appalachian region, consisting of the Gaspé to the east and the Eastern Townships to the south of the populated centre. The settlement and economic development of these peripheral regions reflected both the availability of resources and external demand for them, and both demand and availability were influenced by changes in technology, capital availability and political decisions.

The Shield region's first staple commodity was beaver fur. The fur trade did little to promote permanent settlement, although it led to the establishment of a network of trading posts. By Confederation, the fur trade's most important contribution to the provincial economy was the detailed knowledge of the region's rivers and lakes passed down by fur traders, which provided transportation for other resources.

Throughout the latter half of the nineteenth century, the focus of employment in the Shield region was the timber industry, which depended on river systems both for transportation and for hydraulic power in the form of water wheels, used mainly in sawmills. Although the initial stimulus, in the early 1800s, was British demand, by mid-century the main external market for British North American forest products was the United States. White pine, red pine, ash, and oak were the bases of an expanding industry that was now producing charcoal and barrel staves in addition to squared timber, lumber, and logs.

Agriculture was not absent from the Shield. As was noted earlier in this chapter, some of the farmers pushed out of the St Lawrence Valley because of land shortages were specifically encouraged to move to the clay belts. One advantage of having farms located near forest industry operations was that they could supply the fodder needed to feed the oxen and horses that represented the main short-haul transportation mode. In addition, some subsistence farmers were able to earn income from employment as loggers during the winter.

Technological innovations were important spurs to new industrial activity in the first half of the 1900s. The many river systems emptying into the St Lawrence gave Quebec an advantage in the development of hydroelectric power; there were fourteen dams with generating stations in place by the 1920s and another seven were added over the next 20 years. These early dams were not particularly important in terms of generating capacity, but they were the key to attracting industries that used electrical energy, such as pulp and paper milling and aluminum smelting. The pulp and paper industry, which used mainly spruce, took off in the early 1900s, largely in response to American newspaper demand. In fact, the demand was so great that newsprint was allowed into the United States duty-free in 1911. This change stimulated further investment in Canadian pulp and paper, from Americans as well as Canadians. Meanwhile, the lumber product side of the industry was beginning to experience shortages of wood, particularly the high-value pine, because earlier generations had made no effort to replace the trees they cut down. (Reforestation would not become government policy until the 1950s.)

Although one early pulp and paper mill was established at Hull, on the Ottawa River, most were located in the St Lawrence Valley core, wherever the necessary water, electricity, and rail transportation were available. Soon, however, the network of rail lines and pulp mills was extended into the Témiscamingue region, up the Saint Maurice and Saguenay Rivers, and south into the Eastern Townships.

As successful as this industry was, it was not immune to world events as they affected market prices. For example, the value of pulp and paper production exceeded $240 million by 1929, but dropped to half that by 1933 (Statistics Canada, 11–516–XIE). These reductions had disastrous consequences for the industry, for the communities dependent on it for employment, and for the province dependent on resource revenues and taxes. With the outbreak of the Second World War, however, prices once again rose and mills went back into production.

Exploitation of Quebec's mineral resources did not begin until the 1870s, and was initially limited to deposits of phosphate, asbestos, and placer gold (nuggets, as opposed to gold bound in ore, which is much more expensive to extract) in the southern part of the province. One reason for the delay in tapping the rich metal resources of the Shield was the need for railways to transport the heavy, relatively low-value ore. Another was the high capital cost of developing the necessary technology: lode or hardrock mining involved crushing the rock and using chemical processes such as cyanidation or, later, electrolytic separation to extract the valuable minerals from it.

The first rail line into the Canadian Shield came not from Montreal or Quebec City but from Toronto. Opened in 1902, the Temiskaming and Northern Ontario Railway (see p. 165; renamed the Ontario Northland Railway in 1946) was a direct link between Toronto and the silver-rich cobalt region on the border between Ontario and Quebec. It made economic sense to extend this line across the border to the valuable gold mine of Val-d'Or (1934) and, later, the copper mine of Rouyn–Noranda (1939).

Another metal industry—aluminum production—got its start around the turn of the twentieth century. The key material in aluminum production is bauxite, which had to be imported (mainly from the Caribbean); equally critical, however, is the electrical energy used to refine the bauxite into aluminium. Cheap hydroelectricity became available the 1890s, and in 1901 Canada's first aluminum plant opened at Shawinigan. A second plant was established in 1925 in the Jonquière–Arvida region, where the Roberval Saguenay Railway had been serving pulp-and-paper interests since 1908.

With the economic boom that followed the Second World War came the era of resource mega-projects: huge, capital–intensive ventures in resource development. Quebec was a major beneficiary of this era, in which increasing consumer demand stimulated multi-million-dollar investments in resource industries. Demand for the steel used in automobile production, for example, increased dramatically just as American supplies of iron ore were becoming seriously depleted. The rich iron-ore belt of Quebec and Labrador had been well known since the turn of the century, but the cost of the infrastructure required to exploit it—railways, mining equipment, port facilities, and the like—had been considered too high. Now, in the 1950s, investment in those facilities would be richly rewarded. The first rail line, running from the port of Sept-Îles north through Labrador City (and nearby Wabush) to Schefferville on Quebec–Labrador border, opened in 1954 (Fig. 5.8). A second line, the Quebec–Cartier Railway, opened under separate corporate auspices in 1960, linking Port Cartier to the mines at Gagnon and Fermont.

Figure 5.8   Iron ore communities of Quebec and Labrador

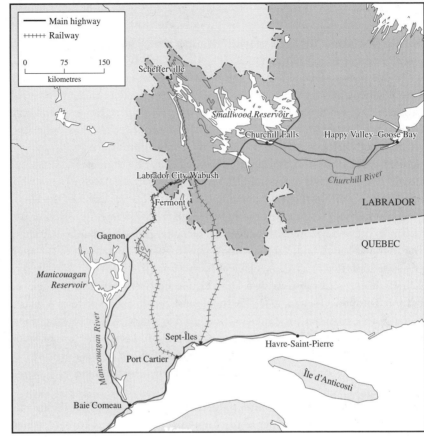

The opening of the St Lawrence Seaway in 1959 facilitated the shipping of iron ore from Quebec to Ontario's steel centres such as Hamilton and Sault Ste Marie, as well as American centres on the Great Lakes. This shipping activity in turn gave rise to new spatial patterns as the carriers of iron ore delivered their cargoes and continued west to Thunder Bay, where they would load up with wheat from the Prairies before returning to Quebec. As a consequence, Quebec ports such as Baie Comeau and Port Cartier erected some of the largest grain elevators in Canada, facilitating the trans-Atlantic grain trade.

Among the other mining regions that received massive infrastructure investments in the 1950s were Chibougamau (copper, gold, and zinc), and Rouyn–Noranda (copper and gold) and Val-d'Or (gold). In addition, a large open-pit copper mine was opened at Murdochville in the Gaspé.

Demand for pulp, paper, and wood products also increased in this period, attracting investment by large multinational corporations. As Table 5.12 shows, Quebec was responsible for a significant share of Canada's pulp and paper production, making this a key industry for both the province's periphery and for the core region where many pulp mills are located.

Table 5.12 Production of pulp, newsprint and other paper products,[1] Quebec and Canada, 1951–2001

Year	Quebec			Canada		
	Pulp	Newsprint	Other Paper	Pulp	Newsprint	Other Paper
1951	3,885	2,617	569	8,450	5,045	1,510
1956	4,363	3,021	675	9,738	5,847	1,834
1961	4,153	2,880	616	10,686	6,094	1,861
1966	5,463	3,579	1,178	14,477	7,739	2,795
1971	5,666	3,609	1,348	16,542	7,733	3,428
1976	5,881	3,931	1,447	17,990	8,063	3,728
1981	6,458	4,287	1,857	19,391	8,950	4,666
1986	6,854	4,199	2,395	21,798	9,202	6,065
1991	7,243	3,883	3,206	23,213	8,855	7,720
1996	7,795	3,978	3,942	24,352	9,027	9,429
2001	7,180	3,561	4,704	24,918	8,373	11,277

[1]Pulp production is reported in thousands of tonnes; newsprint and other paper in thousands of tons.

Sources: Natural Resources Canada, (http://www2.nrcan.gc.ca); Government of Quebec, 'The Pulp and Paper Industry: Highlights' (http://www.mrn.gouv.qc.ca/english/publications/forest/publications/stat_edition_resumee/chap11a.pdf).

Expansion in forestry and mining went hand-in-hand not only with transportation improvements, but also with massive increases in hydroelectric power. Between the 1950s and 1990s, 27 dams were constructed in Quebec, adding more than 30,000 megawatts of electricity to a provincial grid that until the 1960s had a total capacity of only 3,660 megawatts. Other industries requiring large amounts of electricity, such as pulp and paper mills and smelters for minerals and especially aluminum production, located in Quebec, where electricity rates were among the lowest in the world.

Even though the 1950s and 1960s were profitable, workers in the resource industries faced an uncertain future. New technologies in mining and smelting, pulp and paper, and even energy production were capital-intensive, requiring fewer and fewer workers. And the 1970s brought a new set of pressures. Environmental groups forced a near-end to the asbestos industry; called for restrictions on the effluents produced by pulp and paper mills; and demanded that smelters reduce their emissions. Together, environmental concerns and the global energy crisis changed the nature of automobile production. As demand for smaller, lighter, more fuel-efficient cars grew, heavy steel was increasingly replaced with much lighter aluminum and plastic. The decline in demand for steel, and hence iron ore, had a devastating effect in Quebec. Schefferville closed in 1982, Fire Lake in 1985; today all that is left of the company town of Gagnon is a boulevard and a few sidewalks in the wilderness.

One of the most contentious mega-projects involved hydroelectric development. The enormous James Bay project set First Nations and environmental groups against Hydro-Québec and Québécois nationalism, raising fundamental questions about sovereignty, minority rights, and how best to preserve Aboriginal lands and ways of life. The project, announced in 1971 by Premier Robert Bourassa, was a grand scheme to use the water resources of northern Quebec to generate electrical energy both for use in the south and for sale to customers outside the province. The project was divided into two parts, James Bay I and James Bay II, and within these divisions there were several phases (see Figure 5.9).

Figure 5.9   Phases of James Bay hydroelectric development

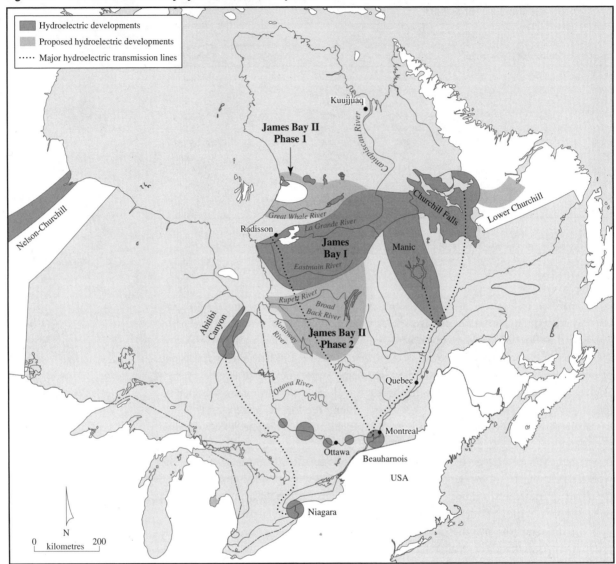

Legend:
- Hydroelectric developments
- Proposed hydroelectric developments
- Major hydroelectric transmission lines

Source: Adapted from P. Dover, 'US Groups Fight James Bay II', *Probe Post* (Summer 1991): 6–12.

James Bay I focused on the La Grande River and its tributaries along with several diversions, such as the Caniapiscau River (which flows to Ungava Bay) and the East-main River (which lies south of the La Grande River). Ten dams were slated to be built and some 10,500 square kilometres of land to be flooded—an area roughly twice the size of Prince Edward Island (Diamond, 1990: 26). James Bay II had two separate phases. The first phase was centred on the Great Whale River, north of the La Grande River, where three dams would produce nearly 3,000 megawatts of electricity. The second phase was to harness the hydroelectric potential (over 8,000 megawatts) of three rivers to the south—the Nottaway, Rupert, and Broadback—by erecting eight dams (see Figure 5.9).

James Bay I and II would require the flooding of approximately 25,000 square kilometres of land. Environmentalists argued that the plan paid scant attention to the environmental consequences of diverting and changing the discharge rates of rivers, the changes to salinity, sediment loading, and the flooding of productive river valleys and wetlands. The Cree and Inuit of the region, who were informed of the provincial government's plans via the media, were incensed that their traditional homeland—on which many still relied for food—was to be altered without consultation, let alone a treaty agreement.

As was noted in Chapter 3, the federal government's 1969 White Paper on Indian Policy had sparked an unprecedented reaction, mobilizing Aboriginal people to protect their interests. Resistance to the White Paper proposals was so strong that in 1973 Ottawa finally withdrew them. In the same year, the Supreme Court of Canada ruled in the Calder case that Aboriginal peoples did indeed hold title to their ancestral lands. In this atmosphere of heightened awareness of Aboriginal rights, the James Bay Cree were granted a court injunction in November 1973 forbidding construction of the hydro project until Aboriginal claims to the land were settled. The injunction was overturned a week later, but it opened the way to negotiations, and two years later the first modern-day treaty in Canada was concluded.

Under the terms of the James Bay and Northern Quebec Agreement, the Cree and Inuit ceded most of the disputed territory in exchange for $225 million in compensation (to be paid over 20 years); guarantees of continuing rights to the use of certain areas for hunting, fishing, and trapping, as well as the right to participate with the government in resource management; and various provisions concerning self-government, education, and local responsibility for health and social services. There were also promises of

Hydro transmission lines in northern Quebec.   *Photo B. McGillivray.*

employment for the local Aboriginal people. (In 1978 the Northeastern Quebec Agreement made similar arrangements for the Naskapi people to the east.)

With this agreement the project proceeded. Dams were built, water was diverted and impounded, and the land was changed substantially, with unforeseen consequences. Productive wetlands and river edges were damaged or lost entirely; caribou calving areas were destroyed; populations of fish and game decreased; and the migratory paths of many animals were altered. Some 10,000 caribou drowned in 1984 when heavy rains caused the dammed Caniapiscau River to flood. In some places dam construction exposed local Cree to the neurotoxin methyl mercury, created when flooded vegetation released naturally occurring mercury into the water: through **bioaccumulation**, small quantities of a toxin can become dangerous concentrations for animals at higher levels in the food chain (Dover, 1991: 7). A new community, Radisson, was established to house the hydroelectric workers. Roads and airports were built, linking this isolated northern region to the south and facilitating an influx of southern hunters, fishers, and tourists, along with alcohol and drugs (Hornig, 1999).

In effect, the province of Quebec reaped the economic benefits of James Bay I and the local Aboriginal people paid the price. The Cree did not even receive the benefit of the jobs they had been led to expect; Chief Billy Diamond charged that the JBDC had 'adopted a racist mandate to drive the Crees out of regional development' (1990: 29). By 1985, when Hydro-Québec announced the beginning of James Bay II, the Cree were determined to resist. In 1989 Quebec signed a contract to sell James Bay electric power to New York State. To bring media attention to their objections the Cree, with the help of the Sierra Club in Washington, DC, organized a campaign that included building a large canoe (the Odeyak) and transporting it, first by dogsled over ice and then by river, from Chisasibi on James Bay to Ottawa and eventually New York City. As a result of Cree pressure, the New York State Power Authority cancelled its contract with Hydro-Québec in 1992.

The James Bay projects became embroiled in the larger turmoil of Quebec politics after 1994, when the Liberal government of Robert Bourassa was defeated by the Parti Québécois under Jacques Parizeau. With a provincial referendum on separation scheduled for 29 October 1995, the Cree held their own vote a few days earlier to determine whether, in the event of separation, they would go with Quebec or remain within Canada. The Cree made it clear that they would choose to stay within Canada. Accordingly, the federal government was obliged to include the Cree issue among the fundamental questions about separation that it posed to the Supreme Court (see p. 150 below).

The story of the Cree people's successful struggle to prevent the damming of the Great Whale River is well documented in the National Film Board's *Power: One River, Two Nations* (1996). Meanwhile, James Bay I has other potential dam sites; for example, an agreement was signed in 2002 under which the Cree agreed to another dam on the Eastmain River in exchange for 'more than $3.4 billion from the Quebec government over 50 years for badly needed services and economic development' and greater 'powers of self-government in certain economic and social-development areas, such as trapping and tourism' (*Montreal Gazette,* 2002; Hydro Québec, 2005). A question that might arise here is why the Cree would agree to further dam-building (as they did in a secret ballot). One argument was that they might as well seek more concessions, since the

bioaccumulation

the process in which trace elements of toxic materials, such as mercury, accumulate in organisms at the lower end of the food chain, such as plankton As animals at higher levels in the food chain, such as fish, eat the plankton, mercury accumulates in their bodies, so that humans who eat contaminated fish consume dangerous concentrations of mercury.

Table 5.13   Electrical energy produced in Quebec, 2001

Source	Production (megawatts)
Hydro (48 dams)	34,466.9
Oil-fired (1 plant)	600.0
Gas-fired (3 plants)	851.2
Nuclear (1 plant)	675.0
Total	36,593.1

Source: Natural Resources Canada (http://www2.nrcan.gc.ca).

Table 5.14   Electricity consumption and sales by Hydro-Québec, 2001

Consumption	Kwh[1]	$million
Residential farm	50,850	3,131
General and institutional	30,360	1,973
Industrial	66,343	2,482
Other	4,659	217
Total within Quebec	152,212	7,803
Sales outside Quebec	42,814	3,120
Total	195,026	10,923

[1]Millions of kilowatt hours

Source: Natural Resources Canada (http://www2.nrcan.gc.ca).

Eastmain had already been 'ruined'. Today Quebec is the largest producer of hydro-electricity in Canada and its rates are among the lowest in Canada; see Tables 5.13–5.15.

Most peripheral regions in Quebec have depended on a single staple, but Chicoutimi-Jonquière in the Lac St-Jean–Saguenay River region has hydroelectricity, aluminium plants, pulp and paper mills, and agriculture. The population of this Census Metropolitan Area grew until 1991 and then declined (Table 5.11), largely because of market uncertainty and a trend towards capital-intensive investment requiring fewer workers.

Sherbrooke, in the Eastern Townships, has done better, partly because it is relatively close to the St Lawrence core and has good transportation links there, and partly because its economic base is more varied, including universities as well as tourism and recreation. Forestry continues to be an important employment sector, but agriculture employs far fewer people than it did in the past, as does asbestos mining. Labour-intensive industries such as clothing, textile, and shoe manufacturing have a long history in this region but in recent years have declined in the face of free trade and global competition.

The maritime periphery of Gaspé is much more distant from the core centres of Quebec City and Montreal. Historically, it was populated by Acadians, Loyalists, and French Canadians, many of whom were 'pushed' out of the St Lawrence Valley. Most of these early settlers were farmers and fishers. Later, when forest products came into demand, lumber along with pulp and paper mills provided employment. With the opening of a large copper mine at Murdochville in 1953 this industry became the region's largest single employer. However, all of these industries employed fewer and fewer people over time, and for many, employment was seasonal. As farming became less economically viable, the government encouraged displaced agricultural workers to work in the ground fishery; but when the cod stocks collapsed in 1991 unemployment again increased. When the Murdochville mine closed in 2002, the region's unemployment rate jumped to more than 20 per cent.

Agriculture has also had a long history in the region. While the main agricultural belt was the Matapedia Valley, there were also many farms on the coastal

Table 5.15   Residential electricity rates for selected Canadian cities[1], 2004

City	750 kW.h	¢/kW.h
Charlottetown	97.11	12.948
Toronto	79.57	10.609
Halifax	75.41	10.055
Regina	72.79	9.705
Saint John	69.42	9.256
St John's	68.62	9.149
Edmonton	65.53	8.737
Vancouver	50.13	6.684
Montreal	**49.32**	**6.576**
Winnipeg	46.04	6.139

[1]Based on 750 kilowatt hours per month.

Source: Manitoba Hydro, 'Residential–Comparison@750 Kw.h per month' (http://www.hydro.mb.ca/your_service/er_residential_750.html). Reprinted by permission.

periphery. By the 1960s, however, agriculture, particularly in the dairy industry, mirrored the decline of marginal farming in many other regions of Canada. In a study of the region, Diane Lamoureux (1985) identified several key factors that led individual dairy farmers to abandon farming. First, new health regulations required the use of modern milking machines, which small dairy farmers could not afford to buy. Second, large corporations controlled the purchasing of milk and wanted to deal only with farms producing high volumes. Third, aging farmers were retiring, while younger family members, with more education and therefore more options for employment, were choosing to go into occupations other than marginal farming.

Quebec Separatism

> Do you agree that Quebec should become sovereign, after having made a formal offer to Canada for a new economic and political partnership, within the scope of the Bill respecting the future of Quebec and of the agreement signed on June 12, 1995? (CBC Newsworld, n.d).

Many people found the question posed by the referendum of October 1995 confusing. The second referendum on separation since 1980, it ended in a victory for the 'No' side, but the margin was slim indeed: 50.6 per cent to 49.4. While separation has emerged as a real possibility only since the 1970s, Quebecers have been struggling to protect their rights and resist assimilation for well over two centuries.

The Quebec Act of 1774 enshrined a number of important rights for the people of Quebec: language, religion, civil law, continuation of the seigneurial system. But the legislative system established by the Constitutional Act of 1791 gave political control to a small group of wealthy merchants, most of them English-speaking, and left the French-speaking majority virtually powerless. Following the rebellions of 1837–8, the Durham Report clearly stated that French Canadians should be assimilated to the majority culture, leading to the establishment of a legislative structure in which the two provinces of Upper and Lower Canada were united as one. The British North America Act of 1867, which established Canada and reserved a number of powers for the provinces, allayed some of Quebec's fears of assimilation. Still, Quebec was only one province in a country dominated by anglophones, and even within its borders, anglophones continued to dominate the economy.

At the national level, the political dominance of the English-speaking population led to serious divisions between Quebec and the rest of Canada. One of the most contentious issues was conscription (compulsory military service) in time of war. Whereas English-speaking Canadians at the time of the First World War generally saw themselves as members of the British Empire and supported Ottawa when it introduced conscription in 1917, many French-speaking Canadians saw the war as Britain's affair and strongly opposed the idea that Canadians should be forced to participate in a foreign conflict. When the issue arose again during the Second World War, the country was similarly divided.

The Quiet Revolution is the name given to the remarkable social changes that Quebec experienced in the 1960s, but its roots dated back to the Second World War. In Quebec as elsewhere, there were not enough men available to meet the huge wartime demand for labour, particularly in the munitions and other war-related industries in the Montreal area, and women were recruited to fill the gap. For many French Canadian women, entering the work force marked a major break from their traditionally rural, church-dominated lives (Lévesque, 1972).

The economic prosperity that followed the war saw many rural Quebecers leave their farms and join the modern urban (or suburban) world of cars and televisions. At the same time values were shifting: more importance was attached to higher education, for example, and less to the rules laid down by the Catholic Church regarding matters such as birth control. Urbanization went hand-in-hand with much smaller families. With the election of Jean Lesage as premier in 1960, the change accelerated. A general trend towards secularization was reflected in massive investment in public education. All electric utilities were nationalized under the umbrella of Hydro-Québec (originally established in 1944). The provincial government began to support French-Canadian artists, filmmakers, and publishers, encouraging a sense of specifically Québécois nationalism that demanded constitutional amendments to protect and strengthen provincial powers.

For the more radical elements in Quebec, however, change was not coming fast enough. After a series of relatively minor terrorist actions in the 1960s, the Front de Libération du Québec (FLQ) in October 1970 kidnapped the British Trade Commissioner, James Cross (later released in a police raid) and murdered the provincial minister of Labour, Pierre Laporte. In response, Prime Minister Pierre Trudeau (at the request of Premier Bourassa) invoked the War Measures Act, which allowed the suspension of civil liberties. Some 465 citizens (in particular those sympathetic to the recently formed Parti Québécois) were arrested without warrants and denied access to lawyers, although in the end only 62 were ever charged, and just 18 pleaded guilty or were convicted. For many Quebecers, even among those who had not previously embraced Quebec nationalism, the October Crisis represented a powerful argument in favour of liberating Quebec from the control of Canada.

In 1976 René Lévesque and his Parti Québécois were elected on a separatist platform. In 1977 the PQ government enacted Bill 101, making French the official language of the province. At the same time it drew attention to the second-class status of French-speaking Quebecers in their own province. As Table 5.16 shows, the economic disparities between those (mainly anglophones) at the top of the income scale and those

Table 5.16 Income levels by ethnic and employment categories, 1976

Income (family or single)	% of total	Characteristics
$100,000 and more	3%	90% English-speaking; large industrialists, financiers, merchants
$20,000 to $100,000	12%	40% English-speaking and 50% bilingual; managers, professionals, businessmen
$7,000 to $20,000	30%	20% English-speaking, 20% bilingual, 60% French-speaking; smaller professionals, organized workers, large farmers
$4,000 to $7,000	35%	5% English-speaking, 30% bilingual, 65% French-speaking; unorganized workers and small farmers
$4,000 and less	20%	95% French-speaking; unemployed, welfare recipients, students, pensioners

Source: Adapted from Statistics Canada, Census of Canada, 1976.

(mainly francophones) at the lower levels were dramatic. Levesque's proposal of sovereignty-association was intended not only to gain greater autonomy for Quebec, but also to restructure its economy. Although the 1980 referendum was defeated (60 per cent 'no' to 40 per cent 'yes'), the federal government was sufficiently shaken to promise constitutional reform.

In 1982 Canada 'patriated' its Constitution, which until then had required the consent of the British parliament for any amendment. After a long battle over the conditions for future amendments, centring on Quebec's demand for a veto, the nine other provinces ratified the new Constitution Act, enacted in 1982, but to this day Quebec has never accepted it. In 1987 Prime Minister Brian Mulroney gained the assent of all ten provincial premiers, including Quebec's Robert Bourassa, to a new constitutional arrangement—the Meech Lake Accord—but several provincial legislatures failed to ratify it before the deadline expired in 1990. Two years later, another attempt at satisfying Quebec's desire for 'distinct society' status within Canada produced the Charlottetown Accord, but it too was defeated, this time in a national referendum. It was in the context of these failures that the stage was set for the 1995 referendum.

The narrow margin of the federalist victory in 1995 gave rise to questions about the status of the territories added to Quebec in 1898 (to the 52nd parallel) and 1912 (north to the Hudson Strait): should they be obliged to separate along with the territory that constituted Quebec in 1867? This issue becomes even thornier given the clear desire of the Cree people, who are the majority population of James Bay region, to stay within Canada. The ambiguity of the referendum question—which essentially required that those who wanted to stay in Canada vote 'No'—was another problem. It was also suggested that there is a fundamental difference between joining the country (as Newfoundland did) and leaving it. Should Quebec, unilaterally, be able to hold a referendum and, by simple majority (50 per cent plus one), leave Canada and become a separate sovereign nation?

A number of these questions were referred to the Supreme Court of Canada, including the question of whether a province has a legal right to secede without Canada's consent. In 1998 the court ruled that there is nothing in international law that would permit unilateral secession 'from a democratic country such as Canada'. In addition the Court ruled that, if Quebec does hold another referendum regarding secession, and 'if there is a clear majority on a clear question', then the province must negotiate with the rest of Canada because secession would involve a change to the Constitution (Dept. of Justice Canada, 1998). This ruling may have helped to discourage pursuit of the separatist option, at least in the short run.

Summary

Quebec is the largest province in Canada and has abundant natural resources. Its Aboriginal people belong to three groups: Iroquoian, Algonquian, and Inuit. Although Cartier led three early expeditions to the St Lawrence (1534–42), European activity in the region did not begin in earnest until 1608, when Champlain established a fur-trading post at Quebec. The impact of the fur trade on First Nations was profound. Populations were drastically reduced by European diseases, warfare intensified, and traditional ways of life changed as Aboriginal people came to depend on European trade goods.

French agricultural settlement along the St Lawrence began in the 1640s, structured along the lines prescribed by the seigneurial system. By 1760, when Britain officially took control of New France, its French-speaking population numbered approximately 70,000. Life for the Canadiens changed little at first, largely because the British—anxious to gain and keep their allegiance at a time when the Thirteen Colonies to the south were becoming restless—guaranteed them the rights to their own language, religion, civil law, and seigneurial tradition. By the 1830s, however, the dominance of the English-speaking elite had become intolerable for many francophones. Following armed rebellions in 1837–8, Britain determined that the French Canadians must be assimilated to British culture, and to that end joined Lower and Upper Canada together in a single legislative unit that by the mid-1860s was in a state of permanent deadlock. By the time Confederation created Quebec as a separate province, agricultural land in the St Lawrence core had become so scarce that many were forced to move away: some to the peripheral regions of Quebec, some to other parts of Canada, and many to the neighbouring states of New England. While urban centres industrialized, and Montreal in particular developed labour-intensive manufacturing industries, the peripheral regions focused on staples—pulp, paper, and wood products, metal mining and smelting, and agriculture. By the 1960s the generation of hydroelectric power had become a major part of the provincial economy.

The years since the 1960s have been turbulent. In addition to facing the same economic uncertainties as every other part of the country, Quebec has had to deal with the fallout from the threat of separation, which led many anglophones to flee the province. Toronto surpassed Montreal as the largest city in Canada, and Quebec's percentage of the Canadian population declined.

Today Quebec's peripheries continue to rely largely on resource industries, many of which have become high-risk as a result of volatile world market prices, global competition, foreign ownership, deregulation, and the rising costs of establishing essential environmental safeguards. Tourism has provided some much needed diversification, but it is seasonal. Meanwhile, the core region faces other pressures because many of its industries are labour-intensive and face competition from regions of the world where labour costs are much lower. At the same time, Quebec has a solid banking, financial, and administrative sector. It is also home to many high-tech industries and a thriving film and television industry. Maintaining its distinctive culture within North America is a great advantage for Quebec's growing tourist industry.

References

Bertram, G.W. 1967. 'Economic Growth in Canadian Industry, 1870–1915: The Staple Model'. Pp. 74–98 in Easterbrook and Watkins (1967).

Billington, R.A. 1960. *Westward Expansion: A History of the American Frontier*. 2nd edn. New York: Macmillan.

Canadian Manufacturers and Exporters. 2004. 'Manufacturing 20/20: Manufacturing in Ontario' and 'Manufacturing in Québec'. http://www.cme-mec.ca/mfg2020/dates/ONReport.pdf; http://www.cme-mec.ca/mfg2020/dates/QCReport.pdf.

Canadian Museum of Civilization. N.d. 'New France: A New World'. http://www.civilization.ca.

Canadian Pulp and Paper Association. N.d. 'Growing Up: The History of Pulp and Paper in Canada'. http://www.cppa.org.

CBC Newsworld. N.d. 'Flashback: Québec Referendum'. http://www.newsworld.cbc.ca/flashback/1995/quebec2.html.

Creighton, D. 1956. *The Empire of the St Lawrence*. Toronto: Macmillan.

Department of Justice Canada. 1998. 'Québec Secession Reference'. http://canada.justice.gc.ca.

Diamond, B. 1990. 'Villages of the Dammed'. *Arctic Circle* (November–December): 24–34.

Dover, P. 1991. 'U.S. Groups Fight James Bay II'. *Probe Post* (Summer): 6–12.

Easterbrook, W.T., and M.H. Watkins, eds. 1967. *Approaches to Canadian Economic History*. Toronto: McClelland and Stewart.

Francis, R.D., R. Jones, and D.B. Smith. 2000. *Origins: Canadian History to Confederation*. 4th edn. Toronto: Harcourt.

Frideres, J.S. 1988. *Native Peoples in Canada: Contemporary Conflicts*. 3rd edn. Scarborough: Prentice-Hall.

Government of Québec. N.d. 'The Pulp and Paper Industry Highlights'. http://www.mrn.gouv.qc.ca/english/publications/forest/publications/stat_edition_resumee/chap11a.pdf.

Hamelin, L.-E. 1969. *Canada: A Geographical Perspective*. New York: Wiley.

Harris, R.C. 1966. *The Seigneurial System in Early Canada*. Kingston and Montreal: McGill-Queen's University Press.

———. 1990. 'The Extension of France into Rural Canada'. Pp. 94–109 in G. Wynn, ed. *People, Places, Patterns, Processes: Geographical Perspectives on the Canadian Past*. Mississauga: Copp Clark Pittman.

——— and J. Warkentin. 1991. *Canada Before Confederation: A Study in Historical Geography*. Ottawa: Carleton University Press.

Heidenreich, C.E. 1987. 'The Great Lakes Basin, 1600–1653'. In R.C. Harris, ed. *Historical Atlas of Canada: Vol. I From the Beginning to 1800*. Toronto: University of Toronto Press.

Hornig, J., ed. 1999. *Social and Environmental Impacts of the James Bay Hydroelectric Project*. Montreal: McGill-Queen's University Press.

Hydro-Québec. 'Eastmain-1-A Powerhouse and Rupert Diversion'. http://www.hydroquebec.com/eastmain1a/en/index.html.

Indian and Northern Affairs Canada. 'The James Bay and Northern Québec Agreement and The Northeastern Québec Agreement'. http://www.ainc-inac.gc.ca.

Innis, H.A. 1930. *The Fur Trade in Canada: An Introduction to Canadian Economic History*. Toronto: University of Toronto Press.

——— 1967. 'The Fur Trade'. In Easterbrook and Watkins (1967).

Isacsson, M., director. 1996. *Power: One River, Two Nations*. Glen Salzman, producer. National Film Board of Canada.

Lamoureux, D. 1985. *The Abandonment of Agricultural Land in Gaspé, Québec: The Causes and the Impacts on Land Use*. Environment Canada, Working Paper No. 29.

Latouche, D. 1985. 'Quebec'. In *The Canadian Encyclopaedia*. Edmonton: Hurtig.

Lévesque, R. 1972. 'Why Québec Should Separate'. *Canada and the World*, 37, 8 (April).

McKnight, T.L. 2001. *Regional Geography of the United States and Canada*. 3rd edn. Upper Saddle River, NJ: Prentice-Hall.

McGuigan, G.F. 1967. 'Administration of Land Policy and the Growth of Corporate Economic Organization in Lower Canada'. Pp. 99-109 in Easterbrook and Watkins (1967).

Manitoba Hydro. April 2004. Residential–Comparison @ 750 Kw.h. per month. http://www.hydro.mb.ca/your_service/er_residential_750.html.

Marsh, J. 1985. 'Stadacona'. P. 1749 in *The Canadian Encyclopedia*. Edmonton: Hurtig.

Mathieu, J. 1985. 'New France'. P. 1239 in *The Canadian Encyclopedia*. Edmonton: Hurtig.

Mills, D. 1985. 'Durham Report'. Pp. 525–6 in *The Canadian Encyclopedia*. Edmonton: Hurtig.

Montreal Gazette. 2002. 'Keep an Eye on Eastmain'. 5 Feb. http://canada.com.

Morton, D. 1992. *A Military History of Canada*. Toronto: McClelland and Stewart.

Patterson, E.P. 1972. *The Canadian Indian: A History Since 1500*. Don Mills, Ont.: Collier-Macmillan.

Nader, G.A. 1976. *Cities of Canada*. Vol. II. *Profiles of Fifteen Metropolitan Centres*. Toronto: Macmillan.

Natural Resources Canada. N.d. http://www2.nrcan.gc.ca.

Ouellet, F. 1980. *Economic and Social History of Quebec 1760–1850*. Ottawa: Carleton University Press.

Sitwell, O.F.G., and N.R.M. Seifried. 1984. *The Regional Structure of the Canadian Economy*. Agincourt, Ont.: Methuen.

UNI. 1999. 'Fine Distinctions'. From the July 1999 Economist Survey on Canada. http://www.uni.ca/economist_survey.html.

Vancouver Sun. 2002. 'Belugas' Forebear Found Intact'. 15 Feb.: A5.

Wallace, I. 2002. *A Geography of the Canadian Economy*. Don Mills, Ont.: Oxford University Press.

6

Ontario: The Dominant Half of the Core

Ontario, the second largest province in area, has the largest population and exercises a powerful influence, both economically and politically, over the whole of Canada. Although the Canadian Shield and Hudson Bay Lowlands account for roughly 90 per cent of the province's land mass, most of the people are concentrated in the triangular area from Georgian Bay across to Kingston and south to Windsor.

The boundaries of the region we know as Ontario have undergone a number of changes. The southern portion was officially part of the extended Quebec from 1774 until 1791, when the Constitutional Act created the separate provinces of Upper and Lower Canada. From 1840 to 1867 the two once again formed a single province of Canada (West and East), and Ontario finally acquired its current name with Confederation. At the time, however, Ontario was considerably smaller than it is today, because the northern area draining into James Bay and Hudson Bay was still part of Rupert's Land. In 1870 the Dominion of Canada purchased Rupert's Land from the Hudson's Bay Company, and in 1876 Ontario's borders were extended westward and north to the 50th parallel. Further extensions in 1889 moved the boundary line west to Lake of the Woods and north along the Albany River to James Bay. The province took its present form in 1912, when its northern border was extended to Hudson Bay.

Economically, Ontario has been the dominant half of the industrial heartland, capturing many of the forward and backward linkages outlined by staples theory. Among the factors that have contributed to its economic success are a base of good agricultural land, an extensive network of natural waterways, available energy supplies, proximity to the industrial centres of the United States, and a large population concentrated in a relatively small area. Political support, both federal and provincial, for the business sector has also benefited Ontario. For many years Toronto lagged slightly behind Montreal in both population and economic influence. But it pulled ahead in the 1970s and since then has clearly established itself as the country's dominant urban centre.

Physical Characteristics and Resources

In many ways Ontario's landscape resembles Quebec's, though Ontario's share of the Hudson Bay Lowlands is considerably larger. Much of the province is covered by the Canadian Shield, which contains minerals—nickel, gold, silver, zinc, copper, uranium—that have been major economic assets.

Figure 6.1   Map of Ontario

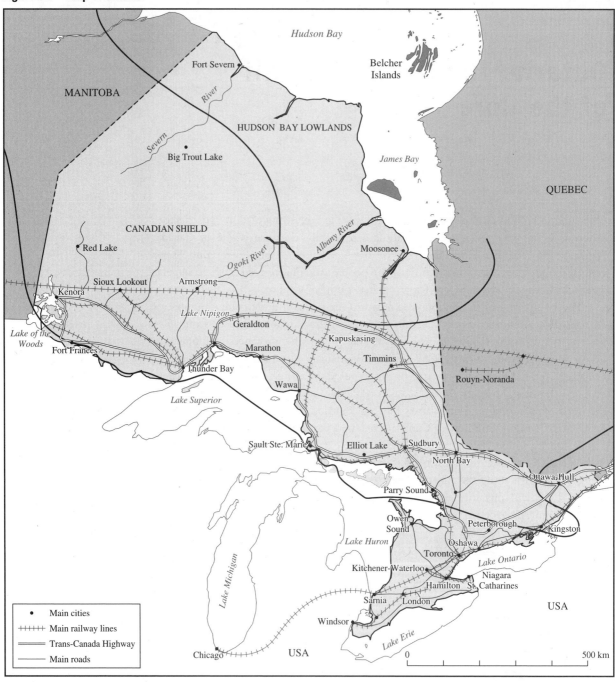

South of the Shield, the landscape is relatively flat, with one exception: the Niagara escarpment is a massive ridge running more than 700 kilometres from Niagara Falls around the end of Lake Ontario and up the Bruce Peninsula into Lake Huron, where it forms a number of islands, including Manitoulin. More than 300 metres high in some locations, the escarpment marks the boundary of what was, 400 million years ago, a large inland sea. Its cliff face consists of harder sedimentary rock (such as limestone and dolomite) over top of more easily eroded shale and sandstone, which rivers such as the Niagara continue to wear away at a rate of one metre per year (University of Waterloo, n.d.; Klivo, 1999).

Glaciation profoundly modified the landscape of southern Ontario. Prior to the last ice age the Great Lakes drained into the south-flowing Mississippi. Then, as the glaciers retreated, isostatic rebound caused the drainage pattern to change direction, so that the lakes now flow northeast into the St Lawrence. The enormous volume of water left behind as the glaciers melted accounts for the remarkable network of lakes and streams that provided the province's first transportation system, while glacial sediments are responsible for the fertile land that made southern Ontario a prime agricultural location. Drumlins, eskers, and moraines are among the other postglacial features of Ontario's landscape.

Ontario's climate is primarily continental. Winters can be extremely cold—Hudson Bay regularly freezes over—and summers extremely hot. In the south, the Great Lakes are large enough have a significant influence, producing high humidity in the summer months, considerable amounts of snow in winter, and one of the longest growing seasons in the country. In summer it is not uncommon for southern Ontario to experience tornadoes. The province's many rivers drain in two directions: northward into James and Hudson Bay, and southward into the Great Lakes and St Lawrence. A few rivers, such as the Abitibi, generate moderate amounts of hydroelectric power, and Niagara Falls is an important source. For the most part, however, Ontario's rivers do not have the elevation required for significant hydro production.

Historical Overview

Until Europeans began dividing up the land for their own purposes, the only territorial divisions in central Canada were those established by physical geography and the semi-nomadic Aboriginal peoples who for thousands of years had moved freely throughout the region. It was only in the late eighteenth century that the Royal Province of Quebec was divided into Upper and Lower Canada. Accordingly, the Chapter 5 overview of Aboriginal peoples and European activities to the time of the American Revolution covered both sides of what is now the Quebec–Ontario border; see pp. 122–30.

Historically, European fur traders had been operating in the future Ontario since the early 1600s. In 1749, under the French regime, several farms were established along the Detroit River (Baskerville, 2005: 38–9). But non-Native settlement in the region did not really get underway until Americans loyal to the British Empire began moving north during the Revolutionary War. It was at this point that British officials, needing land to settle the newcomers on, started making agreements with the Aboriginal peoples in the area west of the Ottawa River. By 1791 the non-Native population had reached roughly 14,000, and by the time the War of 1812 began, that number had grown to 70,000.

The pressure on the Aboriginal population only increased after 1815, when Britain began actively encouraging immigration to its remaining North American colonies. The fertile land of southern Ontario was especially attractive to prospective settlers, but soon white interests began encroaching on more northerly peoples as well, drawn initially by the forests of spruce and pine and then by the rich mineral deposits of the Shield. Thus in 1850 the government set out to acquire land in the area north of Lake Huron and Lake Superior through a more formal treaty process that became the model for the numbered treaties later negotiated in the west (see Chapter 3). Together, the Robinson–Huron and Robinson–Superior treaties acquired 140,000 square kilometres of territory for the government—land that it could then lease to commercial forest and mining companies. In return, the government promised the bands concerned that it would provide a sum of money, a reserve (which could not be sold, except to the government), an annual payment to band members (not indexed), and permission for band members to continue hunting, fishing and trapping over traditional lands that were not occupied. By 1906 similar agreements would be negotiated for all of western and northern Ontario; but there are still parts of southern and eastern Ontario where no treaty has ever been negotiated (see Fig. 3.13, p. 82).

In 2001 the Canadian Census recorded 188,315 persons of Aboriginal heritage (Indian, Métis, or Inuit) in Ontario—an increase of almost 25 per cent from the 1996 figure of 141,525 (*Atlas of Canada,* 2001). There are 134 bands in Ontario and nearly 200 reserves, many of which are plagued by problems such as poor water quality. One of the worst cases came to light in October 2005, when hundreds of residents of the Kashechewan reserve, on the banks of James Bay, had to be evacuated to Sudbury, Timmins, Cochrane, and Ottawa because of deadly E. coli bacteria in their water supply. In this case, the federal government has committed to correcting the problem.

Settlement Patterns to 1867

Historically, Ontario was central to the fur-trading interests of both France and Britain and therefore the site of many skirmishes between the two competing factions. With the British conquest of New France the territorial rivalry ended, but new tensions emerged with the Thirteen Colonies after the Quebec Act of 1774 redrew Quebec's boundaries to include what is now Ontario and a significant portion of the American midwest (see Fig. 5.5, p. 130).

Of the roughly 35,000 Loyalists who moved to British territory before the end of the American Revolutionary War (1776–83), approximately 7,500 settled in the western part of Quebec, mainly in the Kingston area but also around Niagara Falls and along the east side of the Detroit River. By 1790 that number had grown to between 14,000 and 20,000 (Baskerville, 2005: 41, 48). When the Loyalists demanded representative government, British authorities were quite prepared to give it to them, if only because an elected assembly would be able to levy taxes and thus relieve the mother country of a considerable financial burden. Accordingly, the Constitutional Act of 1791 divided Quebec into Upper and Lower Canada (Fig. 3.6, p. 65) and gave each new colony an elected assembly with the right to impose taxes. Other settlers soon followed, converting what had been fur-trading 'Indian' territory to farmland.

Settlement proceeded rapidly as immigrants from the United States (sometimes known as 'Late Loyalists') continued to arrive through the 1790s and early 1800s, attracted by free grants of prime agricultural land (see Table 6.1, p. 158 below). Wheat and potash (fertilizer produced from the ashes of the trees burnt as the forests were cleared for agriculture) became the main export items.

Like all Britain's remaining colonies in North America, Upper Canada was vulnerable to political and economic factors beyond its control. In 1793 Britain and France were at war again; the conflict tapered off for a while but revived in 1803, with both positive and negative consequences for Upper Canada. On the positive side was Britain's need for timber supplies from North America. Initially, this demand stimulated the forest and shipbuilding industries in the Maritimes and Lower Canada, but before long the forests of Upper Canada were also playing an important part in the trade. On the negative side was Britain's imposition (in 1807 and 1809) of barriers to trade between the British North American colonies and the United States.

Another major interruption of trade came with the War of 1812. When the United States declared war on Britain, it expected a warm welcome from the former Americans who made up the majority of Upper Canadians. In fact, roughly half the men called for militia duty did not appear, and some who signed up deserted later on (Baskerville, 2005: 88). But the support the Americans had anticipated failed to materialize, and together British regular troops, Aboriginal warriors, and Upper Canadian militias did succeed in repelling the much larger American forces. In the aftermath of the war, some Upper Canadians became strongly anti-American, and gradually a sense of a distinct identity, neither American nor British, began to emerge, along with a general belief that the credit for defeating the Americans belonged above all to the local militiamen rather than the British troops and Aboriginal fighters. Pierre Berton describes this belief as 'more mythic than real', but suggests that it 'helped to germinate the seeds of nationalism in the Canadas' (Berton, 1985: 1919).

The Treaty of Ghent put an end to the border conflict in 1814, and for a time peace was restored between the Americans and British in North America. In 1818 the boundary between the two territories was officially established and extended, dividing four of the five Great Lakes (Ontario, Erie, Huron, and Superior), running west to Lake of the Woods, and from there following the 49th parallel as far as the continental divide in the Rockies. At this stage the fur-trading territory west of Upper Canada was the domain of the Hudson's Bay Company, but it would be of vital importance to the future Ontario.

After the War of 1812, the main source of immigration to Upper Canada shifted from the United States to the British Isles. As the population increased, so did discontent with the colony's political system, for—as in Lower Canada—the elected assembly had virtually no decision-making power. Instead, two councils (executive and legislative), whose members were appointed by the lieutenant governor, controlled the business of government. The ruling elite, known as the Family Compact, was composed almost exclusively of wealthy British landowners firmly opposed to any democratic reform of the kind adopted by the United States. It 'reserved nearly all jobs for its own members and its hangers-on, . . . directed economic development for its own profit, [and] tried to monopolize much of the public land for the advantage of one religious denomination'—that denomination being the Church of England (Craig, 1963: 201). Finally, in December 1837 a Toronto newspaper editor and Reform politician named William Lyon Mackenzie led roughly a thousand poorly armed citizens down Yonge Street in an unsuccessful attempt to overthrow the government. A few days later, an attempted uprising near Brantford also failed. Nevertheless, these actions, together with the rebellions in Lower Canada, clearly signalled the need for political change. Lord

Table 6.1   Population, 1785–1871

Year	Population	Year	Population	Year	Population
1785	6,000	1817	83,000	1842	487,000
1791	14,000	1821	118,000	1848	726,000
1796	25,000	1826	166,000	1851	952,000
1805	46,000	1831	237,000	1861	1,396,000
1811	60,000	1836	374,000	1871	1,621,000

Sources: Statistics Canada, Census of Canada, 1605–1784, Cat. no. 98-187-XIE; 'Historical Statistics of Canada', Cat. no. 11-516-XIE, Series A2–14.

Durham was dispatched to the colonies as their new governor general, with instructions to investigate and report on the best way to approach reform.

Following Durham's recommendations, in 1841 the Act of Union rejoined Upper and Lower Canada in a single province and established an elected assembly with equal representation from both sections, even though Canada East (formerly Lower Canada) had the larger population. Quebec City and Toronto alternated as the capital of the new united province of Canada.

Much of the population increase outlined in Table 6.1 can be explained by reference to the staples theory. For example, in order to start a farm, the land had to be cleared of trees: burning the wood from those trees produced potash, which then could be sold, providing the income required to buy seed, equipment, and so on. The economic activity generated in this way encouraged the development of communities, basic manufacturing industries, and transportation networks linking Canada West to Canada East and the United States.

Transportation was critical to the growth of the future Ontario. At the local level, farmers needed wagon roads to get their produce to market. These roads were often in a poor state of repair, and often impassable in the spring, but they were the essential first link in the transportation network. The introduction of steam-driven vessels to Lakes Ontario and Erie in 1818 dramatically increased the movement of goods and people between ports such as Kingston and York (Toronto). Canals were another important backward linkage. The Rideau Canal, linking Kingston to Bytown (Ottawa) and Bytown to Montreal via the Ottawa River (completed in 1832), does not fall into this category—its main purpose was to move troops—but a number of other canals constructed in the first half of the 1800s were specifically motivated by the needs of trade. For example, while the Great Lakes provided a significant advantage in shipping, to move goods from Lake Ontario to Lake Erie initially required portaging around Niagara Falls. That barrier was removed in 1829, with the completion of the Welland Canal. By 1848 other canals, such as the Lachine, on the St Lawrence made it possible for vessels to sail from Quebec City to the far end of Lake Superior.

But the Americans were also building canals in this period. The Erie Canal, completed in 1825, became the favoured route for the movement of American goods, and after the 1840s, when Britain adopted free trade and abandoned its Navigation Acts, the canal also siphoned off a significant amount of Canadian shipping. The completion of the Welland Canal, bypassing Niagara Falls, only strengthened the Upper Canada–New York City connection, to the detriment of Montreal. From the 1840s on, Canada West was increasingly drawn into the economic orbit of the United States.

The Welland Canal links Lake Ontario and Lake Erie, allowing ocean-going vessels to travel up the St Lawrence Seaway into the heart of North America.   *Photo B. McGillivray.*

In the case of railways as well, the Americans were quick to recognize the advantages of investment in new technology. The first railways in Canada West were short-haul portage systems designed to facilitate Great Lakes shipping. For example, the 14-kilometre Erie and Ontario Railway, built in 1839, was designed merely to transport goods around Niagara Falls. Longer rail lines were not constructed until the 1850s; see Fig. 3.9 (p. 70 above) for some of the main rail and canal routes through Upper Canada.

Agriculture stimulated some local manufacturing of products such as fertilizer and farm implements, as well as items such as buggies and wagons. In addition, some agricultural produce itself required processing: wheat had to be ground to produce flour (grist mills); barley had to be mashed to brew beer or distil liquor; wool had to be carded (combed so that it could be spun into strands) and then fulled—('thickened and felted by a process of washing and beating'; McCalla, 1993: 100); and hides needed tanning before they could be used to manufacture shoes and boots. But except for flour, some of which was exported to Britain, all these products were for local markets: in other words, they represented final demand linkages. The forest industry was much more export-driven. Until the 1840s forestry in Upper Canada was concentrated in the Ottawa River region and most of the wood was shipped to Britain. Gradually, however, mills were opened farther west and many were linked by rail to ports on Lake Ontario. After Britain's move to free trade, United States became the principal market for Canada West's forest exports, although there were also local markets for everything from barrel staves to furniture to cord wood for heating homes and firing the furnaces of steam engines. Among the communities directly related to forest industries was Bytown, founded in 1826 and renamed Ottawa in 1855. Table 6.2 outlines the main industries in Upper Canada in the mid-1800s.

Table 6.2   Industries in Upper Canada, 1842 and 1871

Industries	1842	1871
Grist mills	455	951
Saw mills	982	1,837
Carding mills	186	–
Fulling mills	144	–
Carding and fulling mills	–	158
Woollen mills	–	233
Distilleries	147	18
Breweries	96	105
Tanneries	261	426
Foundries	22	258

Source: Adapted from D. McCalla, *Planting the Province: The Economic History of Upper Canada* (Toronto: University of Toronto Press, 1993), 275.

Montreal and Quebec City continued to be the largest centres in Canada. But Canada West's population was growing, and as resource industries and transportation networks developed, the competition for urban supremacy within Canada West became intense. Kingston, at the eastern end of Lake Ontario, had the earliest advantage because of its administrative and military functions, along with its port facilities. One reason the focus gradually moved west to York (renamed Toronto in 1834), Hamilton, and London was the search for good agricultural land, which Kingston lacked. Increasingly, ports such as York, Hamilton, and St Catharines engaged in trade with the United States via the Erie Canal, which undermined Kingston's role in shipping just as it did Montreal's. A major advantage for York was the monopoly on financial dealings it gained with the charter of the Bank of Upper Canada in 1822. Table 6.3 traces population growth in the main urban centres of Upper Canada, compared with the much older centres of Montreal and Quebec City.

Improvements in transportation gave even further advantages to cities such as Toronto and Hamilton. The Burlington Canal (1832) opened up Hamilton's harbour to shipping, and the deepening of the Welland Canal, in 1845, made it possible for the city to import 'low-cost coal from Pennsylvania which contributed to its growth as an industrial centre' (Nader, 1975: 175). Railways provided other locational advantages. Toronto in particular benefited from multiple rail lines, which allowed it to capture trading opportunities in various directions by the 1850s. In 1851 there were five centres in Canada West with populations of more than 5,000, another seven in the 2,500–4,999 range, and 21 with populations of between 1,000 and 2,499. By 1861 many more centres were linked by railways, the top five cities all had more than 10,000 people, and four more centres had grown to over 5,000 (Brantford, Guelph, St Catharines, and Belleville). Canada West was becoming urbanized.

The census of 1851 revealed that the balance of population in the united Canada had shifted: the mainly English-speaking, Protestant western section had overtaken

Table 6.3   Population, major centres in Upper Canada, 1820–1871

City	1820	1825	1830	1834	1840	1851	1861	1871
York (Toronto)	1,240	1,700	2,860	9,300	13,092	30,775	44,821	75,903
Hamilton				2,155	3,413	14,112	19,096	26,716
Bytown (Ottawa)						7,760	14,669	21,545
London					2,000	7,035	11,555	15,826
Kingston	2,336		3,587		4,828	11,585	13,743	12,407
Brantford						3,877	6,251	8,107
St Catharines						4,368	6,284	7,864
Belleville						4,569	6,277	7,305
Guelph						1,860	5,076	6,878
Port Hope						2,476	4,162	5,114
Montreal	19,000	22,000		36,000	40,000	58,000	90,323	107,225
Quebec City	16,000	22,101				42,052	59,990	59,699

Sources: G. A. Nader, *Cities of Canada*, vol. I, *Theoretical, Historical and Planning Perspectives* (Toronto: Macmillan, 1975), 161–80; Statistics Canada, Census of Canada, 1871.

its mainly French-speaking, Roman Catholic partner (see Table 6.4). Now that the positions were reversed, Canada West demanded proportional representation, but Canada East refused. The deadlock was not broken until 1867, when Confederation broke the unworkable union and created two separate provinces: Quebec and Ontario.

The Industrial Foundations: Confederation to the 1960s

With the largest population, a dynamic industrial base, and strong economic links to the United States, Ontario was the dominant province in Confederation from the start. Agriculture in southern Ontario was diversifying into corn, hogs, and dairying for export as well as local markets, although wheat was still an important export crop. Increasingly, farm roads were connected to rail lines, which in turn were connected to the Great Lakes ports. It was the age of the railway and Canada was rapidly laying down track. From less than 4,000 kilometres in 1867, the total quickly rose to more than 11,000 in 1880, more than 21,000 in 1890, and more than 28,000 kilometres in 1900 (Nader, 1975: 203). As the focus of rail expansion moved onto the prairies, Ontario was able to provide most of the construction materials, and it became the main beneficiary of the raw materials shipped over the new lines from the west. In short, the west was Ontario's hinterland much more than it was Quebec's.

In the century after Confederation Ontario became the dominant part of the industrial heartland, attracting entrepreneurial investment and capturing much of the manufacturing in Canada. Steel was essential to rail lines and rolling stock, agricultural equipment, and, later, to the automobile and many other consumer goods. With its large population base, Ontario also became a centre for food production, breweries, distilleries, textiles, clothing, footwear, printing and furniture. Accompanying these many industries were banks, insurance companies, the stock market and other financial institutions, along with marketing, advertising, wholesaling, warehousing, and retailing activities.

At the time of Confederation, Ontario was one of only four provinces, but within six years there were seven—Manitoba joined in 1870, British Columbia in 1871, and Prince Edward Island in 1873—and the North-West expanded significantly with the federal government's purchase of Rupert's Land from the Hudson's Bay Company in 1870. At that time Ontario consisted of little more than the southern Great Lakes–St Lawrence region west of the Ottawa River, but the northern boundary was moved up to the 50th parallel in 1876. A boundary dispute with Manitoba ended in 1889 with Ontario expanding west to Lake of the Woods, and in the same year Ontario acquired another chunk of northern territory when its upper border was shifted to follow the Albany River. After Alberta and Saskatchewan gained provincial status in 1905 with their northern borders (like British Columbia's) set at the 60th parallel (see Fig. 3.12, p. 76), Manitoba, Ontario, and Quebec wanted to extend their northern boundaries as well, and all three acquired their present configurations in 1912. In the course of these expansions Ontario gained an enormous amount of territory, much of it rich in both forests and minerals.

Table 6.4 Population, Upper and Lower Canada, 1806–1861

Year	Upper Canada	Lower Canada
1806	71,000	250,000
1814	95,000	335,000
1825	158,000	479,000
1831	237,000	553,000
1840	432,000	717,000
1851	952,000	890,000
1861	1,396,000	1,112,000

Source: Adapted from D.G.G. Kerr, ed., *Historical Atlas of Canada* (Toronto: Thomas Nelson, 1961), 5.

Another significant advantage for the heartland was the Bank Act of 1871, which allowed financial institutions to establish branches across provincial boundaries. Whereas American banks were prohibited by law from establishing branches outside their states of origin, Canadian banks were free to expand at will. Through mergers, buy-outs, and takeovers, small independent banks in peripheral regions were replaced by branches of banks with their head offices in either Toronto or Montreal. 'The number of banks in Canada was reduced from fifty-one in 1875 to thirty-six in 1900; thereafter, a steady rate of amalgamation reduced the number to eleven by 1926, while the number of branches increased from 230 in 1874, to 708 in 1900 and to 3,840 in 1925' (Nader, 1975: 215). The consolidation of banking benefited the southern Ontario–southern Quebec core, but left the peripheral regions of Canada without local alternatives to the large banks, which tended to be seen as insensitive to local needs.

Perhaps the greatest boon of all for Ontario was the National Policy. By imposing heavy tariffs on imported (mainly American) consumer goods, the National Policy ensured that Canadians from coast to coast would have little choice but to buy products manufactured in Canada—and the centre of Canadian manufacturing was Ontario. At the same time, as we saw in Chapter 4, the National Policy led many American manufacturers to establish branch plants in Canada so that they could avoid paying duties, and here again the main beneficiary was southern Ontario. The reasons included not only its proximity to major industrial centres such as Pittsburgh, Chicago, Detroit, and Buffalo, and its existing industrial base, but also the fact that—unlike southern Quebec—it was predominantly English-speaking. In addition Toronto benefited from an extensive transportation network. The Grand Trunk Railway provided a link with Montreal by 1856 and with Buffalo by 1873. Although the CPR itself by-passed the city, a line was built from Toronto to North Bay in 1886 to intercept the transcontinental flow of trade goods and people.

As the west opened up to settlers, demand for consumer goods increased. Again, government assisted the core region in supplying these outlying areas by subsidizing both postal and railway freight rates. Thus the T. Eaton Company, headquartered in Toronto, could afford to mail its catalogue across the country and deliver the goods ordered from it with little additional transportation cost. In this way downtown Toronto became the retail centre for the whole of Canada.

In Ontario the energy production crucial to all industries came under government scrutiny and control from an early time. When the Niagara Falls were harnessed to produce hydroelectricity in 1896, there was some concern that a private power company would sell the energy to American firms, leaving Canadian manufacturers to find other, more expensive energy sources. Ontario Hydro was formed in 1906 to regulate the supply and distribution of electricity 'at the lowest feasible cost' throughout the province (Whiteway, 1985: 1328). Similarly, the cost of coal was subsidized to encourage industry to locate in southern Ontario.

Global events also had their impact, of course. Both the First and Second World Wars had positive economic repercussions in that many of the goods needed in wartime, from transport vehicles to uniforms, were manufactured in southern Ontario. And despite the damage done by the Depression, one institution made important gains during the 1930s: the Toronto Stock Exchange attracted a great deal of investment in mining stock, especially in the area of gold, which was one of the few metals to increase in price during that period. In the years that followed, the TSE outpaced the Montreal Stock Exchange by an increasingly wide margin, as Figure 6.2 shows.

Industrialization went hand-in-hand with the growth of urban centres and overall population growth. Toronto led the way with its financial institutions, transportation links, which in turn promoted warehouses and wholesaling, and—above all—manufacturing, particularly after 1895. Together, local manufacturers and American branch plants employed 35 per cent of the city's work force by 1911 (Nader, 1976: 200). Heavy industry such as iron and steel plants, however, located elsewhere. As the home of the two largest steel corporations in the country—the Steel Company of Canada (Stelco), founded in 1897, and Dominion Foundries and Steel Company (Dofasco), founded in 1912—Hamilton became known as 'Steel Town', while Sault Ste Marie was home to the Algoma Steel Corporation; founded in 1899, it became a major supplier for railway construction to the west.

Figure 6.2   Value of Montreal and Toronto Stock Exchange transactions, 1937–1967

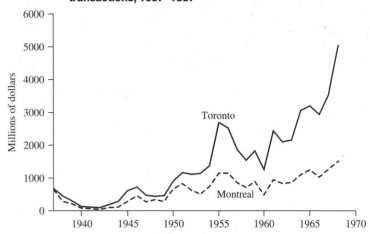

Source: Adapted from G.A. Nader, *Cities of Canada,* vol. I, *Theoretical, Historical and Planning Perspectives* (Toronto: Macmillan, 1975), 212.

As essential as steel was for railways, it became even more important in the early 1900s with the growth of the automobile industry. Production grew steadily until 1929; approximately 200,000 passenger vehicles were produced in that year alone. New automobiles became an unaffordable luxury during the Depression of the 1930s, but military demand during the Second World War revitalized the industry, and production was up to 283,000 vehicles per year by 1951 (Sitwell and Seifried, 1984: 71). Cities such as Oshawa, Windsor, Guelph, London, and Kitchener all acquired factories with assembly lines for vehicles and parts.

Throughout southern Ontario, industry encouraged urban growth: Brantford manufactured agricultural implements; Peterborough attracted General Electric and Quaker Oats; Kingston built locomotives and produced textiles; and the discovery of oil near Sarnia made that town the petrochemical centre of Canada. As industry grew, so did related activities such as finance, insurance, wholesaling, marketing, advertising and retailing, and these too contributed to the process of urbanization. Ottawa and its neighbour across the river, Hull, also experienced significant increases in population, reflecting the growth of government services. In addition, most of the larger cities had universities active in technological research and development. Table 6.5 outlines the overall growth of Ontario from 1871 to 1961, while Table 6.6 lists the main urban centres in Ontario over the same period.

Industrial activity in Quebec was concentrated in Montreal. In Ontario, by contrast, manufacturing and related activities were distributed across a variety of centres, most of them not far from Toronto, and this contributed to Ontario's strength. Well connected by roads, rails, and waterways, these cities became highly integrated

Table 6.5   Population, Ontario, 1871–1961

Year	Population	Year	Population
1871	1,620.9	1921	2,933.7
1881	1,926.9	1931	3,431.7
1891	2,114.3	1941	3,787.7
1901	2,182.9	1951	4,597.5
1911	2,527.3	1961	6,236.1

Source: Adapted from Statistics Canada, 'Historical Statistics of Canada', 1983, Cat. no. 11-516, 29 July 1999, Series A2-14.

Table 6.6   Urban centres (over 25,000 in 1961), Ontario, 1881–1961

City	1881	1891	1901	1911	1921	1931	1941	1951	1961
Toronto[1]	86,415	174,414	208,040	376,471	521,893	631,207	667,457	1,262,000	1,919,000
Ottawa[1]	27,412	38,942	59,928	87,062	107,843	126,872	154,951	312,000	457,000
Hamilton[1]	35,961	47,245	52,634	81,969	114,151	155,547	166,337	382,000	401,000
St Catharines[1]	9,631	9,170	9,946	12,484	19,881	24,753	30,275	189,000	258,000
London[1]	19,746	27,891	37,976	46,300	60,959	71,148	78,264	168,000	227,000
Windsor[1]	6,561	10,322	12,153	17,829	38,591	63,108	105,311	183,000	217,000
Kitchener[1]	4,054	7,425	9,747	15,196	21,763	30,793	35,657	108,000	155,000
Sudbury	–	–	2,027	4,150	8,621	18,518	32,203	42,410	80,120
Oshawa	3,992	4,066	4,394	7,436	11,940	23,439	26,813	41,545	62,415
Brantford	9,616	12,753	16,619	23,132	29,440	30,107	31,948	36,727	55,201
Kingston	14,407	19,263	17,961	18,874	21,753	23,439	30,126	33,459	53,526
Sarnia	3,874	6,692	8,176	9,947	14,877	18,191	18,734	34,697	50,976
Peterborough	6,812	9,717	11,239	18,360	20,994	22,327	25,350	38,272	47,185
Fort William	692	2,176	3,633	16,499	20,541	26,277	30,585	34,947	45,214
Port Arthur	1,275	2,698	3,214	11,220	14,886	19,818	24,426	16,899	43,639
Cornwall	4,468	6,805	6,704	6,598	7,419	11,126	14,117	16,899	43,639
Sault Ste Marie	780	2,414	7,169	10,984	21,092	23,082	25,794	32,452	43,088
Guelph	9,890	10,537	11,496	15,175	18,128	21,075	23,273	27,386	39,838
Chatham	7,873	9,052	9,068	10,770	13,256	14,569	17,369	21,218	29,826

[1]Includes CMA for 1951 and 1961.

Source: Statistics Canada, Census of Canada, 1881, 1891, 1901, 1911, 1921, 1931, 1941, 1951, and 1961.

Figure 6.3   The Golden Horseshoe

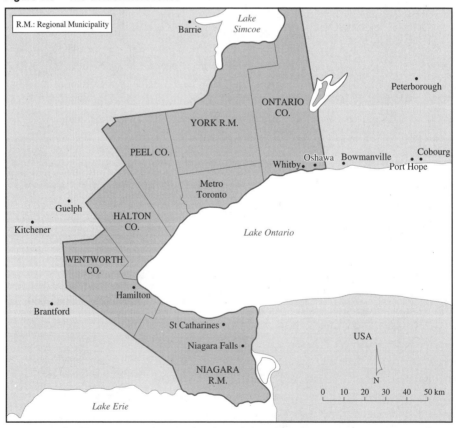

Source: Adapted from G.A. Nader, *Cities of Canada,* vol. I, *Theoretical, Historical and Planning Perspectives* (Toronto: Macmillan, 1975), 234.

economically, and provided southern Ontario with a large domestic market close at hand. Growth in population, industrial activity, and the overall economy was greatest in the area around the western end of Lake Ontario, known as the 'Golden Horseshoe' (Fig. 6.3 and Table 6.7). With the greatest concentration of population in Canada, this small geographic region represents a major commercial and industrial market and a prime location for both goods- and service-producing industries.

The Ontario Periphery to the 1960s

Outside the relatively small triangular core where population, urbanization, and industrialization were con-

Table 6.7 Population of the 'Golden Horseshoe', 1871–1971

Year	Population	As % of Ontario	As % of Canada
1871	323,387	19.9	8.8
1881	380,315	19.7	8.8
1891	475,043	22.5	9.8
1901	495,683	22.7	9.2
1911	718,848	28.4	10.0
1921	1,011,814	34.5	11.5
1931	1,298,285	37.8	12.5
1941	1,442,944	38.1	12.5
1951	1,842,068	40.1	13.1
1961	2,737,797	43.9	15.0
1971	3,647,425	47.4	16.9

Source: Adapted from G.A. Nader, *Cities of Canada*, vol. I, *Theoretical, Historical and Planning Perspectives* (Toronto: Macmillan, 1975), 235.

centrated was a vast hinterland, rich in forest and mineral resources. At the time of Confederation, settlement in Ontario's periphery was sparse. First Nations continued to fish, hunt, and trap; loggers were active along the Ottawa River and around the northern fringes of the Great Lakes; and some farms were established in the upper Ottawa clay belt extending from Lake Temiskaming into Quebec and west into Ontario. To seriously tap the region's valuable timber and mineral wealth, however, railways were needed.

When the last spike of the CPR was driven in 1885, the line ran from Montreal to Ottawa, then west to North Bay, along the northern fringes of Lakes Huron and Superior to the rail–port centre of Port Arthur and Fort William (amalgamated as Thunder

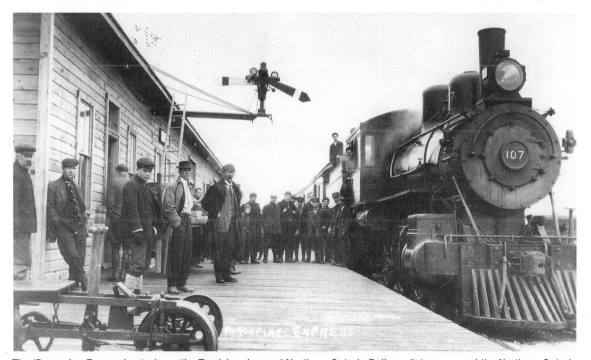

The 'Porcupine Express': a train on the Temiskaming and Northern Ontario Railway (later renamed the Northern Ontario Railway), in the early 1900s. *Library and Archives Canada, PA-119904.*

Figure 6.4   Railways in northern Ontario, 1930s

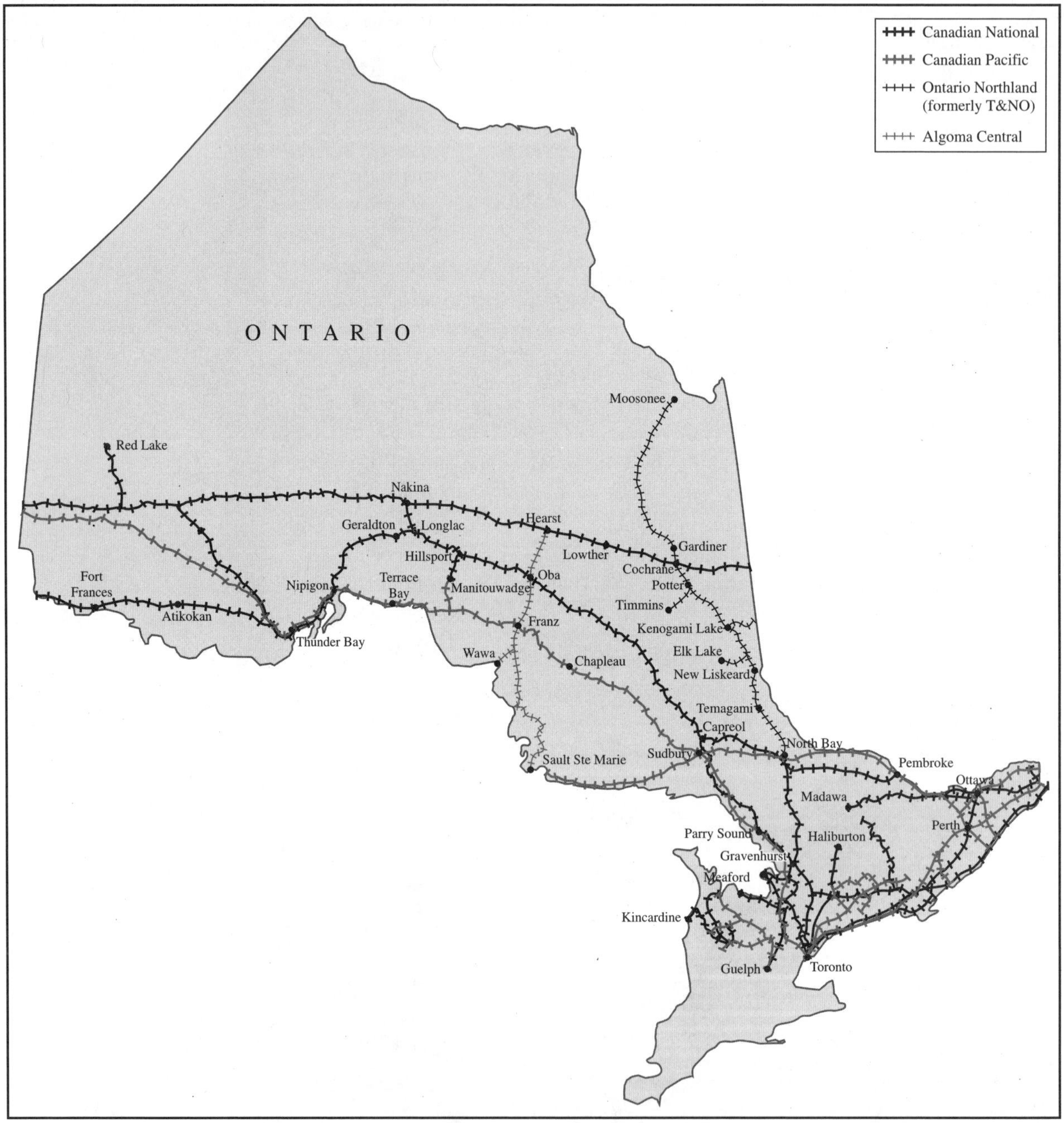

Source: Adapted from J.L. Robinson, *The Geography of Canada* (Toronto: Longmans, 1950), 80.

Bay in 1970) and from there to Winnipeg, across the prairies, and on to Vancouver. By the early 1920s a second transcontinental rail system was operating under the name Canadian National Railway. An amalgam of numerous smaller lines across the country, the CNR took a more northerly route than the CPR. Its Ontario section (formerly the National Transcontinental Railway) connected Quebec City to Winnipeg by 1913 and linked the northern Ontario towns of Cochrane, Kapuskasing, Hearst, and Sioux Lookout (Fig. 6.4).

That line was only one of several constructed in the early decades of the twentieth century to reach the resources of the Canadian Shield and transport them to centres in the south of the province. The CNR built a branch line from Sioux Lookout to Port Arthur to compete with the CPR in transporting wheat from the prairies to the Great Lakes vessels that would carry it east. The Algoma Central and Hudson Bay Railway, linking Sault Ste Marie to Hearst, supplied iron ore for Sault Ste Marie's steel mill and wood for its pulp mill. The provincial government invested in the Temiskaming and Northern Ontario Railway (now the Ontario Northland Railway) to promote farming in the clay belt, as well as forestry and mining. From North Bay, which was connected to Toronto, the Temiskaming and Northern Ontario Railway ran to Cobalt (1903) and Cochrane (1908). A branch line was established to access the valuable Porcupine gold fields and the town of Timmins (1912), the pulp and paper at Iroquois Falls (1913), and more gold at Kirkland Lake (1920). In the 1920s the TNOR extended into Quebec, and a line to Moosonee on James Bay was completed by 1932 (Fig. 6.4).

These railways were essential both in opening up the resource frontiers of Ontario, Quebec, and western Canada and in funnelling those resources through southern Ontario. Some communities got their start when railway construction revealed the presence of valuable minerals: Sudbury, for example, was founded after railway workers discovered copper there in 1883; later, with the development of smelting technology; Sudbury became the largest source of nickel in the world. Similarly, construction of the Temiskaming and Northern Ontario Railway revealed the presence of silver on the shores of Cobalt Lake, setting off a mining stampede into the region. The town of Cobalt was also a mining centre (mainly silver, but also cobalt). Some rail centres flourished; others fell victim to the busts that so often followed booms. Thunder Bay became an important transshipment centre for grain in particular, but also for forest products and minerals. Sault Ste Marie was another shipping centre, though it also supplied steel rails and produced pulp and paper. Sudbury became the largest single-resource town in Canada with its nickel and copper smelters; it also developed many services for northern Ontario. North Bay, the Gateway to the North, had the advantage of being both a major rail centre and an important location for the forest industry.

Many other communities relied on a single resource. Those centred on pulp mills tended to be more enduring than mining towns, which had no reason to exist at all once the metal they mined ran out, but all these communities were subject to the vagaries of the marketplace. Farms in the clay belt of northeastern Ontario were relatively marginal, with poorly drained soils and a much shorter growing season than those at more southerly latitudes. In a region where logging was the major industry, hay (for the horses that hauled the logs) became the main cash crop. Once logging became mechanized, many of these farms diversified into dairying. Here, as elsewhere in Canada, small farms were eventually replaced by large consolidated operations, and labour-intensive practices such as hand milking gave way to more efficient—and costly—milking machines. Agriculture was also practised on the southern fringes of the Canadian Shield, in the vicinity of communities such as Dryden, Fort Frances, and Thunder Bay in the west, and across the northern edges of Lakes Superior and Huron to the North Bay area. For the most part, these were small farms serving local markets. After the 1920s an additional source of revenue for some resource towns was tourism: local hotels and cafés, hunting and fishing lodges, and guiding outfits catered to city folk keen to experience the wilderness for themselves.

As in Quebec, the forest industry in Ontario experienced a number of industrial phases based on external demand, technological developments, and political policies. Until the early 1900s, trees were cut down by hand in the fall and winter; then horses hauled the logs over the snow to frozen rivers. With the spring thaw, the logs would be floated downstream to sawmills or bundled into rafts to be transported across the Great Lakes to American purchasers. Although numerous tree species were in demand, white pine—used for furniture—was the most valuable. Little thought was given to conservation before the passage of the Conservation Authorities Act in 1946.

Politics played the most important role in developing forward linkages in the forest industry. By the 1890s the Americans were importing great quantities of logs to their mills in Wisconsin and Michigan, and in 1897 they imposed a duty on lumber from Ontario in an effort to limit imports to raw logs. Ontario responded by amending its Crown Timber Act to prohibit such exports. Sawmilling boomed, encouraging the growth of communities from Kenora to Ottawa.

Another phase of the forest industry, and one that produced even more forward linkages, was the development of the pulp and paper industry. The technology to break down softwood fibres and turning them into paper was in place before Confederation, but the industry did not take off until the early twentieth century, when depletion of American spruce stocks led the United States to look to Canada for supplies, especially of newsprint. Recognizing an opportunity to stimulate pulp mill activity in Canada, in 1902 Ottawa imposed restrictions on the export of pulp logs; in 1909 the US reduced its tariff on newsprint imports; and by 1913 Canadian newsprint was entering the United States duty-free (Nader, 1975: 209; Canadian Pulp and Paper Association, n.d.).

A lake freighter in port at Thunder Bay, 2001.   *Photo Andrew Leyerle.*

As a consequence pulp and paper mills were built throughout northern Ontario, often by American companies.

Some of these mills were located in existing communities that already had an economic base, such as Sault Ste Marie (pulp, 1896; paper, 1911), Kenora (pulp and paper in the 1920s), and Thunder Bay (a first pulp mill was built there in 1914, a paper mill was added by 1918, and two more mills by the mid-1920s). More often, though, the mill was the heart of the town: Dryden, Espanola, Fort Frances, Iroquois Falls, Kapuskasing, Smooth Rock Falls, and Sturgeon Falls were all mill towns. Among the factors considered in deciding where to locate a pulp mill were the availability of rail transport, access to fresh water, and supplies of hydroelectric power.

The stock market crash of 1929 and the Depression that followed curtailed pulp mill expansion and forced a number of pulp mill corporations to declare bankruptcy. Some mills worked at reduced capacity and some shut down altogether: single-mill towns faced economic disaster. But global demand revived after the Second World War, and Ontario had the raw materials, transportation, and other inputs in place to meet this demand. Mills that had shut down in the 1930s re-opened and new mills such as Red Rock (1944), Marathon (1945) and Terrace Bay (1948) were built, adding new single-resource communities to the map of northern Ontario.

Mining was another catalyst for economic development and settlement in the periphery of Ontario. From the late 1800s to the mid-1900s, a wide variety of metals were discovered in various parts of Ontario's Shield region, including gold, silver, copper, nickel, cobalt, platinum, and iron ore. Mining is a complex and risky industry. Because vast amounts of capital are required at every stage, from exploration and discovery through extraction, concentrating, and smelting, stock markets play a vital role in raising funds.

The Shield region is rich in minerals, which tend to be concentrated not in the Shield's ancient granitic rock but in 'sedimentary and volcanic rocks called greenstones' (Robinson, 1989: 150). Sophisticated technologies are required to break down those rocks so that the metal can be extracted. Lode or hard rock mining is costly, and the metals it produces must often be combined with other metals before they can be used to manufacture consumer products.

Numerous metal mines have located in Ontario's periphery. In the far west of the province, many gold discoveries have been made around Lake of the Woods; Kenora and Rainy River are the main gold mining centres in this region. The Thunder Bay area has a considerable history of silver and iron ore mining. In Sault Ste Marie, the Algoma Steel Corporation acquired much of its iron ore from a mine in Wawa. The largest metal-producing community is Sudbury, where the INCO refinery, opened in 1916, used the latest technology to separate nickel from copper. Another region rich in gold, silver, copper, and cobalt was the clay belt area of northeastern Ontario; Timmins and Kirkland Lake became the main centres for these mining ventures. Common to all these operations was access to rail lines capable of moving large quantities of heavy rock at manageable cost. Only the mines at Red Lake (1890s) and Pickle Lake (1920s), which produced low-bulk, high-value gold, could afford to operate without rail connections, using boats and eventually airplanes. Many mining communities survived only until their ore was exhausted; communities with smelters, such as Sudbury and Timmins, were more stable—at least until the Depression, when a severe decline in the prices paid for most metals (except gold) caused even smelters to reduce production or shut down. A surplus of iron and steel, when demand fell off after the end of the First World War, resulted in a similar situation. Again, a number of mines and blast furnaces shut down and no iron ore was mined in the whole of Canada between 1923 and 1939 (Natural Resources Canada, n.d.) Conversely, war stimulated the development of new uses for metals such as nickel (used to strengthen steel) and uranium (used to build the atomic bomb).

Mining-related industry in Ontario has not been limited to the periphery. Hamilton is the largest, most important producer of iron and steel in the whole of Canada. Before 1900 the Kingston area produced iron from the iron ore mines at Eldorado, and a copper smelter operated at Madoc by the mid-1800s. INCO, the main operator of the smelters in Sudbury, built another nickel refinery at Port Colborne, on Lake Erie, in 1916. Uranium was mined and refined at Port Hope beginning in the 1930s. In addition, non-metallic substances including gypsum, barite, fluorite, sand, and gravel have been mined in the core region, and Sarnia has natural gas as well as oil.

By the 1960s, Ontario's periphery was well connected to the core by rail lines and road systems were branching off to more remote regions. Forestry and mining were the key economic activities and were expanding in response to increased world demand.

Southern Ontario: 1970s to the Present

Following the Second World War, most economies in the Western world experienced dramatic growth. The combination of the baby boom and increased disposable income had profound implications in Canada. The spread of freeways signalled the decline of rail services. Suburbs and shopping centres proliferated, and new house construction resulted in growing demand for consumer goods—all of which required raw materials and massive energy resources.

Fordism was at its peak. Automated assembly lines were producing everything from automobiles to household electrical gadgets. The majority of these industries were located in southern Ontario, and many were branch plants of large American corporations. Until the 1970s, manufacturing was the foundation of the economy of southern Ontario.

Chapter 4 outlined the many unpredictable political, economic, and technological events that since the 1970s have fundamentally shifted Canada from a largely national–continental industrial economy to one centred on services and global in its scope. One of the most fundamental changes was the time–space convergence that came with the revolution in transportation and communications. The ability to move people, goods, and information rapidly, in some cases instantly, changed not only the way business was done and goods were manufactured, but how and where people lived and worked. At the same time international events shook the foundations of existing economies. In the 1970s the gold standard collapsed and an energy crisis revealed the risk of depending on oil. The 1980s were marked by a serious economic recession, freer trade globally with a shift in trade from Europe to the Asia–Pacific region, the negotiation of a Free Trade Agreement between Canada and the US, and the end of the Cold War. The 1990s saw more periods of recession (including a major recession in the Asian countries), the signing of a North American Free Trade Agreement, and expansion of the sphere of global trade and investment as formerly communist countries shifted to capitalism. Since the millennium, regional recessions have continued, terrorist attacks have led to restrictions on the movement of goods and people, and the ongoing conflict in Iraq has increased feelings of unease and uncertainty around the world.

In the course of these changes, the Fordist model of production—in which vertically integrated, highly centralized firms owned and controlled many aspects of the assembly process—became outmoded. Time–space convergence and fragmentation of the production process made it possible to produce goods and services virtually anywhere, and the relaxation of trade barriers encouraged transnational corporations to practise flexible specialization. The new growth sector was services, which by 1961 had overtaken manufacturing as the largest sector of the economy. For industrial regions such as southern Ontario, new technologies and globalization have resulted in major restructuring of both manufacturing industries and services related to manufacturing.

Already by the 1970s, goods produced in Japan and other Asian nations (especially cars and electronics) were presenting a serious challenge to domestic producers of these items in North America generally, and the competition only increased through the 1980s. Beginning in 1973, the energy crisis drove up the price of oil, the main source of energy at that time, forcing manufacturers dependent on oil to raise the prices they charged for their products. In 1981 the price of oil began to collapse, along with the demand for many goods, as the world slid into a recession similar to the Depression of the 1930s. Corporations responded to these highly uncertain times by shutting plants down, contracting out, and moving some or all of their production processes to other parts of the world where costs (of labour, energy, etc.) and/or government policy were more favourable. By the end of the 1980s economies were beginning to recover, but the signing of the Free Trade Agreement in 1989 and another recession at the beginning of the 1990s had serious consequences for Ontario's manufacturing sector. The tariffs that had protected Canadian manufacturing since the days of the National Policy ended with the signing of the Canada–US Free Trade Agreement. Most tariffs were phased out, and American companies were no longer required to operate branch plants in Canada in order to sell their products here. The combination of the FTA and recession, in the early 1990s, brought further restructuring: many Canadian firms well as branch plants left Ontario for places like Mexico or the southern United States, where wages were lower and labour was not unionized. Table 6.8 outlines the loss of some of the firms in Ontario during the late 1980s and 1990s. Other plants remained open but downsized, adopted leaner production practices, and contracted out more of their work.

As Table 6.9 shows, manufacturing accounted for 23.2 per cent of all jobs in Ontario in 1976 and by 2002 that proportion had fallen to just 18.5 per cent. In the same period employment in services increased from 64.9 per cent to 73. Overall employment in manufacturing, however, actually increased. Many of the firms that left Ontario were branch-plant operations; others were older, labour-intensive, or no longer competitive. They have been replaced by newer firms, more sensitive to current economic conditions, in areas such as auto production, transportation equipment, and fuel cell technologies.

The website of Ontario government's Ministry of Enterprise, Opportunity and Innovation (2005) lists the manufacturing investments made in Ontario from 2001 to 2005, including both new plants and expansion projects on the part of existing firms. Many of these investments are related to the auto industry. For example, Cami Automotive, a joint venture between General Motors and Suzuki, invested half a billion

Table 6.8   Selected plant closures and relocation from Ontario, 1987–2004

Company	Community	Products	Relocation	Job loss
Bata Shoes	Quinte West	Shoes and boots	?	?
CAMCO	Hamilton	Appliances	?	800
Canada Packers	Elora and Harrison	Meat	?	231
Dominion Fabrics	Long Sault	Weaving and textiles	Malaysia/Tunisia	365
Dylex	Toronto	Garments	New Jersey	45
Freudenber	Kingsville	Textiles	New Jersey	57
General Tire	Barrie	Tires	US	872
Inglis	Cambridge	Appliances	US	?
J.H. Warsh Ltd.	Toronto	Garments	?	30
Levi Strauss	Cornwall & Brantford	Jeans	China	600
Libbey Inc.	Wallaceburg	Glassware	Mexico/US	560
Monaco Group	Toronto	Garments	?	85
Phil Carry	North York	Garments	?	300
Playtex Ltd.	Renfrew	Underwear	Mexico/Philippines	160
SciCan Scientific Inc.	Cobourg	Glassware	US	100
T.A.G. Inc.	Cambridge/Woodstock London	Clothing	US	1,250
Vogue Bra Canada	Cambridge	Underwear	Mexico	50
Warnaco	Carleton	Swimwear	Kentucky	7
Westinghouse	Mount Forest	Appliances	US	250

Source: Canada NewsWire, 2004, 'Camco appliance plant another victim of free trade' ⟨http://www.newswire.ca/en/releases/archive/October2003/17/c2106.html⟩; R. Kowaluk, 'Stability Prevails in the Canadian Clothing Industry' (Ottawa: Statistics Canada, 1998); Statistics Canada, 'Growth perseveres in the Canadian Primary textile industry Catalogue # 34–250-XIE; S. Jones, 'Jeans maker Levi Strauss to cut 5,900 jobs in the US and Canada' ⟨http://www.wsws.org/articles/1999/ feb1999/ levi-f26.shtml⟩; T. Davies, 'Where the Jobs Go', *Maclean's* 113, 33 (14 Aug. 2000): 23; D. McMur, 'Three for the Show', *Maclean's* 105, 31 (3 Aug. 1991): 22–4; D. North, 'Never Cry Wolf', *Canadian Business* 71, 15 (25 Sept. 1998): 78–86.

Table 6.9   Employment structure, Ontario, 1976–2002 (jobs in thousands and as % of total)

	1976		1981		1991		2002	
	Ont	%	Ont	%	Ont	%	Ont	%
All Industries	**3,752.9**	**100**	**4,289.6**	**100**	**5,015.7**	**100**	**6,068.0**	**100**
Goods-producing sector	**1,320.9**	**35.1**	**1,497.3**	**34.9**	**1,419.9**	**28.3**	**1,635.5**	**27.0**
Agriculture	109.5	2.9	134.4	3.1	112.3	2.2	76.4	1.3
Forestry, fish, mining, oil, gas	60.0	1.6	72.1	1.7	53.0	1.1	34.4	0.6
Utilities	41.9	1.1	50.1	1.2	64.0	1.3	50.9	0.8
Construction	238.6	6.4	228.9	5.3	285.2	5.7	354.1	5.8
Manufacturing	870.9	23.2	1,011.7	23.6	905.3	18.0	1,119.7	18.5
Service-producing sector	**2,431.9**	**64.9**	**2,792.4**	**65.1**	**3,595.9**	**71.7**	**4,432.5**	**73.0**
Trade	610.9	16.3	640.1	14.9	758.6	15.1	920.8	15.2
Transportation and warehousing	182.1	4.9	200.5	4.7	222.7	4.4	284.7	4.7
Finance, insurance, real estate, leasing	229.7	6.1	270.6	6.3	381.8	7.6	398.2	6.6
Professional, scientific, and technical services	106.7	2.8	155.5	3.6	268.9	5.4	435.6	7.2
Management admin. and other support services	69.8	1.9	88.1	2.1	142.8	2.8	254.8	4.2
Education services	242.3	6.5	231.5	5.4	333.2	6.6	378.6	6.2
Health care and social assistance	298.2	7.9	336.6	7.8	481.8	9.6	563.5	9.3
Information, culture, and recreation	142.3	3.8	183.1	4.3	204.4	4.1	288.3	4.8
Accommodation & food services	149.1	4.0	223.0	5.2	271.6	5.4	363.9	6.0
Other services	148.0	3.9	193.4	4.5	214.3	4.3	252.7	4.2
Public administration	252.8	6.7	269.9	6.3	315.6	6.3	291.2	4.8

Source: Statistics Canada, 1976, 1981, 1991, and 2002, table 282-0008, and Catalogue no. 71F004XCB; also CANSIM Table 281-0025.

dollars at Ingersoll in 2002 to build an assembly line for the Equinox sports utility vehicle. Other manufacturing investments were directed at a broad range of goods, from high-tech pharmaceuticals, aerospace components, and communications equipment (including semi-conductors and fibre optics) to common household items such as blinds, insulation, windows and doors, and electric heaters.

The auto industry has in many ways been the backbone of manufacturing in Ontario. It has been operating in the province since the beginning of the twentieth century, and generated many linkages that have also benefited Ontario. The Canada–US Auto Pact, signed in 1965, guaranteed Canadian producers a share of the North American market. As Iain Wallace describes it, the agreement was an example of 'managed' trade in which the 'Big Three'—Ford, Daimler/Chrysler, and General Motors—were able to benefit from economies of scale in producing vehicles for the North American market (2002: 114). This agreement brought increased investment from these corporations to both Ontario and Quebec, and allowed both vehicles and the parts used in their manufacture to cross the border duty-free.

Even with the Auto Pact, however, the auto industry was not immune to economic uncertainty. The energy crisis of the 1970 prompted dramatic change in consumer demand, and assembly lines had to be completely retooled to produce smaller, more fuel-efficient vehicles. Meanwhile, foreign competition increased significantly through the 1970s and 1980s as overseas producers established plants in Ontario: Toyota in Cambridge and Honda in Alliston, in addition to the Cami plant at Ingersoll. Automobile production—a traditionally labour-intensive industry—was transformed beginning in the 1970s, becoming more capital-intensive with the introduction of robots and computer-assisted production systems. Not only was the work force downsized, but production was fragmented with the growth of vehicle-parts producers capable of responding to the 'just-in-time' demands of the auto producers. One consequence of these changes was a shift in employment away from the assembly side to the parts side of the industry: 'Between 1992 and 1997, motor vehicle employment in Ontario dropped by 9 per cent to 44,000, whereas, auto parts employment increased by 17 per cent, to 91,000' (Wallace, 2002: 115).

Ontario auto producers have enjoyed a number of comparative advantages over their American counterparts, including a relatively low Canadian dollar, relatively low-cost health benefits, proximity to the largest share of the North American market, and stable, industry-facilitating governments at both the provincial and federal levels. In 2001, however, Auto Pact was abandoned after the World Trade Organization found that it discriminated against imported vehicles. Since then two Canadian plants have been closed (Daimler/Chrysler in Windsor and General Motors at Ste-Thérèse). Other operations have been more fortunate: in 2004 the federal and provincial governments each contributed $100 million to entice Ford to invest $1 billion in updating its Oakville assembly plant, and the International Truck plant at Chatham was saved when Navistar International Corporation invested $150 million to build new truck cabs (*Canadian Driver*, 2004; Community of Chatham-Kent, 2004). Still, the automobile industry is not guaranteed an easy ride. Now that vehicles are being built to last longer, demand for new models has slowed, while competition from Japanese manufacturers has increased. In addition, the tightening of border security since the terrorist attacks of September 2001 has made it difficult to guarantee 'just-in-time' delivery of parts.

Table 6.10   Ontario's population, 1971–2001

	1971	1981	1991	2001
Ontario	7,703.1	8,625.1	10,084.9	11,894.9
% Urban	80.3	81.7	82.0	84.7
Canada	21,515.1	24,343.2	27,296.9	31,110.6
Ont. as % of Canada	35.8	35.4	36.9	38.2

Source: Adapted from Statistics Canada, CANSIM database
⟨http://cansim2.statcan.ca⟩, Table 051-0001.

Table 6.11   Population of largest 20 Census Metropolitan Areas and Census Agglomerations in Ontario (× 1,000), 1971–2001

City	1971	1981	1991	2001
Toronto	2,628.0	2,998.9	3,898.9	4,682.9
Ottawa–Hull	602.5	717.8	941.8	1,063.7
Hamilton	498.5	542.1	599.8	662.4
London	286.0	283.7	381.5	432.5
Kitchener	226.8	287.8	356.4	414.3
St Catharines–Niagara	303.4	304.4	364.5	377.0
Windsor	258.6	246.1	262.1	307.9
Oshawa	120.3	154.2	240.1	296.3
Sudbury	155.4	149.9	157.6	155.6
Kingston	85.9	115.0	136.4	146.8
Thunder Bay	108.4	121.4	125.6	122.0
Guelph	62.7	78.5	97.7	117.3
Chatham	35.3	47.2	67.1	107.3
Barrie	38.2	61.3	97.2	103.7
Peterborough	63.5	85.7	98.1	102.4
Sarnia	78.4	84.0	87.9	88.3
Belleville	35.1	46.4	92.9	87.4
Brantford	80.3	88.3	97.1	86.4
Sault Ste Marie	81.3	82.7	85.0	78.9
North Bay	49.2	57.1	65.2	63.7

Source: Adapted from Statistics Canada, CANSIM database
⟨http://cansim2.statcan.ca⟩, Table 051-0034.

The picture is brighter on the service side of the economy. Ontario, and more specifically Toronto, has become the financial centre of Canada. Five of the six national banks—the Bank of Nova Scotia, Bank of Montreal, Canadian Imperial Bank of Commerce, Royal Bank, and Toronto Dominion—have their head offices in Toronto (the sixth, the National Bank of Canada, is based in Montreal). Besides the thousands of branch offices throughout Canada, these banks 'operate about 300 international offices and a variety of subsidiary and agency offices in almost 60 countries. Thirty-eight of Canada's 52 banks operate from Ontario and 48 of the 53 foreign banks that operate in Canada have their Canadian head offices in Toronto' (Ontario Strategic Infrastructure Finance Authority, n.d.) Toronto's stock exchange (TSX) is another important financial institution where billions of dollars are invested each year.

The service sector is largely urban-centred, and southern Ontario, with its highly integrated network of cities in relatively close proximity to one another, was well suited to attract service industries. Table 6.10 traces Ontario's population change from the 1970s, and Table 6.11 shows how the main cities have grown over the same period. These increases in population and urbanization are all indicators of economic growth.

Increasing centralization of population in the largest centres is typical of the transition to a service-oriented economy. But there are some interesting dynamics to industry location, which in turn influences urban growth. The decisions of Japanese auto manufacturers to locate their assembly plants at Alliston, Cambridge, and Ingersoll represent decentralization from the larger cities. These relatively small towns are within commuting distance of Toronto. Such locations, in the **commutershed** of a major urban centre, offer a number of advantages for corporations, including relatively low land values—essential for industries that require large production facilities—and easy access both to inputs (such as parts) and to markets. For workers, such communities have all the attractions of a small town: people know one another; houses are more affordable, and lots considerably larger, than in big cities; there is less crime and less smog; traffic problems are rare; and one can still have access to big-city amenities such as major league sports and cultural activities.

For other industries, however, there are distinct advantages to locating in the central business district of the downtown core. In services such as banking, finance, and insurance, face-to-face contact remains crucial (Gad, 1991). The same forces that attract these services and their employees to the city also increase the demand for hotels, conference centres, restaurants, entertainment, high-rise apartments, and condominiums.

commutershed
the area within commuting distance of a major centre

Table 6.12   Selected farm statistics, Canada, Ontario, and Saskatchewan, 1981–2001

	1981			1991			2001		
	Cda.	Ont.	Sask.	Cda.	Ont.	Sask.	Cda.	Ont.	Sask.
Number of farms	318,361	82,448	67,318	280,043	68,633	60,840	246,923	59,728	50,598
Area (ha. $\times$ 10^3)[1]	65,889	6,039	25,947	67,754	5,451	26,866	67,502	5,466	26,266
Average size (ha.)	207	73	385	242	79	442	273	92	519
Farms with receipts of $2500 or more	271,604	68,960	64,342	256,182	61,432	58,651	230,540	55,092	48,990
Cash receipts ($\times$ 10^6)	18,534	4,837	3,994	22,030	5,585	4,130	36,196	8,488	6,567
Farm Type[2]									
Dairy	15.4	18.6	2.5	11.3	15.9	1.3	8.1	11.6	0.7
Cattle (beef)	22.1	28.4	11.0	25.9	27.4	15.4	29.4	24.8	24.7
Hog	4.5	7.2	1.0	4.1	6.2	1.3	3.1	4.5	0.6
Poultry and egg	2.0	2.7	0.4	1.6	2.6	0.2	1.9	2.9	0.2
Wheat	20.5	1.0	63.9	16.8	0.9	50.8	6.6	0.7	18.4
Grain and oilseed (except wheat)	19.2	20.3	15.8	18.5	18.6	24.2	22.8	23.3	44.4
Other field crops	2.8	4.6	0.4	4.6	5.8	1.6	7.5	8.2	4.2
Fruit	2.4	3.5	0.0	2.5	3.4	0.0	2.8	3.1	0.1
Vegetable	1.3	2.6	0.0	1.4	2.7	0.0	1.3	2.2	0.1
Misc. specialty	4.3	5.5	0.7	9.0	11.9	1.6	12.3	13.3	3.5
Livestock comb.	3.3	3.5	2.6	2.7	3.1	2.4	2.2	2.9	1.5
Other comb.	2.1	2.0	1.7	1.6	1.5	1.1	2.0	2.3	1.7

[1] 1 ha (hectare) = 2.471 acres.

[2] Percentage of all farms with gross receipts of $2500 or more.

Sources: Statistics Canada, Census of Agriculture 2001, CANSIM Table 002-0001; Census of Agriculture 1981; 1991.

The tendency for housing, shopping centres, and industrial parks to move away from the city and into the countryside began in the 1950s and was directly related to increases in car ownership and improvements to road systems. One significant effect of this urban sprawl is that much of the excellent agricultural land that drew population to southern Ontario in the first place has now disappeared.

Table 6.12 presents a number of statistics that allow us to compare farming dynamics in Ontario with those in Canada generally as well as in the predominantly agricultural province of Saskatchewan. If it comes as a surprise to learn that Ontario has more farms than Saskatchewan, check the 'average size' row and you will find that on average Saskatchewan farms are nearly six times the size of those in Ontario. Across Canada as a whole the number of farms has decreased, and both Ontario and Saskatchewan have followed this trend, with reductions of more than twenty per cent. Ontario farms may be considerably smaller than those in Saskatchewan, but the relatively mild climate allows them to grow a great variety of crops, which bring in the highest cash receipts anywhere in Canada. The 'farm types' section shows considerable variation between 1981 and 2001; it also underlines how much greater the mix of agriculture is in Ontario than in Saskatchewan.

Another advantage for farms in southern Ontario is the proximity of major urban markets for high-value fresh produce such as fruit, vegetables, meat, and dairy products. The Golden Horseshoe is one of the rare regions in Canada where climate and soil combine to allow soft fruit such as peaches to thrive. In 2001 the Niagara Regional Municipality grew 85 per cent of the grapes used in Canada's rapidly expanding wine industry (Statistics Canada, 2002). These excellent agricultural lands were threatened by urban sprawl, but are now protected under the province's Greenbelt Act, passed in 2005.

Northern Ontario: 1970s–Present

The economic changes that have taken place since the 1970s have not been easy on northern Ontario. The forest and mining industries that continue to be the economic base of most hinterland communities largely depend on external markets, and have faced fluctuations in demand; new technologies have displaced many workers; and most operations are owned and controlled by large transnational corporations.

Only two centres in the region—Sudbury and Thunder Bay—have more than 100,000 residents; only Sault Ste Marie and North Bay are in the 50,000 to 100,000 category. The rest have relatively small populations (see Table 6.13), and most of them depend on a single sawmill, pulp mill, mine, or smelter. Most of these towns and cities are relatively isolated and have few economic links with communities down the road. The four largest cities also have strong ties to resource development; however, they are located at major transportation junctions and have become important regional centres, providing hospitals and health care, government services, and educational training (including universities), as well as serving as gateways for tourism and recreation.

The population statistics in Table 6.13 point to a number of trends. Between 1971 and 1991 many of these communities grew, though in some cases the growth stopped after 1981. After 1991 only four gained population, and all these communities were relatively small. Interim census figures are not included in Table 6.13; however, it is worth noting that with one exception (Sioux Lookout) all the communities listed lost population between 1996 and 2001. Elliot Lake, Kirkland Lake, Red Lake, Atikokan, and Cobalt all experienced losses of more than ten per cent. A series of developments in the mining industry during this period helps to explain this pattern.

Around the world, the mining industry has undergone a major transition over the past three to four decades. By the 1970s, most new mines were mega-projects requiring multi-million- and even billion-dollar investments by large, often foreign, transnational corporations. New technologies were introduced at all levels of mining. For example, sophisticated computer technologies were applied to the concentration, smelting, and refining of ores, making it possible to produce more with fewer employees. The loss in employment was particularly hard on communities where the mine was the main employer.

Mining is a high-cost and high-risk industry. By definition, the resources that mining depends on are non-renewable; inevitably, every mine will run out. But mines can also close before the ore is exhausted: the processes used may become too expensive; competition may make an individual mine uneconomic; labour disruptions may be too costly; or world market prices may collapse.

Table 6.13   Population of selected northern Ontario communities, 1971–2001

Community	1971	1981	1991	2001
Sudbury	90,535	149,923	160,488	155,219
Thunder Bay	108,411	121,379	124,925	121,986
Sault Ste Marie	81,270	82,697	85,008	78,908
North Bay	49,187	51,268	65,222	63,681
Timmins	28,542	46,114	47,461	43,686
Kenora	10,952	9,817	15,910	15,838
Elliot Lake	9,093	16,723	14,089	11,956
Kapuskasing	12,834	12,014	10,344	9,238
Kirkland Lake	–	12,219	10,440	8,616
Fort Frances	9,947	8,906	8,891	8,315
Dryden	6,939	6,640	6,505	8,198
Cochrane	4,965	4,848	4,585	5,690
Espanola	6,045	5,836	5,527	5,449
Sioux Lookout	2,530	3,074	3,311	5,336
New Liskeard	5,488	5,551	5,431	4,906
Marathon	2,456	2,277	5,064	4,791
Red Lake	–	2,120	2,268	4,233
Atikokan	6,087	5,641	4,047	3,632
Terrace Bay	1,860	2,644	2,477	2,324
Cobalt	2,197	1,759	1,470	1,229

Source: Statistics Canada, Census of Canada, 1971 and 1981; 'Community Profiles', 1991; 2001.

Table 6.14   World prices for selected metals (annual averages, in Canadian dollars), 1996–2004

		1996	1997	1998	1999	2000	2001	2002	2003	2004
Copper	$/lb	1.42	1.43	1.11	1.05	1.22	1.12	1.11	1.13	1.69
Gold	$/oz	528.47	458.34	435.74	412.75	414.90	419.68	486.62	507.60	531.75
Nickel	$/lb	3.50	3.22	2.18	2.75	3.99	2.83	3.10	4.45	8.35
Silver	$/oz	7.06	6.77	8.19	7.77	7.42	6.80	7.22	6.82	8.65
Zinc	$/lb	0.70	0.90	0.76	0.78	0.83	0.68	0.55	0.54	0.62

Source: Natural Resources Canada (http://mmsd1.mms.nrcan.gc.ca/mmsd/prices/Table_15.htm).

The high costs of production and volatility of the world market have led many mines to close. Table 6.14 shows that world market prices for the principal metals mined in Ontario have fluctuated between 1996 and 2004, while Table 6.15 presents 1996, 2001, and 2004 figures on the quantities of metal mined and the revenues received. The overall trend between 1996 and 2001 was clearly downward; even gold revenues fell off significantly in 2001. This trend reflected the downward trend in prices over the same period: shut-downs and closures meant that less metal was mined, and revenues dropped accordingly. As a result, mining companies had less revenue to cover the costs of production—costs that continued to rise—and make a profit. Although metal prices recovered somewhat in 2004, the only metal besides gold that showed increases in both quantity and revenue between 1996 and 2004 was silver. Fortunately for mine owners, silver is often found along with gold. The mines at Sudbury, Timmins, and Thunder Bay, which produce mainly copper and nickel, also contain quantities of gold and silver, and the Falconbridge copper mine at Timmins has all these metals as well as zinc and cobalt. This diversity is the strength of metal mining in Ontario.

Mines producing a single mineral are much more vulnerable, and so are the communities that rely on them. Elliot Lake is an example of single-resource dependency. The town's population (Table 6.13) illustrates the classic boom and bust pattern. In fact, Elliot Lake experienced two such cycles. Its first boom lasted from the mid-1950s to mid-1960s, when the proliferation of nuclear weapons during the Cold War increased demand for uranium. With the development of nuclear power generation, demand revived in the 1970s; the price of uranium reached US$40.21/lb by 1976, and demand continued to grow until 1980. But from that year it slowly declined and in 1988 'fell sharply'; the price reached US$8.84/lb by 1991 (Leadbeater, n.d.: 7). Finally, by 1989 the last of Elliot Lake's uranium mines closed down. The reasons are not hard to explain: costs of production were high because the mine was underground (as opposed to open-pit); the ore was low-grade, and uranium mining demands extra precautions because of its radioactivity. In addition, as Robert Bone points out, 'open-pit uranium mines in northern Saskatchewan could produce uranium oxide at a much lower price' (2002: 254).

Elliot Lake is by no means the only single-resource community in Canada that has had to reinvent itself after losing its economic base. However, it has a number of advantages that other communities do not have. Its setting is ideal for recreation and tourism; it is well connected by road (only a couple of hours from Sudbury or Sault Ste Marie and a day's drive to

Table 6.15   Metals production and value, Ontario, 1996, 2001, and 2004

	1996	2001	2004
Cobalt			
tonnes	1,778	1,402	1,343
$'000	136,357	53,737	97,033
Copper			
tonnes	221,341	102,330	176,137
$'000	698,551	455,656	660,161
Gold			
grams	75,074	79,860	71,476
$'000	1,276,402	1,073,317	1,225,094
Nickel			
tonnes	146,844	117,140	115,883
$'000	1,545,977	1,129,694	2,133,182
Silver			
tonnes	183	146	185
$'000	41,641	32,113	51,808
Zinc			
tonnes	118,802	77,776	83,473
$'000	166,086	109,586	113,106

Source: Natural Resources Canada (http://mmsd1.mms.
nrcan.gc.ca/mmsd/production/production_e.asp).

Table 6.16   Elliot Lake population by age, 1991–2001

Age	1991 Pop.	1991 %	1996 Pop.	1996 %	2001 Pop.	2001 %
14 and under	3,515	24.95	2,595	19.10	1,710	14.30
15 to 24	1,875	13.31	1,630	12.00	1,175	9.83
25 to 44	4,575	32.47	3,355	24.69	2,370	19.82
45 to 64	2,875	20.41	3,680	27.08	3,695	30.81
65 to 74	965	6.85	1,730	12.73	2,060	17.23
75 and over	310	2.20	590	4.34	945	7.90
Total	14,089	100.0	13,588	100.0	11,955	100.0

Source: Statistics Canada, 'Community Profiles', 1991, 1996, 2001.

Toronto); and it has a small airport. It is also larger than most single-resource communities; offers many attractive facilities (golf, tennis courts, ice arenas, indoor pool, recreation centre, theatre, and a transit system); and is within easy reach of lakes for fishing, rivers for canoeing, cross-country ski trails, and downhill skiing. The community has launched an aggressive marketing strategy to attract retirees and new knowledge-based industries related to the deactivation of uranium mines and reclamation of uranium tailings. Table 6.16 shows how the age structure of the population changed between 1991 and 2001; by 2001 the majority of residents were over 45.

Forest-based communities in northern Ontario have fared only slightly better. Like mining, the forest industry has undergone massive changes in the technologies used to harvest, process, and manufacture its products, employing fewer and fewer people over the past 35 years.

According to Natural Resources Canada, the lumber, pulp and paper, and other forest industries directly employed 94,300 people in 2004 and was the economic base of more than fifty Ontario communities (Natural Resources Canada, 2005). Because, like other staple industries, they depend on exporting their products (mainly to the United States), Ontario's forest industries are vulnerable to external demand, fluctuations in market prices, and political efforts to restrict trade. They also face competition from other producers in Canada and around the world, as well as growing public concern over their impact on the environment.

Table 6.17 provides a 30-year overview of the main wood-based goods produced by Ontario and Canada as a whole. Several trends can be observed. At the national level, production of softwood lumber (spruce, fir, pine, cedar, etc.) has increased greatly and the same is true of paper products other than newsprint. Ontario's share of softwood

Table 6.17   Ontario's softwood lumber, newsprint, other paper, and paperboard production, 1971–2001

	Softwood (thousands of m³)			Newsprint (thousands of tons)			Other paper and paperboard (thousands of tons)		
	Ont.	%	Cda	Ont.	%	Cda	Ont.	%	Cda
1971	1,658	5.7	28,965	1,609	20.8	7,733	1,220	35.6	3,428
1976	2,277	6.4	35,638	1,411	17.5	8,063	1,181	31.7	3,728
1981	3,717	9.5	39,236	1,774	19.8	8,951	1,755	37.5	4,675
1986	5,324	10.0	53,400	1,773	19.1	9,288	2,150	36.0	5,973
1991	4,058	8.0	50,644	1,555	17.3	8,977	2,374	31.2	7,598
1996	6,121	9.6	63,898	1,701	18.8	9,025	2,793	29.7	9,394
2001	8,104	11.8	68,824	1,620	19.3	8,373	3,204	28.4	11,277

Source: Adapted from Natural Resources Canada, 'Lumber Production by Province and Species Group, 1950–2001' 〈http://www2.nrcan.gc.ca/cfs-scf/selfor/section1New/I4Categ_e.asp〉; 'Basic Paper and Paperboard Production by Category and Region, 1950–2001' 〈http://www2.nrcan.gc.ca/cfs-scf/selfor/historique/section1/I-13-E.htm〉.

production fluctuated during the 1990s, but overall there has been a significant gain in production since the 1970s. Newsprint, which dominated all paper production, has remained fairly consistent at 8,000 to 9,000 million tons per year and Ontario has been able to retain its share of this market. Other paper and paperboard—cartons, bags, corrugated boxes, paperboard, building paper, and so on—has seen a substantial increase in production. Ontario, which had more than 35 per cent of this market during the 1970s and 1980s, has increased its production overall, but lost some of its market share since the 1990s. Still, wood panels, other paper and paperboard, and converted paper accounted for over 40 per cent of Ontario's $9.0 billion forestry products exports in 2004, compared to only 13 per cent for newsprint and 8 per cent for softwood (Natural Resources Canada, 2005).

The prices paid for the various wood-based products have not been stable, reflecting overall economic uncertainty and global competition. In Table 6.18, the annual average price of lumber, pulp and paper has been standardized, with 1997 representing a price of $100. Note that prices can vary considerably within a single year, let alone between years; newsprint prices fell dramatically between 2001 and 2002, for example.

In response to the many factors that have changed the costs of production, forestry companies have restructured their industry, adopting new technologies, engaging in flexible specialization, and integrating their operations. Companies specializing in pulp or paper have found it advantageous to combine or integrate their operations with sawmilling and/or the production of other wood products; in this way sawmill 'waste' can be used to make pulp or oriented strand board. This move to vertical integration has been accompanied by disintegration of many segments in the production process. Often it is more cost-effective for large lumber companies to contract out tasks such as transportation and the drying of lumber than for these companies to own and operate trucks and kilns themselves.

A single corporation may produce many different wood products, and each operation faces different challenges. One of the problems for the pulp and paper industry in Ontario is that the existing mills are old. Many date to the early 1900s, and even mills built in the 1960s and 1970s need upgrading, for two reasons. The first is that they are not as competitive as newer mills in western Canada or 'new producers in Chile, Brazil, and Indonesia' (Mackenzie and Norcliffe, 1997: 2). The second is the danger posed by industrial pollution both to the environment and to human health. In 1969–70, for example, it was discovered that Reed Paper at Dryden had dumped tons of methyl mercury into the English–Wabigoon river system, where it became part of the food chain. As a result, many members of the local White Dog and Grassy Narrows First Nations suffered brain damage. The Grassy Narrows band had to be relocated to a new village site, and commercial fishing in the area was destroyed, along with fishing-based tourism The mercury has never been cleaned up: every spring, even today, the run-off disturbs the mercury and re-injects it into the waterways (Ecosuperior, n.d.). Pressured to set higher standards for emissions, the provincial government has commissioned studies and introduced a program to collect batteries (one source of mercury) in the region; and in

Table 6.18 Selling price indexes for Ontario's softwood lumber, pulp, and newsprint, 1981–2003 (1997 = $100)

	Lumber	Pulp	Newsprint
1981	43.2	81.7	66.3
1986	53.1	80.1	81.6
1991	44.9	84.8	83.9
1996	95.4	103.6	115.5
2001	80.2	105.4	123.0
2002	80.6	95.0	96.2
2003	72.5	96.2	89.3

Source: Adapted from Natural Resources Canada, 'Selling Price Indexes – Wood Pulp and Paper Products, 1981–2002 (1977 = 100)' (http://www2.nrcan.gc.ca/cfs-scf/selfor/members/section5/prtV3.asp?lang=en); 'Selling Price Indexes – Lumber Products, 1981–2002 (1977 = 100)' (http://www2.nrcan.gc.ca/cfs-scf/selfor/members/section5/prtV2.asp?lang=en).

1998 Canada and the United States reached an agreement to reduce mercury in Lake Superior. But pulp and paper companies are reluctant to adopt costly pollution abatement measures that add nothing to productivity, especially when prices are volatile.

In addition, the newsprint industry is required by law to use one-quarter recycled paper in its products. Since there is relatively little recycled paper produced in peripheral areas themselves, many mills have to import de-inked newsprint. This has reversed the traditional pattern of locational advantage in the newsprint industry: now mills closer to the core region have the advantage over those deep in the hinterland. Logging operations have also faced increasing pressure on environmental grounds. Modern technology such as the feller-buncher—a large machine that uses hydraulics to shear a tree near the ground, strip off the branches, and bundle them for pickup—has created massive clear-cuts, with consequences that range from soil erosion to reduction in biodiversity, destruction of animal habitat, and loss of old-growth forests. Environmental groups have drawn national and international attention to wilderness areas such as Temagami, north of Toronto. But forest companies see old-growth trees as vital to keeping their logging operations viable, and the provincial government itself is reluctant to lose the tax revenue it receives for licensing logging operations on Crown land ('stumpage').

Most of Canada's lumber exports are destined for the American house-building market, and those from Ontario are no exception. As Table 6.16 points out, Ontario produces less than 10 per cent of the softwood lumber in Canada, but it too was affected by the long-running softwood lumber dispute with the United States. US lumber producers claimed that Canadian licensing and leasing fees were too low and therefore that Canadian lumber was entering the US at a subsidized rate and undercutting American producers. Despite the Free Trade Agreement, strong lobby groups persuaded the American government to impose barriers on wood imported from Canada.

Before 2001, Canada's quota was set at 14.7 billion board feet per year of lumber, and each province was allocated a portion of this trade based on its traditional cross-border trade. When the quota agreement expired in 2001, Canada claimed there should be no quota restrictions. But the US imposed a 19.3 per cent countervail duty, followed by a 12.57 per cent anti-dumping duty.

Decisions reached through the Free Trade Agreement appeal mechanisms and the World Trade Organization have all found in favour of Canada. But the Americans appeal the decisions, time passes, and nothing is resolved. Meanwhile, duties amounting to more than thirty per cent meant that many mills had to shut down across Canada, although the low Canadian dollar helped the more efficient operations to continue exporting to the United States.

Another problem for northern Ontario has been the tendency for the southern core to gain most of the forward linkages in the forest industry: 'The north has 96 per cent of Ontario's logging jobs, but southern Ontario has two-thirds of all value-added manufacturing jobs' (Runesson, n.d.). The north tends to be limited to producing dimension lumber ('two-by-fours', etc.), offering jobs only for a diminishing number of loggers and sawmill workers, while southern Ontario has the more labour-intensive wood-based industries such as the production of doors, windows, and furniture. A simple but essential strategy for northern communities is to diversify their economic base by attracting other industries or services. Most such efforts have concentrated on tourism. The vast wilderness of lakes, rivers, rock, and forest offers a range of recreation activities for any season: from camping, hiking, bicycling, swimming, boating, canoeing, and kayaking to bird watching, fishing, hunting, cross-country skiing, downhill skiing, snowmobiling, and ice-fishing. Sports tournaments, tennis, First Nations heritage centres, and mining and forestry museums also attract tourists to the north. Some centres focus on a particular activity— Atikokan, for example, bills itself as the 'Canoe capital of Canada'. Others, such as Red Lake, promote fly-in fishing camps, emphasizing their remoteness.

As southern Ontario and North America generally become increasingly urban, more and more people look to northern Ontario for a temporary escape, and thousands of vehicles head out each Friday for the 'cottage country' north of Toronto. But not all recreation activities are compatible, and cottage country has divided into two polarized camps. Those who want to relax and enjoy the scenery, take quiet walks in the woods, canoe on the lake, or cross-country ski are often offended by those who partake in noisy outdoor activities such as jet skiing or snowmobiling. Efforts to limit noise pollution by restricting the size of boat motors or banning motorized activities on trails have so far not been successful. Meanwhile, all cottage owners have seen their tax assessments rise sharply since the mid-1990s. A much more fundamental conflict involves the different perspectives held by those who live in the north and those who do not. Whereas northerners see the lands and forests as the source of their livelihood, southerners see them as natural treasures that must be preserved from assaults such as clear-cutting and open-pit mining. With ten times the population of the north, the south can and does exert considerable pressure on government to place restrictions on forestry and mining activities.

If tourism is an important part of northern Ontario's economy, however, it is even more important for southern Ontario. Two events in particular have shown the vulnerability of the tourist industry in recent years. The terrorist attacks of September 2001 not only caused many people to cut back on air travel, but complicated the process of crossing the border by car, with the result that many potential visitors to Canada were deterred. Then in 2003 an outbreak of SARS (Severe Acute Respiratory Syndrome) in Toronto frightened many others away: concerts, conferences, and many other events were cancelled, and attendance was reduced at all public venues, including sports events and restaurants. These unfortunate events remind us that tourism is just as vulnerable as any other industry to global events and uncertainties.

The Conservative predecessors of Ontario's current Liberal government applied 'Smart Growth' strategies to northern Ontario, assessing the strengths and weaknesses of communities within each Census Division and developing action plans to improve social and economic conditions for the future. As Figure 6.5 shows, most northern Census Divisions are declining in population, and many of them are projected to decline by the year 2021 (Table 6.19, p. 183).

The Smart Growth program has disappeared, but the strategy continues: to reverse the trend towards population loss and enhance economic development through various partnerships between local, provincial, federal governments, First Nations, non-government organizations, and the private sector. To accomplish these goals there is a new Northern Ontario Heritage Fund Corporation that incorporates six funding strategies (Government of Ontario, 2005a).

Although the projections show overall increases in population for both regions by 2021, some districts, such as Algoma, Cochrane, Greater Sudbury, and Rainy River, are expected to experience only minor increases over the 1996 levels, and Temiskaming is

Figure 6.5   Census division boundaries, Ontario, 2001

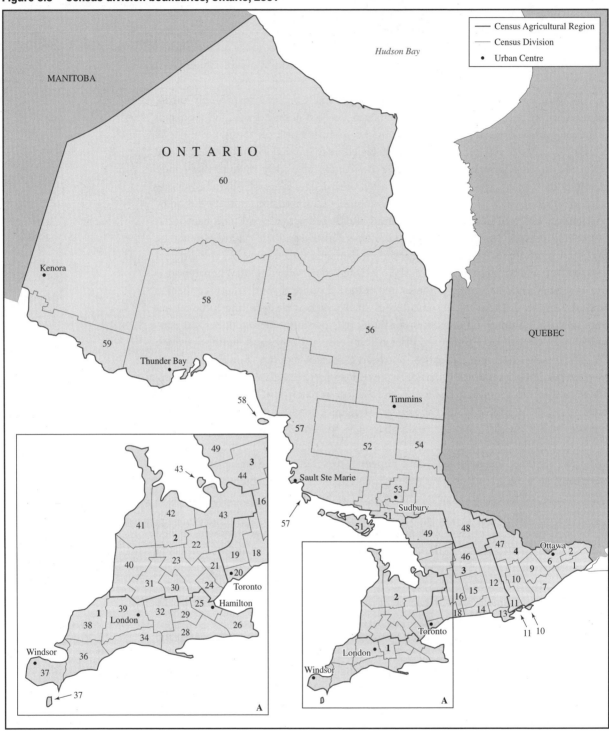

Source: Adapted from Statistics Canada (http://www.statcan.ca/english/freepub/95F0301XIE/maps/ontcar.pdf).

Table 6.19 **Population trends for the northeast and northwest regions of Ontario 1996–2021**

	1996	2001	% Change	2021
Northeast				
Algoma	125,455	118,567	−5.5	125,900
Cochrane	93,240	85,247	−8.6	94,900
Manitoulin	11,747	12,679	+7.9	16,000
Muskoka	50,463	53,106	+5.2	72,600
Nipissing	84,832	82,910	−2.3	87,900
Parry Sound	39,885	39,665	−0.6	46,500
Greater Sudbury	165,618	155,601	−6.0	166,100
Sudbury District	23,832	22,894	−3.9	26,600
Temiskaming	37,807	34,442	−8.9	36,000
Total	**632,879**	**605,111**	**−4.4**	**672,500**
Northwest				
Kenora	63,360	61,802	−2.5	77,700
Rainy River	23,138	22,109	−4.4	24,300
Thunder Bay	157,619	150,860	−4.3	160,000
Total	**244,117**	**234,771**	**−3.8**	**262,000**

Source: Statistics Canada, 'Community Profiles', 1996 and 2001 (http://www12.statcan.ca/english/profil01/PlaceSearchForm1.cfm).

predicted to remain below that level. The popular cottage country destinations of Muskoka and Manitoulin Island are the only census divisions that gained population between 1996 and 2001, and are predicted to grow significantly by 2021.

In short, northern Ontario is a hinterland region that is losing population, especially young people, as jobs in the traditional staple industries disappear. As the remaining population ages, there will be fewer and fewer people to support the businesses that remain—and to pay the taxes needed to support the services that people need more and more as they age. The region's economic future depends on developing alternatives to staple industries. But this task is complicated by the fundamental conflict between traditional extractive industries and the wilderness-centred tourism that at present is the only substantial alternative. Many other peripheral regions of the country face similar problems, as we will see in the following chapters.

Ontario and Its Environment

'We all live downstream'
—Bumper sticker

Today every region of Canada is experiencing environmental degradation that threatens the economy and in many cases human health. Ontario has had its share of environmental crises involving toxic industrial wastes, acid rain, and contaminated drinking water. The various environmental predicaments faced by Ontario reflect a number of factors. To the toxic wastes produced by heavy industry, past and present, must be added the pollution from coal-fired power generation (still an important source in Ontario, despite the move towards nuclear power) and a general reliance on the automobile; the latter is especially significant in southern Ontario because of its high concentration of population.

The list of industrial processes that produce toxic wastes is long, ranging from the smelting and refining of metals to the production of consumer goods such as pesticides, paints, and batteries; even the 'environmentally friendly' practice of recycling involves processes such as bleaching and de-inking and thus becomes another source of pollution. Ontario, as Canada's industrial core, has a great number of industries that contaminate the land, water and air, and its location next to the American industrial heartland compounds the problem, since air and water circulate freely between the two countries. The dangers posed by toxic waste came to wide public attention in 1978, following the discovery that residents of a suburb of Niagara Falls, New York, were being poisoned by chemicals in the ground their community was built on, which had been used as a dump for chemical wastes in the 1940s and 1950s. The 'Love Canal' affair prompted a search for similar sites throughout the United States and Canada. 'Almost 800 dump sites previously unknown to the Ontario government were discovered' in 1979 (Jackson et al., 1982: 18). At that time Ontario generated more than 1.6 million tonnes of hazardous wastes a year—half of the Canadian total—and Toronto and Hamilton together accounted for half of them. Since the companies that dumped the wastes had largely disappeared, the costs of cleaning up the sites were borne by the public.

The Great Lakes continue to be the main source of drinking and irrigation water for the adjacent populations. They also serve many other purposes, as a source of fish, a major transportation route for ocean-going vessels, and a waste disposal site. 'Over 360 compounds have been found in Great Lake waters, more than one-third of which have been shown to be toxic to humans and wildlife' (Draper, 2002: 227). Sewage, pesticides, polychlorinated biphenyls (PCBs), and toxic metals such as cyanide are the most common pollutants in the Great Lakes system. When fish began to die and people became worried about the risks to their health, international agreements were negotiated to improve the quality the water. Plenty of legislation has been passed and many sources of pollution have been banned outright (e.g., PCBs) or severely restricted (e.g., use of 2,4-D as a pesticide), and the quality of Great Lakes water has improved significantly over the past thirty years. 'Contrary to what many people believe,' however, 'industrial companies still legally dump toxic waste directly into the lakes and their tributaries' (Leighton, 1993: 94).

Another persistent problem for Ontario and eastern Canada generally is acid precipitation, produced when sulphur dioxide (SO_2) and various forms of nitrogen oxide (NO_x) permeate the atmosphere and combine with water vapour to form solutions of sulphuric or nitric acid. When these solutions descend (as rain, snow, dust, etc.), they decrease the pH (increase acidity) of the soil and water, killing vegetation and becoming a risk to human health. The main sources of SO_2 are smelters and refineries, pulp mills, and the burning of fossil fuels, while NO_x also come from burning fossil fuels (a primary source is vehicle exhaust). Randee Holmes (2000) relates the good news–bad news story of acid rain in Pollution Probe's 'The Acid Rain Primer'. The good news is that pollution abatement measures have significantly reduced sulphur emissions. For example, INCO and Falconbridge, located at Sudbury, installed some of the highest smokestacks in the world, and reduced their SO_2 emissions by more than 90 per cent by the mid-1990s (Draper, 2002: 371). The bad news is that nitrogen oxide emissions have remained largely unchanged. One problem here is the general dependence on gasoline-powered vehicles: even though vehicles are now equipped with controls to reduce exhaust emissions, the overall number of vehicles on the road has continued to increase. Another problem is the use of coal to generate hydro power: in the 1990s, 40 per cent of the electricity produced by Ontario Power Generation came from coal-fired generators. In 2003 the provincial Liberal party promised as part of its election platform to eliminate all the coal-fired units by 2007, and in 2005 one plant was closed down. But closing of the giant Nanticoke plant has now been postponed until 2009.

The contamination of ground water is a continuing fear for people who depend on wells for their drinking water. In May 2000 the town of Walkerton, in southwestern Ontario, made headlines when it suffered the worst case of E. coli contamination in Canada. The source of the contamination was manure spread on fields near one of the city's wells. Heavy rains washed the waste into the well, and the town's water supply was tainted; seven people died and another 2,300 became seriously ill (CBC, 2002). Walkerton's water managers faced criminal charges and the provincial government was widely criticized for having cut back on its maintenance of water standards. Finally, recognition of the need to clean up the legacy of industrial pollution has led to the development of new high-tech service industries. Developing effective methods for cleaning up contaminated soil or disposing of toxic mine tailings requires a great deal of research and development (R&D). Ontario's universities, in partnerships with private corporations and branches of government, have led all Canadian provinces in R&D expenditures (Government of Ontario, 2005b).

Summary

Several related factors enabled Ontario to become the dominant core region of Canada. The Great Lakes allowed for easy transport of both people and goods, and a large base of good agricultural land attracted many settlers to a relatively small region. These advantages facilitated the creation of many linkages, which in turn led to the development of a diversified, highly urban, and integrated economy. At the same time, the concentration of population gave southern Ontario the political influence necessary to capture a large portion of the country's manufacturing, financing, wholesaling, and retailing activity. Also in southern Ontario's favour is its proximity to the American heartland. Even though economic and political conditions, both internally and externally, have changed radically over the past two hundred years, Ontario has led Canada in population, manufacturing, banking and financial activity, as well as research and development and new patents.

Historically, southern Ontario was able to attract a great number of people because of its favourable physical characteristics: excellent soil and climate allowed the production of a wide range of agricultural products. These products stimulated forward, backward, and final demand linkages, and became the basis of manufacturing. The Great Lakes provided a natural transportation system, which was only enhanced when political and economic decision-makers promoted the construction of canals, ports, railways and road systems connecting the region to other parts of North America and, eventually, the world. Among the other government actions that have benefited Ontario are the Bank Act of 1871, subsidized rail freight and postal rates, and the protective tariffs introduced by National Policy of 1879. In addition, the expansion of the province's borders to incorporate more of the Canadian Shield gave Ontario tremendous economic advantages.

Population growth—from approximately 1.5 million at Confederation to more than 6 million in 1961 and nearly twice that in 2001—reflects Ontario's economic success. The shift to the service economy has been accompanied by major changes in the way goods and services are produced. Southern Ontario manufacturers continue to experience pressure to restructure and adapt to an economic and political playing field that is global in scale. Some industries have relocated or dissolved. But others have adjusted, and new service industries—especially in areas such as computer maintenance, finance, real estate, information and culture, and tourism, as well as professional and administrative services—have found southern Ontario to be the most desirable location in Canada.

Northern Ontario has not shared in the dynamic growth and prosperity of the south. The north is a peripheral region, dependent on the export of staples—mainly forest and metal products—and vulnerable to any number of forces, both external (world market prices, new technologies, foreign ownership) and internal (environmental regulations, changes in taxation, land-use regulations, or simply depletion of the resource), that can shut a mine or mill down. For single-resource communities, the consequences of a shut-down are devastating. Although some parts of northern Ontario have been able to diversify their economies by attracting tourists and retirees, the population is slowly decreasing, and those who are left behind are aging.

In addition, Ontario's industrial growth has entailed widespread contamination of air, water, and land. Investigations into environmental issues, often prompted by human tragedies, have increased public awareness and pressure to reduce and in some cases ban the use of toxic substances. Improving the quality of the environment, however, requires international cooperation.

References

Baskerville, P. *Sites of Power: A Concise History of Ontario*. Toronto: Oxford University Press, 2005.

Berton, P. 1985. 'War of 1812'. P. 1919 in *The Canadian Encyclopedia*. Edmonton: Hurtig.

Bone, R.M. 2002. *The Regional Geography of Canada*. 2nd edn. Toronto: Oxford University Press.

Canada Newswire Group. 2003. 'Camco Appliance Plant Another Victim of Free Trade'. http://www.newswire. ca/en/releases/archive/October2003/17/ c2106.html.

Canadian Driver. 2004. 'Ford Invests $1 Billion in Oakville Assembly Plant'. 29 Oct. http://www.canadiandriver.com/ news/041029-1.htm.

Canadian Pulp and Paper Association. N.d. 'Growing Up: The History of Pulp and Paper in Canada'. http://www. cppa.org/english/info/grow.htm.

CBC (Canadian Broadcasting Corporation). 2002. 'Walkerton Report Highlights'. http://www.cbc.ca/news/ background/walkerton/walkerton_report.html.

Community of Chatham-Kent. 2004. 'International Truck and Engine Awarded New Class 8 Truck'. 16 Dec. http://www.chatham-Kent.ca/business+resources/ business+news/good+news+stories/International+Truck+a nd+Engine++Awarded+New+Class+8+Truck.htm.

Craig, G.M. 1963. *Upper Canada: The Formative Years 1784–1841*. Toronto: McClelland and Stewart.

Draper, D. 2002. *Our Environment: A Canadian Perspective*. 2nd edn. Scarborough: Nelson Thompson Learning.

EcoSuperior. N.d. 'Mercury and Lake Superior'; 'The Whitedog First Nation and Mercury Poisoning in Northern Ontario'. http://www.ecosuperior.com/env_news.html.

Francis, R.D., R. Jones, and D.B. Smith. 2000. *Origins: Canadian History to Confederation*. 4th edn. Toronto: Harcourt.

Gad, G. 1991. 'Toronto's Financial District'. *Canadian Geographer* 35, 2: 203–7.

Government of Ontario, 2005a. 'Ontario's North—Select Government Programs. http://www.2ontario.com/ software/government_programs.asp?gonorth=y)

———. 2005b. 'Ontario Has the Largest Concentration of Industry and Public R&D Expenditure in Canada'. http://www.2ontario.com/welcome/bcrd_501.asp.

Holmes, R. June 2000. 'The Acid Rain Primer'. Pollution Probe. http://www.pollutionprobe.org.

Jackson, J., P. Weller, and the Waterloo Public Interest Research Group. 1982. *Chemical Nightmare: The Unnecessary Legacy of Toxic Wastes*. Toronto: Between the Lines.

Kerr, D.G.G., ed. 1961. *Historical Atlas of Canada*. Toronto: Thomas Nelson.

Leadbeater, D. N.d. 'The Development of Elliot Lake, "Uranium Capital of the World": A Background to the Layoffs of 1990–96'. Department of Economics, Laurentian University. http://inord.laurentian.ca.

Leighton, T. 1993. *Canadian Regional Environmental Issues Manual: Bringing Environmental Issues Closer to Home*. Toronto: Saunders College Publishing.

McCalla, D. 1993. *Planting the Province: The Economic History of Upper Canada*. Toronto: University of Toronto Press.

McIlwraith, T.F. 1990. 'The Adequacy of Rural Roads in the Era before Railways: An Illustration from Upper Canada'. Pp. 196–212 in G. Wynn, ed. *People, Places, Patterns, Processes: Geographical Perspectives on the Canadian Past*. Toronto: Copp Clark Pitman.

Mackenzie, S., and G. Norcliffe. 1997. 'Restructuring in the Canadian Newsprint Industry'. *Canadian Geographer* 41, 2: 2–6.

Nader, G.A. 1975. *Cities of Canada. Vol. I: Theoretical, Historical and Planning Perspectives*. Toronto: Macmillan.

Natural Resources Canada. 2005. 'The State of Canada's Forests, 2004-2005: Profiles Across the Nation—Ontario'. http://www.nrcan-rncan.gc.ca/cfs-scf/national/what-quoi/sof/sof05/profilesON_e.html.

———. 'A Chronology of Mineral Development in Canada'. http://www.nrcan.gc.ca/mms/stude-etudi/chro_e.htm.

———. 'Lumber Production by Province and Species Group, 1950–2001'. http://www2.nrcan.gc.ca/cfs-scf/selfor/section1New/I4Categ_e.asp.

———. 'Basic Paper and Paperboard Production by Category and Region, 1950–2001'. http://www2.nrcan.gc.ca/cfs-scf/selfor/historique/section1/I-13-E.htm.

———. 'Selling Price Indexes—Wood Pulp and Paper Products, 1981–2002 (1977 = 100)'. http://www2.nrcan.gc.ca/cfs-scf/selfor/members/section5/prtV3.asp?lang=en.

———. 'Selling Price Indexes—Lumber Products, 1981–2002 (1977 = 100)' http://www2.nrcan.gc.ca/cfs-scf/selfor/members/section5/prtV2.asp?lang=en.

Ontario Ministry of Enterprise, Opportunity and Innovation. 2005. 'Look Who's Investing in Ontario'. http://www.2ontario.com.

Ontario Strategic Infrastructure Finance Authority. N.d. 'Financial Infrastructure'. http://www.osifa.on.ca/default.asp?active_page_id=2.

Robinson, J.L. 1950. *The Geography of Canada*. Toronto: Longmans, Green and Co.

———. 1989. *Concepts and Themes in the Regional Geography of Canada*. Vancouver: Talonbooks.

Runesson, U.T. N.d. 'Forestry Facts'. Faculty of Forestry and Forest Environment, Lakehead University. http://www.borealforest.org.

Sitwell, O.F.G., and N.R.M. Seifried. 1984. *The Regional Structure of the Canadian Economy*. Toronto: Methuen.

Statistics Canada. 1996 and 2001 Censuses.

———. 2002. '2001 Census of Agriculture: Farm Operations in the 21st Century'. *The Daily*. 12 June.

Wallace, I. 2002. *A Geography of the Canadian Economy*. Don Mills: Oxford University Press.

Whiteway, J.R. 1985. 'Ontario Hydro'. P. 1328 in *The Canadian Encyclopedia*. Edmonton: Hurtig.

7

The Maritimes: Settlements on the Eastern Periphery

Canada's Maritime region (see Fig. 7.1) comprises Prince Edward Island, New Brunswick, and Nova Scotia; these three provinces together with Newfoundland and Labrador make up what is commonly known as Atlantic Canada. Although the four provinces—all former colonies of Britain—have much in common, Newfoundland and Labrador is often treated separately from the Maritimes, largely because it did not become part of Canada until 1949.

The Maritime provinces are part of the Appalachian mountain chain. The Appalachians are considered old mountains—older, for instance, than the Rocky Mountains, though not as ancient as the Canadian Shield—and the landscape of the Appalachian region is, as a result of glaciation and other weathering and erosion agents, one of rounded mountains, uplands, lowlands, river valleys, and a highly indented coastline. Many small rivers and streams as well as forests of both hardwoods and softwoods are found throughout the three Maritime provinces. Maritime soils are often acidic and poorly drained, though there are exceptions in Prince Edward Island, in Nova Scotia's fertile Annapolis Valley, in the Saint John River Valley of New Brunswick, and in other pockets in the highlands and lowlands.

Compounding the challenges to Maritime agriculture is the Atlantic Ocean. The cold Labrador Current, descending from Greenland and Baffin Island, means that this region has a relatively short growing season and is able to produce a smaller range of crops than southern Ontario. Harbour ice during the winter, offshore fog, and the potential of hurricane-force winds are some of the other challenges offered by the Atlantic. The Appalachians do not possess great stores of mineral wealth, though mining has been and continues to be an important part of the Maritime economy. Coal mining has had the longest history; more recent ventures include the drilling of offshore deposits of natural gas.

Many different peoples have settled in the Maritimes. The Mi'kmaq, who occupied most of the Maritimes, and the Maliseet, whose territory included western New Brunswick, were the earliest inhabitants of the area. Norse explorers visited the region in the eleventh century, but it was the French in the early 1600s who colonized the region, about 70 years after Jacques Cartier had explored the area. Initially it was fish and then furs that attracted the French to this region, which they called 'Acadie'; however, these resources also attracted other Europeans, and Acadia, along with the rest of North America, became embroiled in territorial conflicts that would continue until the early eighteenth century.

Figure 7.1 Map of the Maritime provinces

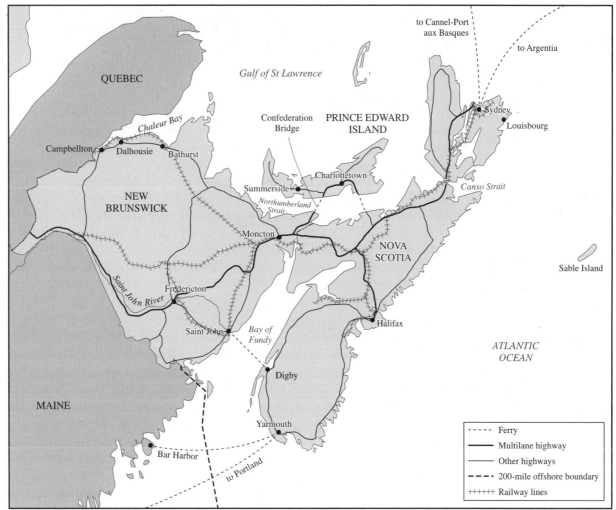

With the signing of the Treaty of Utrecht, which ended the War of Spanish Succession (1702–13), France surrendered most of Acadia to Britain, retaining possession only of Île Saint-Jean (Prince Edward Island), Île Royale (Cape Breton Island), and parts of the territory that would become New Brunswick. A century of conflict had resulted in push and pull factors that influenced the location and relocation of people. For example, many Acadians were chased out of the region; following the War of Spanish Succession, many resettled in the few Atlantic territories that remained in French control. They were replaced, in what became Nova Scotia, by Loyalists from the Thirteen Colonies as well as immigrants from Great Britain and other parts of Europe.

The Maritimes remained a prosperous region until the end of the 1800s. Fishing, forestry, coal mining, and agriculture, together with a pivotal role in Atlantic trade between Britain, the West Indies, and the American seaboard, formed the basis of an economy that gained backward, forward, and final demand linkages. Population growth sparked the growth of communities, which for the most part developed along a linear coastal pattern. With Confederation in 1867 came the promise of a rail line that would link these communities and, more important, link the Maritimes to central Canada. This, it was hoped, would promote regional trade and make the Maritimes the main transportation route for trans-Atlantic shipping.

But although the Intercolonial Railway was completed in 1876, it did not fulfill the promise of sparking economic growth in the region. Just as new manufacturing industries were beginning to develop, the Maritime economy fell into a recession that lasted from the 1870s to the 1890s. During this time investors and workers turned to other parts of the country that were experiencing greater prosperity. At the turn of the century, as central Canada was becoming stronger, the Maritime region was becoming marginalized. The economic stagnation continued through much of the twentieth century, as the two wars, the devastating Halifax explosion of 1917, the depression, and the global shift in trade and investments, among other factors, combined to weaken the Maritime economy and gain the region a reputation for out-migration (particularly of young people), overexploitation of resources, and dependency on federal transfer payments. One of the Maritimes' leading industries today is tourism, as the region's rich history, its natural beauty, and the famed warmth and amiability of its people draw large numbers of visitors from all over the world.

Physical Characteristics

The Appalachian mountain chain is a complex geological structure formed between 475 and 275 million years ago (Wheeler, 1996). Much of the eastern portion of North America was shaped by processes associated with sea floor spreading, which caused the folding, faulting, and uplifting of both the oceanic floor and the continental crust. During the past four hundred million years, weathering and erosion have removed 'several kilometres of rock revealing once deeply buried structures' (Brooks, 1985: 1414). This material, removed and then deposited in the ocean, became the Atlantic continental shelf: the fishing banks that were the centre of the Maritime fishing industry until the 1980s. Glaciation has also played an enormous role in altering the Maritime landscape, leaving upland regions with a thin soil base or, in some instances, bare rock. When the glaciers subsided, just 10,000 years ago, ocean levels rose. At the same time, as a result of isostatic rebound, the land rose as well, leaving an irregular, indented coastline with many protected harbours.

The physical landscape of the Maritimes today is made up largely of uplands and lowlands composed of igneous, metamorphic, and sedimentary rocks, which have been mined and quarried for various purposes. Granite has been quarried as a building stone, as has slate, which is commonly used for roofs. A number of metals, including copper, silver, lead, and zinc, have also been mined. But by far the most valuable mining activity—and the one with the longest history in the region—has centred on the coal deposits formed by the physical process of folding. Above the surface, the physical landscape is heavily forested with softwoods—spruce and pine, with some hemlock, fir, and cedar—mixed with hardwoods (maple and birch).

Of the many rivers and streams found throughout the Maritime region, few are large. The largest is the Saint John River, whose watershed stretches from northern Maine and southern Quebec into northwestern New Brunswick, where it runs the length of the western part of the province and empties into the Bay of Fundy at Saint John.

Despite their size, the river systems of the Maritimes have been important sources of hydraulic energy and irrigation, and their river valleys have provided fertile land for agriculture. There is also some farming activity on the coastal marine terraces created through isostatic rebound.

Other Maritime soils are complex but are generally classed as spodosols. Spodosols have accumulations of iron and aluminum but are heavily leached and acidic, and therefore have 'limited agricultural potential' (McKnight, 2001: 26). A major exception is Prince Edward Island, where distinctive red sandstone soil means that the whole province has agricultural potential.

The weather and climate of the Maritimes vary between inland regions and the coast. The prevailing westerly winds bring Arctic air masses in winter and considerably warmer ones in summer. However, the cold Labrador Current tends to modify temperatures, and its collision with the warm, northward-moving waters of the Gulf Stream produces the offshore fog so common in the Maritimes. Precipitation is fairly even throughout the year, though cities such as Halifax and Saint John record slightly lower amounts in summer. Precipitation frequently forms as snow in winter, when it is cold enough that the harbours freeze. The Maritimes are also on the storm track for hurricanes originating as far south as the Gulf of Mexico, such as Hurricane Juan, which began south of Bermuda as a tropical storm but had developed into a category 2 hurricane by the time it reached the coast of Nova Scotia in September 2003.

The Maritime region records some of the highest tides in the world, particularly in the Bay of Fundy, where they can exceed 15 metres. Visitors can walk among the remarkable 'flowerpot' formations of the Hopewell Rocks at low tide, then fish or kayak among them when the tide comes in. *Photo by Brett McGillivray.*

An interesting road sign on Highway 102 in Nova Scotia, between Halifax and Truro, reminds travellers that they are halfway between the Equator and the North Pole. Indeed, this region is one of the most southerly in Canada. Although the Maritime region is not large in area—the three provinces make up only 1.34 per cent of the country's total area (Natural Resources Canada, n.d.)—its many forests and rivers, plentiful resources, pockets of excellent agricultural land, and many fine protected harbours, together with its location on the Atlantic trade routes, have historically made it attractive for settlement and development.

Settlement and Development to 1763

Archaeological evidence of human inhabitation of the Maritime region dates back as far as 10,600 years, when the last continental ice sheets were retreating. At the time of the first European visits, the Mi'kmaq occupied most of the region, although the Maliseet and Abenaki occupied eastern parts of present-day New Brunswick. These First Nations belong to the Algonquian language group, which predominated throughout what are now Ontario, Quebec, and the Maritimes, as well as the New England states. They were skilled hunters and fishers who adapted well to their environment, using snowshoes and toboggans in winter and birchbark canoes in summer. Before the arrival of Europeans, these First Nations groups were quite large; for instance, Sultzman (1999) estimates that the Mi'kmaq population may have been as high as 30,000, before the infectious diseases brought by European explorers and settlers ravaged their numbers.

The first Europeans to visit North America were likely the Norse, who explored the eastern coast of the continent from camps established in southwestern Greenland around 1000 CE. The Norse sagas offer details of Leif Ericsson's exploration of a region he called 'Vinland' because of its wild-growing grapes. The exact location of Vinland is not known: though archaeological evidence found at L'Anse aux Meadows, on the northern tip of Newfoundland, points to this location as a candidate for Vinland, the territory may in fact have been much larger, extending to New Brunswick and Nova Scotia. Norse attempts to settle in Vinland were short-lived, likely owing to its remote location and the hostility of its Native inhabitants (Conrad and Hiller, 2001: 38).

European voyages of 'discovery' to North America likely began with John Cabot's expedition in 1497. Like Columbus before him, he had hoped to find a passage to Asia; when, instead, he landed on the North American coast—most likely in Newfoundland or on Cape Breton Island—he became the first European since the Norse to reach present-day North America. The Italian-born Cabot, in the service of the English King Henry VII, believed he had reached Asia and led a second, larger expedition the following year, but he and his ships were lost at sea.

The knowledge gained on these early voyages of discovery inspired similar excursions by other European explorers. The realization, in the early 1500s, that what Cabot had believed was Asia was in fact a previously unknown land mass did not deter efforts to find a navigable passage through or around it. Giovanni da Verrazzano, an Italian in service of the French king, made an important contribution to what was known about the continent when he explored the coast between the Carolinas and Cape Breton in 1524. He gave the name 'Arcadia' to a portion of this coastline near present-day Delaware; by the early 1600s, the name had come to be applied to the region claimed by the French as 'Acadie'.

The French claim to this part of North America (already called 'New France' by Verrazzano) was established through the voyages of Jacques Cartier (see Chapters 3 and 5). Although his attempt to establish a permanent settlement failed, French and other European fishermen and whalers spent months every year fishing off North American shores. Maritime harbours became important as locations to dry and cure fish, to escape from storms, and to repair boats and fishing gear. During these times, Europeans traded with the Native peoples who summered along the Gulf of St Lawrence. In exchange for their metal goods the Europeans received furs, which they took back to Europe. By the end of the sixteenth century, beaver fur had become the most coveted resource, since it could be used in the manufacture of the felt hats then fashionable in Europe.

In order to gain a toehold on the increasingly competitive fur-trading industry, the French in the early 1600s began establishing permanent settlements in 'New France' (as the region had been known since Cartier's journeys there). Among them was Port-Royal, established in 1605 at the mouth of the Dauphin (now the Annapolis) River. Port-Royal quickly became the centre of New France, as others followed the initial settlers to the fledgling settlement to fish, establish farms, and engage in the fur trade. Yet just two years later the settlement had been all but abandoned. The French, recognizing that the St Lawrence watershed was a more central and convenient location for gathering furs, established a colony in Quebec City, and Acadia became a backwater to the fur-trading empire on the St Lawrence.

In 1610 the settlement at Port-Royal was revived, and by the mid-seventeenth century it had been captured by the English and returned to French possession. The Acadian settlers built dikes and used sluices to drain the salt marshes and successfully raise crops. They also formed amicable partnerships with the Mi'kmaq, many of whom abandoned their traditional way of life—fishing—in favour of trapping furs. The colony boasted a number of Jesuit priests, who endeavoured to convert the Native population. Most important, the Acadian population had spread throughout the Baie Française (the Bay of Fundy), and in 1631 Fort La Tour (Saint John) was established at the mouth of the Saint John River.

The French were not alone in staking claims in North America. Among the other European nations to have maintained an interest in the continent since the fifteenth century, one of the most aggressive was England. The English too had been searching for the illusive seaway to Asia while maintaining a hold on Newfoundland for its stocks of cod and establishing forts on the southeastern coast of North America, primarily to pillage the silver-laden Spanish cargo ships coming out of Central America. But in the early 1600s, a number of factors caused the English to concentrate their colonization efforts farther north on the continent. The Treaty of London, a peace agreement that ended the 20-year Anglo–Spanish War in 1604, put an end to British piracy in the Spanish Main. By this time, England had also become aware of the importance of securing territory in North America for the valuable fur trade.

During the first half of the seventeenth century the British established a number of colonies along the Atlantic coast, populated by, among others, farmers displaced as a result of the British enclosure movement and Puritans leaving to escape the tensions of the English Reformation. Then in 1670 the Hudson's Bay Company obtained a royal charter giving it rights to Rupert's Land, the vast northern region surrounding Hudson Bay and James Bay. Roughly corresponding to all of modern-day Manitoba and parts of

Alberta, Saskatchewan, Ontario, Quebec, the Northwest Territories, and Nunavut, this region gave Britain access to a secure and extensive supply of furs in North America, and it was inevitable that the French territories of the Maritimes, along with the St Lawrence settlements, would become embroiled in a battle for continental domination of the fur trade.

The English captured Acadia three times in the 1600s (1613, 1654, and 1690), but the territory was returned to the French after each invasion. (It was during the first of these periods of British possession, in 1621, that the colony was named 'New Scotland', or Nova Scotia.) Conflicts and conquests continued into the 1700s, as the British became more determined to win control over North America. The capture of Port-Royal in 1710, when the name of the settlement was changed to Annapolis Royal, was more earnest than previous conquests, as the British had no intention of returning the captured territory to the French. The Treaty of Utrecht, which ended the War of Spanish Succession in 1713 and brought peace between these two warring nations for a time, transferred the territory of peninsular Nova Scotia to Great Britain. This was cause for concern among the Acadians, the majority of whom suddenly found themselves living under British control. Nevertheless, many Acadians chose to remain in the British territory rather than relocate to other French possessions, and the first half of the eighteenth century was a period of prosperity for the colony, as reflected in its dramatic increase in population after only moderate growth during the 1600s (see Table 7.1).

The Treaty of Utrecht clarified the status of Acadia as an English possession, but was vague about where the boundary lines actually lay, leaving parts of New Brunswick in dispute. Having secured possession of Acadia (which they renamed Nova Scotia), the British did not contest France's rights to two of its neighbouring islands, Île Royale and Île Saint-Jean (present-day Cape Breton Island and Prince Edward Island, respectively), and the French immediately began to shore up these two Atlantic positions. In 1718 the French constructed the Fortress of Louisbourg on the northeastern tip of Île Royale in order to protect their interests in the disputed regions of Acadia, the St Lawrence settlements, and of course, the valuable staple commodities: fish and fur. Louisbourg flourished as a fishing port and commercial centre and quickly became the largest community in the Atlantic, with a population nearing 3,000 in 1744 (Conrad and Hiller, 2001: 76). The French also began settling on Île St-Jean, though at a considerably slower pace than on Île Royale. By the mid-1700s, however, fighting resumed, and in 1745, during the War of the Austrian Succession, Louisbourg was captured by forces from New England. Many of the French settlers were banished from Louisbourg, though a number of them returned to Île Royale when the fort was restored to the French three years later, under the terms of the Treaty of Aix-la-Chapelle. As a military counter-measure to Louisbourg, the British in 1749 built a naval base at Halifax, which then supplanted Annapolis Royal as the capital of Nova Scotia, and became more serious about encouraging British settlement in the colony. They also renewed their demand for an oath of loyalty from those Acadians living under British rule, fearing that the local French inhabitants might become rebellious and draw French forces from Quebec and Louisbourg, and even their allies the Mi'kmaq, into a battle for Nova

Table 7.1   Approximate Acadian population, Maritimes, 1671–1871

Year	Population	Year	Population
1671	500	1755	12,500
1707	1,400	1758	10,700
1711	2,500	1765	10,150
1749	16,000	1771	8,442
1752	17,175	1871	92,740

Sources: Statistics Canada, Census of Canada 1665–1871, Cat. no. 98-187-XIE (http://www.statcan.ca/english/freepub/98-187-XIE/1800s.htm); and R.D. Francis, R. Jones, and D.B. Smith, *Origins: Canadian History to Confederation*, 4th edn (Toronto: Harcourt), 144.

Scotia. Many Acadians would have been willing to pledge neutrality but were reluctant to put themselves into a position where they would be expected to take up arms in a conflict against the French.

The situation came to a head in 1755, when the British issued a deportation order to Acadians living in Nova Scotia. The 'rousting of the Acadians' lasted from 1755 until 1763, coinciding with the end of the Seven Years' War. During this time over 6,000 Acadians were rounded up and exiled, their farms and villages burned. Many died in the conflict, and of those who were deported to British colonies along the Atlantic seaboard, many were turned away by the colonial authorities there, then forced to sail to Britain and eventually back to France. Some who were fortunate enough to escape into the woods joined those who had relocated in the years leading up to 1755 in the French possessions of Île Royale, Île St-Jean, the newly built fort of Beauséjour in present-day New Brunswick, and the St Lawrence, where before long, many of them were captured and deported by the British.

The Treaty of Paris, in 1763, ended the Seven Years' War, a war waged by Britain with aim of seizing French colonies and eliminating France as a commercial rival in North America. France's once vast colonial holdings in North America were reduced to the tiny islands of St Pierre and Miquelon and limited fishing rights in the Atlantic. The colony of Nova Scotia grew with the addition of New Brunswick, Île Royale (renamed Cape Breton), and Île St-Jean (the Island of Saint John, or Saint John's Island; eventually renamed Prince Edward Island).

Through the various wars between the French and English in North America, the continent's First Nations were the ones to lose the most territory and lives. Sultzman (1999) estimates that the Mi'kmaq population may have numbered as many as 30,000 but had declined to just 1,800 by 1823. Certainly the illnesses carried by European settlers had a devastating effect on the Native North American population. But disease was not the only threat to the traditional ways of life of Aboriginal peoples in the Maritime region.

While many First Nations groups had been understandably wary of the early explorers, the Mi'kmaq appear to have been eager to form trading partnerships with Europeans from early on (Conrad and Hiller, 2001: 45). Anxious to acquire the metal and cloth trade goods offered by their visitors from overseas, many Mi'kmaq abandoned fishing to trap the furs so coveted by the Europeans. The developing commercial relationship between the Mi'kmaq and the French was accompanied by a degree of cultural assimilation: the French relied on Aboriginal experience and practices to help them adapt to the foreign environment and cope with the rigours of its harsh climate, while many Mi'kmaq converted to Catholicism. There was also extensive intermarriage, which strengthened French–Native commercial ties, since 'Amerindian society, with its stress on kinship, much preferred this type of relationship as a basis for its trading alliances' (Dickason, 2002: 147).

But although the Mi'kmaq were closely aligned with the French through commercial, military, and personal ties, their alliance was not formalized in any treaty that recognized Native title to the land. The British, after conquering parts of Acadia, initiated treaties 'of Peace and Friendship' in 1725, 1752, and 1760; however, these treaties, as the name suggests, were merely intended to end hostilities in exchange for gifts (such as tobacco, blankets, and gunpowder), as well as to acknowledge Mi'kmaq hunting and fishing rights (Mi'kmaq Resource Guide, 2000). They were not designed to recognize Mi'kmaq rights to land or to compensate them for their loss of it. The ongoing Marshall case (see p. 225 below) and the continuing conflict over Maritime fishing rights, particularly at Burnt Church, New Brunswick, have their legal roots in the Peace and Friendship Treaty of 1760. Without formal title to their land, the Mi'kmaq would be pushed aside as the British encouraged settlement.

In 1763, the year the Treaty of Paris formalized the British conquest of French territory in North America, King George III signed a Royal Proclamation that formally established the boundaries and political system of Britain's new North American territories. It also contained several articles addressing the status of the North American Native peoples and their rights to the land. Under the terms of the proclamation, all lands west of Quebec and the Thirteen Colonies (not including the territory of the Hudson's Bay Company) as well as those parts of the settled territories 'not having been ceded to or purchased by Us' were reserved for the exclusive use of the Native population, who could dispose of the land only through negotiations with the Crown, thereby preventing the sale of Native lands to individual entrepreneurs.

The Royal Proclamation had both immediate and lasting significance to those First Nations groups situated west of the British colonies. But it did not improve the situation for many Native groups in the former French colonies of the Atlantic coast—particularly the Mi'kmaq. As Conrad and Hiller explain, 'Conceived with the western frontier in mind, these policies were deliberately ignored by administrators in Nova Scotia, who were slow to establish reserves and only minimally involved in land transactions with the Mi'kmaq and Maliseet' (2001: 89). Not until the 1780s were a number of 'licences of occupation' (essentially reserves) issued to reduce friction between colonists and the Mi'kmaq. Still, since the Mi'kmaq did not farm the land, there were incursions and loss of land. The fractionalization of Nova Scotia into four separate colonies added other problems. For example, New Brunswick, which had been part of Nova Scotia before being defined as a separate colony in 1784, refused to recognize licences of occupation made by the authorities of Nova Scotia in 1783. Prince Edward Island, which became a colony in 1769 (still with the name Saint John's Island), had no land reserved for the Mi'kmaq. These issues created new tensions between Aboriginal people and European settlers, tensions that would be exacerbated when Loyalists opposed to the American Revolution flooded into the region in the 1780s.

Settlement and Development, 1763–1867

With France largely eliminated from continental North America, the former French territories in the Atlantic region were reorganized as a single colony, Nova Scotia, though New Brunswick and Saint John's Island would become separate colonies before the end of the century. The British allowed Acadians to return in 1764, although those who did so found their property repossessed, and most were relegated to the 'vacant' land along the northern coast of New Brunswick. Others returning to North America joined earlier Acadian exiles in the Cajun community in the south of the colony of Louisiana. The largest group of immigrants to the region during this time was made up of colonists from New England. These 'planters', as they were known, had been recruited by Nova Scotia Governor Charles Lawrence with the promise of free land—land vacated by the exiled Acadians—and passage; of particular importance to these colonists, many of whom were dissenting Protestants, was the promise of freedom of worship.

The settlement of Saint John's Island took a different course. In 1765, two years before it became a separate colony, it was surveyed and divided into 67 'cantons' or 'townships' of 20,000 acres (8,094 ha) each. These were given out to 'military officers and others to whom the British government owed favours' (Robb and Holman, 1985: 1480). As a result most of the land was owned by absentee landlords, to whom those actually living on the island had to pay rent.

British-controlled North America was not entirely harmonious. British and American merchants soon filled the void left by the departing French to challenge the Hudson's Bay Company for domination of the North American fur trade, sparking a cut-throat rivalry that would last until the demise of the NWC in 1821. The departure of the French had a different significance for First Nations like the Mi'kmaq, who had aligned themselves so closely with the French and now saw their historic territory on the Atlantic coast in what they regarded as enemy hands. But the most contentious issue for the British was the increasing independence and rebelliousness of the Thirteen Colonies. The Quebec Act of 1774, which extended the southern boundary of Quebec to well south of the Great Lakes, represented in part an attempt to prevent the Thirteen Colonies from spreading westward; however, by enraging American colonists who felt that the territory given to Quebec was theirs by right, it became one of several griev- ances that ultimately led to the American War of Independence (1776–83).

For the Maritimes that conflict was something of an economic boon. British ships, bypassing the American harbours, brought increased trade to the region, while Halifax and other ports were beneficiaries of military spending by both warring parties. By far the most significant consequence of the war, however, was the influx into the Maritimes of more than 35,000 civilian refugees and disbanded soldiers from the United States, drawn by the promise of land grants and other assistance (such as seed and tools) and a new life in a land still controlled by Britain. Most of the Loyalists settled in Nova Scotia (19,000) and New Brunswick (15,000); considerably fewer settled in Cape Breton and Saint John's Island (about 500 each), the latter being especially unattractive because of the land ownership question.

The vast majority of Loyalist immigrants were white Anglo-Saxons, but there were also as many as 3,000 black Loyalists who were promised freedom in exchange for their support of the British military efforts. The parcels of land they received, however, were not only smaller than those granted to whites, but were located in areas unsuited for agriculture. Unable to establish themselves as farmers, many soon left the Maritimes for the new African colony of Sierra Leone (Conrad and Hiller, 2001: 103). Following the 1783 Treaty of Paris, in which Britain formally recognized the independence of the United States, other immigrants—mainly Scots (both Presbyterian and Catholic)— joined the Loyalists. Immigration peaked between 1782 and 1784, but tailed off towards the end of the century, when renewed fighting between France and Britain stemmed the flow of settlers from Europe.

At the start of the nineteenth century, the Maritimes comprised four colonies with a total population of between 75,000 and 80,000 living mainly along the coast, with some inland settlement following river valleys. Urbanization was limited to a handful of small, mainly port communities and just two cities: Halifax, with a population of 8,000, and Saint John, with a population of 3,000 (Harris, 1987: 296). Yet the region was poised for a century of significant population and economic growth.

Table 7.2   Timber exports from New Brunswick, 1807–1824

Year	Tons
1807	27,000
1810	88,000
1819	247,000
1822	266,000
1824	321,000

Source: G.A. Nader, *Cities of Canada*, vol. I, *Theoretical, Historical and Planning Perspectives* (Toronto: Macmillan), 144.

As in the late 1700s, when Britain's northern Atlantic colonies had capitalized on new economic opportunities during the War of Independence, wars played a major role in the expansion and diversification of the Maritime economy in the early 1800s. The Napoleonic Wars (1803–15), in which France attempted to extend its European empire against Britain and a coalition of European armies, were largely responsible for the dramatic growth of the forest industry in Canada. The blockade by which Napoleon attempted to isolate Britain from continental Europe prevented the British from accessing their usual timber suppliers in the Baltic, forcing them to turn to the North American colonies for wood. In the Maritimes, it was New Brunswick that gained the greatest share of this trade, and forestry quickly became the mainstay of its economy. Saint John, whose location at the mouth of the Saint John River was well suited for gathering rafts of timber, became the centre of the timber trade and associated industries, including the manufacture of the ships required to transport wood (among other things) to Britain. In the north of the colony, Miramichi, at the mouth of the Miramichi River, was another key location for gathering and exporting timber. Table 7.2 charts the growth of New Brunswick's timber exports to Britain, the West Indies, and other parts of the Atlantic trading area during the first quarter of the nineteenth century. Nova Scotia (including Cape Breton, reunited with the colony in 1820) and, to a minor degree, Prince Edward Island (as Saint John's Island was renamed in 1799) also benefited from increased demand for North American timber, though their share of the trade never rivalled New Brunswick's.

The War of 1812 was an offshoot of the Napoleonic Wars, a trade war between the United States and Britain. But even this conflict, though it was close to home, could not slow the thriving Maritime economy. As Conrad and Hiller explain, 'Buffered by New England, whose leaders refused to participate in the war, the Atlantic region was spared military invasion and became the centre of a vigorous clandestine trade between the two belligerents' (2001: 106). One of the cities benefiting most from the conflict was Halifax, whose role as a trans-shipment centre was enhanced. Food products, tobacco, cotton, and other goods destined for Europe, as well as European goods destined for the United States, were shipped via Halifax. Halifax also prospered because of its role as a military centre: with nearly 10,000 troops stationed in the city, its population doubled (Nader, 1975: 186).

Immigration following the Napoleonic Wars was aided by the turbulent economic conditions in Europe generally. In Britain, where growing numbers of workers found themselves displaced by the Industrial Revolution, many saw in the colonies a chance to begin a new life. The single greatest wave of immigration during this period, however, followed the Irish potato famine in 1845, when more than 300,000 destitute Irish arrived in British North America (Conrad and Hiller, 2001: 111). Immigrants also continued to come to the Maritimes from other parts of North America. For instance, immediately following the war, 2,000 African Americans joined the earlier black Loyalists to settle in the Maritimes. In all, nearly 800,000 immigrants came to Canada between 1815 and 1850, and though most of them moved on to settle in Upper Canada, the majority arrived first in the Maritimes, and many remained. Table 7.3 and Figure 7.2 illustrate the population changes for each of the Maritime colonies between 1806 and 1871.

The Maritime economy during this time was based on the production and export of staple commodities, which in some cases created backward and forward linkages. The fish that had attracted the earliest European visitors to the region remained an important part of the economy, but the fur trade had largely disappeared from the Maritimes by the 1800s. Most Maritimers were employed in farming, and though most of this activity was subsistence-level, agricultural exports from the region increased throughout the century. As mentioned above, exports of timber products, including everything from barrel staves to spar poles for ships, grew with external demand, but forestry also generated important final-demand linkages, as wood was essential not only for heating and cooking but for manufacturing everything from ships and houses to furniture and tools.

Table 7.3   Population, Maritimes, 1806–1871

Year	PEI	NB	NS[1]	Total Maritimes	Total BNA[2]
1806–7	9,676	35,000	65,000	109,676	430,394
1817			81,351		
1822	24,600				
1824		74,176			
1827			123,630		650,644
1834		119,457			
1838			202,575		
1840		156,162			
1841	47,042				
1851	62,678	193,800	276,854	533,332	2,375,597
1861	80,857	252,047	330,857	663,761	3,171,418
1871	94,021	285,594	387,800	767,415	3,579,782

[1]Nova Scotia includes Cape Breton Island.

[2]British North America includes Upper and Lower Canada and the 3 Maritime colonies.

Source: Adapted from Statistics Canada, 'Introduction to Censuses of Canada, 1665 to 1871', Cat. no. 98-187 (http://www.statcan.ca/english/freepub/98-187-XIE/1800s.htm).

Among the Maritime colonies, Nova Scotia led the way in population. Its economy was relatively diverse, based on fishing and maritime trade. Ideally located for handling the flow of goods between Britain and the United States and between Britain and the West Indies, the colony's ports were also home to a number of privateers: privately owned warships licensed to raid foreign vessels (particularly active during the War of 1812). Nova Scotia's role in these economic enterprises fostered an active shipbuilding industry using local timbers and sawmills, and while Halifax, Lunenburg, and Yarmouth were the main shipbuilding centres, 'nearly every fishing port had a shipyard' (Nader, 1975: 146). The colony's commercial and administrative centre, Halifax, was also a military centre, housing a garrison of British troops and serving as a base for the Royal Navy's North Atlantic fleet.

By contrast, New Brunswick's economy was largely dependent on forestry and wood products, including forward linkages such as sawmilling and backward linkages such as shipbuilding. Like Nova Scotia, New Brunswick developed important Atlantic trade relationships and had a substantial farming population, particularly in the fertile

Figure 7.2   Population, Maritimes, 1806–1871

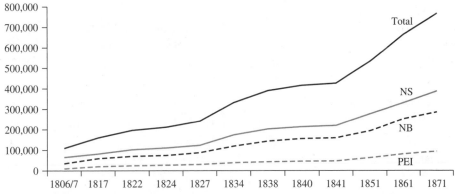

Source: Statistics Canada, 'Introduction to Censuses of Canada, 1665 to 1871', Cat. no. 98-187.

Saint John River valley, where the capital, Fredericton, was located. But throughout the 1800s, it faced the challenge of how to link its isolated northern communities to the growing commercial centre of Saint John in the colony's south. One solution was to build a canal across the Isthmus of Chignecto, like the Shubenacadie canal (completed in 1861) cutting across peninsular Nova Scotia from Halifax Harbour to Cobequid Bay; however, engineers were unable to satisfactorily address concerns about the challenges posed by the enormous tides of the Bay of Fundy. An alternative proposal involved a marine railway—a sort of overland canal—that would carry ships drawn by locomotive over the Isthmus of Chignecto to the Northumberland Strait. Construction began in the 1880s, but the project was abandoned within ten years because of practical and financial difficulties.

Prince Edward Island saw farming and agricultural products supplant fishing as the colony's most important industry during the first half of the 1800s. The handicap for the island colony was the ongoing land question. Almost none of the island's landowners resided on the island, and few had fulfilled the conditions under which the land had been granted to them. This prompted the island's residents, most of whom were tenant farmers paying high rents to the absentee proprietors, to demand *escheat*, the reversion of land to the Crown. The British government was unwilling to provoke the furious response among landowners sure to come from repossessing land without compensation, though they did manage to buy back some of the land and make it available for purchase by tenants. The situation would not be fully resolved until 1873, when Prince Edward Island joined Confederation. Nevertheless, PEI's population grew by 50,000 during the first half of the century, as many settlers, attracted by the island's excellent farmland, came in spite of the adverse political situation.

By the 1850s, the majority of the half-million residents of the Maritimes were rural, living in small and isolated fishing communities, farm settlements, and lumber camps. There were few overland connections between these communities, and the supply of goods and services, along with trade, was conducted mainly through shipping. Of the few cities in the region, Saint John was, by mid-century, slightly ahead of Halifax in population, and these two emerging industrial centres were considerably larger than any others in the Maritimes at this time (see Table 7.4).

Another characteristic of the Maritime population was its lack of cohesion, which was due in large part to the cultural and religious differences of the various immigrants. Though most of the immigrants were British, they had come from all parts of the British Isles, including Scotland, Ireland, Wales, and England. The result was a mix of Protestants, Presbyterians, Wesleyans (Methodists), Baptists, and Catholics. The Maritime population also included immigrants from Germany and other European countries,

Table 7.4   Population of Maritime urban centres, 1817–1871

City	1817	1824	1827	1834	1838	1840	1841	1848	1851	1861	1871
Saint John		8,488		12,073		19,281			22,745	27,317	28,805
Fredericton										5,652	6,006
Halifax	11,156		14,439		14,420				20,479	25,026	29,582
Charlottetown							3,896	4,717		6,706	7,872

Sources: G.A. Nader, *Cities of Canada*, vol. I, *Theoretical, Historical and Planning Perspectives*, and vol. II, *Profiles of Fifteen Metropolitan Centres* (Toronto: Macmillan, 1975, 1976); Statistics Canada, Census of Canada 1871, vol. 4.

Acadians of French background, Native North Americans, and a small number of African-American settlers. The ancient animosities brought by these divergent groups became sources of ethnic hostility, racism, and occasional clashes. In addition, though English was the dominant language, it was not the only language: the Scottish and Irish often spoke Gaelic, the Acadians spoke French, the Europeans often retained the languages of their homelands, and the Mi'kmaq and Maliseet used their respective Algonquian languages. The people of the Maritimes settled in separate, and even segregated, communities according to their ethnic, religious, and linguistic backgrounds, giving rise to a landscape covered with institutional structures that reflected their beliefs: churches, schools, graveyards, and community centres.

Towards Confederation

The half-century from the end of the War of 1812 to Confederation was mostly one of peace and prosperity in the Maritimes. New Brunswick, however, had one ongoing conflict that the other Maritime colonies did not have. Ever since the end of the American War of Independence (1783), the boundary between the State of Maine and New Brunswick had been a source of dispute that in 1839 erupted into the Aroostook War. Both sides had claimed the territory around the Aroostook River valley, but the matter did not become contentious until Maine, shortly after having been granted statehood in 1820, began promoting the region for agricultural settlement, even though it was already home to a number of Acadian settlers and itinerant New Brunswick loggers. When several of these lumbermen began cutting timber in the region, the dispute reached a crisis point and, with both sides sending in the militia, threatened to evolve into something much more serious. The bloodless skirmish ended with the signing of the Webster–Ashburton Treaty in 1842, which awarded approximately 18,000 km^2 of the disputed territory to the Americans and 13,000 km^2 to the British, leaving New Brunswick with a narrow ribbon of land attaching it to central Canada (see Fig. 7.3).

A number of other international conflicts in Europe and in North America had both negative and positive consequences for the Maritime colonies and were among the main forces that pushed them into Confederation. The Crimean War (1853–6) pitted Britain against Russia in an attempt to halt Russian aggression against Turkey. Like the Napoleonic Wars, it increased the demand for timber from the Maritimes and the Canadas. The war came at a time when the British North American colonies were adapting to a new free trade partnership with the United States, following the signing of the Reciprocity Treaty (1854). This agreement was especially advantageous to the Maritime colonies, cementing their trading relationships with New England and other coastal states at a time when they were adjusting to a new set of free trade policies in which Britain no longer gave preference to its colonies.

The Crimean War had ended by the late 1850s, but a new war soon erupted on North American soil. The American Civil War (1861–5) involved Britain to the extent that the British supported the American South and supplied arms to the Confederate army. Because of their British colonial status, the Maritime colonies found it extremely difficult to remain neutral. In fact, the southern Confederates viewed the Maritimes as a friendly base from which to launch attacks on the North, and several incidents occurred that stoked tensions along the border. Even though a number of men from

Figure 7.3   Maine boundary dispute and settlement (1842)

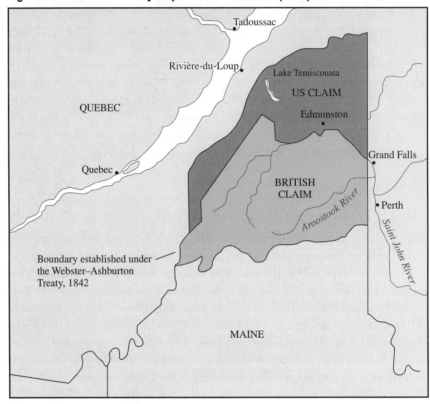

Source: Adapted from R.D. Francis, R. Jones, and D.B. Smith, *Origins: Canadian History to Confederation*, 4th edn (Toronto: Harcourt, 2000).

British North America had fought with the victorious Union army, the end of the Civil War brought numerous calls for annexation and retaliation against the colonies.

At the same time the Fenians—a group of Irish nationalists in the United States who shared the veterans' anti-British sentiments—aspired to drive the British from the continent. In 1866 they launched a series of raids across the border, the first of which was aimed at New Brunswick. Though it stalled at the border, the threat of attack from the south helped persuade New Brunswick and Nova Scotia to agree to proposals for a new union of the British North American colonies.

Another factor that helped to make the idea of Confederation attractive to the Maritimes was the American government's decision, in 1866, to cancel the Reciprocity Treaty. The loss of trade with the United States might be offset by increased trade with the Canadas—as long as the necessary rail links were put in place. Railways could accomplish what canals could not. It was the Saint John to Shediac line, completed in 1860, that gave Saint John access to northern New Brunswick. Nova Scotia already had two rail lines out of Halifax in place by 1858, running northeast to Truro and northwest to Windsor. But these three lines were merely short-haul routes, and what the region really needed was a line linking its population centres both to each other and to those of Canada East and Canada West. Proposals for an 'intercolonial' railway had first emerged in the 1840s, but it was not until the 1860s, when the Fenian raids and the threat of

American annexation underlined the value of such a line for transporting troops, that the tremendous costs of engineering and construction were seen as justified. During the London Conference, in the fall of 1866, Nova Scotia's premier Charles Tupper secured a promise that those costs would be written into the terms of Confederation. Thus the Intercolonial Railway, completed in 1876, was financed by the Government of Canada, with the help of the British government.

The promise of an intercolonial railway was not enough to sway all Maritimers in favour of Confederation. Opposition was especially strong in Nova Scotia, where many believed that a union of the Atlantic colonies would be more advantageous. In addition to the factors that made Confederation an attractive option, however, there was pressure from the British, who were anxious to shed the costs of establishing infrastructure and maintaining a military presence in the North American colonies.

Ultimately the cards were stacked against the anti-Confederate voices in the Maritimes. In 1867 Nova Scotia and New Brunswick joined Ontario and Quebec as the founding provinces of Canada, and within six years Prince Edward Island, hoping for relief from the debts incurred in a spree of railway building and ongoing disputes over the land issue, would join as well.

Boom to Bust: Confederation to 1900

The colonies that united to form Canada were driven together by a variety of factors: a collective fear of American annexation, Britain's desire to offload its colonial costs, and in some cases a genuine belief that Confederation would be economically beneficial. What few understood were the new dynamics that Confederation would bring, including interprovincial competition for industrial activity, and the rapid rise to corporate and political dominance of southern Ontario and southern Quebec, which had a decided advantage in the young dominion. By the 1870s, central Canada had four times the population of the three Maritime provinces, and with its proximity to the American industrial heartland, the Great Lakes–St Lawrence seaway, and the resource-rich Canadian Shield, it was rapidly developing a solid base in manufacturing.

By contrast, the economic base in the Maritimes was mercantile, or commercial, activity carried out in coastal communities scattered throughout the region; Maritime Canada had no manufacturing base comparable to that of central Canada. Acheson (1977: 93) argues that towards the end of the nineteenth century, the Maritime provinces represented 'the classic ideal of the staple economy', depending on fish, forest, and food products, which they exchanged, along with sailing ships, for finished goods from Britain and sugar and cotton from the West Indies and the United States.

Certainly there was some industry, including shipbuilding, sawmilling, food processing, the refining of imported sugar cane, and the turning of imported cotton into cloth. In addition, Nova Scotia responded to the demands of the new age of steam and steel by developing its coalfields and advancing its iron and steel production. But these industrial enterprises were similar to its commercial ventures in that they were mostly isolated, operating in separate communities, often in competition with one another. This pattern went against the Industrial Revolution model of production in centralized factories, where the steam engine could be used to turn a lathe, grind grain, mill lumber, or spin cotton. The technological innovations of the Industrial Revolution brought other economic pressures to bear on the Maritimes. By the mid–1800s, the steam engine had transformed the movement of goods and people, which could now be carried by rail as well as by steam-powered ships. These inventions represented not only time–space convergence but a fundamental shift in the resources demanded, and sparked the emergence of new urban patterns. The growing popularity of steam-propelled ships with steel hulls put much of the shipbuilding industry in jeopardy, not only because the new ships required different materials (coal and iron ore rather than wood), but also because sailing vessels could not compete with the larger and much faster mechanical vessels. The use of the steam engine for railway transportation became a growing challenge to traditional Maritime 'shipping'. Once the Intercolonial Railway was completed in 1876, a journey within the Maritimes that had taken a full week by ship could be completed by rail in just 27 hours (Woods, 1992: 89). Overland transportation routes soon replaced many sea routes and gave the economic advantage to centres through which the railway passed. Since telegraph lines were often erected along rail lines, moving messages between centres instantaneously, railway towns such as Moncton gained a dual advantage.

The growing dependence on the steam engine had another impact on the Maritimes, lessening the region's reliance on its waterways. In the past, the energy source for much of the region's manufacturing industry had been hydraulic power; thus, industrial centres tended to be located on streams and rivers that could be harnessed to turn the water wheels connected to lathes, saw blades, and grinding wheels. The steam engine—infinitely faster than a water wheel, with the locational advantage of not needing a water source—rendered many of these operations obsolete.

In hindsight, it seems obvious that these new technologies would increase productivity while compressing space and time; until the end of the nineteenth century, however, they were largely experimental, both expensive and risky. Furthermore, the people who owned sailing ships, or water-powered mills, were often reluctant to simply abandon their tried-and-true ways of doing things. Unfortunately, by compressing time and space, the new technologies had the added effect of increasing competition from distant locations, challenging the old means of production and patterns of trade, and making it difficult for industries operating in the traditional way to remain competitive.

By the time Prince Edward Island entered Confederation in 1873, the global economy had fallen into a recession that would last until 1895. Canada, like many other nations, responded to the depression with an economic strategy based on protectionist measures. In 1879 Sir John A. Macdonald's Conservative government instituted the National Policy, which attempted to foster local industry by imposing tariffs on foreign-made goods. As Chapter 6 pointed out, southern Ontario was the main beneficiary of this policy, which encouraged American branch-plants to jump the tariff barrier and locate in central Canada. But the Maritimes also benefited from increased industrial investment on the part of entrepreneurs anxious to use the recently completed Intercolonial Railway to supply the rest of the country with manufactured goods from the Atlantic provinces.

Nova Scotia led the way in this period of prosperity, outstripping all the other Maritime provinces in industrial growth between 1881 and 1891 (Acheson, 1977: 93–4). But there was no one centre of industrial development. On the contrary, there were many centres, and these were often determined by the location of individual entrepreneurs. Saint John, noted for its sawmilling and wood products, added a foundry and rolling mill to produce metal goods such as rail cars. Likewise, New Glasgow and Sydney used their abundant supplies of coal to produce steel and metal products. Amherst was home to a number of factories producing goods ranging from railway cars—the first to be built in Canada (Conrad and Hiller, 140)—to shoes, textiles, and even pianos (McCann, 1982: 106). Halifax, which continued to receive imports of cotton and sugar, had two sugar refineries and plants for producing cotton textiles, as well as a rolling mill. Moncton, with its advantage as a rail centre, established a sugar refinery along with textiles and iron works. Fredericton, another sawmill town, and St Stephen had large mills for producing cotton cloth. Acheson sums up the Maritime industrial position by 1885: 'With less than one-fifth of the population of the Dominion, the region contained eight of the twenty-three Canadian cotton mills . . . , three of five sugar refineries, two of seven rope factories, one of the three glass works, both of the Canadian steel mills, and six of the nation's twelve rolling mills' (1977: 105–6).

By far the most important component of the Maritime economy remained the Atlantic-based trade, especially exports of fish, forest, and food products and imports of the staples (such as raw sugar and cotton) that formed the basis of much of the region's

Lumber mills like this one in Newcastle (now part of Miramichi), photographed in 1895, were kept busy at the turn of the century supplying markets at home and abroad with New Brunswick lumber products. *Provincial Archives of New Brunswick, P6-182.*

manufacturing industry. But as the depression of 1873–95, together with the protectionist National Policy, weakened these international trading relationships, the region was forced to shift its focus towards new rail-based relationships within Canada. In the beginning, the Maritimes adjusted well to this transition. Shortly after the Intercolonial Railway was completed in 1876, the Canadian Pacific Railway extended a much more direct line from Montreal through Maine (where it was originally supposed to terminate) to the all-season port of Saint John. The CPR expanded its holdings in the Maritimes by leasing a number of existing railways (such as the New Brunswick Railway between Woodstock and Edmunston, built in 1870), adding a ferry system across the Bay of Fundy between Saint John and Digby, and making sure it had access to Halifax, where its rails could meet Canadian Pacific cruise and cargo ships. By the turn of the century, the region was criss-crossed with rail lines linking ports, resources, and manufacturing centres to central Canada. Even Prince Edward Island had its promised railway, although it was narrow-gauge.

By the mid-1880s, the Maritimes had gained a significant share of the Canadian manufacturing industry while maintaining an important role in Atlantic shipping and trade. But in the middle of the decade, a host of external and internal economic and political factors began to sabotage this industrial and commercial positioning. It is important to understand that the favourable economic conditions created by the National Policy were largely artificial, built on a foundation of tariffs and subsidized rail rates. Further, even these measures could not ensure totally protected markets, especially for Maritime producers. In the cotton industry, for example, cotton factories reached **overcapacity** by the mid-1880s, thus setting up competition between factories. The situation became worse when American producers began reducing the price of their surplus cotton textiles to the point that, even after paying the Canadian duties, they were able to flood the Canadian market. The consequences were disastrous for Maritime producers, who lost control of the domestic cotton industry to producers in Montreal.

Operators of Maritime sugar refineries faced a similar shock when the price of sugar collapsed in the mid-1880s. Sugar cane plantations in the West Indies had been lucrative largely because they relied on inexpensive slave labour. But as slavery was abolished in most parts of the world in the nineteenth century, these sugar plantations became increasingly costly to operate. European countries, and even the United States, began cultivating sugar beets as an alternative source of sugar, causing the price of traditional cane sugar to plummet and leaving Maritime refineries at overcapacity. As the sugar plantation economies of the West Indies went bankrupt, these colonies ceased to be a destination for Maritime exports such as wood and fish.

The depression also affected the trading partnership between the Maritime provinces and Britain. British demand for timber declined, and stiff tariffs made it all the more difficult for Maritimers to acquire the British-made finished goods traditionally obtained in exchange for timber. As a result, southern Ontario and southern Quebec became the main sources of finished goods sold to the Maritimes. This created an imbalance in trade, however, since the economic balance, for the Maritimes, had always rested on the surpluses gained in Atlantic shipping and trade. As the depression continued to slow international trade through Maritime ports, the disparities between central and Maritime Canada broadened.

overcapacity
the situation in which a particular factory, or industry, is unable to sell as much of its product as it is capable of producing.

Industry after industry felt the effects of the economic downturn as Maritime businesses were forced either to shut down or to merge with well-financed central Canadian businesses. Mergers and buyouts were not restricted to traditional industries: the Bank Act of 1871 allowed branch banking throughout the Dominion, and it was only a matter of time before banks in the Maritimes were consumed by financial interests based in Montreal and Toronto. By the early 1900s, the Bank of Nova Scotia had shifted its operations to Toronto, and the Royal Bank—originally incorporated as the Merchant Bank of Halifax—had moved its headquarters to Montreal.

The Maritimes in the Twentieth Century

By the start of the twentieth century, the global economy had recovered from the depression of 1873–95. But the dreadful market conditions of the late nineteenth century had undermined the foundations of the traditional Maritime economy based on Atlantic trading. Though the National Policy had made it profitable for Maritime entrepreneurs to invest in industrial activities that commanded a share of the national market, there was never any serious doubt that central Canada would become the industrial heartland of the young dominion. The capitalist emphasis on economies of scale, corporate control, and shareholder profit combined with government policies to create a situation that favoured the centralization of the national economy, leaving the Maritime economy in shreds and Maritimers harbouring considerable animosity towards central Canada.

During the early twentieth century, the emergence of new technologies—such as electricity and the automobile—together with Fordism and mass production had a tremendous effect on manufacturing and contributed to the growth of the economy in Canada and abroad. But the national economic landscape was changing literally as well as figuratively. The West was the new market, and central Canada was well positioned to supply this rapidly growing region. The Maritimes were on the periphery, far from central Canada, not to mention the West. And Maritime industry was not profitable: Maritime firms were smaller than their counterparts in central Canada, and the materials they used cost considerably more. Even lower labour rates could not offset these disadvantages (McCann, 1982: 111). The failure of industry is one of the main reasons the Maritime provinces failed to gain a large resident population (see Table 7.5).

Table 7.5   Population, Maritimes, 1871–1971

Year	PEI	NB	NS	Total Maritimes	Total West[1]	Total Canada
1871	94,021	285,594	387,800	767,415	109,475	3,689,257
1881	108,891	321,233	440,572	870,696	168,165	4,324,810
1891	109,078	321,263	450,369	880,737	349,646	4,833,239
1901	103,259	331,120	459,574	893,953	598,169	5,371,315
1911	93,728	351,889	492,338	937,955	1,720,601	7,206,643
1921	88,615	387,876	523,837	1,000,328	2,480,664	8,787,949
1931	88,038	408,219	512,846	1,009,103	3,047,789	10,376,786
1941	95,047	457,401	577,962	1,130,410	3,239,766	11,506,655
1951	98,429	515,700	642,584	1,256,713	3,712,980	14,009,429
1961	104,629	597,900	737,007	1,439,536	4,807,900	18,238,247
1971	111,621	634,600	788,960	1,544,181	5,726,957	21,568,311

[1]Manitoba, Saskatchewan, Alberta, and British Columbia.

Source: Adapted from Statistics Canada, 'Historical Statistics of Canada', 1983, Cat. no. 11-516, 29 July 1999, Series A2-14.

Figure 7.4   Population growth, Maritimes and Western Canada, 1871–1941

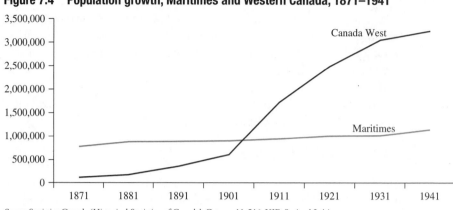

Source: Statistics Canada, 'Historical Statistics of Canada', Cat. no. 11-516-XIE, Series A2-14.

Figure 7.4, comparing population growth in the Maritimes and the West, is telling. The rate of increase in the Maritimes was never large, and by the turn of the twentieth century the population of Prince Edward Island was actually declining. The West, on the other hand, was the new focus of attention and immigration: the Canadian Pacific Railway had reached the west coast in 1885, land was being made available for homesteads, and gold—discovered in the Yukon at the end of the century—was drawing prospectors and miners from around the world. The creation of two new provinces—Saskatchewan and Alberta—in 1905 reflected the rapid population growth on the prairies. The vivid contrast between rates of population growth in the two regions reflected economic and political shifts in the country over the seventy years between 1871 and 1941.

As the population and prosperity of the West grew, the Maritimes were left behind, continuing to depend on the traditional staples: fish, forests, food products, and a few minerals. The new technologies of the twentieth century, for the most part, only increased the vulnerability of this staples dependency. For example, refrigeration—common in ships by the turn of the century—and canning made it possible to transport perishable foods such as meat and fish around the world. European diets now included meat and dairy products from as far away as South America, Australia, and New Zealand. The result was a decrease in demand for salt cod from the Maritimes; even the exports of Maritime butter and cheese to Britain faced considerable competition. Meanwhile, the introduction of large steam-driven trawlers made it possible to catch great quantities of fish with fewer fishers. Fish-processing jobs also disappeared as many small processing plants were replaced by a few centralized facilities. And the opening of the Panama Canal in 1914 enabled the west coast to challenge the Maritimes' trade not just in fish products but in lumber as well.

Maritime agriculture also had to adjust in the face of international competition. Marginal farms, often on marginal soil, were abandoned, and Maritime farmers moved away from wheat, which could not compete with the higher-quality wheat grown in central Canada and the Prairies, in favour of apple growing (in the Annapolis and Saint John valleys) and dairy farming. In Prince Edward Island, the potato began to dominate agricultural crops, as the Island became a major producer of both seed potatoes and table stock. Maritime farms generally became larger, employing more mechanical equipment and requiring fewer farmhands. But with growing efficiency came job losses; Prince

Edward Island in particular was affected by the decrease in employment opportunities, which contributed to its drop in population (see Table 7.5).

Nova Scotia saw considerable growth in its iron and steel industry. Blast furnaces, used to make steel from iron ore, coke, and limestone, were transferred to Sydney on Cape Breton Island from the New Glasgow–Trenton–Stellerton area of Pictou County on the mainland, largely because the high-quality coal of Sydney was better suited for making coke. Iron ore was imported from Bell Island in Newfoundland, and the steel mills of Sydney, along with the rolling mills retained in Trenton, supplied rail cars, locomotive wheels, and track for railway expansion in western Canada. In addition to being used in the local production of coke, Sydney's coal was exported to the Montreal market, resulting in further employment for Sydney coal miners.

Railways were expanding in the Maritimes as well, in part to meet the demand of the forest industry. Rail lines were used to carry logs to the sawmills, and a third major railway—the National Transcontinental, completed in 1913—gave Moncton even greater access to both local and national markets. Most of the valuable pine forests had already been harvested by the early 1900s, leaving less valuable softwoods such as balsam, fir and spruce in a declining lumber industry. However, new growth in the forest industry came with the development of pulp and paper mills. There had been pulp mills in the Maritimes since the 1890s, but by 1911 the value of pulp manufactured in the region had reached $1.4 million.

The First World War sparked a brief resurgence in the Maritime economy. Products such as coal, steel, and even textiles for uniforms were vital to the war effort, stimulating those industries, and Halifax, as the key naval base on the Atlantic, was one of the principal beneficiaries of military spending. But the war also brought a dramatic decline in transatlantic shipping. Reduced international competition meant increased demand for the Maritimes' fish, forest, and agricultural products. But the brief period of wartime prosperity could not compensate for the devastation caused on 6 December 1917, when two ships, one of them carrying munitions, collided in Halifax Harbour. The ensuing explosion levelled a good part of the cities of Halifax and Dartmouth, killing over 2,000 people and leaving nearly 6,000 residents without homes.

The end of the Great War brought the return of economic woes for the Maritimes. International shipping and competition resumed, railway expansion slowed, and the Ontario city of Hamilton became the principal supplier of steel to the rapidly growing automobile industry. Sydney was clearly a peripheral producer, and in 1921 it was taken over by British interests, only to be transferred back to North American hands by the end of the decade with no improvement in the conditions for the industry.

Perhaps the greatest blow for the Maritime economy came in 1919, when the Intercolonial Railway was taken over by the federal government and incorporated into the Canadian National Railway system. Until this time, freight rates had been subsidized, albeit in an erratic fashion that took into account distance travelled, goods transported, and assorted other regulations. All this changed when the Intercolonial (followed a couple of years later by the National Transcontinental) became part of the CNR and rates were harmonized with those of central Canada. As a result, some rates on the Intercolonial tripled. The new rates made it nearly impossible for goods from the Maritimes to remain competitive with those from central Canada, and many small businesses were forced to shut down long before the 1927 Maritime Freight Rates Act

Figure 7.5   Coal production, Nova Scotia, 1869–1978

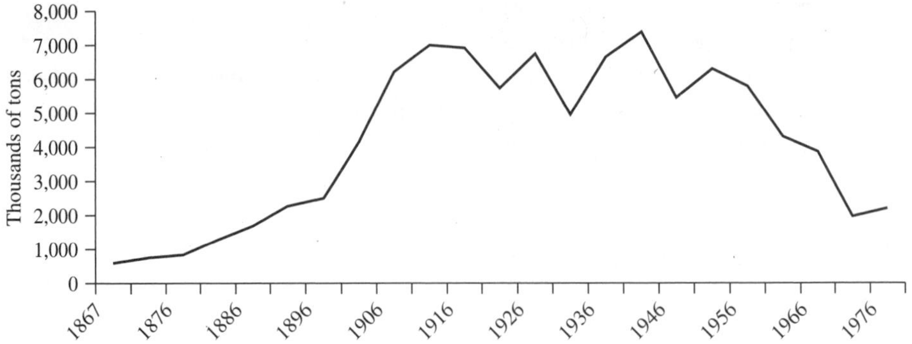

Source: Statistics Canada, 'Historical Statistics of Canada', Cat. no. 11-516-XIE, Series Q1-5.

brought some relief. Adding insult to injury, much of the management of the Maritime railways was transferred from Moncton to central Canada in 1919.

The increase in rail rates certainly had a negative effect on Nova Scotia's coal industry, which had grown with railway expansion. But this was not the sole reason for a collapse in coal production in the mid-1920s. Sydney's coal seams descend under the ocean floor, and extraction became a costly venture around this time. Figure 7.5 charts the ups and downs of Nova Scotia's coal production from just after Confederation to the late 1970s.

The economic situation was not much better in the region's fisheries, where the appearance of large European trawlers fishing the Atlantic banks contributed to a de-cline in the price of cod. New American tariffs on fish and other food products in 1921 aggravated the situation, forcing many Maritime fishers out of the industry.

The one area of economic and industrial expansion during this period was in the pulp and paper industry. North American demand for paper products was increasing, and this brought increased investment to both New Brunswick and Nova Scotia, where many pulp and paper mills were located. The growth of this industry increased the demand for hydroelectricity, although the potential for hydroelectric power in the Maritimes was nowhere near that of central Canada.

The 'Roaring 20s' thus were not kind to the Maritimes, and the Depression of the 1930s made the dismal economic conditions even worse. International demand for Maritime staples declined further, and any industrial production that remained was cut back or ceased altogether as companies went out of business. Maritime cities held little promise of employment, forcing many Maritimers back to the land or to the sea to eke out a subsistence living, or else to Montreal or Toronto, where the prospects for employment were slightly better.

The Second World War, like the Great War before it, brought short-lived relief to the Maritime provinces, which benefited from military spending on coal and steel for munitions. The troops stationed in centres such as Halifax led to increased employment and demand for local resources, and the suspension of international trade and commerce made the short-haul routes profitable again. But the relatively long period of prosperity that followed the war in most of North America eluded the Maritimes. The return of global shipping and trade brought increased competition and challenges to wartime trade routes once dominated by Maritime ships. Foreign trawlers were harvesting cod in the region and cornering the European market. New, more efficient uses for oil and electricity steadily eroded the need for coal, as diesel engines replaced steam engines and many factories installed electric motors. The coal industry was beset by other problems as well: for instance, Sydney's coal, high in sulphur content, continued to come from tunnels that would eventually extend some seven kilometres under the ocean, making it difficult and harmful to extract. Much more difficult were conditions for coal miners. Most miners lived in company-owned towns; working conditions were hazardous, wages were low, and efforts to unionize did little to improve the conditions. Moreover many workers were killed by explosions, fires, and other mining disasters (see Table 7.6).

Table 7.6   Selected coal-mine disasters in Nova Scotia, 1917–1992

Location	Year	Cause	Died
New Waterford	1917	Explosion	65
Stellarton	1918	Explosion	88
Sydney	1938	Broken cable	20
Sydney	1938	Runaway mine tractor	19
Stellarton	1952	Fire	19
Springhill	1956	Explosion	39
Springhill	1958	Cave-in	75
Westray	1992	Explosion	26

Source: R.L. Jones, 'Canadian Disasters: An Historical Survey' (http://www.ott.igs.net).

As the century wore on, the Maritime provinces became increasingly isolated, cut off from the rest of Canada both literally and figuratively. With the rise of the automobile, trucking proved to be a more flexible means of transporting goods and people and soon replaced rail traffic. In the Maritimes, however, near-bankrupt provincial governments could not afford the cost of highways and major road infrastructure; consequently, roads were narrow, winding, and often in poor condition, which increased the transportation costs for consumer products. The opening of the St Lawrence Seaway in 1959 and the use of ice-breakers on the St Lawrence in the early 1960s made it possible for American goods to reach central Canada without going through the Maritime ports of Halifax and Saint John.

The Maritime provinces did benefit from a host of federal government programs and funding schemes that established basic levels of health and education across the country. Unemployment insurance gave some measure of year-round income to those involved in seasonal industries, such as fishing. The federal Trans-Canada Highway Act (1949) guaranteed money for highway building, and federal funding for improvements to port facilities and airports soon followed, all of which helped establish modern transportation networks linking all parts of the country. In 1957 the federal government introduced an equalization program to ensure that the per-capita tax revenues of all provinces were roughly equal to those of the two wealthiest provinces at the time, Ontario and BC. There were also a number of federal government grants designed to kick-start the economies of less wealthy provinces through job creation. These grants, most of which were consolidated in 1969 under the Department of Regional Economic Expansion (DREE), consisted of industrial investments that partnered provincial governments with private enterprises; most of these schemes turned out badly.

By the end of the 1960s there was little industrialization in the Maritimes. Few Maritime goods found their way to central Canada, since there were few products from the region, apart from fish and coal, that could not be produced at a lower cost in Ontario and Quebec. As Table 7.7 shows, the populations of Prince Edward Island, New Brunswick, and Nova Scotia remained predominantly rural, particularly in comparison with populations in the rest of Canada, which were rapidly urbanizing. In terms of personal income and level of education, Maritimers lagged behind the rest of the country, while unemployment was considerably higher in the region (Atlantic Development Council 1972). The Maritimes had become a have-not region dependent on the federal government.

Fishing nets are hung to dry in a Nova Scotia farming and fishing community in the 1950s. Communities such as this, combining family-based fishing and agriculture, were not uncommon in the mid-twentieth century Maritimes.   *Nova Scotia Archives and Records Management, Norwood #175.*

Table 7.7   Rural–urban population distribution (%) by province (excluding Newfoundland), 1941–1971

Province	1941		1951		1961		1971	
	R	U	R	U	R	U	R	U
Prince Edward Island	77.9	22.1	74.9	25.1	67.6	32.4	61.7	38.3
New Brunswick	61.3	38.7	57.2	42.8	53.5	46.5	43.1	56.9
Nova Scotia	48.0	52.0	45.5	54.5	45.7	54.3	43.3	56.7
Quebec	38.8	61.2	33.2	66.8	25.7	74.3	19.4	80.6
Ontario	32.5	67.5	27.5	72.5	22.7	77.3	17.6	82.4
Manitoba	54.3	45.7	35.0	65.0	36.1	63.9	30.5	69.5
Saskatchewan	78.7	21.3	69.6	30.4	57.0	43.0	47.0	53.0
Alberta	68.1	31.9	52.4	47.6	36.7	63.3	26.5	73.5
British Columbia	36.0	64.0	31.4	68.6	27.4	72.6	24.3	75.7
Canada[1]	44.3	55.7	37.1	62.9	29.8	70.2	23.4	76.6

[1]Excluding Newfoundland.

Source: Adapted from G.A. Nader, *Cities of Canada,* vol. I, *Theoretical, Historical and Planning Perspectives* (Toronto: Macmillan, 1975), 206.

The 1970s to the Present

Employment in Canada has shifted over time, from jobs concentrated in resource extraction to jobs in the manufacturing industry and, since the 1970s, to jobs in service-related activities. This is an urban-oriented transition. But as Table 7.8 shows, the three Maritime provinces have a higher percentage of rural residents than other provinces in Canada, and over the past thirty years this percentage has actually increased in New Brunswick and Nova Scotia—running counter to the overall trend for Canada. The Maritime population has slowly increased (see Table 7.9), but the region's share of the overall Canadian population has declined as the pattern of emigration from the Maritimes to more prosperous parts of the nation has continued.

Given the total population of the three Maritime provinces, it is not surprising that the cities of the region are not large. Halifax, with nearly 360,000 residents (2001 Census), is by far the largest centre. Saint John (123,000) is the only other Census Metropolitan Area (CMA), and only nine other centres exceed 10,000 in population. As Table 7.10 shows, the population numbers for many of these cities have remained relatively stable; however, there are exceptions. One is Sydney, which is part of the regional municipality of Cape Breton (also including Dominion, Glace Bay, Louisbourg, New Waterford, North Sydney, and Sydney Mines, all on the eastern side of the island). Sydney shows a notable decline in its population, owing in large part to the collapse of its coal mining and steel mill operations (see p. 215 below). On the other hand, the population of Halifax increased considerably through amalgamation with neighbouring Dartmouth and the Bedford–Sackville areas. Saint John has not yet amalgamated with the adjacent commuter

Table 7.8　Rural–urban population distribution (%), by province, 1971–2001

Province	1971 R	1971 U	1981 R	1981 U	1991 R	1991 U	2001 R	2001 U
Prince Edward Island	61.7	38.3	64.0	36.0	60.0	40.0	55.5	45.5
New Brunswick	43.1	56.9	49.0	51.0	52.0	48.0	49.8	50.2
Nova Scotia	43.3	56.7	45.0	55.0	46.0	54.0	44.4	55.6
Newfoundland	42.8	57.2	41.0	59.0	46.0	54.0	42.3	57.7
Quebec	19.4	80.6	22.0	78.0	22.0	78.0	19.6	80.4
Ontario	17.6	82.4	18.0	82.0	18.0	82.0	15.3	84.7
Manitoba	30.5	69.5	29.0	71.0	28.1	71.9	28.1	71.9
Saskatchewan	47.0	53.0	42.0	58.0	37.0	63.0	35.7	64.3
Alberta	26.5	73.5	23.0	77.0	20.0	80.0	19.1	80.9
British Columbia	24.3	75.7	22.0	78.0	20.0	80.0	15.3	84.7
Canada[1]	23.4	76.1	24.0	76.0	23.0	77.0	20.4	79.6

[1]Excluding Newfoundland.

Source: Statistics Canada, Census of Canada 1971, 1981, 1991, 2001.

Table 7.9　Population (×1,000), Maritime provinces and Canada, 1971–2001

Year	PEI	NB	NS	Total Maritimes	Total Canada	% of Canada
1971	112.6	642.5	789.0	1,535.2	21,962.1	7.1
1981	122.5	696.4	847.9	1,666.8	24,342.6	6.7
1991	129.8	723.9	899.9	1,753.6	27,296.9	6.3
2001	138.9	756.0	942.9	1,837.8	31,110.6	5.9

Source: Adapted from the Statistics Canada CANSIM database (http://cansim2.statcan.ca), Table 051-0012.

Table 7.10 Urban centres with populations over 10,000, 1991–2001

Province	Urban centre	1991	1996	2001
PEI	Charlottetown (city)	31,541	32,531	32,245
	Summerside (city)	13,636	14,525	14,654
NS	Halifax (CMA)	320,501	332,518	359,183
	Sydney (Cape Breton reg. mun.)	117,403	114,733	105,968
	Truro (town)	11,683	11,938	11,457
	Yarmouth (mun. district)	10,827	10,722	10,476
NB	Saint John (CMA)	125,838	125,705	122,678
	Moncton (city)	56,823	59,313	61,046
	Fredericton (city)	46,466	46,507	47,560
	Riverview (city)	16,270	16,653	17,010
	Bathurst (city)	14,409	13,815	12,924

Source: Statistics Canada, 2001 Community Profiles (http://www12.statcan.ca/english/profil01/CP01/Index.cfm?Lang=E).

communities, but it may do so, as it continues to lose residents from its core to these outlying regions.

Some other urban dynamics in the Maritimes are worth noting. Halifax, with its international airport, its large, protected, ice-free harbour, and its many universities, dominates not just Nova Scotia but the entire Maritime region. New Brunswick revolves around three centres—Saint John, Moncton, and Fredericton—each of which has developed in response to a different set of economic and political factors. Saint John is the industrial centre, influenced largely by Irving family interests in pulp and paper, oil refining, shipyards, and service stations; it also has a large tourism industry, drawing visitors to see its harbour, historic centre, and interesting architecture, including a glassed-in city marketplace. Moncton is the 'Acadian capital' of Canada, and with its large bilingual population has become a major telemarketing centre; the province's investment in modern telecommunications technologies has been the key to the development of this industry. At the same time, the city's location at the hub of the province's transportation network, together with its large military airport, has helped to make Moncton a major service centre for New Brunswick. Fredericton, the province's capital and administrative centre, is home to the main campus of the University of New Brunswick. Finally, Charlottetown may be Canada's smallest provincial capital, but it is by far the largest city in Prince Edward Island and is the main administrative and service centre for PEI. Summerside, with its harbour facilities and attractions for tourists, became a city through amalgamation in 1995.

The economies of the Maritime provinces continue to be driven by staples. Unfortunately, economies that depend on natural resources face predictable problems: at some point, non-renewable resources will run out, and even renewable resource industries will fail when demand for those resources dries up. Chapter 4 outlined some of the unpredictable events that have hurt regional economies since the 1970s, including the energy crisis, major recessions, the shift in trade and investment to the Asia–Pacific region, the end of the Cold War, free-trade agreements, and increasing globalization. In the Maritimes, the resource industries and the people who depend on them for employment have been adversely affected by global change. But this problem is not new. The region has a long history of resource industries that have become unsustainable as a result of declining demand. A prime example is the Cape Breton coal and steel industry.

Coal and Steel

By the mid-1960s, declining demand had pushed Cape Breton's coal and steel industries to the point where they were on the verge of shutting down. In an effort to ease the transition for a region with few other employment options, the federal government formed the Cape Breton Development Corporation (Devco) to take over the coal mines, while the provincial government formed the Sydney Steel Corporation (SYSCO) to take over the steel mill. The plan was to gradually reduce the scale of these operations until they could be shut down without causing massive unemployment. In the 1970s, however, the energy crisis sparked a sudden increase in demand for coal. In response, the federal and provincial governments, instead of reducing operations, began to expand and modernize them. Even so, in the long run neither industry could be sustained. Cape Breton coal was costly to mine because of its subterranean location; its high sulphur content made it a major contributor to acid rain; and when the North American Free Trade Agreement removed the tariff barrier, it became less expensive for Devco's main customer, Nova Scotia Power, to purchase its coal from the US. In the late 1990s Ottawa decided to close the Devco mines, the last of which, the Phalen mine, was shut in the fall of 2001. Laid-off workers were offered an $111 million support package, which covered early retirement, severance, and a training allowance (Natural Resources Canada). Meanwhile, efforts to sell the provincially owned SYSCO to private interests had come to nothing, and the steel mill also closed in 2001. The impact was devastating for a region that by then was already struggling to adjust to dramatic cutbacks in the fishing industry.

In addition to its economic problems, the coal industry has been the object of scrutiny over environmental issues and concerns about worker safety. Residents of Sydney living near the sites of old blast furnaces and coke-ovens must contend with toxic wastes—including PCBs and heavy metals such as lead and mercury—leaching into both the surface and subsurface water systems. This environmental contamination caused the closure of the lobster fishery in 1982. And though some steps were taken to clean up the tar ponds in the mid-1980s, recent evidence of contaminated water and air and unusually high rates of cancer in the region has drawn federal attention and promises of a much more extensive clean-up.

In the 1990s Nova Scotia was hit by another coalmine disaster. The Westray Mine at Plymouth, near New Glasgow, which had a history of explosions and fatalities, was the scene of explosion that took the lives of 26 miners on 9 May 1992. While this may not have been the greatest mining disaster to strike the province, it gained considerable national attention because of accusations that the mine's operators had deliberately ignored safety warnings that might have prevented the accident. After a six-year public inquiry, the federal government introduced legislation designed to hold corporations criminally responsible if they fail to provide a safe work environment.

Other Mining and Energy

Despite the decline of the coal industry, mining continues to be integral to the economy of the Maritimes. Together, for example, the mine in Bathurst (zinc, lead, gold, and copper) and the metal refinery in nearby Belledune employ almost a thousand workers.

Unfortunately, a mine's life is limited, and production at the Bathurst mine is expected to come to a stop sometime in 2006; poor world market prices for metals mean that the smelter could close sooner. A proposed truck ferry between Belledune and Corner Brook, Newfoundland, could offset some of the job losses, but likely not all of them.

The expansion of mining activities has focused on offshore natural gas. The Sable Offshore Energy Project has a history of oil and gas exploration going back to the 1960s and became particularly active with the energy crisis of the 1970s. In 1999, a pipeline was laid to take natural gas from the Sable Island drill sites below the Atlantic, then overland across the Nova Scotia peninsula and southern New Brunswick to St Stephen, where it leaves the country for the American market. The Sable Island project represents only a small percentage of the overall Canadian (mainly Alberta) production of oil and gas, but there are large proven reserves of natural gas, and production is expected to increase.

Maritime natural gas exploration is controversial and, like the coal and steel industries, has attracted its share of critics. Environmentalists and fishers have voiced concerns about the impact of drilling on aquatic life in the region. An issue that gained more headlines, however, is the dispute between Newfoundland and Nova Scotia over the boundary line that, for minerals, extends 200 nautical miles offshore (see Fig. 7.6). The two provinces have been in disagreement about the boundary since 1964, but the dispute came to a head with the rise in offshore oil and gas prices. A court settlement

Figure 7.6   Nova Scotia territory transferred to Newfoundland, 2002

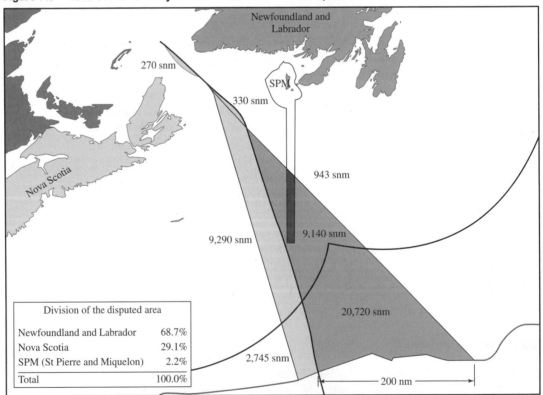

Source: Government of Newfoundland and Labrador (http://www.releases.gov.nl.ca/releases/2002/mines&en/0402n01.htm).

largely favoured the Newfoundland position, as that province ended up with nearly 70 per cent of the disputed area, giving Newfoundland access to a greater share of potentially lucrative offshore oil and gas reserves.

Another controversial aspect of the Sable Offshore Energy Project is the fact that all of the natural gas is being exported to the United States, leaving Canadian customers such as New Brunswick out of the market for Canadian natural gas. The availability of energy has been an ongoing problem for the Maritimes. Oil pipelines from western Canada do not run beyond Quebec; therefore, all oil must be imported from elsewhere. There are no large river systems to dam for hydro generation, although dams on the Saint John and other, smaller rivers produce limited quantities of electricity. Nova Scotia has 33 small hydroelectric stations. Most of the electricity used in the Maritimes is produced via thermal plants, which burn coal (or, less often, oil) to produce steam, which turns turbines to produce electricity. In New Brunswick, the Point Lepreau nuclear power plant (the only nuclear power plant in the Maritimes) supplies 30 per cent of the province's electricity. Nova Scotia has experimented with a small tidal power plant on the Bay of Fundy, while Prince Edward Island has invested in wind turbines, though it still imports most of its electricity from out of province.

Overall, the region has relatively limited access to energy, and as a result electricity rates in the three provinces are relatively high. As Figure 7.7 shows, New Brunswick's rate of 9.96 cents per kilowatt-hour is slightly lower than Nova Scotia's 10.05 cents, and Prince Edward Island is considerably higher at 12.95 cents; however, Quebec, paying just 6.3 cents/kilowatt-hour, has an important advantage.

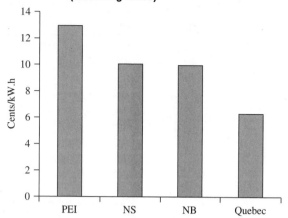

Figure 7.7 Residential electricity rates, April 2003 (excluding taxes)[1]

[1]Based on 750-kW.h/month

Source: New Brunswick Power, 'Residential Electricity Rates, April 2003' (http://www.nbpower.com).

Forestry

The forests of the Maritimes have been another important staple, particularly for New Brunswick. Not surprisingly, large multinational interests, including the home-grown K.C. Irving (headquartered in Saint John), have been involved in all aspects of this industry. Table 7.11 outlines the production of softwood lumber and pulpwood for the Maritimes. New Brunswick's lumber production has increased steadily since 1971, but its pulpwood supply has fallen off over the past fifteen years. Still, there are numerous sawmills and pulp and paper mills in the province, and forestry is an integral part of the economy of at least a hundred New Brunswick communities, a handful of which depend entirely on forestry operations to survive (Province of New Brunswick, n.d.). Nova Scotia maintains three pulp and paper mills and, like New Brunswick, has increased its output of lumber while seeing its production of pulpwood decline. Prince Edward Island has no pulp or paper mills and only a few small sawmills; consequently, its production figures are negligible.

Compared with the rest of Canada, all three Maritime provinces have much more of their forests in private hands. Prince Edward Island, although its has few forests left, leads the list with 92 per cent private ownership, while New Brunswick has 51 per cent, and

Table 7.11   Lumber[1] and pulpwood[1] production, 1971–2000

Year	Prince Edward Island		New Brunswick		Nova Scotia	
	Lumber[2]	Pulpwood	Lumber	Pulpwood	Lumber	Pulpwood
1971	29	66	603	4,913	361	2,467
1976	28	132	686	5,394	429	2,396
1981	35	60	865	5,165	379	2,932
1986	–	41	1,649	5,745	495	2,515
1991	–	39	1,350	4,133	450	2,914
1996	–	132	2,787	3,968	912	3,502
2001	–	130	3,499	2,799	1,474	2,392
2004	–	145	3,881	2,742[3]	1,783	3,069[3]

[1]Thousands of cubic metres

[2]Softwood only; thousands of cubic metres

[3]2003 figure

Source: Natural Resources Canada, 'Forestry Statistics' ⟨http://www.nrcan.gc⟩.

Nova Scotia 28 per cent. Many of these private forestlands are woodlots where individuals cut cordwood—usually in the winter—to supply pulp mills. Producers in Prince Edward Island and many of those in Nova Scotia send their pulpwood to New Brunswick. From a provincial government perspective, private forestland means fewer controls on the rate of cutting and less influence over the forward linkages.

Forestry and forestry products face the usual set of modern global pressures. World market prices are volatile, and dropping prices often bring layoffs and mill closures. Competition drives investment in new technologies that frequently reduce the labour component in production, or force companies out of business altogether. Provincial environment ministries insist on more stringent regulations for effluent emissions, which increase the cost of production. The softwood lumber dispute with the United States represents an enormous tariff barrier to Canada's major export market, while the recent strength of the Canadian dollar has made international trade conditions even more difficult. These conditions create uncertainty for the industry as a whole and the people who depend on forests for employment.

Another forestry concern, especially in New Brunswick, is forest management. At issue is how to combat pests (such as the spruce budworm) that kill trees, and how to eliminate broadleaf species (such as birch and maple) that, once a forest has been clearcut, retard the growth of the more valuable softwoods (spruce and fir). In 1952 New Brunswick opted to combat bugs and unwanted broadleaf species by aerial spraying of pesticides and herbicides, which are a risk to human health. Although critics such as the Sierra Club of Canada have suggested that spraying for budworm is actually counterproductive (because it kills the budworm's natural predators), New Brunswick has continued its spray program, although it has stopped using certain pesticides—such as DDT and, more recently, Fenitrothion—that pose unacceptable health risks to humans and other animals.

Fisheries

The staple that first attracted Europeans to eastern North America was fish, especially cod. But decades of mismanagement and overfishing reduced the stocks to dangerously low levels, leading to a moratorium on cod fishing in 1992. The situation has

Table 7.12   Maritime fish harvests by catch and value (× 1,000), 1991–2004

Year	Volume (tonnes) Cod	Other groundfish	Value of groundfish	Pelagic Volume	Value	Shellfish Volume	Value	Total wild fish Volume	Value
1991	111,250	203,776	224,281	292,433	45,831	153,369	392,147	693,965	666,004
1992	96,531	175,442	206,783	209,192	52,528	156,600	433,753	666,794	696,137
1993	35,481	141,623	133,462	202,025	59,347	167,141	461,238	567,840	658,587
1994	20,064	88,063	99,578	210,977	60,963	180,639	606,312	529,959	772,447
1995	11,087	69,524	88,211	190,148	73,533	154,568	670,605	451,999	836,146
1996	13,889	75,789	89,128	186,127	70,379	140,265	562,729	440,392	725,087
1997	16,001	70,149	93,705	185,210	63,710	163,108	610,437	469,060	771,663
1998	13,039	75,116	101,637	188,463	56,907	167,655	645,334	471,748	806,888
1999	13,721	61,176	93,651	204,064	60,071	179,388	786,916	488,938	943,958
2000	11,674	62,322	90,170	194,490	59,924	213,750	815,528	497,045	967,671
2001	12,588	70,693	101,021	195,265	68,367	232,348	923,095	525,825	1,094,312
2002	11,363	66,767	90,992	189,748	66,920	231,782	958,532	499,660	1,116,444
2003	8,226	58,424	86,820	194,125	67,024	224,209	977,319	484,985	1,131,163
2004	8,482	66,405	75,192	170,338	57,386	188,077	874,413	424,819	1,006,992

Source: Fisheries and Oceans Canada, 'Commercial Fisheries: Atlantic Region: Quantities and Values' (http://www.dfo-mpo.gc.ca/communic/statistics/commercial/landings/seafisheries/index_e.htm).

pitted individual fishers against large corporate interests; low-tech, low-yield methods against highly sophisticated, productive but destructive, technologies; and Canadian fleets against foreign ones. The cod crisis has been disastrous for many coastal communities whose residents—both the fishers themselves and those who worked in fish processing plants—were put out of work and forced to rely on government assistance (see Chapter 8).

Although the ban on cod fishing has been partially lifted, the 40,000 tonnes taken in the Atlantic region (including Newfoundland and Labrador) in 2001 was less than one-tenth the hauls recorded in the late 1980s (Agriculture and Agri-Food Canada, n.d.). Catches of pelagic fish (species found near the surface, such as herring) declined from the 1991 catch, but have maintained an average of 180,000 to 200,000 tonnes per year; unfortunately, the dollar value of pelagic species is not great. The major shift among Atlantic fishers has been to shellfish, and with the exception of a few years in the mid-1990s, catches of lobster, crab, shrimp, and scallops have steadily increased. Accounting for 58 per cent of the Maritime fisheries' overall value in 1991, shellfish rose to nearly 87 per cent by 2004.

Table 7.12 reveals the substantial decline in the cod fishery, and in the ground fishery generally, and consequent revenue losses for the three Maritime provinces. Figures 7.8 and 7.9 give a visual representation of the volumes of fish and their values between 1991 and 2004. Overall, the total volume of fish caught has declined, but their total value has actually increased. Cod fishers have largely been forced out of the industry, while those specializing in shellfish—which requires separate licences, vessels, and gear—have done quite well.

Another development in this industry has been the rise of **aquaculture**, or fish farming. Figure 7.10 traces Maritime production in this industry from 1991 to 2003. It records a steady growth both in finfish (mainly Atlantic salmon raised in net pens) and shellfish culture to the turn of the century, followed by a levelling-out period. As in the wild fishery, where Nova Scotia leads the Maritime provinces with 75 per cent

aquaculture
the breeding of fish or shellfish for food.

Figure 7.8   Volume of Maritime wild fish harvest, 1991–2004

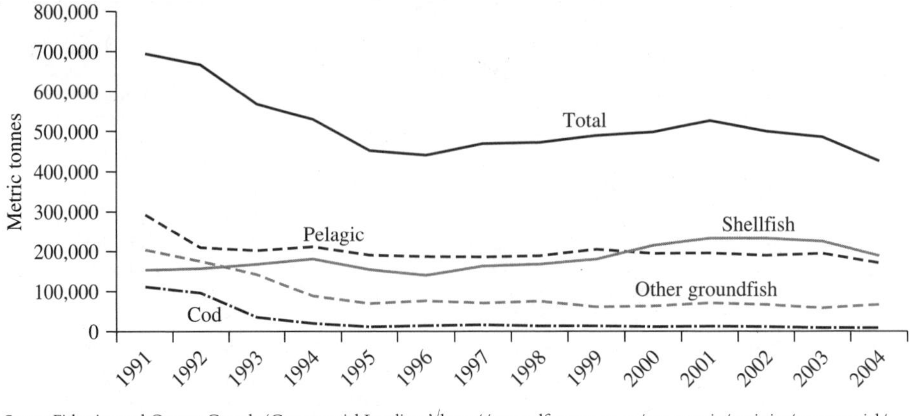

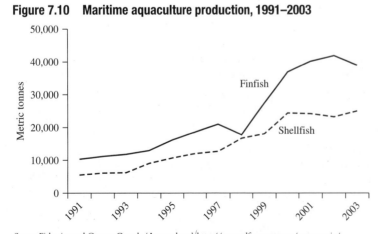

Source: Fisheries and Oceans Canada, 'Commercial Landings' (http://www.dfo-mpo.gc.ca/communic/statistics/commercial/landings/index_e.htm).

Figure 7.9   Value of Maritime wild fish harvest, 1991–2004

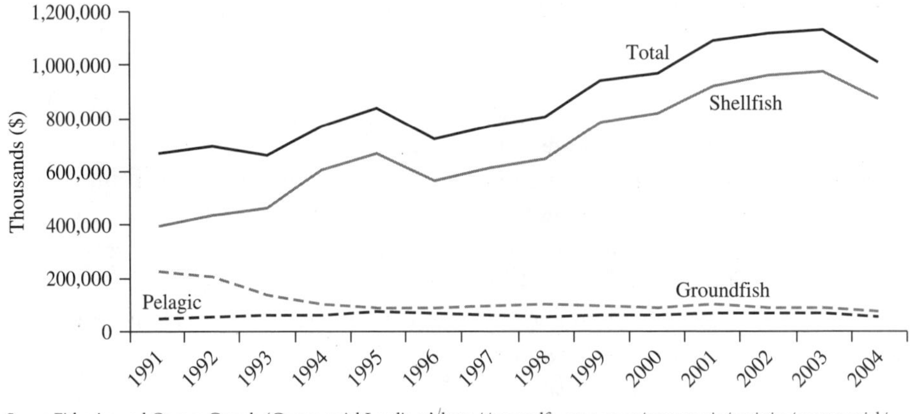

Source: Fisheries and Oceans Canada, 'Commercial Landings' (http://www.dfo-mpo.gc.ca/communic/statistics/commercial/landings/index_e.htm).

of the value harvested, followed by New Brunswick with 15 per cent and PEI with 10 per cent, there are great differences in the importance of aquaculture to each of the three provinces. Prince Edward Island is the leading shellfish producer in Canada and has specialized in mussels. New Brunswick, by contrast, has few shellfish farms but is the leading Maritime producer of salmon (although its total is considerably lower than British Columbia's). There are corresponding differences in revenues, with New Brunswick accounting for 75–80 per cent of the total aquaculture revenues in Maritime Canada because of its large salmon production (see Fig. 7.11).

Disputes over territorial boundaries and ocean resources have been common ever since Europeans began exploring the Atlantic

Figure 7.10   Maritime aquaculture production, 1991–2003

Source: Fisheries and Oceans Canada. 'Aquaculture' (http://www.dfo-mpo.gc.ca/communic/statistics/aqua/index_e.htm).

Figure 7.11   Maritime aquaculture value, 1991–2003

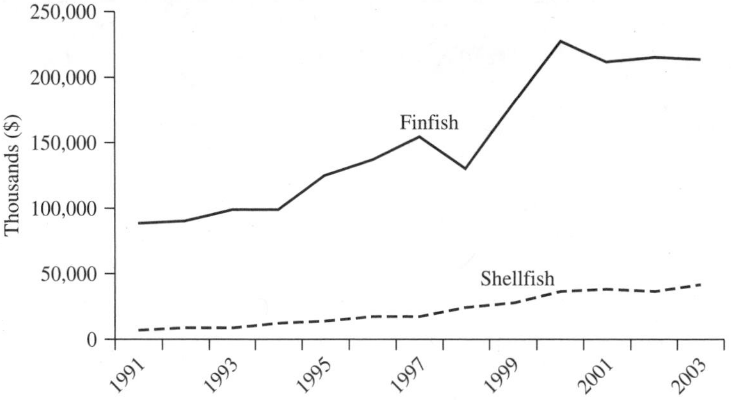

Source: Fisheries and Oceans Canada, 'Aquaculture' (http://www.dfo-mpo.gc.ca/communic/statistics/aqua/index_e.htm).

coast of North America in the fifteenth century. International boundary lines will be addressed in detail in the next chapter, on Newfoundland. One conflict that will be discussed here, however, is the dispute over the location of the Canada–US offshore boundary in the 1970s and 1980s. At stake were fishing rights on the lucrative Georges Bank, south of Nova Scotia (see Fig. 7.12). The Americans claimed the whole of the Bank, while the Canadians claimed essentially half of it. The dispute was settled by international court hearings at The Hague in the Netherlands, with a boundary line (as shown in Fig. 7.12) giving Canada the northern tip of Georges Bank. As it turned out, much of the highly valued scallop harvest is now within Canadian territory. However, Canada's limited naval resources have to be regularly deployed in this region to prevent poaching by American fishers.

Agriculture

Working the land is a long tradition in the Maritimes, but today the small family farm is largely a thing of the past. Agriculture has become 'agri-business', and farming, like other primary industries, has had to adapt in order to remain economically viable—mostly by increasing the size of farms and adopting costly new technologies. As Figures 7.13 and 7.14 show, farms have decreased in number while increasing in size.

Maritime farmers have also adapted by moving away from traditional products. Dairy and hog farming have decreased in favour of beef cattle, field crops (mainly potatoes), fruit, and specialty crops (see Table 7.13).

Large multinational corporations have also played a role in the changes to Maritime agriculture. McCain Foods Ltd, with its head office in Florenceville, NB, is the largest producer of French fries in the world. Another large New Brunswick multinational is Irving, in Saint John; while the company is best known for its oil refinery, service stations, pulp and paper mills, shipyard, transportation interest, and various media outlets, it also has large investments in Prince Edward Island's potato production. The increase in field crop production shown in Table 7.13 is largely a consequence of increased international demand. The potato industry has suffered occasional setbacks. In 2000, for instance, the discovery of a potato wart fungus in a single field in Prince Edward Island was enough for the United

Figure 7.12   Gulf of Maine boundary dispute

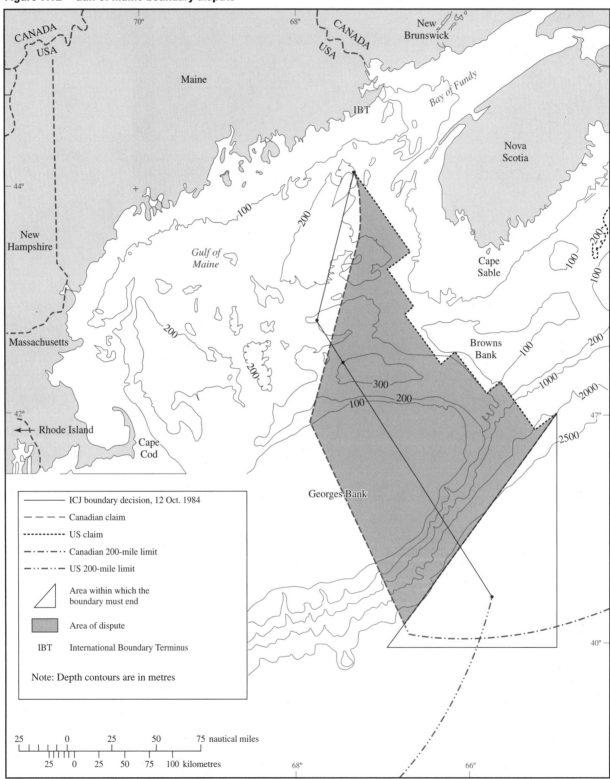

Figure 7.13   Number of farms, Maritime provinces, 1981–2001

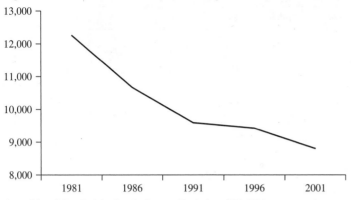

Source: Adapted from Statistics Canada, Census of Agriculture 1981–2001.

Figure 7.14   Average farm size, Maritime provinces, 1981–2001

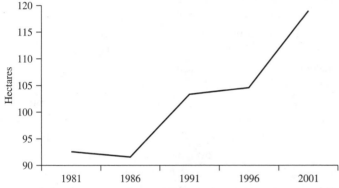

Source: Adapted from Statistics Canada, Census of Agriculture 1981–2001.

States to ban PEI potato imports for over a year. Potato farmers have also drawn criticism for their increasing use of fertilizers and pesticides, which pose a threat to human, fish, and animal populations when they leach into water systems.

Tourism

One industry that has enjoyed steady growth in the Maritimes is tourism. While the number of tourists fluctuates from year to year, there has been an overall increase in visits to the Maritimes both from abroad (mainly from the US) and from elsewhere in Canada. The region has numerous attractions that appeal to tourists year-round, including historic sites (Louisbourg, Kings Landing, Hartland's covered bridge, Acadian Historical Village, museums, and community heritage sites), spectacular

Table 7.13   Agricultural production by province (%), 1981–2001

Agricultural product	Prov.	1981	1986	1991	1996	2001
Dairy	PEI	29.7	23.8	23.2	16.7	17.8
	NS	26.2	22.0	19.2	13.9	11.3
	NB	27.1	22.7	19.1	14.4	12.5
Cattle (beef)	PEI	21.2	26.5	22.8	29.4	26.2
	NS	29.9	30.9	30.6	25.3	25.0
	NB	26.8	26.6	30.6	27.3	28.0
Hogs	PEI	9.9	9.0	9.5	5.1	5.4
	NS	6.2	4.2	3.0	2.6	2.0
	NB	4.3	4.5	2.6	2.7	3.1
Field crops (excluding grains)	PEI	17.9	19.3	24.7	26.2	26.5
	NS	2.3	1.4	2.5	4.9	7.3
	NB	16.2	13.8	14.0	16.2	16.9
Fruit	PEI	1.0	1.2	2.3	2.8	5.2
	NS	11.1	11.6	15.7	16.9	19.7
	NB	5.0	5.8	7.4	8.4	11.9
Miscellaneous specialty	PEI	3.4	6.1	6.7	6.2	6.6
	NS	10.2	15.2	16.5	24.1	22.8
	NB	6.1	11.3	15.0	19.5	19.3

Source: Statistics Canada, Census of Agriculture 1981–2001.

Table 7.14   Tourist travel to the Maritimes (× 1,000), 1996–2004

Prov.	Travel	1996	1997[1]	1998	1999	2000	2001	2002	2003	2004
PEI	Non-residential	518	NA	651	601	321	595	702	556	562
	Intraprovincial	160	NA	251	288	314	312	423	341	349
NS	Non-residential	1,059	NA	1,237	1,282	1,150	1,275	1,516	1,313	1,117
	Intraprovincial	4,567	NA	4,954	5,523	5,740	5,686	6,772	5,833	5,749
NB	Non-residential	930	NA	1,279	1,284	1,088	1,164	1,470	1,316	1,251
	Intraprovincial	3,545	NA	3,636	3,924	3,514	4,219	4,605	4,297	3,787

[1]Totals for this year were suppressed in order to meet the confidentiality requirements of the Statistics Act.

Source: Adapted from the Statistics Canada CANSIM database ⟨http://cansim2.statcan.ca⟩, Table 426-0003.

natural landscapes (the Cabot Trail, the Hopewell Rocks, the Reversing Falls, Magnetic Hill, the red sandstone soil of Prince Edward Island, and beaches such as Cavendish); special events (music festivals, writers' festivals, fiddlers on the Tobique), and recreational activities (golf, walking, cycling, hiking, kayaking, canoeing, skiing, whale watching, bird watching, and so on). Sites such as the home of *Anne of Green Gables* author L.M. Montgomery in Prince Edward Island and the Nova Scotia fishing village of Peggy's Cove have become internationally famous as icons of a romanticized past.

Tourism depends on more than just attractions. For instance, improved highway systems throughout the Maritimes have made tourist travel easier than it was in the past. Transportation infrastructure also includes Halifax's international airport, ports visited by cruise ships, ferries (crossing the Bay of Fundy, the Northumberland Strait, and the Cabot Strait), and the Confederation Bridge (over the Northumberland Strait), which now carries more than a million tourists per year from New Brunswick to Prince Edward Island. In addition, there has been considerable investment—both private and public—in marketing the Maritimes, and many American tourists in particular have been attracted by favourable exchange rates on US currency.

First Nations

One group that has not been allowed to capitalize on Maritime resources, including land, is the region's Aboriginal community. The Mi'kmaq, who were among the first to sign historic treaties of Peace and Friendship with Europeans, have struggled to maintain a foothold on their traditional lands. In total there are 30 bands or tribal councils throughout the Maritimes: most are Mi'kmaq, but the Maliseet are also represented in Table 7.15. Of the region's 72 reserves, few are larger than 1,000 hectares, and some, like the Margaree #25 Reserve of the Wagmatcook Band, northwest of Sydney, are less than one hectare in size. Table 7.15 puts into perspective just how little land First Nations have managed to retain in the Maritimes. The Aboriginal populations (the statistics include Indian, Métis, and Inuit) in each province are increasing, but job opportunities on reserves remain minimal, and therefore many have left reserves.

Disputes over the right to harvest resources have occasionally erupted into bitter and violent confrontations between Native and non-Native Maritimers. Burnt Church

Table 7.15   Aboriginal populations, bands/tribal councils, area of reserve lands (ha), and area of provinces (ha), 1996–2001

Province	1996	2001	Number of bands	Area of reserve	Area of province	Reserves as %
PEI	950	1,395	2	674.8	566,000	0.1
NS	12,380	17,065	13	12,389.1	5,528,400	0.2
NB	10,250	17,155	15	18,957.5	7,290,800	0.3
Total	23,580	35,615	30	32,021.4	13,385,200	0.2

Source: Statistics Canada; Mi'kmaq Resource Centre, 'Band Governments in Prince Edward Island, Nova Scotia, and New Brunswick' (http://mrc.uccb.ns.ca).

(Esgenoôpetitj), on New Brunswick's Miramichi Bay, was the scene of a confrontation in 2000 over the number of lobster traps that local Mi'kmaq were setting out. Non-Native fishers argued that any increase in the number of Mi'kmaq traps would force non-Native fishers to set fewer traps or risk putting the fishery in jeopardy. The Mi'kmaq, while recognizing the need for conservation, claimed they were merely exercising their treaty rights by trying to make a living from this lucrative fishery. The band, which had carried out its own assessment of the number of traps that were sustainable, was backed by a 1999 Supreme Court decision (the Donald Marshall case) that 'affirmed the treaty rights of Indian band members to earn a moderate livelihood from fishing, hunting and gathering' (Harvey, 2000). Angered by the ruling, non-Native fishers destroyed some Mi'kmaq traps and fish plants. The issue continues to be a source of resentment and hostility on both sides to this day.

Native groups are also fighting to assert their land rights. The Mi'kmaq, like Aboriginal groups in other parts of Canada, maintain that they have never ceded their title to the land and that they should be able to harvest trees on Crown forest-land. Again, with provincial and federal governments reluctant to negotiate, the courts are being asked to rule on the modern-day implications of historic treaties of peace and friendship, as well as on the fundamental question of whether Aboriginal title has been extinguished in the Maritimes. The issue does not appear likely to be settled anytime soon.

Summary

The Maritimes were home for the Mi'kmaq and Maliseet First Nations, who were traditionally hunters and gatherers but became increasingly involved in trading furs for European goods once the French colonized the region in the early 1600s. They formed fairly strong bonds with the French and often assisted them in their military activities against the British. When the British eventually conquered the territory, they negotiated treaties of peace and friendship with the Mi'kmaq. But here, as elsewhere in the 'new world', these First Nations were devastated by European diseases. They were pushed onto small reserves, and only recently, mainly with the help of the courts, have they asserted their historic rights to land and resources.

The 400 years of European settlement in the Maritimes have been turbulent, notably for the original Acadians who lived under the constant threat of British invasion.

By the mid–1700s, most Acadians had been expelled from the Maritimes, as the British took over French territories throughout North America. An interesting relocation diffusion process brought the return of many Acadians, not to their original homesteads on the Bay of Fundy, but mainly to northern New Brunswick.

For the past hundred years, the Maritimes have been the gateway to Canada for people from many different backgrounds. Although many came from Great Britain, they were hardly a homogeneous group: Scots and Irish came with different religions and languages, though they shared an animosity toward the English. Other Europeans came, bringing with them a variety of languages and religions, and Loyalists, including many Blacks, fled from the United States. Many of these immigrants passed through the Maritimes on their way to other parts of the country. But others stayed, attracted by the prospects for agriculture, forestry, fishing, and coal mining. The region became famous for shipbuilding, and during the 1800s, manufacturing industries were established. The most important part of the region's economy, however, was the commercial activity associated with Atlantic trade routes.

Political and economic events at both the national and international levels tied the Maritimes to central Canada through Confederation and railways. Maritimers believed that the cities of Halifax and Saint John would become major transportation centres for the rest of Canada, particularly in winter, when the frozen St Lawrence became impassable by ship. This hope did not materialize, as central Canada frequently used American ports.

The protective tariffs that Canada adopted in response to the worldwide depression of the late nineteenth century initially spurred industrial development throughout the Maritimes. But as the depression continued, Atlantic trade was drastically reduced, and more and more of the Maritime economy—industry, retailing, transportation, banking, and finance—came under the control of Montreal and Toronto interests.

By the early twentieth century the focus of population and economic expansion had shifted to western Canada, leaving the Maritimes as a peripheral economy dependent on its natural resources and international trade. New technologies that compressed space and time created greater competition for Atlantic trade routes. While developments in pulp and paper benefited the Maritime economy, the introduction of new technologies meant that fewer workers were required in the traditional industries—sawmilling, fishing, agriculture, and coal mining—and the result was widespread unemployment.

The two World Wars brought military spending to the region and, by limiting trans-Atlantic shipping, reinvigorated Atlantic trade. But in the years following 1945, the Maritime economy became increasingly dependant on transfer payments from the federal government and government programs designed to promote manufacturing. Unfortunately, few of these programs were successful.

Since the 1970s, massive economic and political changes have created a great deal of uncertainty in the trade and investment sectors. In this modern global economy, the services industry is the biggest employment provider, and most business is conducted in large urban centres. However, much of the Maritime population continues to live in rural areas, depending on resources that are quickly becoming scarce. Halifax, with a population of approximately 360,000, is the dominant urban centre in a region with a total population of less than two million. The fact that this small domestic market is spread across three provinces means that economic opportunities are often fragmented. Moreover, the provinces are closer to the New England states than to the economic core of Canada.

The Maritimes offer a vast range of natural and historical attractions, and their landscape, juxtaposing the old and the new, has great appeal. As a result, tourism has become a major industry, especially in recent years, when favourable exchange rates and lingering fears of another 9/11-style terrorist attack have led many Americans to take their holidays closer to home. At the same time, the region's reputation for a relatively relaxed pace of life, affordable land values, and above all, friendly people is attracting new residents from other parts of Canada.

References

Acheson, T.W. 1977. 'The National Policy and the Industrialization of the Maritimes, 1880–1910'. Pp. 93–124 in G.A. Stelter and A.F.J. Artibise, eds. *The Canadian City: Essays in Urban History.* Toronto: McClelland and Stewart.

Agriculture and Agri-Food Canada. N.d. 'Atlantic Cod'. http://atn-riae.agr.ca.

Atlantic Development Council. 1972. 'A Strategy for the Economic Development of the Atlantic Region, 1971–1981'. In R.M. Irving, ed. *Readings in Canadian Geography.* Revised edn. Toronto: Holt, Rinehart and Winston, 424–40.

Brooks, I.A. 1985. 'Appalachian Region'. Pp. 1414–15 in *The Canadian Encyclopedia.* Edmonton: Hurtig.

Canada's Digital Collections. N.d. 'Black Loyalists: Our History, Our People'. http://collections.ic.gc.ca.

Conrad, Margaret R., and James K. Hiller. 2001. *Atlantic Canada: A Region in the Making.* Toronto: Oxford.

Dickason, Olive Patricia. 2002. *Canada's First Nations: A History of Founding Peoples from Earliest Times.* 3rd edn. Toronto: Oxford.

Fisheries and Oceans Canada. N.d. 'Commercial Fisheries: Atlantic Region: Quantities and Values'. http://www.dfo-mpo.gc.ca/communic/statistics/commercial/landings/seafisheries/index_e.htm.

———. N.d. 'Aquaculture'. http://www.dfo-mpo.gc.ca/communic/statistics/aqua/ index_e.htm.

Francis, R.D., Jones, R., and Smith, D.B. 2000. *Origins: Canadian History to Confederation.* 4th edn. Toronto: Harcourt.

Francophonie Connection, The. N.d. 'The Acadians of Nova Scotia'; 'The Acadians of New Brunswick'. http://www.fracophonie.gc.ca.

Government of Newfoundland. 2002. http://www.gov.nf.ca.

Harris, C. 1987. 'The Pattern of Early Canada'. *The Canadian Geographer* 31, 4 (Winter): 290–8.

Harvey, J. 2000. 'DFO Out of Line at Burnt Church'. *Telegraph Journal.* 17 May. http://www.nbnews.com.

History of Canada, The. N.d. 'The Colonies Grow Up'. http://www.linksnorth.com.

Jones, R.L. 2003. 'Canadian Disasters: An Historical Survey'. http://www.ott.igs.net.

Kurlansky, M. 1997. *Cod: A Biography of a Fish that Changed the World.* Toronto: Alfred A. Knopf.

McCann, L.D. 1982. 'Staples and the New Industrialism in the Growth of Post-Confederation Halifax'. Pp. 84–115 in G.A. Stelter and A.F.J. Artibise, eds. *Shaping the Urban Landscape: Aspects of the Canadian City-Building Process.* Ottawa: Carleton University Press, 84–115.

McKnight, T.L. 2001. *Regional Geography of the United States and Canada.* 3rd edn. Upper Saddle River, NJ: Prentice-Hall.

McVey, W.W., and Kalbach, W.E. 1995. *Canadian Population.* Scarborough: Nelson.

Margaret's Museum (film). 1995. M. Ransen, director. British–Canadian co-production.

Mi'kmaq Resource Centre and Mi'kmaq Resource Guide, 2000. 'Band Governments in Prince Edward Island, Nova Scotia, and New Brunswick'; 'Treaty of 1725'; 'Treaty of 1752'; 'Treaty of 1760'. http://mrc.uccb.ns.ca.

Nader, G.A. 1975. *Cities of Canada.* Vol. I. *Theoretical, Historical and Planning Perspectives.* Toronto: Macmillan.

———. 1976. *Cities of Canada.* Vol. II. *Profiles of Fifteen Metropolitan Centres.* Toronto: Macmillan.

Natural Resources Canada. N.d. 'Facts about Canada'; 'Future Direction Set for the Cape Breton Development Corporation'; 'Forestry Statistics'. http://www.nrcan.gc.ca

New Brunswick Power. N.d. 'Residential Electricity Rates, April 2003'. http://www.nbpower.com

Nova Scotia CBC. 2003. 'Ottawa legislates safety in workplace'. 12 June. http://www.novascotia.cbc.ca.

Province of New Brunswick N.d. http://new-brunswick.net.

———. Aboriginal Affairs. N.d. '10,000 Years of History'. http://www.gnb.ca.

Robb, S.A., and Holman, H.T. 1985. 'Prince Edward Island'. Pp. 1474–81 in *The Canadian Encyclopedia*. Edmonton: Hurtig.

Sierra Club of Canada. N.d. 'Pesticide Facts'. http://www.sierraclub.ca.

Sultzman, L. 1999. 'Micmac History'. http://www.dickshovel.com.

Wheeler, J.O. 1996. 'About the Geology of Canada'. Natural Resources Canada. http://www.nrcan.gc.ca.

Woods, S.E. 1992. *Cinders and Saltwater: The Story of Atlantic Canada's Railways*. Halifax: Nimbus.

8

Newfoundland and Labrador: Resource Dependency

The province of Newfoundland and Labrador is unlike any other part of Canada in many regards, including its physical characteristics, its history of settlement, its entry into Confederation, its economy, and its people. Accessible only by ferry or by plane, the island of Newfoundland—affectionately known as 'the Rock'—is relatively isolated. But it has had a long history of exploration and settlement, much of it revolving around the lucrative stocks of fish, mainly cod, off its shores. The land and the adjacent waters have been the scene of many conflicts that, over the years, have involved Newfoundlanders in territorial battles, concessions, and agreements that have left a legacy very much in evidence today.

Labrador, with its single road (much of it unpaved) connecting it to Baie-Comeau in Quebec, is remote by Canadian standards. The greatest influences on its settlement and development have been its resources—iron ore, hydroelectricity, forests, and, more recently, nickel—although the facilities at Happy Valley–Goose Bay, including a military airport, NATO headquarters, and port at the western end of the Hamilton Inlet, have also influenced settlement in the region.

One of the principal challenges for Newfoundland and Labrador has been economic management, a challenge made especially difficult by the fact that codfish—a single species of a single staple commodity—represents such an important part of the province's income. But the former British colony has faced many challenges over its history, including building a railway, persevering through depressions, and diversifying the economy. The decision to join Canada in 1949 was extremely divisive for Newfoundlanders, and the union had both positive and negative consequences, for although Confederation brought transfer payments and other aid from the federal government, in return for those benefits Newfoundland surrendered control of the waters on which it has always depended. By the early 1990s the cod stocks had been depleted to the point that a moratorium was imposed on the cod fishery. The cod moratorium has essentially eliminated the economic base in a thousand or more isolated outports, radically changing the way of life for many of the island's residents and leaving the province in need of strategies to provide alternative employment and curtail the flow of Newfoundlanders out of the province in search of work. There are other, 'newer' resources and developments, including the planned nickel mine at Voisey's Bay and the proposed smelter at Argentia, as well as offshore oil production. Fishing continues, but—as in the

Figure 8.1   Map of Newfoundland and Labrador

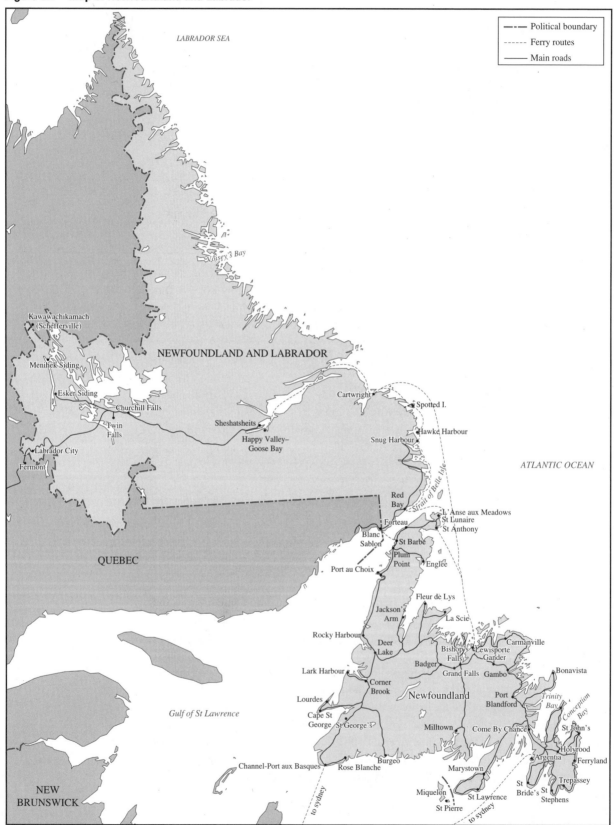

Maritimes—is now focused on other fish species and especially shellfish (lobster, crab, and shrimp); in addition, aquaculture (fish farming) is becoming an important industry.

Through all these developments, the First Nations of Newfoundland and Labrador have not fared well. The indigenous Beothuk of Newfoundland are extinct, and the island's Mi'kmaq population lives without officially recognized title to the lands they occupy. The Innu and Inuit of Labrador have also not signed treaties. These Aboriginal communities have largely been pushed aside through resource and military developments.

Physical Characteristics

The province of Newfoundland and Labrador occupies three physiographic regions: Labrador is part of the Canadian Shield, Newfoundland is situated along the Appalachian Uplands, and the Atlantic Continental Shelf lies offshore. The Shield and Appalachians are old and weathered formations, and consequently the rugged landscape has almost no towering elevations. The exception is found in the Torngat Mountains of northern Labrador and Quebec, where Mount D'Iberville, the highest peak in the Canadian Shield, stands at 1,729 metres—more than twice the height of the highest peaks in the Long Range Mountains in the western part of the island, which barely exceed 800 metres.

The most famous parts of the Continental Shelf are the Grand Banks: a series of undersea plateaus created by billions of years of erosion. Because the relatively shallow depth of the banks, combined with the ocean currents that meet over them—the cold Labrador current clashing with the warm Gulf Stream—promotes the growth of plankton, this region has been one of the most productive habitats in the world for fish, codfish especially. Oil, discovered on the Grand Banks in 1979, is another resource that has generated interest in the region, sparking development of the Hibernia oilfield along with plans for future offshore developments.

As in most regions of Canada, glaciation left little soil for agriculture but enough for forests. Much of the interior of Newfoundland is swampy and poorly drained, but with its many lakes (called 'ponds') it has been an excellent habitat for wildlife. Highly indented shorelines of fjords and inlets along the coasts of both Newfoundland and Labrador offer well-protected harbours that have attracted settlers who make their living from the sea.

The rivers of Newfoundland are small by comparison with those of other provinces, but they are numerous and are important sources of fish (especially salmon) and hydroelectricity. The largest by far is the Churchill River in Labrador, which has been dammed to create the Smallwood Reservoir. The hydroelectric generators at Churchill Falls produce a great deal of electricity, and there is the potential for more dams further downstream.

Most of Labrador lies north of 52° latitude, and the cold northern climate is frequently exacerbated by the Labrador Current. This current is known for carrying icebergs from the Arctic to the shores of Newfoundland, where they become hazards to vessels navigating the northeastern Atlantic. In contrast to Labrador, all of Newfoundland lies below the 52° mark; nevertheless, it, too, experiences the effects of the Labrador Current, which modifies both summer and winter temperatures. The collision between the Labrador Current and the Gulf Stream is responsible for the fog banks so typical of Atlantic Canada.

The entire region of Newfoundland and Labrador is affected by westerly flows of winds. Labrador receives these air masses mainly from the northwest, and Newfoundland also experiences its share of 'northwesterlies', but its southern shores are often in the path of much warmer air from the southwest. The collision of these two air masses results in a low-pressure zone that is responsible for a considerable amount of precipitation year-round. In winter harbours freeze over, and some locations receive substantial amounts of snow.

Early Settlement and Development

Shananditti (or Shawnawdithit), who was born in 1801, was captured by English fur traders in 1823, and died of tuberculosis in 1829, was the last of the Beothuk in Newfoundland. The Beothuk had inhabited the island long before the arrival of Europeans, living mainly along the coasts, where they fished and hunted seals and other marine animals. But they were not the first Native society to call the region home. Artefacts dating back 7,500 years have been found at L'Anse Amour, on the shores of the Strait of Belle Isle in Labrador (McGhee, 1985: 1468), and the evidence of island settlement dates back some 5,000 years. Dorset Inuit replaced the original inhabitants between 4,000 and 2,500 years ago and made the territory home until approximately 1,500 years ago, when the Beothuk began to inhabit the island. Evidence of the Mi'kmaq's presence in Newfoundland dates back to approximately 1600 (Pastore, 1998). In present-day Labrador, the Thule replaced the Dorset in the north, while southern Labrador was occupied by the Montagnais–Naskapi (known as Innu in Labrador).

The Norse were the first Europeans to arrive in Newfoundland, and their recorded history suggests that they made several voyages to Newfoundland and coastal Labrador between the tenth and fourteenth centuries CE. It is believed that Bjarni Herjolfsson was the first European to reach Newfoundland when, setting out for a new Norse colony in Greenland around 986, he was driven south by a storm. The Norse *Sagas* record later expeditions led by (among others) Leif Ericsson, who identified three distinct regions: Helluland, a region of ice and rock, and the heavily forested Markland were probably parts of present-day Labrador, while Vinland, a place of wild grapes, may have been along the coast of present-day New Brunswick and northern Nova Scotia. Archaeological evidence, including the remains of several buildings, at L'Anse aux Meadows on the northern tip of the Northern Peninsula of Newfoundland confirms that the Norse attempted to establish a colony there; the primitive dwellings have been restored and today give an excellent representation of early Norse settlement. It is believed that the Norse were attracted to the region by its abundant timber, but conflict with the Aboriginal people, whom the Norse called Skraelings and who are thought to have been Dorset Inuit, apparently caused them to abandon the colony.

Mark Kurlansky (1997: 24) suggests that Basque fishers were sailing to the waters off Newfoundland at least as early as the Norse, but most historians place their movement into this part of the Atlantic much later. The British interest in Newfoundland dates from the late 1400s and the voyages of the Italian-born English explorer John Cabot, who, like so many other adventurers from Europe, was searching for a sea route to Asia and found North America instead. In June 1497 he made landfall on the North American coast; the exact site of his landing is a matter of dispute, but there is a good chance it was in Newfoundland.

Cabot found no seaway to Asia and no riches, but he returned with stories of massive amounts of codfish to be had off the shores of this 'new isle', or 'Terra Nova'. This was an important discovery for the British, since it meant they would no longer have to rely on Iceland for their supply of fish. As Kurlansky explains, codfish was extremely important to the European diet, accounting for 60 per cent of all fish eaten in Europe in the mid-sixteenth century (1997: 51). It is not surprising, then, that fishers were drawn from all over Europe to the Grand Banks.

Almost as important to the fishers as the fish themselves were the protected bays and inlets of Newfoundland's coast. Fishers using the 'wet' method of preserving their catch would salt it heavily and store it in the ship's hold, but those using the 'dry' method needed a land base where they could set up racks called 'flakes' to dry the fish in the sun. This was the method used by British fishers, who had limited supplies of salt (Innis, 1956: 27). All fishers, however, also needed some base on land for tasks such as mending nets and repairing boats.

It was on these shores that the Europeans encountered the Beothuk. Whereas European fur traders were to depend on Aboriginal partners to conduct their business, the early fishers saw no benefit to cultivating friendly relations with the local people. As Frideres bluntly notes, 'In the fisherman's eyes the Indians were of no use' (1988: 45). The Europeans considered the Aboriginal people thieves and pilferers, and the punishment for such crimes was often death.

The hostility between the two groups would be aggravated when British fishers began establishing settlements on the island and competing for the same resources—fish, seals, and other maritime wildlife—that the Beothuk, as a coastal people, had traditionally relied on. The ensuing conflicts pushed the Beothuk inland, where food was much more difficult to find. Shananditti's stories, recorded after her capture, indicate that many of her people died of starvation after they were forced inland, although European diseases also took their toll, and at times the Beothuk were even hunted down for sport or for bounty. It is estimated that as many as 50,000 Beothuk once lived in Newfoundland; all were extinct by 1829 (Winter, 1975).

Although the English explorer Sir Humphrey Gilbert had claimed the island of Newfoundland for England in 1583, the process of settlement was slow. One reason was the harsh physical environment, which was not favourable to agriculture. Another was the opposition of the powerful West Country merchants who sponsored the seasonal fishery. Fearing that their fleets would not be able to compete with a resident population fishing the Banks year-round, they pressured the government to prohibit settlement on the island. British officials did not want to anger the merchants; but they also realized that if Britain did not settle Newfoundland, then France would do so instead. Thus an anti-settlement policy was adopted in 1671, but no serious effort was made to enforce it: in effect, settlement was tolerated, though it was not encouraged. Britain's ambivalent approach meant that the island's permanent population remained low throughout the seventeenth century, though a number of settlements—home to both permanent residents and seasonal fishers—were established along the eastern coast of the peninsula. As Table 8.1 illustrates, the population of Newfoundland did not really begin to grow until the middle of the 1700s.

Table 8.1 Population, Newfoundland, 1650–1830

Year	Population
1650	500
1680	2,000
1730	2,300
1783	10,000
1789	16,000
1800	20,000
1830	40,000

Sources: R.D. Francis, R. Jones, and D.B. Smith, *Origins: Canadian History to Confederation*, 4th edn (Toronto: Harcourt), 404, 409; J. Rusted, *Tolerable Good Anchorage* (St John's: Creative Book Publishing, 1995), 18.

The Struggle for Autonomy, 1700s–1900s

The early pattern of settlement on Newfoundland was very much influenced by the nature of the fishery. Small vessels called dories—narrow, high-bowed rowboats with flat bottoms and pointed at both ends—were used to catch the cod when they came inshore to spawn (generally from spring until fall). These boats could not venture far from shore; consequently, local fishing grounds easily became overcrowded. As the population increased, therefore, the tendency was to start a new settlement in the next unsettled bay or inlet rather than to expand the existing hamlet. The result was a linear pattern of settlement consisting of small outports strung out along the coastline.

Yet despite the scattered nature of the settlements, a powerful sense of nationalism began to emerge for Newfoundlanders during the eighteenth century, in part because of the constant threat posed by the French. With the Treaty of Utrecht, signed in 1713 to end the War of Spanish Succession, France officially recognized Newfoundland as British territory and abandoned its base at Plaisance; however, Britain allowed the French fishery to continue in North America and granted the French the right to fish off the northern shore of Newfoundland, from Cape Bonavista to Point Riche. The treaty precluded settlement, but it recognized that the French fishers could use the various bays and inlets on the 'French Shore' to dry and cure their fish (see Figure 8.2).

Figure 8.2   The French Shore, 1713

Source: Map by Tanya Saunders. © 2001 Newfoundland and Labrador Heritage Web Site. Reprinted by permission.

Initially these provisions had little impact on Newfoundland fishers, who for the most part were settling on the eastern coast of the Avalon peninsula. But the treaty also did little to quell the hostility between Britain and France, who were locked in a struggle for control of North America and its valuable resources of furs and fish. During the Seven Years War (1756–63) the British captured New France and Acadia. The French in 1762 managed to capture St John's, but the British military forces gained it back. The Treaty of Paris (1763) officially recognized British sovereignty over much of eastern North America, including Labrador, the administration of which was immediately assigned to the governor of Newfoundland. The French negotiated the right to continue fishing in the Gulf of St Lawrence and off the northern shore of Newfoundland, and to occupy the islands of St Pierre and Miquelon as unfortified bases for the Grand Banks fishery.

With Labrador now in British possession, Newfoundland fishers became interested in the rich fishing grounds off its coast. They also recognized that the French presence on the island's northern shore was hampering settlement and restricting the fishing rights of Newfoundlanders. But their requests that Britain extinguish France's rights to the northern shore were to no avail. Having seen its migratory fishery fleet—which had served as an excellent source of experienced naval recruits—shrink as more and more fishers settled permanently in its North American colonies, Britain had no interest in doing anything that might promote settlement opportunities in Newfoundland. In 1775, the British government passed Palliser's Act, which made settlement within six miles of the Newfoundland coast illegal.

By then, however, Britain had more serious issues to contend with. The outbreak of the American War of Independence in the same year meant that Palliser's Act went largely unheeded and unenforced. One consequence of the American revolution was a provision concerning the French Shore in the Treaty of Versailles (1783), which recognized the various territorial changes in North America following the war. French fishing rights were moved from the northern coast of Newfoundland to the western coast, including much of the northern peninsula, extending from Cape St John in the north to Cape Ray on the southwest (see Fig. 8.3). St Pierre and Miquelon, which had been ransacked by the British during the revolution, remained French possessions, although fortifications were still not allowed.

The revolution had other implications for Newfoundland as well. The war interrupted both fishing and trade, which brought great hardship to the island communities that depended on these two vital aspects of the local economy. Once the war was over, however, the United States was prohibited from trading with British colonies in the Caribbean, and this opened the door for a significant increase in trade between the US and Newfoundland. Britain's involvement in the Napoleonic Wars between 1793 and 1815 benefited Newfoundland fishers greatly, increasing both the demand for codfish and the price paid for it.

These were prosperous times for Newfoundland, and its population increased significantly. St John's, with its natural harbour and favourable location with respect to both the north shore and south shore fishery, emerged as the commercial, military, and administrative centre, and Britain, realizing that the population of Newfoundland would only increase, finally awarded Newfoundland the official status of colony in 1811. Unlike Britain's other colonies, however, Newfoundland would not have local government representation until 1832, and would not achieve internal self-government until 1855.

Figure 8.3 The French Shore, 1783

Source: Map by Tanya Saunders. © 2001 Newfoundland and Labrador Heritage Web Site. Reprinted by permission.

Newfoundland's lack of autonomy became apparent twice in the nineteenth century. The first incident occurred shortly after the War of 1812, when the British and American governments signed the British–American Convention in 1818. The US, which had long wanted a share of the valuable cod banks, successfully negotiated for the right for American fishers to use the southern shore of Newfoundland for their fishing operations. This was a devastating setback for Newfoundlanders, who were already annoyed with French fishing off the island's northern and western coasts. Many Newfoundlanders felt that the British were essentially giving away their southern coast at a time when the colony's population—a population engaged almost exclusively in fishing—was expanding.

The second incident occurred late in the century, when Newfoundland, with British permission, negotiated a free-trade agreement with the United States. Canada, which had recently adopted its protectionist National Policy, objected strongly. Arguing that this arrangement would undermine Canada's economy and provoke anti-Confederation sentiment, Ottawa put great pressure on Britain to prevent it from going forward. The British government backed the Canadian demands and did not ratify the treaty, sparking bitterness in Newfoundland and straining its trade relations with Canada. In 1902, after petitioning the British government, Newfoundland was once again allowed to negotiate a free-trade agreement with the US. But again the treaty failed to be ratified, this time because of the objections of American fishers, who felt that it would threaten their fishing interests. The question of fishing rights off the Newfoundland coast was not settled until the early twentieth century. By this time, the French migratory fishery using the west shore of the island had substantially diminished. 'Where once, in the late 1820s, more than 9,000 French nationals had fished on the French Shore, only 133 French fishermen showed up in 1898' (Janzen, 1998). As a result, in 1904, as part of an effort to settle Anglo–French disputes throughout the world, the French government agreed to surrender its fishing rights on the French Shore, giving Newfoundland unrestricted access to its western coast. The Americans were not so willing to abandon their rights to fish off Newfoundland's southern coast. Britain, reluctant to open up a messy international incident, turned to The Hague for an international ruling on the south shore issue. In 1910 an international tribunal ruled in favour of Newfoundland, and the Americans were forced to depart from the southern shore.

Another issue involving Newfoundland's sovereignty arose in 1902, when the province of Quebec objected to Newfoundland's granting timber rights on Labrador's Churchill River to a Nova Scotia company, arguing that the land belonged to Quebec and not Newfoundland. No boundary between Quebec and Labrador had ever been marked or surveyed, and Labrador was defined merely as the northeastern 'coast'. From the Canadian perspective, this meant only the coastal fringe involved in the Newfoundland fishery; but Newfoundland argued that it meant the height of land from the 52nd parallel north. An appeal to the Privy Council of Great Britain to rule on this territory was submitted in 1914, and 13 years later, in 1927, Britain ruled that Newfoundland's interpretation was correct. The border between Quebec and Labrador was set at the watershed where the rivers flowing into the Atlantic begin, and Newfoundland secured an extremely valuable resource region.

These successes were immense, especially for a small colony of fishers who, for a considerable period of their history, were not even legally allowed to settle in Newfoundland. Newfoundlanders were determined, and through their perseverance won the essential battles—the ones threatening their sovereignty over the land. These unifying conflicts, some of them centuries old, became the foundation of a powerful nationalism. Winning the rights to the French and American shores soon resulted in settlement of the many bays and inlets, which led in turn to economic problems associated with the proliferation of dispersed, isolated outports dependent on a single resource. Politicians in Newfoundland could easily rally support when other nations encroached on their land and threatened their rights to fish; few, however, could offer solutions to an economy based almost entirely on one staple.

The Staple Economy

Gaining self-government in 1832 was a major achievement for Newfoundland; losing it barely a century later was a serious economic, political, and emotional shock. In 1934 Newfoundland was forced to declare bankruptcy and Britain took over, ruling the island by what was officially called Commission of Government. Why did Newfoundland's economy fail?

There are many reasons, including

- reliance on one industry,
- failure to increase productivity in that industry,
- unpredictable world market prices,
- geographically scattered communities,
- the seasonal nature of fisheries employment,
- over-extension of credit,
- the giveaway of land-based resources,
- debt incurred from infrastructure projects,
- debt incurred from First World War commitments, and
- changing global economic conditions.

Before considering these factors, however, it is important to have some understanding of the industry that was the mainstay of Newfoundland's economy for so long.

Throughout the 1800s and the first half of the 1900s, the population of Newfoundland increased substantially, from approximately 40,000 in 1830 to more than 120,000 by the 1857 census and twice that figure by 1911 (see Table 8.2). During this time there was a corresponding increase in the number of settlements: mostly small (fewer than 200 people) outports spread along both the northern and southern coasts of Newfoundland as well as the coast of Labrador. Table 8.2 shows that more than three-quarters of these were small outports; however, from 1857 to 1945, between 44 and 57 per cent of the population lived in communities of 500 people or more. Even more revealing are the figures showing the value of exported fishery products and this value in relation to total exports. Two things are worth noting: first, that the value of exported fish did not increase to any extent from 1870 until after the First World War, and that the Depression of the 1930s devastated the industry; and second—perhaps more telling—that the economy was utterly dependent on exports of fish products, which represented over 90 per cent of all exports until the early 1900s.

Table 8.2   Population, settlements, and fish exports, 1857–1945

Year	Population	Number of settlements	% of settlements 0–199	% of population living in settlements of 500 or more	Value of exported fishery products[1]	Fish as % of total exports
1857	122,638[2]	615	79.8	56.7	1,591[3]	96.4
1869	146,536	662	74.7	56.6	5,807	95.9
1874	161,374	801	77.8	55.5	7,042	96.0
1884	197,335	1,052	81.0	52.9	6,409	97.6
1891	202,040	1,183	82.2	48.4	6,680	89.8
1901	220,984	1,372	81.5	44.7	6,908	82.6
1911	242,619	1,447	81.1	43.8	8,799	73.5
1921	263,033	1,440	78.5	47.3	15,943	71.0
1935	289,588	1,387	75.2	51.0	8,288	30.4
1945	321,819	1,379	72.6	51.5	21,869	44.9

[1]In thousands of dollars

[2]Labrador not included

[3]Value in Newfoundland monetary pounds

Source: Statistics Canada, Census of Canada 1665–1871, Cat. no. 98-187-XIE, Series No. 130–1; Census of Newfoundland 1874, 1884, 1891, 1901, 1911, 1921, 1935, 1945.

A family stands outside a 'tilt' (shack) in Logy Bay, near St John's, around 1900. Because of the seasonal nature of the cod fishery, Newfoundlanders would spend the summer at temporary fishing settlements and move inland for the winter.
Provincial Archives of Newfoundland and Labrador, C2-37/NA-3698.

Not only did Newfoundland depend overwhelmingly on a single resource, but it depended on a single species of that resource: cod. The fact that the nature of the fishery promoted the expansion of small, isolated communities accessible only by water, which relied primarily on a seasonal resource, created a fundamental weakness in the Newfoundland economy: while codfish could be caught only during the few months when they came inshore to spawn, the people depending on cod for their livelihood needed to support themselves year-round.

There were other fisheries at other times of the year, but they were often in locations requiring considerable travel. For example, the seal fishery, which was active in late winter and in spring, when the ice floes served as the birthing grounds for seals, was located primarily on the northern coast of Newfoundland and off Labrador. At times of year when these important fisheries were not active, families survived by living off the land, hunting game, picking berries, and cultivating gardens for essential food supplies. As well, most families ran up debts for credit provided by the merchant fish buyers.

Cod fishers used hook and lines until 1865, when the invention of the cod trap made it possible to catch large quantities of fish without having to bait hooks. But while Newfoundland fishers became more efficient, the overall amount of fish and their export value remained more or less constant during the late nineteenth and early twentieth centuries, even though the population was continuing to increase. The result was diminished productivity. In short, there were too many fishers in small dories catching too few fish, a situation that left the population more and more marginalized. What the industry required were new technologies, like the cod trap, that would make it possible to catch more cod with fewer workers. Technological advances were affecting other staple industries at the time, such as farming on the prairies. However, these new technologies, if they could be found, would only push more fishers into unemployment in an isolated community dependent on fishing.

One factor contributing to the stagnation of fish products in the late nineteenth century was the decline of the seal fishery, which had played a much larger role in fish exports during the early to mid-1800s. Seal oil was the most valuable product of this industry, although the hides also had value. But as Hiller (2001) explains, seal oil, which had represented 84 per cent of the value of exported seal products in the late 1840s, represented just 54 per cent of seal products exported in the 1890s.

Both seal exports and the numbers of vessels involved in the seal hunt declined sharply in the mid-1800s. Much of the decline in this industry can be attributed to the lack of regulations governing the seal hunt, which led to over-exploitation. The decline in sailing vessels was related to a change in technology. Until the 1860s, the seal fishery used wooden sailing vessels sailing out of a variety of communities: most of these, including St John's, were located on the eastern coast of the Avalon peninsula, but there were other communities involved in the seal hunt on Conception Bay, such as Brigus, Harbour Grace, and Carbonear, and on Bonavista Bay, such as Greenspond, Brookfield, and Wesleyville. When the sailing vessels were replaced by large steamers, the number of communities taking part in the fishery dropped sharply. Hiller (2001), for example, notes that 'Harbour Grace in Conception Bay had sent 58 schooners and 2,400 men sealing in 1868; 18 years later it sent no sailing vessels at all.' As a result, investment and employment became concentrated in larger centres like St John's.

The sealing industry was largely unregulated until the mid-1800s, when the Newfoundland government began limiting sailing dates and banning second trips. Unfortunately for the workers, reducing the size of the catch did not increase its value. Demand for seal oil dwindled as kerosene and other petroleum products came into use, and seal pelts had plenty of competition from other hides available on the market.

Newfoundland also faced other economic woes at the end of the nineteenth century. St John's, where most of the buildings were constructed of wood, was prone to fire. After serious fires in 1817, 1819, 1846, in 1892 nearly 80 per cent of the city was incinerated, and rebuilding was expensive. Two years later, the over-extension of credit to fishers by St John's merchants caused a bank crash that led to devaluation of the currency and the failure of many businesses.

Newfoundland politicians recognized the need for diversification into land-based industries such as mining and forestry. But they knew this would require considerable investment in land-based transportation systems. Much of this investment, like the capital required to open mines and build pulp mills, came mainly from private corporations outside Newfoundland. These companies were able to negotiate favourable economic terms that allowed them to harvest most of the profits, leaving only a small portion of revenues for Newfoundland itself.

Some roads had been built by the mid-1800s, but the largest enterprise, from both a financial and a logistical standpoint, was the construction of an 882-kilometre railway line from St John's to Port aux Basques, on the southwestern corner of the island. With its branch lines, the Newfoundland Railway comprised more than over 1,400 kilometres of track. Although initially financed by private investors, the project received considerable government assistance. Construction was very slow: beginning in 1881, it took nine years for construction to move beyond the Avalon Peninsula, and the line did not reach Port aux Basques until 1898.

The financial drain of the railway did not end with its construction: running it was another burden. Because it was narrow-gauge, cars that ran on it were not compatible with tracks in Canada and the United States. Narrow gauge also meant a smaller carrying capacity, which increased the cost of shipping goods (Cuff, 2001). By 1921 freight rates on the Newfoundland Railway were roughly ten times those on the CPR. The government's decision to buy out the railway in 1923 only added to its financial stress. The railway did benefit the colony in several ways. Linking the main population centres on the Avalon Peninsula to the western portion of the island certainly contributed to population increases in that region. The railway was also instrumental in opening up the mining and forest industries, helping to create employment in industries other than the fishery.

Some mining had begun on the northeastern coast of Newfoundland even without a railway. For example, there were copper and even gold mines in locations such as Tilt Cove, Terra Nova, Bett's Cove, Little Bay, and Pilley's Island. But these mines, some of which had been in operation since the 1860s, had for the most part shut down by the early 1900s (Rennie, 1998). The railway made it possible to open up other mines, such as the one on Bell Island, which between 1895 and 1966 supplied iron ore for steel mills in Sydney, Nova Scotia, as well as mills in Germany and the United States. In 1927 the rich deposits of lead, zinc, copper, gold, and silver ore led to the establishment of the company town of Buchans to house the miners. In 1933 a fluorspar (used mainly in aluminium production) mine opened at St Lawrence on the Burin Peninsula. Mines like these did provide employment, but they offered little in the way of royalties, taxes, or other benefits to Newfoundland's economy. Workers at the Bell Island mines were hired only for six months at a time, so that the company avoided paying benefits; thus employment in the colony continued to be largely seasonal.

As in the mining industry, there were sawmills operating in Newfoundland prior to the construction of the railway, but most served only local builders. The railway was essential for opening up the forest industry for export markets. The Anglo Newfoundland Development Company built a pulp and paper mill at Grand Falls in 1909, and in 1925 another major pulp and paper operation opened at Corner Brook. With these new pulp mills came the demand for energy, leading to the construction of several hydro dams that generated electricity for both industrial and residential users. In this sector too, the colony basically gave away the rights to the resource and received few benefits in return.

Meanwhile, the railway had devastating consequences for the island's Mi'kmaq, bringing settlers, forest workers, and hunters to the interior and giving them access to the caribou herds on which the Mi'kmaq depended. Ralph Pastore (1998) suggests that caribou stocks declined from perhaps 300,000 in 1900 to near-extinction by 1930.

During the First World War, Newfoundland was generous in its support for Britain, supplying and funding more than 5,000 soldiers. Nearly 1,500 troops died and many more were wounded. Beyond the human cost was the financial cost of supporting the returned soldiers. By 1929 the colony's debt was $87.7 million—eight times its annual income. The value of exported codfish, which had reached a wartime peak of $25 million per annum, had fallen to just $12 million per annum (Chadwick, 1967: 154). These were disastrous conditions on the eve of the Great Depression, and they led to a major economic crisis. Debts continued to mount, while demand for Newfoundland's staple exports was declining. Worldwide protectionism made trade even more difficult, and the 'new' industries such as pulp and paper and mining paid no direct taxes.

In 1934 Newfoundland declared bankruptcy, forcing Britain to govern the colony by Commission. The move was a disappointment for many, but it underscored the need for Newfoundland to restructure its economy. The Commission introduced changes to the civil service and to the tariff structure. It also looked for ways to modernize the fishing industry and established a Fisheries Board to improve trading arrangements. It also tried to encourage unemployed Newfoundlanders to take up farming—an effort that had limited success among people who had traditionally lived by the sea.

When the Commission of Government was instituted, few could have anticipated the military role that would be foisted onto Newfoundland in 1939. The time–space convergence that came with the introduction of long-range bombers and submarines made the island a critical site for Britain, Canada, and the United States. Accordingly, two major naval bases were established (at St John's and Argentia) along with five airports, including one in Gander (the largest of the five) and one in Goose Bay, Labrador.

The employment that the war brought to Newfoundland provided an economic boost that continued after the war. As Table 8.2 (p. 238 above) indicates, dependence on fish declined significantly during this time; by 1949 fish products accounted for only 31.2 per cent of the total value of exports (Statistics Canada, n.d.). Forest products and minerals were becoming more important, and with the increased price of staples during the war years and after, the Commission of Government managed to pay off the colony's debts and slowly began accumulating a surplus.

Canada's Tenth Province: From 1949 to the 1990s

The Commission's work had carried on much longer than expected, and now that the colony had emerged from its financial crisis, Britain was ready to give Newfoundlanders a voice in determining how they would be governed. Having experienced a period of prosperity unlike any in their history, Newfoundlanders wanted to continue improving their standard of living. However, it was estimated that the colony required $100 million for economic development, infrastructure improvements, and health and social improvements (Hiller, 1998: 18). Britain itself was in difficult financial straits as a result of the war, and, with no capital to spare, was keen to see Newfoundland either go on its own or join Canada.

The first referendum to decide the future of Newfoundland was held on 3 June 1948. The ballot presented voters with three options:

1. continue with a Commission of Government;
2. return to responsible government; or
3. enter Confederation as Canada's tenth province.

The Confederation option was put on the ballot by Britain in a move that many Newfoundlanders considered manipulative. The first ballot favoured responsible government, but not by a majority, making a second ballot—with the least popular option removed—necessary.

Table 8.3 indicates the narrow margins in both cases. Votes split along geographic lines, as Newfoundlanders in the peripheral outports largely supported Confederation, while most urban voters, concentrated on the Avalon peninsula, opposed the idea. With the majority voting in favour of union with Canada, Joey Smallwood, the champion of the Confederation option, became the first premier of Canada's newest province.

The Commission had left Newfoundland with a surplus of more than $40 million (Summers, 1985: 1252). This sum, combined with generous transfer payments from a federal government eager to make a good impression, gave Newfoundland plenty of money to invest in hospitals, schools, road building, and electrification. Even the debt-ridden Newfoundland Railway was removed from the province's budget, when it was taken over by the Canadian National Railway. Through monthly family allowance and old-age pension cheques, Canada also put cash into the hands of individual Newfoundlanders, many of whom, with little disposable income prior to Confederation, had been accustomed to trading fish for such basic supplies as flour and sugar. These were among the immediate benefits of Confederation, and they helped to keep Smallwood in the premier's office for 23 years, from 1949 to 1972.

But for many Newfoundlanders Confederation's disadvantages outweighed its benefits. The economic mainstays of Newfoundland's economy prior to 1949 had been import duties and the fishing industry. The terms of Confederation, however, dictated that international trade and oceans were a federal responsibility. Consequently, it was Ottawa that received the revenues from any taxes levied on the imported goods. Furthermore, the federal control over oceans meant that Ottawa rather than St John's was in charge of managing the fishery. Not understanding the external forces at play, Ottawa did not consider the cod fishery a priority, and it suffered as a result.

The population of Newfoundland, which had risen slowly through 1945, experienced a marked increase of over 200,000 people in the 26 years between 1945 and 1971—a sign of better economic times ahead (see Table 8.4). This was a relatively prosperous time for Newfoundland, and its economy was diversifying.

As the demand for aluminum increased, the fluorspar mines at St Lawrence boomed. Meanwhile, asbestos was discovered at Baie Verte, on the eastern side of the Verte Peninsula, and a mine was in operation by 1955, while the old Bell Island mines, not far from St John's, continued to produce iron ore until 1966. By far the largest mining and resource investments, however, went to Labrador, where iron ore, needed to produce the steel required for an expanding auto industry and industrialization generally, was in high demand. The North Shore and Labrador Railway, completed in 1954, ran through the western portion of Labrador and linked the iron ore mines of Schefferville, Quebec (on the Labrador border) to Sept-Îles. In 1956 one of the richest iron ore deposits in the world was discovered in the Carol Lake region of Labrador. The Iron Ore Company of Canada established a concentrator and pelletizer plant, and the new community of Labrador City was incorporated nearby in 1961. Wabush mines, only 5 kilometres away, set up a similar plant, and the community of Wabush was incorporated in 1969.

These were not the only resource investments in Labrador. The iron ore mines required energy, and initially this was supplied by the Twin Falls hydroelectric project, situated on a tributary of the Churchill River, which supplied 225 megawatts of electricity (Churchill Falls Labrador Corporation). The Twin Falls plant was closed in 1974, and its reservoir was combined with the enormous Smallwood Reservoir. The much larger project was based at

Table 8.3   Referendum results (%), 1948

	Responsible government	Confederation	Commission government
3 June 1948	44.6	41.1	14.3
22 July	47.7	52.3	

Source: J.K. Hiller, *Confederation: Deciding Newfoundland's Future 1934 to 1949* (St John's: Newfoundland Historical Society, 1998), 54.

Table 8.4   Newfoundland population (× 1,000), 1901–1991

Year	Population	Year	Population
1901	221.0	1951	361.4
1911	242.6	1961	457.9
1921	263.0	1971	522.1
1935	289.6	1981	567.2
1945	321.8	1991	568.5

Sources: Statistics Canada, Census of Canada, Historical Statistics of Canada, Cat. no. 11-516-XIE, Series A2-14; CANSIM Table 051-0001; Newfoundland and Labrador Census 1901–45.

Churchill Falls in south central Labrador, which began producing electricity in 1971; by the time its eight generators were in place, in 1974, it had the capacity to generate over 5,000 megawatts of electricity.

The concept of 'mega-projects' like Churchill Falls was not unique to Newfoundland and Labrador. Provincial governments across Canada, often with the assistance of federal government programs (such as grants from the Department of Regional Economic Expansion, or DREE), firmly believed that attracting corporate investment (often foreign) was the path to industrialization, modernization, employment, and security. Premier Smallwood's Liberal government, with its new connections in Ottawa, vigorously pursued resource exploitation throughout Newfoundland and Labrador as a means of industrializing, modernizing, and diversifying the economy. Unfortunately, Smallwood was not unlike earlier Newfoundland leaders who had given away rights to resources (for instance, forest tenures and mineral rights) or had squandered government funds on unprofitable ventures (such as the Newfoundland Railway); in fact, he did

The infamous oil refinery at Come-By-Chance was one of the boondoggles that led to the fall of Premier Joey Smallwood's government. *Photo by Brett McGillivray.*

both. Among the disastrous industrialization schemes for which he has been blamed were a failed linerboard manufacturing plant at Stephenville, a failed oil refinery at Come By Chance, and long-term contracts in which he essentially gave away the hydroelectricity revenues from Churchill Falls.

The linerboard plant appeared to be a good idea in 1967. The raw material (wood) would come from the Happy Valley–Goose Bay area, generating forestry jobs in that region of Labrador. The wood would then be manufactured into the sheets of paper containing cardboard corrugations at Stephenville, providing much needed employment for that area as well. But cost overruns more than doubled the initial estimated cost of $53 million for the plant (Reid, 2002). The government took over the mill, but a serious downturn in linerboard prices in the mid-1970s, together with a major strike, forced the plant to close in 1977.

Come By Chance, located at the end of Placentia Bay, was the site of another Smallwood mega-project. In 1968 John Shaheen, an American industrialist, acquired the contract to construct an oil refinery at Come By Chance. The goal was to produce 100,000 barrels of oil per day and a whole range of petroleum products from jet fuel to asphalt. The provincial government bankrolled the construction of wharf facilities and offered loan guarantees. The grand opening of the refinery in 1973 was a story in itself, as Shaheen rented an ocean liner, the *Queen Elizabeth II*, to accommodate the invited guests. Unfortunately, structural problems meant that the refinery could not produce the high-end fuels, and the Shaheen interests were reluctant to spend millions of dollars on reconstruction. These problems coincided with the world energy crisis, which increased uncertainty with respect to price and supply of crude oil. By 1976 Come By Chance had become a financial disaster, 'the largest bankruptcy in Canadian history' (Memorial University, n.d.).

Churchill Falls became home to a massive hydroelectric project at a time when the American market was eager to import electricity from Canada. However, in order to serve this market, high-capacity transmission lines would have to be extended to the US across the province of Quebec. For a number of reasons, including a longstanding grievance concerning the 1927 ruling on the Labrador boundary, Quebec objected to this plan. In 1969 a long-term agreement was negotiated to allow Quebec to purchase power from the Churchill Falls plant for its own increasing provincial demands and sell the surplus to the United States. In addition to setting a favourable rate for the electricity, the agreement stipulated that the price was to remain fixed for 65 years. Quebec ended up profiting greatly from this arrangement when energy prices soared in the 1980s. As Jeffrey Simpson commented in *The Globe and Mail*, 'The deal might have been fair when signed, but when world energy prices skyrocketed, Quebec kept buying Newfoundland power for a pittance, as provided in the original contract, and then resold for a king's ransom' (2003: A25).

Another project with disastrous consequences was Smallwood's 'resettlement' scheme. Providing services such as health care, education, electricity, and roads to Newfoundland's widely dispersed population was an enormous and costly challenge. Consequently the premier proposed closing down many small, isolated outports and relocating their inhabitants in larger, more central communities.

There were two resettlement plans, both of which were divisive for the targeted communities. Under the first relocation plan, every family that relocated would receive a financial incentive of $2,000—but all members of the community had to agree to the move. Needless to say, this condition pitted neighbour against neighbour. Nevertheless, between 1954 and 1965 approximately 8,000 people were moved from 110 communities.

The second resettlement program began in 1965 and was sponsored jointly by the provincial and federal governments. This time, larger centres were identified as destinations for those to be relocated, and just 90 per cent of the residents of an outpost had to agree to resettlement (this figure was lowered to 80 per cent in 1966), and the head of each family received a moving grant of $1,000, plus $200 for each additional family member. Between 1965 and 1970, another 116 communities were closed and 3,242 families relocated.

When the Smallwood era ended, the incoming Conservative government (1972–89) inherited the tasks not only of resolving the financial troubles at Stephenville and Come By Chance, but of establishing a new economic direction for the province. In 1977 the government closed the linerboard plant, though it encouraged new investment in the existing facility. In 1981 the plant was taken over by Abitibi Price, which retooled the facility and converted it into Newfoundland's third bleached Kraft and newsprint mill.

It took longer to bring the Come By Chance oil refinery out of mothballs. Petro-Canada, a federal Crown corporation, acquired the refinery in 1980 but decided that it was not worth reactivating. Plans to demolish the enormous structure were cancelled in 1986, when a Bermuda-based company, Newfoundland Energy Ltd, offered to buy the

Resettlement was not always a simple matter of packing up the family's belongings and moving to a new community. The house in this photo was floated from Fox Island to Bonavista Bay, where it stayed moored until the tide rose and it could be hauled ashore.   *Photo by B. Brooks, Library and Archives Canada, PA-154123.*

refinery and its equipment for the grand total of $1. Reopened a year later, the refinery created much needed employment opportunities.

Meanwhile a number of mines were forced to shut down. The long-productive Bell Island iron ore mines closed in 1966, and twelve years later Alcan closed the fluorspar mine at St Lawrence as a result of foreign competition and declining prices. The asbestos mines at Baie Verte fared no better and were finally forced to close in 1990 because of the health risks associated with asbestos. During the 1970s and 1980s, the federal government began to take an interest in the potential for offshore oil and natural gas in the Atlantic region. There had been earlier exploration off the shores of Newfoundland, but the energy crisis of the 1970s and widespread fear of a looming petroleum shortage spurred the government to provide generous concessions to promote gas and oil exploration. As a result, the Hibernia oil field was discovered in 1979, followed by Hebron in 1981, Ben Nevis in 1982, and Terra Nova in 1984. With these discoveries came dreams of Newfoundland becoming 'the Alberta of the east'.

There were setbacks, however. The loss of 84 crewmembers of the Ocean Ranger, a floating oil rig platform, in February 1982 was a tragic blow. Another setback was of a political nature. The Newfoundland government, in a bid to wrest control of the offshore oil reserves from the hands of the federal government, went all the way to the Supreme Court for a decision on ownership of the ocean floor. In 1984 the court ruled in favour of Ottawa. But although this decision represented a loss for Newfoundland and Labrador, the province gained an important concession from the federal government in the Atlantic Accord, a plan for revenue sharing.

By 1989 Newfoundlanders were again ready for a political change, and the Liberals were returned to power in the provincial election that year. In many ways, the population statistics for the census years 1981 to 1991 (Table 8.4, p. 243) tell the tale: high unemployment, significant out-migration, and slowing population growth all indicated that the economy was not doing well. For the newly elected Liberals, a crisis of major proportions was looming. The industry that had been the lifeblood of Newfoundland and Labrador had been so abused and mismanaged over time that in 1992 it had to close down.

The Cod Fishery: From the 1940s to the Present

The history of Newfoundland and Labrador is inseparable from that of the cod fishery. Traditionally, the cod fishery had operated out of small outport communities: the cod were caught when they came inshore to spawn by fishers working in small boats, then cleaned, dried, salted, and exported around the world. Several factors brought this way of life to an end in the second half of the twentieth century. Offshore vessels, using dragger technology, became larger and more efficient; fewer cod came inshore to spawn; freezing (rather than salting) became the preferred method of preserving the catch; and the market narrowed primarily to the United States. The management of the ocean, its fish stocks, and the industry as a whole shifted to the federal government, according to the terms of Confederation.

Steam-powered fishing trawlers—mainly of European origin—dragging large nets over the bottom of the Grand Banks were already common before the First World War, and steam gave way to diesel power during the 1930s. By the 1960s, these foreign trawlers had become larger, more numerous, and much more sophisticated, with technological gadgetry, including radar, fish finders, and satellite navigation, that enabled them to fish at greater depths and to operate year round, and they were often accompanied by factory freezer ships, where the catch could be processed and preserved immediately. As the offshore industry became more sophisticated, inevitably the inshore cod catch began to decline. As Harris (1998: 65) explains, 'Between 1956, when the first factory-freezer arrived on the Grand Banks, and 1977, when Canada's 200-mile limit closed the barn door after the horse was gone, inshore cod catches in Newfoundland plummeted by two-thirds.' William Warner points to 1974 as the turning point, explaining that 'In that year alone 1,076 Western European and Communist-bloc fishing vessels swarmed across the Atlantic to fish North American waters. Their catch of 2,176,000 tons was ten times the New England and triple the Canadian Atlantic catch' (1983: 58). The demise of the cod stocks meant that Newfoundland fishers increasingly came to depend on unemployment insurance.

Fish are a renewable resource, but they are also highly mobile, and governments have no authority to control the behaviour of fishers outside their jurisdiction. These realities make fish one of the most difficult resources to manage. In the case of the Atlantic cod, a large part of the problem was that there was no way to curb the increased intensity of fishing in the international waters of the North American continental shelf. The International Commission of the North Atlantic Fisheries (ICNAF) had been formed in 1949 to monitor catches, collect scientific data on fish stocks, set mesh sizes for nets, and, beginning in the 1970s, establish Total Allowable Catch (TAC) limits on certain species, including cod and haddock. Unfortunately, the ICNAF was only an advisory body, with the authority to recommend regulatory measures but no power to enforce them (Blake, n.d.).

Protecting the 3-mile limit to territorial waters had been a problem for many maritime nations, and following the Second World War a number of them had unilaterally extended their control over adjacent waters to protect their offshore interests in oil and fish, and to prevent pollution. Canada was relatively slow to extend its boundary, declaring a 9-mile limit in 1964 and extending it to 12 miles in 1970. Since this did little to control the extensive fishing off the Grand Banks, in 1977 Canada finally declared a 200-nautical mile (322 km) territory. These boundary lines are shown in Figure 8.4.

Even the 200-mile limit, however, did not guarantee that fish stocks could be saved; in this as well as other matters the federal government did not appear to understand the complexities of fisheries management. The difficulties facing Ottawa were compounded by tensions with the governments of the Atlantic provinces. As the 'gatekeeper' of this resource, the federal government controlled the licensing of vessels as well as the openings and closings of the fisheries, but the provincial governments controlled the processing plants. This arrangement led to some nasty confrontations between the two levels of government. For example, the provincial government would issue a licence and often assist in building a new processing plant, thereby setting up expectations of much needed employment opportunities. But if Ottawa cut back on openings, the catch would be reduced and local members of Parliament would take the blame for the loss of the expected jobs and run the risk of losing their seats (Harris, 1998: 70).

The establishment of the 200-mile limit raised hopes that much of the catch formerly taken by foreign fleets would now go to Canadian fishers, and the federal and provincial governments (mainly that of Nova Scotia) encouraged the building of a fleet of large trawlers. There were similar hopes for Newfoundland's inshore fishery, reflected in the increase of registered inshore fishers from 13,736 in 1975 to 33,640 in 1980 (Harris, 1998: 69). New fish processing plants were built in preparation for the anticipated bounty.

In fact, the Canadian catch of codfish did increase after 1977, but only in the short run. In the first two years after the 200-mile line was established, Canada's share of the catch increased by more than 21 per cent, accounting for 73 per cent of the international total. In Newfoundland and Labrador, the total catch increased by 27 per cent in the four years following the establishment of the new boundary. Over the same period, this upturn brought increases in both the fishers (41 per cent) and registered

Figure 8.4   Canada's offshore Atlantic territory

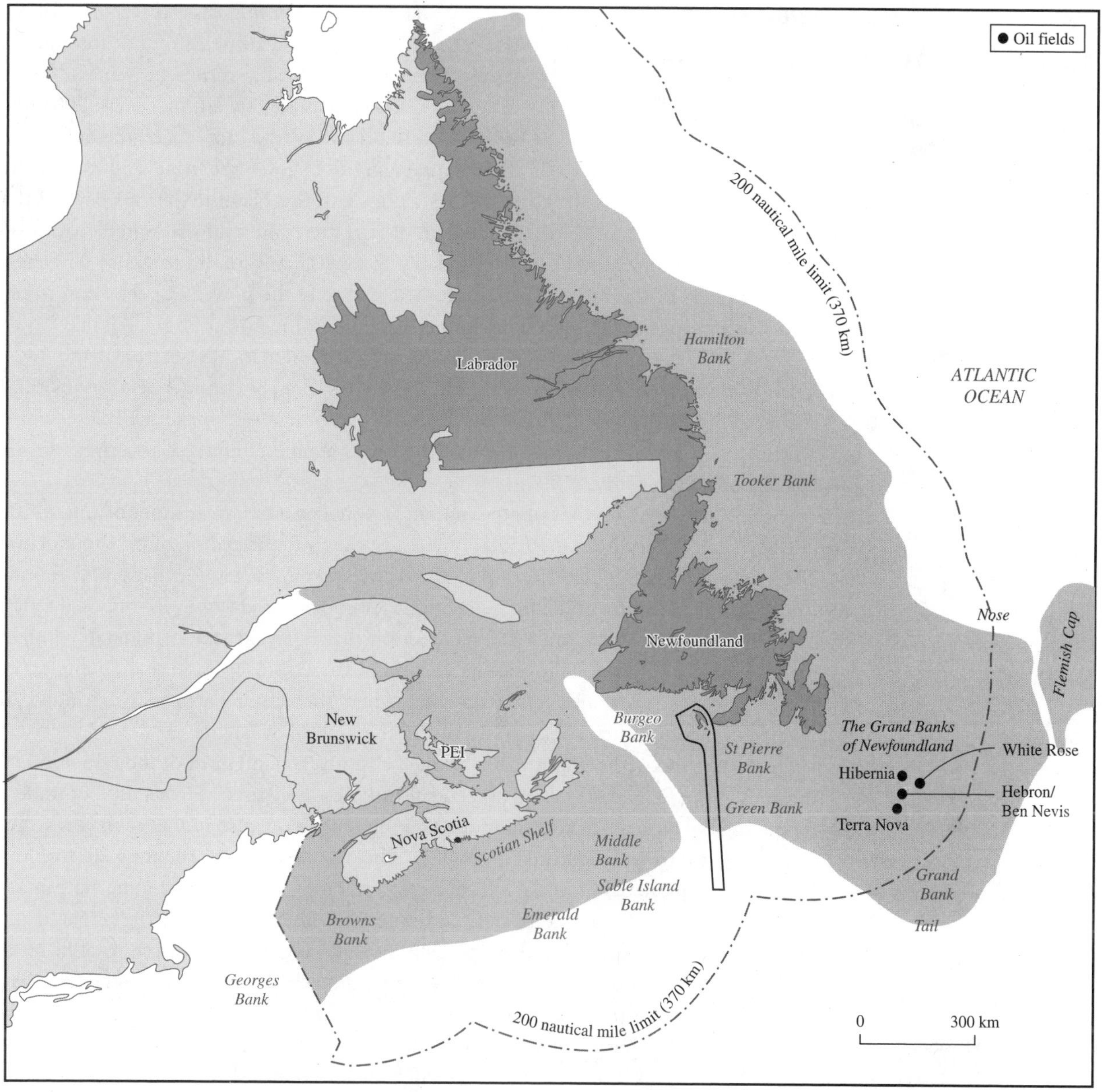

Source: Adapted from P.M. Saunders, 'Policy Options for the Management and Conservation of Straddling Fisheries Resources' (paper prepared for the Royal Commission on Renewing and Strengthening our Place in Canada, 2003) ⟨http://www.gov.nf.ca/publicat/royalcomm/research/Saunders.pdf⟩.

vessels (23 per cent) participating in the Newfoundland fishery (Blake, n.d.). Table 8.5 shows the Canadian catch of Atlantic groundfish for selected years from 1978 to 1992.

The real issue, which ultimately brought the industry to the point of crisis, was the continued harvest of groundfish, including cod, beyond their sustainable limits off the coasts of Newfoundland and Labrador. Neither Canada nor the new North Atlantic Fisheries Organization (NAFO), which replaced the ICNAF, addressed this issue seriously. Certainly scientists issued warnings, but these were either ignored or disbelieved. In fact, the federal government sped up the demise of its own fishery by giving foreign fleets

Table 8.5   Canadian catch of cod and other groundfish (× 1,000 tonnes), 1978–1992

Species	1978	1982	1986	1988	1990	1992
northern cod	102	211	207	245	188	21
other cod	169	297	268	216	196	162
other groundfish	264	267	273	227	220	225
total catch	535	775	748	688	604	418

Source: Department of Fisheries and Oceans (http://www.dfo-mpo.gc.ca).

permission to fish within the 200-mile limit. The conflicts were many and inevitable, pitting inshore versus offshore fishers, foreign versus Canadian vessels, and community processing plants versus federal government quotas.

Even if Canada had strictly enforced its 200-mile jurisdiction, this boundary did not cover the whole of the fishery. As Figure 8.4 shows, the 'nose' and 'tail' of the Grand Banks along with the Flemish Cap are beyond the 200-mile limit. It is in these international waters that NAFO set TAC quotas for its members. Regrettably, for NAFO and for Canada, not all fishers were members of the organization, and NAFO had only the power of persuasion to restrict the activities of the many vessels operating under the power of greed. Table 8.6 illustrates how even NAFO members consistently and dramatically exceeded the TACs. Mark Kurlansky comments on this trend: 'Fishermen rarely consider regulations their responsibility. As they see it, that is the duty of government—to make the rules—and it is their duty to navigate through them. If the stocks are not conserved, government mismanagement is to blame' (1997: 171).

On 2 July 1992 the federal government announced a two-year moratorium on the northern cod fishery from the Labrador coast to the southeastern tip of Newfoundland. This was a devastating blow for the province, overturning what, for many Newfoundlanders, had been a way of life for generations. Although the closure was supposed to last only two years, there was a general recognition that it would take considerably longer for the cod stocks to return to acceptable levels. Concerns over the size and duration of the moratorium grew the following year, when the closure area was expanded to include Newfoundland's southern shore and the Gulf of St Lawrence.

Needless to say, the moratorium sparked controversy, and most of the criticism was directed at the federal government. Federal fisheries biologists were accused of underestimating the biomass of codfish in the sampling technique used to set each year's TAC. According to Tony Leighton (1993: 32), 'The TAC was set at roughly 20% of the "estimated exploitable biomass". As it turns out, biologists were operating with inaccurate information, using collection and sampling methods that overrepresented the real stocks. Fishing fleets may have actually been taking 45–50% of the total biomass (the weight of all cod in the system).' Compounding these problems was the fact that, since the mid-1980s, the size of the cod being caught had been decreasing, but this had not been noted. Consequently, not only were the biomass estimates inaccurate, but they were based on the biomass of what were for the most part immature cod (between the ages of 4 and 7, before they begin to reproduce). As Gillmor (1993: 38) explains, 'We are, in essence, eating away the biological capital of the cod stock, no longer living off the interest.'

With the moratorium on cod, fishers turned to other species such as capelin and turbot. These fish, however, were part of the diet of the remaining cod. This led to further disaster, since cod become cannibalistic when their food supplies are reduced (Harris, 1998: 194). At the same time, pressure from environmentalists led governments to impose drastic restrictions on the seal hunt. Yet another hit to the economy of

Table 8.6   European Community's NAFO quotas versus actual catch,[1] 1986–1991

Year	Quotas	Catch
1986	25,665	172,163
1987	23,170	140,842
1988	19,010	85,353
1989	15,155	93,476
1990	15,377	97,750
1991	20,049	58,350

[1]Tonnes of northern cod and other groundfish

Source: M. Clugston, 'Sky Patrols over the Grand Banks', in Leighton (1993), 48.

Newfoundland, this move also contributed to the demise of the cod fishery, since seals eat cod, among other fish species. Species do not live in isolation; they are part of complex **food webs** in an ecosystem, and efforts to manage the population of one species always has implications for other species sharing the ecosystem.

Restoring groundfish stocks to acceptable levels may require governments to place restrictions on the kinds of equipment used for fishing. For instance, dragger technology—dragging heavy nets along the ocean floor—has been shown to 'churn up the seafloor and destroy the plants and small animals essential for healthy marine life' (Myers, 1992: 22). At the same time dragger technology 'pulls huge volumes of unwanted species—known as "by-catch"—along with the preferred catch. Trawlers looking for shrimp, for example, will commonly catch nine pounds of other species, including baby cod, for each pound of shrimp. The bycatch is thrown back into sea, dead' (Leighton, 1993: 32). In short, dragger technology leaves fish with no place to hide, and is not compatible with a sustainable fishery.

Banning dragger technology and going back to long lining and cod traps is just one of the suggestions that have been made to address concerns over diminishing groundfish stocks. Another is to convert this common property resource into a private property resource through a quota system that would be allocated by vessel or by community (Myers, 1992). Others have recommended that Canada extend its jurisdiction beyond the 200-mile boundary to include the entire continental shelf. All these suggestions are predicated on the assumption that the cod stocks will recover to a point where they can once again be fished; the truth is that they may not.

The demise of the groundfishery is only one side of the story; the other is what happened to the people of Newfoundland and Labrador who had depended on it. Following its imposition of the moratorium in 1992, the federal government made funds available to offset the loss of income due to the closure. When the federal government realized that the moratorium was not going to be a short-term measure, a new $1.9 billion program was launched in 1994. Administered by Human Resources Development Canada and the Department of Fisheries and Oceans in collaboration with the provincial government, The Atlantic Groundfish Strategy, or TAGS, had a number of objectives, among them:

1. retraining in such areas as adult basic education, literacy, and entrepreneurial skills;
2. income support;
3. relocation for employment opportunities;
4. early retirement with benefits for those aged 55 to 64; and
5. retirement of groundfish licences through buyouts.

Approximately 40,000 people, most of them fishers and fish processors, were displaced by the moratorium. Some 22,530 residents of Newfoundland and Labrador—nearly 70 per cent of all those who qualified throughout the Atlantic region—applied for assistance through the TAGS program (Government of Newfoundland, 1997: 6). Of the applicants, of whom approximately two-thirds were male, only 30 per cent had grade 12 education and even fewer (10 per cent) had other skills training. (1997: 6). The TAGS program ended in 1998, when all the money ran out; it was replaced by a $750 million federal support program, which was designed to help not just the Atlantic fishery but the ailing West Coast salmon fishery also.

food web
a system of interlocking and interdependent food chains.

Table 8.7   Newfoundland and Labrador fish harvest (tonnes) and value (×1,000), 1990–2004

| Year | Volume (tonnes) | | Value of groundfish | Pelagic | | Shellfish | | Total wild fish | |
	cod	Total groundfish		volume	value	volume	value	volume	value
1990	245,654	336,560	134,600	160,424	29,937	47,259	78,253	544,243	283,449
1991	179,570	270,868	148,913	105,130	20,518	48,948	88,888	424,945	258,319
1992	75,123	156,199	85,049	69,770	12,822	57,320	93,924	283,289	191,794
1993	37,068	97,650	50,882	80,108	26,404	67,060	118,429	244,818	195,714
1994	2,285	35,370	19,177	23,182	6,309	78,524	196,973	137,076	222,459
1995	914	22,182	19,866	25,004	5,917	91,407	313,559	138,594	339,343
1996	1,147	27,542	27,184	53,491	13,339	108,562	233,539	195,347	289,759
1997	12,317	39,335	34,093	44,040	11,757	131,313	260,688	220,287	325,530
1998	22,764	51,666	60,368	62,894	15,379	145,893	299,932	265,052	386,255
1999	38,663	68,078	84,173	40,524	11,815	162,950	424,800	276,456	533,044
2000	30,216	69,109	74,706	42,913	11,890	162,961	490,839	278,141	584,319
2001	23,774	67,421	68,465	46,242	9,617	152,368	431,169	267,959	519,027
2002	21,079	60,107	62,298	50,200	13,365	163,799	440,337	274,936	535,664
2003	14,290	58,539	63,261	71,884	15,790	178,123	455,874	308,547	534,925
2004	14,521	51,677	52,100	97,858	24,433	206,940	517,618	356,201	594,151

Source: Fisheries and Oceans Canada (http://www.dfo-mpo.gc.ca).

Was the program successful? Certainly some Newfoundlanders and others through-out the Atlantic region benefited from retraining, new job opportunities, early retire-ment, and supplements to their meagre incomes. Michael Harris (1998: 203) suggests that there were plenty of inefficiencies in the program. Few people (just over 7,000) actually signed up for retraining, and even fewer relocated. The number of groundfish licences bought out was relatively small, translating into only a small reduction in the capacity for groundfish harvesting.

Since the implementation of the moratorium, which has continued uninterrupted except for a short opening prior to the 1997 federal election, the fishing industry of Newfoundland and Labrador has undergone dramatic changes. Table 8.7 breaks down the various species of fish caught and the values gained.

Codfish catches are a fraction of what they were before the moratorium. Pelagic fish (mainly herring, mackerel, and capelin in Newfoundland) are caught in consider-able quantity but do not command a high price per kilogram. The most significant change has been in the volume and value of shellfish catches. The sum of these changes has been a dramatic decline in the overall volume of catch but only a short-term decline in value of the catch. In addition, the fact that the number of fishing licences issued for shellfish is much lower than the number of groundfish licences issued has resulted in a shift in the distribution of income, as far more dollars are concentrated in the hands of far fewer fishers (see Table 8.8). Figure 8.5 presents graphically the change in volume of fish caught, and the graph in Figure 8.6 indicates how the value of the commercial har-vest has grown since 1990.

Table 8.9 confirms the trend toward fewer fishers and fewer vessels. One reason for this trend is the introduction of 'non-core' licences that were not transferable; the hope was that many of these would disappear upon buyout or retirement. However, as Table 8.9 also shows, this policy has recently changed, leading to a modest increase in licences and mid-sized vessels. A report published by the Department of Fisheries and Oceans in May 2002, entitled *Evaluation of the Canadian Fisheries Adjustment and Restructuring*

Table 8.8   Licences by fishery, 1990–2002

	1990	1991	1992	1993	1994	1995	1996
Groundfish	9,871	9,447	9,202	7,269	7,255	7,029	6,747
Pelagic	10,181	7,400	7,458	7,472	9,229	9,376	9,411
Shellfish	6,686	8,853	7,679	7,920	8,907	8,671	8,902
Total	26,738	28,292	24,339	22,661	24,197	23,892	23,834
	1997	**1998**	**1999**	**2000**	**2001**	**2002**	
Groundfish	6,682	6,680	5,323	5,039	4,714	4,693	
Pelagic	8,396	8,367	7,009	6,678	6,384	6,491	
Shellfish	10,154	9,139	8,317	8,042	7,701	7,695	
Total	24,169	24,186	20,649	19,759	18,799	18,879	

Source: Fisheries and Oceans Canada (http://www.dfo-mpo.gc.ca).

Program Licence Retirement Programs, states that the number of groundfish licences issued since 1992 has fallen by 50 per cent, from 9,441 to 4,681. The number of non-groundfish licences has also decreased, owing largely to the policy of retiring licences: lobster licences are down by 35 per cent, capelin licences by 44 per cent, and herring by 32 per cent. For those fishers with licenses to harvest shrimp and crab, the potential for wealth is great; but the number of licences that have been bought out suggests that many other people are now unemployed and have lost a way of life.

Figure 8.5   Volume of commercial fish, Newfoundland and Labrador, 1990–2003

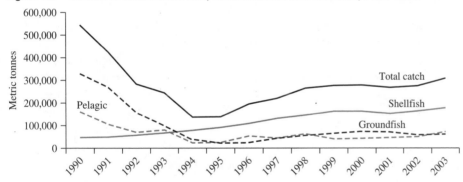

Source: Fisheries and Oceans Canada, (http://www.dfo-mpo.gc.ca).

Figure 8.6   Value of commercial fish, Newfoundland and Labrador, 1990–2003

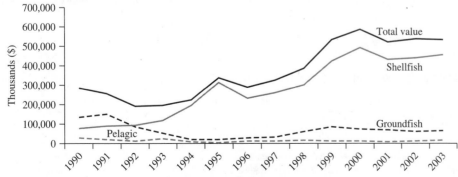

Source: Fisheries and Oceans Canada (http://www.dfo-mpo.gc.ca).

Table 8.9   Licensed fishers and vessels, Newfoundland and Labrador, 1996–2002

	1996	1997	1998	1999	2000	2001	2002
Fishers							
Core	5,359	5,445	5,488	4,514	4,271	4,057	4,154
Non-core	12,251	7,849	8,778	8,403	9,831	10,328	11,161
Total	17,610	13,294	14,266	12,917	14,102	14,385	15,315
Vessels							
<35 ft	10,659	10,357	10,245	8,605	8,219	7,693	7,640
35–100 ft	949	962	971	986	466	993	1,562
>100 ft	28	23	21	22	24	26	25
Total	11,636	11,342	11,237	9,613	8,709	8,712	9,227

Source: Fisheries and Oceans Canada ⟨http://www.dfo-mpo.gc.ca⟩.

In a more recent report, entitled *The Fish Processing Policy Review Commission* (4 Feb. 2004), Eric Donne identifies a number of persisting problems, including the fact that 'two species, crab and shrimp, now account for over 75% of the total earnings from harvesting' (p. I). Donne's report also shows that the number of active facilities within the processing sector declined from 221 in 1990 to just 122 in 2003, leading to a 42 per cent drop in employment (p. I). Equally disturbing were income levels: between 1990 and 2001 the average annual income declined by 4 per cent to just $10,220, in spite of the fact that average plant incomes increased by 18 per cent over the same period (p. III).

A recent development in the industry is the revival of sealing. One reason is the dramatic increase in the population of harp seals, which has nearly tripled from less than two million in the early 1970s. The hunting of seal pups has been banned, and since 1997 there has been a quota of 275,000 allocated for mature harp seals (Dept. of Fisheries and Oceans, n.d.). (A few grey seals and approximately 10,000 hooded seals are also harvested.) There has also been intense public pressure to discontinue the seal hunt, and international protests have gained wide media attention, most recently in March 2005. But as Table 8.10 indicates, sealing continues to be an important source of income for approximately 12,000 Newfoundlanders, especially those still living in isolated outports who can no longer participate in the groundfishery.

A relatively new fishing industry for Newfoundland and Labrador is aquaculture. Although much smaller (in production and dollar values) than the commercial fishery, aquaculture increased by 300 per cent between 1996 and 2002, and it will be interesting to see whether it can continue to grow. As Table 8.11 shows, steelhead operations have been the most successful, but salmon and mussels have also done well.

Table 8.10   Newfoundland seal fishery, 1998–2004

	1998	1999	2000	2001	2002	2003	2004
Seals (#)	275,000	241,552	92,000	226,493	312,000[1]	283,497	365,971
Seals ($)	8,750,000	7,500,000	4,300,000	8,400,000	20,000,000	12,139,000	n.a.

[1]Sealers were permitted to exceed the pre-season quota in 2002.

Sources: Government of Newfoundland, 'Fisheries and Aquaculture Statistics', ⟨http://www.gov.nf.ca/Fishaq/Statistics⟩; Department of Fisheries and Oceans (http://www.dfo-mpo.gc.ca).

Table 8.11 **Newfoundland and Labrador aquaculture production and value (tonnes × 1,000 and $ × 1,000), 1996–2004**

		1996	1997	1998	1999	2000	2001	2002	2003	2004
Fin fish	Salmon (t)	295	613	401	399	670	1,092	1,270	1,450	–
	Salmon ($)	1,665	2,714	2,925	2,462	4,962	5,200	6,132	6,670	–
	Steelhead (t)	734	355	1,316	2,078	842	1,719	1,600	1,150	–
	Steelhead ($)	3,210	1,475	6,919	11,402	5,494	9,752	8,800	6,324	–
	Trout (t)	24	14	48	10	–	–	–	–	–
	Trout ($)	154	93	197	80	–	–	–	–	–
Total fin fish (t)		1,053	982	1,765	2,487	1,512	1,512	2,870	2,600	3,329
Total fin fish ($)		5,029	4,282	10,041	13,944	10,456	10,456	14,932	12,994	17,000
Shellfish	Mussels (t)	377	752	946	1,700	1,051	1,452	1,700	1,300	2,300
	Mussels ($)	333	635	815	3,800	2,700	3,929	5,500	4,200	–
	Scallops (t)	19	12	9	–	–	–	–	–	–
	Scallops ($)	104	54	53	–	–	–	–	–	–
	Other (t)	1	4	7	–	–	–	–	–	–
	Other ($)	19	40	32	–	–	–	–	–	–
Total shellfish (t)		397	768	962	1,700	1,051	1,051	1,700	1,300	2,300
Total shellfish ($)		456	729	900	3,800	2,700	2,700	5,500	4,200	5,055
Total aquaculture (t)		1,450	1,750	2,727	4,187	2,563	2,563	4,570	3,900	5,629
Total aquaculture ($)		5,485	5,011	10,941	17,744	13,156	13,156	20,432	17,194	22,055

Source: Fisheries and Oceans Canada ⟨http://www.dfo-mpo.gc.ca⟩.

Newfoundland and Labrador from the 1990s to the Present

The urban pattern of Newfoundland and Labrador revolves around one main centre—St John's—which, with a population of 170,000, is not large in comparison to Census Metropolitan Centres in other parts of Canada. Corner Brook, with 25,000 residents, is the next largest centre. On the other hand, there are numerous communities with populations under 5,000. The loss of nearly 60,000 people from the province between 1991 and 2001 has affected the urban pattern in almost all communities, as Table 8.12—which includes only those communities of 5,000 or more—illustrates. These communities, for the most part, rely on resource harvesting and, in some instances, processing,

Table 8.12 **Census Metropolitan Areas (CMA), Census Agglomerations (CA), and Communities over 5,000, 1991–2001**

Community	1991	1996	2001
St John's CMA	171,848	174,051	172,918
Grand Falls–Windsor CA	21,053	20,378	18,981
Gander CA	12,037	12,021	11,254
Corner Brook CA	28,559	27,945	25,747
Labrador City CA	11,392	10,473	9,638
Bay Roberts	5,474	5,472	5,237
Carbonear	5,259	5,168	4,759
Channel-Port aux Basques	5,644	5,243	4,637
Deer Lake	5,161	5,222	4,769
Happy Valley–Goose Bay	8,610	8,655	7,969
Marystown	6,739	6,742	5,908
Placentia	5,515	5,013	4,426
Stephenville	7,621	7,764	7,109

Source: Adapted from Statistics Canada, 2001 Community Profiles ⟨http://www12.statcan.ca/english/profil01/CP01/Index.cfm?Lang=E⟩.

Table 8.13   Population, Newfoundland and Labrador, 1991–2004

Year	Population	Year	Population
1990	578,037	1998	539,932
1991	579,518	1999	533,409
1992	580,029	2000	528,043
1993	579,939	2001	521,986
1994	574,469	2002	519,449
1995	567,442	2003	518,350
1996	559,807	2004	517,027
1997	551,011		

Note: From 2002 to 2004 these are preliminary statistics.

Source: Government of Newfoundland Census Data and Information ⟨http://www.nfstats.gov.nf.ca⟩.

Table 8.14   Population in selected age categories (%), 1991 and 2003

Age group	1991	%	2003	%
65+	55,746	9.6	65,250	12.6
55+	98,104	16.9	124,991	24.1
40+	199,906	34.5	254,048	48.9
0–14	128,404	22.2	84,716	16.3
15–55	251,208	43.3	180,806	34.8

Source: Government of Newfoundland, Census Data and Information ⟨http://www.nfstats.gov.nf.ca⟩.

both of which require fewer people today than they did in the past. Those communities that used to rely on the groundfishery have suffered even greater unemployment. St John's is something of an exception in that its 2001 population has actually increased slightly over the 1991 census. This growth reflects the diversification of its economy, which relies to a greater extent on services; St John's is also the capital and administrative centre of Newfoundland and Labrador. The population loss documented in figures in Table 8.13 is a clear indication of the economic difficulties that the province has faced since the 1992 codfish moratorium.

Table 8.14 indicates that it is young people who are moving away, leaving older residents behind. In 2003, nearly one-quarter of the people of Newfoundland and Labrador were 55 years of age or older, and close to one-half of the population were 40 or more. Residents over the age of 55 made up a much larger percentage of the population than in 1991, and there were fewer children (0–14 years) and people aged between 15 and 55 in the more recent census.

What are the underlying economic and political conditions that have led to the downward swing in population? The most important cause is unemployment. The restructuring of the fishing industry was a major contributor to unemployment, and while the TAGS program compensated many for the loss of income and provided others with early retirement, it did little to create new employment opportunities. The extent to which fishing represents a way of life not just to individuals but to whole communities cannot be overstated; for this reason, the loss of fishing licences and processing plants means that the prospects for the survival of these communities are bleak.

Mining

The long-term outlook for mining in Newfoundland and Labrador is more optimistic. The mining industry can be divided into three categories: metal mining, non-metal mining, and energy. Table 8.15, which lists the production quantities and dollar values of the various metals mined, highlights the dominance of iron ore pellet production at Labrador City and the next-door community of Wabush. Non-metals mined include such materials as sand and gravel, limestone, and stone, many of which are used locally. Their value, also shown in Table 8.15, is relatively low. Offshore oil began to be produced in the Hibernia oilfields in 1997, and with the Terra Nova rig coming on-stream in 2002, there was a jump in the production and value of oil in the province. The good news for Newfoundland and Labrador is that there will be more offshore wells producing in the near future.

The province's mining industry has faced a number of obstacles. For instance, the discovery of a very rich body of nickel at Voisey's Bay in 1993 raised hopes of a megaproject that could create many jobs. The International Nickel Company (Inco), one of the largest producers of nickel in the world, with smelters at Sudbury, Ontario, and Thompson, Manitoba, acquired the mineral rights to Voisey's Bay in 1996, but became

Table 8.15 Newfoundland and Labrador metal, non-metal, and oil production and value (× 1,000), 1995–2004

Year	Copper kg	Copper $	Gold kg	Gold $	Iron ore 846,407	Iron ore $	Silver $	Total metals $
1995	1,247	846,407	2,685	45,516	871,217	795,839	38	846,407
1996	5,159	871,217	2,813	47,827	966,218	806,784	325	871,217
1997	662	966,218	2,858	42,121	1,046,063	921,893	107	966,218
1998	–	1,046,063	1,381	19,388	778,135	1,026,517	158	1,046,063
1999	–	778,135	1,314	17,507	921,611	760,482	146	778,135
2000	–	921,611	1,455	19,353	818,514	902,134	124	921,611
2001	–	818,514	1,503	20,203	918,429	798,238	72	818,514
2002	–	918,429	1,477	22,897	810,057	895,477	54	918,429
2003	–	810,057	1,176	19,263	773,860	790,927	49	810,057
2004	–	773,860	466	7,989	14,946	765,848	24	773,860

Year	Total non-metals $	Oil m³	Oil $	Grand total $
1995	31,891	–	–	878,299
1996	34,984	–	–	905,901
1997	42,054	202	29,900	1,038,173
1998	48,471	3,795	444,962	1,539,496
1999	42,139	5,786	997,518	1,817,792
2000	45,510	8,394	2,203,326	3,170,447
2001	44,686	8,633	2,038,204	2,901,398
2002	48,156	16,457	4,086,031	5,052,616
2003	35,104	17,826	4,839,300	5,684,461
2004	37,650	16,640	5,700,000	6,511,510

Note: 2003 are preliminary figures and 2004 are estimates.

Sources: Natural Resources Canada, 'Mining and Mineral Statistics Online' ⟨http://mmsd1.mms.nrcan.gc.ca/mmsd/intro_e.asp⟩; Government of Newfoundland and Labrador, 'Mines and Energy Statistics' ⟨http://www.nr.gov.nl.ca/mines&en/statistics/#energy⟩.

involved in a showdown with the provincial government when the latter refused to grant mining permits unless a new smelter for the ore was constructed at Argentia on Placentia Bay. Inco also faced opposition from Labrador's Inuit and Innu communities, who claim Voisey's Bay as their traditional territory. The two Aboriginal groups went to court to seek an injunction on any development and insisted that an Impact Benefit Agreement be completed before they would permit mining to go ahead. In 2002 the Labrador Inuit Association and the Innu Nation signed an Impact Benefits Agreement. While the details have yet to be ironed out, the benefits will likely include employment opportunities, revenue sharing, environmental protection and rehabilitation, and perhaps joint ventures. In addition, an agreement signed by the provincial government and Inco calls for an $800-million processing plant to be built at Argentia (Innu Nation) once the mine begins production. Figure 8.7 offers another perspective on the metal and non-metal mining sectors, where the introduction of technologies to increase productivity has led to a general reduction in employment.

Meanwhile, offshore oil production, which is tripling the province's mining revenues, has created new jobs; however, this employment is associated less with actual drilling operations than with the construction of the platforms, which has been done at

Figure 8.7   Metal and non-metal mining employment, 1994–2003

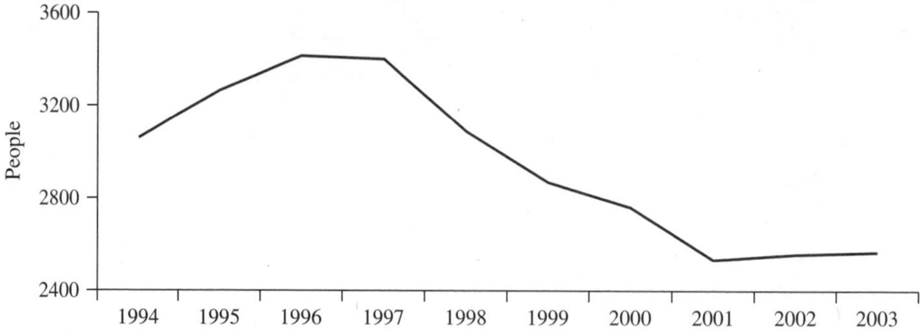

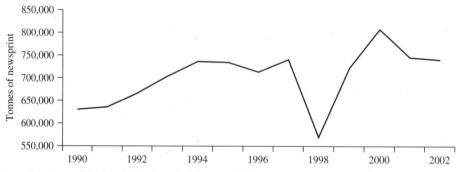

Source: Government of Newfoundland, 'Mining Industry Average Employment 1994–2003' ⟨http://gis.gov.nf.ca/minesen/ avg_employment/⟩.

Bull Arm. Consequently, in 2002, when the Terra Nova rig was ready for production, employment decreased even as revenues increased. Fortunately, in 2003 the operators of the White Rose project contracted the Bull Arm facilities to build their offshore drilling platform. In early 2005, the issue of revenue sharing sparked a bitter dispute between the federal and provincial governments. Newfoundland and Labrador Premier Danny Williams, in a move that rekindled the sentiment of the anti-Confederation movement, had the Canadian flag taken down from provincial buildings. The Atlantic Accord was signed in February 2005, guaranteeing that both Newfoundland and Nova Scotia will receive one hundred per cent of the oil and gas revenues until 2012, with no impact on federal–provincial revenue sharing agreements.

Forestry and Agriculture

The forest industry, which revolves primarily around the production of newsprint, has maintained output at all three paper mills in Newfoundland (see Figure 8.8). In this industry, the main source of uncertainty is the world market price for newsprint. For example, the average price per tonne of newsprint in 2001 was US$585, but in 2002 it dropped to US$465 (Government of Newfoundland, n.d.).

Farming is not a major enterprise in Newfoundland and Labrador, where neither the soil nor the climate is favourable for agriculture. Table 8.16 uses Census data to trace

Figure 8.8   Newsprint production, Newfoundland and Labrador, 1990–2002

Source: Government of Newfoundland, 'Industry Statistics: Quarterly Shipments of Newsprint, Newfoundland and Labrador, Tonnes, 1990–2003' ⟨http://www.stats.gov.nl.ca/Statistics/Industry/Newsprint.asp⟩.

farming since 1981. It shows that the number of farms in the province increased until 1996, but has dropped off considerably since then.

Hydroelectricity

The massive Churchill Falls hydro project remained contentious throughout the 1990s because of the unfair advantage Quebec gained from its 65-year contract to buy the power produced there at a very low fixed price. Towards the end of the 1990s, several developments made a resolution to this inequitable situation possible. In 1997, the US electricity market was deregulated. One of the terms of deregulation was that Hydro-Québec, as a condition for continuing to sell electricity to the US, be required to open its transmission grid to outside power suppliers. This made it possible for Newfoundland to consider other power developments in Labrador, which could be operated without Quebec's cooperation and could compete with Quebec for a share of its sales to the US. With this new leverage, the province was able to strike a new deal with Quebec in 1998, whereby Newfoundland and Labrador will receive a greater share of the electricity revenues and will develop a further 3,200 megawatts of hydroelectricity downstream from Churchill Falls (Canadian Electricity Association, n.d.).

Tourism

Newfoundland and Labrador's tourism industry has enjoyed considerable growth in recent years, especially since 1997, when the five hundredth anniversary of John Cabot's landing on the coast of Newfoundland attracted many tourists. As Table 8.17 shows, in 1997 there was a 22 per cent increase over the previous year's tourist numbers. What is perhaps more remarkable is that the province has been able to increase the number of tourists each year since then, even though tourism in other parts of North America has

Table 8.16 Number of farms and farm size, Newfoundland and Labrador, 1981–2001

	1981	1986	1991	1996	2001
Farms	679	651	725	742	643
Area (hectares)	33,454	36,561	47,353	43,836	40,578
Average farm size	49	56	65	59	63

Source: Data adapted in part from Statistics Canada, Census of Agriculture, 2001.

Table 8.17 Non-resident visits and expenditures, by mode of travel, 1990–2004

Year	Automobile Visitors	Automobile $million	Airline Visitors	Airline $million	Cruise ship Visitors	Cruise ship $million	Total Visitors	Total $million
1990	114,334	45.1	175,910	85.3	–	–	290,244	130.4
1991	111,267	46.7	154,741	79.9	–	–	266,008	126.6
1992	110,778	46.8	153,432	79.8	–	–	264,210	126.6
1993	114,682	45.5	192,752	105.0	–	–	307,434	150.4
1994	114,629	46.2	214,800	119.0	–	–	329,429	165.2
1995	118,133	48.5	204,363	119.9	–	–	322,497	168.4
1996	109,626	46.3	195,436	118.2	–	–	305,062	164.5
1997	122,425	56.2	247,265	175.5	–	–	369,690	231.7
1998	127,960	60.3	244,253	177.8	10,344	0.5	382,557	238.6
1999	140,864	68.0	256,600	195.4	15,511	0.8	412,975	264.2
2000	149,975	75.3	266,480	212.1	9,792	0.5	426,247	287.9
2001	141,675	72.2	266,276	215.1	19,755	1.0	427,706	288.3
2002	161,442	85.2	259,467	216.0	25,410	1.3	439,444	302.5
2003	140,400	74.2	269,900	224.7	14,100	1.0	424,400	299.9
2004	126,200	66.6	305,400	262.1	17,700	1.3	449,300	330.0

Source: Government of Newfoundland, 'Annual Non-Resident Visitation and Expenditures by Mode Newfoundland and Labrador: 1973 to 2002' (http://www.nfstats.gov.nf.ca).

decreased in response to factors such as the attack on the World Trade Center, the outbreaks of SARS and the West Nile Virus, and the weakening of the US economy.

Since 2003 there has been talk of building some sort of permanent link across the Strait of Belle Isle, which separates Newfoundland from the eastern coasts of Labrador and Quebec. This is not a new idea: in 1986 a bridge was proposed that would open up Labrador, northeastern Quebec, and the Northern Peninsula of Newfoundland. But the Conservative government of Danny Williams appears to be treating the latest proposal seriously, and has gone as far as commissioning a study to examine a number of options, including tunnel, causeway, bridge, and variations on these, all with differing costs and timetables. Such a fixed link, if it were built, would be a great advantage to trucking and road transportation generally, as well as a boost to tourism.

Summary

From its colonial origins, the province of Newfoundland and Labrador has had a history of political conflict and economic vulnerability, mostly related to its reliance on a single resource. The Norse adventurers who are thought to have been the first Europeans to land on Newfoundland were less concerned with fish than with grazing land and trees, but they abandoned the idea of settlement when they came into conflict with the local Aboriginal people. The next wave of Europeans came to fish and eventually settle near the Grand Banks. Britain attempted to control the colony, but France acquired the islands of St Pierre and Miquelon and occupied the north shore of Newfoundland, while American fishers gained access to the island's southern shore. Canada also played a role in these conflicts, as Quebec attempted to annex Labrador. Meanwhile the population gradually increased to the point where Newfoundlanders were able to extinguish the French, American, and Canadian claims to their territory.

These long and ultimately successful battles contributed to a strong sense of nationalism among Newfoundlanders. But though these external struggles gave the people a common cause, they diverted attention away from some fundamental weaknesses in their economy. As the population expanded, so did the vulnerability that came with dependence on a single species of a single commodity. The very nature of the cod fishery meant that much of the population lived in remote coastal settlements of fewer than two hundred people, all of whom relied on one seasonal resource.

It was a serious moral blow when, just over a hundred years after gaining autonomy in 1832, the colony went bankrupt. Certainly, the collapse of cod prices and declining productivity in the industry were major contributors to the bankruptcy, but there were other factors as well. The Newfoundland Railway and the First World War represented huge financial burdens, and efforts to diversify the economy by promoting mining and forestry generated little revenue for the colonial government. The 'keys' to Newfoundland were returned to Britain. The Commission of Government ruled for longer than expected, primarily because of Newfoundland's military importance to Britain and its allies during the Second World War. From an economic standpoint, the new government brought a number of positive changes: the fishing industry was reorganized, the civil service was reformed, and the tariff structure was overhauled. These changes, along with massive military spending by the United States, Britain, and Canada, steered Newfoundland's economy from deficit to surplus.

By 1948 the time had come for Newfoundlanders to decide whether they would continue under British control, return to the pre-1934 status quo, or join Canada. Following two referendums, Newfoundland agreed by a narrow margin to enter Confederation in 1949. Provincehood brought some immediate benefits. Family allowances, old age pensions, and, later on, unemployment insurance put dependable cash into the hands of families. Transfer payments and other federal monies allowed the provincial government to develop infrastructure such as roads, hospitals, schools, and lines for electricity and telephones. The economy was diversifying with the expansion of mining, forestry, and hydroelectricity, and the population increased considerably until the 1980s.

From the perspective of many Newfoundlanders, however, there was a negative side to Confederation. The federal government was now in control of both the revenues from international trade and the management of ocean resources. By the 1990s, overfishing (largely as a result of new technologies) and poor management, by Canada and the many other countries fishing the Grand Banks, would have virtually destroyed the cod stocks. Furthermore, several of the province's efforts to diversify and expand the province's economy were controversial. Attempts to establish a linerboard plant and oil refinery were costly mistakes, as was a long-term agreement with the province of Quebec to sell massive amounts of hydroelectricity at a fraction of its worth. The province's scheme to close down remote outports and relocate their residents was equally contentious. Even the development of the province's offshore oil deposits looked less than promising until the federal government agreed to revenue sharing and the building of the drilling platforms in Newfoundland.

The moratorium on cod fishing in 1992 was a new low for the province. The fishing industry had already begun its decline when Newfoundland joined Canada in 1949. Still, many continued to rely on the fishery for their income. Since the early 1990s young people in particular have been leaving the province. The economy is improving, however. The fishing industry brings in more revenues today than in the past, but now it focuses mainly on shellfish, and provides much less employment. Offshore oil drilling and production is expanding, and the long awaited nickel mine at Voisey's Bay is poised for production now that issues with the local First Nations have been resolved. A new deal concerning the Churchill Falls hydroelectricity plant is bringing greater revenues to the provincial government, and plans to build more dams and produce more energy are being negotiated. Pulp, paper, and other forestry activities continue, along with a small number of commercial farms, and the economy is becoming more diversified, especially as the tourism industry expands.

References

Blake, R. N.d. 'Canada's Fishery: North Atlantic Fisheries Organization'. http://www.nafo.ca.

Canadian Electricity Association. N.d. http://www.canelect.ca.

Chadwick, St. John. 1967. *Newfoundland: Island into Province.* London: Cambridge University Press, 1967.

Churchill Falls Labrador Corporation. 2003. 'History of Churchill Falls'. http://www.cflco.nf.ca.

Clugston, M. 1993. 'Sky Patrols over the Grand Banks'. Pp. 46–9 in Leighton (1993).

Cuff, R. 2001. 'Railway'. http://www.heritage.nf.ca.

Department of Fisheries and Oceans. N.d. 'Aquaculture Production Statistics'; 'Canadian Landings Information'; 'Licensing Statistics: Fishers and Vessel Information'; 'Evaluation of the Canadian Fisheries Adjustment and

Restructuring Program Licence Retirement Programs'. http://www.dfo-mpo.gc.ca.

———. Fisheries and Aquaculture Management. 'RECENT CANADIAN HARVEST LEVELS'. http://www.dfo-mpo.gc.ca/seal-phoque/reports-rapports/facts-faits/facts-faits2004_e.htm#RECENT%20CANADIAN%20HARVEST%20LEVELS.

Draper, D. 2002. *Our Environment: A Canadian Perspective*. 2nd edn. Scarborough: Nelson.

Frideres, J. 1988. *Native Peoples in Canada: Contemporary Conflicts*. 3rd edn. Scarborough: Prentice Hall.

Geo-Help Inc. 2003. 'History of the Canadian Oil Industry'. http://www.geohelp.ab.ca/history.htm.

Gillmor, D. 1993. 'A Fine Kettle of Fish'. Pp. 34–9 in Leighton (1993).

Government of Newfoundland and Labrador. N.d. 'Fisheries and Aquaculture Statistics', 1998–2002. http://www.gov.nf.ca/Fishaq/Statistics/.

———. 1997. 'An Overview of TAGS Clients'. http://www.gov.nf.ca/publicat/tags/text/page6.htm

———. 2005. Atlantic Accord. Arrangement between the Government of Canada and the Government of Newfoundland and Labrador on Offshore Revenues. http://www.gov.nl.ca/atlanticaccord/agreement.htm.

———. 2005. Final Report. Fixed Link between Labrador and Newfoundland Pre-feasibility Study. http://www.gov.nf.ca/publicat/fixedlink/.

———. N.d. 'Mining Industry Average Employment 1994–2003'. http://gis.gov.nf.ca/minesen/avg_employment/.

———. N.d. 'Industry Statistics: Quarterly Shipments of Newsprint, Newfoundland and Labrador, Tonnes, 1990–2003'. http://www.stats.gov.nl.ca/Statistics/Industry/Newsprint.asp

———. N.d. 'The Economy 2003'. http://economics.gov.nf.ca.

———. N.d. 'Annual Non-Resident Visitation and Expenditures by Mode Newfoundland and Labrador: 1973 to 2002'. http://www.nfstats.gov.nf.ca.

———. N.d. '2001 Census Data and Information'. http://www.nfstats.gov.nf.ca.

———. N.d. Mines and Energy. Statistics. http://www.nr.gov.nl.ca/mines&en/statistics/#energy.

Harris, M. 1998. *Lament for an Ocean*. Toronto: McClelland and Stewart.

Hiller, J.K. 1998. *Confederation: Deciding Newfoundland's Future 1934 to 1949*. St John's: Newfoundland Historical Society.

———. N.d. 'The Treaty of Versailles, 1783'. http://www.heritage.nf.ca.

———. 2002. 'Reciprocity with the United States of America'. http://www.heritage.nf.ca.

———. 2001. 'The Sailing Seal Fishery'. http://www.heritage.nf.ca.

———. 2001. '19th Century Steamer Seal Fishery'. http://www.heritage.nf.ca.

———. 2001. '20th Century Steamer Seal Fishery'. http://www.heritage.nf.ca.

———. 1997. 'The Labrador Boundary'. http://www.heritage.nf.ca.

Innis, H.A. 1956. 'An Introduction to the Economic History of the Maritimes, including Newfoundland and New England'. Pp. 27–42 in *Essays in Canadian Economic History*. Toronto: University of Toronto Press.

Innu Nation. N.d. 'Innu Nation Mounts Court Challenge Over Voisey's Bay'. http://www.innu.ca.

Janzen, O. 1998. 'French Presence in Newfoundland'. http://www.heritage.nf.ca.

Kurlansky, M. 1997. *Cod: A Biography of the Fish that Changed the World*. Toronto: Alfred A. Knopf.

Leighton, T. 1993. 'Introduction: The Atlantic Cod Fishery'. Pp. 32–3 in Leighton, ed. *Canadian Regional Environmental Issues Manual: Bringing Environmental Issues Closer to Home*. Toronto: Harcourt Brace.

McGhee, R. 1985. 'Prehistory'. Pp. 1466–9 in *The Canadian Encyclopedia*. Edmonton: Hurtig.

MacKenzie, D.C. 1985. 'Commission of Government'. P. 379 in *The Canadian Encyclopedia*. Edmonton: Hurtig.

Memorial University K to 12 Internet On-ramp. N.d. 'History of the Gas and Oil Refinery'. http://www.k12.nf.ca.

Mowat, F. 1965. *Westviking: The Ancient Norse in Greenland And North America*. Boston: Little, Brown.

Myers, O. 1992. 'The Corporate Rape of Canada's Cod Fishery'. *Canadian Dimension*. September: 22–4.

Natural Resources Canada. N.d. 'Mining and Mineral Statistics Online'. http://mmsd1.mms.nrcan.gc.ca/mmsd/intro_e.asp.

Newfoundland Historic Trust. 1975. *A Gift of Heritage: Historic Architecture of St John's*. St John's: Valhalla Press.

Pastore, R.T. 1998. 'The History of the Newfoundland Mi'kmaq'. http://www.heritage.nf.ca.

Reid, K. 2002. 'The birth and re-birth of Stephenville's paper mill'. http://www.town.stephenville.nf.ca.

Rennie, R. 1998. 'Mining'. http://www.heritage.nf.ca.

Rusted, J. 1995. *Tolerable Good Anchorage*. St John's: Creative Book Publishing.

Ryan, S. 1990. 'History of Newfoundland Cod Fishery'. http://www.stemnet.nf.ca/cod/history5.htm.

Simpson, J. 2003. 'There's the light in the east: Take note Ontario'. *The Globe and Mail*. 16 Aug.: A25.

Statistics Canada. N.d. 'Value of exports of fisher products in relation to total exports, Newfoundland, 1858 to 1949'. Series N130-131. http://www.statcan.ca.

———. '2001 Census of Agriculture'. http://www.statcan.ca.

Summers, W.F. 1985. 'Newfoundland'. Pp. 1244–52 in *The Canadian Encyclopedia*. Edmonton: Hurtig.

Warner, W.W. 1983. *Distant Water: The Fate of the Atlantic Fisherman*. Boston: Little B.

Webb, J.A. 2001. 'Representative Government, 1832–1855'. http://www.heritage.nf.ca

Wheaton, C. 1999. 'Trade and Commerce in Newfoundland'. http://www.heritage.nf.ca

Winter, K. 1975. *Shananditti: The Last of the Beothucks*. North Vancouver: J.J. Douglas Ltd.

Wright, M.E. N.d. 'Freedom of Mobility: A Historical Perspective'. http://www.stemnet.nf.ca/cod/history5.htm.

9

The Prairie Provinces

Manitoba, Saskatchewan, and Alberta are grouped together as the Prairie provinces because of the flat, treeless grassland that characterizes the southern portions of all three. This landscape is typical of the sedimentary region known as the Great Interior Plains. In addition, however, the northern portions of all three provinces are part of the Canadian Shield.

Despite these similarities, there are considerable physical contrasts both within and between the provinces. Geological processes and the receding of glaciers have produced variations in topography as well as surficial geology. These elements, in combination with weather and climate, have produced a wide range of soil and vegetation patterns, and resource development has varied accordingly.

The pattern of human settlement in the Prairie region has been equally varied. Aboriginal peoples have occupied the land for at least 10,000 years, evolving from nomadic to semi-nomadic hunting and gathering societies whose populations increased with their expertise in living off the land. But in the seventeenth century the region was opened to the fur trade, and in 1670 most of the Prairies came under the control of the newly created Hudson's Bay Company under the name of Rupert's Land. By the end of the next century the HBC was challenged by the much more aggressive North West Company, touching off a bitter rivalry that did not end until the two companies merged in 1821.

The fur traders were dependent—both for their survival and for the success of the trade—on the knowledge they gained from the region's First Nations. Over time, relationships between traders and Aboriginal women gave rise to a distinct community of mixed European (especially French and Scottish) and Aboriginal (mainly Cree, Ojibway, and Saulteaux) ancestry: the Métis. This group soon dominated the Prairie fur trade as suppliers both of hides and of the staple food: the mixture of dried meat, fat, and berries called pemmican. Although Métis settlements developed across the prairies, the largest was located at the forks of the Red and Assiniboine rivers. As the fur trade diminished, the people of this community established small farms that took the same long-lot form as the seigneurial lands in Quebec. By the time of Confederation, the new country was anxious to see agricultural settlement begin on the prairies in order to prevent the United States from annexing the region. Accordingly, it arranged to purchase Rupert's Land from the HBC and, even before the transfer was completed, began surveying the Red River district in preparation for distributing the land to settlers—despite the

Figure 9.1   Map of the Prairie provinces

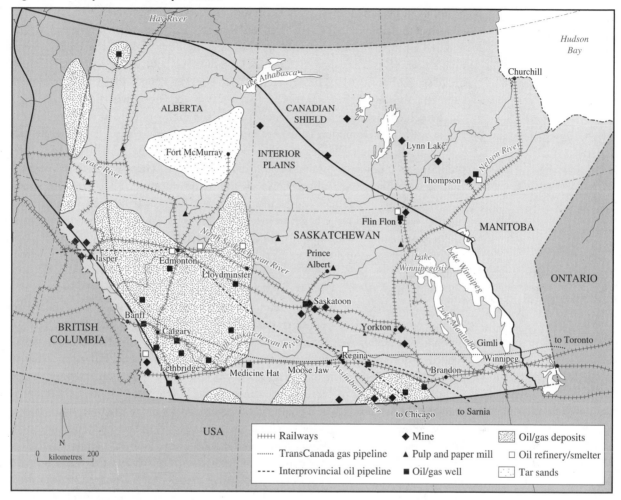

long-established presence of the Métis community there. Although the Métis under Louis Riel eventually succeeded in negotiating the terms of Manitoba's entry into Confederation, their execution of a troublesome prisoner outraged Anglo-Protestant Ontarians, and to pacify them the federal government sent troops to quell the supposed 'rebellion'. Most of those involved in the resistance were granted amnesty, but Riel himself was forced into exile, and many Métis were pushed out of Red River as Canadian settlers moved in.

Settlement of the Prairies was slow, in part because construction of the transcontinental railway was delayed. Nevertheless, by 1885 life was becoming increasingly difficult for all the region's Aboriginal peoples. The buffalo were rapidly disappearing, and the people who depended on them were facing starvation. Meanwhile, many of the Métis displaced from Red River had moved west and settled along the South Saskatchewan River, only to find their land holdings once again under threat. In June 1884 they appealed to Riel, who was then living in Montana, for help. He agreed, and in December the Métis sent a petition to Ottawa requesting, among other things, title to the lands they occupied and provincial status for the North-West. By the time the government promised to establish a commission, however, frustrations had built to the point that the more militant Métis were ready to take matters into their own hands. Riel declared a provisional government, and in March fighting broke out at Duck Lake. A military force was sent west—via the new Canadian Pacific Railway—and after a number of skirmishes the Métis surrendered in May. Riel was hanged for treason six months later. The Aboriginal resistance to Canada's westward expansion was all but finished.

Settlement began to increase following the land survey of the North-West Territories in 1887. The Dominion Lands Act of 1872, in addition to specifying how the survey would be undertaken, set out the conditions for granting homesteads to settlers promising to cultivate a certain amount of land per year. There were serious physical challenges to prairie agriculture, however, and it was not until the early 1900s, when new agricultural techniques and hardier strains of wheat made farming less risky, that the population could really begin to increase. It also took aggressive recruitment efforts in Europe to attract a stable population that would continue to grow. By 1905, the population was large enough to warrant the creation of two new provinces, Saskatchewan and Alberta.

By the time the stock market crashed in 1929, prairie farmers had developed a dependency on wheat that was approaching Newfoundlanders' dependency on codfish. As a result, when the price of wheat crashed and the southern Prairies endured ten years of drought, this region was among the hardest hit. However, the Prairies enjoyed an extended period of prosperity during the post-war economic boom. From the 1950s to the 1970s the growing demand for resources was met with a series of mega-projects that included the building of hydroelectric dams and the development of open-pit mines to extract and process metals and potash. Farming diversified and in time was transformed, with ever fewer people on ever larger plots of land producing ever greater quantities of agricultural products. Most important, development of the Prairies' energy resources—oil, natural gas, and coal—for export to other parts of Canada and the world brought huge revenues, particularly to Alberta. The energy crisis of the 1970s led Ottawa to impose a National Energy Program (1980) that created enormous resentment in Alberta and continues to fuel a significant movement for separation from Canada. To the present day, resource developments have been accompanied by a shift to more service-oriented industries, which have drawn rural residents to the major urban centres of each province.

The Physical Environment

The ancient and mineral-rich rock of the Canadian Shield cuts a swath from the southeastern corner of Manitoba northwest across the northern half of Saskatchewan and into the northeastern corner of Alberta. Throughout its long geological history, the region has been subject to rising and falling ocean levels, tectonic forces that have moved both continental and oceanic plates, and advancing and receding ice sheets. The agents of weathering and erosion that wore down the Canadian Shield deposited the layers of sediments that form the Great Interior Plains: the geophysical region lying to the south and west of the Shield in these three provinces. This layering process buried plant and animal remains, which through heat and pressure were converted to oil, natural gas, and coal. The ancient seas that covered the Prairies were also responsible for deposits of potash, an alkaline potassium compound used in the manufacture of fertilizer and soap, among other things.

Across the three provinces, the Great Interior Plains comprise three distinct land-forms that differ in both age and elevation. The First Prairie Plain is the oldest—formed more than 500 million years ago—and lies 200 to 300 metres above sea level, although there are higher elevations such as the Pembina, Riding, Duck, and Porcupine mountains. The Second Prairie Plain, formed approximately 300 million years ago, rises 500 to 600 metres above sea level. The Third Prairie Plain, which is the most extensive, is the most recent (approximately 100 million years old) of the three prairie plains as well as the highest, rising more than 1,000 metres above sea level.

Two other physiographic regions lie on the fringes of the Prairies. The northeastern border of Manitoba occupies part of the recently uplifted Hudson Bay lowlands. On the western side of the Prairies, the drainage pattern of the Rocky Mountains (part of the Cordilleran physiographic region) defines the southern half of the boundary between Alberta and British Columbia.

Glaciation has greatly modified the landscape of all three Prairie provinces. The giant bulldozers of ice moved huge quantities of material, depositing them as moraines of till. The relatively recent (in geological time) melting and receding of these continental ice sheets, some 12,000 years ago, produced large glacial lakes such as Lake Agassiz, which stretched from central Saskatchewan through most of southern Manitoba and southeastern Ontario and south into the United States. There were other large and small glacial lakes throughout Alberta and Saskatchewan, many of which overflowed their banks and became glacial spillways that carved deep channels out of the soft sedimentary layers.

For the most part, the river systems of the Prairies run west to east. For example, the North and South Saskatchewan rivers and the Nelson River, which together formed a major 'highway' for fur traders, flow eastward. But the northern parts of Alberta and Saskatchewan belong to a different drainage pattern, where rivers flow north as part of the Mackenzie River drainage basin. The drainage system in the southern part of Alberta and Saskatchewan is tied in with the Mississippi and eventually flows south to the Gulf of Mexico. These southern rivers eventually became important for agricultural irrigation and, later, as sources of hydroelectricity.

The weather and climate on the Prairies can be extreme. With no major mountain chains to block either northern or southern air masses, extremely harsh Arctic air can descend in winter, while exceedingly hot weather can move up from the Gulf of Mexico in the summer; the latter is responsible for the tornados that sometimes strike the region. The western margin of Alberta experiences chinooks—warm, dry winds that descend from the eastern side of the Rockies and can raise temperatures 15 to 20 degrees Celsius within a few hours. One of the main drawbacks to farming has been the short growing season: the annual total of frost-free days ranges from approximately 120 in the south to 100 or fewer in the Peace River District to the north. The number of growing-degree days (the average number of days with temperature 5 °C or above) ranges from 180 to 160, south to north. Planting in time for crops to ripen before winter has always been a challenge on the Prairies.

Precipitation in the region occurs mainly in the summer, when the convection process brings hail as well as rain. The pattern of precipitation varies from south to north and west to east. Southern Alberta and southern Saskatchewan receive the least precipitation; Medicine Hat, in southern Alberta, averages approximately 350 mm per year, whereas Edmonton, to the north, averages around 465 mm and Winnipeg, to the east, receives an average of more than 500 mm. The Cypress Hills, which rise to nearly 1,500 metres and were free of ice during the last glacial period, are an exception to the semi-arid pattern of southern Alberta and southern Saskatchewan: they receive more precipitation and support a mixed coniferous and deciduous forest.

The vegetation of the Prairies is influenced by both climate and soil characteristics. The dry grasslands of the south support few trees, while the north receives enough precipitation for forests of aspen to grow. The area farther north and east, including the Canadian Shield, is covered by coniferous boreal forest. The soils of the Prairies are also varied. The most fertile, the rich black chernozemic soils, form a crescent arching from southern Manitoba through Saskatchewan and mid-Alberta (see Fig. 9.2). The dark brown chernozemic soils lie inside this crescent, while the less fertile light brown chernozemic soils are found at the southern core. In the Peace River region of Alberta and British Columbia, decaying aspen forests produce rich, black soils.

Two surveyors, John Palliser and Henry Hind, were sent out to the Prairies in the mid-1800s to assess the physical characteristics of the region and its potential for agricultural development. Palliser, who surveyed the dry southern region, commented in his journal: 'soil poor, herbage scanty, no wood except on northern exposures' (Finlay and Sprague, 1997: 172); this area, south of the Saskatchewan River in southwestern

Figure 9.2   Prairie soil and vegetation patterns

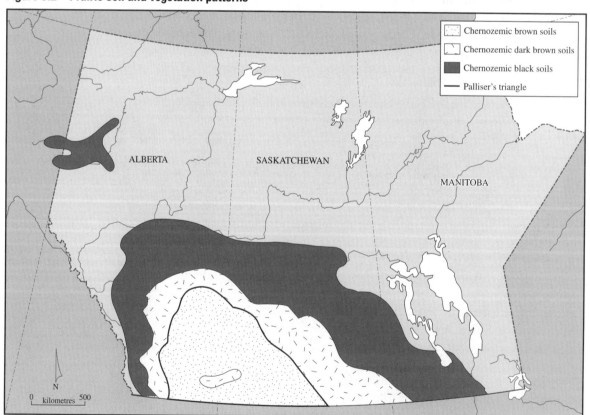

Sources: Adapted from R.M. Bone, *The Regional Geography of Canada,* 3rd edn (Toronto: Oxford University Press, 2003), 409, 410.

Saskatchewan and southeastern Alberta, is known as Palliser's Triangle. Hind mapped out the more northerly regions, where the soil was much better and where there were trees; this became known as Hind's Fertile Belt (see Fig. 9.2). Although this information was available before the majority of farmer settlers began establishing homesteads, early settlement patterns on the Prairies had more to do with the interests of the Canadian Pacific Railway than with the physical characteristics of the region.

Early Patterns of Occupation

There is archaeological evidence of the presence of Aboriginal groups on the Prairies as long ago as 10,000 years. These earliest inhabitants survived mainly on buffalo, caribou, and various plants. Between 5,000 and 2,000 years ago they developed more efficient means of hunting, including the use of buffalo pounds (corrals into which buffalo were chased and penned) and jumps (steep precipices over which the buffalo were stampeded to their deaths). Within the past 2,000 years, prairie peoples made contact with farming groups much farther south, from whom they learned about growing crops. It was through Spanish settlers in southwestern portions of North America that horses were introduced to northern Aboriginal groups (McGhee, 1985: 1467-8). This example of the spatial diffusion process was especially important, since horses made it possible for the Plains peoples to increase their take of buffalo for food and hides.

The numerous semi-nomadic tribes of the Prairie provinces belong to three separate linguistic families, whose geographical borders tended to overlap. To the north were the Athapaskan-speaking peoples: Chipewyan, Slavey, Beaver, and Sarcee. The southern Prairies were dominated by peoples of the Siouan language family: Assiniboine, Peigan, Blackfoot, Blood, and Stoney. The eastern portion of the prairies was occupied by Woodland Cree, Plains Cree, and Ojibwa, all belonging to the Algonquian language family (see Fig. 9.3).

A Plains Cree camp south of Vermilion, Alberta, September 1871.   *Photo by Charles Horetsky. Library and Archives Canada, C-5181.*

Figure 9.3   Semi-nomadic Aboriginal territories on the Prairies

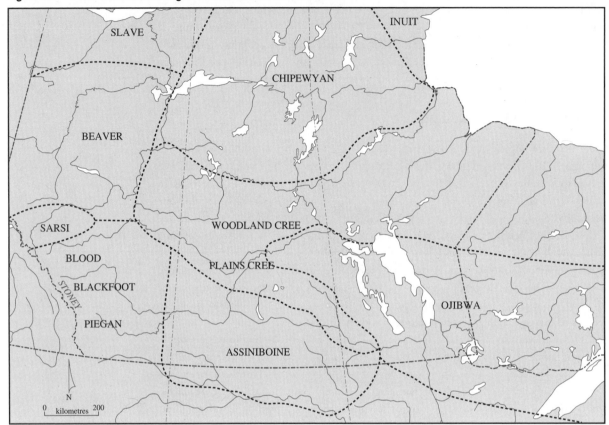

Sources: Adapted from R.C. Harris and J. Warkentin, *Canada Before Confederation: A Study in Historical Geography* (Ottawa: Carleton University Press, 1991); G. Friesen, *The Canadian Prairies* (Toronto: University of Toronto Press, 1984).

The fur trade brought Europeans to the Prairies in the seventeenth century, when the Hudson's Bay Company's acquisition of Rupert's Land in 1670 shifted the Anglo–French competition for furs from the Atlantic region to the northern forts of the territory defined by the river drainage pattern of Hudson Bay and James Bay. These forts traded hands several times before the French formally recognized Rupert's Land as British territory in the Treaty of Utrecht (1713). These forts, including Fort Prince of Wales (later Fort Churchill) at the mouth of the Churchill River, and Fort York (later York Factory) at the mouth of the Hayes and Nelson Rivers, were the entrepôts where Native-trapped furs were exchanged for European trade goods. It was not necessarily the trappers themselves who traded them, however: the Chipewyan and Woodland Cree people of the areas where the forts were situated jealously guarded their territories against the encroachment of more distant tribes, acting as middlemen who controlled and profited from the trade. On the Prairies as elsewhere, contact with Europeans had devastating consequences for Aboriginal populations and ways of life. The introduction of guns dramatically skewed the balance of power between various bands. But it was the spread of European disease that did the most damage. According to Harold Innis, a smallpox epidemic that began at York Factory and Fort Prince of Wales in 1781–2 'wiped out' nine-tenths of the 'Northern Indians' (1930: 152). The same epidemic weakened local Native populations to the point where they were unable to prevent the encroachment of trespassing non-Native fur traders (Francis et al., 2000: 427). The fur trade itself felt the consequences when those who survived the illness deserted the forts. A subsequent outbreak of smallpox, in 1836, resulted in the death of '4,000 or more Assiniboines' (Patterson, 1972: 95). By this time a vaccine for smallpox had been developed, and the Cree, who lived in proximity to the Hudson's Bay Company (unlike the Assiniboine), were largely spared because of the Company's vaccination program. This enabled the Cree to take over the disease-decimated territories (Francis et al., 2000: 440).

York Factory became the dominant trading post because of its location in relation to the Nelson and Saskatchewan rivers, which drained into and served as a transportation system through the southern half of the Prairies. But the HBC's fortunes fluctuated in response to smallpox epidemics and wars with the French. Even after the British takeover of New France in 1760, the rivalry between the two countries hampered the British fur-trading enterprise. In 1783, for example, the French, who supported the Americans in their War of Independence against the British, captured and destroyed Fort Prince of Wales. A far greater threat to the fortunes of the Hudson's Bay Company, however, was the formation of the rival North West Company in 1783.

An amalgam of individual fur-trade interests headquartered in Montreal, the North West Company changed the nature of the fur trade in western Canada. Unlike the HBC, whose forts on the shores of Hudson Bay provided easy access to ocean shipping, the Nor'Westers had to transport trade goods by boat from Montreal to the west via the Great Lakes and St Lawrence River and then make the return journey laden with furs. They made up for this disadvantage with their aggressive strategy, establishing forts across western Canada and intercepting Native traders carrying furs to the Hudson's Bay Company forts.

The bitter rivalry between the two companies had a major influence on the spatial pattern of occupation on the Prairies. The NWC's forts gave Native people in areas far from Hudson Bay direct access to European goods, including guns and ammunition, which altered the dynamics among various bands. Native middlemen were no longer required as intermediaries. But some groups, such as the Woodland Cree, took on a new role as suppliers of pemmican—the chief source of food in the western fur trade. As the competition increased, the populations of fur-bearing animals near the existing trade routes were rapidly depleted, forcing the trade to keep moving farther west and north. In the process, more and more Aboriginal groups became involved in the trade.

Together, European diseases, changing power relations between bands, and the establishment of trading forts on the prairies led to many changes in traditional territorial boundaries. The addictive properties of trade goods such as whisky and tobacco ensured that many Native people became increasingly dependent on Europeans. Perhaps the most significant change of all, however, came about as a result of the North West Company's favourable attitude towards relationships between its employees and Aboriginal women. Whereas the Hudson's Bay Company discouraged such unions, the Nor'Westers saw them as a way of securing alliances with Native fur traders. The offspring of these relationships were certainly not the first of mixed Aboriginal–European parentage in North America, but they soon formed a distinct Prairie community. The Métis became central participants in the fur trade, hunting buffalo, transporting hides and furs, and supplying pemmican to European traders. Many were also part-time farmers, cultivating long lots modelled on the pattern established under the seigneurial system in New France.

By 1795, scarcely ten years after the creation of the North West Company, the Hudson's Bay Company's profits had been dramatically reduced: in that year, according to E.E. Rich, the Nor'Westers controlled an estimated '11/14 of the trade, the Hudson's Bay Company 2/14 and opposition traders 1/14' (1960: 186). The HBC began establishing new forts in the western interior in order to remain competitive, but this was not enough to narrow the chasm in profits between the two companies: in 1800 'the Hudson's Bay Company sent £38,000 in furs to London, the Nor'Westers' £144,000' (Friesen, 1987: 62). But the HBC's largest grievance by far was the NWC's intrusion on Rupert's Land—the territory granted to the HBC by royal charter in 1670. In the early 1800s, Thomas Douglas, the Earl of Selkirk and principal HBC shareholder, launched a plan to reinforce the company's title to Rupert's Land. Figure 9.5 shows the extent of

Figure 9.4   Selkirk settlement boundaries

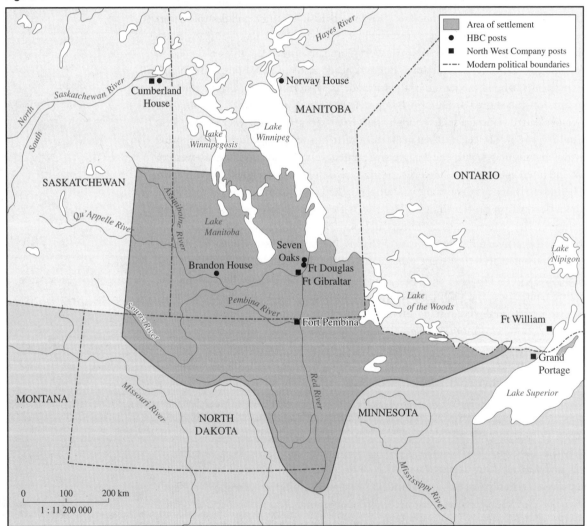

Sources: Adapted from J.M. Bumsted, 'Selkirk, Thomas Douglas, 5th Earl of', *The Canadian Encyclopedia* (Edmonton: Hurtig, 1985), 1674; G. Friesen, *The Canadian Prairies* (Toronto: University of Toronto Press, 1984).

the 300,000 square kilometres that made up the Red River colony (also known as the Selkirk Settlement), established in 1811 as a destination for emigrants displaced from the Scottish Highlands. This land, called Assiniboia by the HBC, was the subject of the first numbered treaty, under which the Saulteaux and Cree surrendered their Aboriginal title for 'the annual payment of one hundred pounds of tobacco to each Nation' (Frideres, 1988: 70).

Besides asserting the HBC's title to the region and fulfilling Selkirk's philanthropic wish to resettle his displaced countrymen, this new agricultural colony had two ostensible purposes: to produce food for HBC traders and to serve as a place where former HBC employees—especially those married to Aboriginal women—could retire (Thompson, 1998: 19). But the new colony threatened the existing Métis holdings, especially in 1814, when the governor of Assiniboia, Miles Macdonell, prohibited the export of pemmican from the district. The rationale for this embargo was that the new settlers, who had not been able to grow enough crops to sustain themselves over the winter, needed the food. But it was a serious blow to North West Company traders, who obtained most of their pemmican from Assiniboia, and to those Métis traders who profited from this exchange (Thompson, 1998: 19). The Red River colony thus became the focal point in the rivalry between the two companies. After enduring harsh agricultural conditions and repeated skirmishes with local Métis, most of the Selkirk settlers were soon persuaded to relocate in Upper Canada, which they did with assistance from the North West Company. The settlement was burned and the crops destroyed. But in the fall of 1815, despite continuing hostilities, the HBC managed to persuade another group of colonists to settle in the area under the governorship of Robert Semple, an HBC employee. It was Semple who, on 19 June 1816, led a group of colonists into confrontation with a party of Métis horsemen led by Cuthbert Grant. The Battle of Seven Oaks resulted in the deaths of approximately twenty colonists, while only one or two (reports vary) of the Métis were killed. Although the incident was often characterized as an ambush and used to highlight the supposed 'savagery' of the Métis, Thompson argues that 'the Semple party fired first, and the fighting took place with the Métis dismounted' (1998: 21). In any event, the Battle of Seven Oaks marked the beginning of a Métis nationalism.

The rivalry between the Hudson's Bay Company and the North West Company did not end until 1821, when the two companies merged. The merger, which followed ten years of clashes and lawsuits that nearly bankrupted both companies, was made possible in large part by the death in 1820 of Lord Selkirk, one of those most opposed to the union (Thompson, 1998: 22).

The establishment of a monopoly imposed a new order on the Prairies. Many of the Prairie forts were no longer needed. Similarly, it no longer made economic sense to transport furs via the Great Lakes and St Lawrence River, so this route was largely abandoned in favour of the route to York Factory. While Aboriginal populations were ravaged by disease, the numbers of Métis were growing rapidly (see Table 9.1). Their location close to trading forts, their knowledge of various languages (including French and English), and their Christianity gave them access to European ways of preventing disease, including smallpox vaccine; they may also have inherited genes that gave them some protection against European diseases.

Table 9.1 Red River Métis population, 1821–1869

Year	Population
1821	500
1831	1,300
1843	2,600
1856	3,230
1869	10,000

Source: Heritage Canada, 'The Virtual Museum of Métis History and Culture' (http://www.metismuseum.ca/main.php).

Figure 9.5   Decline of the Plains buffalo

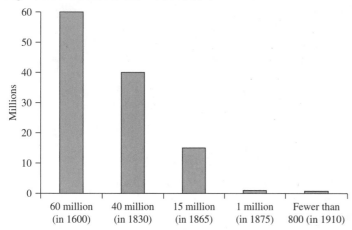

Source: Adapted from P.C. Newman, *Caesars of the Wilderness: Company of Adventurers*, vol. II (Markham: Penguin, 1987).

Another factor contributing to the decline of the some Native populations was the diminishing population of the Plains buffalo as the fur trade expanded. Extremely high in protein, and easily preserved, buffalo meat was the fundamental ingredient in pemmican, and the increasing demand for it put increasing pressure on the Plains buffalo herds (Symington, 1969: 222). In time, railway workers and new settlers also came to rely on buffalo meat as part of their diet, and a market developed for buffalo skins, used to make leather belts, boots, and clothing.

Unfortunately, these uses were not the only motives for hunting buffalo. Many animals were killed expressly to reduce what was thought to be a superabundant population. According to Young and Préfontaine (2003)—who note that rail travellers were encouraged to shoot buffalo from train windows as sport—killing buffalo was also part of 'the American military's initiative to destroy the American Indian's food source'. The result, outlined in Figure 9.6, was the near-extinction of the species.

From Fur Trade to Agriculture

By the time the Hudson's Bay Company had gained its monopoly, the fur trade was in decline. Changing fashions in Europe meant that the prices paid for beaver pelts fell even though the supplies available were dwindling. Meanwhile, the nomadic way of life on the prairies was about to be transformed. Despite the discouraging experience of the Selkirk colonists at Red River, the west was coming to be seen as the new agricultural frontier.

South of the 49th parallel, settlers were already establishing farms on the American plains; by the mid-1800s, there were well over 100,000 settlers in North Dakota, South Dakota, and Wisconsin, with a railroad running west all the way to St Paul, Minnesota, and 'modern' paddle wheelers on the Red River. As these new transportation systems drew the southern region of Manitoba and the remnants of the fur trade into St Paul's sphere of influence, that city 'gradually replaced York Factory on the Hudson Bay as the Red River's major entrepôt' (Francis et al., 2000: 438). This development aroused concern in the Canadas that the United States would try to annex the territory north of the 49th parallel. Agricultural settlement would help to secure the land for British North America, and Hind's favourable report on the 'fertile belt' supported the idea.

There were a number of hurdles that had to be overcome before settlement could occur. The greatest was the fact that most of the prairies were part of Rupert's Land and therefore would have to be bought back from the Hudson's Bay Company. Fear of American annexation grew when the US purchased Alaska in 1867. While the newly created government of Canada saw the necessity of purchasing Rupert's Land, the initial plan was to do so in stages, the first of which was to take over the District of Assiniboia. After concluding negotiations with the Hudson's Bay Company in 1867, the government dispatched surveyors and road builders to the Red River district, ignoring the existing land holdings of the Métis. The Métis were not the only inhabitants of Rupert's Land opposed to Ottawa's presumptuous plans to annex and colonize the territory without consulting its residents, but they mounted the stiffest challenge. They organized an armed resistance that produced a few minor clashes and, under the leadership of Louis Riel, formed a provisional government that drafted a bill of rights and set out to nego-tiate terms of Confederation with Canada. The result was the Manitoba Act, which took effect in July 1870, creating Canada's fifth province in an area that essentially followed the boundaries of the Red River settlement. Under the Manitoba Act, Métis land title was recognized, and the children of Métis parents received a federal land grant of 1,400,000 acres (566,580 ha) in all. The rights to speak either English or French and to be taught in either Protestant or Catholic schools were also guaranteed. However, Ottawa retained control over all the public lands and natural resources of the new province.

On the surface, Riel and the Métis appeared to have attained most of their objec-tives. But one tactical error would have devastating consequences. In the spring of 1870, before the Manitoba Act received royal assent, an Irish immigrant with Protestant sympathies named Thomas Scott, who had gone to Red River from Ontario, was court-martialled and executed by the Métis with Riel's approval. Although Scott had been arrested on a number of occasions and was a boisterous and violent prisoner, his execu-tion outraged the largely Protestant population of Ontario in particular. The Canadian military were sent to the region, and although most of those involved in the resistance were given amnesty, Riel and his closest supporters went into exile in the United States.

In the new province of Manitoba the incoming settlers, most of whom were English-speaking Protestants, resented the presence of the French-speaking Catholic Métis, who received little support from the new political administration. Of the roughly 10,000 Métis in Red River, at least two-thirds are thought to have left the province over the next few years, either 'pushed' out by persecution (Brown, 1985: 1126) or 'pulled' farther west and north because they were still attached to the buffalo hunts and the fur trade (Pannekoek, 2001: 115). The map in Figure 9.7 shows the spatial diffusion of the Métis in the two decades after 1870.

The Métis of the Red River region had developed a powerful sense of nationalism, which was dampened but not extinguished as the community was dispersed. The solidarity of those who relocated in what is now central Saskatchewan was reinvigorated in the mid-1880s, when the Métis once again feared that they were about to be dispos-sessed by Ottawa. This time, however, the Métis had allies in their dispute with Ottawa, including several Plains bands that were close to starvation because of the dramatic drop in the buffalo population, and some aggrieved white settlers in the region.

Once again the Métis turned to Louis Riel to lead their cause. The exiled leader agreed, but he was not the same person he had been fifteen years earlier; having un-dergone a number of religious experiences, he now considered himself a prophet with a mission and was much more anxious to take up arms, which cost him the support of some white settlers and of the influential Catholic clergy. The first confronta-tion of the North-West Rebellion occurred on 26 March 1885 when a group of Métis led by Gabriel Dumont encountered a detachment of the North-West Mounted Police at Duck Lake. The federal government was quickly informed by tele-graph and responded at once, sending troops west on the new railway to subdue the

Figure 9.6   Dispersal of the Métis, 1870–1890

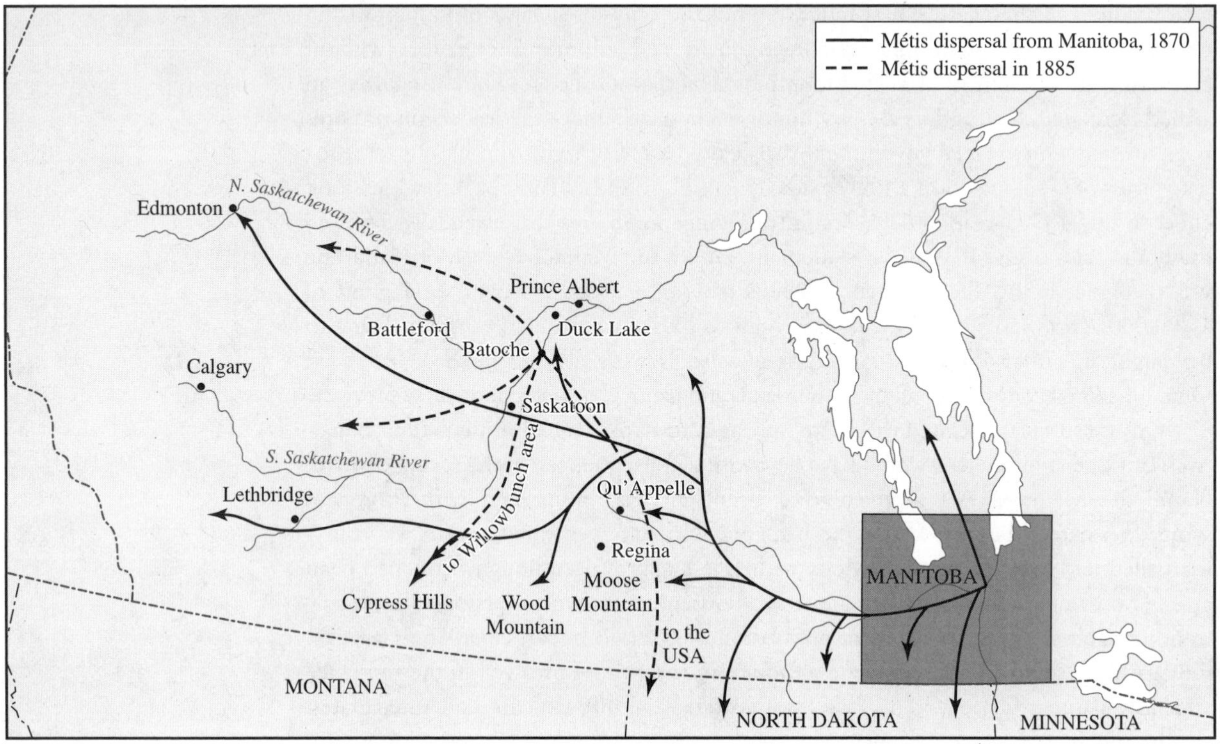

Source: D.B. Sealey and A.S. Lussier, *The Métis: Canada's Forgotten People* (Winnipeg: Manitoba Métis Federation Press, 1975).

uprising. The decisive battle took place on 12–15 May at Batoche, where militia regiments led by Major General Frederick Middleton wore down the Métis force during a four-day siege. Riel surrendered on 15 May and was later tried and hanged for treason. The government's decisive suppression of the resistance eased the way for treaty negotiations with First Nations bands on the Prairies, while forcing many of the Métis even farther west and north (see Fig. 9.7).

The Métis were not the only group to be pushed aside by Ottawa's settlement plans. A publication by the Ontario department of education expressed a view of the Plains Indians that was common in central and eastern Canada in the latter half of the nineteenth century. While recognizing the presence of the Plains peoples, it claimed that they 'were not fond of labor, and did little to cultivate the soil', and characterized the region as 'an unoccupied wild' (Dept. of Education, 1887: 32). Within a few years of Confederation the Canadian government was working to replace the region's Native inhabitants with settlers who would turn the 'wild' prairie into productive agricultural land. First, however, it had to negotiate treaties extinguishing the various Plains groups' Aboriginal title to the land. Between 1871 and 1877, therefore, Canada made seven numbered treaties covering approximately 34,000 people across the Prairies (Thompson, 1998: 48). Once the Native people had been assigned reserve lands, the way was clear for the rest of the territory to be surveyed for railways, homesteads, and other uses.

Treaties 1 through 7 were the ones that the federal government was most eager to complete to make way for settlement. Treaties 8 through 11 were concluded later, motivated by the prospect of valuable minerals in the northern portions of the North-west Territories. The various treaties were largely the same, but there were some differ-ences. For instance, while all the numbered treaties allowed for reserves, the formulas used to determine the size of the reserves varied. Thus Treaties 1, 2, and 5 allotted only a quarter-section, or 160 acres (65 ha), for a family of five, whereas the other numbered treaties provided a whole section (640 acres/260 ha) for a family of the same size. There were cash awards paid in yearly instalments as well as payments for signing and, in some instances, separate payments for band chiefs and headmen; again, these amounts varied from treaty to treaty. Most of the treaties also provided for the Native people concerned to continue hunting, fishing, and trapping, although Treaties 1 and 2 did not, and Treaty 5 included some restrictions on these rights. Agricultural aid was promised for groups planning to establish farms. Some of the treaties promised clothing for chiefs and head-men, some covered yearly ammunition and twine, as well as medals and flags, and Treaty 6 included an unusual agreement regarding medical assistance (Frideres, 1988; Frideres and Gadacz, 2001; Friesen, 1987).

Were these treaties fair? From the perspective of the federal government, it was important to avoid conflict and live up to the conditions laid out in the Royal Proclamation of 1763, which required that Aboriginal people be compensated for extinguishing their title to the land. But there is no doubt that the government negotia-tors were bargaining from a position of strength: widespread famine and the encroach-ment both of settlers from the east and of traders from the south made many Native people desperate to sign treaties, which they considered 'peace alliances', in order to gain some control of the chaotic situation of the time. Complicating the matter of translation was the fact that the various Plains peoples belonged to four distinct language groups. There is also some question about how much Aboriginal leaders understood of the arrangements they agreed to. The Treaty 7 tribal council and elders have suggested that perhaps as little as one-sixth of this treaty was translated, and there were no Native words for such key terms as 'reserve', 'mile', 'square', 'Canada', 'Treaty', or 'surrender' (Treaty 7 El-ders and Tribal Council, 1996: 24). Thus, the tribal Elders conclude, their ancestors did not understand that by signing a document with an 'X' they were surrendering their land.

Unlike First Nations, the Métis did not qualify for reserves. They were dealt with individually and through government policies that left them with little land of their own. Many Métis were issued 'scrips'—certificates entitling them to a certain amount of land or money—but these often ended up in the hands of unscrupulous speculators (Boldt and Long, 1985; Frideres, 2001; Goyette, 2003). Frits Pannekoek suggests that scrip 'was designed to benefit the speculator, not the Métis', and that the federal government 'was guilty of breach of trust' (2001: 118).

One of Ottawa's goals in settling the land issue quickly was to designate lands for a transcontinental railway, which it saw as critical to ensuring that the west did not fall into American hands. Concerns over that possibility increased after 1869, when the Union Pacific Railroad began carrying ever-greater numbers of settlers to the American west. The vision of a transcontinental railway on the Canadian side of the boarder came closer to reality in 1871, when British Columbia joined Confederation, but a political scandal delayed its construction for ten years.

Figure 9.7   Townships, ranges, and meridian lines for the Dominion Land Survey

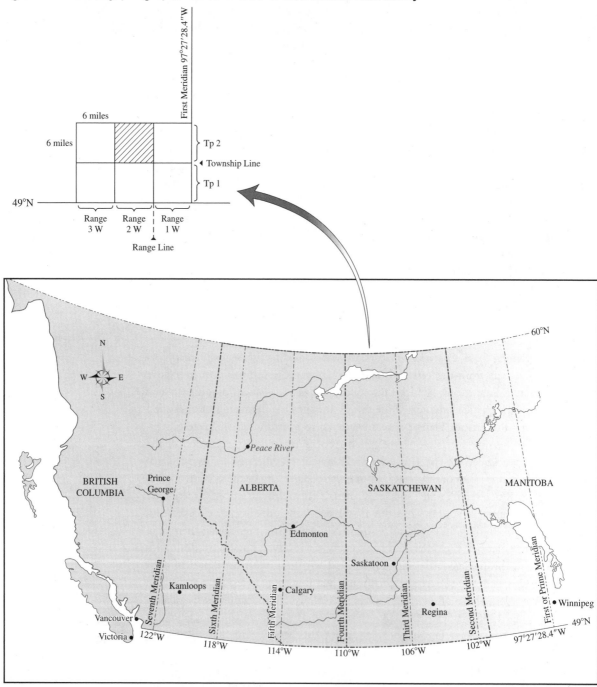

In any case, before the railway could be built, a process for surveying and subdividing the treaty lands had to be established. The Dominion Land Survey system, introduced in 1870, was similar to the one used in the American west. Square blocks of land called townships were laid out at 6-mile intervals, starting at the 49th parallel. Lots were measured west from seven north–south meridians established by the Dominion surveyors; each column of lots was referred to as a range. The combination of ranges and townships produced a grid pattern of 36 blocks of land across western Canada (see Fig. 9.7).

One problem was that the distance between ranges narrowed as the surveyors moved north. To keep the sizes of the townships roughly equal, the north–south lines had to be adjusted at regular intervals: thus the northern boundary of every fourth row of townships (every 24 miles) became a 'correction line' where the edges of the next row would jog west (for ranges to the west of a meridian) and east (for ranges to the east). Each township and range, representing 36 square miles or 36 sections, could be divided and subdivided into smaller and smaller units. Sections measuring one square mile (640 acres; 260 ha) were commonly divided into quarters of 160 acres (65 ha) each. In this way the quarter-section became the main unit used for allocating land across western Canada (Fig. 9.8).

The Dominion Land Survey established a rigid geometry that took no account of physical features such as rivers, lakes, or marshes. It became the basis for allocating lands not only for farming homesteads and schools but for the railway, Aboriginal reserves, and the purchase of Rupert's Land from the Hudson's Bay Company. In many ways, this survey system was the instrument that converted the Prairies from a mobile hunting-and-gathering economy to one based on individual land-owners practising various forms of agriculture.

After many delays, the transcontinental railway became a priority for the Conservative government of John A. Macdonald towards the end of the 1870s, and was an important part of the National Policy introduced in 1879. However, it is important to keep in mind that the Canadian Pacific Railway was operated by a private company whose most important goals were high profits and satisfied shareholders. In other words, though the company gained many concessions from the government, including $25 million, 25 million acres (more than 10 million hectares) of land, the existing railway line in Ontario (worth $37.8 million), a 20-year property tax exemption, and a 20-year monopoly (Friesen, 1987: 177–8; Chodos, 1973: 22), its operations were designed to serve private interests and therefore did not necessarily serve the public good.

A case in point was the railway's route across the Prairies. The agricultural potential of the Prairie region was well known after Palliser and Hind completed their surveys in the mid-1800s. Certainly it was natural to expect that the CPR line would be designed to carry settlers to the Fertile Belt—but it did not (see Fig. 9.9). Instead, it took a more southerly route through Palliser's Triangle. The reasons reflected the interests of the CPR: a more southerly route meant lower construction costs (because it was shorter route and required fewer large bridges); it was closer to the southern coalfields of Alberta; it was in a better position to compete with the American railways; and the company would realize far greater profits by creating supply centres in Brandon, Regina, and Calgary, where it owned most of the valuable urban land (Friesen, 1987: 178–9). As a result, settlers were effectively invited to establish farms on land with some of the worst growing conditions the Prairies had to offer. In spite of these problems, the CPR (and accompanying telegraph lines) represented an enormous technological advance. The railway was an instrument of time–space convergence, capable of moving goods, people, and information. It also served to stimulate the Canadian economy during a time of depression, and was crucial to the settlement and development of the west.

Figure 9.8   Sections and quarter-sections in the Dominion Land Survey

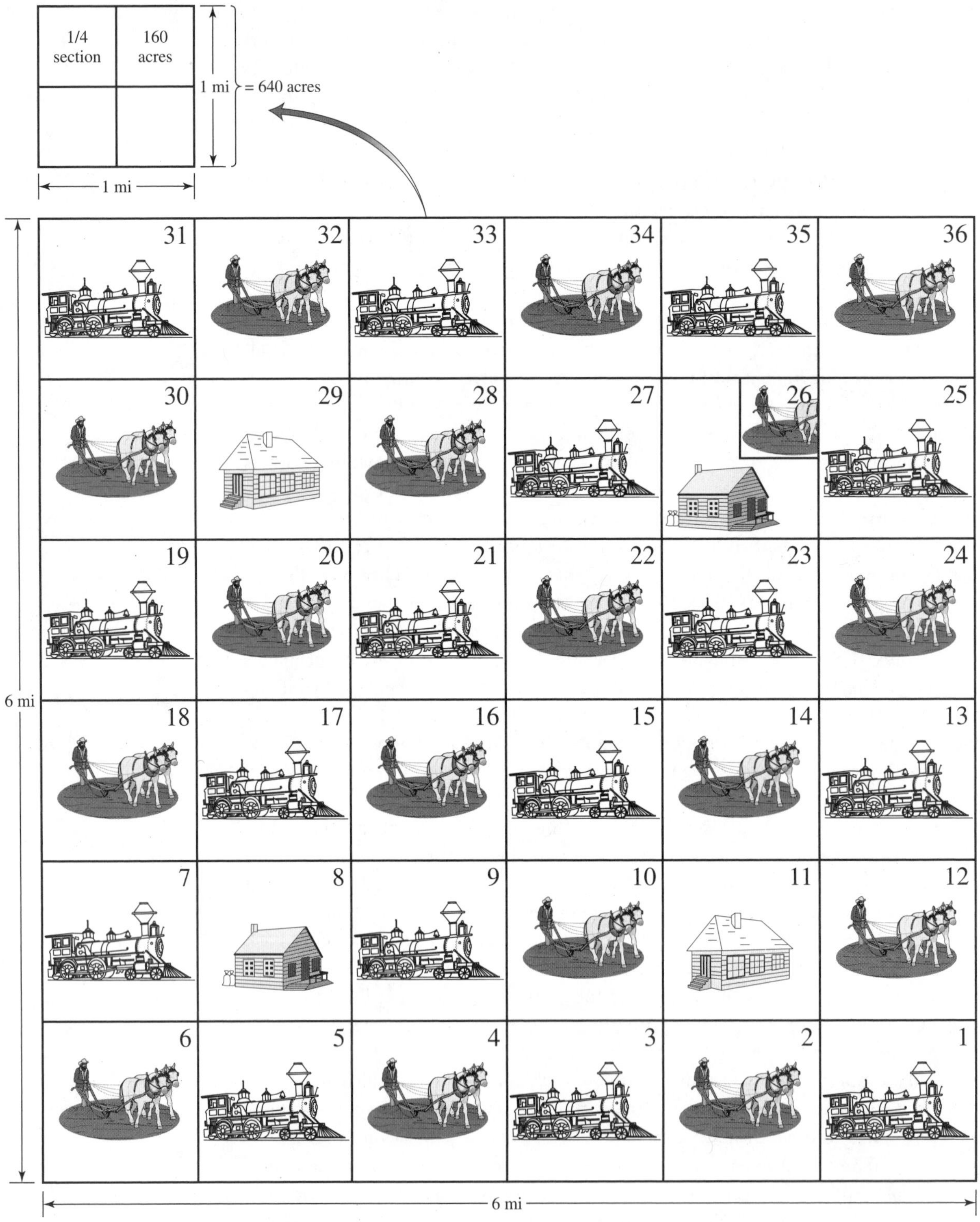

Figure 9.9　The CPR route across the Prairies

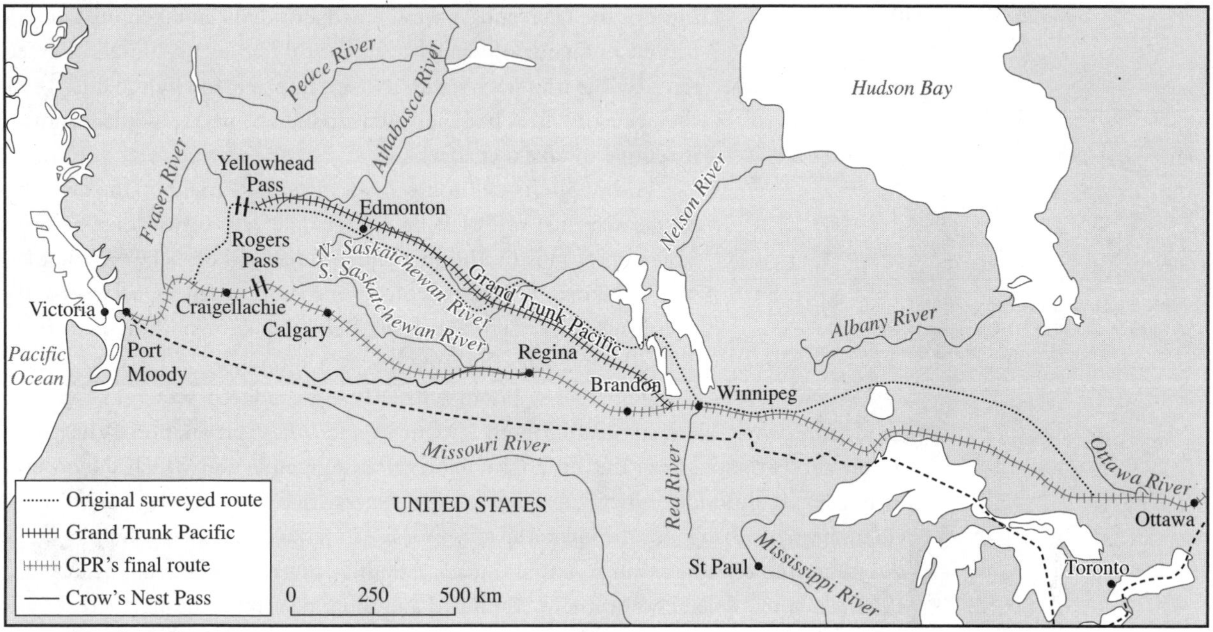

Source: G. Friesen, *The Canadian Prairies: A History* (Toronto: University of Toronto Press, 1984).

Agriculture and Settlement: 1860–1950

Lord Selkirk had advanced the vision of farming on the Prairies by persuading desperate families from Scotland to come to the Red River in the early 1800s. But as they soon discovered, farming on the southern Prairies was not easy. The climate offered little chance of crops maturing before the first frost, and the landscape was subject both to major floods and to plagues of grasshoppers. Many of the original settlers were unable to sustain themselves.

Making this landscape fit for farming would take people willing to invest a great deal of time and effort. The federal government began promoting the settlement of the Canadian Prairies throughout Europe, offering would-be settlers homesteads in exchange for just ten dollars and a promise that they would cultivate a certain amount of land each year. Yet until the late 1890s, emigration was higher than immigration, primarily because of the overwhelming lure of the United States (see Table 9.13). The US Homestead Act of 1862 preceded the Dominion Lands Act by ten years; the American west had railways in place early, and prices for both land and farm equipment were lower

Table 9.2　Population (× 1,000), Canada, 1871–1921

Years	Natural increase	Immigration	Emigration	Net migration	Total population
1871–1881	720	353	438	−85	4,325
1881–1891	714	903	1,108	−205	4,833
1891–1901	719	326	507	−181	5,371
1901–1911	1,120	1,782	1,066	715	7,207
1911–1921	1,349	1,592	1,360	233	8,788

Source: G. Friesen, *The Canadian Prairies: A History* (Toronto: University of Toronto Press, 1987), 248.

Table 9.3   Railway expansion in Western Canada, 1897–1949

Year	Track (in miles)	Track (in km)
1897	3,300	5,311
1901	4,000	6,437
1906	6,000	9,656
1911	8,000	12,874
1916	14,000	22,530
1949	18,000	28,967

Source: K. Buckley, 'Capital Formation in Canada, 1896–1930', in W.T. Easterbrook and M.H. Watkins, eds, *Approaches to Canadian Economic History* (Toronto: McClelland and Stewart, 1967), 176.

than in Canada. By the end of the nineteenth century, however, most of the farmland in the US had already been taken up. The tide turned in favour of Canada, which still had plenty of land for settlers. By the mid-1880s, the CPR was in place, and by the mid-1890s the price of wheat had increased, giving prospective settlers another incentive to take a chance.

Although the CPR route encouraged settlement on the drought-prone marginal soil of Palliser's Triangle, it was not long before a labyrinth of rails (both independent lines and branches of the CPR) was extended to the north, giving homesteaders access to the rich black soils of Hind's Fertile Belt (also known as the Park Belt). Table 9.3 indicates the rapid increase in track.

The railway boom on the Prairies reduced the cost of moving goods and people alike, stimulating both settlement and wheat production. Wheat producers also benefited from the 1897 Crow's Nest Pass Agreement, in which the government agreed to subsidize a new CPR line into the mineral-rich Kootenay region of British Columbia in exchange for the rail company's promise to reduce its rates for shipping grain and flour from the Prairies into central Canada. Another railway development occurred in 1918, when the federal government combined a number of central and northern Prairie railways into a second transcontinental railway with a western terminal at Prince Rupert: the Canadian National Railway, or CNR. The effects of these developments on the wheat market were clear: between 1900 and 1911 wheat production expanded from 40 million bushels to 230 million bushels (Sitwell and Seifried, 1984: 51), and by 1928 sales of Canadian wheat represented close to half of the world export market (Friesen, 1987: 301).

Prairie farming was never easy, but several innovations reduced the risk of having no crop to harvest. The development of new varieties of wheat helped farmers cope. Marquis wheat, for example, which ripens in a relatively short growing season, was introduced in 1909, and Thatcher wheat, a strain resistant to rust (a fungus that can destroy wheat crops) in the 1930s. Irrigation systems helped to counteract the arid conditions on the southern Prairies; barbed wire separated farms from ranches, keeping cattle away from crops; machines cut, stacked and threshed the wheat; and the practice of summer fallow retained soil moisture and reduced weeds. Together, these innovations brought significant improvements to Prairie farming.

Sir Clifford Sifton, federal Minister of the Interior from 1896 to 1905, gained much of the credit for settling the Prairies through aggressive—though discriminatory—immigration policies. His list of immigrants ranged from 'Most Wanted' to 'Acceptable' and finally 'Need Not Apply'. The first category included British, French, and white American farmers. The 'Acceptable' category included most Europeans: Belgians, Dutch, Scandinavians, Swiss, Finns, Russians, Germans, Austro-Hungarians, Ukrainians, and Poles. Among those considered least desirable were Italians, South Slavs, Greeks, Jews, Blacks, Asians, and Gypsies (Canadian Human Rights Commission). 'Bounty hunters' were paid a commission for every immigrant they signed up, at rates that varied according to the candidate's perceived value: a Ukrainian man was worth almost three times as much as a British farmer. Sifton recognized the reality of the tough physical conditions of Prairie farming as well as the background and experience of the various immigrants: British settlers, after a difficult year or two, often abandoned their homesteads to seek

A family of Polish settlers harvesting the potato crop on their Manitoba farm around 1928. The CNR commissioned photos like this to use in advertising for prospective immigrants in Europe.   *Photo Canadian National Railways/Library and Archives Canada, c-016926.*

work in the city, whereas Ukrainians represented Sifton's ideal: 'the "stalwart peasants in sheepskin coats" who were turning some of the most difficult areas of the West into productive farms' (Hall, 1985: 1695).

The recruitment campaign reflected the long-standing myth of Canada as an empty land waiting to be settled. It also promised a year-round pleasant climate, soil that was universally excellent for farming, a society that recognized no social distinctions, and certain prosperity for those who were prepared to work (Friesen, 1987: 303). Glossing over the harsh physical realities, these myths served as 'pull' factors for immigrants. But there were also many 'push' factors, including war, famine, religious persecution, insufficient land, poverty, and natural disaster. One example of migration prompted by natural disasters involved a group of 1,400 Icelanders who came to Canada between 1874 and 1876, 'pushed out' of their native land by the failure of cod stocks and the threat of volcanic activity. With the encouragement of the Canadian government, this group established New Iceland on the edge of Lake Winnipeg, north of the new postage-stamp province of Manitoba. This block of land comprised nearly 13 townships covering 462 square miles (1,197 sq. km); the town of Gimli became the administrative centre, and the residents of the region had their own form of governance until the area became part of Manitoba

Table 9.4   Population, Prairies, 1901–1951

Year	Manitoba	Saskatchewan	Alberta	Total
1901	255,211	91,279	73,022	419,512
1911	461,394	462,432	374,295	1,298,121
1921	610,118	757,510	588,454	1,956,082
1931	700,139	921,785	731,605	2,353,529
1941	729,744	895,992	796,169	2,421,905
1951	776,500	831,700	939,500	2,547,700

Source: Adapted from Statistics Canada, 'Historical Statistics of Canada', 1983, Cat. no. 11-516, Series A2-14.

in 1881. The soil was good for farming, there were trees for fuel and building in abundance, and Lake Winnipeg provided a means of transportation as well as a commercial fishery. Even so, harsh winter conditions and diseases such as smallpox took their toll (Lyon, 1985: 741; IceCan, n.d.; Great Canadian Lakes, n.d.; Bye the Lake Communications, 2001).

Religious persecution in Russia was an important push factor for two groups. When some 7,000 Mennonites immigrated to the Prairies in the 1870s, blocks of land were set aside for them, including eight townships in southern Manitoba and two reserves comprising 22 townships in what would become Saskatchewan. More than 7,400 Doukhobors arrived in 1898–9, during Sifton's tenure, and like the Mennonites they were granted land in Saskatchewan, where they lived communally. However, once Sifton was no longer Minister of the Interior, the federal government insisted that they swear allegiance to Canada. When they refused, thousands of their homesteads were cancelled; many then moved to the Kootenay region of British Columbia (Woodcock and Avakumovic, 1968; Doukhobor History to 1930).

Table 9.4 documents the rapid increase in the Prairie region's population during the first half of the twentieth century. As a result of this growth, as well as improvements in technology affecting all aspects of agriculture, from planting to harvesting, farms increased both in number and in size during this period (see Table 9.5).

To help manage the flow of immigrants to the Prairies the federal government in 1905 created the provinces of Saskatchewan and Alberta, and in 1912 it extended the northern boundary of Manitoba to the 60th parallel. The boundaries for the new provinces had been the subject of much debate. Some proposals would have divided the territory in four; others would have made it single province—although that idea was seen as potentially threatening to central Canada. As in Manitoba, the federal government retained control over Crown lands—and the resource revenues derived from them—in Saskatchewan and Alberta. The three Prairie provinces would not achieve equality with the older provinces in this respect until 1930.

monoculture
the cultivation of a single crop

Over time, more and more Prairie farmers began growing nothing but wheat. This **monoculture** meant that unfavourable climatic conditions or a sudden drop in the

Table 9.5   Total farms, farm area, and average farm size (acres), 1901–1951

	Manitoba			Saskatchewan			Alberta		
	Farms	**Area**[1]	**Avg.**[2]	**Farms**	**Area**	**Avg.**	**Farms**	**Area**	**Avg.**
1901	32,252	8,843	274	13,445	3,833	285	9,479	2,736	289
1911	43,631	12,184	279	95,013	28,099	296	60,559	17,359	287
1921	53,252	14,616	274	119,451	44,023	369	82,954	29,293	353
1931	54,199	15,132	279	136,472	55,673	408	97,408	38,977	400
1941	58,024	16,891	291	138,713	59,961	432	99,732	43,277	434
1951	53,251	17,730	333	117,781	61,663	524	77,130	44,460	576

[1]Farm area in thousands of acres.

[2]Average farm size in acres.

Source: Adapted from Statistics Canada, 'Historical Statistics of Canada', 1983, Cat. no. 11-516, Series M12-33.

'Dust bowl' was the term used to describe the dry regions of the Prairies during the great drought of the 1930s. This photograph, taken south of Regina, was one of a series commissioned by the Saskatchewan Wheat Pool to dramatize the effects of the drought. *Saskatchewan Archives Board, R-A 15077-1.*

world market price could have serious consequences for the farming community. These two situations occurred together during the 1930s Depression, when the price of wheat plummeted from a high of $1.60 a bushel to just 28 cents in 1932, and overall farm income in Saskatchewan dropped from $419 million in 1929 to $109 million in 1933 (Saskatchewan Interactive, 2002). At the same time, drought caused crops to dry up, while winds created devastating dust storms that carried away huge quantities of topsoil. With waves of grasshoppers devouring what little grain survived, wheat yields declined by close to 90 per cent in some cases (Saskatchewan Interactive 2002).

Saskatchewan was particularly hard hit, and as Table 9.4 shows, its population declined. But not all farms and farmers suffered equally. While communal societies such as the Hutterites practised mixed farming and managed to weather the adversities, where conditions were worst—in the dry southern portion of the Prairies—many farms were abandoned altogether. But some important lessons were gained from this disastrous experience. Until that time, it had been common practice to use a plow and then harrows to break up the topsoil into fine particles before planting; but when it was recognized that this had helped to dry out the soil to the point where it could be blown away, new 'zero tillage' methods were developed—for example, drilling into the topsoil and dropping a seed. Other important innovations included diversification (growing crops other than wheat), practising summer fallow, increasing irrigation, and planting rows of trees ('shelter belts') to cut down on wind and to preserve snow for valuable spring moisture.

In addition, the farming community's experience of the Depression sparked many social, cultural, political, and economic changes. Prairie women's organizations initiated many social changes, from the recognition of women as 'persons' eligible to sit in the Senate to the building of the social safety net and the provision of the kind of education that many Canadians presently enjoy. Two political parties emerged in response to the Depression. In Alberta, William Aberhart's Social Credit party came to power on the strength of the idea that citizens should be given money to spend their way out of economic conditions. The Co-operative Commonwealth Federation (CCF), the fore-runner of the New Democratic Party, took the opposite direction, advocating the replacement of capitalism with a social system that would include programs for health and welfare insurance, unemployment insurance, children's allowances, worker's compensation, and old-age pensions, among others. The party's first convention was held in Regina in 1933.

Most immigrants went to the Prairies intending to farm or ranch, but there were other resources and sources of employment. The coalfields of southern Alberta and Saskatchewan, the minerals of the Canadian Shield in Manitoba, and the forests in the northern portions of all three provinces provided for some economic diversification. As well, urban centres were emerging, and many immigrants were drawn to them in search of work.

The urban pattern of the Prairies began with Winnipeg, the 'Gateway to the West'. It was a transportation hub: both the CPR and the CNR passed through the city, and it gained a considerable share of the wholesale and retail trade. Winnipeg became home to a number of banks and insurance companies that provided services to the entire Prairie region. Other urban centres—Regina, Saskatoon, Calgary, and Edmonton—grew in response to railway extensions and immigration promotion, and they too developed retail trade and important services, such as health and education. Increasingly, however, Winnipeg found itself in competition with Vancouver. The completion of the Panama Canal in 1914 and rail rates that facilitated the movement of grain to the west coast made Vancouver's international port especially attractive. And with its growth as a shipping centre, Vancouver developed wholesaling, retailing, financial, insurance, and legal services that competed with similar economic activities in Winnipeg. Table 9.6, comparing the growth of the main urban centres on the Prairies from the turn of the twentieth century to 1951, highlights the dominant position of Winnipeg. The rapid rise of Vancouver points to the advantage of having an international port linked to two national railways.

Table 9.6   Urban populations, Prairies and Vancouver, 1901–1951

Year	Winnipeg[1]	Regina	Saskatoon	Edmonton[2]	Calgary	Vancouver[1]
1901	42,340	2,249	113	4,176	4,152	29,432
1906	90,153	6,169	3,011	14,088	11,967	
1911	136,035	30,213	12,004	31,064	43,704	120,847
1916	163,000	26,127	21,048	53,846	56,514	
1921	179,087	34,432	25,739	58,821	63,305	231,542
1926	191,998	37,329	31,234	65,163	65,513	
1931	218,785	53,209	43,291	79,197	83,761	348,519
1936	215,814	53,354	41,734	85,774	83,407	
1941	221,960	58,245	43,027	93,817	88,904	409,262
1946	229,045	60,246	46,028	113,116	100,044	
1951	235,710	71,319	53,268	159,631	129,060	587,635

[1]Census Metropolitan Area (1971) boundaries used.

[2]Includes Strathcona

Source: G.A. Nader, *Cities of Canada*, vol. II, *Profiles of Fifteen Metropolitan Areas* (Toronto: Macmillan, 1976), 272, 298, 317, 337, 358, 381.

Diversifying the Prairie Economy: The 1950s to the Present

The Prairie provinces' reliance on agricultural commodities diminished after the Second World War. New resources, technological innovations, improvements to transportation, and the shift to a more global (Pacific-oriented) economy brought considerable diversification. But this has not occurred to the same degree in all three provinces. Staples still play an important role, and events beyond the control of the provinces, or even the country, still influence supply and demand. Table 9.7 shows the populations of the three provinces over the last half of the twentieth century. The region's overall population has doubled in that time, but Alberta has experienced a far greater increase than Saskatchewan. As Table 9.8 shows, the percentage of the population living outside urban centres has decreased, reflecting the shift to manufacturing and service-based employment that has occurred across the Prairies, although one-third of the population of Saskatchewan remains rural. Most Prairie residents (57 per cent) live in the five major cities, and Calgary and Edmonton have overtaken Winnipeg in terms of population (see Table 9.9).

The communities a tier below the five major cities—those with populations between 10,000 and 100,000—have faced different pressures. In Alberta all these centres, with the exception of Fort McMurray, experienced population increases between 1991 and 2001. Cochrane, for example, has become a commutershed for the rapidly growing city of Calgary, while Canmore is becoming a popular destination for skiers. Much of the growth in other centres reflects developments in the oil and natural gas industries.

Communities in Saskatchewan and Manitoba, by contrast, have tended to experience population decreases or at best sluggish growth. Lloydminster, situated right on the

Table 9.7   Prairie population (× 1,000), 1951–2003

Year	Manitoba	Saskatchewan	Alberta	Total
1951	776.5	831.7	939.5	2,547.7
1961	921.7	925.2	1,331.9	3,178.8
1971	988.3	926.2	1,627.9	3,542.4
1981	1,026.2	968.3	2,237.7	4,232.2
1991	1,091.9	988.9	2,545.6	4,626.4
2001	1,150.7	1,017.7	3,059.1	5,227.5
2002	1,155.5	995.5	3,114.4	5,265.4
2003	1,162.8	994.8	3,153.7	5,311.3

Source: Adapted from Statistics Canada, CANSIM Table 051-0001.

Table 9.8   Rural–urban population (%), Prairies, 1971–2001

	Manitoba		Saskatchewan		Alberta	
Year	Rural	Urban	Rural	Urban	Rural	Urban
1971	30.5	69.5	47.0	53.0	26.5	73.5
1981	28.8	71.2	41.8	58.2	22.8	77.2
1991	27.9	72.1	37.0	63.0	20.2	79.8
2001	28.1	71.9	35.7	64.3	19.1	80.9

Sources: Statistics Canada, 'Population urban and rural by province and territory', Census of Population 1851–2001
⟨http://www40.statcan.ca/l01/cst01/demo62a.htm⟩.

Table 9.9   Population of major Prairie urban centres and rank order, 1961–2001

City	1961	1971	1981	1991	2001
Winnipeg	476,543 (1)	540,262 (1)	592,061 (3)	652,355 (3)	671,274 (3)
Regina	113,749 (4)	140,734 (4)	173,226 (5)	191,695 (5)	192,800 (5)
Saskatoon	95,564 (5)	126,449 (5)	175,058 (4)	210,025 (4)	225,927 (4)
Edmonton	359,821 (2)	403,319 (3)	740,882 (1)	839,920 (1)	937,845 (2)
Calgary	279,062 (3)	495,702 (2)	625,966 (2)	754,030 (2)	951,395 (1)

Sources: W.W. McVey and W.E. Kalbach, *Canadian Population* (Scarborough: Nelson, 1995), 163; (1961–81); Statistics Canada, Community Profiles ⟨http://www12.statcan.ca/english/profil01/CP01/Index.cfm?Lang=E⟩ (1991–2001).

Table 9.10   Prairie communities of 10,000–99,000, 1991, 1996, and 2001

Province	Community	1991	1996	% change 1991–1996	2001	% change 1996–2001
Alberta	Fort McMurray	36,771	35,213	−4.2	41,466	+17.8
	Grande Prairie[1]	28,271	31,353	+10.1	36,983	+18.0
	Cold Lake[2]	n.a.	27,139	—	27,935	+2.9
	Wetaskiwin	10,657	10,959	+2.8	11,154	+1.8
	Camrose	13,420	13,728	+2.3	14,854	+8.2
	Red Deer	58,145	60,080	+3.3	67,707	+12.7
	Canmore	5,681	8,353	+47.1	10,792	+29.2
	Cochrane	5,267	7,424	+41.0	11,798	+58.9
	Medicine Hat	52,681	56,570	+7.4	61,735	+9.1
	Lethbridge	60,974	63,053	+3.4	67,374	+6.9
Saskatchewan	Lloydminster	17,283	18,953	+9.7	20,988	+10.7
	Prince Albert	41,257	41,706	+1.1	41,460	−0.6
	North Battleford	18,455	17,987	−2.5	17,512	−2.6
	Yorkton	18,023	17,713	−1.7	17,554	−0.9
	Moose Jaw	35,552	34,829	−2.0	33,519	−3.8
	Swift Current	16,429	16,437	0.0	16,527	+0.5
	Estevan	12,178	12,656	+3.9	12,083	−4.5
Manitoba	Thompson	14,977	14,385	−4.0	13,256	−7.8
	Brandon	39,897	40,581	+1.7	41,037	+1.1
	Portage la Prairie	20,994	20,385	−2.9	20,617	+1.1

[1]Boundary change.   [2]Amalgamation of three former communities in 1997: Grand Centre, Medley, and Cold Lake.
Source: Adapted from Statistics Canada, 2001 Community Profiles ⟨http://www12.statcan.ca/english/profil01/CP01/Index.cfm?Lang=E⟩.

border between Saskatchewan and Alberta, is an exception, with significant population growth related in large part to increased oil production in the region. (As a border community, Lloydminster is also unique in that laws regarding everything from drinking age to taxation differ from one side of town to the other.) Many of the larger communities in Saskatchewan and Manitoba have been important service centres for agriculture, but are suffering with the decrease in the number of active farms. Even more vulnerable are centres (such as Thompson) that rely on nickel mining and smelting. The most important development by far for the Prairies was the discovery of oil and natural gas in the early twentieth century. The geographic distribution of these resources favours Alberta. Oil was discovered in the Turner valley, near Calgary, at the beginning of the First World War, and by 1930s this region was producing both oil and natural gas, although at that time Canada relied primarily on the United States for oil. It was after the Second World War that rich oil fields were discovered in Leduc, near Edmonton; pipelines were constructed to carry oil from the region west to Vancouver in 1953 and east to Sarnia, Ontario, in 1954, although the region from Montreal east continued to import oil from Venezuela and the Middle East. Meanwhile, Canada, like other industrialized countries of the world, was becoming more and more reliant on oil. Table 9.11 shows the increase in production of oil and natural gas and the differences in production among the three Prairie provinces prior to the energy crisis of the 1970s.

Table 9.11   Production of crude petroleum (thousands of barrels) and natural gas (millions of cubic feet), 1951–1971

	Alberta		Saskatchewan		Manitoba	
Year	Oil	Natural gas	Oil	Natural gas	Oil	Natural gas
1951	45,915	69,877	1,249	860	11	—
1961	157,657	424,146	56,020	26,327	4,480	—
1971	370,604	1,664,613	87,992	57,306	5,618	—

Source: Statistics Canada, 'Historical Statistics of Canada', Cat. no. 11-516-XIE, Series Q13-18 and Q26-30.

The energy crisis caught the world by surprise. It was sparked by conflicts in the Middle East, especially the Yom Kippur War of 1973, in which Egypt and Syria attacked Israel over Israel's takeover of Palestinian lands. This and other conflicts throughout the 1970s made the supply of oil from the Middle East unstable. The OPEC nations, led by Saudi Arabia (and encouraged by the major oil companies) cut back on the supply of crude oil, forcing prices to escalate dramatically through to 1981—from \$2.80US per barrel in October 1973 to \$10.84 by January 1974 and \$35.00 by 1981 (Earth Net, 1999; Mintz, 2003).

Table 9.12 Canadian oil production, imports, and exports, 1978

Oil supplies	Barrels per year (millions)
Canadian production	524
Imports	225
Exports	98
Available oil	652

Source: J. Marmorek, *Over a Barrel: A Guide to the Canadian Energy Crisis* (Toronto: Doubleday, 1981), 7.

The energy crisis was a financial windfall for oil-rich Alberta, but it was devastating for other regions of Canada (and the world) that depended on imported oil. Table 9.12 shows Canadian oil production, imports, and exports in 1978; in that year oil accounted for 52 per cent of all the energy used in Canada (Marmorek, 1981: 7). Rising oil prices affected all costs related to petroleum, including gasoline and home heating. Businesses were similarly affected. The petrochemical industry, producing everything from plastics and fabrics to paints and cosmetics, was particularly hard hit, and provinces that used oil to produce electricity also faced increased costs. Inflation increased along with unemployment, and it was the industrial heartland of Canada that was most threatened.

Facing great pressure, especially from the manufacturing sector, the Trudeau government froze oil prices and increased the taxes paid by western oil producers and the Alberta government. This policy, designed primarily to benefit manufacturers in Quebec and Ontario, was not well received in western Canada, and Albertans in particular were outraged when the Liberals introduced the National Energy Program (NEP) in 1980. Designed to stabilize oil prices and make Canada more self-sufficient in energy, the NEP included measures to promote research into alternative energy sources, to stimulate oil exploration in the Arctic and off Newfoundland, and to encourage development of Alberta's tar sands—but these efforts were to be financed by imposing even higher taxes on western oil. Alberta cried foul, claiming that it was being robbed of the resource revenues that, according to the Constitution, belonged to the province. Even though the profits that Alberta received were enough to create a Heritage Fund worth billions of dollars, resentment of the NEP contributed directly to the rise of the Reform party and the western separatist movement, and the federal Liberal party was for many years unable to elect a single member of Parliament in Alberta.

Oil prices plummeted in early 1980s with the onset of a worldwide recession that proved to be almost as damaging to the global economy as the Depression of the 1930s. Trade, investment, and production fell off, and unemployment rose. The National Energy Program was shelved by the incoming Conservative party in 1984, but the 'made-in-Canada' pricing system meant that the provincial and federal governments alike now relied on oil taxation revenue. As a consequence, Canadians paid more than the world market price for oil, which remained at the \$15–20 (US) level throughout the 1980s, until world events once again intervened. The Gulf War of 1990 caused oil prices to spike, and although the collapse of the Japanese and other Asian economies caused the price to fall to just \$11US a barrel in 1997, the US-led invasion of Iraq in 2003 brought another spike. More recently, an especially bad hurricane season in the summer and fall of 2005 had devastating effects on the Caribbean and US Gulf states, wreaking havoc on oil refineries located there and driving oil prices to all-time highs. How has the volatility of oil

Table 9.13 Production of crude petroleum (thousands of barrels/day) and natural gas (millions of cubic feet/day), 1996–2004

Year	Alberta Oil	Alberta Natural gas	Saskatchewan Oil	Saskatchewan Natural gas	Manitoba Oil	Manitoba Natural gas	Total Prairies Oil	Total Prairies Natural gas
1996	1,557	12.8	359	0.6	11	–	1,927	13.4
1997	1,638	13.0	402	0.6	11	–	2,051	13.6
1998	1,649	13.3	399	0.6	11	–	2,059	13.9
1999	1,550	13.7	374	0.6	10	–	1,934	14.3
2000	1,541	13.8	417	0.6	11	–	1,969	14.4
2001	1,544	13.6	418	0.7	11	–	1,973	14.3
2002	1,566	13.4	421	0.7	11	–	1,998	14.1
2003	1,534	13.1	420	0.7	11	–	1,965	13.8
2004	1,743	13.2	424	0.7	11	–	2,178	13.9

Source: Canadian Association of Petroleum Producers, 'Industry Facts and Figures: Alberta, Saskatchewan and Manitoba' ⟨http://www.capp.ca/default.asp?V_DOC_ID=40⟩.

Table 9.14 Canadian energy demand by energy type, 1997

Energy type	%
Oil	33
Natural gas	30
Coal	10
Hydroelectricity	9
Nuclear	9
Renewable	6
Natural gas liquids	3

Source: National Energy Board, *Canadian Energy Supply and Demand to 2025*, Cat. No. NE 23-15/1999E: 83.

prices affected energy production in the Prairie provinces? Production of oil and natural gas has remained steady throughout the last half of the 1990s and early 2000s, as illustrated in Table 9.13. What the table does not show is that the amount of the total produced by Alberta's conventional oil wells has been decreasing, from 942,000 barrels a day in 1996 to 629,000 in 2003 (Canadian Association of Petroleum Producers). The shortfall has been made up by increasing production from Alberta's tar sands, which new technology has made much less expensive to extract. No doubt the rising prices of both oil and natural gas will stimulate further exploration and development on the Prairies as well as in other regions of Canada.

In late 2002 Canada ratified the Kyoto Protocol on climate change, indicating that the country recognizes the connection between emissions from burning fossil fuels (coal, oil, and natural gas) and global warming. The protocol commits Canada to reducing greenhouse gases to 6 per cent below 1990 levels by 2008–12. Naturally Alberta, the country's leading producer of fossil fuels, feels somewhat threatened by this commitment, not only because the province's economy depends on its exports of fossil fuels but because it is also a major consumer of fossil fuels. As Table 9.15 shows, coal and natural gas are the main sources of electricity, although wind generation is increasing.

Table 9.15 Alberta electrical generation (GWh) by resource, 1992–2002

Year	Coal	Natural	Hydro gas	Wind	Biomass/ waste	Others[1]	Total
1993	39,187.2	7,771.6	1,799.4	1.8	–	16.5	48,776.5
1994	42,269.8	8,047.4	1,771.3	35.6	16.3	16.1	52,156.5
1995	42,460.8	7,219.8	2,006.5	54.3	129.3	14.3	51,885.0
1996	41,220.3	8,228.3	1,973.4	59.1	229.8	13.0	51,723.9
1997	43,054.3	8,724.6	1,830.5	62.0	232.2	26.7	53,930.3
1998	41,267.7	11,467.7	2,044.6	49.4	279.1	32.1	55,140.6
1999	40,276.7	12,126.2	2,188.2	64.6	335.5	19.7	55,010.9
2000	40,459.2	15,219.9	1,756.3	71.8	273.8	57.0	57,838.0
2001	41,713.3	18,792.9	1,453.3	183.1	255.2	82.0	62,479.8
2002	42,541.8	19,462.1	1,675.4	323.2	281.3	44.8	64,328.6

[1]Includes oil, diesel, geothermal, and solar.

Source: Alberta Energy and Utilities Board: ST28-2002: Alberta Electric Industry, Annual Statistics for 2002.

It is interesting to note how the production of electricity in the other Prairie provinces differs from that in Alberta, owing largely to differences in population (hence demand) and the availability of other energy options. Saskatchewan, which has significant quantities of lignite coal, uses this for 78 per cent of its electricity production; 21 per cent comes from hydro, and the remaining 1 per cent from 'other' sources. Manitoba, on the other hand, derives 97 per cent of its electricity from hydro, while 2.8 per cent is generated by natural gas and 0.2 per cent by diesel (Natural Resources Canada, 2003).

Coal, natural gas, and oil are all important parts of the Prairie mining industry, which has helped to diversify the economies of the three provinces. Geophysical characteristics, including the position of the Canadian Shield relative to the Interior Plains, have the greatest influence on the kinds of mining undertaken (and, ultimately, the mining revenues received) in each province. Manitoba, which is largely occupied by the Shield, is the largest metal producer of the three, with smelters at Thompson and Flin Flon; it generates few revenues from non-metals and fuels. Saskatchewan, which also includes a large portion of Shield terrain, is a major producer of uranium, but tops the non-metal category with its dominance in potash, which is mined in the southern part of the province, on the Interior Plains. However, the province's greatest revenues come from fuels, and these figures pale compared to those of Alberta. Table 9.16 summarizes the revenues received by each province for metals, non-metals, and fuels.

Table 9.16   Mineral revenues (× 1,000), 1998–2004

	Years	Manitoba	Saskatchewan	Alberta
Metals	1998	808,445	551,444	118
	1999	727,879	549,489	224
	2000	989,319	501,726	292
	2001	791,519	661,263	520
	2002	753,962	669,856	1,128
	2003	791,249	488,709	1,106
	2004	1,127,496	719,398	1,200
Non-metals	1998	84,713	1,748,901	623,834
	1999	82,700	1,634,596	668,936
	2000	79,487	1,645,577	670,162
	2001	93,577	1,649,948	600,067
	2002	96,497	1,673,338	666,809
	2003	94,985	n.a	384,586
	2004	105,118	n.a	n.a
Fuels	1998	73,912	2,495,903	21,262,403
	1999	96,553	3,812,729	28,560,378
	2000	165,259	6,267,238	49,296,666
	2001	138,166	5,422,519	48,707,579
	2002[1]	100,000	5,700,000	43,284,586
	2003[1]	200,000	6,500,000	57,330,462
	2004[1]	200,000	7,300,000	64,400,000
Total	1998	967,070	4,796,247	21,886,355
mineral	1999	907,132	5,996,814	29,229,537
revenues	2000	1,234,065	8,414,541	49,987,120
	2001	1,023,259	7,733,519	49,308,167
	2002	950,459	8,043,194	43,952,523
	2003	1,086,234	n.a.	57,716,154
	2004	1,432,614	10,118,176	65,599,579

Sources: Canadian Association of Petroleum Producers, 'Industry Facts and Figures: Alberta, Saskatchewan and Manitoba' ⟨http://www.capp.ca/default.asp?V_DOC_ID=40 2002, 2003 and 2004⟩; Natural Resources Canada, 'Minerals and Mining' ⟨http://mmsd1.mms.nrcan.gc.ca/mmsd/production/production_e.asp.1998–2004⟩.

Table 9.17   Softwood and hardwood lumber production (cubic metres × 1,000), 1961–2004

Year	Alberta	Saskatchewan	Manitoba
1961	680	189	85
1971	1,180	286	164
1981	1,945	451	222
1991	4,130	451	230
2001	6,866	757	566
2002	7,232	953	739
2003	7,559	1,056	542
2004	8,053	1,184	637

Source: Natural Resources Canada, 'Lumber Production by Province and Species Group, 1950–2004 ⟨http://mmsd1.mms.nrcan.gc.ca/forest/members/section1/I-4print.asp?lang=en&categ=99⟩.

Forestry is another resource industry that has helped to diversify the Prairie economy. Many sawmills, pulp mills, and paper mills are located in an arc north of the Fertile Belt. Alberta is the leading producer, with 11 pulp, paper, and paperboard mills; Saskatchewan has 3 and Manitoba only 2 (Statistics Canada, June 2003). Table 9.17 indicates the overall production of lumber in each of the three provinces; here again, Alberta is far in the lead. Table 9.18, tracing sales of lumber products to the US, highlights differences between the provinces; it also shows the abrupt decline in sales that followed the end of the softwood lumber agreement (see Chapter 10 for more detail).

Perhaps the greatest changes to the resource landscape of the Prairies since the 1950s have occurred in the industry that attracted most people to the Prairies in the first place: agriculture. Between 1981 and 2001 the overall number of farms on the Prairies has decreased—by an astonishing 17,000 in Saskatchewan alone (see Table 9.19). Many farmers have had to declare bankruptcy, and the overall depopulation of rural communities throughout the Prairies has hurt the agriculture industry. Certainly farms today employ much more technology to plant and harvest crops. As Table 9.19 shows, farm size has increased, but farmers are still vulnerable to a host of unpredictable conditions: climate and the physical environment, market conditions, and large multinational corporations affect all aspects of farming, from inputs to retail pricing of agricultural commodities.

A telling sign is the gradual disappearance of the grain elevator, so long the symbol of Prairie agriculture. In the 1930s there were more than 5,500 grain elevators in

Table 9.18   Softwood lumber exports to the US ($Cdn × 100,000), 1990–2004

Year	Alberta	Saskatchewan	Manitoba	Year	Alberta	Saskatchewan	Manitoba
1990	161.2	15.0	55.6	1998	600.8	180.6	86.1
1991	124.5	16.2	49.3	1999	752.1	215.0	128.0
1992	95.2	51.2	54.9	2000	616.7	190.1	137.3
1993	89.1	57.6	96.9	2001	634.7	140.5	97.2
1994	100.8	31.9	92.9	2002	612.2	106.6	89.0
1995	126.4	35.4	99.9	2003	511.3	84.2	53.9
1996	548.1	112.4	57.6	2004	657.4	98.4	73.7
1997	638.0	185.4	71.9				

Source: BC Stats, 'Softwood Lumber Exports to the USA by Province' ⟨http://www.bcstats.gov.bc.ca/data/bus_stat/busind/trade/SWLprov.asp⟩.

Table 9.19   Numbers of farms and average farm size (acres), Prairies, 1981–2001

Year	Alberta		Saskatchewan		Manitoba	
	Farms	Avg. size	Farms	Avg. size	Farms	Avg. size
1981	58,056	813	67,318	951	29,442	640
1986	57,777	885	63,431	1,035	27,336	699
1991	57,245	899	60,840	1,092	25,706	744
1996	59,007	880	56,995	1,151	24,383	783
2001	53,652	971	50,598	1,282	21,071	892

Source: Adapted from the Statistics Canada website http://www40.statcan.ca/101/cst01/econ124h.htm.

western Canada, linked by a spider web of rail lines that was instrumental in enabling individual farmers to transport their grain to the market. In 1991 only some 1,500 primary grain elevators remained, and by 2002 this figure had dropped to just 429 (Drew, 2002).

The disappearance of grain elevators coincided with the abandonment of thousands of kilometres of rail lines. The Crow Rate, which subsidized the transportation of grain to ports such as Thunder Bay and Vancouver, was abandoned in 1995, compounding the financial woes of Prairie farmers. Heavy trucks replaced rail cars for transporting grain, but this brought increased costs to the provincial and municipal governments for structural upgrades to roads and bridges. The downward spiral has continued as small communities that lost rail lines and elevators also lost customers for other services, resulting in the closure of various stores and other facilities, and continued depopulation.

The three Prairie provinces differ in the range of agricultural commodities they produce, and their agricultural revenues differ as well (see Table 9.20). Alberta receives much of its income from the beef cattle industry. The discovery of bovine spongiform encephalopathy (BSE), or 'mad cow disease', in two Canadian-born cows, in May and December 2003, has had a devastating effect on Canadian beef exports, and Alberta, which produces 42 per cent of Canada's beef, has been particularly hard hit (see Table 9.20).

Alberta also produces wheat and canola, but Saskatchewan remains the major producer of crops, including wheat, canola, barley, dried peas, lentils, oats, and flax seed. Both Saskatchewan and Manitoba, like Alberta, gain considerable revenues from livestock. But Table 9.20 also documents how net cash income has fallen for each of the provinces, with especially disastrous results for Alberta and Saskatchewan. Darrin Qualman argues that the main reason for the erosion of farm income is not the much larger subsidies given

Table 9.20   Agricultural receipts and net income, 2002–2003

	Years	Alberta	Saskatchewan	Manitoba
Crop receipts	2002	2,168.7	3,625.7	1,884.2
$ Million	2003	1,925.0	2,768.1	1,689.7
Livestock receipts	2002	5,120.1	1,726.6	1,722.5
$ Million	2003	3,819.8	1,303.3	1,575.9
Total receipts	2002	7,288.7	5,352.2	3,608.8
$ Million	2003	5,744.8	4,071.4	3,265.6
Net cash income	2002	2,090.1	1,534.8	898.2
$ Million	2003	894.1	498.3	504.5

Source: Statistics Canada, Agriculture economic statistics, Cat. nos. 21-010-XIE to 21-018-XIE.

Figure 9.10 Agricultural subsidies ($CDN per tonne) for wheat production, 2000

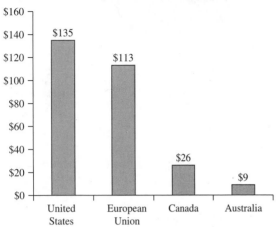

Source: Canadian Wheat Board, 'No teeth in recent U.S. trade ruling' ⟨http://www.cwb.ca/en/publications/farmers/mar-apr-2002/03-04-02.jsp?pm=1⟩.

out to farmers in the United States and the European Union (see Fig. 9.14) but rather the power of large corporations to increase their prices and extract high profits: 'In 1975, 13% of the retail value of bread went to farmers, [while] today a mere 4% does' (2001: 23). Qualman goes on to document how fertilizer companies unilaterally increased their prices during the mid-1990s, not because their costs had increased but because the prices of commodities such as wheat, corn, soybeans, and other crops had gone up (23–4).

Unpredictable weather conditions make farming on the Prairies a risky venture. Farmers are well aware of the differences between average annual rainfall statistics and what actually happens in any given year. Global warming has had a marked effect in this regard. In 1988, for example, a 40 per cent shortage in rainfall resulted in 29–50 per cent decreases in crop production and the loss of $4 billion in exports (Herrington et al., 1998: 36). Other severe droughts occurred in 1992 and 2001–3. Among the other potential disasters for farmers are grasshoppers, hail, early or late frosts, plant diseases such as rust, and massive floods (such as the ones that occurred in Manitoba in 1950 and 1997). Fortunately, crop insurance and off-farm employment give farmers some protection from random events.

Tourism is an industry with less inherent risk, although the threat of terrorism has hurt travel and tourism in the Prairie provinces, as elsewhere, in recent years. The decline in travel

Table 9.21 Domestic travel, Prairie provinces[1] (× 1,000), 1998–2003

	Alberta				Saskatchewan			
	Person trips	Non-resident trips[2]	Intra-provincial trips[2]	Reallocated expenditures	Person trips	Non-resident trips[2]	Intra-provincial trips[2]	Reallocated expenditures
1998	20,193	2,287	7,293	3,018,622	8,211	1,215	2,895	895,829
1999	20,296	2,463	7,365	3,135,557	8,434	1,114	3,032	942,592
2000	19,338	2,426	6,806	3,414,852	7,919	1,117	2,652	1,024,053
2001	17,332	2,844	6,596	3,895,231	7,108	1,042	2,932	1,151,025
2002	19,186	2,446	7,514	4,068,107	8,029	1,220	2,663	1,112,872
2003	15,775	2,294	5,549	3,071,985	7,413	1,106	2,498	1,076,599

	Manitoba			
	Person trips	Non-resident trips[2]	Intra-provincial trips[2]	Reallocated expenditures
1998	7,207	870	2495	858,749
1999	6,875	751	2252	871,953
2000	6,700	832	2,220	865,858
2001	6,366	794	2,132	1,033,426
2002	6,265	677	2,238	905,212
2003	5,938	713	2,043	919,443

[1]Estimates based on the 1996 Census population counts.

[2]Based on over-night trips.

Source: Adapted from Statistics Canada, CANSIM Tables 426-0001 and 426-0002.

in all three provinces can be observed in Table 9.21. Also of note are the differences between the three provinces. Manitoba and Saskatchewan are fairly close in both number of trips taken and expenditures, but Alberta, with its larger population, is considerably ahead.

Tourists travel for many reasons: to visit friends or relatives, to shop or sightsee, to attend cultural or sporting events, to visit national and provincial parks, to participate in recreational activities, and so on. The Prairie provinces have all of these attractions, but Alberta has gained a 'destination' reputation for millions of tourists visiting Banff (more than 4.6 million visitors in 2003) and Jasper (more than 1.8 million visitors in 2003) (Alberta Economic Development). More than a million tourists also visit the Calgary Stampede every year.

Summary

There have been some formidable changes to the Prairie landscape over the past two hundred years. Initially populated by the First Nations and, later, Métis, the region was heavily influenced by the fur trade and the competition between the two principal fur-trading companies. Following Confederation in 1867, the Canadian government set out to settle the west in order to prevent encroachment by the Americans. The purchase of Rupert's Land from the Hudson's Bay Company, the marginalization of the First Nations and Métis, the establishment of the Dominion Land Survey system, and the awarding of major concessions of land and money to the Canadian Pacific Railway were critical steps in Ottawa's Prairie settlement program. Settlers, drawn by the promise of virtually free homesteads, came to the Prairies from other parts of Canada as well as from Europe and the United States. Settlement started slowly, but new agricultural technologies, rail construction, and government promotion from the end of the 1890s to the mid-1900s brought dramatic population growth.

Reliance on a single staple commodity is risky. Initially, Prairie farmers were encouraged to grow wheat, and they did so with great success: the price of wheat was relatively high during the 1920s, and the cost of shipping wheat by rail to ports was subsidized. But the Depression of the 1930s was catastrophic, particularly for farmers in the Palliser's Triangle region, where drought combined with falling world market prices to drive many into bankruptcy. Both wheat prices and weather conditions improved during and after the Second World War, but the most important development was the advent of the mega-project era. The Prairie provinces had begun to develop coal, oil, metals, and forest products earlier in the century, but beginning in the late 1950s, all three provinces saw enormous resource development. The Canadian Shield offered metals, hydroelectricity, and forest products, while the Interior Plains produced potash and, most important, oil, natural gas, and coal. Alberta was the most fortunate, with enormous pools of oil and natural gas; it also led the way in agriculture, and tourism—and its population growth reflected these advantages.

Table 9.22 summarizes employment statistics for the Prairies and Canada overall. There are several notable differences: primary industry on the Prairies employs more than twice as many people (mainly in agriculture and oil and gas) as it does in Canada as a whole. Manufacturing, on the other hand, accounts for a considerably smaller proportion of people on the Prairies than in Canada generally, although the percentages for service industries are similar. On the Prairies as elsewhere, technological developments

Table 9.22   Selected labour force characteristics (× 1,000), Prairies and Canada, 2002

NAICS[1]	Alta.	Sask.	Man.	Prairies Total	Prairies %	Canada Total	Canada %
Total	1,673.8	482.0	567.0	2,722.8	100.0	15,411.8	100.0
Goods-producing	459.7	125.8	138.6	724.1	26.6	3,942.6	25.6
Primary	172.7	70.8	44.7	288.2	10.6	733.6	4.8
Agriculture	61.3	50.7	32.0	144.0	5.3	330.0	2.1
Forestry	3.7	1.1	1.3	6.1	0.2	74.8	0.5
Mining plus oil and gas	90.1	14.7	4.7	112.5	4.1	169.2	1.1
Secondary	287.0	55.0	93.9	435.9	16.0	3,209.0	20.8
Manufacturing	147.1	29.5	68.8	245.4	9.0	2,326.2	15.1
Service-producing	1,214.2	356.2	428.4	1998.8	73.4	11,469.3	74.4
Trade	252.8	78.0	87.8	418.6	15.4	2,430.0	15.8
Transportation	98.6	24.7	34.9	158.2	5.8	756.2	4.9
FIRE[2]	84.5	27.6	28.6	140.7	5.2	895.6	5.8
Professional, scientific, and technical	121.8	17.7	23.5	163.0	6.0	993.3	6.4
Education	105.2	36.7	41.0	182.9	6.7	1,015.9	6.6
Health	158.4	57.9	73.9	290.2	10.7	1,607.0	10.4
Tourism-related[3]	187.5	51.4	60.4	299.3	11.0	1,708.7	11.1
Public administration	67.0	27.0	34.0	128.0	4.7	778.0	5.0

[1]North American Industrial Classification.

[2]Fire, Insurance, Real Estate and Leasing.

[3]Information, culture, recreation, accommodation, and food services.

Source: Adapted from the Statistics Canada CANSIM database ⟨http://cansim2.statcan.ca⟩, Table 282-0008.

allow resource industries to operate with fewer and fewer workers. Meanwhile, free-trade agreements and improvements in transportation are increasing global competition. When these economic conditions combine with unpredictable global events (wars, recessions) or local conditions (drought, BSE), the result is continuing uncertainty.

Table 9.23 traces interprovincial migration from the recession of the 1980s to the twenty-first century. Of course there are many reasons for people to move within Canada, but an especially powerful 'push' factor is lack of economic opportunity. Conversely, good economic opportunities may 'pull' people to other regions. Both Saskatchewan and Manitoba are still experiencing out-migration, which slows overall growth. These two provinces continue to rely on resources that have been exploited for a considerable time: agricultural products, metals, non-metals, and some hydrocarbons and forest products.

For Alberta, the 'oil patch' has become the most important part of the provincial economy, which has been expanding since the 1990s. Unprecedented increases in oil and gas prices in the early part of the twenty-first century have sparked increased exploration and expansion of the tar sands. Alberta's growing economy is reflected in its population numbers (see Table 9.7, p. 287). However, if the world market price of oil and natural gas were to collapse, as it did for much of the 1980s, Alberta too would face plant closures, unemployment, and out-migration.

Another factor that could have a dramatic effect on the fossil fuel industry is the effort to meet Canada's obligations under the Kyoto Protocol. Increasing pressure to reduce

Table 9.23   Interprovincial migration, 1982–2004

Years	Alberta	Saskatchewan	Manitoba
1982–86	–82,737	–7,057	–2,395
1987–91	–13,198	–69,397	–39,533
1992–96	14,142	–20,578	–21,615
1997–02	163,928	–31,450	–25,385
2003–04	22,805	–8,042	–4,970

Sources: Statistics Canada, 1996–2001, Table 051-0012; and S. Girvan, 'Where Canadians Move Within Canada', *The Canadian Global Almanac 2003* (Toronto: John Wiley and Sons, 2004), 66.

emissions from the burning of fossil fuels should stimulate research into less polluting ways of using these resources, as well as development of alternative 'green' forms of energy, such as wind power—and the Prairies are windy. Other problems are associated with natural gas and coal-bed methane. Some natural gas contains hydrogen sulphide, a substance that is toxic even at low levels. Although this 'sour' gas can be 'sweetened', when gas companies burn it off (a common practice with gas that cannot be profitably sold) the hydrogen sulphide is released into the air, threatening the health of nearby communities. In addition to releasing methane, drilling can damage agricultural land by bringing contaminated water (often saline) to the surface.

There are large profits to be made in agriculture, but they rarely go to individual farmers. It is the large (often multinational) companies—oil companies, transportation companies, suppliers of seed, fertilizer, and farm equipment, food retailers—that receive most of the profits. The move to genetically modified food will only increase corporate domination of agriculture, particularly as government regulation is reduced. Like mining, farming has many environmental issues to contend with as well, including soil erosion, the detrimental effects of artificial fertilizers, pesticides, and herbicides, and the contamination of both surface and groundwater. The increasing popularity of organically grown food, which has so far been produced mainly by small operations, gives some hope for the family farm, however.

The three Prairie provinces continue to live with the legacy of their early settlement. The treaties that paved the way for settlement have recently given rise to court challenges by First Nations who maintain that the historic treaty process was flawed and that the federal government has not lived up to its fiduciary obligations. These treaties are likely to come under increasing scrutiny in future, especially as the educational opportunities for Aboriginal people improve. Many of the most important issues facing the Prairie provinces today involve land-use conflicts, and these tend to accelerate during periods of rapid growth. Both Saskatchewan and Manitoba are likely to experience slow growth as service-based industries develop in their major urban centres. Meanwhile, rural communities, whether farm- or mineral-based, will likely continue to lose population even as they seek alternative sources of employment and investment. Alberta's growth, powered by oil and natural gas, may level off as prices for these commodities stabilize or even decline.

References

Alberta Economic Development. 'Frequently Requested Alberta Tourism Statistics'. http://www.alberta-canada.com/statpub/pdf/td_book2.pdf.

BC Stats. 2003. 'Softwood Lumber Exports to the USA by Province'. http://www.bcstats.gov.bc.ca/data/bus_stat/busind/trade/SWLprov.asp.

Boldt, M., and A. Long. 1985. *The Quest for Justice: Aboriginal People and Aboriginal Rights*. Toronto: University of Toronto Press.

Brown, J.S.H. 1985. 'Métis'. Pp. 1124–7 in *The Canadian Encyclopedia*. Edmonton: Hurtig.

Buckley, K. 1967. 'Capital Formation in Canada, 1896–1930'. Pp. 169–82 in W.T. Easterbrook and M.H. Watkins, eds.

Approaches to Canadian Economic History. Toronto: McClelland and Stewart.

Bumsted, J.M. 1985. 'Selkirk, Thomas Douglas, 5th Earl of'. P. 1674 in *The Canadian Encyclopedia*. Edmonton: Hurtig.

Bye the Lake Communications, 2001. 'Town of Gimli Community Profile'. http://www.communityprofiles.mb.ca/cgi-bin/csd/index.cgi?id=4618033.

Canadian Association of Petroleum Producers. 'Industry Facts and Figures: Alberta, Saskatchewan and Manitoba'. http://www.capp.ca/default.asp?V_DOC_ID=40.

Canadian Human Rights Commission. N.d. 'The Plight of Immigrants'. http://www.chrc-ccdp.ca/en/index.asp.

Canadian Wheat Board. 2002. 'No teeth in recent U.S. trade ruling'. http://www.cwb.ca/en/publications/farmers/mar-apr-2002/03-04-02.jsp?pm=1.

CBC Jan. 6, 2004. 'Mad Cow in Canada: The science and the story'. http://www.cbc.ca/news/background/madcow/#top.

Chodos, R. 1973. *The CPR: A Century of Corporate Welfare.* Toronto: James Lorimer.

CNN Apr. 5, 2005. 'Greenspan: Oil prices should cool'. http://money.cnn.com/2005/04/05/news/economy/greenspan_oil.reut/?cnn=yes.

Department of Education, Ontario. 1887. *Public School Geography.* Toronto: Canada Publishing Co.

Drew, W. 2002. Canadian Transportation Agency—The Canadian Wheat Board. http://www.cta-otc.gc.ca/rail-ferro/disputes/submissions/cwb_e.html.

Earth Net. 1999. 'Historical Perspective'. http://earthnet.bio.ns.ca/english/activities/oil/a4diary.html.

Evans, B. 1968. *Prairie Women: the story of farm women and cooperative action 1913 to 1939* (film). Montreal: National Film Board.

Finlay, J.L., and D.N. Sprague. 1997. *The Structure of Canadian History.* 5th edn. Scarborough: Prentice Hall.

Francis, R.D., R. Jones, and D.B. Smith. 2000. *Origins: Canadian History to Confederation.* 4th edn. Toronto: Harcourt.

Frideres, J.S. 1988. *Native Peoples in Canada: Contemporary Conflicts.* 3rd edn. Scarborough: Prentice Hall.

———, and R.R. Gadacz. 2001. *Aboriginal Peoples in Canada: Contemporary Conflicts.* 6th edn. Toronto: Prentice Hall.

Friesen, G. 1987. *The Canadian Prairies: A History.* Toronto: University of Toronto Press.

Girvan, S. 2003. 'Where Canadians Move Within Canada'. *The Canadian Global Almanac 2003.* Toronto: John Wiley and Sons, 66.

Government of Alberta, Energy and Utility Board. N.d. http://www.eub.gov.ab.ca.

Goyette, L. 2003. 'Divided by Treaty'. *Canadian Geographic* 123, 4 (July–Aug. 2003): 70–81.

Great Canadian Lakes. N.d. 'Lake Winnipeg: Icelandic Introduction'. http://www.greatcanadianlakes.com/manitoba/lake_winnipeg/his_page4.htm.

Hall, D.J. 1985. 'Sir Clifford Sifton'. P. 1695 in *The Canadian Encyclopedia.* Edmonton: Hurtig.

Harris, R.C., and J. Warkentin. 1991. *Canada Before Confederation: A Study in Historical Geography.* Toronto: Oxford University Press.

Heritage Canada. N.d. 'The Virtual Museum of Métis History and Culture'. http://www.metismuseum.ca/main.php.

Heritage Wheat Varieties. N.d. http://members.shaw.ca/oldwheat/htwheat.html.

Herrington, R., B. Johnson, and F. Hunter. 1998. *Responding to Global Climate Change in the Prairies.* Toronto: Environment Canada.

IceCan. N.d. The Icelandic Canadian Homepage. http://www.umanitoba.ca/faculties/arts/icelandic/IceCan/.

Innis, H.A. 1930/1956. *The Fur Trade in Canada.* Revised edn. Toronto: University of Toronto Press.

Kamchen, R. 2002. 'Farm Business Communications—Canada's Agricultural Information Centre'. http://www.agcanada.com/custompages/stories_story.aspx?mid=22&id=137.

Lanken, D. 2005. 'Alberta and Saskatchewan: The View in 1905'. Map supplement. *Canadian Geographic* 125, 1 (Jan./Feb.).

Lyon, D. M. 1985. 'Gimli'. P. 741 in *The Canadian Encyclopedia.* Edmonton: Hurtig.

Marmorek, J. 1981. *Over a Barrel: A Guide to the Canadian Energy Crisis.* Toronto: Doubleday.

McGhee, R. 1985. 'Prehistory'. Pp. 1466–9 in *The Canadian Encyclopedia.* Edmonton: Hurtig.

McVey, W.W. Jr, and W.E. Kalbach. 1995. *Canadian Population.* Scarborough: Nelson.

Métis Resource Centre Inc. 'Battle of Seven Oaks'. http://www.metisresourcecentre.mb.ca/history/oaks.htm.

Mintz, S. 2003. 'The Politics of Oil'. The Galt Global Review. http://www.galtglobalreview.com/business/politics_of_oil.html.

Morley, J.T. 1985. 'Co-operative Commonwealth Federation'. In *The Canadian Encyclopedia.* Edmonton: Hurtig Publishers Ltd., Vol. I, 422.

Nader, G.A. 1976. *Cities of Canada.* Vol. II. *Profiles of Fifteen Metropolitan Areas.* Toronto: Macmillan.

National Energy Board 1999. *Canadian Energy Supply and Demand to 2025.* Calgary. Cat. No. NE 23-15/1999E.

Natural Resources Canada. 2003. 'Cross-Country Electricity Snapshot'. http://www.nrcan-rncan.gc.ca/media/newsreleases/2003/2003106a_e.htm.

———. 2003. 'Lumber Production by Province and Species Group, 1950–2002'. http://mmsd1.mms.nrcan.gc.ca/forest/members/section1/I-4print.asp?lang=en&categ=99.

———. 1998–2001. 'Minerals and Mining'. http://mmsd1.mms.nrcan.gc.ca/mmsd/production/production_e.asp.

Newman, P.C. 1987. *Caesars of the Wilderness: Company of Adventurers*. Vol. II. Markham: Penguin.

Patterson, E.P. 1972. *The Canadian Indian: A History Since 1500*. Don Mills: Collier-Macmillan.

Pannekoek, F. 2001. 'Métis Studies: The Development of a Field and New Directions'. Pp. 111–28 in T. Binnema, G.J. Ens, and R.C. Macleod, eds. *From Rupert's Land to Canada*. Edmonton: University of Alberta Press.

Qualman, D. 2001. Canadian Centre for Policy Alternatives. 'The Farm Crisis and Corporate Power'. http://www.policyalternatives.ca/.

Rich, E.E. 1960. *Hudson's Bay Company, 1670–1870*. Toronto: McClelland and Stewart.

Saskatchewan Interactive. 2002. 'Agriculture in the 1930s'. http://interactive.usask.ca/ski/agriculture/history/saskhis_1930.html.

Sealey, D.B., and A.S. Lussier. 1975. *The Métis Canada's Forgotten People*. Winnipeg: Manitoba Métis Federation Press.

Sitwell, O.F.G., and N.R.M. Seifried. 1984. *The Regional Structure of the Canadian Economy*. Toronto: Methuen.

Stanley, G.F.G. 1985. 'Riel, Louis'. Pp. 1584–5 in *The Canadian Encyclopedia*. Edmonton: Hurtig.

Statistics Canada. 2003. 'Major Wood Manufacturing: Pulp, paper and paperboard mills', Cat. No. 31-203. June.

———. Census of Agriculture, 2002. 'Total area of farms, land tenure and land in crops, provinces'. http://www.statcan.ca/english/Pgdb/econ124h.htm.

Symington, F. 1969. *The Canadian Indian: The Illustrated History of the Great Tribes of Canada*. Toronto: McClelland and Stewart.

Thompson, J.H. 1998. *Forging the Prairie West*. Toronto: Oxford University Press.

Treaty 7 Elders and Tribal Council. 1996. *The True Spirit and Original Intent of Treaty 7*. Montreal: McGill–Queens University Press.

University of Calgary. 1997. 'Rupert's Land'. http://www.ucalgary.ca/applied_history/tutor/calgary/rupert.html.

van Herk, A. 'Imagine: One Big Province'. *Canadian Geographer* 125, 1: 40–7.

Wallace, I. 2002. *A Geography of the Canadian Economy*. Toronto: Oxford University Press.

Woodcock, G., and Avakumovic, I. 1968. *The Doukhobors*. Toronto: Oxford University Press.

Young, P., and D.R. Préfontaine. 2003. 'The Virtual Museum of Métis History and Culture: Bison Hunting'. http://www.metismuseum.ca/resource.php/00716.

10

British Columbia: Canada's New Front Door

In most of Canada the history of European exploration and settlement moves from east to west. In British Columbia, however, that process started in the west, where the first European settlers arrived two hundred years after their counterparts on the east coast. At a time when the sailing vessel was the only means of communication between the European and North American continents, British Columbia occupied one of the most remote corners on the earth.

British Columbia is largely a vertical landscape, dominated by the Cordilleran mountain ranges—the youngest and among the highest in Canada. They are also unusually complex because of the tectonic processes through which they were formed: subduction and accretion of offshore terranes. The predominantly westerly flows of wind over the relatively warm Pacific Ocean have a strong influence on the weather and climate of this region, and together the climate and geological structure have influenced soil characteristics and vegetation patterns. The result is a uniquely diverse set of landscapes ranging from coastal fjords and lush coastal rain forests to interior deserts of cactus and sagebrush to alpine meadows and year-round glaciers.

British Columbia's location and rugged landscape did not grant easy access to European explorers seeking the region's plentiful resources. Europeans were drawn to the west coast of North America, as they had been to the east, in hopes of finding the fabled Northwest Passage and exploiting the resource wealth of the 'new world'. The quest for the Passage was fruitless, but furs and gold were discovered, attracting immigrants and sparking territorial conflicts. The discovery of gold in the mid-1800s attracted prospectors not only from eastern Canada but from the American west and overseas, and became the catalyst for road-building and settlement, which in turn began the process of establishing political boundaries. British Columbia entered Confederation and officially joined the rest of Canada in 1871, though it was not until the mid-1880s, when the Canadian Pacific Railway was finally completed, that the province was truly connected to the rest of the country.

The CPR stimulated not just immigration but resource development and international trade and investment. Forestry, fishing, mining, agriculture, and other resource industries each offer a story of changing technologies, developing transportation networks, building communities, and managing resources in the context of unpredictable world events. British Columbia's population growth was rapid but uneven, reflecting the boom and bust cycles that the province was subject to.

Figure 10.1   Map of British Columbia

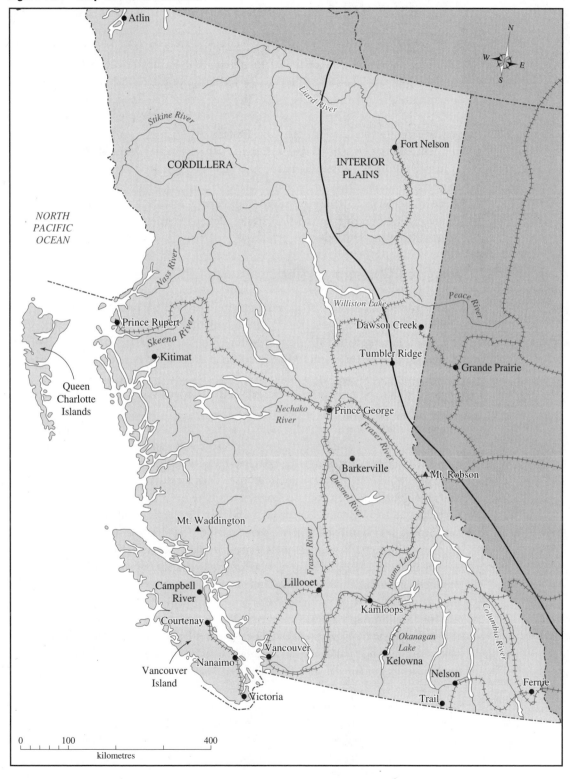

As in other parts of the country, the Aboriginal peoples of the Pacific Northwest were devastated by European exploitation and settlement. Diseases such as smallpox killed up to 95 per cent of the Native population. The survivors were forced onto reserves, and in most cases did not even have the opportunity to negotiate treaties, as the governing authorities—first colonial, then provincial—maintained that Aboriginal land title did not exist. The struggle for legal recognition of Aboriginal rights and land title has been long, but has finally begun to produce results. The modern-day treaty signed with the Nisga'a people of northwestern BC in 1999 was the province's first, and there is now a process in place for others to be finalized.

Until the 1970s, a good deal of Canada's international economic activity involved Britain and Europe, and as a result the east coast served as the front door through which much of the country's business was transacted. Since that time, however, the development of the Asian economy has increasingly drawn trade and investment to the Asia–Pacific region. This shift has made British Columbia Canada's new front door to international trade and investment.

Physical Characteristics

The Cordillera is the main physiographic region of British Columbia. This mainly vertical landscape features two peaks that are approximately 4,000 metres in height: Mount Waddington in the Coast Range and Mount Robson on the BC side of the Rockies. The highest peak, Fairweather Mountain (4,663 m) is in the remote northwestern corner of the province on the border with Alaska. Running through the province from north to south, the mountains historically made east-to-west linkages with the rest of Canada difficult. The exception to this rugged topography is the prairie landscape of the province's northeastern corner, which is part of the Great Interior Plains; wheat is grown here, and the sedimentary layers contain coal, oil, and natural gas.

The Cordillera is geologically complex because of tectonic activity in the subduction zone, which has produced an accumulation of accreted terranes. Some 250 million years ago, the subduction zone lay essentially where the interior plateau is now located. Over time it has migrated westward to its present-day location off the coast of Vancouver Island. The original collision of plates forced the flat-lying sedimentary layers of the Interior Plains upwards to form the spectacular folded Rocky Mountains, and volcanic activity in the interior laid large volumes of lava over a base of sedimentary rock. As the subduction zone migrated westward, fragments of continental and oceanic plates were forced onto the western continental margin. As a consequence, British Columbia's physical composition is like a jigsaw puzzle made up of mismatched pieces: new pieces (terranes), formed in other parts of the globe, were not fitted neatly into place, but smashed up against existing landforms. The terranes differ in their geological composition and age, and many contain valuable minerals (see Chapter 2).

Glaciation has had the greatest influence on the shape of the province. During the last glacial period, ice built up in high elevations and flowed down river valleys, carving them into 'U'-shaped channels. Vast sheets of ice 1,500 to 2,000 metres thick operated like giant bulldozers, creating moraines of sand and gravel, and leaving the landscape scattered with erratics. The scouring out of valleys and subsequent rise of oceans combined with isostatic rebound to create a coastal landscape of deep channels and fjords that serve as excellent harbours.

In terms of its weather and climate, British Columbia is a province of extremes. In the coastal region, conditions are influenced by westerly flows of wind and moderated by the proximity of the Pacific. The mountainous topography produces orographic precipitation on the western slopes and a rain-shadow effect on the eastern side of mountains. With the mildest winter climate in Canada, the southwestern corner of the province attracts retirees from across the country, and its long growing season favours agriculture. Farther inland there are much greater extremes in temperature, and precipitation is often the result of the convection process, although frontal precipitation also occurs.

The wet environment of the west coast produces the largest coniferous trees in Canada, the object of a forest industry that is vital to the economy of the province. The interior also has coniferous forests, but these are smaller, less dense, and subject to many more forest fires. Most of the settlement in the interior has been in the valleys of the Fraser, Thompson, Columbia, and Kootenay Rivers and Okanagan Lake. The climate is dry, and the vegetation in these valleys consists of grasses and sagebrush; the southern Okanagan is known for its desert conditions. Irrigation is necessary for crop production in these interior valleys. In the northeast, the Peace River region has the largest block of good soil, but the short growing season at this latitude limits the range of crops that can be grown.

Historical Overview

The Aboriginal societies of the territory that became British Columbia were extremely diverse, with as many as 34 different languages representing eight distinct language families. Before the arrival of Europeans, the peoples living along the Pacific coast and the salmon rivers of the BC interior were the most numerous in all the northern half of North America, with sophisticated governance structures and clearly defined social roles. Although they were semi-nomadic, relocating as different resources became available at different times of the year, they returned to the same sites year after year, and their political boundaries were well established.

The introduction of European diseases decimated the Native population: Cole Harris suggests that perhaps 90 to 95 per cent of the region's people died (1997: 30). Alcohol, which was introduced as a trade good, further destabilized the traditional way of life. Table 10.1 summarizes the changes in the population of First Nations in comparison to changes in non-Native populations. It must be kept in mind that the table begins only with the census record of 1871, when Aboriginal populations were already greatly reduced by various diseases.

The wave of European exploration that led to the 'discovery' of North America was motivated by the desire to gain access to valuable Asian products such as silk, tea, and porcelain from China, and spices from the Molluccas (Indonesia). The voyage was perilous, but one successful trip was enough to make the survivors rich. At the time there

Table 10.1 Native and European populations,[1] British Columbia, 1871–1951

Year	Total	Native	%	European	%
1871	36,247	25,661	70.8	9,038	24.9
1881	50,387	26,849	53.5	19,348	38.4
1891	98,173	24,543	25.0	64,720	65.9
1901	178,657	25,488	14.3	133,687	74.8
1911	392,480	20,134	5.1	341,899	87.1
1921	524,582	22,377	4.3	462,715	88.2
1931	694,263	24,599	3.5	620,320	89.3
1941	817,861	24,882	3.0	752,264	92.0
1951	1,165,210	28,478	2.4	1,111,693	95.4

[1]Does not include Asians, Blacks, or Hawaiians.

Source: Adapted from Statistics Canada, Census of Canada 1871–1951.

were only two routes to Asia from Western Europe: east around the southern tip of Africa, and west around the southern tip of South America. The journey would be much shorter if a northern route could be established, but despite many efforts the Northwest Passage would not be discovered until the 1850s. As a result, the northwestern coast of North America remained relatively isolated until the late 1700s. By this time, Russian forts ran across the coast of Alaska and down its Panhandle. The Spanish had claimed possession of the territory south of the Panhandle, although their closest fort was San Francisco.

No one knows who was the first European to sail the coast of British Columbia. It may have been the Spanish explorer Juan de Fuca in 1592, though there is some doubt about the veracity of his account of his journey to the northwest coast. It may have been the English explorer Sir Francis Drake, who is said to have visited the region around 1580. The Spanish explorer Juan Perez Hernandez explored the Queen Charlotte Islands and sighted Nootka Sound in 1774. But he never landed, and certainly there were no European settlements or official claims when Captain James Cook arrived in the Pacific Northwest in 1778, nearly 200 years after Drake, in search of the Northwest Passage. Cook and his crew spent a month at Nootka Sound, on the west coast of Vancouver Island, where they traded with the local Nuu-chah-nulth for sea otter pelts. Although Cook was killed a few months later, before he could return to Britain, reports of this episode aroused British interest in the possibilities of the sea otter trade. When a Spanish force arrived at Nootka in 1789 to establish a fort, they found several British ships there, which they seized. The diplomatic crisis that followed was resolved with the signing of the Nootka Sound Convention in 1790, and within a few years the entire coastline had been surveyed by British Captain George Vancouver with the cooperation of the Spanish captains Quadra, Valdes, and Galiano. In 1794 the Spanish surrendered their claim on this territory to the British, but left a legacy of Spanish names that are still on the maps of coastal British Columbia.

The sea otter trade was intense, with Russian, British, and American traders competing to control this highly lucrative commodity destined for trade with China. Inevitably, by the early 1800s the species was nearly extinct and with it the trade. By then, however, the overland fur trade had made its way across the Rockies. Following Alexander Mackenzie's epic journey to the Pacific coast in 1793, the North West Company began erecting forts throughout the interior and as far south as the Columbia River. Here the fur traders faced challenges they had not experienced in other parts of Canada. With hundreds of distinct territorial jurisdictions ruled by hereditary chiefs, trade negotiations were complicated. The birchbark canoe, which had been used for two hundred years to transport furs, was difficult to construct in British Columbia, where birch is not common, and many of the rivers were too treacherous for navigation by canoe. Trails were used and some furs were carried overland by horses, but this was an expensive alternative to river transportation. Although the 1821 merger of the two rival fur companies eliminated the costs of competition, over-trapping soon brought the population of fur-bearing animals in the region close to extinction.

Once the United States' interest in the interior had been attracted by the Lewis and Clark expedition of 1804–6, Americans built a number of fur trade forts on the Columbia River. Britain's control of the territory east of the Rockies and north of the forty-ninth parallel had been established in 1818, but the land from the 42nd parallel north to the bottom of the Russian panhandle (54°40′), known as Oregon Territory, was administered jointly by the Britain and the United States (see Fig. 3.7, p. 67). By the 1830s and 1840s, American settlers were moving into Oregon and aggressively occupying lands that had formerly been Spanish possessions. The notion that it was the United States' 'manifest destiny' to occupy the entire continent of North America became a key issue of the presidential race of 1844, when Democratic candidate James K. Polk's slogan '54–40 or Fight!' became the rallying cry for the American push to take over all of the Oregon Territory. Polk won the election, but the situation was resolved diplomatically with the Oregon Treaty of 1846, which extended the border between British and American lands west along the 49th parallel from the Rockies to the Georgia Strait. Vancouver Island, which dips below the 49th parallel, remained British and became a British colony in 1849. The British lost the most navigable portion of the Columbia River, however, which dealt a further blow to the failing fur trade.

The discovery of gold in California in 1848 sparked North America's first major gold rush. Gold fever soon spread throughout western North America. The next major discoveries were centred on the Thompson and Fraser rivers. Beginning in 1858, gold-seekers poured into the colony from California, central and eastern Canada, and beyond, including many Chinese prospectors, some moving north from California and some coming across the Pacific directly from southern China. Existing communities like Victoria (founded as a fur-trade post in 1843) expanded to take on new roles as administrative, supply, and transportation centres, and new mining towns such as Barkerville were quickly established, along with transportation systems based on portages, trails, paddle wheelers on rivers and lakes, and—as the rush moved on to the Cariboo district of south-central BC in the 1860s—the Cariboo Road.

Until this time there had been comparatively few non-Native people in the region. The gold rush opened the way for settlement. In 1858, when British Columbia officially became a British Crown colony, it included the mainland territory only from the continental divide in the Rockies to the watersheds of the Columbia, Fraser, and Skeena rivers, but further gold finds on the Stikine (1862) and Peace (1863) rivers saw the mainland boundaries extended to their present configuration (see Figure 10.2).

The gold rush also brought more detrimental alterations to the land. One of only a few metals that occur in pure form as nuggets (though it also occurs 'bound' with other minerals), gold was accessible in a way that most metals are not: with very little investment—a shovel and a gold pan—an individual prospector could actually strike it rich. This was the allure of the gold rush for the many (predominantly single) men who came to the region in order to exploit it and had no intention of staying. The 'frontier mentality' of these men prompted many environmentally destructive activities. In placer mining, for instance, shovels and gold pans soon gave way to sluices; streams and rivers were dammed and diverted, and the habitat of the salmon on which many Aboriginal communities depended was destroyed. Miners trespassed on First Nations territories, introducing diseases and alcohol. Forests were cut down; haphazard, fire-prone settlements were erected; and cattle, brought in to feed the miners, so overgrazed the southern interior valleys that sagebrush replaced bunch grass as the dominant vegetation.

Not everyone in British Columbia during this early period subscribed to the frontier mentality, however. Some did come to stay, and they demonstrated their desire for permanence by laying the foundations for a 'proper' British colony. Institutions of law and order, education, transportation, and government were put in place to impose some order on the chaos. Before long, settlers came to farm the land and raise families, and they too left their mark on the landscape.

Figure 10.2   Boundaries of British Columbia, 1858–1863

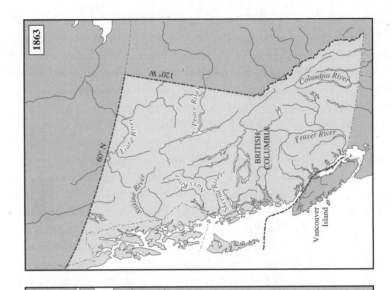

Source: Adapted from D.G.G. Kerr, *Historical Atlas of Canada*, 3rd edn (Toronto: Thomas Nelson, 1975), 32.

By the mid-1860s, however, the gold rush had ended. Now out-migration exceeded immigration. To reduce administrative costs, Britain decided to unite the colonies of British Columbia and Vancouver Island in 1866. Even so, heavy investment in the Cariboo Road had left the colony in considerable debt, and with the United States' purchase of Alaska in 1867, Americans in the colony began demanding a vote on whether to join the United States. Finally in 1870 the terms of confederation were negotiated, and in July 1871 British Columbia joined Canada.

Confederation brought several immediate benefits to the new province: the debt was erased, a transcontinental railway was promised, and lingering concerns about the possibility of incursions by the United States were put to rest. But Ottawa was slow to fulfill its promise to build the railway, largely because of the Pacific Scandal of 1873 and the collapse of Sir John A. Macdonald's administration. Although the contract with the Canadian Pacific Railway was not signed until 1880, the line from Montreal to the Pacific was completed in November 1885, when the symbolic 'last spike' was driven at Craigellachie, in the Rockies.

This spectacular trestle bridge at Mountain Creek, on the eastern slope of the Selkirk mountains, gives a hint of the challenge involved in building the railway through the Rockies. Completed in 1885, the bridge was 331 metres (1,086 ft) long and stood 41 metres (164 ft) over the Illecillewaet River. *Canadian Pacific Limited/A.11385. O. Lavallée Collection.*

The boom-and-bust pattern of the British Columbia economy was established early on. The downturn that followed the end of the gold rush lasted until 1881, when the construction of the CPR created a boom that lasted until 1886. The linkage between the transcontinental railway and the international port of Vancouver was a major influence on resource development in the province, making it possible to transport 'high-bulk', low-value commodities such as lumber, canned salmon, and copper, lead, and zinc concentrates over great distances at relatively low cost. But this was only the beginning of the railway era in British Columbia; many other lines were soon constructed. Some were short lines dedicated to a specific resource—for example, silver in the West Kootenays, forestry on Vancouver Island, or agriculture in the Fraser Valley—and built by small private railway companies. The CPR extended a branch line south to Lethbridge and through the Crow's Nest Pass (see Chapter 9) to the rich coalfields of the East Kootenays and the more lucrative metal mines of the West Kootenays, and developed a lead–zinc smelter at Trail. This Kettle Valley line continued westward, linking the Kootenays to the Okanagan and extending through the Coquihalla district to Hope and Vancouver.

The provincial government also got into the railway business, financing the Pacific Great Eastern (PGE). Built in stages, it connected North Vancouver to Squamish and then headed north to Prince George and eventually to Fort Nelson. The second transcontinental railway—initially known as the Grand Trunk Pacific before being taken over in 1919 by the Canadian National Railway—took a more northerly route across the province: west from Edmonton to Prince George and on to the new port city of Prince Rupert. Later, a branch line of the CNR was built to connect Edmonton to Vancouver via Kamloops. Figure 10.3 shows the main railways, but there were many others. In fact, by 1914 the provincial government had issued 212 railway charters, including some for lines that were never built (Seager, 1996: 209). As incentives, these charters included the rights to the forests and minerals adjacent to the rail line. As Chodos (1975: 55) explains, the CPR eventually bought up many of the smaller lines and dormant charters, acquiring a large portion of the 22 million acres of land the province had handed out to various railway companies.

Resource development went hand in hand with the new transportation systems that were being built throughout the province. New communities sprang up in response to these economic activities, and the province's population soared. Table 10.2 charts British Columbia's population growth compared with Canada's and shows the shift in its distribution from rural areas to urban centres. The increase, from scarcely 50,000 when construction of the CPR began to more than one million by 1951, reflects the province's economic expansion over nine decades, although the pace of growth varied in response to world events—including the Yukon gold rush, the First and Second World Wars, and the depression of the 1930s—that affected economic conditions.

By 1951 the province's urban profile included both resource towns and regional service centres. Victoria, as the capital, was the main administrative centre, but Vancouver had the largest population. Of the handful of towns numbering more than 10,000 people by 1951 (Table 10.3), two (New Westminster

Table 10.2   Population, British Columbia and Canada, with rural–urban distribution (%), 1871–1951

Year	BC	% rural	% urban	Canada	% rural	% urban
1871	36,247	84.8	15.2	3,689,257	80.4	19.6
1881	50,387	72.0	18.0	4,324,810	74.3	25.7
1891	98,173	57.5	42.5	4,833,239	68.2	31.8
1901	178,657	49.5	50.5	5,371,315	62.5	37.5
1911	392,480	48.1	51.9	7,204,838	54.6	45.4
1921	524,582	52.8	47.2	8,787,949	50.5	49.5
1931	694,263	56.9	43.1	10,376,786	46.3	53.7
1941	817,861	45.8	54.2	11,506,655	45.7	54.3
1951	1,165,210	47.2	52.8	14,009,429	38.4	61.6

Source: Adapted from Statistics Canada, Census of Canada 1871–1951.

Figure 10.3 Main railway lines in British Columbia, to 1952

Sources: C.N. Forward, 'Evolution of Regional Character', in Forward, ed., *British Columbia: Its Resources and People,* Western Geographical Series, vol. 22 (Victoria: University of Victoria, 1987), 4; R. Galois, 'British Columbia Resources', in D. Kerr and D. Holdsworth, eds, *Historical Atlas of Canada,* vol. III, *Addressing the Twentieth Century, 1891–1961* (Toronto: University of Toronto Press, 1990), Plate 21.

Table 10.3 Communities over 10,000 in 1951, 1871–1951

Community	1951	1941	1931	1921	1911	1901	1891	1881	1871
Vancouver	344,833	275,353	246,593	163,220	100,401	27,010	13,685	–	–
Victoria	51,331	44,068	39,082	38,727	31,660	20,919	16,841	5,925	4,161
New Westminster	28,639	21,967	17,524	14,495	13,199	6,499	6,641	1,500	1,356
North Vancouver	15,687	8,914	8,510	7,652	8,196	–	–	–	–
Trail	11,430	9,392	3,020	7,573	1,460	1,360	–	–	–
Penticton	10,548	5,777	4,640	3,979	–	–	–	–	–

Source: Adapted from Statistics Canada, Census of Canada 1871–1951.

and North Vancouver) would later be incorporated into the larger Census Metropolitan Area of Vancouver. Vancouver's ascension resulted mainly from its role as a transportation hub, with three rail lines—the CPR, Pacific Great Eastern (PGE), and CNR—although it also served as a centre for lumbering, fishing, and agricultural interests, and as an outlet for western Canada generally.

First Nations: Claiming Back the Land

On the Prairies, the treaty process served as a systematic means of extinguishing Aboriginal title and creating reserves where First Nations could be contained in order to free up land for agricultural settlement (see Chapter 9). In British Columbia, by contrast, the treaty process started with 14 small agreements known as the Douglas Treaties on the southern end of Vancouver Island in the early 1850s and almost ended there—although the Prairie-like northeastern region of the province was covered by Treaty # 8 in 1899. Reserves were considered necessary, however, by colonial administrators and (after 1871) the provincial government, who were keen to move Native people out of the way in order to promote settlement and resource development. As a consequence, BC today has 1,681 reserves—63 per cent of the Canadian total—and all of them are considerably smaller than those on the Prairies: the allotments per family of five were not 640 or even 160 acres but 20 and sometimes just 10 acres (Province of British Columbia, 2004a). As a result, Aboriginal hunting and gathering were severely restricted. Further, the failure to negotiate treaties not only violated Aboriginal rights and title but contravened the Royal Proclamation of 1763.

In 1949 the province granted Native people the right to vote without renouncing their Indian status. The ban on ceremonies such as the potlatch was lifted in 1951, and residential schools were phased out across the country in the 1960s. These changes were progressive and long overdue. But by this time a more serious threat to Native traditions had emerged: the resource mega-project. The provincial government had begun to invite large, often foreign, interests to invest in resource development. This money was used to build new pulp and lumber mills that relied on clearcut logging and enormous open-pit mining operations. Massive hydroelectric dams were constructed on the Columbia, Peace, and Nechako rivers; new service roads were built; railways were extended; and whole new communities were added to the map of British Columbia. Many First Nations felt threatened by these assaults on traditional lands that had never been surrendered.

In the 1970s a series of court decisions forced the federal government to recognize Aboriginal title and begin negotiating comprehensive land claims (see Chapter 3). The provincial government was slower to respond to these decisions: it was not until 1991, when the New Democratic Party was elected on a platform that included recognition of Aboriginal title, that the province began to deal seriously with the issue of land rights. The NDP government established a treaty commission, including government officials at the provincial and federal levels, to negotiate modern-day treaties and to compensate First Nations for all untreated territory. Under this model, Ottawa assumed the primary responsibility for financial compensation, while the province became responsible for land and resource allocation (McKee, 1996). By 2004 there were 42 Native bands or tribal councils at the negotiating table, representing about two-thirds of all the bands in the province (Province of British Columbia 2004b). These negotiations have not been straightforward. Governments have been charged with failing to bargain in good faith, and some bands have turned to the courts instead to resolve their disputes. A landmark decision in the 1997 case known as Delgamuukw, involving the Gitksan and Wet'suwet'en nations, established that 'Aboriginal title is a right to the land itself'; 'encompasses the right to exclusive use and occupation of the land'; cannot be extinguished by the province; and—as the Royal Proclamation stipulated in 1763—can only be transferred, sold, or surrendered to the Crown (Delgamuukw v. British Columbia [1997] 3 S.C.R. 1010).

But court cases are time-consuming, confrontational, and costly; negotiations are the preferred route. Negotiations have also produced many 'interim agreements', mainly concerning economic development, that have been used to resolve disputes over such issues as logging in First Nations territory. One modern-day treaty that has been completed is the Nisga'a Treaty of 2000, and while it claims not be precedent-setting, since it was the product of talks that began before the formal negotiation process was established, it addresses a number of issues in a way that could serve as the basis for future treaty negotiations throughout the province.

Figure 10.4 shows the traditional lands of the Nisga'a people, based on the watershed of the Nass River. The treaty allocates 8 per cent of the traditional area as a land base for the people, and includes both surface and subsurface rights. This land base is centred on the existing communities, and it is no longer reserve land. The Indian Act no longer applies, and the tax exemption for reserve land has disappeared. Cash compensation for the surrender of the remaining 92 per cent of the land in question amounted to $196.1 million, with a further $11.8 million for the Nisga'a to become involved in the commercial salmon fishery. The treaty includes 'an annual treaty-entitlement of salmon, which will, on average, comprise approximately 18 per cent of the Canadian Nass River total allowable catch. In addition, the Nisga'a will receive an allocation of sockeye and pink salmon for commercial purposes under a harvesting agreement outside the treaty' (Nisga'a Treaty Negotiations, 1996:3). The document gives the Nisga'a responsibility for wildlife management within their territory, as well as for establishing environmental standards. The deal also includes funding for education, training, and health and social services, and a provision for self-government and the establishment of justiciability, which means the right to establish policing and court systems (Indian and Northern Affairs Canada, 2004).

These efforts to right the wrongs of the past are long overdue. Use and management of the land and its resources, cash compensation, and self-government are all ways to

Figure 10.4   Nisga'a Aboriginal Homeland

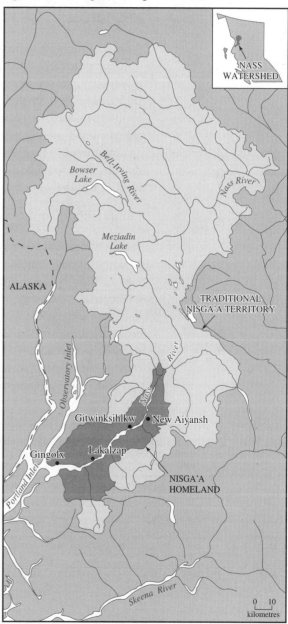

Source: Adapted from British Columbia, Ministry of Sustainable Resource Management, 'Geographical Names' ⟨http://srmwww.gov.bc.ca/bcnames/g2_nl.htm⟩.

establish an economic base for the future and a solid foundation for preserving cultural values. And, as one consulting company's report concludes, ultimately all British Columbians will benefit from these negotiations: 'Completing treaties to settle Aboriginal land claims will bring a net financial benefit of between $3.8 and $4.7 billion to British Columbia over the next 40 years' (Thornton, 2004). Settling land claims and bringing finality to questions of land use and ownership is obviously in the province's best interest, though the economic benefits will take many years to materialize.

Resources

Resources continue to be the strength of the British Columbia economy. Since they are managed primarily by the provincial government, and to a lesser degree by the federal government, the support given to the province's resource industries is liable to change with changes in the political climate. There are also economic factors affecting the way resources are used, or valued. These have varied over time and are influenced by the interrelated and shifting roles of labour, technology, capital, and land. Adding to these complexities are unpredictable events such as wars, economic recessions, and other crises that can affect resource development. This section will examine the historical development of British Columbia's most important resource industries to the present day.

Commercial Fishing

Fish are a renewable resource, but fisheries management is complicated by the difficulty of calculating and monitoring species populations. More than 80 different species of finfish, shellfish, and marine plants found off the coast of British Columbia are harvested commercially (Ministry of Agriculture, Food and Fisheries, 2002). The focus of this discussion is the salmon industry, but the lessons learned here apply to the full range of commercial species. The salmon industry has been affected by overfishing, international disputes, intense competition, changing international markets, technological improvements, a deteriorating aquatic ecosystem, the introduction of aquaculture, and poor management. Pacific salmon dominated the commercial catch until recently, but as Table 10.4

Table 10.4   Commercial and aquaculture landings (metric tonnes) and value (× 1,000), 1981–2004

Commercial species	1981 Volume	1981 Value	1991 Volume	1991 Value	2001 Volume	2001 Value	2002 Volume	2002 Value	2003 Volume	2003 Value	2004 Volume	2004 Value
Groundfish	54,227	27,873	165,913	102,741	115,573	118,875	112,078	118,907	127,755	127,178	181,259	139,954
Pelagic	119,933	193,958	125,605	222,272	52,222	85,020	63,436	102,660	70,160	93,969	57,384	100,997
Salmon	78,921	158,067	85,679	172,440	24,723	37,131	33,269	57,294	38,424	48,091	25,566	52,459
Shellfish	8,347	11,145	24,369	46,279	18,804	123,001	16,771	103,775	19,731	120,335	18,602	110,868
Subtotal Wild	**182,789**	**236,181**	**316,586**	**380,181**	**187,053**	**339,706**	**192,285**	**325,342**	**217,646**	**341,482**	**257,246**	**351,121**
Aquaculture Salmon			24,362	110,913	67,700	269,400	84,200	288,900	70,500	248,500	61,774	212,038
Shellfish			4,651	4,021	8,320	15,700	8,790	14,800	8,630	15,900	9,245	15,036
Subtotal Farmed			**29,126**	**115,472**	**76,120**	**285,600**	**93,090**	**304,400**	**79,230**	**264,900**	**71,147**	**227,788**
Overall total			**345,712**	**495,653**	**263,173**	**625,306**	**285,375**	**629,742**	**296,876**	**606,382**	**328,393**	**578,909**

Source: Fisheries and Oceans Canada, 'Commercial and Aquaculture Statistics' ⟨http://www.dfo-mpo.gc.ca/⟩.

shows, the value of salmon has waned while the value of other commercial catches (shellfish, halibut, cod, and other groundfish) and aquaculture products (mainly farmed salmon and oysters)—has increased.

Of the five species of Pacific salmon—sockeye, chinook (spring, king), coho, pink, and chum—sockeye is the most popular and commands the highest price because of its rich red meat. Chinook is the largest salmon, reaching up to 30 kilograms. Coho vary in size depending on where they are caught: in southern waters, large coho weigh roughly 4 kilos, but farther north that figure can be 10 kilos or more. Coho and chinook are called 'hook-and-line' species because they are the most sought after by anglers; both are central attractions for the sport fishing and tourism industries. Pink and chum salmon are called 'schooling' varieties because they travel together at or near the surface in schools. This makes them accessible to the seiners who encircle these schools with their nets.

Salmon are born in freshwater lakes and streams (where they spend part of their early life) but then migrate to the ocean before returning to the freshwater to spawn and die. While this cycle is common to all five species, it varies. For example, young sockeye spend a year or more in the freshwater lakes and streams before migrating to the ocean. Sockeye from the Fraser River have a four-year life cycle, while those from the Skeena and Nass can live from four to six years (Barker, 1977: 115). Some chinook in the Columbia River system (before it was dammed) migrated 1,400 kilometres or more and lived seven years, while coho complete their cycle in three years and pinks in only two.

Most salmon return to the streams where they were born in order to spawn, and therefore are identified as races or stocks of those streams. Thus the sockeye born in the Adams River are known as the Adams River race—the largest sockeye run in the world. The Quesnel River also has a large race of sockeye that, by coincidence, is on the same four-year cycle. Since both the Adams and Quesnel are tributaries of the Fraser, every four years there is an enormous run of sockeye salmon on the Fraser. Since salmon spawn in specific streams, the physical condition of those streams is obviously critical to the continuation of salmon stocks.

The fact that two habitats—freshwater and saltwater—are involved causes serious problems with respect to management. The federal government is officially responsible for salmon management because the fishery takes place in saltwater. However, other resource activities for which the province is responsible (forestry, mining, and hydroelectricity, for example) can interfere with the salmon's freshwater habitat. There is a long history of abuse of rivers and streams in British Columbia. One of the most catastrophic events occurred in 1913 at Hell's Gate, in the lower Fraser, when construction on the Great Northern Railway triggered a rockslide that piled debris into the river. Tragically, 1913 was the fourth year of the sockeye cycle, and the rockslide occurred just as the salmon were about to return to their spawning grounds. Fish ladders have been built to allow these salmon to get past Hell's Gate, but their numbers have yet to be restored to their historic levels.

The condition of the ocean environment may be the most critical factor of all. Global warming is raising ocean temperatures ever closer to the critical mark—7°C—at which salmon cannot survive. The film *Phantom of the Ocean* documents how Pacific salmon are gradually moving north to remain in cooler waters (Raincoast Storylines, 1997).

An important development in the industry's history was the introduction of canning technology, an innovation that made commercial fishing viable. Canneries began to appear at the mouth of the Fraser River in the early 1870s. Stacey (1982) defines two periods in the development of this technology: the manual era, from 1871 to 1903, and the mechanical era, from 1903 to 1913. Canning technology helped the industry move from labour-intensive to capital-intensive methods of processing fish. In the early years, according to Stacey, 'each can was cut out of sheet tinplate, formed, and soldered, by hand. By 1890 a number of machines had been introduced to punch out body pieces, top, and bottoms and to apply solder, but these were still aids to the hand process' (198: 4). The one-pound tins were shipped in cases, with 24 cans to the case.

Between 1876 and 1905 the number of cases exported increased from 9,847 to 837,489. While it would be reasonable to think that such growth must have been the result of a major change in technology, a more important factor was a sudden expansion of the salmon harvest. Before 1888, only sockeye were harvested; there was no market for the lighter coloured species with lower oil content. This meant that the commercial fishery lasted only five to six weeks, and as a consequence there were just three canneries on the Fraser in 1876. When the market was expanded to include all five species of salmon, in 1888, both the length of the fishing season and the number of canneries involved increased dramatically. The fishing season now lasted five to six months, and by 1901 there were 49 canneries on the Fraser.

The advent of mechanized canning led to increases both in efficiency of the production line and in corporate concentration in the industry. The introduction of electricity for lights and motors and Fordist assembly line techniques reduced the demand for labour at every stage of the process. The Smith Butchering Machine, developed in 1907, was the most important mechanical invention of this era: it could clean and cut up 60 to 75 fish per minute in a procedure that involved just three workers; the butchering gangs it replaced often consisted of as many as 30 workers (Stacey, 1982: 21).

Of the various methods of catching salmon, 'gillnetting' was the most popular. Gillnets were set up in the mouths of the rivers to intercept the salmon as they travelled upstream to spawn. Since the boats used in the gillnet fishery were not designed to travel great distances, hundreds of canneries were located up and down the coast, wherever there were stocks of salmon to be caught. With the proliferation of canneries and fishers, however, the competition became intense and these waters were increasingly crowded. Some of the crowding was relieved with the introduction of the steam-powered tender boat, which some of the larger canneries used to tow gillnetters farther out, where they might intercept the salmon. Likewise, the invention of the gasoline engine in 1907 enabled individual fishers to travel greater distances from the canneries. As the actual fishing moved farther away from the canneries, however, it soon became clear that catches could easily rot before they ever reached the cannery. This problem was solved in 1915 with the development of the diesel-powered packer boat, which used ice for refrigeration. The motorized gillnetters could now unload their catches onto these large vessels while still at sea.

Fishing is a highly competitive industry in which new technologies are constantly sought to gain advantage. Thus many of the technologies developed during the First and Second World Wars were modified for use in the fishing industry, including echo sounders, asdic, sonar, radar, radio telephones, and hydraulic systems. Along with these sophisticated technologies came synthetic nets, the ability to freeze salt water, and a host of other inventions that made commercial fishing easier. As individual vessels got larger, and as the distances they could travel increased, so did their capacity to harvest salmon. But there

Figure 10.5   Licensed commercial fishing vessels, British Columbia, 1985–2002

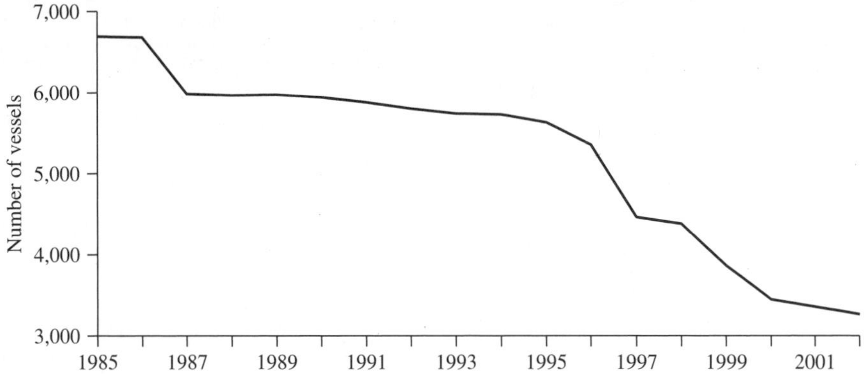

Source: Fisheries and Oceans Canada, 'Pacific Fleet Statistics 1985–2002, by Overall Length' (http://www.dfo-mpo.gc.ca/communic/statistics/commercial/licensing/pacific_info/pactype_e.htm).

was no such increase in the size of the resource itself, and in recent years people have begun to fear that the west coast salmon fishery may meet the same end as the cod fishery on the east coast. Salmon are a common-property resource for which the federal government is the manager, or gatekeeper. The problems associated with this responsibility are enormous. One is the fact that salmon frequently swim through American waters before entering British Columbia's rivers. The province has had salmon treaties with the US in the past, but there have also been bitter 'fish wars'. A new treaty, signed in 1999, regulates the share of the salmon stocks that American fishers are entitled to take.

BC's Aboriginal peoples have the right to catch salmon for food and ceremonial purposes, but they want a share of the commercial activity as well. Under the Nisga'a Treaty a portion of the allowable salmon catch on the Nass River is earmarked as a commercial allotment for the Nisga'a; this portion is set as a proportion of the total run (approximately 26 per cent) in order to ensure the sustainability of the stock. In making salmon a private- rather than a common-property resource, this arrangement has set a precedent that is likely to be followed in modern-day treaties with other First Nations.

In 1996 the federal Department of Fisheries and Oceans launched the 'Mifflin Plan', designed to revitalize the Pacific salmon fishery by designating specific areas for seiners, trollers, and gillnetters, buying back fishing licences, and setting limits on the kinds of gear that fishers could use. Two years later the $400 million Pacific Fisheries Adjustment and Restructuring (PFAR) program, designed to protect and rebuild the salmon habitat, set out to further reduce the commercial fishing fleet through licence buy-backs, while helping fishing communities adjust to the changes to the industry. As Figure 10.5 shows, between 1985 and 2002 there was a 50 per cent reduction in the number of licensed fishing vessels, from 6,690 to 3,363 (Fisheries and Oceans Canada, 2003). A similar decline in the number of licences held can be seen in Table 10.5. Probably the most important factor in these developments was the buyout of 276 seine licences, which has greatly reduced the number of these vessels—which catch enormous quantities of fish, unselectively, with large nets—in BC waters.

Sport fishing accounts for only a small portion—perhaps between 4 and 10 per cent—of the total catch. But there is an important multiplier effect attached to this industry, especially in conjunction with tourism. When things like accommodation, fishing licences,

Table 10.5   British Columbia's commercial fishing licences, 1995–2003

	1995	1996	1997	1998	1999	2000	2001	2002	2003
Gillnet/troller	3,570	2,817	2,813	2,745	2,115	1,578	1,570	1,562	1,562
Seine	536	489	488	442	350	265	264	264	260
Total[1]	**4,364**	**3,596**	**3,628**	**3,505**	**2,786**	**2,172**	**2,173**	**2,168**	**2,166**

[1]Includes special and other licenses.
Source: Fisheries and Oceans Canada, 'Commercial and Aquaculture Statistics' ⟨http://www.dfo-mpo.gc.ca/⟩.

equipment, and beer sales are taken into account, sport fishing realizes a much greater return per fish caught than does the commercial fishery. Thus the sport fishing industry is lobbying the federal government for an even greater share of this dwindling resource.

The future of BC's fishing industry is hard to predict. In response to the decline in salmon catch, federal and provincial governments commissioned the McRae-Pearse Report (2004), which recommended the introduction of an Individual Transferable Quota (ITQ) licence for 25 years (renewable). This would mark a radical departure, making salmon essentially a private-property resource and allocating the commercial fishery on the basis of size of vessel and history of fish catches (McRae-Pearse, 2004). Only time will tell whether this management model will prove to be more sustainable.

Salmon are not the first commercial fish species to be privatized. When halibut stocks were threatened by overfishing—Canadian and American—early in the last century, a 1923 treaty regulated the catch between the two countries. It wasn't until 1991, however, that an Individual Vessel Quota (IVQ) system was introduced under which the licence to fish for an allocated quota is awarded to a particular vessel rather than an individual. Pacific groundfish such as cod had no restrictions until the mid-1990s. Again, depletion of fish species led to IVQs and much tighter management. Similar concerns have arisen over the shellfish, in which the management techniques include closures, quotas, and trap limitations. The McRae-Pearse Report recommends that all of these fisheries implement Individual Transferable Quotas, renewable for 25 years. This would make all fish commercially harvested on the west coast a private-property resource.

Another issue for the commercial salmon fishery is the recent increase in salmon farming. The value of aquaculture now rivals that of the total commercial catch (Table 10.4). Farmed salmon—mostly the foreign Atlantic species, raised in net pens along the coast—brings down the price of wild salmon. Worse, salmon farms expose wild stocks to diseases and parasites, and when the net pens break, they release farmed fish to compete with native species for food and habitat.

Forestry

There are important differences in the BC forestry industry as it operates on the coast and in the interior. On the coast, the dominant species are western red cedar, Douglas fir, and western hemlock; trees of these species can live a thousand years and grow to an enormous size, resulting in a huge volume of wood per hectare. In the interior, by contrast, much greater climatic extremes mean that the dominant species are lodgepole pine in the south and spruce in the central and northern regions, although cedar, hemlock, and fir also occur in some areas. The trees of the interior are, for the most part, smaller in size, spaced farther apart, and much more susceptible to forest fires. Consequently, the volume of wood per hectare is considerably smaller in the interior than on the coast; however, the forested area of the interior is seven times larger than the one on the coast.

Historically, it was the coastal industry that dominated the market, not only because the coastal trees are so large but because the proximity of the ocean offered a cheap and convenient means of transportation to both local and international markets. Logs could be hauled over skid roads by oxen or horses or floated over flumes (artificial channels) to the tide line, then towed from there to mills for processing into lumber as well as shakes and shingles (used for roofs and siding). This set up a linear pattern in which cutting extended only a few hundred metres back from the coast. By the early twentieth century, railway construction throughout Vancouver Island and the southern portion of the mainland made it possible to log in areas far from the coast. The result was a different but still linear pattern of logging. Another important innovation was the steam donkey, or donkey engine: a powerful steam-driven winch that used cables attached to pulleys at the top of a spar tree. This system could haul logs from a wide perimeter to a central point, where it could then lift the logs onto rail cars. Together, these innovations made it possible to cut much greater quantities of trees.

The linear pattern of logging was largely broken with the invention of the combustion engine. Bulldozers were used to build switchback roads in many areas inaccessible by rail, and few forests were so isolated that they could not be reached by road. Trucking became the main means of transporting the forest resource in the 1940s and remains important to this day. The combustion engine also brought about other efficiencies: double-bladed axes and hand saws gave way to the chainsaw, while the mechanical spar pole that could be driven to the logging site replaced the donkey engine. These new technologies made it possible to launch an all-out assault on a resource that appeared to be inexhaustible.

The history of forestry in the interior was quite different. There the commercial forest industry served local markets (representing final-demand linkages). For example, when the gold rush brought prospectors into the Cariboo region in the 1860s, there was a demand for wood for houses and commercial structures such as pit props, sluices, and flumes, as well as for heating and cooking fuel. Once a gold claim was exhausted, the community that had grown up around it was often abandoned, and so the market for forest products disappeared. The interior could not begin to export forest products until railways were in place to transport lumber east to the Prairies and beyond. Eventually the development of roads and truck logging opened up the interior forest industry even more.

Until the middle of the twentieth century, most mills (lumber, plywood, and pulp and paper) were individually owned. In the 1950s, however, a movement towards consolidation and integration began. Large, often foreign corporations bought out existing mills, or built new ones, and increasingly took control of the wood supply and wood products. These large corporations were more versatile, capable of transforming wood 'waste' from sawmilling, for example, into pulp chips, or diverting their wood from lumber to plywood construction if that was what the market demanded. One of the most dynamic developments was the shift in production to the interior, where there had been no pulp mills before 1961. This sparked a boom for communities like Castlegar, Quesnel, Kamloops, and Prince George, where new pulp mills were built. The industry also expanded north of Prince George, spawning a new community, Mackenzie, with pulp, paper, and sawmills. Many of the old coastal pulp and paper mills were refurbished (or, in the case of Ocean Falls, shut down), and new pulp mills were built in Kitimat and the newly created pulp mill town of Gold River.

Every year the provincial government establishes what it calls the allowable annual cut (AAC) for various regions. Although this sounds like a limit, it is really a quota: in fact, companies can be penalized if they fall short of the specified amount. As Figure 10.6 shows, the total increased by more than 300 per cent between 1950 and the 1980s.

Raising the AAC is in the provincial government's interest because it translates into increased revenues. By the early 1990s, however, some commentators were questioning whether such levels of cutting were sustainable (see Drushka et al., 1993; Hammond, 1991; Hayter and Barnes, 1997). In his video documentary *The Falldown Effect* (1993), Mike Halleran graphed the inevitable decline in the timber supplies available for cutting, discussing its causes and speculating about the future of the industry. Areas with a history of intense harvesting are the first to experience the 'falldown effect'. In the coastal forest region, for example, the historic base of old-growth trees has been largely cut, and most of the timber cut in this region now is second-growth (Drushka, 1999). These trees are considerably smaller and produce much lower volumes of wood per hectare. Another factor is the shrinking of the forest base. By the late 1980s many groups were demanding that forests be set aside for uses other than logging, including environmental purposes such as wildlife preservation and recreation, and industrial purposes such as hydroelectricity generation. Some of these arguments have been addressed through the creation of parks in environmentally sensitive areas such as watersheds, but other issues have yet to be resolved. All these 'other' uses of the forest have meant reductions in AACs. The recent increase in AAC reflected in Figure 10.6 was intended to permit the cutting of trees killed by a devastating mountain pine beetle infestation in the interior. Today efforts are underway to increase the volume of wood that will be available for cutting in the future. Basic silviculture, which involves the preparation of clearcuts and the replanting of forests, ensures that new forests will grow to replace old ones. Intensive silviculture goes further and includes spacing, weeding, fertilizing, and commercial thinning of the forest. These processes can triple the volume of wood produced

Figure 10.6   Volume of wood cut from BC coast and interior, 1950–2004

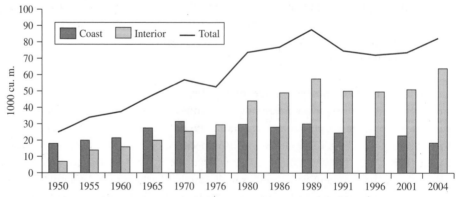

Sources: M.L. Barker, *Natural Resources of British Columbia and the Yukon* (Vancouver: Douglas, David and Charles, 1977); Council of Forest Industries (COFI), *British Columbia Forest Industry Fact Book: 1994* (Vancouver: COFI, 1998); National Forestry Data Base Program ⟨http://nfdp.ccfm.org/compendium/products/tables_index_e.php#tables⟩; Government of BC, Ministry of Forests and Range, Forest Analysis and Inventory Branch, 'Timber Supply Review' ⟨http://www.for.gov.bc.ca/hts/tfls.htm⟩.

per hectare; but they are costly, and the results will not be seen for a minimum of 60 years (M'Gonigle and Parfitt, 1994; Travers, 1993).

There are many other issues that will bring fundamental changes to the forest industry. Among the issues that must be taken into account today are preservation of the remaining old-growth stands, protection of wildlife habitat, stumpage rates (taxes paid on tree harvests), tenure (the means for private companies to access Crown forest land), insect infestations, and forest-fire management.

Another major issue has been the US practice of imposing 'non-tariff barriers' on softwood lumber imports from Canada since 2001. The dispute is not new: it stems from fundamental differences in forest management and taxation between the two countries. In Canada, most lumber comes from Crown land (96 per cent of BC forests are provincial Crown land), and provincial jurisdictions like British Columbia use a tenure system to allow private corporations to cut trees (tree farm licences and forest licences are the most common form of tenure). There is a complex system of taxation, or stumpage, on the wood cut, with stumpage rates varying according to the species of tree, its designated use, and its geographic location. Conversely, the Americans use a bid system, and most wood comes from private lots. Because of these differences, the US has maintained that Canada subsidizes its lumber industry and floods the American market with cheap softwood. In 2001, when an agreement based on provincial quotas ended, the Americans unilaterally slapped an 18.79 per cent levy on all Canadian softwood lumber coming across the boarder, adding an 8.43 per cent anti-dumping duty on top of the original tariff.

Canada has claimed that these duties (in excess of 27 per cent) are unfair, and has found support in rulings by the World Trade Organization and an independent NAFTA tribunal. The dispute has had serious consequences for BC's forestry sector, which has experienced a significant loss in employment, from 85,000 jobs in 2001 to 67,000 in August 2003 (BC Stats 2003a: 2). Nevertheless, as Table 10.6 indicates, there has been some recovery in softwood lumber exports to the US following the slump in 2003, and in December 2005 the US government reduced the rate charged by roughly 50 per cent, though it said it would continue to collect duties until the legal dispute is resolved. Canada, for its part, is continuing to press for repayment of approximately $4 billion the US has collected from softwood producers since 2002.

Metal Mining

British Columbia's metal mining industry is widely credited with opening the province up to non-Native settlement and development. Since the gold rushes of the mid-1800s, mining has had a powerful and permanent impact on the province's landscape. When a non-renewable resource like a mineral is eventually depleted and a mine closes, the community that has depended on that mine for its economic life often becomes a ghost town.

Choosing the right place to look for certain minerals is obviously crucial, but there are numerous other factors that also influence the economic viability of a given mine. Technology is very important to all aspects of mining, from discovery to the end use of the metal. New technological innovations can affect the cost of production as

Table 10.6 Softwood lumber exports to the US ($Cdn), 2001–2004

Year	Exports	Year	Exports
2001	4,962,118,234	2003	3,778,630,564
2002	4,770,883,244	2004	5,189,963,050

Source: BC Stats, 'Softwood Lumber Exports to the USA by Province' (http://www.bcstats.gov.bc.ca).

Table 10.7 Value of selected metals as a percentage of total metals mined, 1860–2004

Year	Gold	Silver	Copper	Lead	Zinc	Moly[1]	Iron
1860	100						
1870	100						
1880	100						
1890	83	17					
1900	42	20	14	23			
1910	44	10	35	10	2		
1920	13	16	40	14	16		
1930	8	11	28	31	17		
1939	41	8	13	22	15		
1950	10	6	7	37	40		
1960	6	6	7	31	41		9
1970	2	3	42	12	15	19	7
1980	13	11	48	4	4	20	
1990	15	8	56	1	8	6	
1997	17	7	47	3	20	6	
2001	23	10	49	2	11	5	
2002	26	12	48	<1	6	2[2]	
2003	28	11	46	<1	4	4[2]	
2004	19	9	48	<1	3	21[2]	

[1]Molybdenum

[2]Estimated value

Source: Natural Resources Canada, 'Mineral Production of Canada, by Province' (http://mmsd1.mms.nrcan.gc.ca/mmsd/production/2001/01prod.pdf).

Figure 10.7 Stages in metals production

well as the supply and demand for the final product. Other influences on the economics of mining include transportation costs (from mine sites that are often remote and isolated), political decisions, the cost of energy, and environmental considerations. The world market price reflects the overall supply and demand for any mineral.

Table 10.7 provides a capsule history of metal mining in British Columbia. Gold dominated the industry until a silver boom hit the Kootenays in the late nineteenth century. New mining techniques and growing demand for other minerals led to the development of copper, lead, and zinc mining. By the 1960s, some iron ore was being mined on Texada Island in the Georgia Strait; the big discovery in the 1970s, though, was molybdenum, an alloy added to steel to harden it.

The flow diagram in Figure 10.7 outlines the essential stages in metals production, from discovery to end use. Each stage is vital to the industry. Although the diagram may suggest that the market is the end point in a progression, in a sense the process is actually circular, since the market (or the world market price) is the key factor motivating exploration and discovery in the first place.

Technological change plays a role at each stage in the process. In the early gold rush era, for example, a gold pan or sluice was used to sift pure gold nuggets out of streambed sediments; this is called placer mining. But not all gold comes in the form of nuggets: sometimes it is 'bound' to other minerals, and extracting it means smashing and crushing the rock in which it is contained. This lode mining calls for more sophisticated technologies, with much higher costs.

Today, as in the past, prospectors need a good understanding of geology, but now they can draw on techniques like remote sensing to assist in the search for valuable metals. Assessing the quality and quantity of the ore body is critical to the next stage, which is production. The development of processing technologies can change the quality–quantity equation considerably. Until the twentieth century, for example, copper extraction became economically viable only at 10 per cent or higher; then new techniques and new demands (e.g., for electrical wire or pipes) made 2 per cent copper ore viable, and by the 1940s, 1 per cent was considered viable. The development in the 1960s of open-pit mining made 0.5 per cent concentrations viable, and today even 0.4 per cent copper may be worth extracting (Barker, 1977: 28; Ross, 1987: 163).

Open-pit technology meant that low-grade ores could be economically processed (though only if there were huge quantities). The low-grade ores are crushed and concentrated, and most are exported at this stage. In the past British Columbia had a number of smelters that refined or smelted concentrates into a pure state. Today there are smelters operating at Trail (mainly lead and zinc) and Kitimat (aluminum), but neither refines minerals mined in the province.

The last two stages of the diagram, 'Manufacturing' and 'Market', refer to end uses. Demand for the end uses affects the world market price, and the world market price is critical to economic viability. But changes in technology can also influence the demand for any metal. For example, manufacturers of copper wire and pipe today must compete with fibre optics (glass threads made from silica) and plastic pipe made from petroleum.

World market price fluctuates—dramatically, in some cases—in response to changes in supply and demand. For example, gold has a very long history as a currency, so that even when paper money was introduced, it was based on gold. The 'gold standard' had been widely adopted by most countries by 1900, and though it was abandoned in the 1930s, the price of gold remained fixed until 1970. Table 10.8 shows the dramatic increase in the price for gold when the market was allowed to establish its own level. By 2001 the average annual price for metals was generally lower than it had been in the mid-1990s, but the costs of transportation, energy, labour, and other inputs increased. The figures for 2004 are much more promising—if they can be sustained.

One of the strengths of BC's large copper mines is that they frequently produce gold, silver, and molybdenum in addition to copper. It has been gold in particular, with its relatively high price per ounce, that has kept some of these mines operating. High fixed operating costs and volatile world market prices make metals mining a high-risk industry, and as a result, over the past twenty years far more mines have closed than opened. It will be interesting to see whether the resurgence in metal prices since 2004 encourages the development of any new mines.

Table 10.8 World market prices for selected minerals and years, 1971–2004

Year	Gold US$/oz.	Silver US$/oz.	Copper US$/lb	Lead US$/lb	Zinc US$/lb	Moly US$/lb
1971	35	1.56	0.38[1]	0.12	0.13	1.39
1974		166[1]	4.98[1]	0.70	0.16[1]	
	0.29[1]	1.65[1]				
1980	708	23.95	0.94	0.32	0.27	9.63
1985	434	8.40	0.72	0.13	0.38	3.55
1990	469	5.60	1.13	0.30	0.67	2.68
1991	362	4.04	1.06	0.25	0.53	2.35
1992	343.73	3.94	1.03	0.25	0.58	2.18
1993	359.77	4.30	0.87	0.18	0.46	2.28
1994	384.00	5.28	1.05	0.25	0.49	4.50
1995	383.98	5.21	1.33	0.28	0.53	7.42
1996	387.70	5.18	1.04	0.35	0.51	3.61
1997	331.10	4.89	1.03	0.28	0.65	4.18
1998	294.16	5.53	0.75	0.24	0.51	3.31
1999	278.77	5.25	0.72	0.23	0.49	2.59
2000	279.77	5.00	0.84	0.21	0.51	2.50
2001	270.99	4.41	0.74	0.21	0.45	2.31
2002	310.03	4.60	0.71	0.21	0.35	3.59
2003	363.35	4.88	0.81	0.23	0.39	5.21
2004	409.35	6.66	1.30	0.40	0.48	15.92

[1]The average price has been used since 1970 for copper and 1974 for gold, silver, lead, zinc, and molybdenum.
Sources: Minister of Mines, Annual Reports; BC Stats ⟨http://www.em.gov. bc.ca/mining/miningstats/⟩; Natural Resources Canada ⟨http://mmsd1. mms.nrcan.gc.ca/mmsd/production/production_e.asp⟩.

Energy Resources

British Columbia has supplied energy resources in many forms, both locally and to markets abroad, and the demand for these resources has changed considerably over time. The earliest resources used in the province—animal power, wood, and water wheels—gave way to coal, electricity, oil, and natural gas. In British Columbia, as elsewhere, there are spatial patterns of supply and demand: not all energy resources are available uniformly throughout the province, nor are the demands for energy the same in each part of the province.

Coal was an early energy resource exported from British Columbia. Some of the first coal mines were on Vancouver Island, and in the early 1900s coal was discovered in the east Kootenays. Demand for coal fluctuated widely, largely because of technology. Historically, it was used mainly to power the steam engine, and also as fuel for cooking and heating, but with the discovery and development of petroleum and other energy sources in the 1960s, demand for coal fell sharply. During the 1970s coal demand

Table 10.9   Coal production (× 1,000 tonnes), 1951–2004

Year	Production	Year	Production
1951	1,578	1986	20,837
1956	1,196	1991	24,848
1961	797	1996	26,179
1966	786	2001	26,482
1971	4,142	2002	24,398
1976	7,538	2003	23,099
1981	11,753	2004	27,107

Source: Natural Resources Canada, 'Mineral Production of Canada, by Province' (http://mmsd1.mms.nrcan.gc.ca/mmsd/production/2001/01prod.pdf).

Table 10.10   Production (× 1,000 tonnes) and value (× $1,000) of metallurgical and thermal coal, 1981–2001[1]

Year	Metallurgical Quantity	Metallurgical Value	Thermal Quantity	Thermal Value	Total Quantity	Total Value
1981	10,812	515,428	941	35,844	11,753	554,271
1986	16,690	828,539	4,147	105,875	20,837	934,414
1991	21,773	854,784	3,075	83,052	24,848	937,836
1996	23,615	1,030,318	2,564	79,263	26,179	1,109,581
2001	25,173	1,026,895	1,309	40,928	26,482	1,067,823

[1]For reasons of confidentiality, coal is no longer separated into metallurgical and thermal after 2001.

Source: BC Stats, 'British Columbia Coal Production: 1970 to 2001' (http://www.bcstats.gov.bc.ca).

rebounded as metallurgical coal (or coking coal) used to create steel and as thermal coal to produce electricity in countries such as Japan (see Table 10.9). Table 10.10 charts the production of thermal and metallurgical coal (the more important of the two) since 1981 and suggests the importance of coal to the BC economy, given that almost all the coal it produces is exported.

As Figure 10.8 shows, the price of metallurgical coal was relatively low in the 1990s, which resulted in the closure of two coal mines at Tumbler Ridge (Bullmoose in 1999 and Quintette in 2003). These closures seriously undermined the economic base of the Tumbler Ridge community. Since 2004, however, prices have rebounded, and two new mines are scheduled to open in the northeastern part of the province, one of them (Wolverine) quite close to Tumbler Ridge.

The story of BC's oil and natural gas industry is quite different. Until the early 1950s, the province imported all its oil from California. In 1954, however, after huge quantities of oil were discovered in Alberta, and smaller quantities in BC's Peace River region, the Transmountain Pipeline was constructed to supply the Vancouver-area re-fineries. As the demand for oil in BC increased with increases in population, transporta-tion demands, and industrial development, the province's demand always exceeded its

Figure 10.8   Value of metallurgical coal, British Columbia, 1972–2004

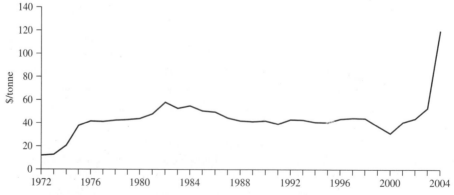

Sources: BC Stats, 'British Columbia Coal Production: 1970 to 2001' (http://www.bcstats.gov.bc.ca.2002); Northern Energy and Mining, 'The Future of Coal in BC' (http://www.nemi-energy.com).

supply. Exploratory drilling for oil most often revealed the presence of natural gas, which until 2000 was considered much less valuable. The province has tried to use natural gas (of which there was a surplus) instead of oil wherever possible in order not to overtax its diminished oil reserves.

Table 10.11 shows BC's production and consumption of natural gas and oil from 2000 to 2004. Natural gas production (largely for export) increased somewhat during this time. The price of this energy had risen considerably by 2003, as Table 10.12 shows. Oil production has also increased, although consumption continues to out-strip production. Much of the oil extracted from BC is exported to Alberta for refining and then imported back into the province. As of 2005, the federal government still had not yet decided whether to allow offshore drilling in one of the most seismically risky regions of Canada.

The demand for electricity in BC has been met largely through the building of dams and the generation of hydroelectricity. During the early twentieth century, the increase in demand for electricity was slow because the province was home to a small population and only a few large industries. Demand increased rapidly after the Second World War, however (see Figure 10.9). The province's first mega-project was Kemano 1, a large hydroelectric generating station using water diverted from the Nechako River, built by a private company (Alcan) to produce aluminum at Kitimat. Completed by the end of the 1950s, it established an industrial model for the provincial government: build hydroelectric dams, and industrial expansion will follow. The provincial government encouraged the expansion of the forestry and mining industries, and created BC Hydro to supply the electricity.

During the 1960s a number of hydroelectric dams were built on the Peace and Columbia rivers, under BC Premier W.A.C. Bennett's 'two-river policy'. The Columbia River dams required the cooperation of the United States, since the river is an international waterway, and this led to the Columbia River Treaty, signed in 1964: the Americans agreed to pay for a number of dams in BC in exchange for receiving the benefit of hydroelectricity from the Columbia River. During the 1970s BC Hydro considered building dams on other waterways in the province, including the Fraser, Skeena, Nass,

Table 10.11   Production, consumption and exports of natural gas and crude oil, 2000–2004

	2000	2001	2002	2003	2004
Natural gas (billion cu. ft./d.)					
Production	2.2	2.5	2.7	2.5	2.6
Consumption	0.8	0.8	0.8	0.7	0.7
Exports	1.0	1.1	1.2	1.1	1.1
Crude oil (thousand barrels/d.)					
Production	55	55	52	52	48
Consumption	187	187	191	195	208
Exports	11	1.5	2.7	2.3	2.1

Source: Canadian Association of Petroleum Producers ⟨http://www.capp.ca/default.asp?V_DOC_ID=674⟩.

Table 10.12   Value of fuels (× $1,000), 1996 and 2001–2004

Fuel	1996	2001	2002	2003	2004
Coal	1,109,581,000	959,292,000	1,034,860,000	999,986,000	1,127,025,000
Natural gas	816,524,000	4,832,221,649	3,468,168,707	5,366,499,627	n.a.
Oil	441,499,000	554,305,574	550,750,169	544,236,058	n.a.
Total oil and gas[1]	1,335,806,000	5,632,682,368	4,251,421,812	6,184,636,798	7,100,000,000
Total fuels	2,445,387,000	6,591,974,368	5,286,281,812	7,184,622,798	8,227,025,000

[1]Includes oil and natural gas by-products.

Sources: BC Stats, 'All Minerals Production and Values: 1998 to 2003' ⟨http://www.bcstats.gov.bc.ca⟩; Natural Resources Canada, 'Mineral Production of Canada, by Province' ⟨http://mmsd1.mms.nrcan.gc.ca/mmsd/production/2001/01prod.pdf⟩; Canadian Association of Petroleum Producers ⟨http://www.capp.ca/defalt.asp?V_DOC_ID=674⟩.

Figure 10.9   Electrical generation, including hydro and thermal (gigawatt-hours), 1920–2003

Sources: M.L. Barker, *Natural Resources of British Columbia and the Yukon* (Vancouver: Douglas, David and Charles, 1977), 54; BC Stats, 'Financial and Economic Review: 2004', p. 32 〈http://www.bcstats.gov.bc.ca〉.

Stikine, and Liard rivers. But the energy crisis of the 1970s caused prices to rise and prompted industrial consumers to find other sources of energy; for example, pulp mills—major consumers of electricity—began creating electricity from wood waste ('hog fuel'). The recession of the 1980s further reduced the demand for hydroelectricity, all but putting an end to plans for additional hydro dams in the province. Opposition

The W.A.C. Bennett Dam on the Peace River, near Hudson's Hope in northeastern BC. Opened in 1967 and named for the premier who authored the 'two-river policy', it stretches 2 kilometres across the head of the Peace River Canyon. The hydroelectric generating station there is capable of producing more than 13 billion kWh of electricity a year (BC Hydro, http://www.bchydro.com/recreation/northern/northern1198.html).   *Photo Brett McGillivray.*

from environmental groups concerned about the damage caused by flooding river valleys also played a role in the decision to put these plans on hold.

As the population of the province increases, so does the demand for electricity. BC Hydro's Energy Smart Program has helped to persuade consumers to conserve energy, and energy conservation is becoming essential to reducing consumption costs in BC as elsewhere. In addition there are a number of 'Green Energy' projects that will increase the supply of electricity, but as recently as 2004 BC Hydro was looking again at the viability of developing Site 'C'—one of the projects shelved 1970s, which would be constructed on the Peace River, close to Fort St John. If built, it will flood some of the finest agricultural land in the province.

Other Resource Industries

Except in the Peace River region, the agricultural landscape of British Columbia is very different from that of the Prairies. Agricultural land is mostly confined to valley bottoms, and the interior plateau is used as grazing land for cattle. These areas constitute the total of British Columbia's arable land, which is approximately 3 per cent of the land base, though another 30 per cent is considered to have some agricultural capability (BC Stats 2002b: 8). Agriculture is thus restricted to small pockets; however, the warm climates of the southern and coastal regions allow them to grow an exceptional variety of agricultural crops (more than 200). Table 10.13, comparing the numbers of farms across Canada, shows that despite the small portion of the province that is suitable for agriculture, BC still has more farms than all of Atlantic Canada. BC was for many years the only province to have adopted legislation (in 1972) protecting farmland against conversion to non-agricultural uses (Ontario has recently followed suit).

British Columbia has much to offer tourists, from the unique topography, flora, and fauna of its coastal and interior landscapes to the many year-round recreational activities associated with those landscapes. A successful tourism industry requires coordination between government and tourist-related private businesses. Conflicts have arisen, however, around the traditional resource industries: fish, minerals, and forests. Restrictions on

Table 10.13 Census farms[1] in Canada, 1991, 1996, and 2001

Province	1991 Farms	1996 Farms	% Change 1991–1996	2001	% Change 1996–2001
Newfoundland	725	731	0.8	643	−13
Prince Edward Is.	2,361	2,200	−6.8	1,845	−17
Nova Scotia	3,980	4,021	1.0	3,923	−12
New Brunswick	3,252	3,206	−1.4	3,034	−11
Quebec	38,076	35,716	−6.2	32,139	−11
Ontario	68,633	67,118	−2.2	59,728	−12
Manitoba	25,706	24,341	−5.3	21,071	−14
Saskatchewan	60,840	56,979	−6.3	50,598	−11
Alberta	57,245	58,990	3.0	53,652	−9
British Columbia	**19,225**	**21,653**	**12.6**	**20,290**	**−7**
Canada	280,043	274,955	−1.8	246,923	−11

[1]Refers to a farm, ranch, or other agricultural operation that produces agricultural products for sale.

Sources: Adapted from the Statistics Canada website ⟨http://www40.statcan.ca/101/cst01/agrc42a.htm⟩ and Statistics Canada, 'The Daily', Cat. no. 11-001, 14 May 1997 ⟨http://www.statcan.ca/Daily/English/970514/d970514.htm⟩.

Table 10.14   British Columbia tourism revenue and volume, 1997–2004

	1997	1998	1999	2000	2001	2002	2003	2004
Tourist revenue and volume								
Revenue ($ millions)	8,471	8,731	9,080	9,449	9,242	9,336	8,953	9,473
Visitors (thousands)	21,313	21,753	22,053	22,491	22,381	22,571	21,870	22,450
Visitor entries (thousands of persons)								
USA	5,893	6,549	6,862	7,006	6,895	6,591	6,137	4,994
Europe	449	449	485	498	466	412	410	616
Pacific Rim	920	771	842	893	864	882	702	859
BC tourists	10,654	10,654	n.a.	10,761	10,761	10,869	10,884	11,032

Sources: BC Stats, 'Tourism Industry Monitor', Annual 2003, p. 3; 'Financial and Economic Review', 2004, p. 8; ⟨Tourism Performance Preliminary Estimate', all at ⟨http://www.bcstats.gov.bc.ca⟩.

catches of some salmon species, for instance, have led some sport fishing lodges to close, which has hurt restaurants and other businesses in communities associated with sport fishing. Other conflicts have involved clearcutting of forestland and open-pit mining operations, which are not conducive to tourism. The provincial government's efforts to create more parks and protected areas indicate that it recognizes the necessity of preserving the natural setting in order to promote tourism.

Tourism has grown steadily in British Columbia since Expo '86, in part because the relatively low value of the Canadian dollar in relation to other currencies (especially the US dollar) has made the country a 'good buy'. British Columbia's geographic position and growing economic attachment to the Asia–Pacific region have also contributed to increases in international visitors. Unpredictable events can drastically change the fortunes of this industry, however. An example is the severe recession that hit several Asian economies in 1997, which hurt many aspects of British Columbia's economy, including tourism. Fear of terrorism in the wake of the September 11 attacks has also had a negative impact on the numbers of tourists choosing BC. On the positive side, Vancouver's successful bid to host the 2010 Winter Olympics should provide a major boost for tourism.

Table 10.14 traces the ups and downs of BC's tourist industry from 1997 to 2004. The most significant change has been the decrease in international visitors since 2000. Figure 10.10 focuses on the downturn in international cruise ship passengers visiting the port of Vancouver. Seattle's development of cruise ship facilities has played a role in this downturn, as many American travellers now depart from within their own country instead of beginning their cruise in Vancouver.

Urbanization and the Global Economy

Settlement patterns changed dramatically in the years following 1950. British Columbia experienced prosperity until the 1970s, when a series of unpredictable global economic

Figure 10.10   Cruise ship revenue passengers, port of Vancouver, 1992–2004

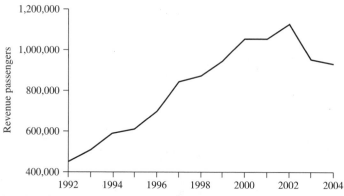

Source: Port of Vancouver, 'Five Year Statistical Summaries: 2000 and 2004' ⟨http://www.portvancouver.com/statistics/2000_statistical.html⟩.

Table 10.15   Population and urbanization, BC and Canada, 1951–2001

Year	B.C.	% Rural	% Urban	Canada	% Rural	% Urban
1951	1,165,210	47.2	52.8	14,009,429	38.4	61.6
1961	1,629,082	27.4	72.6	18,338,247	30.4	69.6
1971	2,184,621	24.3	75.7	21,568,311	23.9	76.1
1981	2,744,465	22.0	78.0	24,343,181	24.3	75.7
1991	3,282,061	19.6	80.4	27,296,859	23.3	76.6
1996	3,724,500	18.0	82.0	28,846,761	22.1	77.9
2001	4,101,579	15.3	84.7	31,110,565	20.3	79.7

Source: Adapted from the Statistics Canada website (http://www40.statcan.ca/l01/cst01/demo62a.htm).

events, mostly negative, disrupted the economy of the province and the world. Even so, the province's population more than tripled in size between 1951 and 2001. As Table 10.15 shows, growth was accompanied by a distinct shift to urban areas.

The 'long boom' from the 1950s to the 1970s was a period of unprecedented growth in North America, fuelled by rising disposable incomes, increasing automobile use, new homes in the suburbs for the post-war baby boom, and new consumer goods, all of which reflected changing living conditions and increasing urbanization.

Rising standards of living throughout North America translated into rising demand for resources, including many resources found in British Columbia. Oil, natural gas, and electricity became the most important forms of energy, and regions like the Peace River had all three. There were several wood-processing plants in the interior but no pulp mills until 1961, when the increased demand for pulp, paper, lumber, and other wood products made it economically feasible to exploit the mainly untapped forests of the interior. There was also a major expansion in mining during this time, as world prices for copper, molybdenum, silver, lead, and zinc increased. The massive investment in developing these resources during the long boom was felt both in existing towns and in the new communities like Kitimat, Fraser Lake, Granisle, and Sparwood that were built around this new industrial activity.

The initial expansion and upgrading of road systems in the 1950s became 'pavement politics' in the 1960s and 1970s. Not only were new roads, highways, and bridges built: the whole transportation system was transformed as the provincial and federal governments became involved in airport expansions, ferry systems, and the extension of the PGE (renamed the British Columbia Railway, or BCR, in 1971) from Prince George to Fort St James in 1967 and to Fort Nelson in 1971. Another major rail expansion involved improvements in the CPR line to the coal sources in the southeast, linking the area around Fernie to the new coal port of Westshore Terminals at Roberts Bank in 1970. These transportation developments aided the growth of the expanded urban system.

Suburbanization went hand in hand with highway and freeway expansion and increasing automobile ownership. The move to the rural–urban fringe was sparked by the desire for single-family dwellings, which were becoming difficult to find and costly to own in the established communities of the cities, where land prices were climbing. At the same time many shops and services were motivated to find new suburban, commutershed locations in shopping centres and industrial parks. These relocated services in turn became catalysts for further growth.

The development of high-growth regions such as the Lower Mainland, the Victoria–Saanich peninsula on Vancouver Island, and the Okanagan Valley resulted in enormous problems. Agricultural land, never in abundance in British Columbia, was being consumed for urban and industrial uses at a rapid rate, and providing low-density regions with services such as water and sewer facilities presented another set of challenges. The need for planning was obvious.

The provincial government responded to this sudden growth with a number of measures, including the Instant Town Act of 1965, which allowed for the building of new resource towns for the booming resource industry. 'Instant towns' like Gold River, Mackenzie, Logan Lake, and Sparwood were designed as 'permanent' incorporated communities and deliberately not structured on the old company-town model. But as single-resource communities they were equally vulnerable to the vagaries of world market conditions.

Regional Districts were also created in 1965, making British Columbia a federation of incorporated and unincorporated electoral areas, all with political representation and municipal powers under the Municipal Act. This allowed the unincorporated areas of regional districts to become involved in planning, as well as in public utilities and other functions—from solid waste management to parks and recreation—that had previously been controlled by the province. In 1972 the Agricultural Land Commission Act created an agricultural zone (the Agricultural Land Reserve) in an effort to prohibit the conversion of agricultural land to urban uses. The province also encouraged the amalgamation or annexation of communities, with the result that many urban centres (including Kamloops, Prince George, Kelowna, and Nanaimo) expanded their boundaries. Vancouver, the largest city, became a Census Metropolitan Area, though it was more practical to view the Greater Vancouver Regional District (GVRD)—Vancouver and its rapidly growing adjacent communities (North Vancouver, Burnaby, Richmond, Surrey, etc.)—as one large metropolitan area. Vancouver's role in the province was changing as it took more and more control of resource development throughout the province (Robinson and Hardwick, 1968; Denike and Leigh, 1978). Victoria, the main urban centre for the Capital Regional District (CRD), became the second Census Metropolitan Area in the province.

The production of goods and services began shifting from a national to a global scale in the 1970s, though the transition was complicated by numerous unpredictable and mostly negative market conditions that created economic uncertainty and instability. In general, the 1970s were a period of high inflation, increased wages, and speculation in land. By contrast, the first half of the 1980s was marked by a recession that brought high unemployment and a major reduction in demand for resources. In BC, the use of capital-intensive technologies in the mines and mills had begun to reduce the number of unionized workers in the province. Restructuring, downsizing, and adjusting to the new world order of business meant uncertainty for far more than the resource industries of BC, as the province's manufacturing and services industries were increasingly challenged by global competition. In short, British Columbia felt the effects of the recession more than any other province.

There was a partial recovery in the latter half of the 1980s, fuelled in part by major government investments designed to kick-start the economy. The provincial and federal governments invested heavily in extending the British Columbia Railway from Chetwynd to Tumbler Ridge, the centre for northeastern coal, and double-tracking the

CNR line to Prince Rupert, where the new coal port of Ridley Island was constructed. Other major projects supported by government investments included the building of the Coquihalla Highway and Expo '86—both of which contributed significantly to tourism in the province. Another area that became increasingly important in this period when many of the traditional industries were cutting back was the retirement industry. There had always been a retirement population in BC, but with the baby boomers moving towards retirement age, this population increased significantly. The Okanagan, the southeastern part of Vancouver Island, and the Lower Mainland became popular destinations for retirees from across Canada.

The Canada–US Free Trade Agreement (FTA) of 1989 created further economic uncertainty leading into the 1990s. The change in the territorial status of Hong Kong, which was scheduled to revert from British control to the People's Republic of China in 1997, resulted in increased immigration of Hong Kong Chinese to British Columbia, along with substantial transfers of capital and investment, mainly to the Lower Mainland region. By the end of the 1990s, however, the 'Asian economic flu' had weakened the strong economic links between British Columbia and the Asia–Pacific countries, resulting in another recession in the province. Overall, in spite of the boost provided by the wave of immigrants from Hong Kong, population growth had slowed considerably since 1971: whereas the number of British Columbians had doubled between 1951 and 1971, the rate of increase over the next 20 years was only half as great, in part because of the economic turbulence of the period (see Table 10.15).

The 1990s also saw a widening of the economic gap between the highly urban and integrated core—the Lower Mainland and the southern end of Vancouver Island— and the rest of the province. The core, characterized by knowledge-based and information-based employment, value-added manufacturing, and administrative functions, gained an ever greater share of the incoming population. Vancouver was no longer just a port city with strong links to the rest of the province and western Canada: it had become an integrated part of the Asia–Pacific region and a world city.

The rest of the province, the resource-dependent periphery, struggled through the 1990s and continues to struggle today. The forest industry has had to face both reductions in the amount of wood available and increases in labour costs, which together have produced some of the highest costs in the world for products like pulp. Mining has followed a similar pattern, as low world market prices (until 2004) for metals such as copper and for energy minerals such as coal led to mine closures and threatened the survival of communities such as Granisle, Logan Lake, and Tumbler Ridge.

Table 10.16 gives the rank order (based on 2001 population data) for communities of 10,000 or more people in British

Table 10.16 Municipalities with populations over 10,000 (in 2001) by rank, 1996, 2001, and 2004

Municipality	1996	2001	2004
1. Vancouver, CMA	1,831,665	1,986,965	2,132,824
2. Victoria, CMA	304,287	311,902	331,491
3. Kelowna CA	136,541	147,739	162,555
4. Abbotsford CMA	136,480	147,370	161,304
5. Kamloops CA	85,407	86,491	91,739
6. Nanaimo CA	82,691	85,664	90,988
7. Prince George CA	87,731	85,035	91,227
8. Chilliwack CA	66,254	69,776	76,566
9. Vernon CA	49,701	51,530	55,327
10. Courtenay CA	46,297	47,051	51,597
11. Penticton CA	41,276	41,574	44,294
12. Duncan CA	38,464	38,813	41,549
13. Campbell River DM	28,851	33,872	35,737
14. North Cowichan CA	25,305	26,148	28,065
15. Port Alberni CA	26,893	25,396	26,569
16. Mission DM	30,519	31,272	33,970
17. Quesnel CA	25,074	25,486	25,766
18. Williams Lake CA	24,992	25,122	26,735
19. Parksville CA	22,629	24,285	25,696
20. Cranbrook CA	24,151	24,275	25,792
21. Terrace CA	20,941	19,980	21,002
22. Powell River CA	18,402	18,269	19,232
23. Dawson Creek CA	18,039	17,444	18,624
24. Fort St. John CA	15,021	16,034	17,280
25. Prince Rupert CA	17,414	15,302	15,678
26. Salmon Arm DM	14,664	15,210	16,466
27. Squamish CA	14,236	14,435	15,604
28. Comox T	11,069	11,172	12,394
29. Summerland DM	10,584	10,713	11,776
30. Kitimat CA	11,136	10,285	10,449

CMA = Census Metropolitan Area; CA = Census Area; DM = District Municipality; T = Town

Source: BC Stats, 'Sub-Provincial Population Estimates' ⟨http://www.bcstats. gov.bc.ca.2004e⟩.

Columbia. With 30 communities in this category, the 2001 list stands in marked contrast to the one for 1951, when only six made the grade (see Table 10.3). In the 50 years since 1951 the urban system had evolved into 28 regional districts and 154 incorporated communities, and the proportion of the population based in rural areas had shrunk from 48 per cent to approximately 20. A comparison of 1996 figures with those for 2001 and 2004 shows how many of the communities in the core region have grown in population. Few of the resource-dependent communities, on the other hand, have fared well: Prince George, Port Alberni, Terrace, Powell River, Dawson Creek, and Kitimat all lost population between 1996 and 2001, although they made gains by 2004. The core region of British Columbia, extending from Victoria to Nanaimo and the Lower Mainland, now contains more than 60 per cent of the province's population, and will likely have an even greater share in the future.

Summary

The processes of settlement and development in British Columbia were delayed, not only because of the region's rugged topography but also because of its relative isolation during the colonial phase of Canada's history. The Aboriginal peoples who had inhabited the region for more than 10,000 years were extremely diverse, speaking as many as 34 different languages, and by the time of contact the population density of the coastal region was the highest anywhere in the territory that would become Canada. But their numbers were drastically reduced by disease within a few years of the Europeans' arrival. In the latter part of the 1800s the survivors were forced onto reserves (much smaller than the reserves provided elsewhere in the country), in most cases without the benefit of treaties. It has been a long struggle for BC's First Nations to gain legal recognition and the right to reclaim their land through modern-day treaties. Only the Nisga'a Treaty has been completed to date, and so the struggle continues, both at the negotiating table and in the courts.

Non-Natives were drawn to British Columbia in hopes of making a fortune from its resources: first furs and then gold. There was little settlement during the fur trade period, but the discovery of gold opened the province for development and set it on a boom-and-bust course. When British Columbia joined Confederation in 1871 its population was barely more than 36,000; there were only two incorporated communities, and just 15 per cent of the province was urban. By 2001 the province had more than four million inhabitants occupying 154 municipalities, and the population was 85 per cent urban. Regional patterns of urbanization and population growth followed resource discoveries and the development of transportation systems. The completion of the CPR marked the beginning of the railway era and represented the development of technologies that made it possible to exploit the resources found throughout BC's mountainous landscape.

Since 1960, world events have played a greater role in shaping the geography of British Columbia, largely because of transportation technologies that have shrunk the international scale of business transactions and commerce. The services that are at the centre of the new global economy for the most part favour large urban centres. This has resulted in tremendous growth for the core region centred on Victoria and, especially, Vancouver. The rest of the province continues to function as periphery, and the economies of hinterland communities still depend on resource extraction. As the world shrinks and the pressure for free trade becomes greater, demand for service-related industries will increase, and the advantages will accrue to large urban centres capable of mounting international events such as the 2010 Winter Olympics. For communities in the vast geographic hinterland, the challenge will be to find new ways to diversify their economies.

References

Barker, M.L. 1977. *Natural Resources of British Columbia and the Yukon*. Vancouver: Douglas, David and Charles.

Bawlf, R.S. 2003. *The Secret Voyages of Sir Francis Drake 1577–1580*. New York: Walker.

British Columbia, Ministry of Finance and Corporate Relations. 1998. *Financial and Economic Review*.

BC Stats. 2005. 'Softwood Lumber Exports to the USA by Province'. http://www.bcstats.gov.bc.ca.

———. 2004a. Small Business Quarterly. 'Lumber Dispute Big Issue for Small Business'. Issue 04-3. http://www.bcstats.gov.bc.ca.

———. 2002b. 'All Minerals Production and Values: 1998 to 2003'. http://www.bcstats.gov.bc.ca.

———. 2004c. 'British Columbia Financial and Economic Review: 2004'. http://www.bcstats.gov.bc.ca.

———. 2004d. 'British Columbia 2004 Tourism Performance Preliminary Estimate'. http://www.bcstats.gov.bc.ca.

———. 2004e. 'Sub-Provincial Population Estimates'. http://www.bcstats.gov.bc.ca.

———. 2003a. 'Earnings & Employment Trends'. 'How Has the Forestry Sector Fared?'. Issue 00-09. http://www.bcstats.gov.bc.ca.

———. 2003b. 'Tourism Industry Monitor, Annual 2003'. http://www.bcstats.gov.bc.ca.

———. 2002a. 'British Columbia Coal Production: 1970 to 2001'. http://www.bcstats.gov.bc.ca.

———. 2002b. 'Quick Facts about British Columbia'. 'Agriculture': p. 8. http://www.bcstats.gov.bc.ca.

CBC Radio. 2004. 'Major Overhaul of B.C. Salmon Fishery'. 5 May. http://vancouver.bc.ca/regional/servlet/View?filename=British Columbia_fish20040505.

Chapman, J.D. 1960. 'The Geography of Energy: An Emerging Field'. *Occasional Papers in Geography*. Vancouver: Tantalus, Canadian Association of Geographers, BC Division, No. 1: 31–40.

Chodos, R. 1975. *The CPR: A Century of Corporate Welfare*. Toronto: James Lorimer.

Council of Forest Industries (COFI). 1994. *British Columbia Forest Industry Fact Book: 1994*. Vancouver.

Davis, H.C., and T.A. Hutton. 1994. 'Marketing Vancouver's Services to the Asia Pacific'. *The Canadian Geographer* 38, 1: 18–27.

Denike, K.G., and R. Leigh. 1972. 'Economic Geography 1960–1970'. Pp. 139–45 in J.L. Robinson, ed. *British Columbia*. Toronto: University of Toronto Press

Drushka, K. 1999. 'British Columbia's Forests: A New Way to Grow'. *The Vancouver Sun*. 31 Mar.: D1, 2, 19, 20.

———, B. Nixon, and R. Travers, eds. 1993. *Touch Wood: B.C. Forests at the Crossroads*. Madeira Park: Harbour.

Fisheries and Oceans Canada. 'Commercial and Aquaculture Statistics'. http://www.dfo-mpo.gc.ca/.

———. 2003. 'Pacific Fleet Statistics 1985–2002, by Overall Length'. http://www.dfo-mpo.gc.ca/communic/statistics/commercial/licensing/pacific_info/pactype_e.htm.

Halleran, M. (producer). 1993. The Falldown Effect. Westland Television Series. Kaslo, B.C.

Hammond, H. *Seeing the Forest Among the Trees*. Vancouver: Polestar. 1991.

Harris, C. 1997. *The Resettlement of British Columbia: Essays on Colonialism and Geographic Change*. Vancouver: University of British Columbia Press.

Hayter, R., and T. Barnes. 1997. 'The Restructuring of British Columbia's Coastal Forest Sector: Flexible Perspectives'. *B.C. Studies* (Spring): 6–34.

Hutton, T.A. 1997. 'The Innisian Core-Periphery Revisited: Vancouver's Changing Relationships with British Columbia's Staple Economy'. *BC Studies* 113: 69–98.

Indian and Northern Affairs Canada 2004. 'Fact Sheet: The Nisga'a Treaty'. http://www.ainc-inac.gc.ca/pr/info/nit_e.html.

M'Gonigle, M., and B. Parfitt. 1994. *Forestopia: A Practical Guide to the New Forest Economy*. Madiera Park: Harbour.

McKee, C. 1996. *Treaty Talks in British Columbia: Negotiating a Mutually Beneficial Future*. Vancouver: University of British Columbia Press.

McRae, D.M., and P.H. Pearse. 2004. *Treaties and Transition: Towards a Sustainable Fishery on Canada's Pacific Coast*. Report for Fisheries and Oceans Canada. ⟨http://www-comm.pac.dfo-mpo.gc.ca/publications/jtf/tint_e.htm⟩.

National Forestry Data Base Program. http://nfdp.ccfm.org/ compendium/products/tables_index_e.php#tables.

Natural Resources Canada 2005. 'Mineral Production of Canada, by Province'. http://mmsd1.mms.nrcan.gc.ca/ mmsd/production/2001/01prod.pdf.

Northern Energy & Mining. 2005. 'The Future of Coal in BC'. http://www.nemi-energy.com.

Port of Vancouver. 2004. 'Five Year Statistical Summary'. http:// www.portvancouver.com/statistics/2004_statistical.html.

———. 2000. 'Five Year Statistical Summary'. http://www. portvancouver.com/statistics/2000_statistical.html.

Province of British Columbia. 2005. Ministry of Energy and Mines. 'British Columbia Coal Mine Gate Prices: 1970 to 2001'. http://www.em.gov.BC.ca/Mining/MiningStats/ 31coalsold.htm.

———. 2004a. 'Frequently Asked Questions'. http://www.gov. bc.ca/arr/FAQ/default.htm#top.

———. 2004b. 'BC Treaty Negotiations'. http://www.gov. British Columbia.ca/tno/negotiation/.

Raincoast Storylines Ltd. 1997. In association with the Canadian Broadcasting Corporation. 'Phantom of the Ocean: The Mystery of Global Climate Change' (video). Kelowna: Filmwest Associates (distributor).

Robinson, J.L., and W.G. Hardwick. 1968. 'The Canadian Cordillera'. Pp. 438–72 in J. Warkentin, ed. *Canada: A Geographical Interpretation*. Toronto: Methuen.

Ross, W.M. 1987. 'Mining'. Pp. 162–76 in C.N. Forward, ed. *British Columbia: Its Resources and People*. Victoria: Western Geographical Series, Vol. 22.

Seager, A. 1996. 'The Resource Economy 1871–1921'. Pp. 205–52 in H.J.M. Johnston, ed. *The Pacific Province: A History of British Columbia*. Vancouver: Douglas and McIntyre.

Stacey, D. *Sockeye and Tinplate*. Victoria: BC Provincial Museum, 1982.

Statistics Canada. 2002. 'Farming Facts: 2002'. http://www. statcan.ca.

Thornton, G. 2004. 'An Update to the Financial and Economic Analysis of Treaty Settlements in British Columbia'. Government of British Columbia, British Columbia Treaty Commission. March.

Travers, O.R. 1993. 'Forest Policy: Rhetoric and Reality'. Pp. 171–224 in Drushka et al. (1993).

11

The North: Resource Frontier and Native Land

The history of the land north of the 60th parallel has taken a very different course than the history of the southern provinces. As elsewhere, so in the North, Aboriginal people had sustained themselves for thousands of years before Europeans arrived. Non-Natives went to the North, as they had gone to other parts of the continent, to explore, trade, and exploit resources, bringing their diseases and dependencies and altering the landscape in many ways. What sets the northern landscape apart is that non-Natives were unable to transform it into an agricultural landscape; as a consequence, relatively few non-Natives have made their home in the North, and it has remained Native land.

Figure 11.1   Map of the North

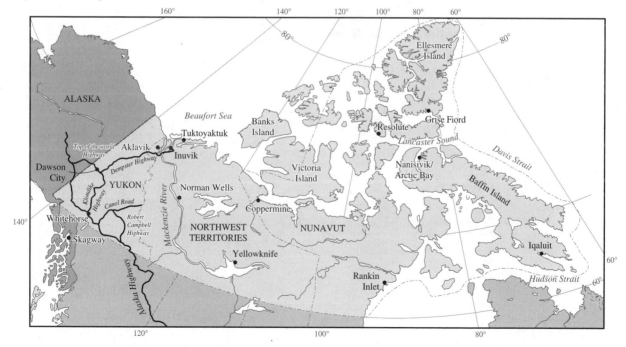

For much of Canada's existence the North has been a neglected landscape. To be sure, Ottawa asserted its political authority over the region, largely to thwart American expansion. The Klondike gold rush of the late 1890s temporarily attracted swarms of miners to the Yukon, and when international events threatened Canadian sovereignty in the North, during the Second World War and the Cold War, non-Natives again invaded the region. But they too left once the conflict ended. The legacy of these incursions was altered political boundaries, new communities and transportation systems, and considerably more knowledge about the land.

Following the Second World War, the federal government set out to remake the North in the image of southern Canada, establishing permanent communities with schools, healthcare facilities, and the whole array of social programs. It also set out to exploit the region's resources. These policies profoundly altered the traditional ways of life of the North's Native peoples. The influx of southerners during the mega-project era of the 1960s and 1970s sparked many conflicts. The Berger Inquiry was established to resolve just one conflict, surrounding the construction of a natural gas pipeline down the Mackenzie River valley, but it accomplished much more. In effect, it exposed the incompatibility of the southern and northern ways of life. The first revolved around resource exploitation and wage employment. The second revolved around subsistence land use by Aboriginal people, who remained the dominant population in the Northwest Territories. As Berger saw it, the 'solution' lay in negotiating treaties that would give northern Aboriginal people greater autonomy. The federal government, which by this time had accepted the idea that Aboriginal title still existed in untreatied regions, agreed. By the end of the 1990s a number of settlements had been concluded, and a new political territory—Nunavut—was created. Resource extraction has continued and will continue in the future; now, however, it will not be done without the approval of the people whose home this has been from time immemorial.

Defining the North

There is more than one way to define the North. For most Canadians it is simply everything 'north of 60'—'60' being the latitude that marks the southern boundary

Figure 11.2   Evolution of the northern territories, 1870–1999

Sources: Adapted from Q. Stanford, ed., *Canadian Oxford World Atlas,* 5th edn (Toronto: Oxford University Press, 2003), 37; E. Struzik, 'Changing Courses', *Canadian Geographic* 122, 5 (Sept.–Oct. 2002), 44–5.

of mainland Yukon, Northwest Territories, and Nunavut. The political boundaries of the region have been adjusted and readjusted many times since Confederation, when it was still British territory (see Figure 11.2). Most of the region officially became part of Canada in 1870, when the Dominion purchased the North-Western Territory and Rupert's Land from the Hudson's Bay Company, but possession of the Arctic Islands was not transferred to Canada from Britain until a decade later. The Yukon became a separate territory in 1898, in the wake of the Klondike gold rush, with its southern limit set at the 60th parallel. This rather arbitrary dividing line was first used to separate north from south when British Columbia joined Confederation in 1871, but it was not extended east until Alberta and Saskatchewan were created in 1905 and Manitoba's border was adjusted in 1912, the year the northern boundaries of both Ontario and Quebec were also extended to their present locations.

Another way of defining the North is in terms of its physical characteristics. Three of the physiographic regions discussed in earlier chapters—the Canadian Shield, the Great Interior Plains, and the Cordillera—extend into the North. The Innuitian Mountains and the extensive Arctic Continental Shelf, however, occur exclusively in the North (see Figure 2.6, p. 32). Climatically, the main distinction is between the treeless Arctic, where permafrost is continuous, and the subarctic, where trees can grow and permafrost is discontinuous (see Figures 2.5 and 2.10, pp. 31 and 40). The western Arctic is part of the Cordilleran climate region; here temperature, precipitation, and vegetation vary widely, depending on elevation and latitude.

Hamelin (1973: 37) combined physical variables such as climate and vegetation with human variables such as accessibility and economic activity to produce an index of what he called 'nordicity' (i.e., northernness). On the basis of this index he identified three distinct northern zones defined less by latitude (though latitude is a contributing factor) than by perception. Thus the line marking the bottom of the 'Middle' nordicity zone reaches as far north as Prince Rupert on the mild west coast and as far south as Winnipeg in the harsh continental climate region (Fig. 11.3). The middle north has relatively few human inhabitants compared to southern Canada, and population numbers decrease dramatically in the 'Far North', while the 'Extreme North' is virtually unpopulated.

Figure 11.2   (*continued*)

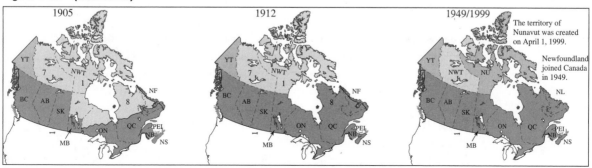

Figure 11.3   Nordicity zones

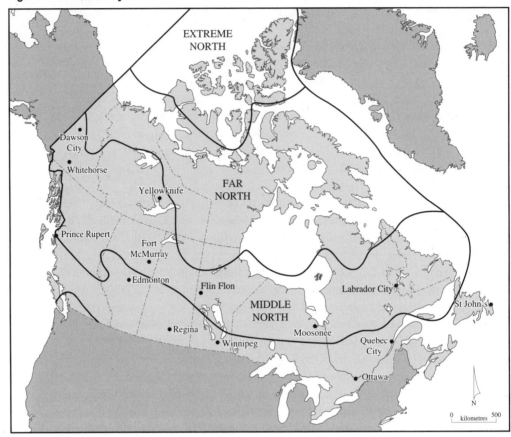

Source: Adapted from L.-E. Hamelin, *Canada: A Geographical Perspective* (New York: Wiley), 37.

Physical Characteristics

The North comprises five physiographic regions (see Fig. 2.6, p. 32). In the North, as elsewhere, rock formations of the Canadian Shield do not reach high elevations, having been subjected to weathering and erosion for billions of years. This mineral-rich region is noted for its deposits of iron ore, copper, nickel, lead, zinc, gold, silver, and most recently its diamonds.

The Great Interior Plains consist of layers of sediments that accumulated when this region was covered by water. Over time, heat and pressure acted on these layers to produce sedimentary rock, and as ocean levels decreased and tectonic forces pushed up the Cordilleran Mountains, the western plains were elevated as well. The last glacial age left a mark on these soft sediments when massive amounts of meltwater ran off the land, scouring out huge channels and leaving behind the enormous Great Slave and Great Bear lakes. This region is not a large part of the North, but it is an economically important one, as these sediments contain oil and natural gas.

The Cordilleran region makes up nearly all of Yukon as well as the western portion of the Northwest Territories. The Cordilleras are the highest and youngest mountains in all of Canada—products of the most recent episodes of mountain building. Mount Logan, the highest peak in Canada at nearly 6,000 metres, stands with other towering mountains of the Saint Elias chain in the southwestern corner of Yukon. The Cordilleran landscape is one of accreted terranes—fragments of other tectonic plates pushed together (see Chapter 2)—which makes this physiographic region particularly complex. It is also seismically active, rich in minerals, and difficult to traverse.

The Innuitian region is part of the permanent ice cap covering the most northerly islands of Canada. Geologically this is a sedimentary region in which mountains predating the Rockies peak at less than 3,000 metres. This is one of the most remote locations in Canada, but extensive exploration has confirmed the presence of hydrocarbons.

The final physiographic region, the Arctic Continental Shelf, which consists mainly of low-lying islands, also has oil and natural gas within its sedimentary layers. Ocean depths are relatively shallow here, and the land is still in the process of isostatic rebound since the relatively recent withdrawal of the last ice sheet.

There are three weather and climate regions in the North: Arctic, Subarctic, and Cordilleran. The Arctic climate region—and, in fact, most of the North—is strongly influenced by the Arctic high-pressure zone and latitude. It is a landscape of extremes when it comes to daylight: the High Arctic—any point north of the Arctic Circle (66°33′)—will see 24 hours of daylight on the summer solstice and just the opposite on the winter solstice. However, even in the summer the low angle of the sun means that there is relatively little incoming solar radiation; hence temperatures are frigid in winter and cool (by southern Canadian standards) in summer, and the most northerly extremities remain ice-bound year-round. Essentially, the Arctic is a polar desert. The little precipitation that does occur comes only in the summer months, once the sea ice has melted, and is concentrated in the eastern Arctic (especially Baffin Island), because of its proximity to large bodies of water. With little moisture and very low temperatures, the Arctic, which makes up approximately one-third of Canada, cannot support trees, although grasses, wildflowers, and shrubs, along with mosses and lichens, are able to grow during the very short summer season.

The 10° **isotherm** for July demarcates the boundary between Arctic and Subarctic. The Subarctic is truly a continental climate regime, with typically warm, dry summers and cold winters, although temperatures are heavily influenced by the high latitude. During the summer, convectional precipitation ensures sufficient moisture to support the growth of trees. With no physical barriers to prevent the Arctic air masses from descending into this region, winter temperatures are especially cold.

The vertical landscape of the Cordilleran climate region acts as a barrier against the penetration of more moderate Pacific air masses. Latitude and elevation are important influences on temperature, precipitation, and vegetation. Higher elevations feature year-round alpine glaciers, while plateaus and river valleys at lower elevations feature boreal forests.

Associated with the cold Arctic temperatures and somewhat milder Subarctic and Cordilleran temperatures are areas of continuous and discontinuous permafrost (see Figure 2.5, p. 31). The Arctic sub-surface is frozen year-round, as are large portions of the Subarctic and Cordilleran regions. Only the top layer (the active layer) thaws in summer, when incoming solar radiation has sufficient energy. In the Arctic these

isotherm
a line on a map connecting points that have the same temperature at a particular time or on average, over a given period.

conditions are responsible for unusual formations such as pingos (raised mounds with an ice core). Because permafrost is sensitive to disturbances that can cause it to thaw unevenly, extra care must be taken when planning human development of permafrost landscapes. Providing basic infrastructure—water and sewage systems, solid waste (garbage) disposal, housing construction, home heating, road-building, and pipeline construction—requires considerably more planning in the North than in other parts of Canada.

In fact, the entire northern ecosystem is extremely sensitive. Because the summers are so short and the winters so frigid, there are very few species of plants and animals that can live here, and they often take much longer to grow than would be the case in the south. Food webs and food chains are much less complex in the North than in the south, but simplicity means greater vulnerability to change, whether natural or human-induced. In fragile northern ecosystems, the risks associated with economic development—oil spills, mine tailings in water systems, disturbance of the permafrost—can be catastrophic for all members of those systems, including the Aboriginal people who make their living from the land.

Historical Overview

If the Beringia theory is true, North America's first human inhabitants passed through Canada's western Subarctic region following the ice-free corridor south. It would be thousands of years before the glaciers retreated enough for people to move into the Arctic, but the ancestors of the Dene—the collective name for the Athapaskan-speaking peoples of the Subarctic—were probably established in the region by the end of the last ice age. Living in semi-nomadic hunting and gathering communities in a forested landscape of lakes and rivers, and plenty of snow in winter, the Dene used canoes made of birchbark or moose hide in summer, and snowshoes and toboggans in winter. Fish, caribou, moose, and buffalo were among the mainstays of their diet.

The drier, treeless Arctic was home to a succession of peoples before the Thule people—the ancestors of the modern Inuit—moved into the region from Alaska. Traces of the original Paleoeskimo culture have been dated to approximately 3000 BCE. The descendents of the Paleoeskimos, the Dorset people, were displaced by the Thule roughly 1,000 years ago, and the modern Inuit emerged around 1500 CE. Living on fish, seal, whale, walrus, caribou, and muskox, these peoples developed extensive hunting territories and a linear pattern of settlement along the mainland and island coastlines. The kayak, harpoon, dog sled, igloo, and oil lamp were important innovations in this cold environment.

The first Europeans to visit the Canadian North were likely Norse from the Greenland settlement (established in 986 CE by Leif Ericsson), whose sagas suggest that they may have sailed along the coasts of Baffin and Ellesmere islands and traded with the Aboriginal people there (Mowat, 1985: 1267). It was some five hundred years later that the quest for the Northwest Passage brought other European sailors into Arctic waters. Of the many unsuccessful expeditions that ventured into the North over the following centuries in the effort to find a shortcut to Asia, perhaps the most famous was that led by Sir John Franklin in 1845. Although Franklin and all his crewmen were lost, his maps, along with the ones made by the expeditions sent to find them, produced a much more accurate picture of the North and strengthened the British claim to this territory.

Early efforts to find precious gold and silver in the North were also unsuccessful, but furs were available in abundance. The most valuable beaver pelts came from the Subarctic, where the cold climate encouraged the growth of the thickest fur. From its base on the St Lawrence, the French fur trade extended its tentacles into the Subarctic. Not to be outdone, the British, through a grant to the Hudson's Bay Company in 1670, defined the territory of Rupert's Land, an enormous region that included the river drainage system of Hudson Bay and James Bay. The inevitable rivalry between the French and British did not end until 1763, when Britain took control of New France. The Hudson's Bay Company continued to dominate the North until the 1780s, when the rival North West Company arrived on the scene. To intercept the furs destined for HBC forts, this aggressive company established fur trading posts across the North as well as the Prairies and British Columbia (see Chapter 9). This strategy forced the Hudson's Bay Company to establish positions in both the west and the north, and the rivalry continued until the two companies were amalgamated in 1821.

The fur trade had a significant impact on the Athapaskan-speaking peoples of the North. In the early years of the trade the HBC set up forts on Hudson Bay, at places like Fort Churchill at the mouth of the Churchill River, and in exchange for furs offered Aboriginal traders European goods such as firearms and alcohol, which, together with European diseases, brought dramatic changes to Aboriginal ways of life. Traditional patterns of hunting and gathering were altered to include trapping, and some Native peoples, such as the Chipewyan, cultivated a stronger relationship with the European traders—and acquired a more powerful status—by acting as middlemen for bands farther west and north.

The Inuit of the Arctic region had a different experience with non-Natives, but the outcome was similar. European–Inuit contact occurred accidentally in many instances, when European ships seeking the Northwest Passage became trapped by the ice floes. A more organized commercial relationship developed when Europeans and Americans involved in the whaling industry traded with the Inuit for food such as caribou. Until 1889, when American whalers moved into the Beaufort Sea, the whaling industry was an eastern Arctic endeavour. Francis (1985: 1935) identifies the period from 1820 to 1840 as the peak of the eastern Arctic whale hunt, 'when there were sometimes almost 100 vessels in the Davis Strait area'. With the annual catch exceeding 1,000 in some years, whales became an endangered species.

The same was true for some Inuit communities. Many whaling vessels and their crews would winter over at whaling stations in the Arctic so that they could hunt as soon as the ice broke up. The resulting contact with the Inuit was often disastrous. The population of the Mackenzie Delta Inuit, estimated to be 2,000 in 1865, was reduced to 10 by 1930, and only intermarriage saved the band from extinction (Bone, 2003: 63). The Sadlermiut of Hudson Bay 'were annihilated by disease (*typhus*) in 1902–03' (Briggs, 1985: 1614). As the whaling industry subsided, the Arctic fox, prized for its shiny white fur, became the next target species. The Hudson's Bay Company established a number of fur trade forts in the North the early 1900s, exposing the Inuit to many of the same problems experienced earlier by the people of the Subarctic. The near-extinction of the muskox during the early 1900s was a direct result of the introduction of the rifle to the region, and only a ban imposed by the Canadian government saved the species from extinction.

Economic activities in the Arctic had a political aspect as well. With the American purchase of Alaska in 1867 and the appearance of American whaling vessels in the North, sovereignty became a concern, and although Canada's purchase of Rupert's Land in 1870 and acquisition of the Arctic Islands from Britain in 1882 established Ottawa's authority over the territory in theory, Canada had virtually no presence in the region to establish its sovereignty in practice.

From the Klondike Gold Rush to the 1930s Depression

In 1897 news of the Klondike gold find sparked a stampede of some 30,000 prospectors to the Yukon. The gold rush changed the landscape of the western Arctic and forced governments to establish some control over what until then had been a very isolated location.

There were few ways in the 1890s to gain entry to the Yukon. Booking passage up the Yukon River to Dawson City was the simplest way to get to the gold fields, but it was also the most expensive, and relatively few prospectors took it. Another, much more difficult route was over land from Edmonton, but fewer than 800 prospectors and 4,000 horses set out from this starting point; none of the horses survived, and only 160 prospectors completed the difficult journey; many more turned back or died along the way (Klondike Trail Society, 2000–4). By far the most popular method of reaching the gold fields was to take a boat from San Francisco, Seattle, Victoria, or Vancouver to Skagway, Alaska. From here prospectors had a choice between two trails: the longer but lower-elevation White Pass, and the shorter but steeper Chilkoot Trail.

Packhorses and mules could be used on the White Pass, although so many animals died of exhaustion and lack of fodder that the route came to be known as the 'dead horse pass'. For those who could not afford a pack animal, however, the Chilkoot was the only choice. After a climb of nearly 1,200 metres (3,739 feet), miners entered Canadian territory (British Columbia), where they found a Northwest Mounted Police post. Canadian authorities required all those entering to register and to show they had enough food—1,100 pounds (550 kg)—to sustain them for one year; as a result most of the prospectors had to make many trips back and forth with a heavy pack. Both the White Pass and Chilkoot Trail led miners to the town of Bennett, BC, which became the largest tent-town in the world in 1898. At Bennett the miners would construct rafts—or anything that would float—to carry them over Lake Bennett, on to the Yukon River, and into Whitehorse, where they could catch a paddlewheeler to Dawson City, the centre of the gold rush. At gold-bearing streams like Bonanza Creek (originally Rabbit Creek) and of course the Klondike River itself, miners staked claims (only one per person in those days) and set out to search for gold, mostly with shovels, gold pans, and hand-made sluices. This was not an easy task in a landscape where summers were short, winters were brutally cold, and much of the gold was roughly three metres below the surface. Any digging soon ran into permafrost. The initial solution was to use fires to melt the permafrost and scrape up the potentially gold-bearing muck into piles that would be put through sluices during the summer season. Soon, however, a new and much more destructive technique was developed in which large dredges used steam to thaw the permafrost and then scrape up the streambeds, destroying fish habitat not only on these local streams but also, because of the heavy increase in **siltation**, throughout much of the Yukon River.

It was not long before would-be miners were arriving only to find that there were no more claims to be had. Some ended up working as labourers, others entered the service industries, many returned home, and quite a few moved on to Nome, Alaska, where in 1899 there were rumours of another gold strike. Those who had claims in the Dawson City region reaped handsome rewards: $10 million in gold came out in 1898, $2.5 million in 1899, and more than $22 million in 1900 (Tourism Yukon, 2001).

The Klondike rush, like the Cariboo rush of the 1860s in British Columbia, transformed a wilderness into a landscape of permanent trails, well-established river

siltation
the deposition of fine sand, clay, or other material carried by running water into another waterway, often a harbour or channel.

Dawson City, Queen Street looking west from Second Avenue; photo taken at midnight on 1 July 1904. The new town's sidewalks may still have been made of planks, but the architecture was quite sophisticated, with metal shutters and siding on the bank and prominent bay windows on several of the shops. Unfortunately, Dawson began to decline as soon as the gold rush had ended. *Library and Archives Canada, C-14546.*

transportation, new communities, and by 1900, the narrow-gauge White Pass and Yukon Railway, running between Whitehorse and Skagway. Renewed fear of American annexation led to the establishment of the Yukon as a separate Canadian territory in 1898.

The gold rush and its aftermath also transformed traditional Aboriginal ways of life in the region. Destruction of the salmon habitat and over-hunting depleted the food available for Aboriginal people in many parts of the territory. Some Native people became packers on the trails, while others found wage employment in chaotic new communities such as Dawson, at least until the gold rush subsided. In 1898 as many as 30,000 people were recorded as residing in the Yukon, but by 1901 that number had fallen to just over 27,000, and ten years later another 19,000 people had left (Fig. 11.4), plotting a trend that would continue until the Depression of the 1930s.

The Yukon gold rush was a classic boom-and-bust situation, and the 'bust' triggered a mass exodus. Not all mining ended, though. Dredging for gold continued into the 1960s, and a number of mines opened up in the Yukon early in the century, including a coal mine at Carmacks and silver (along with lead and zinc) mines at Mayo, Elsa, and Keno Hill. But none of these operations did much to create employment.

The Northwest Territories had its own mining ventures in the early twentieth century. Gold was found on the shores of Great Slave Lake near Yellowknife, but no gold rush occurred until the mid-1930s, when Yellowknife became a boomtown. Another important ore deposit was found in the 1930s at Port Radium on Great Bear Lake. This discovery included radium (used to treat cancer) and silver. Oil was discovered in 1920 at Norman Wells on the Mackenzie River, but it was not developed until a small refinery was established in the 1930s. This oil discovery had significant ramifications for the First Nations of the Mackenzie region, whose title to the land was 'negotiated' away under Treaty 11 (1921). By the 1930s the North was being recognized as an important mining frontier.

At a time when few roads existed in the North, the airplane became essential for moving people (including prospectors, administrators, and police), information (including mail), and goods across the vast landscape. On the other hand, as transportation improvements brought more southerners into the North, local people were increasingly exposed to diseases they had no defences against. In 1928 close to one-sixth of the Dene population died in a flu epidemic (Indian and Northern Affairs Canada, 2004). Another problem was the introduction of registered trap lines—a concept akin to fencing off private farmland (or turning land from a common-property resource to a private-property resource). This policy was introduced in British Columbia during the 1920s and was eventually extended to 'all parts of northern Canada excluding the high Arctic' (Brody, 1981: 88). This new restriction on traditional ways of life became especially difficult when non-Natives acquired traplines, and the collapse of fur prices in the 1930s dealt another economic

Figure 11.4   Population, Yukon, 1901–1941

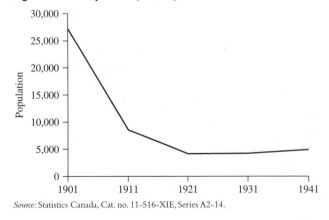

Source: Statistics Canada, Cat. no. 11-516-XIE, Series A2-14.

blow to the North. But it was as that decade came to a close that the North experienced its most unexpected transformation: from sparsely populated hinterland to important military and strategic position.

From the Second World War to the 1950s

At its outset, the Second World War was largely a European war, although Canada's participation in support of Britain extended the fighting across the North Atlantic. The United States did not enter the war until 7 December 1941, when the Japanese attacked a US naval base at Pearl Harbor, Hawaii. The war was now to be fought across the Pacific as well as the Atlantic, and the Americans, who until then had been bystanders, were now fully engaged in the conflict.

Following the attack on Pearl Harbor, a series of Japanese raids on American bases in the Aleutians—two of which, Attu and Kiska, were captured in 1942—only reinforced American and Canadian fears of an attack on the mainland West Coast. A map showing the northern polar projection (see Figure 11.5) gives an indication of how close these islands off the coast of Alaska are to East Asia. With few people, poor transportation, and little in the way of defences, both the Canadian and the American North were vulnerable.

In 1943, after the US, with help from Canadian forces, had managed to gain back the two Aleutian islands, the Americans set out to fortify the North. They had recognized their largely defenceless position in Alaska in 1941, when they had begun to build a military supply road through Canada in order to strengthen their existing Alaskan air force base at Fairbanks. The Alaska Highway was 2,446 kilometres (1,520 miles) in length, stretching from Dawson Creek on the BC–Alberta border to Fairbanks. The American military engineers built this road over some incredibly difficult terrain in a very short time so that it was in use by 1943; it was turned over to the Canadian government in 1946 and opened to the public in 1948 (Morris Communications, 1998).

Whitehorse boomed during the war, becoming an important air force base and the sole supplier of aviation fuel for the northern war effort. At the same time as the Alaska Highway was being built, the Americans built the 1,000-kilometre Canol Pipeline linking the oil fields at Norman Wells to Whitehorse, where a refinery (abandoned almost immediately after the war) was built. This was not the only military infrastructure development in the North. In the eastern Arctic, Iqaluit (then known as Frobisher Bay) was the site of a major American air force base that was part of an air shuttle system linking Europe and North America.

The Cold War that followed 1945 placed Canada squarely between the adversaries in the race for nuclear superiority: the United States and the Soviet Union. The perspective shown in Figure 11.5 (see also Fig. 1.1, p. 4) highlights Canada's vulnerable (or, from an American point of view, strategic) position between the two belligerents. By the mid-1950s, three lines of radar ('radio detection and ranging') stations had been built across Canada, the last and most northerly of which, the Distant Early Warning (DEW) Line, ran along the Arctic coast from Alaska to Baffin Island at approximately the 69th parallel.

The DEW Line represented more than just a military presence in the Arctic. Although the United States paid the construction costs, Canadian labour was used wherever

Figure 11.5   Canada, the United States, and the Soviet Union

possible. In essence, each radar station became a new community, staffed by military personnel (mainly American) and connected to the rest of North America through new airports, roads, and sea-lifts. For the Inuit, the stations became important as sources of medical supplies.

Until the 1930s the federal government's policy had been essentially to leave the Inuit to look after themselves. In 1934, however, in response to severe food shortages, it began relocating families from Banks and Baffin islands to Devon Island, where game was more abundant. It was supposedly for similar reasons that, beginning in 1953, 17 Inuit families, mainly from northern Quebec, were sent to Grise Fiord on Ellesmere Island and Resolute on Cornwallis Island. The scheme was a disaster, made worse by suspicions that it was motivated, at least in part, by the desire to strengthen Canada's claims to sovereignty in the high Arctic. The video *Broken Promise: High Arctic Relocation* (1995) traces what eight of those families endured, exiled in a harsh and unfamiliar environment. (More than forty years later, in 1996, the federal government would award the survivors compensation in the amount of $10 million; yet as the Nunatsiaq News pointed out in 1999, 'no apology' was ever offered.)

Reshaping the North

Before the middle of the twentieth century, most Canadians knew very little about the North and its people. In the late 1950s, however, the rapidly increasing demand for minerals sparked a wave of northern mega-projects that drew many southerners north. The energy crisis of the 1970s produced yet another 'gold rush' in which the prospectors were large corporations searching the sedimentary layers of the northern landscape for hydrocarbons. When deposits were found, further mega-projects were required to build the necessary transportation infrastructure. All this activity took a serious toll on the land and the people who still lived on it. Yet the indiscriminate exploitation of northern resources continued until the Mackenzie Valley Pipeline Inquiry (1975–7) headed by Justice Thomas Berger focused attention on traditional ways of life in the region and made recommendations that set a new, more autonomous direction for the Aboriginal people of the North.

The years following the Second World War brought an end to restrictions on the right of Native people to vote and conduct traditional ceremonies. There was also a growing expectation that government should take responsibility for the well-being of citizens generally. By the mid-1950s Ottawa's preferred solution to problems such as food shortages was to encourage industrial development in the North and try to help its Native people develop the skills to participate in the wage economy (Indian and Northern Affairs Canada, 1996). To that end, it began encouraging Aboriginal people to abandon their semi-nomadic way of life in favour of permanent settlement in a number of new government-established communities.

But adjusting to life in a permanent community was not an easy transition, and settlements without an economic reason for existence offered very few opportunities for wage employment. As a result, intensive hunting and fishing in the vicinity of the community soon depleted local wildlife populations, and the people became increasingly dependent on government assistance. Ottawa expected that northern Native people would leave their small, isolated communities and seek work in the new service and administrative centres such as Yellowknife, or the new resource-based communities like Pine Point. But as Table 11.1 shows, most northern Aboriginal people continued to live far from any resource activity, trying to support themselves by hunting, fishing, and trapping, and relying heavily on social programs. Table 11.1 also reflects the changing demography of the North, as many non-Native southerners ventured north to pursue employment opportunities created by the growth associated with mining and oil and gas exploration in the 1960s, 1970s, and 1980s.

Table 11.1   Population distribution of NWT population by ethnicity and community type (%), NWT, 1961 and 1981

Community type	1961		1981	
	Native	Non-Native	Native	Non-Native
Regional centre	15	68	22	75
Resource town	2	5	3	13
Native community	83	27	75	12

Source: Adapted from P.J. Usher, 'Indigenous Management Systems and the Conservation of Wildlife in the Canadian North', *Alternatives Journal* 14, 1 (1987): 4.

A float plane lands between Latham Island and Yellowknife. The discovery of gold in 1934 turned the tiny community of Yellowknife into a boom town that was still thriving when this photo was taken in 1947.   *Library and Archives Canada, PA-116541.*

Mega-projects and Land-use Conflicts

The tremendous increase in demand for mineral resources after the Second World War pushed the mining frontier to the North. By the late 1950s, the era of the mega-project was beginning, and in the years that followed multi-million dollar investments led to the establishment of in open-pit mines, new roads, and in many cases new communities. In effect, the south was moving into the North.

Most of the non-Native and southern Canadian interest in the North since the end of the Second World War has been focused on its non-renewable resources—metals, oil, and natural gas. Developing these resources has not been easy: the **friction of distance** is enormous, particularly because of the extremes in topography and climate. By definition, non-renewable resources will at some point be exhausted, and there are no guarantees that demand for a particular mineral will not disappear before the supply itself runs out. Mining is a high-risk venture involving enormous capital outlays, and—in the North particularly—many mining operations would never have been commercially viable without millions of dollars in government subsidies. Gurston Dacks, who has documented the importance of metal mining in the North, argues that many of the mines north of the 60th parallel would not be operating at all without government support: 'the Cyprus Anvil mine at Faro in Yukon benefited from a more than \$25 million federal-government investment in infrastructure and the Nanisivik lead-zinc mine on

friction of distance
the additional costs associated with operating in remote locations (e.g., shipping supplies in and transporting minerals out).

Baffin Island received an estimated $16.7 million in the form of direct grants and infra-structure' (1981: 127).

The discovery of oil at Norman Wells in 1920 proved that hydrocarbons were avail-able in the North; however, at the time the value of oil was low, and the cost of trans-port to the industrial south was prohibitive. The Energy Crisis, beginning in 1973, changed everything, as oil prices rose from $2.80 per barrel to $35 by 1981 (see Chap-ter 9). These soaring oil prices, combined with the fear that oil-producing regions else-where were running out, sparked a whole new interest in northern gas and oil ex-ploration. Still, it was not until after the 1970s, when the priority was transporting the large and proven reserves of natural gas from the Beaufort Sea to markets in the United States, that these northern reserves were developed.

Oil and gas exploration combined with various mining ventures to produce an eco-nomic boom in the North from the 1960s to 1980s. But resource development can have serious consequences for the environment. Roads and pipelines may divert migrating herds of caribou away from their traditional routes. If a pipeline causes the permafrost to thaw in uneven patches, the line itself may rupture, spilling oil into surrounding land and water. Placer mining with dredges and hydraulics produces enormous quantities of silt, which can contaminate rivers and streams, causing major damage to fish and their spawning habitat. Other kinds of metal mining leave tailings of acid-laden rock or toxic chemicals such as arsenic that can leach into water systems with serious consequences for the ecosystem. Oil spills have occurred from offshore exploration, and the sonic shock waves produced by oil and gas exploration drive away seals and whales.

There is also a legacy of environmental damage resulting from the mega-projects as-sociated with military installations. For example, many of the DEW Line radar stations have been abandoned, leaving behind everything from old transformers to PCB-laced paint. All these industrial and military activities have placed greater stress on wildlife populations by disturbing traditional migration paths and reducing the fish and game populations that remain an important source of food, income, and connection to the land for Aboriginal people in this region.

The Berger Inquiry: 'Northern Frontier, Northern Homeland'

The federal government has full control over the North. Yet even today the government consists almost entirely of southern Canadians, and its actions with regard to the North inevitably reflect southern attitudes, values, and interests. It is not surprising, therefore, that Ottawa's primary purpose in promoting mineral development in the northern hin-terland in the 1960s was to benefit the south. In short, the relationship between the south and the North was a classic example of the core–periphery relationship.

By the mid-1970s, however, the federal government was becoming aware that re-source development in the North was having a negative impact both on the land and on the lives of the Inuit and Dene. It had also, as a result of the Calder decision in 1973, ac-cepted the principle that Aboriginal title continues to exist on untreatied land until it is surrendered by treaty—which meant that it would have to do something about the un-surrendered Aboriginal title to the lands in the North where it had already permitted min-eral exploration and development. A number of environmental regulations (including the Arctic Waters Pollution Act, the Northern Inland Waters Act, and the Canada Oil and Gas

Drilling Regulations) were in place by the early 1970s, but most people recognized that such rules could be circumvented. Certainly the Aboriginal people of the North had little faith in these safeguards and were well aware that when environmental damage occurred, they paid the price without compensation. It also became clear to northern Aboriginal people that treaty negotiations would give them a chance both to address environmental and land-use conflicts and to take some control over their lands and their lives.

One proposed mega-project that would have profound consequences for northern Aboriginal communities was the Mackenzie Valley Pipeline. In response to concerns raised by the Inuit and Dene of the region, in 1977 an inquiry was launched under the direction of Justice Thomas Berger, whose mandate was to examine the social, environmental, and economic impacts of building the pipeline. To put the Dene and Inuit on an even playing field with the wealthy multinational corporations that wanted to build the pipeline, the federal government provided funding for professional representation (lawyers, geographers, anthropologists), and separate hearings were held in every community along the pipeline route.

The inquiry exposed the long history of inequity in relations between non-Natives and Native people in the North. Canadians discovered that their government had encouraged and even subsidized the non-renewable mining sector while paying little attention to renewable resources; they also learned how important the land still was to the people of the North. Native people told the inquiry about their experience of previous resource extraction and military projects, bringing to light the many social problems—including alcohol and drug abuse, violence, crime, suicide, and family breakdown—that could be expected during the construction phase.

In his report, issued in April 1977, Berger concluded that a 'larger issue' surrounding Treaty 11 needed to be resolved before the construction of the pipeline could be carried out. The Aboriginal people who signed Treaty 11 in 1921 believed they were signing a peace treaty and not a treaty to surrender their title to the land. Berger thus recommended a ten-year moratorium on the pipeline, during which the government could negotiate treaties with the various Native communities that would be affected by the pipeline. In this way Aboriginal people would have a say in any land development, and would benefit financially if a pipeline were to be built.

Like all public inquiries, the Berger Inquiry was empowered only to make recommendations to the government; it could not prevent the project from going ahead. But in the end the pipeline was not built, for a variety of interrelated reasons: the federal government would not allow the gas from the sensitive Mackenzie delta to be tapped; the pipeline companies had not secured firm contracts; new surpluses of gas were being discovered in Alberta and British Columbia; and the National Energy Program of 1980 increased taxes on production (Dacks, 1981: 131). Although an alternative pipeline route to parallel the Alaska Highway was approved in 1982, the recession of the 1980s drove down the demand and the price for natural gas, making construction of the line uneconomical. An oil pipeline was built, however, connecting Norman Wells to the Alberta feeder lines. The Dene and Métis of this region were not pleased as this project conflicted with their land claim; nevertheless, they negotiated an interim agreement in which they received nearly $21 million in compensation. The pipeline, completed in 1985 with the support and encouragement of the federal government, only emphasized the importance of negotiating modern-day treaties throughout the North.

Modern-Day Treaties and First Nations Autonomy in the North

The legal basis for negotiating the surrender of Aboriginal land title through treaties derives from the Royal Proclamation of 1763. Treaties were completed in many regions of the country, especially in the late nineteenth and early twentieth centuries, when much of western Canada and some of the Northwest Territories were covered by the numbered treaties (see Fig. 3.13, p. 82). This treaty process did not extend to the rest of the NWT, however, or to Yukon. The pressure to begin negotiations there increased after 1971, when the US government signed a precedent-setting agreement with Native groups in Alaska, covering 65,000 square miles (168,350 sq. km) and providing $962.5 million for 'some 60,000 beneficiaries' (Crowe, 1990:17).

The federal government negotiated its first comprehensive claims treaties in the mid-1970s in northern Quebec, to resolve the conflict over the James Bay hydroelectric project (see Chapter 5). Although the need for a parallel process in the Mackenzie Valley was obvious, there was a potential obstacle in the fact that Aboriginal title in most of that region had already been surrendered through two of the numbered treaties (treaties 11 and 8). On the other hand, no reserves had ever been established there, and by allowing non-Natives to acquire trapline permits, Ottawa had failed to protect the land base that the Native people needed to pursue their traditional way of life. Accordingly, it was decided that the comprehensive claims process could be undertaken there after all. The way was then clear for the Inuit, Dene, and Métis of the Mackenzie Valley to engage in a process that would give them a voice in the future development of their homeland.

Table 11.2 outlines the comprehensive claims agreements that have been negotiated in the North (see also Fig. 11.6). The first of them, the Inuvialuit Final Agreement (1984), covered approximately 2,500 people living in the western Arctic, and provided for a land base (mainly around the communities of Aklavik, Inuvik, Tuktoyaktuk, Paulatuk, Holman, and Sachs Harbour), sub-surface land rights (hence full mineral royalties), a cash settlement for the area of land surrendered, grants for economic enhancement and social development, and wildlife and fisheries management rights, such as setting quotas, assigning hunting and trapping areas, and protecting wildlife habitat.

At the time of the Inuvialuit Final Agreement the federal government separated negotiations on land claims from negotiations on self-government. However, following sustained pressure by First Nations groups, Ottawa in the mid-1990s agreed to negotiate self-government. What self-government means in practice varies widely but generally involves matters such as land and resource management, healthcare, education, policing and court services, housing, and marriage. As a result, each self-government agreement is unique and has to be individually negotiated. The Yukon Umbrella Agreement was the first comprehensive agreement to include self-government, and four First Nations in Yukon have secured the right to self-government, while others are in the negotiating phase. The Sahtu Dene and Métis Final Agreement was recognized as a two-stage process, and these two groups are presently negotiating self-government. The territories of the Inuvialuit and Gwich'in overlap, and they are negotiating a unique regional self-government agreement that covers the Beaufort and Mackenzie Delta. Negotiations by the Tungavik Federation of Nunavut—an enormous land base that includes all of the eastern Arctic—led to the creation of a separate territory, Nunavut, in 1999.

Table 11.2   Completed northern comprehensive claims, 2005

Agreement	Year	People/Land/Cash compensation/Conditions
Inuvialuit	1984	2,500 people; 91,000 km^2 of land; 13,000 km^2 sub-surface; $152 million over 13 years; $10 million for economic enhancement; $7.5 million for social development; wildlife harvesting rights; right to participate in regional decisions on wildlife management, conservation, and environmental protection
Gwich'in	1992	2,400 people; 24,000 km^2 of land in NWT and 1,554 km^2 in Yukon; 4.299 km^2 sub-surface in NWT only; $75 million over 15 years; royalties from Mackenzie Valley; wildlife harvesting rights; right to participate in regional decisions on wildlife management, conservation, and environmental protection
Yukon Umbrella	1993	8,000 people; 41,439 km^2 of land; some sub-surface rights; $243 million over 15 years; $3 million for wildlife enhancement; mineral resource royalties; wildlife harvesting rights; right to participate in regional decisions on wildlife management, conservation, and environmental protection; 14 separate agreements with individual nations.
Tungavik Federation of Nunavut	1993	17,500 Inuit; 351,000 km^2 of land; 37,000 km^2 sub-surface; $1.148 billion over 14 years; a share in mineral and energy royalties; mineral resource royalties; right to participate in regional decisions on wildlife management, conservation, and environmental protection.
Sahtu Dene and Métis	1994	2,700 people; 41,537 km^2 of land; 1,813 km^2 sub-surface; $75 million over 15 years; share in resource royalties; right to participate in regional decisions on wildlife management, conservation, and environmental protection; exclusive trapping rights.
Tlicho (Dogrib) Agreement-in-Principle	2003	2,003 people; 39,000 km^2 of land with sub-surface rights; $152 million over 15 years; royalties from Mackenzie Valley; wildlife harvesting rights; right to participate in regional decisions on wildlife management, conservation, and environmental protection; NWT's first combined land claim and self-government agreement.
Deh Cho	Ongoing	4,500 people; 210,000 km^2; framework and interim measures agreements; participation in Mackenzie Valley resource management and regional land-use planning; involvement in Nahanni National Park management; overall resource management.
NWT Métis Nation (South Slave)	Ongoing	Interim measures agreement (2002). Ongoing negotiations on land, resources, and self-government.

Source: Adapted from Indian and Northern Affairs Canada, 'Agreements' (http://www.ainc-inac.gc.ca/pr/agr/index_e.html#FinalAgreements2).

Figure 11.6   Northern comprehensive claims, 2005

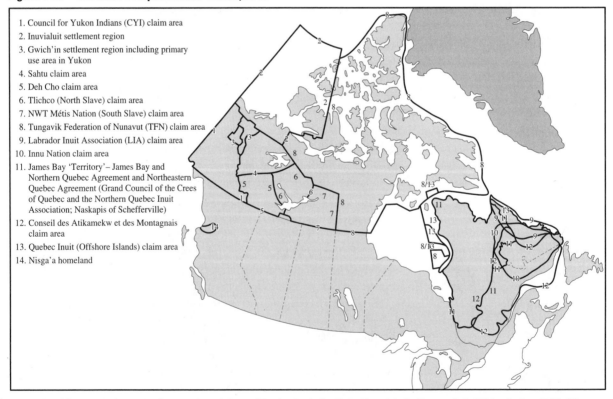

1. Council for Yukon Indians (CYI) claim area
2. Inuvialuit settlement region
3. Gwich'in settlement region including primary use area in Yukon
4. Sahtu claim area
5. Deh Cho claim area
6. Tlichco (North Slave) claim area
7. NWT Métis Nation (South Slave) claim area
8. Tungavik Federation of Nunavut (TFN) claim area
9. Labrador Inuit Association (LIA) claim area
10. Innu Nation claim area
11. James Bay 'Territory'– James Bay and Northern Quebec Agreement and Northeastern Quebec Agreement (Grand Council of the Crees of Quebec and the Northern Quebec Inuit Association; Naskapis of Schefferville)
12. Conseil des Atikamekw et des Montagnais claim area
13. Quebec Inuit (Offshore Islands) claim area
14. Nisga'a homeland

Source: Adapted from O.P. Dickason, *Canada's First Nations: A History of Founding Peoples from Earliest Times,* 3rd edn (Toronto: Oxford University Press, 2002), 380.

As the term 'comprehensive' suggests, these agreements represent much more than resolutions to disputes over land use. Taking into account people and their communities, sacred and unique landscapes, renewable and non-renewable resources, education, employment, and self-government, they give Native people a measure of control over their future. Resource development can continue in the North, but not without consideration of the land and the people whose home it is.

Current and Future Issues

The North has been a mining frontier since the Klondike gold rush, but mining is not the region's only resource industry. Fur trapping, commercial fishing, and tourism are also important sources of revenue and employment. Nevertheless, as political power has devolved from the federal to the territorial level, the service industry has grown dramatically, and it now provides many more jobs than the resource sector. Together, employment opportunities and government policies have led to the development of three types of communities: urban administrative–commercial centres, resource-based communities, and Native-based communities. The North is no longer as isolated—or insulated—it once was from southern Canada or the rest of the world, and global influences are becoming increasingly evident.

Minerals

Following the 1960s–1970s boom, the 1980s and 1990s were largely a bust for mineral exploration and production. However, the early twenty-first century has seen a turnaround in world market prices for gold, oil, and natural gas, and this is attracting new investment. Some of the dynamics of the northern mining industry can be seen in Table 11.3, which shows great variance in revenues among the three territories. Placer gold mining continues in Yukon, but natural gas brings in the most revenues. In the Northwest Territories the big mining story is diamonds, with two mines generating huge revenues for the territory; oil and natural gas also bring in substantial revenues. Nunavut's mining revenues, with the closure of the Polaris and Nanisivik mines in 2002, fell sharply in 2003. Figure 11.7 shows sites of present, past, and future mining activity.

Table 11.3   Mineral revenues (× 1,000), 2001 and 2004

Mineral	Yukon		NWT		Nunavut	
	2001	2004	2001	2004	2001	2004
Gold	37,298	54,233	54,314	8,928	59,351	35,493
Lead	–	–	–	–	23,837	–
Silver	193	222	207	27	3,326	119
Zinc	–	–	–	–	234,396	–
Total metals	**37,491**	**54,455**	**54,522**	**8,956**	**320,910**	**35,612**
Diamonds	–	–	717,780	2,140,123	–	–
Total non–metals[1]	**3,646**	**7,178**	**725,008**	**2,147,890**	**0**	**0**
Natural gas	98,081	n.a.	207,278	164,165	–	–
Natural gas by-products	–	n.a.	1,524	–	–	–
Crude oil	–	n.a.	337,619	336,651	–	–
Total fuels	**98,081**	**n.a.**	**544,897**	**500,816**	**0**	**0**
Overall total	**139,218**	**n.a.**	**1,323,427**	**2,657,662**	**320,910**	**35,612**

[1]2003 figures

Source: Natural Resources Canada, 'Mineral Production of Canada, by Province and Territory' 〈http://mmsd1.mms.nrcan. gc.ca/mmsd/production/production_e.asp〉.

Figure 11.7   Mines in the Northwest Territories

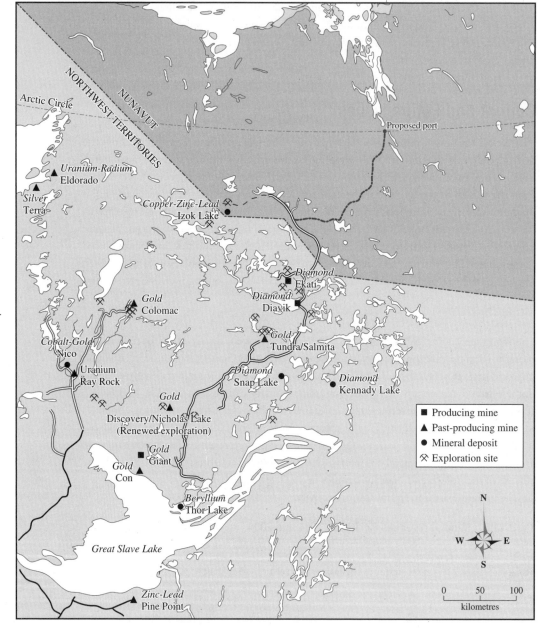

Sources: Adapted from R. Boychuk, 'The Road from Bathurst Inlet', *Canadian Geographic* 124, 2 (Mar.–Apr. 2004), 43; E. Struzik, 'Changing Courses', *Canadian Geographic* 122, 5 (Sept.–Oct. 2002), 44.

In the North as elsewhere, volatile markets make metal mining a risky business. Canada's largest (and for a time only) tungsten mine (located in the Northwest Territories, next to Nahanni National Park) closed down in 1986 because of falling metal prices, and with it the company town of Tungsten; 16 years later, prices rebounded and in 2002 the mine re-opened—but only until December 2003. Other mining ventures have followed a similar path, and the generally downward path of gold prices (until recently) led to the closing of a number of gold mines (see Figure 11.8). The large open-pit lead and zinc mine at Faro, Yukon, closed in 1987 and re-opened in 1992, only to close again in 1997 in response to falling prices, which eventually led to the closing of the Polaris and Nanisivik mines in Nunavut (both in September 2002); as Figure 11.9 shows, lead and zinc prices have recovered somewhat since 2003.

There appears to be no shortage of metals in Yukon, the Northwest Territories, or Nunavut, but few of these metals mines will go into production when relatively low world market prices are weighed against the friction of distance. An interesting example is the mineral-rich region south of Bathurst Inlet. There is currently a plan to build a $164 million port and a 290-kilometre all-weather road to 'serve whatever mines eventually spring into operation' (Boychuk, 2004: 42). The proposed port and road (seen in Figure 11.7) may well open up this region, create new jobs for local people, and generate economic wealth. But some question whether it is appropriate to spend public money for non-renewable resource development, and some fear that any development would harm tourism opportunities, interfere with migrating caribou herds, and increase the risk of oil spills.

The northern oil sector weathered the early part of the global recession of the 1980s thanks to heavy subsidies through the National Energy Program. But when these subsidies dried up in 1984, so did hydrocarbon exploration. Figure 11.10 shows the wild ride

Figure 11.8 Average annual values, gold, ($US/oz.), 1985–2005

Source: BC Stats, Quick Facts, 'Weekly Metal Prices' ⟨http://www.em.gov.bc.ca/mining/miningstats/⟩.

Figure 11.9 Annual values, lead and zinc ($US/lb), 1992–2005

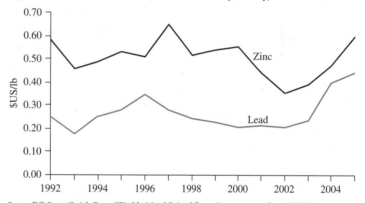

Source: BC Stats, Quick Facts, 'Weekly Metal Prices' ⟨http://www.em.gov.bc.ca/mining/miningstats/⟩.

Figure 11.10 World market price, crude oil ($US/bbl), 1970–2005

Source: US Department of Energy, Energy Information Administration, 'Light Crude Oil Price ($/bbl)' ⟨http://www.eia.doe.gov/neic/historic/hpetroleum.htm⟩.

Figure 11.11   Wellhead price, US natural gas ($/Mcf), 1980–2004

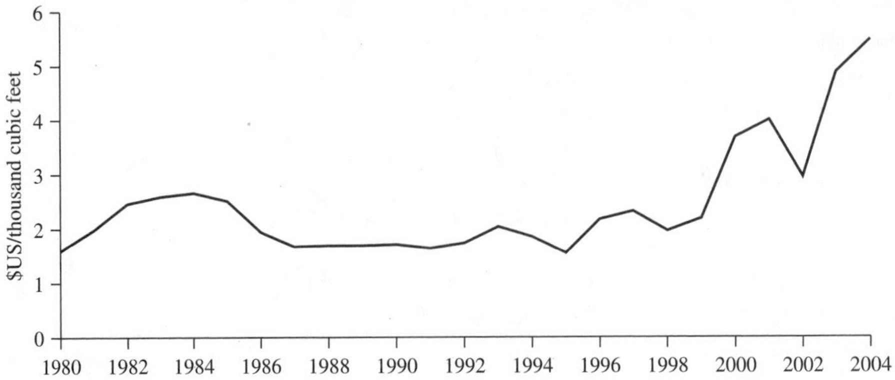

Source: US Department of Energy, Energy Information Administration, 'U.S. Natural Gas Wellhead Price ($/Mcf), ⟨http://tonto.eia.doe.gov/dnav/ng/hist/n9190us3a.htm⟩.

that crude oil prices experienced between 1970 and 2005, when increased conflict in the Middle East pushed prices to record highs. Demand for natural gas has not been as volatile as demand for oil, and prices have been more stable; on the other hand, the value of this commodity was fairly low until the industry was deregulated in the early 2000s, when prices escalated (see Figure 11.11).

The resurgence in oil and natural gas prices has sparked renewed interest in the hydrocarbons of the Beaufort Sea and Mackenzie Valley regions. There are currently a number of proposals for a pipeline through the Mackenzie Valley, which remains the most expedient route to markets in the south. These proposals have reopened the debate that gave rise to the Berger Inquiry; but the circumstances today are very different. In the 1970s Aboriginal people were left out of the decision-making process; they had no opportunity to voice their concerns about the impact of the pipeline on the environment and what this would mean to their traditional way of life. Today they are no longer marginalized, and it appears that the economic advantages of a pipeline—including a share in ownership, as well as training and construction jobs—may outweigh the environmental concerns.

There may also be a sense in the Aboriginal communities involved that any environmental concerns can be addressed through technology. But this is not the opinion of environmental organizations (such as the Sierra Club of Canada), which have issued dire warnings about the consequences of a pipeline both for the northern environment and for global warming. The Canadian Arctic Resources Committee (CARC) has released a mapping study on the *Cumulative Effects of the Mackenzie Valley Gas Project* (2005). One of the myths this study attempts to disprove is that a pipeline would represent only a narrow ribbon through the Mackenzie Valley: when wells, linking pipelines, roads, compressor stations, camps, and equipment are taken into account, the footprint would be substantial.

The discovery of diamonds in the ancient rock of the Canadian Shield sparked a new mining boom in the Northwest Territories in the 1990s. The kimberlite pipes in which they were formed developed some 50 million years ago, when molten material finding its way to the surface of the Shield rock produced funnel-shaped pipes. These formations are not easy to locate because they are often under water (Canadian Museum of Nature, 2000). In 1991, a very rich deposit of kimberlite diamonds was discovered at Lac de Gras, a remote area 300 kilometres northeast of Yellowknife and close to the NWT–Nunavut border. Two mines—Ekati and Diavik—are now in operation, and a third, Snap Lake, is expected to open in 2008 (McDonald, 2004: 51). The two mines currently in operation have brought new employment opportunities to Native communities—in particular, the Dogrib First Nation—both directly (the Ekati mine employs approximately 800, and the Diavik, 630) and indirectly, in contracts for construction and hauling. An important forward linkage is the cutting and polishing of diamonds, and two of the three independent firms contracted to perform this work have Aboriginal ownership (McDonald, 2004: 54). Local First Nations have also benefited from education and training programs sponsored by the mining companies.

A big change from past mining practices has been the introduction of rotational employment, in which workers are flown into a camp near the mine to work two-week shifts, then flown out to spend two weeks at home. It is hoped that this system will be easier on families than the old system, in which a community (usually a company town) would be built near the mine. Those single-resource communities gave the illusion of permanence, but the inevitable closure of the mine would result in tremendous hardship for families. There have been some social problems with rotational employment: McDonald (2004: 55) notes that 'Local communities are reporting more separations and divorces, and children can find it more difficult to focus on school when the primary wage earner is away from home.' Nevertheless, the fly-in camp model has the advantage of allowing Native workers to participate in hunting, fishing, and trapping during their two weeks off.

By far the biggest difference in the northern mining industry today is that the people who will be most affected by mining development now have the opportunity to approve or reject mining proposals, depending on whether they believe they will bring increased employment and economic benefit to their communities. The prospect of more diamond mines, gold mines, and oil and natural gas developments will require enormous investment not just in these ventures themselves but in infrastructure, including pipelines, roads, ports, and sea-links. The experience of past mining activities should not, however, be forgotten: proactive policies are essential to minimizing the risk of environmental catastrophes.

Other Resource Industries

Trapping continues to be a source of income in the North, although incomes have diminished considerably since the 1980s (see Fig. 11.12), when anti-fur campaigns began to make real inroads into the demand for furs. For many First Nations, however, trapping, like hunting and fishing, is a traditional tie to the land, and it continues to be part of the local or domestic economy.

There are a few northerners employed in fishing, forestry, and farming. Commercial fishing is centred on the large inland lakes (such as Great Slave and Great Bear) and focuses on species such as whitefish, pike, char, and trout. Forestry occurs in the Subarctic region, where the wood is used mainly for lumber and as fuel for cooking and heating. Farming is an activity not normally associated with the territory 'north of 60', but the 2001 Census recorded 175 farms in Yukon and 35 in the Northwest Territories

Figure 11.12   Fur values, Northwest Territories, 1993–2003

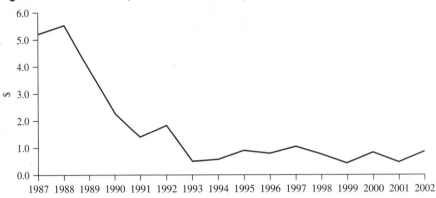

Source: Northwest Territories, '2004 NWT Socio-Economic Scan' (http://www.stats.gov.nt.ca/Statinfo/Generalstats/Scan/scan.html).

(Statistics Canada). Most of these operations (primarily ranches) are located in the south of the region, near the large urban centres of Whitehorse and Yellowknife.

Tourism is an increasingly important industry in all three territories. There are some spectacular landscapes and an abundance of recreational opportunities, from hunting and fishing to whitewater rafting, kayaking, canoeing, and bird and game watching. The Northwest Territories has been successful in attracting visitors (mainly Japanese) in the winter to experience the aurora borealis (northern lights); and hunters, while they account for only 4 per cent of all visitors, account for '30 per cent of overall spending' (Northwest Territories, 2002). Other tourists are attracted to the North for its history (especially connected with the Klondike gold rush), its cultural heritage (including, most famously, the arts and crafts of the Cape Dorset community), or simply its remoteness.

Access is one of the main variables in the northern tourist industry. Yukon receives a great number of tourists (over 360,000 travellers in 2002) because of the Alaska Highway and its extensive road network. In southern Yukon the Robert Campbell Highway and Canol Road provide access to hunting, fishing, canoeing, and wildlife viewing (see Figure 11.1). Travellers can go north from Whitehorse along the Klondike Highway to Dawson City and, from this historic gold rush community, travel the Top of the World Highway to Alaska. Dawson City also has tourists arriving via Yukon River cruises. The Dempster Highway, with spectacular views, begins just south of Dawson City and links Yukon to Inuvik (at nearly 70° north latitude) at the mouth of the Mackenzie River.

In the northern part of the Northwest Territories the only road is the Dempster Highway—although the Mackenzie River also provides a link to the south. From British Columbia the Liard Highway can lead travellers as far north as Wrigley on the Mackenzie River. Yellowknife, the capital of the NWT, is accessible from Alberta via the Mackenzie Highway. These roads give access to Wood Buffalo National Park and Nahanni National Park, which are unique tourist attractions. Some communities that in summer can be reached only by air become more accessible in winter: **ice roads** provide the only land connection between Inuvik and Aklavik and Tuktoyaktuk.

Nunavut has no road access. For a limited time in summer there is ocean access to coastal communities, but most tourists fly into one of the three centres that provide regular air service: Cambridge Bay, Rankin Inlet, and the capital, Iqaluit. The advertising

ice road (winter road) a secondary road made of compacted snow or ice, often plowed over a frozen lake, river, or muskeg that is impassable in the summer.

Beginning near Dawson City, the Dempster Highway runs 720 kilometres across northern Yukon and into the Northwest Territories, ending at Inuvik. Located on the Mackenzie Delta, south of the Beaufort Sea, Inuvik is the largest community north of the Arctic Circle. *Photo Brett McGillivray.*

slogan for Nunavut aptly describes the appal of the North in general: 'Untamed, unspoiled, undiscovered'. Those qualities are likely to become all the more attractive to travellers as most of the world becomes increasingly urbanized.

Urban Patterns, Employment, and Demographics

The earliest permanent settlements that grew up in the North—Hudson's Bay Company forts, whaling stations, mining communities—were all directly related to resources. The Second World War and Cold War added military communities; a number of settlements were created in the 1950s and 1960s as part of the federal government's Native resettlement program; and a resurgence in mining from the 1960s to 1980s produced a new generation of northern mining towns. Another development that has contributed to the population growth shown in Figure 11.13, especially in urban centres, is the transfer of powers from Ottawa to the territorial governments, which has generated civil-service employment in the administrative centres of the territories.

Both Native and non-Native populations have increased, the former mostly through natural increase, and the latter mostly as a result of employment-related migration from southern Canada. As Table 11.4 shows, Yukon has the lowest percentage of Native people, while in Nunavut more than 80 per cent of the population is Aboriginal (almost all Inuit).

Figure 11.13   Population, Yukon and Northwest Territories,[1] 1951–2005

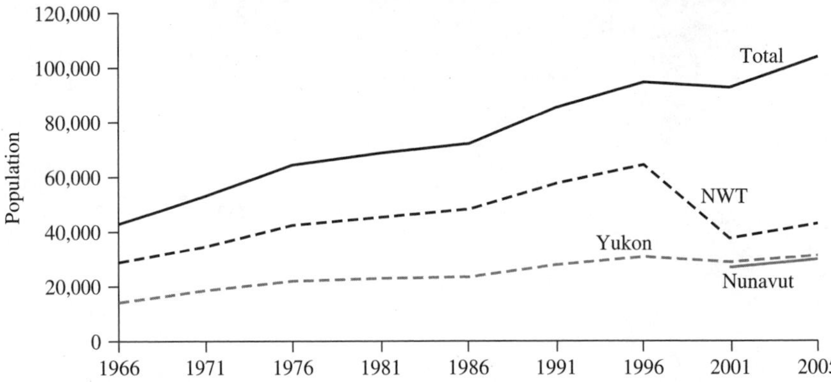

Sources: Statistics Canada, 'Historical Statistics of Canada', Cat. no. 11-516-XIE, Series A2-14; CANSIM Table 051-0001 and matrix TM01-0001.

Table 11.4   Population, total and Native, and Native population (%) by territory, 2001 and 1991

Territory	Total 2001	Total 1991	Native 2001	Native 1991	% Native 2001	% Native 1991
Yukon	28,674	27,797	6,545	6,385	21.6	23.0
NWT	37,360	57,649	18,730	35,390	45.8	61.4
Nunavut	26,745		22,725		80.8	
Total	92,779	85,446	48,000	41,775	48.4	48.9

Source: Adapted from Statistics Canada, Cat. no. 97F0011XCB2001005.

Much of the overall population increase has gone to the territorial capitals. Whitehorse, the capital of Yukon since 1953 (when it replaced Dawson City), is clearly the dominant centre in Yukon, accounting for 75 per cent of the territory's population in 2001. Whitehorse is expected to grow steadily in the lead-up to the 2007 Canada Winter Games, which it will be hosting. Yellowknife, designated the capital of the Northwest Territories in 1967, enjoyed consistent population growth until 1999, when Nunavut became a separate territory. Still, the population of Yellowknife represents 26 per cent of the total population of NWT (see Table 11.5). Although the historic gold mines of Yellowknife have closed, diamonds, gold, and (most likely) natural gas will almost certainly contribute to the city's population in the years ahead.

Communities with populations below those of the capital cities are for the most part quite small: of the 77 communities that exist today across the North, only a few have more than a thousand residents (see Table 11.6). Peter Usher classifies communities of more than 1,000 in four categories: 'capital cities', 'regional administrative centres', 'resource communities', and 'historic aboriginal communities' (1998: 381). One of the main distinctions among these categories is ethnic composition: over 80 per cent of the population of the capital cities is non-Native, and non-Natives dominate the resource communities as well. The administrative centres are more balanced, but over 80 per cent of the Native population resides in the historic aboriginal communities (381).

Richard DiFrancesco (2000: 116) takes a similar approach when he labels northern communities as either 'developed' or 'underdeveloped': developed communities 'are either

Table 11.5   Population, Whitehorse, Yukon, and Yellowknife, 1971–2001

Year	Whitehorse	% of Yukon	Yukon	Yellowknife	% of NWT	NWT
2001	21,405	74.6	28,674	16,541	44.3	37,360
1996	21,808	70.9	30,766	17,275	26.8	64,402
1991	19,157	68.9	27,797	15,179	26.3	57,649
1986	17,925	76.2	23,504	11,753	24.2	48,488
1981	14,814	64.2	23,075	9,483	20.8	45,535
1976	13,311	61.0	21,836	8,256	19.4	42,609
1971	11,217	61.0	18,388	5,867	16.9	34,807

Source: Statistics Canada, Cat. no. 11-516-XIE, Series A2-14; CANSIM Table 051-0001; T-stat matrix TM01-0001.

regional centres (administratively, or for the purposes of commerce—e.g. Yellowknife) or they are resource communities (e.g. Norman Wells, and Nanisivik)'. A highly educated, well-paid, non-Native population dominates the developed communities, whereas the underdeveloped communities have largely Native populations and are characterized by poor transportation links, low levels of education and skills, and high unemployment.

Nunavut, which contains the majority of historic Aboriginal communities, is unique among the three territories in having been created with the aim of decentralizing government. As a consequence, the capital, Iqaluit, accounts for less than 20 per cent of Nunavut's population, and ten regional centres have been designated to perform administrative functions. Nine of the ten are listed in Table 11.6 (Gjoa Haven, with a population of 960, is not included), and all of these centres have increased in population in every census since 1981, some of them significantly.

Another interesting population dynamic is the large proportion of young people (under 15 years of age) making up the Native population, compared with a relatively small proportion of people over the age of 65 (see Table 11.7). These young people are being brought up and educated in an environment that has changed radically from the one their parents and grandparents grew up in. Already there is considerably more mobility as Aboriginal people gain education and skills and move to larger urban centres. Of the 32 communities in the Northwest Territories, only three were predominantly non-Native in 2001 (Yellowknife, 77.5 per cent; Norman Wells, 70.6 per cent; and Hay River, 53 per cent). Part of the decline in the non-Native population is related to the disappearance of various mining communities.

Table 11.8 offers a breakdown of jobs in the North and includes statistics for all of Canada for comparison. Primary resource activities such as hunting, trapping, fishing, forestry, and agriculture account for relatively little employment, but most Aboriginal people take part in these activities on a part-time and recreational basis. Mining jobs, however,

Table 11.6 Communities of 1,000 or more, Yukon, NWT, and Nunavut, 2001

Yukon	Northwest Territories	Nunavut	
17 communities	*32 communities*	*28 communities*	
Whitehorse 21,405	Yellowknife 16,541	Iqaluit	5,236
Dawson 1,251	Hay River 3,510	Rankin Inlet	2,177
	Inuvik 2,894	Arviat	1,899
	Fort Smith 2,185	Baker Lake	1,507
	Rae-Edzo 1,552	Cambridge Bay	1,309
	Fort Simpson 1,163	Igloolik	1,286
		Pangnirtung	1,276
		Kugluktuk	1,212
		Pond Inlet	1,220
		Cape Dorset	1,148

Source: Adapted from Statistics Canada, 2001 Community Profiles.

Table 11.7 Total population and age structure for Native population (× 1,000), 2001

	Yukon		NWT		Nunavut	
Population	Native	%	Native	%	Native	%
Total	6.5	100.0	18.7	100.0	22.7	100.0
0–14	2.0	30.8	6.4	34.2	9.4	41.4
15–65	4.3	66.2	11.3	60.4	12.7	55.9
Over 65	0.3	3.0	1.0	5.4	0.6	2.7

Source: Adapted from Statistics Canada, Census of Canada 2001.

Table 11.8 Selected labour-force characteristics, 2001

NAICS[1]	Yukon	NWT	Nunavut	North Total	North %	Canada %
Total	**17,950**	**20,785**	**11,355**	**50,090**	**100.0**	**100.0**
Goods-producing	**2,650**	**3,920**	**1,610**	**8,180**	**16.3**	**25.6**
Primary	**715**	**1,725**	**470**	**2,910**	**5.8**	**4.8**
Agriculture, forestry, fishing, and hunting	285	305	125	715	1.4	2.6
Mining plus oil and gas	430	1,420	245	2,095	4.2	1.1
Secondary	**1,935**	**2,195**	**1,140**	**5,270**	**10.5**	**20.8**
Manufacturing	385	260	185	830	1.7	15.1
Construction	1,400	1,530	730	3,650	69.2	9.8
Service-producing	**15,300**	**16,865**	**9,745**	**41,910**	**83.7**	**74.4**
Trade	2,275	2,205	1,390	5,870	11.7	15.8
Transportation	770	930	200	1,900	3.8	4.9
FIRE[2]	570	660	395	1,625	3.2	5.8
Pro., sci., technical	740	930	200	1,870	3.7	6.4
Education	1,180	1,565	1,440	4,185	8.4	6.6
Health	1,585	2,005	1,045	4,635	9.2	10.4
Tourism-related[3]	2,850	2,040	990	5,880	11.7	11.1
Administrative	4,315	4,910	2,795	12,020	24.0	5.0

[1]North American Industrial Classification. [2]Fire, Insurance, Real Estate and Leasing.
[3]Information, culture, recreation, accommodation, and food services.

Source: Adapted from the Statistics Canada CANSIM database ⟨http://cansim2.statcan.ca⟩, Table 281-0025.

number above the national average, and as long as metal and oil prices increase, this employment sector will grow as well.

Since few of the North's primary industries involve forward linkages, manufacturing in the region is minimal; construction accounts for almost 90 per cent of the jobs in secondary industry. In fact, services account for an even greater percentage of jobs in the North (almost 84 per cent) than they do in Canada as a whole. The proportions of service jobs in areas like trade and transportation are relatively small, but the figures for education and tourist-related services are above the Canadian average, and administrative functions account for a much higher proportion of service jobs in the North than elsewhere (almost 25 per cent, compared to just 5 per cent for the country as a whole). Many of these services are paid for by the federal government.

Future Issues

The northern environment is ecologically fragile, and many factors mentioned earlier in this chapter—including active and abandoned mines, oil and gas pipelines, and abandoned military radar stations—pose a serious threat. An issue of particular concern is global warming. The Kyoto Protocol recognizes the severity of the problem caused by emissions from the burning of fossil fuels, and there is mounting evidence that the summer ice pack has retreated and that southern species such as salmon and dragonflies are moving into the warming western Arctic.

A warmer North has many implications. The boreal forest would extend farther north, and with it pests like the mountain pine beetle and events such as forest fires. There would be more precipitation, but also more rapid melting of snow and glaciers, increasing the risk of flooding for communities near rivers as well as those on the coastline, where ocean levels would rise. The potential for agriculture would increase, and the historic dream of an easily navigable channel linking the Atlantic and the Pacific would come closer to reality. The prospect of regular ship transportation across the North has considerable appeal to many industries, including tourism, though many fear the increased risk of oil spills and other environmental disasters. An Arctic shipping lane could also open up the still unresolved issue of sovereignty, as the United States considers such a route to lie in international waters (Draper, 2002: 129; Maduro, 2000: 64; David Suzuki Foundation, 2002; Maxwell, 1987).

Recent years have brought many economic, political, and social changes to the North. Comprehensive claims agreements have given northern Native communities control over large areas, including sub-surface rights. Aboriginal northerners have also secured the right to self-government, and are successfully using this new autonomy to establish their own economic, political, and social priorities (Saku and Bone, 2000: 268).

The territorial governments have gained more autonomy as well, though unlike the provinces they do not control Crown land and resources within their borders. Many writers on the North agree that the territories are unlikely to gain provincial status as long as they continue to depend on federal government funding (Bone, 2005: 528; DiFrancesco, 2000: 131; Usher, 1998: 392). But with more diamond and gold mines and increasing oil and gas development, revenues for the federal government will only increase. Thus Ottawa has agreed to negotiate 'provincial-like powers' for the Northwest Territories (Canadian Press, 2005; *Globe and Mail*, 2005: A10).

New technologies for overcoming time and space have also brought change, giving many 'isolated' northern communities access to the same consumer goods available in the south—though at much higher prices. Northern chain stores offer the same movies available elsewhere in North America. Wired and wireless communications—radio, television, telephone, fax, e-mail, and the Internet—are all here, as are drugs, alcohol, junk food, and the latest fads and fashions. All of this has brought increasing social change and pressure as the allure of assimilation challenges the desire to preserve traditional values.

Improvements in health and education and the financial benefits accruing from comprehensive claims are helping northern Native people overcome 'the lack of an entrepreneurial heritage' (DiFrancesco, 2000: 131). Aboriginal people have formed their own corporations and are taking over administrative functions. Increased education and skills development have brought increased employment. The Aboriginal population is young and accustomed to change. At the same time, just as many in the south are determined to hold on to values that they believe distinguish Canada from the United States, northern Aboriginal people are determined to retain the values important to their society.

Summary

In southern Canada, the first resource industry—the fur trade—had profound consequences for Aboriginal societies, but in itself did little to interfere with traditional ways of life. It was only with agricultural settlement and the development of other resource industries requiring the construction of elaborate transportation systems that Aboriginal people were pushed out of their traditional territories and onto reserves.

In the North there was no phase of agricultural settlement. Waves of non-Native gold-seekers arrived in the North in the late 1890s, but most left when the gold finds dwindled. A significant portion of the land north of 60 was included in Treaty 11, the last numbered treaty, but no reserves were established in the region, because the traditional hunting, trapping, and fishing way of life was not seen as impeding development. It was not until the mid-twentieth century, in the aftermath of the Second World War, that large numbers of non-Natives began to arrive in the North, first in a military capacity and then, in the 1960s and 1970s, to work in mining and oil and gas exploration. Federal government programs, beginning in the 1950s, brought a number of non-Native administrators, teachers, nurses, and business people into the region. But the non-Native population was small, and Native people remained the dominant population in many parts of the territories.

Two separate economies evolved in the North, representing conflicting relationships with the land. The Berger Inquiry set in motion the process of negotiating comprehensive claims to protect certain lands for Native use while providing compensation for the lands taken for development. Northern Aboriginal communities stood up for their view of the North and forged modern-day treaties, many of which included the right to self-government.

Safeguarding the fragile northern environment in the face of increasing pressure to exploit the North's non-renewable resources—gold and diamonds as well as oil and gas—will be a major challenge. Unlike earlier rounds of resource development, however, this one will involve First Nations as decision-makers and even partners. In this context, preserving traditional values may be an even greater challenge.

References

BC Stats. 2005. Quick Facts. 'Weekly Metal Prices'. http://www.em.gov.bc.ca/mining/miningstats/.

Berger, T.R. 1977. *Northern Frontier, Northern Homeland: Report of the Mackenzie Valley Pipeline Inquiry.* 2 vols. Ottawa: Supply and Services Canada.

Bone, R.M. 2003. *The Geography of the Canadian North: Issues and Challenges.* 2nd edn. Toronto: Oxford University Press.

———. 2002. *The Regional Geography of Canada.* 2nd edn. Toronto: Oxford University Press.

Boychuk, R. 2004. 'The Road from Bathurst Inlet'. *Canadian Geographic* 124, 2 (March–April): 38–56.

Briggs, J.L. 1985. 'Sadlermiut Inuit'. P. 1614 in *The Canadian Encyclopedia.* Edmonton: Hurtig.

Brody, H. 1981. *Maps and Dreams.* Vancouver: Douglas and McIntyre.

———. 2000. *The Other Side of Eden: Hunters, Farmers and the Shaping of the World.* Vancouver: Douglas and McIntyre.

Canadian Arctic Resources Committee (CARC). 2005. *Cumulative Effects of the Mackenzie Valley Gas Project.* http://www.carc.org/2005/mapping_cumulative.htm.

Canadian Museum of Nature. 2000. 'Amazing Story: The Haystack: Kimberlite Pipes'. http://www.nature.ca/discover/treasures/trsite_e/trmineral/tr3/tr3amaze2.html.

Canadian Press. 2005. 'N.W.T. to get provincial-like powers'. 3 March. http://www.canadainfolink.ca/nwtmap.htm.

Coates, K.S., and W.R. Morrison. 1986. 'Treaty Research Report: Treaty No. 11 (1921)'. Indian and Northern Affairs Canada. http://www.ainc-inac.gc.ca/pr/trts/hti/t11/index_e.html.

Crowe, K.J. 1990. 'Claims on the Land'. *Arctic Circle* (Nov.–Dec.): 14–23.

Dacks, G. 1981. *A Choice of Futures: Politics in the Canadian North.* Toronto: Methuen.

David Suzuki Foundation 2002. 'Parks in the Greenhouse: Canada, Climate Change, and Nature'. http://www.davidsuzuki.org/files/Parks_Brochure_Eng.pdf.

DiFrancesco, R.J. 2000. 'A Diamond in the Rough?: An Examination of the Issues Surrounding the Development of the Northwest Territories'. *The Canadian Geographer* 44, 2 (Summer): 114–34.

Dolho, L. 2003. First Nations Drum. 'Mackenzie Valley Pipeline a Go, But . . .'. Summer. http://www.firstnationsdrum.com/Aug02/CovHollywood.htm.

Draper, D. 2002. *Our Environment: A Canadian Perspective.* 2nd edn. Scarborough: Nelson Thomson Learning.

Efron, S. 2003. 'Nunavut Winds'. *Canadian Geographic* 123, 6 (Nov.–Dec.): 26.

Francis, D. 1985. 'Whaling'. Pp. 1935–6 in *The Canadian Encyclopedia.* Edmonton: Hurtig.

Frideres, J.S. 1988. *Native Peoples in Canada: Contemporary Conflicts.* 3rd edn. Scarborough: Prentice Hall.

Globe and Mail. 2005. 'Resource-revenue deal to be discussed, NWT says'. 7 April: A10. http://www.theglobeandmail.com.

Hamelin, L.-E. 1973. *Canada: A Geographical Perspective.* New York: Wiley.

Indian and Northern Affairs Canada. 2004. 'Dene First Nations: Yellowknives'. http://nwt-tno.inac-ainc.gc.ca/youthbuzz/dfn-yk_e.htm.

———. 1995. Federal Policy Guide: Aboriginal Self-Government'. http://www.ainc-inac.gc.ca/pr/pub/sg/plcy_e.html.

———. 1996. *Report of the Royal Commission on Aboriginal Peoples Volume 1—Looking Forward Looking Back.* Chapter 11—Relocation of Aboriginal Communities. http://www.ainc-inac.gc.ca/ch/rcap/sg/sg38_e.html.

Klondike Trail Society. 2000–2004. 'Trail of 98'. http://www.klondiketrail.ca/.

McDonald, D. 2004. 'The Diamond Frontier'. *Time.* 5 April: 48–55.

McGhee, R. 1985. 'Prehistory'. Pp. 1466–9 in *The Canadian Encyclopedia.* Edmonton: Hurtig.

Maduro, M. 2000. 'Northern Shortcut'. *Canadian Geographic* 120, 7 (Nov.–Dec.): 64.

Maxwell, B. 1987. 'Atmospheric and Climatic Change in the Canadian Arctic: Causes, Effects, and Impacts'. *Northern Perspectives.* Canadian Arctic Resources Committee. http://www.carc.org/pubs/v15no5/2.htm.

Mine Watch Canada. 2003. 'CanTung Closes: NWT Mine Reclamation Policy Shown to be Farce'. 9 Dec. http://www.miningwatch.ca/publications/CanTung_closure.html.

Morris Communications. 1998. 'History of the Alaska Highway'. http://www.themilepost.com/history.html.

Mowat, F. 1985. 'Norse Voyages'. Pp. 1266–7 In *The Canadian Encyclopedia.* Edmonton: Hurtig.

Northwest Territories. 2004. '2004 NWT Socio-Economic Scan'. http://www.stats.gov.nt.ca/Statinfo/Generalstats/Scan/scan.html.

———. 2002. 'Tourism Outlook' 1, 1 (Fall). http://www.iti.gov.nt.ca/parks/tourism/2002tourismoutlook.pdf.

Nunatsiaq News. 1999. http://www.nunatsiaq.com/archives/nunavut991030/editorial.html.

Nutaaq Média Inc. in co-production with the National Film Board of Canada. 1995. *Broken Promises: The High Arctic Relocation* (video). Directed by P.V. Tassinari.

Saku, J.C., and Bone, R.M. 2000. Pp. 259–70 in *The Canadian Geographer* 33, 3 (Fall).

Savage, C. 2001. 'Caribou Shuffle'. *Canadian Geographic* 121, 3 (May–June): 28–36.

Sierra Club of Canada. 2004. 'Mackenzie Valley Pipeline and Alberta Oil Sands'. 28 April. http://www.sierraclub.ca/national/programs/atmosphere-energy/energy-onslaught/campaign.shtml?x=307.

Statistics Canada. Population of Canada, by province, census dates, 1851 to 1976. Catalogue 11-516-XIE, Series A2. http://www.statcan.ca.

Struzik, E. 2003. 'Discovery: Orphan Mines'. *Canadian Geographic* 123, 3 (May–June): 25.

Tourism Yukon. 2001. 'Gold Rush History'. http://www.writeyukon.com/klondike/gr_history.asp?i=*D2*C4&a=*99*94T*7D*29.

US Department of Energy, Energy Information Administration. 2005a. 'Light Crude Oil Price ($/bbl)'. http://www.eia.doe.gov/neic/historic/hpetroleum.htm.

———. 2005b 'U.S. Natural Gas Wellhead Price ($/Mcf)'. http://tonto.eia.doe.gov/dnav/ng/hist/n9190us3a.htm.

Usher, P. J. 1987. 'Indigenous Management Systems and the Conservation of Wildlife in the Canadian North'. *Alternatives Journal* 14, 1: 3–9.

Yukon Government. N.d. 'Facts'. http://www.gov.yk.ca/facts/.

Part III

Canadian Issues from a Geographic Perspective

12

A Nation of Regions

This final chapter begins with a broad overview of the factors that have shaped Canada's regional landscapes, both physical and human. It concludes with a look at some of the most important issues facing the country today—from global warming to economic relations with the United States to the possibility that at least one of its regions may break away to form a separate nation.

The Regional Development of Canada

The history of Canada's physiographic regions begins nearly four billion years ago with the formation of the Canadian Shield. Over time, erosion built platforms on its outer edges, and tectonic forces attached new terranes along the edges of the craton. Because Canada is so large, the range of landscapes contained within its borders is extremely varied in terms of climate, soils, vegetation, and resources.

Canada's human history is much shorter, beginning perhaps 15,000 years ago when nomadic hunters-gatherers from Asia made their way across the Beringia land bridge near the end of the last ice age. As the ice retreated, the land gradually stabilized, reaching its present form approximately 6,000 years ago. Now Aboriginal peoples in the various regions were able to establish more permanent territorial boundaries and develop more settled ways of life, along with more sophisticated technologies, cultural practices, and institutional structures.

The first Europeans to reach North America were probably the Norse. They established a small settlement on the northern tip of Newfoundland around the year 1000 CE, but did not stay long—perhaps because of conflict with the local Aboriginal people. By the late 1400s, however, sailors from a number of European nations were making their way across the Atlantic first to fish and then to search for the fabled Northwest Passage. Before long Europeans were arriving armed with 'guns, steel, and germs' (Diamond, 1999) to colonize new lands, exploit their resources, and convert their indigenous peoples to Christianity. In the northern half of North America, the main European rivals were France and Britain, each of which had its own interests in the new land and was prepared to fight at home and abroad to defend them.

Staples theory maintains that European demand for resources strongly influenced the course of the colonies' development. On the east coast, seasonal fisheries gradually led to the establishment of permanent communities along the shorelines. In the process, the local Beothuk people were pushed to the barren interior of the island. Over the following centuries, disease, starvation, and conflict with Europeans reduced their numbers to the point that the entire population was exterminated by the early 1800s.

In the early 1600s European demand for furs sparked the development of a new land-based staple industry in which Aboriginal fur trappers and traders played an integral part. From their base on the St Lawrence the French traders pushed west towards the Great Lakes and down the Mississippi Valley, while the British, initially based on the eastern seaboard, looked north to Hudson Bay. Granted a royal charter in 1670 giving it control of the vast region newly named Rupert's Land, the Hudson's Bay Company established a series of forts at the mouths of the rivers draining into the bay. Although participation in the fur trade offered Native people material benefits, it also created dependency on European goods, involved them in the territorial conflict between the two main rivals, and exposed them both to devastating European diseases and to Christian missionaries whose influence undermined their spiritual traditions and weakened their social bonds.

Meanwhile a small French colony had become established along the St Lawrence, but it was much less successful in attracting new settlers than its counterparts in the British-held territory to the south. Land distribution followed the long-lot model established in France under the seigneurial system.

In 1713 the British gained control of a large part of the French colony of Acadia, which it renamed Nova Scotia, but for several decades it made no effort to bring in British settlers. Thus the French-speaking, Roman Catholic Acadians remained the dominant population, and although they refused to swear allegiance to Britain, they maintained a careful neutrality where France was concerned. It was only with the establishment of Halifax, in 1749, that Britain undertook to recruit its own colonists. In 1755 British authorities began systematically deporting the Acadians. The following year Britain and France were once again officially at war.

Having captured Quebec in 1759 and Montreal in 1760, the British took possession of New France in 1763. Within months a Royal Proclamation was issued that established the boundaries of Britain's newest possessions, reserving the land west of Quebec and the Thirteen Colonies for Aboriginal people. This document would eventually become the foundation both of the treaty process and of modern Aboriginal rights in Canada. A decade later, the Quebec Act (1774) guaranteed the French-speaking people of Quebec the rights to their own language, religion, and civil law. It also extended Quebec's boundaries to the west and south—infuriating the American colonists who wanted that territory for themselves, and intensifying their desire for independence from Britain. Within two years the American Revolution had begun, and by the early 1780s Loyalist refugees from the new United States were pouring into Britain's remaining North American colonies. So many Loyalists—more than 30,000—went to Nova Scotia that in 1784 it was divided to create the new colony of New Brunswick. Another 7,500 or so settled in the western part of Quebec, and by 1791 the English-speaking population in this region was substantial enough that Quebec too was divided to create Upper and Lower Canada.

In the early 1780s—as the American Revolutionary War was ending and the Loyalists were moving north—several independent rivals of the Hudson's Bay Company had formed their own company based in Montreal. The NWC traders pressed aggressively across the Prairies, building forts, establishing close relationships with local Aboriginal groups, and compelling the HBC to do the same.

Meanwhile, on the far side of the continent, British sailors searching for a western entrance to the elusive Northwest Passage were charting the Pacific coast and discovering the rich trading potential of its sea otter populations. But they were not the first Europeans in the region. Russian fur traders already controlled Alaska, and the Spanish had already claimed the territory from Alaska south to Mexico, mainly in hopes of preventing other nations from gaining a foothold there. In the early 1790s, however, under the Nootka Sound Conventions, Spain formally recognized Britain's right to trade in the area and soon withdrew entirely; today the only traces of its presence are the many Spanish place names along the Pacific coast. By that time Alexander Mackenzie of the NWC had already completed his epic overland journey to the Pacific (1793), and by the early 1800s the competition between the NWC, the HBC, and, increasingly, American fur traders, was raging on both sides of the mountains.

The border between British North America and the United States was established as far west as the Rockies in the aftermath of the War of 1812. Although British troops and Aboriginal warriors probably played a greater role in repelling the invaders, the idea that the French- and English-speaking people of the two Canadas had joined forces against the Americans played an important part in the development of Canadian nationalism. It would take the threat of another war—over the Oregon Territory ('54-40 or Fight')—to see the remaining section of the boundary set in 1846.

British North America in the middle decades of the 1800s was not a single entity but a collection of colonies. Although most of its people—with the notable exceptions of the Canadiens and Acadians—traced their origins to the British Isles, their cultural backgrounds varied widely. Irish and Scottish immigrants might have been able to communicate in Gaelic, for instance, but were often separated by religious differences; both groups were also internally divided between Catholics and Protestants. British authorities preferred Protestant Loyalists in any case, and encouraged them to take up the prime farmlands of the Annapolis Valley, the Saint John River Valley, and—as good land became scarce in the Maritimes—southern Ontario (Upper Canada). Thus although the French-speaking Catholic Acadians expelled in the 1750s were allowed to return to the Maritimes, they had to settle on the more marginal farmland of northern New Brunswick, far from their original homes around the Bay of Fundy.

As for the majority population in Quebec (Lower Canada), the French-speaking Catholic Canadiens, their society was still almost exclusively rural; economically and politically, the colony was overwhelmingly dominated by the English-speaking Protestant elite of Montreal. When frustration with this imbalance of power erupted in 1837–8, the rebellion was quickly put down and British authorities, following the advice of Lord Durham, decided to hasten the process of assimilating the troublesome francophones of Lower Canada by forcing them into a legislative union with the rapidly growing English-speaking population of Upper Canada.

When the Act of Union took effect, in 1841, Canada West (the former Upper Canada) was still a good deal smaller than Canada East, yet the two sections were required to have the same number of representatives. A decade later the balance of population was reversed. Now Canada West began to demand the proportional representation that had been denied to Canada East when it had the larger population. Although the equal-representation rule remained in place, the divisions between the two sections became increasingly entrenched, and no party from either side was able to form a majority government. The resulting stalemate became one of several persuasive arguments for Confederation.

In agreeing to the union plan, Nova Scotia and New Brunswick hoped to benefit from increased trade with Ontario and Quebec. But within a few years of Confederation it was clear where the power was concentrated. Southern Ontario and southern Quebec were the uncontested core, dominating both the manufacturing and the service sectors. Railway expansion had been expected to give the port of Halifax a pivotal role in the flow of goods between central Canada and Europe, but most of that trade went through American ports instead. Meanwhile, mergers and takeovers inspired by the principle of economies of scale meant that the Maritimes lost industrial activity and jobs, while the Bank Act of 1871, which allowed banks based in the larger provinces to set up branches outside their borders, led to the loss of established local financial institutions. By the 1890s few manufacturing industries remained in the Maritimes, and the region was relegated to the status of a staple-dependent periphery. Young people looking for work increasingly had little choice but to leave, and traces of bitterness towards central Canada have remained in the Maritimes ever since.

There was bitterness on the Prairies as well. It was the French-speaking, Roman Catholic Métis of Red River, under the leadership of Louis Riel, who negotiated the terms of Manitoba's entry into Confederation. But Ottawa's heavy-handed response to the uprising of 1870, and the influx of mainly Protestant, English-speaking settlers from Ontario that followed, drove the Métis away from Red River. The Northwest Rebellion erupted 15 years later, when those who had resettled along the South Saskatchewan River feared that they would once again be pushed out. It culminated in the hanging of Riel and the further marginalization of the Métis. Meanwhile, to make room for settlers and railways, treaties were negotiated whereby the First Nations of the Prairies were removed from their traditional territories and confined to reserves. Converting the Prairies to an agricultural landscape was not easy. But the government made a concerted effort to recruit experienced farmers from Eastern Europe, and the wheat economy of the Prairie provinces was well established by 1930—just in time to be devastated by economic depression and drought. The disaster was made all the worse by the fact that—because it had been economically advantageous for the CPR to take a more southerly route—farms were concentrated in the Palliser's Triangle region, where the soil was poor and dry, rather than in Hind's Fertile Belt. It was little wonder if farmers were disillusioned and bitter towards the powers that had manipulated their lives.

British Columbia also experienced rapid growth in the first half of the twentieth century, largely as a result of resource development and Vancouver's emergence as a major international port linked to a transcontinental railway system. But not all people in the province were equal. Aboriginal people were not given the opportunity to negotiate treaties. The Chinese workers who had built the BC section of the CPR were not wanted once the job was done. In 1914 a ship (the *Komagata Maru*) carrying Sikh immigrants was turned away from Vancouver. And in 1942, following the bombing of Pearl Harbour, Canadian citizens of Japanese descent living near the Pacific coast were removed from their homes and sent either to the interior or to farms on the Prairies, their possessions confiscated by the government. They were not permitted to return to the coast until 1949.

As for the North, the interest generated by the Klondike gold rush was short-lived, and it was not until the 1940s that the infrastructure was established to make it accessible to southerners. The roads and airports built by the US military opened the way for resource exploration and development, which by the 1970s would necessitate serious efforts to protect both the region's fragile ecosystems and the rights of its Aboriginal peoples.

Wartime military activity also brought significant change to Newfoundland, allowing it to pay off the heavy debts that had led Britain to take charge of its governance during the Depression. Two referendums were held to allow the people of the formerly self-governing colony to decide whether they wanted to return to responsible government, continue with Commission government, or join Canada. Although only 52 per cent of voters favoured the last option, Newfoundland became Canada's tenth province in 1949. In the years to come, Ottawa's mishandling of the cod fishery would provide ample justification for the fears of those who had opposed Confederation. Overall, however, the 1950s–1970s period was a prosperous one for Canada. Both the 'needs' and, increasingly, the 'wants' of a consumer society were fulfilled by large corporations—including many American branch plants—that invested heavily in new technologies.

The national population increased from 14 million to 21.5 million between 1951 and 1971. The distribution of this growth—Ontario and Quebec together gained 5 million, the west 2.1 million, and Atlantic Canada just 0.4 million—reflected the core–periphery divide, although the peripheries did benefit from the booming demand for resources—from forest products and minerals to hydro generation. The one region that did not experience any significant benefit was Atlantic Canada.

The post-war economic boom was accompanied by social and political change. Aboriginal and Asian Canadians gained the voting rights they had been denied; restrictive immigration laws were liberalized; a wide-ranging social safety net (old-age pensions, family allowances, unemployment insurance) was developed to assist have-not people; and in 1957 the federal government introduced an equalization program to ensure that have-not regions could provide public services (such as health care and education) comparable to those available in the better-off provinces.

In Quebec the Quiet Revolution loosened the grip of the Roman Catholic Church, challenged the virtual monopoly of anglophones in the economic realm, and stimulated the development of a powerful Quebec nationalism. The infamous White Paper on Indian Policy (1969) spurred Aboriginal people to organize and begin pressing for their rights. At the same time Canadians generally began to recognize the impact on the environment—and hence human health—of the industries devoted to resource exploitation and the production of consumer goods. From the early 1970s to the present, economic stability has increasingly given way to uncertainty. A host of economic and political factors have contributed to this uncertainty. The roots of the political factors go back to the end of the Second World War, when (under the leadership of the United States) global institutions were established to promote free trade and reduce tariff barriers between nations. Meanwhile, technologies were developed that made it possible to move goods, people, capital, and information ever more rapidly, encouraging the fragmentation of production processes. As increasingly powerful transnational corporations extended their operations around the world, many core regions, including Canada's, found that their manufacturing industries were subject to ever-greater global competition, particularly with the rise of Asian economies and the movement towards global free trade under the direction of the World Trade Organization. Feelings of insecurity were only intensified by events such as the energy crisis of the early 1970s, the recessions of the 1980s and 1990s, the Asian 'economic flu' of 1997, the terrorist attacks of 2001, and the Iraq war of 2003.

The shift in emphasis from manufacturing to services (such as banking, finance, real estate, insurance, research, tourism, health, education, legal and administration services) was well underway by the mid-1960s, and only accelerated over the following decades. Large urban centres with international airports, major port facilities, convention centres, and business and tourist infrastructure expanded accordingly, while resource-dependent regions faced ever-greater competition from around the world. As the Asia–Pacific region emerged as the new economic powerhouse in the 1980s, the focus of international trade shifted from the east coast to the west. At the same time, government cost-cutting widened the gaps—and heightened the tensions—between 'have' and 'have-not' regions.

Canada's population increased by more than 9 million between 1971 and 2001, and the regional distribution of the growth predictably reflected differences in economic health. More than 58 per cent of the increase (5.3 million) went to Ontario and Quebec—especially the former (4.2 million, or almost 80 per cent). The resource hinterlands of Ontario and Quebec experienced little growth, and some actually lost population. Quebec also had other issues to cope with. The concentration of labour-intensive industries in its southern core meant that it experienced more industrial losses than southern Ontario did as a result of the movement towards free trade. At the same time the threat of separation was a constant source of anxiety for many individuals and businesses, especially after the federalist forces came within a hair of losing the second referendum vote (1995).

The west—especially Alberta and British Columbia—also received a significant share of the population increase between 1971 and 2001. The energy crisis transformed Alberta's economy, although Ottawa's efforts to control oil prices sparked deep and lasting resentment. Resource development also continued in British Columbia, but the main economic catalyst there was the shift in trade towards the Asia–Pacific region, which made Vancouver the new gateway to the rest of Canada.

The energy crisis also spurred oil and gas exploration in the North. The proposal to build a natural gas pipeline across the north slope of the Yukon and down the Mackenzie Valley drew the Aboriginal peoples of the region together in resistance, which (with the help of the Berger Inquiry) led to the negotiation of modern-day treaties that included self-government arrangements. Similarly in the eastern Arctic, the creation of the new territory of Nunavut in 1999 gave the majority Inuit population a significant degree of control over their lives and economy.

Atlantic Canada did not fare well economically in the 1971–2001 period. Overall population growth was small, and Newfoundland actually lost population. The collapse of the cod fishery (1992) was a serious blow to the whole of Atlantic Canada, but especially Newfoundland. The loss of the coal mines and steel mill in Sydney, Nova Scotia, was another economic blow, though on a more local scale. While tourism and offshore oil and gas offered some hope for the future, they were not enough to stop many young people from leaving the region.

Table 12.1 **Total federal transfers, per capita amounts, and estimated contributions to provincial/territorial revenue, 2004–2005**

Province/territory	$ millions	$/capita	% revenue	Province/territory	$ millions	$/capita	% revenue
Nunavut	796	28,061	91	Man.	3,045	2,428	40
NWT	736	17,951	80	Que.	13,865	1,757	26
Yukon	508	16,818	78	BC	6,136	1,383	19
PEI	439	2,930	42	Ont.	16,745	1,332	21
NB	2,220	2,739	39	Sask.	1,859	1,332	28
NS	2,466	2,455	42	Alta	4,325	1,321	16
Nfld/Lab.	1,367	2,449	34				

Source: Adapted from Department of Finance Canada, 'Federal Transfers to Provinces and Territories' ⟨http://www.fin.gc.ca/FEDPROV/mtpe.html#Newfoundland⟩.

There is no denying that regional disparities exist in Canada. However, the principle of equalization introduced in 1957 was enshrined in the Constitution Act of 1982 and continues to ensure that citizens across the country receive comparable public services. Have-not provinces still receive equalization payments, and a similar program is in place for the territories. In addition, two other programs—the Canada Health Transfer and Canada Social Transfer—provide funding for all provinces and territories, including 'have' provinces such as Alberta, British Columbia, Ontario (the only province that to date has never received equalization funding). Table 12.1 shows the total amounts of federal transfers to the provinces and territories under all four programs—equalization, territorial financing, and health and social transfers—listed in order of per capita amounts (highest to lowest). Not surprisingly, federal money accounts for the bulk of revenues in the three territories, while the Atlantic provinces and Manitoba receive substantially more money per capita than their more prosperous counterparts.

From time to time disputes arise over eligibility for equalization payments, and some critics have charged that the program encourages dependency on the part of have-not regions. Nevertheless, the great majority of Canadians support the equalization program—85 per cent, according to a 2004 survey by the Centre for Research and Information on Canada. And even in the province where support was lowest (Alberta), 78 per cent of respondents favoured the program. This suggests that fairness is a value shared across all the nation's regions.

Current Challenges

In colonial times, Canada's development was shaped by external forces operating in a global context. Even as the colonies grew and developed to the point of establishing some local control over the management of their own affairs, the overarching influences that created demand for resources and stimulated the growth of forward, backward, and final demand linkages were still external: British trade policy, international conflicts, the technological innovations of the industrial revolution. As Canada evolved into an independent nation state, it was increasingly pulled into the economic orbit of the United States, and American influence continued to grow once US firms began establishing branch plants here. But Canada was scarcely alone: by 1950, the United States was the dominant influence on national economies throughout the capitalist world.

The engines of capitalist economic life are trade, investment, production, and consumption; the operators that make these engines run are private corporations; and the driving force behind those corporations is the profit motive. Since the days of mercantilism, this system has worked on the laissez-faire principle that competition in the marketplace (rather than government regulation) should provide whatever checks and balances might be necessary. However, competition encouraged the stronger firms to swallow up the weaker ones (through mergers, takeovers, and buyouts), and as technological innovations permitted increasing time–space convergence and fragmentation of the production process, an ever-smaller number of ever-larger corporations wielded ever-greater power in the marketplace. As the popular film *The Corporation* (2004; based on Joel Bakan's book *The Corporation: The Pathological Pursuit of Profit and Power*) pointed out, corporations may be classified in law as 'individuals', but they have no conscience: their only responsibility is to their shareholders, and society pays the price. The role that government plays (or fails to play) in balancing private and public interests is the basis of many land-use conflicts.

High on the list of private–public conflicts are environmental concerns. Many environmental issues today are global in scope—most obviously, the global warming caused in large part by the burning of fossil fuels. The effects of climate change will vary around the globe, and for some regions they could even be beneficial, at least for a while. In the long run, though, the consequences are expected to include rising sea levels, severe flooding, more intense heat waves, droughts, and storms, uncontrollable plagues of pests and disease, and species extinctions. Canada is among the many nations around the world that have ratified the Kyoto Protocol, pledging to reduce their emissions of carbon dioxide and other 'greenhouse gases'. Yet the United States continues to argue against the agreement, and even within Canada it is not universally accepted. Alberta, for example, has expressed strong opposition on a variety of grounds—though many supporters of Kyoto suspect that the primary objection has to do with the huge revenues that the province currently receives from the oil and gas industry (see Chapter 9).

In any event, Canadian emissions have actually increased substantially since Kyoto was signed, and Canada has a very long way to go if it expects to meet the targets set for 2012, when the agreement expires. One major problem at the individual level is dependence on the automobile, which is a significant contributor to greenhouse gases and acid rain. New hybrid cars and hydrogen fuel cells may represent technological 'solutions', but they are too expensive for most people today to consider. Among the alternatives are public transit, car-pooling, walking, and cycling—but to give up the convenience of driving requires a significant attitude change, and is out of the question for people in places where public transit is poor or non-existent.

The utilities, public or private, that supply electricity are expected to do so in the most 'cost-effective' manner. In regions that depend on thermal generation, the burning of coal, natural gas, and oil creates greenhouse gases and contributes to acid rain. Other regions, such as Quebec, can generate electricity without burning fossil fuels, but massive hydro dams create a different set of problems, radically changing regional landscapes and displacing local populations both of wildlife and of people. Those who support the use of nuclear power to generate electricity point out that it does not produce greenhouse gases, and that reactors can be located close to demand. But they often neglect to mention the risk of radioactive contamination, the poor performance record of nuclear generation to date, and the unsolved problem of how to dispose safely of nuclear waste.

If the prime concern is the environment, greater attention must be paid to developing 'green' energy sources: clean, renewable sources that have minimal environmental impact, such as wind, solar, and run-of-the-river hydro generation. Energy production needs to be decentralized, to encourage local regions and individuals to take more responsibility for their own energy needs. Reducing energy demand is also crucial. In a northern country like Canada, the need for heating is unlikely to disappear, but there are many ways of reducing the amount of energy we use for that purpose: governments, for example, can adjust building codes to require better insulation, and individuals can get used to wearing warmer clothing indoors—though that too may require attitude changes on the part of many people.

The demand for consumer goods is a major generator of economic wealth, but it also lies at the root of many environmental problems. The production of consumer goods requires the use of vast quantities of resources, not only in the form of materials but also in the form of energy to power the manufacturing process and transport the goods produced. These processes also tend to produce dangerous pollutants. Governments encourage manufacturing because it attracts capital and technology, creates employment, and generates tax revenues. But are such activities sustainable? Will the same resources be available for future generations? How much industrial waste can the planet absorb before it becomes uninhabitable?

The Plains buffalo barely escaped extinction in the nineteenth century. The sea otter trade on the west coast was another near-disaster, and illegal commercial whalers continue to kill endangered species despite international efforts to control the hunt. Virtually every region of Canada has its own story of environmental catastrophe related to resource exploitation. Perhaps the worst such incident was the poisoning of members of the White Dog and Grassy Narrows First Nation in Ontario by mercury discharged into the water system by a pulp mill. Incidents like this one raise the question of whether any level of industrial pollution can be considered 'safe', and point to the need for government control—not only in establishing regulations but in enforcing compliance.

Canada's fisheries offer numerous examples of the need for stronger government action. On the east cost, the collapse of the cod fishery can be traced in part to the fact that individual nations like Canada are hard-pressed to control the behaviour of foreign fishing fleets in international waters. Yet Canada has also failed to take action in an area that is within its control: although it has known for decades that dragger fishing (using huge nets that scour the ocean floor and do not discriminate as to species or age) was a major factor in the depletion of the cod stocks, it still has not banned the practice. In this 'tragedy of the commons', the public interest in maintaining a valuable natural resource has been traded off against private fish companies' interest in maximizing their profits by using the most cost-effective technology available.

On the west coast, the federal government allows aquaculture operations (fish farms) to raise Atlantic salmon in pens located in the same water that is home to the various wild Pacific salmon species. Such operations threaten the wild native salmon in at least two ways: by exposing them to diseases, parasites, and chemical contaminants, and by making it possible for Atlantic salmon to escape and compete with the native fish for food and habitat (according to the David Suzuki Foundation, an average of 90,000 Atlantic fish escaped every year between 1990 and 2000). The most obvious solution would be to build such pens on land, so that farmed salmon could not escape and mix with wild species. On the other hand, this solution would mean a significant increase in costs, first to fish farmers and then to consumers. Is the public willing to pay a premium for protecting wild salmon stocks?

As for the safety of the food that Canadians eat, there is a general expectation that government regulations and inspection services provide adequate protection against any food-borne illness. Only when cases of diseases such as BSE (bovine spongiform encephalopathy, or 'mad cow disease', found in an Alberta-raised cow in 2003) or avian flu (discovered in BC's Fraser Valley in 2004, leading to the slaughter of millions of healthy chickens and turkeys), are questions raised over the way food is produced and the risks that modern agricultural practices have introduced. Similarly, the safety of water supplies was rarely questioned until seven people in Walkerton, Ontario, died of e-coli contamination in 2000. Incidents such as these underline the need for greater accountability on the part of government. At the same time, the growing market for 'organic' or 'naturally raised' indicates that many consumers are willing to pay extra for food grown without chemical pesticides or genetic modification. There is also increasing interest in ethical considerations of various kinds, evident in the trends towards vegetarianism and, on the global scale, more equitable treatment of food producers in the Third World (paying a premium for 'fair trade' coffee or chocolate, for instance, so that producers can receive a better price).

Resources and environmental safety have also been at the centre of several conflicts regarding Canada–US free trade. For years, the United States continued to impose high duties on imports of Canadian softwood lumber, despite multiple rulings in Canada's favour. Other conflicts, actual or anticipated, have involved the effect of free trade agreements on Canada's freedom to make its own laws and social policies. In 1998, for example, after banning imports of a toxic gasoline additive called MMT, Canada was forced to pay $13 million to the maker of MMT, the US-based Ethyl Corporation. It has often been suggested that Canada may some day be forced to allow bulk exports of water to the US, and many have pointed out that, under WTO rules, even Canada's health care system could be challenged as an unfair 'subsidy'. The fundamental concerns are that, under the rules of free trade, public interests are being sacrificed to private ones, and that Canada's sovereignty is being undermined by the power of American corporations.

A variation on the latter theme is the concern that Canadians are becoming more like Americans. But at least one recent study is reassuring: Michael Adams (2003) found that Canadians are much 'more than unarmed Americans with health insurance' (xii). In his view, 'There is no reason to believe . . . Canada will not continue its trajectory of social liberalism even in the face of powerful forces of American social conservatism' and he underlines the fact that it is 'increasingly a peaceful microcosm of the entire world' (143). Michael Ignatieff (2000) also recognizes the unique character of Canadian multiculturalism: 'We are living in the first human society actually attempting to create a political community on the assumption that everyone—literally everyone—has the right to belong.'

Concerns for human rights and the environment have come together in the modern-day treaty process. After centuries of marginalization, Aboriginal peoples are now in a position to influence the course of resource development, especially in the North. With increasing opportunities for education, skills development, and employment, Aboriginal communities will be increasingly able to set and achieve their own goals and objectives.

The prospects for resource-based communities in Canada's peripheral regions may not be so bright. Established specifically for the purpose of housing workers in resource industries—sometimes in a single industry—these communities were expected to be permanent, and workers invested in them accordingly. But the capitalist emphasis on productivity means minimizing costly inputs and maximizing profits. Thus over time corporations invested more and more in technologies that enabled them to operate with fewer workers, shrinking the employment base. Meanwhile, global competition and volatile world market prices have led many mines and mills to shut down, leaving the communities centred on them with no choice but to find another source of economic activity or else close down themselves. Similarly on the Prairies, economic considerations led to the abandonment of the branch rail lines and local grain elevators that small farm operations had relied on to get their produce to market. As a result, many small communities went into a downward spiral of reduced economic activity and continuing depopulation.

The more people are displaced from the rural periphery, the more Canada's urban centres continue to grow. But big cities have their own problems. The concentration of poverty, unemployment, and homelessness (and all the problems associated with them, from alcohol and drug abuse to crime) in large urban centres is also a product of the capitalist system. Cities have no power to address the root causes of these problems, and because they are constitutionally dependent on the provincial level—with only the powers the provinces give them, and limited ability to raise funds through taxation—providing adequate services becomes more difficult every day.

Finally, one of the most complex regional challenges that Canada faces is the prospect that Quebec will secede and form a separate sovereign state. The British conquest made the people of New France second-class citizens in their own homeland. Two centuries later, as part of the Quiet Revolution of the 1960s, a new Québécois nationalism emerged that by the mid-1970s was powerful enough to see a party advocating independence elected to form the provincial government. Although the first referendum on the subject, in 1980, produced a clear 'no' vote, the second referendum, in 1995, was a virtual draw. Shaken by this result, Ottawa asked the Supreme Court of Canada for its opinion on Quebec's right to secede, and on the basis of the Court's decision drafted the Clarity Act (2000), outlining the conditions under which Ottawa would negotiate the secession of any province (in the West, discontent with Ottawa's perceived interference—especially in the area of resources—has given rise to a variety of secessionist movements). Among other things, the Clarity Act requires that the views of Aboriginal peoples be taken into account, especially in cases where their territorial rights would be affected. This condition is particularly relevant to the Cree people of northern Quebec, since that region did not become part of the province until 1912—45 years after Confederation.

Historical grievances, territorial conflict, regional discontent, control of resources, social and political change, evolution of boundaries, Aboriginal rights: the separation issue brings together many of the recurring themes that this book has explored. Geography is uniquely positioned to help us understand issues of this kind, because its multidisciplinary perspective takes into account the complex interactions of so many different factors. Anyone interested in learning more about the range of current geographic research is encouraged to see the 50th anniversary issue of *The Canadian Geographer* (2001). Dedicated to 'Geographical Interpretations of Canada', it presents contributions from 35 geographers, organized in five sections: 'Canada and the World', 'Contemporary Environmental Issues', 'Population', 'Geographies of Human Rights', and 'Retrospective'. Together, these articles offer a comprehensive overview of the important role that geography can play in contemporary society.

References

Adams, M. 2003. *Fire and Ice: The United States, Canada and the Myth of Converging Values*. Toronto: Penguin.

Bakan, J. 2004. *The Corporation: The Pathological Pursuit of Profit and Power*. Toronto: Penguin.

Centre for Research and Information on Canada (CRIC). 2004. *Opinion Canada* 6, 36. http://www.opinion-canada.ca/en/articles/article_124.html.

David Suzuki Foundation. 'Escaping Farmed Salmon Pose Risks'. http://www.davidsuzuki.org/Oceans/Aquaculture/Salmon/Escapes.asp.

Diamond, J. 1999. *Guns, Germs, and Steel: The Fates of Human Societies*. New York: Norton.

Ignatieff, M. 2000. CBC Massey Lectures. 'The Rights Revolution'. http://www.cbc.ca/ideas/massey/massey2000.html.

Index